THE ARCHITECTURE OF FREEDOM

How to Free Your Soul

TIM CROSS

Austin, Texas

www.thearchitectureoffreedom.com

DEDICATION

This book has evolved far beyond its original intention, a simple letter to my daughters. If, early on, I had any real sense that this project would become a dominant part of my life for more than three years, it is quite possible that I would never have started. As with all heartfelt journeys, it unfolded moment by moment.

I dedicate this effort to my two daughters, Emily and Rachel, and to Merlyn, their mother, who was my partner through much of the early part of this journey.

This book would not have been possible without the endless help and full loving support of Connie Colten, my longtime best friend, life partner and now wife: so, of course, it is also dedicated to her.

There are many others who directly contributed to making this book possible. Thanks to all of you who helped and who continue to be a part of my amazing personal journey.

Since this is a journey of discovering our connections, I also collectively thank all of us, together. We are so beautiful.

FOREWARD

Each of us brings to the world a uniqueness that is our greatest gift. It begs to be discovered, acknowledged, explored and shared. Since this quality is a fundamental aspect of who we are, each of us will eventually have to make peace and embody this essential part of ourselves. We can't avoid this work, because, in the end, we can't avoid the truth. If we engage in this inner journey with integrity, then a deep, peaceful joy will naturally follow.

To see or be seen by others, we have to first be able to see ourselves. One reason this is true is because there really are no others. The process of growth is, ultimately, always a process of self-examination.

To "see" ourselves we must first become "open." This is not the same as being open to an idea or "something" of our own choosing. The path to freedom begins with learning how to be open to the amazing adventure of life itself. This means that we welcome any and every possibility that life sends our way. Only when we are this open, do our perfect choices for each moment become clear and easy to recognize.

As we open, we experience greater freedom and our sea of Truth becomes larger. This also means our sea of Love becomes greater. These seas are the same.

Is that inside voice that we sometimes sense our resistance or our truth? It could be either, and we all have the ability to distinguish the difference. This book is relates some of the things that I encountered while on this journey towards freedom and Love. It is my hope that like-minded souls will find this book to be a helpful guide for their own personal journeys.

"When I let go of what I am, I become what I might be."
Lao Tzu 600 BC

"We must be willing to let go of the life we planned so as to have the life that is waiting for us."
Joseph Campbell

"Whether you think you can, or think you can't—you are right."
Henry Ford

"We don't see things as they are. We see them as we are."
Anais Nin

"Life is what happens to you when you're busy making other plans."
John Lennon lyrics from "Beautiful Boy"

"Out beyond ideas of wrongdoing and rightdoing, there is a field. I will meet you there."
Rumi

"A human being is a part of the whole, called by us 'Universe,' a part limited in time and space. He experiences himself, his thoughts and feelings as something separated from the rest—a kind of optical delusion of his consciousness. This delusion is a kind of prison for us, restricting us to our personal desires and to affection for a few persons nearest to us. Our task must be to free ourselves from this prison by widening our circle of compassion to embrace all living creatures and the whole of nature in its beauty. Nobody is able to achieve this completely, but the striving for such achievement is in itself a part of the liberation and a foundation for inner security."

Albert Einstein in a letter of 1950, as quoted in *The New York Times* (March 1972) and *The New York Post* (November 1972).

TABLE OF CONTENTS

PREAMBLE

Personal freedom can only exist when we each have the freedom to choose from all possibilities–the deepest level of freedom requires that ALL possible options be available for us to explore–this includes absolutely everything–all that we think of as good, right along with those parts of life that we consider to be bad or problematic. In order for us to experience true freedom, all possible choices must be available in our world.

We are currently engaged in a process of discovery, learning that our universe is actually designed and structured to create all these possibilities–a deep and responsive Architecture of Freedom. Our infinite home is built upon a structure that not only permits personal freedom but also one that actually "desires" and instantly responds to our individual free expression. Our purpose here is to discover how to best allow this already existing architecture to guide and move us through our lives.

Throughout the last century, guided by the light of science and math, we have uncovered exciting new understandings about the hidden architecture of our universe. With this growing body of knowledge comes a new awareness of our dramatic, extremely effective and mostly untapped individual power to change our world from within. Not surprisingly, this new understanding meshes beautifully with many of the world's spiritual traditions. ***This book, the Architecture of Freedom, is about this new understanding and how it sets us completely free from our old concepts and ideas about life.***

Everything that we experience in our physical lives begins with our senses and the subsequent processing and interpretation of their signals by our brain. Both our senses and our brains have physiological limitations. We know that there are many animals that can hear, see, smell and feel things that we are utterly incapable of sensing or cognizing. We can't see or sense radio waves or wireless signals, yet we now entirely depend on them to move much of the information that runs our contemporary society. In our day-to-day lives we are only aware of a small proportion of what is really going on around us. Not only do we miss all types of local phenomenon, but also, throughout the last century, scientists have been busy discovering that the vast majority of our physical universe is imperceptible to humans, even when we are using our most sensitive scientific instruments. Something very significant is going on "out there," and most of it is completely hidden from us.

Life on our planet often seems chaotic and contradictory. On one hand we see our culture aggressively testing the limits of what our Earth can support. We face severe social and environmental problems, yet we witness a deepening of these problems through the common patterns of politics infused with fear and greed. Little thought, resource or action ever seems to be directed towards our actual collective welfare or the physical health of our planet. The larger and more affluent nations and corporations contribute to this dysfunction by exercising their own special interests, which are often focused upon financial gain, control and the consolidation of power; they often choose to invest their enormous resources in competitive, but destructive, political gamesmanship. Others add to this general chaos and dysfunction by gaming the system to reap enormous short-term profits at the expense of many. These manipulations often culminate in wars, which ultimately only serve these larger corporate or political interests. How many times have we been told something like "this war will be the war to end all wars"? We also observe that, in some form or another, these same destructive and shortsighted behaviors have been mankind's pattern for thousands of years.

Coincidentally, the very same technology that created our "smart" bombs and laser-guided cruise missiles has also been used to connect people all around the world in ways we never could have

1

imagined in the past. We talk, blog, Skype, Tweet, share ideas and are reminded by this new form of direct intercommunication that we are, at our core, all the same. Through this process we are collectively reminded that all of us, living on this planet are brothers and sisters with similar needs, concerns, desires and dreams. Today, we share our art, music, literature, movies and ideas in amazing ways that we never could have imagined, even twenty years ago. Today, more than ever, we can all witness and recognize our direct interconnectedness. Below the surface of the planet's chaos, something very special is happening. Spirit is evolving, growing and interconnecting. A beautiful chorus is being sung by many shared voices. At this deep level of personal connection, below the surface chaos, we are creating an extremely beautiful and resonant harmony–one that involves our entire planet and much more.

Five hundred years ago, almost everyone on earth was convinced that our world was flat. Copernicus, Galileo and others tirelessly and courageously developed, then presented clear physical evidence for a new vision of our solar system. The cultural paradigm then gradually shifted from the "flat earth" to what it is today. Our understanding of our universe has changed dramatically since the times of Galileo and Newton, but their ideas still shape our cultural paradigm. We are now facing the same type of conceptual challenge that our ancestors did five hundred years ago. Science and our real-world experiments have pushed our old paradigm to the point of dissolution. We find ourselves in the middle of a process that is requiring our culture to dramatically rethink its worldview. *A new way of being is now available and we each, individually, get to choose when to enter into this new paradigm–the architecture of freedom. There is no need to wait for others.*

As a young man, when I focused on the state of world affairs, I always found myself wondering why there wasn't a "better way." I no longer react this way. Today, I am comfortable and satisfied, knowing that the natural world has already provided this "better way." This "better way" already exists and it is being consciously used by millions of people to dramatically change their perception of, and their relationship to, our world and universe. The secret of this new way of living has been hidden from us only because of our old beliefs; they have blinded us from seeing the deeper truths about life. This deep and powerful understanding will always seem strange and impossible when viewed from our old belief system, or paradigm; but, as our newest science rapidly advances our understanding about the hidden architecture of our universe, these once-strange ideas will begin to make a wonderful kind of sense.

Within this new paradigm we discover that any and all ways of living, or any worlds that we might ever imagine, already exist. These worlds and ways of being are always available to us, but they are simply hidden from us because of our limiting perceptions and beliefs. We can access these other realities, but only when we are fully prepared for, and completely open to, all aspects of this new and expanded experience.

Ironically, this new way of living also teaches us that our lives, just as they appear today, are perfect for the purposes of creation and our individual and collective development. The following may seem to be paradoxical, or even impossible, however: *the world is perfect just as it is, and, at the same time, we have the opportunity to experience our lives very differently.* Our ability to experience life differently, in any moment, is a large part of what makes it perfect. We have complete control of our participation in life, but the way we can "control" our life is really quite different from what most of us imagine.

The world, as it appears to us today, is exactly as it has always been. It is "a mixed bag," containing all that we consider "good," along with the "bad," saints along with the sinners, and the lightness with the darkness. *Because of the very nature of existence, life has to be this way. This collection of opposites describes the fundamental nature of duality, and without this duality there would be no life on Earth, or even an Earth!*

Once closed, the doors to this hidden architecture of the cosmos have been recently opened wide by advances in quantum physics, relativity and cosmology. These breakthroughs point to a new and different way of living that involves adjusting our lives, actions and habits to better work with our growing understanding of this hidden architecture. *The most wonderful and empowering implication of this new understanding is that no other person has to be involved for your world to change. Actually, you are the only person who can make this change. There is absolutely no need to wait for others because when you change, the world changes!* This single personal adjustment is much more profound than it initially appears to be. It is completely different from but easily confused with our old ideas about "self-responsibility," and it changes almost everything that we assume we know about life.

An extraordinary irony is built into the very foundation of this new approach: it requires each of us to fully embrace the world exactly as it appears, right now, including all of its apparent problems. To not embrace the world and everything in it, just as it appears, is a personal act of resistance, a focus of energy, and a judgment that ultimately bind us even more deeply to those very aspects that we find most problematic. To the logical mind this is an illogical, and impossible, "Catch 22." To a mind that is prepared to see logic for what it really is–a very functional but still limited tool for three-dimensional conceptual thinking–it is possible to get past the paradox and the limitations of logic to discover the extraordinary and expansive possibilities beyond.

Despite the title and some of the chapter headings, this is not a book about architecture, math or physics. It is, instead, a book about discovering how to develop more-enduring joy, peace, fun, relaxation, purpose, enjoyment, connection and direction in life. In short, it is about one way to live life more fully. It includes just enough contemporary physics to help create a foundation for the recommended life-style changes that are the real message of this book.

The writing of this book served two primary and personal purposes. First, I began this project to help me organize my thoughts so that I could better communicate them to my own children. I taught high school for a few years, and all teachers learn that the process of reviewing material, so it can then be better explained to others, leads to a very substantial deepening of their own understanding; organizing this material helped me to better integrate my own thinking. Second, it is my hope that this project, built throughout a lifetime of directed focus, may also help others as they explore new ways to perceive and respond to life and its apparent daily challenges. I hope that others, including my own children, will find this book helpful because it resonates with something deep within that they already understand.

While many of the ideas in this book are rooted in contemporary science, it is written largely from the experiential perspective. This book asks, *"Why wait for hard scientific proof? If our lives improve by using these principles today, don't we, ourselves, then become 'the living proof' of a better way of being?"* Our lives changing for the better could be all the experimental proof that is required.

This book explains how our short engagement in this adventure within the physical world is only a small part of a much more extensive and timeless existence. Understanding this can and will shift our perspective and, therefore, change our lives. I am attempting to present enough information, scientific and experiential, so that readers will feel supported and comfortable, should they choose to explore some of the recommended lifestyle changes. Some of these changes will seem contrary to much of what we thought we knew about life. ***This book is designed to increase trust and reduce our fear about beginning this particular process of self-change.***

All the life-changing concepts and techniques presented in this book are taught, and practiced, elsewhere in our contemporary world. In addition, many teachers and writers use a host of different, but related, methods and technologies, and some of these are listed in the resource section. This book also explores how and why all of these approaches are ultimately just different names and interpretations of the same fundamental principle, especially when they are all viewed through the lens of our new, growing understanding about the hidden architecture of the universe.

To this end I attempt to always return to the middle ground, where there are connections to both the knowable world of science and the intuitive world of spirituality. There will be some readers who will find the book not scientific enough because I am far too willing to wander into unprovable ideas, feelings and experiential extrapolations. There will be other readers who feel that the science, a critical part of this book's backbone, is too limiting, rigid, and possibly even impenetrable. Throughout this book, I have attempted to find and return to the middle, balanced, and common ground.

Architecture, which has been my profession for almost 35 years, is founded squarely in this middle territory. Our buildings have to stand firm, resist weather, and meet all degrees of technical and functional requirements. At the same time they are created to add delight and beauty to the world and, in the most successful cases, lift our spirits to new heights. "The Architecture of Freedom" is written from this middle ground, while always aspiring to encourage all of us to reach and expand, in all directions, to include more of this amazing human adventure that we call life. For this reason, this book will always be a work in progress.

PART ONE–INTRODUCTION

OUR COMMON JOURNEY

Life continues as it has always been. Since the beginning of recorded history, certain parts of our human adventure have always seemed mysterious, and beyond our reach or understanding. Over millennia, we explored our physical planet and grew a body of scientific knowledge; large parts of this mystery became illuminated as we decoded much of what was once considered unexplainable. Today, we are now able to gaze billions of *light-years* into space–a single light-year is about six trillion miles–and simultaneously peer deep into the smallest known particles.

Much that was previously considered mysterious can now be explained with the help of our newly uncovered understanding about the hidden nature, structure and geometry of our universe. Much of what we used to call supernatural is really quite natural, but just not apparent to us through our senses or our instruments. We all understand that, while we can't see radio waves or wireless signals, they are still very real and functional. In a similar way, even though our bodies and instruments cannot perceive the greatest parts of our own universe, these invisible parts still exist and function beautifully with the known parts.

However, even with all of our new knowledge and tools, there is still an enormous, and even growing, component of unexplained mystery. It is ironic that the more we learn, the more we discover new and even greater, unknown parts of creation, which seem to always hide beyond these newly unveiled regions. Therefore, our universe now appears more extensive and extraordinary than we could ever have imagined just a few dozen years ago. Also, for all of our scientific advances, we still have no satisfactory explanations for many common experiences, including déjà vu, past-life memories, the source of consciousness and awareness, synchronicities, premonitions, precognitions, the miraculous behavior of many of the Earth's creatures, the common sensation of knowing when another person is looking at us, or even something as basic as the miracle of life itself.

The dramatic expansion of our scientific and technical knowledge is beginning to shift our long-standing paradigm. This new knowledge allows a very empowering perspective that, once recognized, understood and integrated, changes our entire relationship to absolutely everything about our lives. This "secret" is built upon the growing body of knowledge which demonstrates that our physical universe is only a small part of a much more expansive creation. Not only does creation turn out to be so much larger and more interesting than we ever believed, but it also is simultaneously completely intimate, interconnected, responsive and interactive. Everything that we once thought of as being "out there" is fully, and always, intimately connected to us. Our science is helping us understand that "out there" and "in here" are really one and the same. *Through this newly discovered architecture, each of us has the mostly undiscovered ability to alter our relationship with our universe in such a way that we can completely change our perception and experience of life. More importantly, once we truly make these changes, the world that we once perceived as only "outside" of us, completely changes its character—it embraces and safely contains us as we realize our connection and integration to this much greater whole.*

Everything in our universe is intimately interconnected and always communicating through direct cause-and-effect interaction; we, however, are usually only able to perceive separation and randomness. Because most of our universe lies beyond our perception and current consciousness (conscious awareness), normally we lack the sensory and conceptual ability to

see and directly participate in this depth of interaction. It still exists, regardless of how we sense it, and its architecture affects and shapes our lives in ways that we are only beginning to understand. Today, because of what we have been taught, most of us spend vast amounts of time and energy fighting or resisting the natural order of this creation. As we grow to better understand and integrate the implications of this newly uncovered architecture, the way that we live our lives will dramatically change.

What we are learning is this: ***To change the way the outside world works or appears, we only need to change ourselves inside. Deep inside we are vibrational beings. The vibrational state of our being is the result of our deeply held, but usually unconscious, beliefs. As our personal subterranean vibrational landscape changes, the appearance of the world outside of us automatically changes. We never have to change the outside world through external action. In fact, we can't change the "outside" world in that way. Instead, by changing only ourselves, we can completely alter the way the world appears to us and this shifts our relationship to it.*** This single and personal shift of perspective makes all the difference. This book discusses our amazing intimate relationship to our universe, why the structure of the universe works this way, and how to change our lives to work best with this structure.

Almost every idea expressed in this book has been said or explained by many others. Little within involves new ideas, and any of what might be considered new is mostly just reorganization or reinterpretation of ideas already said, practiced or uncovered by many others. This book is only unique in that it presents my personal interpretation and compilation of this wider understanding.

Some self-help books promise quick fixes for our problems. However, as we have all discovered, these usually don't work, at least not for long. I make no such promise because inner growth is a natural process and this requires time. As we begin to explore the lifestyle recommendations in this book, we should not expect an instant cure for everything that seems wrong with our lives or the world. While the method is simple and accessible to everyone, it involves embracing and integrating a brand-new paradigm about the fundamental nature of life. As we begin to initiate these recommended deep-level changes, we must understand the nature of the process. It took us many years to become who we are, so it is reasonable to expect that it will also take some time to fully develop a different way of being. While the gradual nature of this change has been my observation, it has not been everyone's experience. Some claim to have undergone this change in an instant and this, as we will discover, is entirely possible.

This new way of living ultimately requires that we each reach the deep recognition that this world, exactly as it appears to us right now, is absolutely perfect for our soul's journey. It is perfect because it precisely reflects and illuminates our current inner state of being, and because of this, life presents each of us with our own, perfectly orchestrated opportunities for growth. This idea may seem strange and may not make sense until later in this book because it contradicts almost everything that we have been taught. For most, embracing this radical idea will require new and deeper levels of understanding, trust, honesty, courage and self-reflection. The complete recognition, acceptance and integration of this idea means that an individual has reached that special place in their evolutionary process where they fully understand that ***"we are the same as everything that is reflected in our experience."*** For most of us, this deeper level of self-knowledge will require a new way of seeing and *being*.

While this critical hurdle might initially seem difficult or impossible, once we start opening to this new way of seeing the world, almost everything about our lives begins to change in ways that are continuously surprising, amazing and beautiful–reinforcement comes quickly. Everyday life becomes an exciting and joyful practice that produces extraordinary and completely unexpected, real-world results. Embracing any new way of living can be a complex and challenging process, and this fundamental lifestyle change is no different–it requires a focused, long-term commitment of time, energy and trust. *However, as mentioned earlier, it is always possible that for those who are fully prepared in every way, this change can effortlessly unfold in an instant.*

Deep within this journey it will be understood that it is not necessary, or even possible, to fix all the world's problems. Problems such as hunger, political corruption, disease and suffering are created by the deep, dualistic nature of life itself. Ironically, as the reader will discover, the manifestation of these problems is actually a critical element of the creation process, and one that helps to make life extremely meaningful. *The world, with all its bumps and rough edges, always forms the perfect gristmill for the evolution of our collective soul.* Due to this deeper nature, the basic processes and relationships that generate these human issues will not disappear as a direct result of any of our problem-solving activities. Local-level functional problems may be mitigated for a short time, but the underlying causative issues will linger because they are an integral part of the human condition. The fundamental causative issues will persist and then simply reappear elsewhere. *Ultimately, to change the world, we each must and will evolve individually, and it is only this internal evolution that shifts everything–inside and outside.*

I am certainly not implying that humanitarian endeavors that are attempting to mitigate the world's problems and crisis are futile, or pointless. They are, in fact, completely the opposite–they are critically important for the evolution of humanity; they serve the dynamic balance on this planet in many ways–they bridge our differences as they illuminate and define the critical focal points. Devoting our attention to these universal problems always will be an extraordinary way to express and share love, become fully engaged in life, and show others, by example, a way to live a fuller and more compassionate life. Along with reducing the suffering from the crisis at hand, humanitarian endeavors help to focus our usually distracted public attention back on these basic issues, so that we all have another opportunity to participate and become more understanding and compassionate. If we find that public-interest work is our deep passion, then we must ultimately express ourselves through this type of service. If we feel called, but choose not to participate, something will seem to be missing from our lives until this act of resistance is rectified. All of life is served best when we each freely follow our heart's desire and vibrantly sing our individual song.

To gain the most benefit from this book, the reader needs to understand and then embrace the idea that our world is only a part of a much greater universe, one that is multi-dimensional, infinite, completely and intimately interconnected and, at the same time, mostly invisible to us. Since this vision meshes naturally with the newest scientific discoveries about the architecture of our universe, understanding the actual science can certainly help the integration of this idea, but it is not a requirement for benefiting from this book. While these ideas are well supported by our contemporary physics, many parts of this vision are technically unprovable and may remain this way for a long time to come. *Science requires "proof," therefore this is not a scientific book.*

The science presented within is only a general summary infused with some history. Explaining the more exacting details of the latest groundbreaking physics theories, such as *string* and *holographic theory*, is a body of work that I shall leave to those authors who are also deeply immersed in that science and have a talent for its presentation. There are a number of physicists and cosmologists who are doing an excellent job of this and if the reader desires more detailed science, many resources are listed at the end of this book.

At one end of the scale of human reason is our science, rooted in provable facts. At the other end is our faith, which is completely built upon our embracement of ideas that are wholly unprovable. Between these two bookends, containing the range of human reason, lie our beliefs, which contain elements of both faith and science. This book is based and built upon this middle way. It was conceived by integrating scientific fact, experience, intuition and faith–making it holistic, but fully human.

My personal journey has guided me through a long and sometimes confusing conceptual labyrinth, to a very clear field beyond. *As I have aged, I have lost some of the physical strength and abilities that once helped me believe that I could "move the world." In their place I have integrated a different type of knowledge and a set of new skills that make it easier for the world to "move me." This has made all the difference.* At every level of my being, I now have a knowing that our lives are a part of something that is much greater, and that we inhabit and understand only a small portion of this creation. I have also happily discovered that I am far from alone in this understanding because I share many parts of this "knowing" with a large part of humanity, probably even a majority. Most of us sense that life operates at levels that we cannot readily understand or easily discuss and this book is my attempt to facilitate more understanding and discussion.

THE VISION AND THE MODEL

The ideas that I will be describing are all built upon a personal vision that has been gradually evolving and moving into a clearer focus over the last 50 years. This is also a vision that closely parallels the new understanding about the structure of our universe that has been forming within the physics community. This science is now leading us to radical new insights and fresh perspectives about what our universe actually is, how it works, who "we" are within it, and what is now possible because of our new knowledge.

The ideas that I explore in this book first began as questions that came into my consciousness when I was a preteen; they continued with my early education in physics and my immersion into the world's social and political environment as a potential military draftee during the Vietnam War. Over time, partial answers first arrived as deep, intuitive feelings and eventually solidified into visual models or vignettes. Only lately have I attempted to describe these "visions" using words.

Relying on language and words for this task is a tremendous challenge–the architecture that I am attempting to describe lies beyond words and ideas. Even when describing simple three-dimensional objects, all words, even the most carefully chosen, are always poor substitutes for feelings and visual images. Since the ideas I am trying to communicate are structural, and they are also attempting to describe aspects of the multi-dimensional nature of creation, words, drawings and even models are inherently inadequate. For describing structural ideas, drawings, which are only two-dimensional—at most they imply a third dimension—are often more helpful than just words, and three-dimensional models usually communicate these ideas better than drawings. However, our words, pictures and forms are all built upon established three-dimensional concepts, so they all fail us when we are trying to explore new ideas that lie beyond our "normal" visual, conceptual and sensory fields. However, while we have no effective tools to understand or describe multi-dimensional space, we can often accurately describe, "what it is not."

Human beings are specifically designed to operate efficiently in our three-dimensional universe. Our brains are fully specialized for this environment. Our dualistic type of conceptual thinking works quite well within three-dimensions; and because we are specialists, we have not developed an effective language or capacity to describe four or more dimensions. Nature usually does not waste energy or resources evolving organs or structures that are not directly useful for species survival. As three-dimensional *beings,* we have not yet evolved an ability to visualize or conceive complete multi-dimensional form. Instead, we only can experience extra-dimensional space through our brief glimpses of the vague "shadows" that it casts upon our three-dimensional realm.

We are not able to visualize or understand the full extent of our universe because it is largely constructed outside of, or beyond, our experiences and concepts about form and time. It is not possible to create understandable models that demonstrate how the multi-dimensional parts of the universe work because there are no available tools or concepts that can describe multi-dimensional space from within our limited conceptual realm. "Form," as we understand it, does not even exist beyond our three-dimensional realm. Instead, we can only model and describe small bits and pieces of this larger idea. Also, we again must resort to language and concepts as we try to understand and explain the small and indirect "shadows"–those parts of the multi-dimensional creation that appear in our three-dimensional realm.

To describe these "shadows," I will use smaller and therefore more understandable pieces–a series of two-dimensional and three-dimensional metaphors, vignettes or analogies. Each of these "partial ideas" is designed to demonstrate different particular aspects, glimpses, slices, or "viewing angles" of the much more extensive and complex whole. These vignettes, along with verbal ideas and concepts that support these partial models, will all work in unison as I attempt to cobble together a patchwork image that communicates a larger vision.

The images and ideas that I am presenting can be thought of as 3D snapshots, taken from different angles, of the same subject–our multi-dimensional universe. Collectively, they allow me to begin to describe something that otherwise is unexplainable. While each vignette only hints at one or two aspects or qualities of the whole, it is my hope that over the course of this book a more complete pattern will begin to emerge from all these smaller pieces.

At best, the piecemeal picture constructed from these smaller models can only provide us with hints about certain aspects of our amazing and expansive universe. The actual universe is, and will remain, almost entirely invisible to all of us; most of creation is constructed in a "place" that exists beyond the range of what our minds and senses can comprehend or see. This "invisible" part of our universe, built upon the infinite and multi-dimensional space of creation, is the single reason so much of life seems strange and mysterious.

As I explain this new "vision," I will necessarily rely on words and drawings because these are the tools we have available. I will repeat and circle back around new ideas that I am trying to communicate; approaching most ideas from various directions to help different readers find the easiest personal entry point for their own understanding. Repetition helps trigger comprehension, especially when ideas being communicated are unexpected or from outside our usual conceptual field. *This access point to comprehension will be different for different readers, so if it appears that I am being too repetitive, then please skip over that particular section because it probably means that you already understand the idea.*

Some repetition is also designed to make each section more self-contained, allowing readers to more easily and freely skip around the book. Because of this, parts four and five of the book do not need to be read in any particular order. While the repetition may be frustrating for some readers who are already familiar with this material, it will be very helpful for others. I found that I needed many layers of repetition before I began to understand this information.

I will also rely on the old standard "shotgun" approach. By presenting a large amount of data and many examples, there is an increased chance that some of it will resonate with a reader's personal experience.

We cherish our system of binary logic–the logic of yes or no, and right or wrong. This type of reasoning is rarely questioned because it is such an integral part of our culture, especially in the West. We rely on it for every aspect of our lives, including when we are digesting and integrating new ideas, such as those in this book. Ironically, it is this logical reasoning that most inhibits us from understanding and integrating this new way of thinking and being. Our reliance upon rational binary logic therefore must be one of the first casualties of our evolution towards our next great paradigm.

As we explore these ideas, we will probably first understand the smaller component pieces as abstract *verbal* concepts. As these new ideas have time and mental space to settle and connect to other pieces, we may then be able to *visualize* some of their forms and eventually we might even start to *feel* aspects of these concepts. The final step of this integrative evolutionary process is when we understand an idea intuitively, knowing it deep in our bones. For most of us, this final level of understanding is likely to remain elusive because, as 3D specialists, we simply have not yet evolved the tools or senses needed to digest and understand creation at this level. However, even though we may not fully understand our universe, we are still an integrated part of it and we are always relying on its hidden, but fully integrated, aspects. We can learn to trust this mystery and flow with it instead of resisting its gifts.

This book discusses and relies upon many new discoveries, ideas and theories proposed by contemporary physicists and cosmologists, which have yet to be scientifically "proven." Modern physics is filled with a dizzying array of constantly evolving theories that most scientists consider "unprovable." *String theory*, and its direct descendent, *M-theory*, are amongst these because they exist in and require a structural space containing 10 or 11 dimensions. How can we possibly run experiments to test ideas built upon 10 dimensions? The type of thinking, and the process that is required for working in 10 dimensions, is completely foreign to our three-dimensional realm. To correctly design such experiments, we would need to understand and manipulate "things" and information beyond our conceptual limitations. Because of this, we expect that these theories will not be directly verifiable through our conventional experiments. Regardless, many physicists are embracing these untested theories as the best possible route to the elusive Holy Grail of modern physics–the *unification* of the four known *forces* within a single theory.

Within this book I also describe that nebulous but meaningful territory where science and spirituality merge. Ultimately they must merge, because they both seek to explain the truth about creation at the deepest levels. As I have explored this material for more than 50 years, I have developed my own personal inner "truth" meter. *To experience something as true, it had to make sense to my scientific mind, my intuition and my real world experience.*

Most physicists will agree with some of my conclusions and some will agree with most of them. A number of physicists have even proposed very similar explanations or interpretations. Others will be bothered by some of my assumptions or connections because these ideas are not yet scientifically verified, or the ideas may not fit their favorite models or theories.

Even though scientists don't know how it all works, they are constantly learning more about what the universe is not. Some of what they once thought to be unquestionable is now understood to be just approximate or only applicable in limited situations, and they always seem to uncover more questions than answers, especially in the leading edge of our scientific explorations.

When I describe what I think that these evolving truths mean for us, these are not just abstract ideas–all of these ideas have evolved and been well tested through personal experiences–some from my own life and even more from the lives of others. At the end of the day, *"The proof is in the pudding."* These ideas need to be more than just an interesting intellectual exercise–they need to have practical applications.

It has become clear to me, along with many others, that this new vision and way of being works very well in our "real" world. This new way of seeing the world brings new types of tools and methods that can be used, today, to make our lives much more joyful, powerful and meaningful. ***The concepts and lifestyle changes that will be discussed, when applied to our day-to-day lives, will produce real results–right here, right now.*** Once incorporated, they completely change our entire understanding about life. They serve to help us develop new tools and illuminate many of our more difficult and long-standing questions about life, our connections, and our unique relationship to the universe.

THIS IS NOT A BOOK ABOUT PHYSICS

This is not a book about physics even though the thoughts were originally birthed during the years that I formally studied this branch of science. I taught physics at the high school level, but I have never practiced as a professional physicist. I began studying *quantum physics* at the university level in 1969. This was before personal computers or calculators were readily available and because of this I spent most of my study time doing the necessary, but very laborious, hand calculations with a slide rule. I really wasn't very interested in spending hours manipulating these practice problems because what I really wanted to know was *"what does this very weird stuff really mean?"*

The classical physics that I studied in high school always came effortlessly. For me, it was just common sense and its application was obvious and, for me, that made it very exciting. However, once I started learning about the *quantum* realm in college that comfortable and direct connection to my logical and mechanistic worldview ended. With *quantum physics*, my professors could no longer provide satisfactory answers to my numerous *"what?"* and *"why?"* questions. This may have been because they were either equally confused or overwhelmed by its mystery and strangeness, or perhaps they also knew that this philosophical pondering was a diversion from the real job at hand, which was learning how to manipulate the equations. From their perspective, I clearly needed more time for my studies, and spending my time and energy on these more philosophical questions did not directly serve this primary academic need.

Being an extremely visual person, I have always been able to understand something once I formed the "picture" in my mind. Until my studies in *quantum mechanics*, those pictures came quickly and automatically. However, no matter how hard, or long, that I tried, I could not visualize this new multi-dimensional space where *quantum particles* lived and behaved in their strange and unexpected ways. I became an extremely frustrated student of *quantum physics*.

Fortunately, I was eventually able to direct my interest in high-school physics and *classical mechanics* towards engineering and architecture, which I found infinitely more understandable and satisfying. For me, this application was very visual, direct, relatively quick, practical and very functional. This change of direction suited my temperament.

However, for me, the questions that were raised in those college physics classes persisted. As the years marched on, an increasing number of philosophically inclined physicists attempted to explain in books and journal articles the possible meanings of the quantum ideas that they were exploring. With this additional help, for the first time during my journey into the *quantum* realm, some of this new physics finally started to make sense.

The physics in this book is presented so that a nonscientific reader can easily understand the most important principles. It is written more like a history book, as it describes the development of the new physics, which is presently re-shaping our paradigm. I include this because, for me, contemporary physics is what first explained parts of the mystery surrounding our existence. This new physics helped me understand why and how the machinery of life works on so many different levels. The physics was a critical part of my journey and is included in this book as part of my attempt to organize and share my personal experience. ***Understanding this physics is not a requirement for understanding and integrating the ideas presented in this book. It is not necessary for all readers to read this section but, for some, it may help them understand terms and ideas that once seemed complicated.*** Just knowing that science generally supports this new worldview will be enough for many readers.

Some readers may see little meaning or value in my desire to understand the hidden physical structure of our universe. We certainly do not need to understand its architecture to benefit fully from its existence. Many great musicians play beautifully without ever understanding music theory. ***This kind of analysis and detailed knowledge can actually become a growth inhibitor, for it can keep us focused and bound within the three-dimensional realm of thought.*** At some point during this process of "freeing our souls," our intellectual concepts will be understood to be a significant limitation–just another way that we shackle ourselves. Our thoughts are always limited to the three-dimensional conceptual framework, and any "thinking" that is to go beyond this boundary must find a way to free itself from this closed self-reflective system.

Therefore, if the physics section is not enjoyable, too difficult, or simply not interesting, the reader should simply skip it without any guilt or even a second thought. This book was not designed to be read cover to cover like a novel. As soon as a reader understands this book's basic ideas, the rest of the book can then, if desired, be approached randomly by just opening the book anywhere.

DON'T SWEAT THE VISUALIZATION

As I describe the architecture of our multi-dimensional "*universe,*" do not become discouraged because it seems extremely strange or impossible to understand or visualize. ***It actually is both strange and impossible for anyone to fully visualize, and it will remain that way.*** No human can really "understand" these ideas in the same way that he or she can understand most of the things in our day-to-day lives. These ideas are, by their very nature, beyond the limits of our conceptual thinking and sensory abilities. Our brains are simply not designed to understand or work directly in these realms. ***At the most, we can relate some of these multi-dimensional concepts to well-understood, three-dimensional analogies. We can also discuss, with a reasonable amount of clarity, ideas that help us to better understand "what our universe is not."***

Over time, I have developed a "feel" for parts of this architecture, but this "feel" is only focused upon the visible but fuzzy near-edge of this expansive reality–the edge that sits very close and adjacent to our three-dimensional realm. This edge is called our *conceptual horizon*. What lies farther or further beyond this gauzy veil is completely invisible to all of my senses. ***While most of the concepts and structures that we will be discussing are beyond our capacity for visualization or understanding, the effects or ripples from this deeper world are extremely visible and understandable. These have a direct impact on our world and our lives right here and now.*** If this were not true, there would be little reason to explore any of these ideas.

CONVENTIONS IN THIS BOOK

Whenever I discuss ideas such as "future," "beginning" and "later," I am referencing concepts that are time-based. *Forward-marching time, as we will explore, is a human creation. The greater universe views time very differently.* We have been trained, throughout our entire lives, to think that concepts built around time and space are absolute and real. They are, in fact, anything but absolute and real. While terms such as "time" and "distance" work for our basic communication purposes, they cannot begin to describe what these concepts become when viewed from the greater perspective of added dimensions.

Our unconditional and unconscious acceptance of the three-dimensional concepts that these words imply is a primary impediment that interferes with our ability to freely interact with the much more expansive reality that lies beyond these ideas and their framework. We will learn that, within the larger geometry of our universe, all temporal things unfold so that they can be seen and understood as always being fully interconnected, interactive and occurring at once. *At the deeper levels of creation there is no "before" or "after" and no "beginning" or "end," as all events unfold "outside" of time. Time, as we think of it, simply does not exist outside of conceptual limits of our thinking minds.* These extra dimensions and what they really mean, form the crux of what will, one day, become our next cultural paradigm. This book is written to encourage the reader to more deeply explore the endless possibilities that lie beyond our concepts and their preconditioned and predefined bounds. To this end, when I use common time-based terms, I am only using them as well understood cultural concepts to facilitate communication. When my meaning of a time-based term is slightly different from our typical usage of that word, or when the concept that a word usually implies is too limited for my meaning, I will add quotation marks (for instance, "future") to remind the reader to try to expand the meaning of the term beyond our usual conceptual boundaries. For the reader, these quote marks are used to provide a reminder that our common understanding of these terms needs to be questioned. I have also placed the most important actions, ideas or focal points in *bold oblique* and I have set apart useful, technical and scientific terms with *italics*.

Throughout this book, I will refer to the space and "time" that we inhabit and best understand as three-dimensional or 3D space. Since Einstein's groundbreaking theories, physicists have referred to the extent that he described as *spacetime.* Some scientists describe this region as containing three and one-half dimensions, or even four dimensions (even though Einstein's Relativity Theory does not actually describe a full four-dimensional *spacetime).* We can manipulate *spacetime* mathematically, and much of today's engineering even requires this added dimensionality, but what we live in, understand, think in, and walk through will be referred to as 3D space. This is the realm in which we live our everyday lives. In 3D space we normally only recognize a one-directional passage of time, which we will refer to as "the arrow of time." Throughout this book I will call this, our most familiar landscape, three-dimensional space or simply 3D.

I will also be speaking about our *universe* in two contexts. The first, which is the most obvious, is all of that which we can see, touch, observe and measure directly. This is our familiar and understandable *universe,* the physical *universe.* The second meaning is much more abstract and expansive. It includes the expanded but hidden aspects of our *universe* that we are just beginning to understand through our new physics. This includes vast regions that we cannot directly see, touch, observe or measure. These new regions exist both, within three-dimensional space and in a place that is beyond the form and structure, which we usually describe as physical. When I am referencing this more abstract meaning of *"universe,"* I will add quotation marks at first but, later in this book, this expanded version will be described using a different name–the *Multiverse.*

WE ARE REALLY ALL ONLY ONE

I will also be using the term "individual," a word that implies separation, even though, as we will discover, this separation is another artifice of our language, culture and limited dimensional awareness. I use these terms with full knowledge that as our perspective evolves, grows and changes to include more breadth and a deeper understanding, it will become understood, by everyone, just how directly connected we all are. ***At our root, we all are actually only different-appearing aspects of a single, throbbing, pulsating, and vibrating being.***

Our Western perspective encourages us to see ourselves as separate, competing individuals. At a deeper level of truth, we are only as separate as the leaves of a tree. From up close these leaves may all appear individual and look like they are in competition with each other for light and nutrients, but when our perspective expands to include the trunk and roots, they are then all seen to be integrated and important component parts of a single, grand organism. The tree metaphor is simple, but very powerful. Like leaves, we also are fully interconnected, but we don't usually see this connection because of our limited senses, perceptions and abilities. As we each evolve and expand our awareness of our extra-dimensionality, our interconnectedness will become much more vivid. Our common "trunk" is not visible to us because it exists beyond the conceptual veil of our three-dimensional worldview–it lies outside of our *conceptual horizon*. This interconnection also extends beyond humans to include all plants and animals, along with everything that exists in creation. ***As we evolve and learn to expand our awareness, these various name and form-based separations will dissolve, and we will naturally come to understand and embrace our full, resonant place within creation.***

We all think that we are separate and competing individuals, but just like the leaves on a tree, we share more than we can imagine.

MODEL HELPS US BETTER UNDERSTAND LIFE

The hidden architecture of the universe can help us to better understand human behavior and our lives. It can help explain why we have wars and profound spiritual opportunities at the same time.

It helps us understand why we build and destroy, why we love and hate, why we are born and die, what heaven and hell might be, what karma is, and even what happens after we "die."

A new understanding, built upon this vision of the universe, makes it completely clear that our "death" is never an "end," but rather it is only a displacement, movement or transition in the ever-changing flow of life. It helps us to understand phenomena like premonitions; past-life memories; time passing quickly, slowly or even stopping; love at first sight; seemingly impossible coincidences; or even the sudden awareness of a deep personal "knowing." It can explain things like why, occasionally, physical things might disappear from our lives, only to later reappear. This new model of our universe helps us to understand all these things, and so much more–many of the very things we have the greatest struggle with in our lives, suddenly make sense when viewed through this new lens.

One of the biggest differences with this new worldview involves our old concept of "time." *As we begin to understand the true nature of our timeless universe, it becomes clear that our sense of "time" is a very functional, but limited, three-dimensional concept. This has very deep implications. If we can learn to navigate within and around "time," and manipulate its flow, then what becomes of gradual aging and death? Within this new architecture, "before" and "after" do not exist as time ordered events– instead they can occur, or unfold in any order. Our old Ideas about the finality of "death" are completely torn asunder. "Before" and "after" actually exist simultaneously within the now moment. Ultimately, all of our concepts that are built upon "time," will be reevaluated.*

This new vision of the universe has been working, for me, very consistently and very well. In retrospect, I realize that since I was a child, understanding this architecture, and what it means on a functional day-to-day level has been a big part of my life's work. Because of this work, I am now a completely different person than I was 35 years ago. While I still have that familiar place inside where I can observe myself as unchanged, my outward personality and temperament are dramatically and fundamentally different from what they were when I first began this quest. Then, I was often troubled, unhappy and feeling very alone in the world. Today, I am not only happy, but I feel completely at peace, safe, settled and very well supported by my extended family of close friends with a shared or similar perspective. Beyond this, I am having tremendous fun, and my happiness is not dependent on having external circumstances go my way. I still feel anger and disappointment, but I do not become angry or disappointed, at least for long. My "reflex" reactions pass quickly as the positive aspects of any and every situation are discovered, witnessed and integrated. Old friends often remark about the difference, especially if they haven't spent time with me in many years. Since this new vision works for me, and many of my friends, it will also work for "others." This same awareness also helps me understand that these "others" and I are not even different *beings*.

PART TWO–THE MODEL

INTRODUCTION

I will now present a verbal description of this architecture: **"The Web of Possibilities,"** even though, as we will learn, this creation cannot be expressed in words–we have to begin somewhere. Following these principles is a list of recommended lifestyle changes that derive directly from this architecture. These are being introduced this early to provide context and direction as new ideas are introduced. Because of the early timing, these concepts are extremely undeveloped and may, therefore, seem rather unsupported, even strange or ridiculous; much of the rest of the book is devoted to describing this architecture and showing why this is actually the best current approximation for how our universe works. If these ideas are unfamiliar, refer back to this section as new concepts are presented–later, these principles and lifestyle changes will begin to make more sense.

If, on the other hand, these principles are already understood, then jump around and explore this book in any order–it has been designed to be approached either way.

THE "WEB OF POSSIBILITIES"–TWELVE PRINCIPLES

The critical concept of this book, the architecture, will now be introduced through 12 fully interconnected ideas that only appear to be separate. These ideas will be dissected and explained thoroughly, using different approaches and methods throughout the book. All 12 represent different three-dimensional interpretations or views of a single multi-dimensional principle–they only appear to be different because of the way our minds function.

1. WE ARE INFINITE–There exists, now and always, an infinite and fully interconnected structure, not unlike a woven web, built from the information for every possible outcome of every situation, choice, or thing that has ever been or will be possible. This is the fabric of all of creation. It exists, now and forever, yet it is always outside of time. It is within this infinite creation that we live our lives, for this is our real home. Within this structure, there is a well-designed place that is home for every possibility of everything that did happen or could have happened–ever.

2. WE ARE MULTI-DIMENSIONAL–This Web is built upon more physical dimensions than the three directional coordinates, plus time, with which we are familiar. We are not able to directly "see" or experience most of this fully interwoven Web; it is invisible to us because it lies beyond our physical senses and ability to conceptualize–it is not physical. This mostly invisible "Web of Possibilities" is the multi-dimensional and infinite fabric that forms the structure of creation: the place where we live and express ourselves in all of life's various forms.

3. WE ARE VIBRATIONALLY BASED–Physical form is of secondary importance in this Web. Everything in creation begins with information that originates as vibration. The entire Web is alive with vibration. Just where in this amazing vibrating Web our individual awareness expresses itself, in any given moment, depends on the resonant qualities of our individual soul. Physical form only appears as an indirect result of the way information is being expressed through vibration.

4. FORM IS AN ILLUSION–All of the forms that we encounter in our physical realm are only shadows or dreamscapes, even though they feel and seem very real. Our world is created with at least 11 dimensions, but we can only participate in that smaller part of creation that can be "seen" from within our own, limited, three-dimensional viewpoint. Form only comes into being through the separation that unfolds within duality. This is only one small aspect of creation. Our real and solid world is not what it seems; there is so much more.

5. TIME IS NOT LINEAR OF ABSOLUTE–Time, as we know and understand it, does not exist. Our sense of time is only because our three-dimensional minds (left hemisphere) must process information in a linear fashion; time is necessary to keep our thinking organized. All moments really only happen in the "now." This "now" moment is always our most direct access point to the fullest possible encounter with life. The "now" moment facilitates access to that part of our being that exists beyond thought and time. The instant we think about anything or try to explain what it means, the "now" is lost, it becomes the past or the future.

6. ALL POSSIBILITIES ALREADY EXIST–All of the potential possibilities for form and life are already expressed in an infinite number of other "worlds." Some of these worlds are identical to ours; others are very similar, and most are very different from our "world." These "worlds" are positioned in the fully interactive and multi-dimensional Web, so that all "worlds" are layered to be always directly adjacent and "parallel" to each other, allowing instant intercommunication and access. From our three-dimensional perspective, we usually only have the ability to consciously observe one of these "worlds" in any moment of "time."

7. OURS IS AN EVOLUTIONARY JOURNEY–We are an integral part of creation designed grow and expand in order to know and become one with everything in existence. Each evolutionary step is an expansion of consciousness; we merge with what lies beyond and our newly expanded beingness always includes all that came before.

8. WE HAVE THE FREEDOM TO CHANGE OUR EXPERIENCE–We can, and do, continuously and automatically move between these parallel "worlds." Every one of us is constantly shifting our viewpoint, or position, within this fully expansive Web. What we imagine is our "world" is actually many different "worlds" that are always shifting, changing and being shuffled continuously. That which is understood by us as the "I" is always expanding, contracting and migrating between different "worlds," which exist in many different locations within this amazing Web. The "I" always vibrates with whatever part of the Web that most resonates with our fundamental core vibration in any given moment. From certain perspectives, this manifests as movement between "parallel worlds." We each have the ability through personal transformation to consciously adjust, or tune, our fundamental core vibration; when we do, we begin to resonate within new locations or "worlds" within this Web. In this way we are always changing our experience within an infinite collection of universes. Since these are truly different "worlds," these shifts can and do completely change the way our outer world appears to us. Because of the way our brains function–employing cognitive dissonance, smoothing and interpolation–most of the time we don't even notice these shifts unless they are extremely dramatic, or the circumstances are just right.

9. WE ARE ALL PART OF ONE VIBRANT LIVING BEING –Everything in creation is alive with vibrational life and intimately connected with everything else. We are so closely connected with everything else, it can be said that at the deepest levels, there is really only one thing in the entire universe. Our appearance as separate beings is important to facilitate the creation of new possibilities. We ultimately all function as a single entity, whether or not this is our direct awareness. As we open to more of this amazing expansiveness, that part of us which is experienced as the "I" will expand to intermix and co-join with "others," but the core awareness of "I" will always remain no matter how much we evolve. That "I" part of our being does not change–it will continue to feel like the same "I." Through our evolutionary expansion we lose nothing except our old ideas and concepts. As we evolve more deeply, we expand and grow to eventually recognize our direct interconnection to all "others." Our direct resonant connection to source is often called "Love." Love is actually a place of being; a place that we can always choose to dwell within. Love is the place of being where we fully experience our deep interconnection.

10. LIFE IS ALREADY PERFECT–Because of this timeless interconnectedness, everyone is always in perfect harmony with the universe, and nothing is ever wrong or out of place. The universe, which includes each of us, is always in perfect dynamic balance. This balance can be found in everything that unfolds. It does not matter how our lives appear; they are always the perfect expression for being.

11. DEATH DOES NOT EXIST–Because time is not linear and form is an illusion, our concepts around the birth and death of our physical body are also only illusions. Birth and death represent one mechanism for shifting positions and journeying through this amazing Web. Death, like time, is only a three-dimensional concept. Our reflexive and unfounded fear of death is one of the main things that block us from experiencing life more fully.

12. WE ARE HERE FOR THE EXPERIENCE–We are here in our physical lives to encounter, embrace and know every corner of this amazing Web. Our only mission is to explore and participate in its every nook and cranny, no matter how wonderful or terrible it may seem. One reason for the appearance of many separate individuals is simply to facilitate this total exploration of creation. Through this diaspora of broadening experience and the eventual embrace of everything that we encounter, together we can all know and become more of an integrated part of "all that is." We will know true freedom only when we no longer experience ourselves as separate physical individuals, living within a limited amount of time, who are also expecting to, one day, die and then disappear. These beliefs are all part of the shadow illusion of our dimensional realm. This process of "knowing and becoming" through our opening to all of creation is the ultimate purpose of this strange and awesome journey that we call life.

This book is designed to develop, build, reinforce and explain these and related ideas for readers, so that they will then be more able to trust, understand and use this new knowledge. Since these twelve statements represent some of the most relevant aspects of this hidden architecture that can be expressed in writing, these ideas will be illustrated, expanded and described in many different ways throughout this book. The reader must keep in mind that the multi-dimensional nature of the universe will always mean that it cannot be fully or accurately described using our three-dimensional concepts and language.

For us to even begin to comprehend this more expansive vision of the universe, we first need to focus upon smaller and more accessible three-dimensional partial views or angles, which is why this book explains and demonstrates these smaller views or partial insights in so many different ways. As the reader moves through the book, a more integrated understanding of the new paradigm can begin to emerge through this collection of glimpses. Eventually, in much the same way that we piece together jigsaw puzzles, pieces will begin to merge and fit, as a map of this new territory forms in each reader's mind. This is exactly how early explorers of our world constructed the first physical maps of the places that they were exploring.

A temporary suspension of our normal rational analysis may help some readers with their process of integrating and understanding these ideas. *It is critical that each reader arrives at the point, where he or she understands, or at least temporarily accepts, the premise that the universe is infinite and multi-dimensional. Once the reader makes the leap and accepts these ideas, then everything else presented within this book will fall into place.*

I do not ask the reader to blindly accept the ideas of this book. Since many of these ideas are unprovable, that would be asking for an act of faith. *Instead, I am suggesting that the readers adjust their lives to better align them with these principles, and then just see how their lives change.* The material in this book is designed to support and explain these lifestyle changes and the "real life" potential of these, once strange, ideas.

This Web is the structural foundation of our universe. It is designed and constructed to support an *infinite* number of possible expressions of life. These expressions are always intimately interconnected, and, therefore, always fully intercommunicating and interactive. It might be more accurate to call it the WIIP or Web of Interconnected and Infinite Possibilities. *However, since the word Web represents such a universally understood visual model for interconnectedness, it is my preferred word symbol for describing the structure.*

I recognize that as our knowledge of the "physical universe" deepens, it is probable that the real structure of the cosmos will be found to include even deeper and more fantastic levels than those that we are discovering today. Evolution is a process; and with each new level of expansion, our explanations, at any given moment, will always be approximate and incomplete. Since our universe exists in a "space" that is built upon many more dimensions than those that we now understand, we will always run into one particular conceptual roadblock. *We are being asked to imagine multi-dimensional things and ideas using fewer dimensions than those that they actually exist within. This is what I will refer to, throughout this book, as "the dimensional problem."* Our human perception is contained within, and limited to, a smaller region of creation. This is the single reason we live lives that are surrounded by great amounts of mystery.

Humans have evolved to function, efficiently and well, in this 3D environment. Being 3D specialists, we have a very limited ability to imagine concepts beyond our known paradigm. We did not develop our ability to function in more dimensions because our expanded imagination was not particularly useful for the basic survival of our species, and species survival is what drives our genetic evolution. Through the greater wisdom of evolutionary design, the deeper shape and structure of our universe has been hidden from our view.

While the secrets and truths that are revealed through a larger dimensional awareness are not critically important for species survival, they still are very useful for our individual happiness, inner guidance and the evolution of our being. A better understanding of the deeper universe provides us with a useful vision and a new set of tools for living. With this added knowledge, instead of simply existing or surviving, we become more able to participate in a fuller expanse of creation; the universe becomes a much more inspiring and supportive playground for the evolution of our individual souls.

THE LIFESTYLE CHANGE RECOMMENDATIONS

In this section I will list practical recommendations that, if adopted, will create dramatic change within our lives. There is no need to understand the physics or even be interested in the science. Believing any of this book's conclusions–mine, or those of others presented here–is not a prerequisite for this personal experiment. If readers seek to dramatically change their lives, or if they just are simply looking for a different way of meeting life, then I suggest that they try out these lifestyle changes.

Other similar suggestions are mentioned throughout this book. *As an experiment, just assume, for a set period of time, that the vision proposed is an accurate and functional representation of the structure of our universe. Live your life from this perspective and just see what then happens.* See if your life–and the world you encounter–seems to shift towards something that feels much more peaceful, joyful, real and empowering; something that maybe feels more like "you." The most basic idea, the one to try out first is *"attitude changes everything."* This is a very powerful idea because it is clear to most of us that we have complete control over our own attitude.

This is a process; patience is necessary. Don't expect it to be fast or easy–for any of us. The attitudinal changes that will make a real difference can't be accomplished by simply changing thoughts–we must examine and modify our core beliefs, both conscious and subconscious. These existing beliefs are often invisible and always deeply rooted within our culture and our paradigm. Most of these core beliefs are rooted so deeply that, over time, they have literally become integrated into our physical bodies. To be fully effective, this process must create change at this deepest levels and this takes time, focus, trust and persistence. As our core beliefs shift, our *resonant vibrational* patterns will also shift. As we will discover, *life is all about vibration and absolutely everything that we perceive begins with vibration.*

As we begin to integrate these ideas, the first changes will probably be subtle. We may only notice a small shift in the ambiance or tonality around our lives–a delicate change of flavor. That initial shift might help us to dive into even deeper waters, and eventually our core belief system will be touched. This way of living then becomes a lifelong process–it is actually an *infinite* process.

As already stated, there is absolutely no need to understand the physics and math in this book. There is also no need to even believe that the vision of the "universe" that is presented in this book is real. All that needs to be done is make certain changes in our life and these will eventually have an impact on our core *vibrational being*.

Some of these changes are... *to:*

-Live our lives without fear, especially the fear of death.

-Live our lives as if we all are a part of one being–treat all others as we wish to be treated.

-Know that Love is always available. It is a place that we can go to any time we are ready for the experience. We miss the richness and depth of this experience only because of our choices and habits.

-Live as if we are creating our universe anew with every thought and feeling–we actually are.

-Learn to feel into ourselves deeply. Learn to find and feel into all of our empty and dark spaces–individual and collective. Feeling illuminates the darkness.

-Learn to also feel "others" deeply. Deeper within, all others are only different expressions of the same "I"–others can be experienced as the expansion of oneself.

-Forgive our self through learning to forgive all "others." There is no difference.

-Always remember and remind ourselves that we are so much more than just our "body and mind."

-Remember that every thought or word has great communicative power and instantly connects to everything in the universe.

-Live as if there is no such thing as a secret. Because everything is so interconnected, there is no place to hide. Learn to be impeccably honest with our self and all "others."

-Always remember that no other person needs to change his or her self for your world to change. You are the only person that can make this change for you—you are the only person who can ever change your own world!

-Live as if there is no such thing as a mistake. Instead, there are only new and different opportunities to deepen and enrich our experience and awareness. Every experience is a chance for learning and an opportunity for growth.

-Live with the knowledge that whenever we participate, everything changes because of our participation. Our focus, intent and attention completely influence the unfolding of events.

-Remember that there is always a natural balance in life. Our physical world requires contrast so all things have "positive" and "negative" aspects. Always seek to realize this balance.

-Practice finding the "positive" aspects that are inherent to every situation—all things in life can be viewed from many different perspectives.

-Always remember that everything is perfect—life is perfect, exactly as it is, right now.

-Stop rushing through life; know that "time" is not what we once thought it was.

-Give our loving attention to whatever is right in front of us in every moment; live fully in each and every "present moment."

-Get out of our own way. Embracing what is in front of us in every moment allows us to flow with the organic changes in life; and...

-Always be grateful for this gift of physical life, no matter how it may appear in any given moment. Develop an enduring "attitude of gratitude."

From this practice alone we learn to love all "others," and ourselves, in surprising new ways, as we fully enjoy this infinite process we call life. This way of walking through the world creates many new challenges for our conditioned minds. However, once this new approach is integrated, and the natural inner shifts begin to happen, everything about our lives will change in wonderful and unexpected ways.

Commit to trying these guidelines for a fixed period of time—there really is nothing to lose. If you try these methods and they don't work for you, the worst that could happen is that your world will not appear to change. There is no potential downside to this experiment.

These changes will initiate a deep and personal process of opening. This will seem difficult at times–it will often be challenging and sometimes it will even seem impossible. However, at other times it will flow so easily and naturally that we will find ourselves wondering why it ever seemed difficult. Growth is rarely an easy or straightforward process. As young children we all had our "growing pains." We banged our heads and skinned our knees because we did not yet fully occupy our bodies. In a similar way we are now discovering and learning to occupy more of our potential *being*. Any frustration and difficulty we experience are only "growing pains."

Many writers, speakers and workshop leaders have encouraged similar life changes through related approaches or technologies. Some of these people are listed in the resource section. Try any of these techniques, for there is no perfect or right practice. They all evolved from the same or similar worldview, and they all point to the same place: a life steeped in a deeper truth, a life of freedom. The absolute truth lies outside the limits of our ability to sense, conceptualize or even imagine, so if we desire to experience a deeper truth, we must be willing to explore far beyond what we once understood as real.

IT ALL EXISTS FOR US

These principles describe an architecture where ***"Everything that did or could possibly exist in what we think of as the present, the past and the future, already exists. It all exists together, as a continuum, in the singular place and time called the "now."*** Included is all of that which is destructive and creative, terrible and wonderful–all of it–along with everything that ever was, ever could be, could have been and will be. There are no exceptions. It all exists at once, now and forever, in the infinite and multi-dimensional "Web of infinite possibilities." This immense expanse of creation is only available to us through the "present moment," and it is the vibration of our "core being" that determines exactly which part of this amazing "everything" we encounter and interact with at any given "moment" in time.

This amazing "Web of Possibilities" has many similarities to the World Wide Web that is built upon the Internet. In this cyber universe we simply type in a new address and instantly we find ourselves shifted to a new place in the web of the Internet. Here, in the "Web of all possibilities," it is much the same, but changing locations requires something much deeper than just typing. Locations are only changed through the shifting of our inner *vibration*. While our thoughts support these changes, our thoughts, by themselves, cannot change our location or the appearance of our world.

Even if we knew how to access an "address" of some imagined place in this Web, we still would not be able to accurately predict the terrain or the type of adventure because of another important principle: **This Web is fully interactive and interconnected so every experience will change completely, and instantly, simply because we are now present and participating.** All experience is shaped by our participation. Each of us is an integrated and critical part of our every encounter and interaction. This also will mean that our personal experience is ours alone. In fact, there is no experience without the experiencer. Because each person's participation is such an integral part of any experience, two people can never share the same experience. Each of us will always experience any event from our own perspective.

As we each learn how to free ourselves from the layers of conditioning that bind us, we can become more like tourists in this Web. We will learn how to consciously explore, observe and participate more freely within this newly expanded playground. Through the expansion of our inner *being*, we will become more aware of all the different aspects and parts of this beautiful, elegant and unlimited creation. Every possibility will still always exist, but we will learn how to better "choose" those experiences that have the most meaning for us in our present vibrational state. *This "choosing" is not executed by the mind, but rather it is a result of the natural flow of our inner being. The best choices will always result from the uninhibited and natural resonant expression of our fundamental vibrational state of being at any given moment. We simply need to learn how to get out of our own way for this to happen.*

The process of learning how to navigate this landscape of many dimensions is not about becoming a "better" person. Understanding and using this model will not make us, or even our lives, better. *Each of us, and everything in the world is already perfect, right now!* This important principle is extremely ironic, paradoxical, and can be very difficult to internalize. *Understanding that everything is always perfect, exactly as it appears, is critical for the expansion of our freedom and self-empowerment.* We are all engaged in this process of evolution and when the "time" is right, each of us will be presented with just the perfect opportunities and challenges for the development of our unique *being*. This is the deep nature of this fully interactive process–all things unfold when the "time" is right. *The "right time" is when our individual inner vibration is perfectly tuned to interact or resonate with these particular experiences.*

When we assign values to our experience, such as good or bad, we are only inhibiting our own evolution and deepening. We have few tools for understanding the bigger picture because ours is an evolutionary journey. All of the elements from our limited 3D reference frame will continue to exist, and will still be present when we operate from an expanded dimensional space–life actually won't feel that different because it involves expansion; this process is inclusive, leaving nothing behind. As we evolve, the conceptual context will change so we will be more able to see the deeper connections and relationships. "Good" and "bad" will then be seen for what they really are–only the misunderstood labeling of critical and integral elements that contribute to the makeup of the whole of our *being* and our lives.

After expansion, we will still be presented with unexpected challenges. However, within this new awareness these challenges can more easily be understood to be fresh opportunities to revisit, explore and develop aspects of our being that are necessary for its full expression. *If we come across a situation that appears particularly difficult, we will understand that this is because some part of us is still resisting the natural flow of life and asking for deep level growth.* Any internal resistance to that which is being offered in the moment will always create difficulties and limit the full expression of our being. If we choose to, we move beyond this resistance by witnessing, learning, knowing, and then, finally, incorporating these resisted parts into a full loving embrace. This is a never-ending process, but it becomes much easier and fluid as we learn how to not resist and how to flow more naturally with life's deeper rhythms.

HERE FOR THE EXPERIENCE

An important living principle derived from this architecture is that we all are, in each and every moment, fulfilling important and integrated functions within this amazing evolutionary process called life. *This means that we are always fulfilling an essential role, no matter how our lives may appear.*

Nothing about our lives ever needs to be changed because we are always growing and evolving through every little thing we do. Personal and collective shifts in evolution happen in a natural and orderly process when the time and circumstances are right. Life is always showing us how to become more compassionate; and this is a continuous influence on our evolution, even if we are not conscious of this. Everything that we meet with in our lives adds to the richness of our adventure and contributes to our evolutionary progress. *One function of our physical world is to provide us with the raw material that will shape our soul to prepare us for the next stages of our evolution. We are living a significant and important lifetime, immersed in this process, and we are always contributing to the whole of creation, no matter how our particular situation appears. We each have an opportunity to live within only a small subset of this amazing creation, but it always contains exactly the encounters, relationships, problems, feelings and information that we require for our evolution. The challenge for each individual is to be authentic and true to our self. That purpose ultimately invites us to live our lives here on Earth as consciously and with as much gratitude and love as is possible. In this way we can always be fully participating in this thing that we call life. We are here to make acquaintance with all of this life, and then use these experiences to continue, and broaden, our evolution.*

We can do no better than to live a grateful and authentic life. Such an existence allows us to become fully acquainted with love, anger, the beautiful, the not-so-beautiful, happiness, sadness, joy, despair, ecstasy and emptiness. Every personality, every sensation, every misstep, every correction– all of it–is important to live and witness. There are never mistakes or wrong turns for, just by having this deep and personal participation in life, we gradually become blessed with a greater wisdom.

Guided by our own inherent wisdom and understanding, we gradually have the experiences and make the changes that affect our evolution. However, we can only make these changes when we are fully prepared. Our honest, conscious and heartfelt participation, in all aspects of life is what provides this preparation. It is precisely this exposure to all aspects of life that will lead each of us towards the next stage in our evolution as our *being* gradually becomes more able to play within a larger piece of this creation.

Understanding that everything is exactly right in each and every moment is a fundamental principle of this book; and the wonderful paradox that we will explore is that, at the same time, we simultaneously have the hidden ability to shape our adventure in very dramatic ways.

THE LIMITS OF WHAT WE KNOW TODAY

Our current physical form is an expression that depends on "time," and it is fully based in dualistic concepts. We usually miss the broader perspective that allows us to fully understand who and what we really are. This is a fundamental truth about our experience and the recognition of this truth is another foundation stone of this book. Because we are physical beings, we are always witnessing, experiencing and describing life from within our own self-defined and limited reference frame. Our size, the *energy* expenditure of our processes, our limited senses, our conceptual abilities and our physical location are all specific to our particular physical expression within the greater expanse of creation. It is impossible for us to fully understand things that exist beyond the natural limits of our senses, abilities and awareness. We simply cannot expect to know the *truth* of everything from where we now experience creation.

We, therefore, have a built-in limit–we are incapable of conceiving or fully understanding things that exist beyond this limit. This is called our "conceptual horizon." To understand our universe in more depth, the extents of our *conceptual horizon* must first expand.

Because of our current level of knowledge and technology, we do understand some things very well, and one of the things we know clearly is "what our universe is not." It is not solid, it is not limited to three dimensions, and it is not limited by the one-directional "arrow of time." We, ourselves, are a part of this universe, and therefore we also are not these things. We are not 3D bound, individual, vulnerable and very separate beings living in a hostile and competitive world. While we may not be able to say with any certainty exactly who or what we are, we can say with the certainty of our physics, knowledge and life experience that we are not limited by time or space in the ways that we once thought.

PARADIGM-BUSTING, OUT-OF-THE-BOX EXPERIENCES

Over the millennia, as we collectively evolved, we formed and solidified a consensus view of how we think our world and the greater universe works. ***This set of assumptions, concepts, values and practices forms our cultural paradigm. Our current paradigm completely determines what we think is possible and how we live our lives.*** A few small subcultures embrace significantly different views but, for the most part, the vast majority of humans are connected by this general agreement. We all have many personal experiences that fit and support this collective and deeply entrenched *paradigm,* and this reinforcement allows our common vision of the universe to seem extremely solid and real.

However, simultaneously, each of us also has a much less-discussed collection of personal experiences that do not easily fit into this collective vision. We all manage these unusual experiences in different ways. Sometimes we may not even recognize the parts of episodes that fall outside of this cultural box. ***Most of the time we are not even consciously aware of those parts of our experience that lie outside of our normal expectations–even if they are well within our conceptual horizon– because we all have, built right into our brains, a filter which psychologists have named cognitive dissonance.*** Our conscious minds are only capable of processing new information if it already fits with everything that we understand and believe: our known worldview. This means that things or experiences that fall outside of this consensus worldview are not even seen, recognized, cognized or processed. ***For all of us, our concepts are always built from the bricks and mortar of older concepts that our minds already understand.*** This unconscious and automatic psychological filter restricts our conscious input–it has evolved for efficiency and survival. *Cognitive dissonance* is our "conscious awareness *damper.*" To allow our minds to work effectively in our three-dimensional universe, strange or unexpected ideas are automatically cast aside and often not even processed by our conscious awareness. Due to *cognitive dissonance,* we may "miss" many of the more unusual aspects of our daily experiences, even though we might still sense aspects of these deeper truths.

At other times we may notice unusual aspects but not understand them, so we choose to remain quiet. If what we notice is unexpected enough to disturb our sense of wellbeing, we can then turn on our self-protective instinct and bury the incident by keeping our minds engaged in a more comprehensible activity. Some of us will recognize our "out-of-the-box" occurrences as the actual "paradigm busters" that they really are, but still consciously choose to forget or ignore them because of personal fear or confusion. We might be embarrassed or uncomfortable about discussing our more unusual encounters because, within our current culture, there is no context for processing these events. Some of us might attend a church or join spiritual or support groups in our attempts to normalize, discover meaning, or provide a language for our own personal "out of the box" experiences.

However, not all unusual encounters are lost in "the prison of our paradigm." There will always be some that break through the veil to become expressed as art, books, poetry, song, movies, insights, spiritual experiences and personal growth. Later in this book I relate specific "paradigm busting" experiences–some from my own life, and some from others.

LIFE IS FOR LIVING

As the reader attempts to piece together this vision, it is important to remember that it is not necessary to know, understand or believe any of this information. Life is created for the adventure of "living" and this is our primary purpose. *We are living our lives to their maximum potential if we live fully in this and every moment–nothing else is necessary. Life is always about engaging with what is being presented in each moment.* Life is perfectly designed for maximizing our engagement and insights and this book will explain why it must be this way. Our lives are always in perfect resonance with the totality of creation because that is the inherent nature of this architecture–it is fully interactive and responsive. Life is the totality of all this experience, every bit if it, all together, at once, resonating as a single vibratory symphony. Life simply "is," and we are here to fully meet with it, exactly as it "is." *Our lives may not always look perfect, wonderful or complete, but they are exactly all of that–perfect in each and every moment.*

For those, like myself, who rely on science and technology, it is possible that a clearer understanding of the hidden architecture of this place, where we are living out our lives, will help make the actual process of living easier, more enjoyable and less stressful. Having this useful model as a reference can help guide us, as we attempt to shift our viewpoints and attitudes about life. The architecture can serve as a framework for vetting our ideas and thoughts.

For me, understanding this structure clarified how we humans always have the potential to change our perspective of any and every encounter in life. Today, I understand that *real change can only be accomplished at the deep, individual, subconscious "root" level. This type of change only occurs when we shift our fundamental vibrational patterns at the very core of our being. This is a level of inner work that is unfamiliar to almost all of us, and yet this is the only place where we actually "create" ourselves and our lives.*

We can't make these fundamental changes with our minds, alone, because this real type of change only happens through direct meaningful experience. This results in an inner shift of our awareness and then, ultimately, our *vibration*. We make these deep-level changes only through living life fully while embracing and engaging in whatever adventure lies before us in each present moment. A well-disciplined mind can be a wonderful aid for this process, by helping us to focus on the "present moment" and guiding us back when we wander. However, our conscious minds can also become a hindrance, directing us away from difficult situations that our soul might actually desire for its own deeper self-knowledge.

In the grand picture–the gestalt–humankind will know the entirety of all possible human experiences. Through our collective availability, we will witness and integrate all our human experiences–all of which are of critical and equal value to *Being*. *Through this process called life, we will become "experienced," together, and know "all that is."* When Jimi Hendrix sang "Are You Experienced," he was asking if we are open and available for this. This is our purpose. This is life's purpose.

PART THREE–THE SCIENTIFIC JOURNEY

OUR AGING PARADIGM

MY EARLY QUESTIONS AND JOURNEY

What is this experience that we call life really all about? Why are we here and what is our purpose? What is death and how can we best live our lives? While these constitute some of the most fundamental questions about our existence, we have become accustomed to a lack of good, or even reasonable, answers to inquiries like these–fully satisfying and resonant answers have been completely lacking. The outside world consumes our energy, we become absorbed in family, finances and friends and then, lacking time, we give up searching as we gradually come to accept the assumption that any real answers must lie beyond our understanding. Instead, we focus our energy on survival and loving those close to us, all the while searching for ways to mitigate the pain of the inevitable suffering that we all experience. Some of us volunteer to work on the front lines, attempting to beat back the endless march of poverty, war, greed, oppression and disease; but still these conditions and old habits of the world persist, and often things even seem to only get worse, causing many of us to develop a sense of acceptance or even hopelessness. We might feel tired, lose hope and isolate ourselves from this world that we believe cannot, and will not, change. At the same time, we recognize that this is not the most ideal way to live our lives.

For whatever reason, much of my life has been centered on a continuous search for the meaning and answers to these fundamental questions. Fortunately, I am, along with everyone else who is reading this book, experiencing a very special period of history. Today, not only are legions of others are actively working to answer these same questions but, scientific advances, technology and interpersonal communication all have contributed to make this sharing much faster, easier and more meaningful. Because of when and where I live, I have received an amazing amount of help and support throughout my journey.

When I was thirteen (1963), my eighth-grade teacher gave our class the open assignment of writing about any topic that we personally found interesting. My chosen topic was titled "The Secret of Life" and was about the mystery, its various scientific and religious explanations, and the lack of cultural resolution between these two perspectives. The paper was either going to be about this or skateboarding because these were my two primary interests at that time; my fascination with skateboarding morphed over time, as it evolved through surfing into windsurfing, but my other pressing interest persisted, unchanged. This book is the updating of that paper and represents the current state of my search, after an additional 50 years of study. During those years much has changed–now we have scores of new tools, discoveries and resources that greatly facilitate this exploration.

I have always learned a tremendous amount about life from friends and others, their lives and their work. By now, however, I have also developed my own powerful and direct understanding, having accumulated more than 60 years of experiential and experimental results observing the transformation of myself and of others. I am fortunate to have spent the bulk of my adult years in Austin, Texas, an important nexus of alternative ideas and thinking. In Austin, I have been exposed to almost every conceivable modality of self-help, healing, and spiritual practice. I also live in the shadow of a wonderful university, The University of Texas at Austin. With the contributions of renowned physicists like John Wheeler, Stephen Weinberg and others, this university has been a leader in the development of the very physics that helps shape this book.

By nature and training, my habit, until recently, has been to not trust my intuition until I discovered repeatable hard data that backed it up. I was always looking for and relying on scientific data to support my thinking, and I was continuously curious and excited about exploring our physical world so that I could understand exactly how it works–science simply made good sense to me. Because high school physics seemed so powerful and logical, I was absolutely sure that someday I would be able learn enough to explain everything through this science. However, in my late teens, I began to have some experiences that were outside the expected or the predicted, and I found that I could not always process them using science alone.

While in college, I studied physics, math and other sciences, and after a half-dozen years working, first as a high school physics and math teacher and then as an environmental ecologist, I went to graduate school to study architecture. With architecture I finally found a wonderful and satisfying blend of hard science, engineering and materials science that was fully integrated with the mysteries of beauty, harmony, human interactions and the extremely intriguing creative process. Along the way I have also explored world religions, music, dance, art and interpersonal relationships and have worked thoroughly to integrate all of this knowledge and personal experience. However, the more I learned about what we do understand, the more I began to discover just how much greater, and still seemingly expanding, were the parts that we don't understand.

As my knowledge grew, at some point it became absolutely clear that it was not possible to understand everything through technology and science alone. I gradually began to understand life as more of a living process, one that is always organically evolving and growing. Because of the nature of creation, life's actual processes and inner workings are also evolving and may, by design, always remain at least one conceptual step beyond our ability to understand and explain. The universe evolves as time marches in the forward direction and therefore, from this, our temporal perspective, much of existence is yet to be created. Because of this, we may never be able to know or understand all of it; we will always be chasing something that is forever evolving. Moving at least one step ahead of our mind's ability to comprehend, it is creation itself that is evolving and expanding. ***From our culturally defining but extremely limited time-based perspective, it can accurately be said that we are creating life and the universe as we go!***

SCIENCE AND PARADIGM SHIFTS

The scientific discoveries derived from *quantum physics* and *relativity* have been rapidly and thoroughly changing our lives and culture for more than 75 years. Although conceptually different and even very "strange," this new physics has consistently proven itself to be quite valid and reliable–it has resulted in the production of a dizzying array of very practical, real-world devices. From this physics, we have discovered, developed and refined transistors, lasers, amplifiers, neon, fluorescent and LED lights, microwaves, CDs, DVDs, computers, atomic bombs, and atomic energy. Using this revolutionary science we have predicted new elements and particles, launched accurate space probes, developed accurate GPS systems, and achieved a much more detailed understanding of our "physical universe."

Along with all of these practical devices, the last 100 years of physics have also uncovered a large number of principles, interpretations and possibilities about our existence that simply don't make sense when viewed from within our existing, but now very old, *paradigm*. Our world has been operating from an old worldview that was based upon scientific understanding that is now over

500 years old, but today we are actively witnessing the emergence of a new and life-changing global paradigm.

The magnitude of this shift will be even more dramatic than the changes introduced by the last great shift, the one that overturned our previous "flat earth" paradigm. Our "flat earth" paradigm, which had been challenged unsuccessfully for about 1500 years, only began its final dissolution 600 years ago. That long-dominant worldview did not disappear quickly or easily; many deeply committed scientists, explorers, rulers and religious leaders gave their full efforts, and often their lives, to help break our conceptual and cultural "flat earth" shackles.

There was then, as there is now, an established, organized resistance to dramatic societal change. This natural type of resistance was, and still is, extremely powerful and enduring. Since changes of this large magnitude will always require enormous societal redirection or restructuring, they will always be strongly resisted by the existing power structures. This is a very natural response because many corporations, institutions and individuals are deeply vested in the status quo and do not want to lose their fortunes or privileged positions. Built-in resistance is not a "bad thing" for society because it functions as a buffer, keeping society operational by reducing or *damping* radical fluctuations or instabilities. This resistance can and should be understood as a natural and organic part of the process of change. Functioning like the shock absorbers of a car, built-in resistance can make the ride smoother for all of us.

Six hundred years ago the "flat earth" paradigm, with the Sun obeying a god's daily command to rise on one side and set on the other, was so much a part of life, that it was impossible for most people to even think about a different model. In 1543, Copernicus introduced a new scientific model for the universe that described a solar system where the Earth was no longer the center physically, philosophically or energetically. He understood that, with this shift, humanity would instantly lose its self-proclaimed position as the most central and important element of the entire universe, and we would become, instead, just a smaller part of a much greater whole. The public had no context from which to visualize this type or degree of change. Naturally, from the perspective of the Christian church that was built upon this "flat earth" paradigm, this new worldview directly threatened to erode the church's absolute authority and its hold on power. Therefore, this revolutionary idea was officially declared to be blasphemous; many brilliant and courageous scientists were persecuted by the church for introducing or spreading these "dangerous" and heretical notions. The once-universal belief that the Earth existed as the center of the universe could not, and would not, die easily.

Galileo, and many others, tirelessly and courageously developed and presented additional clear, physical evidence for this new vision of our solar system. These cosmological pioneers and the new science that they brought to light continued to suffer terribly at the hands of the church and state, but eventually this new worldview began to be seen as potentially advantageous by some of those in power. Largely because of the potential vast economic benefits connected with the plundering of a much more expansive planet, the exploration of this new idea began to be gradually encouraged by a few rulers who had the church's conditional support. Eventually, as real world financial rewards flowed in, adventurers, such as Columbus and Magellan, were granted state- and church-sanctioned permission and financial support, to begin the exploration of "new" lands that might exist beyond the edges of their old paradigm.

Through these direct experiments of physically sailing off the "edge," but returning, these early explorers demonstrated and proved that the world was round, and not flat. As vast riches flowed into the old world, this new paradigm became very real and through practical economics, it continued to solidify. However, even after the first of these successful real-world experiments, the old paradigm continued to persist and resist. Kepler, and then Newton, refined the physical laws of motion. While their contributions did a remarkable job of describing why large physical objects, such as apples and planets, behave as they do, the integration of the complete shift still took many generations. Eventually, the world settled into this new paradigm and mankind's understanding of the universe–and life itself–was forever changed.

Today, this 600-year-old idea is still our dominant current cultural paradigm. Once again we are facing the same type of conceptual challenge–our science and real-world experiments are pushing our old paradigm to the point of dissolution. Again, we find ourselves in the middle of a confusing process; driven by science and economics, our culture is dramatically rethinking its now-obsolete worldview. *We are just now beginning to learn how live with our new paradigm–the architecture of freedom.*

WE MAY ONLY BE TRANSDUCERS

Scientists, philosophers and science-fiction authors have made logical and consistent arguments that human expression might only be an artificial *virtual* adventure generated through something akin to computers or *transducers*. A *transducer* is any device that converts one form of *energy* to another. They propose that we might only be responding to signals from outside of our awareness, or reacting as part of some type of self-informed and self-programmed computer system. The entirety of what we imagine to be "out there" may be nothing more than the *virtual image* created by a "bio-program," or possibly an advanced *Artificial Intelligence* system. We may be participating in a completely programmed simulation, or we may only be video-game characters–it is entirely possible that we might only be computer-generated characters inside an advanced simulation, similar to the once-popular "Sim-City." There would be no obvious way for us ever to know what is really going on, because the program could be designed to make everything seem "real" from our point of view. It would probably be a closed system where "we" could even be programmed to "imagine" that we exist and our existence has meaning.

If we were just programmed, biological computers, then this would drastically shift the meaning of any of our "thinking," especially any analysis of questions like *"what is life all about?"* If our lives were generated by a computer, such queries would essentially become meaningless–at least from a human perspective.

A much more interesting option, at least from our perspective, is to assume that we are, instead, sentient and evolutionary *beings* of some type that are engaged in a meaningful and evolutionary journey. If this assumption is wrong, then even being able to make this assumption had to be an option allowed by the programmers and there is really nothing to lose. There is no downside to living our lives as if we are a part of an amazing evolutionary journey, but there is an enormous potential upside. If we live our lives in this new type of freedom and we are indeed *evolving sentient beings*, then our lives will expand as they become infused with wonderful and unseen possibilities.

For many reasons, this book assumes that we are, in fact, *evolving sentient beings*, and that life is not simply the product of programmed subroutines within some virtual creation.

IMPOSSIBLE TO PROVE

Today, with the scientific tools we have available, it is impossible to prove that the universe is structured and works in the way that I am proposing. It is always difficult or even impossible to test theories that reside outside of our conceptual paradigm–we usually lack even the basic tools to set up the necessary experiments. ***The concepts presented in this book are founded upon the fundamental idea that our universe is constructed from many more physical dimensions than the three we commonly recognize.*** It was difficult to get experimental proof of Einstein's *relativity theory*, and it required only one tiny step into this new and unknown expanse. His theory only incrementally modified our conceptual understanding of space–it required less than a single additional dimension or *coordinate*. With *Relativity*, we expanded our worldview from three cardinal dimensions plus "time" into a more integrated, dimensional system called *spacetime*. Some scientists refer to this as three and one-half dimensional, while others call *spacetime* four-dimensional. However, as we will discuss, it now seems that at least 10 or 11 dimensions are necessary to resolve the lingering issues between *Relativity* and *Quantum Physics*. ***If we are pushing our scientific limits to find the experimental proof for theories that exist in three-and-one-half dimensional space, then how can we possibly test a ten-dimensional concept with only three-dimensional tools?***

Another way to understand why we may not be able to explain the depths of our universe is to recognize that we rely on words and conceptual ideas to form our understanding. Words and conceptual ideas are only products of our current three-dimensional realm and they lack meaning in the multi-dimensional space beyond. The depths of creation lie far beyond what our words and ideas can convey, so alone, they cannot take us into this new landscape. ***However, these limited words and concepts can still be useful to expand our understanding of what creation is not. What remains will then help point us in the direction of deeper truth.***

As three-dimensional beings, therefore, we may never be capable of scientifically testing all of these ideas. We can, however, observe the changes to our lives, as we modify the way we live in our universe to better reflect the meaning of this new geometry. If we find that we get consistent and positive results, then this fact alone might be enough of an interim proof to keep us motivated and focused on this new vision.

LIFE IN A 3D UNIVERSE

FLATLAND–A NOVEL FROM 1884

It is not possible to directly imagine or visualize the expanded space that extends beyond our known three dimensions–we simply do not have the senses, tools or conceptual abilities to understand the amazing extent of creation. What we do have, however, is a direct exposure to and a detailed understanding of one-, two- and three-dimensional space. Using this knowledge, we can observe relationships that can help us understand more about the nature of dimensionally expanded space. The transition from one-dimensional space to two-dimensional space and the transition from two-dimensional space to three-dimensional space are completely comprehensible. Once these transitions are analyzed, we can *extrapolate*, to gain a sense of what types of things and relationships to expect with the next transition: the shift from three dimensions to four.

This process is similar to *reverse engineering*, and it is a valuable tool for helping us understand the types of things to expect as we expand our worldview to include more dimensions. With *reverse engineering*, a product is taken apart by others to determine how it was built. In a similar way, we can go "back" to 2D space, which we understand well, and then look at our present cultural, social or conceptual experience in 3D space and observe what changes. By backtracking to a world of only two-dimensions and then observing what is discovered when we reintroduce the third-dimension, we can predict many possible aspects and qualities of our next transition from three dimensions to four. This is exactly what E. A. Abbott did 125 years ago in his novel titled, *Flatland*.

This transition from two dimensions to three dimensions was thoroughly explored by Abbott in his 1884 English novel *Flatland-A Romance in Many Dimensions*. It is interesting that this Victorian-era novel was written about the same year that Einstein was born. When I first read it as a nineteen-year-old, I experienced a dramatic shift in my awareness as I was first introduced to, and then mesmerized by, the "dimensional problem."

While this work of fiction predates Einstein's theory of *special relativity*, it does not predate the original math that inspired his physics. From about 50 years before Relativity, the foundational mathematics for Einstein's work were described by Bernhard Riemann, James Maxwell, Marcel Grossman and several others less well-known; Einstein was only one participant in a much larger, scientific movement.

Flatland was specifically written to make two very different points. On the social front it was designed as a clever and cutting criticism of the Victorian social caste system, but in the scientific realm it introduced the public to the very new idea of extra dimensions. Abbott's book also does an excellent job of helping readers understand the conceptual and social challenges of a society that is meeting a new spatial paradigm for the first time.

Abbott builds and describes a detailed Victorian social environment and culture as he takes the reader slowly and carefully into the two-dimensional universe that he named Flatland. Throughout the novel he carefully develops his characters' two-dimensional mindsets as he constructs a very believable world around them. His two dimensional characters are so fully developed that, for me, they became completely real and I could fully experience what it would be like to live in this two-dimensional world. As Abbot takes us into this world, our thinking becomes spatially restricted to the point where we start to think, and even feel, like his 2D characters in *Flatland*. We might even have the experience of feeling "trapped" by the constraints of this reduced version of the universe.

Once this two-dimensional perspective is fully internalized by the reader, Abbott introduces a meeting with a three-dimensional character. As we make our acquaintance with this three-dimensional object (a sphere) from the limited two-dimensional Flatland mindset, we begin to see and understand the "dimensional problem." As we watch the lead character struggle to explain his encounter with three dimensions, it becomes easy to understand just how difficult, or even impossible, it is to describe three-dimensional objects from a two-dimensional perspective. Through this cross-dimensional interaction, we easily see that from the perspective of someone living a 2D existence, simple 3D objects will always appear as strange and unexplainable phenomena. At the end of the novel, the reader is then asked to imagine how difficult it would be for three-dimensional humans to make the transition to a world of more than three dimensions. *This means that the concept of extra-dimensional space was fully verbalized and described twenty years before Einstein's Theory of Relativity was published.*

TRY THIS EXPERIMENT

Flatland's 2D world exists on a tabletop-like surface where every person and object is completely flattened. In this world there are only two *coordinates* for movement: movement can be forward or backwards, left or right, or some combination of these. There is no such thing as up and down, so a Flatlander can't look or travel in the directions that we call up or down. *In fact, they can't think of, or even conceive of, an up or a down. From the Flatlander's perspective, this third dimension does not even exist because it lies beyond their senses and outside their ability to comprehend.* Everything within Flatland is seen only from this tabletop level or perspective—a Flatlander would see only objects or parts of objects that are visible at the exact level of this tabletop. Any object that is above or below the actual surface of the tabletop is not visible or discernible. *From the Flatlander's perspective, those parts of the objects do not even exist—they lie outside of their dimensional realm.*

To get a feel for this 2D worldview, sit at your kitchen table, place a chopstick or toothpick on the table and then lower your eye along the table edge until you are looking at the object from the height of an insect walking on the table–you might even imagine that you are that small bug. Close one eye and then slowly spin the stick and observe. What you see is a line that gets longer, and then shorter as the stick turns or rotates. Next, cut a circle, a triangle and a square, all about the same size, from a piece of cardboard and place them flat on the table. Close one eye and lower your other eye so you can see only the thin edges of the objects and observe. The circle, triangle and a line should all look about the same because we only can see a line formed from the closest edges of the object–we lost our depth perception by using only one eye. While this loss of depth perception is not an absolute requirement for a 2D worldview, it does add another useful experimental condition; by sacrificing our depth perception, we can better understand what it means to have sensory limitations. This demonstration illustrates how critical some of our abilities and senses are for perceiving and understanding our own worldview. *If we lack certain senses, we will miss information, even if it is fully present and available.*

LIFE IN FLATLAND

The Flatlanders of Abbott's novel lack depth perception, so, for them, the differences between circles and triangles can only be noticed by touching or feeling the sharpness of the points. As we observed, until they are rotated, all shapes will look similar–they will look like a line. When circles– the priest class in Flatland–are turned or rotated, they don't change shape at all; they always look like unchanging lines. However when triangles–the commoners in Flatland–are turned, they become shorter, then longer and then shorter again, and so on. Rotating squares look much the same as triangles, except their changes would be more frequent for the same number of turns–each time a square rotates, it will change between longer and shorter, four times, instead of the three times for a triangle.

Flatlanders describing the difference between triangles and squares could introduce the idea of "time." For example, Flatlanders might say that the square changes its size more frequently than the triangle. From our broader 3D perspective, we can easily see that it is only their geometry that is different. "Time" has nothing to do with their real differences. "Time" is used to describe these shapes in Flatland only because of the conceptual limitations caused by the 2D geometry. Other qualities of 2D shapes will also be invisible to Flatlanders, because of their limited perspective. Since their senses, perspective and conceptual mindset have no understanding of "above," they cannot observe these simple shapes from above and count the sides. To do so would require an extra dimension. This is one example of *dimensional limitations* that lead to the "dimensional problem."

Flatlanders do have a method for perceiving the differences between shapes. Touching a square, would feel slightly different from touching a triangle because the points are slightly less sharp. Since these differences are very subtle, it would take a great amount of skill and sensitivity to distinguish a ten-sided figure from a nine-sided figure. They might describe the two shapes as "feeling" different.

To add emphasis to his social commentary on Victorian life, Abbott chose the simple 2D line to portray the women of Flatland. The significance of this shape can be demonstrated on our tabletop by using a toothpick or chopstick; the toothpick appears to dramatically change in length as it is rotated. In Victorian England women were seen as inferior partly because they were deemed so mercurial; they often appeared to change emotionally and were extremely "unpredictable." The Flatlander could only see females (lines) easily when they were viewed from the side. When turned so they were pointing their heads or feet towards the observer they became almost invisible. This stealth-like quality and their sharp point meant that the women of Flatland were known to be extremely dangerous; if angered, they could easily use their point as a weapon.

In Flatland–or any two-dimensional system–we are able to describe the differences between different shapes by talking about how they change with "time." Terms like *rate of rotation* or *frequency* might become part of this descriptive vocabulary. If Flatlanders could add one more dimension to their perspective, meaning if they were able to see common objects in 3D as we do, they would easily see that these different classes of citizens are all distinct shapes such as triangles, squares, rectangles and circles. They would also realize that it is not necessary to use *time* as part of the object's description. From this new expanded perspective they would see that these actual shapes do not change over "time."

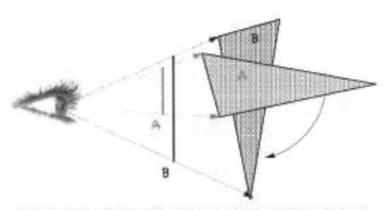

In Flatland the inhabitants lack depth perception and only see what is in their flat plane. Looking from above it is easy to see that triangle A and triangle B are the same shape and size. Their only difference is one is rotated. Flatlanders can not see from above. All they perceive is the line A and the line B, which are different lengths. As the triangle turns the Flatlander perceives a line that changes length as "time" passes.

If Flatlanders could suddenly understand three dimensions, at that moment their entire view of their universe would dramatically change. Of their many potential discoveries, two are of particular importance for this book. First, they would discover that they did not understand or interact with the full extent of objects that occupy their own realm. For example, even though the entire triangle is within their world, they never "see" the shape of a triangle; they only observe a line that changes length. The second discovery is about the role of "time" in their "universe." ***In the dimensionally restricted Flatland, "time" is functioning as a clue or a "window" into the deeper structure and workings of the next dimension!***

Like Flatlanders, we also only interact with that limited part of creation that is visible from within our dimensional realm. Because of the built-in limitations of our 3D reference frame, we also describe many things using "time," not knowing that we are really trying to describe qualities belonging to or beyond our dimensional space that are not visible or describable from within it.

A SPHERE VISITS FLATLAND

Once Abbott fully establishes the nature of the culture, perspective, characters and ordinary life in Flatland, a fully three-dimensional object, a sphere, visits Flatland. Imagine yourself living in a flat land; a tabletop world where you can't look up, and you can't look down. You can't see any parts of an object that lie above or below your tabletop because "above" and "below" don't even exist in two-dimensional space. It is completely impossible for a Flatlander to even understand the idea of "up and down." A Flatlander can only see that which is straight in front of them, and only those parts of the objects that are intersecting the flat plane of their world, the tabletop.

Continue to imagine yourself in this world, as a sphere comes to visit your flat land by moving through 3D space until it almost touches your tabletop world. When it first makes contact, that is, when the sphere just touches or sits on the table, only the bottom tip of the sphere actually touches or intersects the surface plane of Flatland. At this first moment of contact, the observers in this flat world see the sphere as a small point, or dot–remember that the Flatlanders cannot look up and see the rest of the ball that is sitting above the tabletop. All that can be seen from their perspective is that point where the sphere first touches.

Imagine this sphere as a magic ball, one that can pass through a table–or as a ball that is slowly being dipped into a flat pond. This second image might be easier for many readers to understand. The sphere continues to move through Flatland, but as the sphere passes through the plane of the tabletop (or the top surface of the water) that initial single point of contact then grows to become a larger circle. As the sphere or ball continues to move, the Flatlander will see the circle growing bigger because a thicker part of the ball is passing through the tabletop (or the surface of a pond). To the Flatlander, lacking depth perception, this circle looks just like a line that gradually grows longer over time. Once the equator or midpoint of the ball passes through the tabletop, the circle will begin to get smaller. At that point, from the Flatlander's perspective, the line starts getting shorter, until, once again, it becomes only a small point or dot; this is what they see at the very last moment of contact.

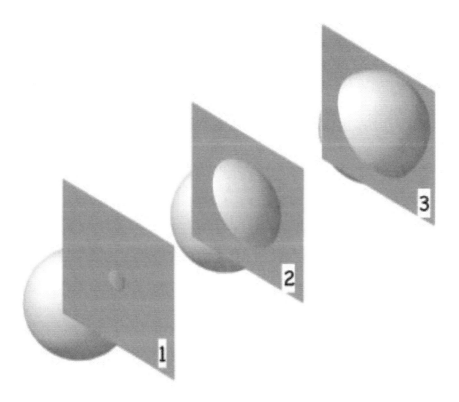

A three-dimensional sphere passes through the flat, two-dimensional world called Flatland. Flatlanders can't see above or below their flat plane of a world. First they see a dot which becomes a very small circle (1). As time passes the circle gets larger (2) until it reaches the middle (equator) of the sphere (3). From this point the circle begins to get smaller and then eventually it disappears entirely.

Then, in the very next instant, the sphere disappears entirely from Flatland, having passed beyond the surface plane of the tabletop (or pond surface). From the Flatlander's perspective, the sphere has mysteriously disappeared. To the three-dimensional viewer, it is still there, but it has simply moved beyond the flat plane of Flatland.

OURS IS A FLATLANDER'S EXPERIENCE

From the Flatlander's perspective, this "alien" visitor to Flatland displayed very unusual behavior, and in their attempts to describe this behavior, the Flatlanders required the concept of "time." They might have said something like *"it grew to a large size in one minute and then shrunk just as quickly before completely disappearing."* This entire event was far beyond their ordinary experience; this strange and curious object broke all the "normal" rules. It came from "nowhere" and "disappeared" just as mysteriously, and while it was visible, even though it was a circle, it continuously changed in size. What was this mysterious object? What happened to it? How did it become invisible? Why did it grow and shrink over time? Describing it and its behavior would be especially confusing for Flatlanders because unlike triangles, squares or lines, normal circles don't normally change size. From their perspective this sphere was clearly a magical or paranormal object not fitting any of their logical "rules." If you lived in a two-dimensional world, but suddenly "saw" three dimensions and then tried to describe this experience to others, you would likely be ridiculed or perceived as crazy. This is exactly what happened to the lead character of the novel.

From our three-dimensional perspective, there is no mystery at all since the physics and geometry of a sphere intersecting a flat surface are quite understandable and explainable. It is neither strange, nor paranormal, and all the mystery can be explained through simple 3D geometry. However, this geometry requires understanding three dimensions and this is beyond the conceptual reach of Flatlanders. The ability to perceive in three dimensions is a type of awareness that only exists beyond their *conceptual horizon.*

I reference this part of his story to illustrate that within our three-dimensional world, phenomena that appear mysterious or seem to be changing in very strange ways over "time," might become quite easy to visualize and understand, if we were suddenly able to employ additional dimensions. This is a key idea to grasp in this book, so I will repeat it in a slightly different way. ***Strange or unexplained phenomena and even our understanding of the way things age or change with "time," may simply be our limited way of glimpsing or understanding the nearest edges of extra-dimensional space.***

Take a moment to contemplate how simple objects such as spheres appear when seen through the eyes of observers who occupy a more dimensionally-limited, reference frame. This Flatland-type exercise demonstrates the difficulty we might have when we are imagining how four-dimensional things would appear to us from within our three-dimensional reference frame. We can only observe odd-looking pieces, parts or views of these "objects" that otherwise exist in more dimensions–no human will ever be able to fully understand a 4D object from a 3D perspective. In fact, as illustrated in Flatland, we are probably not even experiencing the full range or extent of the objects' 3D qualities. Like the residents of Flatland, who don't have depth perception, we lack the senses to even perceive everything in our own (three-) dimensional space–our perceptions that involve "time" are particularly misunderstood.

I have been speaking of "objects" but everything discussed also applies to people, ideas, energy and everything that is part of our three-dimensional reference framework. ***Behavior and phenomena that seem complex or strange from our limited perspective will suddenly become clear, resolved and even simple, when viewed from an expanded, dimensional reference frame.***

OUR WORLDVIEW

VIEWPORTS

Throughout this book I use the expression, *viewport*. This is a wonderful term that I borrowed from a software program used in my architectural practice. Within this software program, *viewport* refers to a special graphic presentation "window" used to hide certain elements in a drawing, so that it becomes easier to understand. The original drawings are typically constructed in three-dimensions, but sometimes showing all three dimensions can be confusing for a presentation to clients or subcontractors because there is too much *information*; the amount of *information* can be so overwhelming that the critical parts become obscured. The *viewport* is then used to simplify and customize whatever *information* is necessary for that particular presentation. It can be set so that only two dimensions are visible at any given time, and any extra data that is not useful (technical notes, dimensions, specifications, etc.) for that specific presentation are also hidden. This ensures a simple and direct presentation of the specific and critical *information* for each viewer. The other *information* isn't gone or lost, but rather, it is simply no longer visible. ***The extra information is still present, but it is now invisible, because it has been placed, in essence, beyond the viewer's senses.*** Everything that we are permitted to see is intentionally controlled by the software settings for the *viewport*.

This metaphor is a useful tool for this book because it can be used to describe our 3D experience within a multi-dimensional universe. We will always have a limited view or *viewport* of the much fuller universe and we are not capable of understanding and processing all of the available information; the number of dimensions we "see" is only three, plus that misty window into the fourth, which we can relate to "time." We experience life from within the limited parameters of our *viewport,* even though we understand from the physics and the math that there are more unseen dimensions. ***To help us function efficiently in our 3D world, our viewport filters out the non-critical or extraneous information.***

The physical size of this *viewport*, our reference frame, is presently limited to 15 billion *light-years*, in any direction, because this is the outer limit of the physical universe that we can presently observe with our astronomical tools; this is also the distance that light has traveled since the cosmological event called the *Big Bang.* Our *viewport* is also limited in size to things that are within the range of our senses and our tools. If we were much smaller or larger, our direct observations would be very different. Additionally, our *viewport* is restricted by the vast reduction of *information* filtered through brain processes, such as by *cognitive dissonance* and the known limitations of our five recognized senses. All of these factors work together to filter the quantity and quality of the *information* that we consciously process. Our "point of view" is always framed by the information that actually gets processed. We interact with very little of what lies "beyond" or "deeper within" because of the preset limitations and parameters of our *viewport*. As a result, we see and participate in only a very small, limited slice of the full creation! We will also discover that "beyond" and "deeper-within" are equivalent ideas if they are understood from a more expansive *viewport*.

Throughout the rest of this book, I will refer to our restricted reference frame as our "viewport." Our "viewport" will be defined as the "window" through which we on Earth meet and experience our particular slice of the universe. Our *viewport* defines our human realm. The precise extents of this *viewport* will be slightly different for each different individual, but generally all of our individual human *viewports* will fall within a defined range of common and expected experiences.

Einstein once described the nature of our *viewport* this way: "Nature shows us only the tail of the lion, but I do not doubt that the lion belongs to it even though he cannot at once reveal himself because of his enormous size."

As quoted by Abraham Pais in *Subtle is the Lord: The Science and Life of Albert Einstein* (1982)

PROJECTIONS

To the residents of Flatland, as the sphere passed through their world, it appeared to be a line that changed length as time passed. Two-dimensional objects, such as triangles and squares, also appeared as lines that changed in length as they turned, and "time" was also used to help describe their differences. These 3D-to-2D relationships can all be described by an important type of mathematical function, called a *projection*. Understanding the concept of *mathematical projections* is integral to understanding many of the ideas within this book. Common examples of different forms of *projections* that we see every day are the images we see in movies, mirrors, maps, photographs and shadows. With all of these, what we experience is never the actual object; instead, we interact with only an image of the original object–movies even use the actual term *projection* to describe this process. With the movie type of *projection,* actors play their roles in three dimensions, but the process reduces the presentation of their roles to only two dimensions, both on the film and on the screen.

In Flatland, the actual "real" visiting object was a sphere, but because their *viewport* was limited to only two dimensions, the sphere appeared to the Flatlanders as a circle that changed size with time. This circle was the *projection* (similar to a shadow) that the three-dimensional sphere "cast" onto the two-dimensional plane of Flatland.

If we were to stand in our backyards and look at our shadows, we would be looking at *projections* of our standing 3D bodies onto the flat (2D) plane of the ground. This *projection* or shadow is not the object, but rather it is the reduced (information) or *flattened image* of the object that has been transferred, intersected or mapped onto another system of *coordinates*. In this case, this "other system" is the flat (two-dimensional) plane of the ground.

*A shadow lying entirely on the flat plane of the surface
of the Earth is a 2D image or projection of a 3D object.*

If there were flat, bug-like *beings* living entirely on the flat surface of the Earth, unable to look up or down, much of their awareness of us would be limited to encountering our shadows. From the bug's perspective, imagine how very difficult, unpredictable and mysterious their understanding of humans would be. How could they even begin to describe us from their encounter with our shadows alone?

On Earth, we see and understand everything from our three-dimensional *viewport,* even though, as we will explore, the universe is actually built from many more dimensions. **What we observe and experience on Earth is only the very limited projection of our full multi-dimensional being. We meet with only the shadows that intersect, interact, or map onto our more dimensionally-limited 3D world. This means that we are seeing and experiencing only a small slice or "image" of the real thing.**

Throughout this book I use the terms *projection, shadow, image* and *dreamscape* to describe the same phenomenon. *Projection* is the mathematical term, while *shadow* more accurately describes our sensory awareness. *Dreamscape* and *image* more closely relate to the psychological aspects. Physicists have recently been referring to the term *hologram* to describe the image quality of our 3D, physical world. This is an excellent metaphor and we will later discuss *holograms* in depth. (*Holograms*, when fully understood, become even more interesting because of the way all *information* may be stored in our universe.)

PROJECTIONS CREATE ARTIFACTS

ARTIFACTS AND ERRORS FROM DIMENSIONAL REDUCTION

As we explore the concepts, ideas and worlds that unfold through extra dimensions, we always need to keep in mind a very important principle–**whenever we interact with or view something in fewer dimensions than its actual full geometry, what we encounter is only a slice, a small piece, of the full expression of the actual object, idea or experience.** We are not capable of visualizing or fully understanding a multi-dimensional object, experience or concept because our input and processing is always limited by the extents of our 3D *viewport*. The parts we make contact with in our *viewport* are only the *projections* of the *projections,* or the shadows of the shadows. They are *projected* or "cast" from the original objects and filtered as their images pass through multiple dimensional realms before they eventually intersect our 3D world. What we eventually see and

40

encounter will not even resemble the real thing because, through this process of "dimensional reduction," it is distilled and simplified. We only experience the shadow aspects that are understandable by us. This is another critical concept in this book. ***This reductive process, which involves multiple levels of projections, can be called our "dimensional filter," and this is the primary reason for the appearance of mystery in our lives.***

For the inhabitants of Flatland, as the three-dimensional sphere passed through their *viewport,* it appeared as a circle that changed in size over "time." "Dimensional reduction" plays tricks on our sensory systems, specifically when it involves our ideas of "time" and space. Later in this book we will discuss Einstein's realization that the *force* we call *gravity* is only a three-dimensional expression of something that is unfolding within a greater geometry–one that integrates both space and "time."

In order for this book to make complete sense, these fully related concepts of "dimensional reduction" and "dimensional filtering" need to be clearly understood. The simple and common task of making a map can help us better understand these ideas. (I use the quotes above because these terms have specific meanings in physics and math that are somewhat different from how I am using them in this book.)

Mapmaking

Mapmaking is useful for demonstrating the profound loss of information that is often the result of processes that include "dimensional reduction." Mapmaking involves taking a three-dimensional (3D) object, such as part of the surface of our curved Earth, and then reducing its information so it can be placed within a flat, two-dimensional representation called a map. This can be accomplished mathematically with special *algorithms* or formulas. Because a two-dimensional map could be drawn on a piece of paper or smartphone screen, we are essentially eliminating or flattening the third dimension. Another way of saying this is, when we use a map, we are viewing a three-dimensional object through only two dimensions–we "lose" *information* from the third dimension. Here is an everyday example of "dimensional reduction" that can be easily understood by all of us.

With mapmaking, the larger the piece of the Earth that is mapped, the greater the information loss and inaccuracies. This is because a bigger part of the Earth's curve is involved and, therefore, we have to flatten more of the third dimension. The larger the extent of the Earth's curve in the piece being mapped, the greater the distortion caused by this "dimensional reduction." There is no fully accurate way to express the entire Earth on a flat piece of paper. The information contained in the Earth first needs to be "filtered" before it can be presented on paper.

When maps are constructed, the only type of map that can be accurate over large distances and in all directions are globes, because these model the actual 3D shape of the Earth–unfortunately globes do not fit in our glove boxes very well. Flat maps function quite well for general directions in small cities, towns, or even state-to-state travel because, with a small part of the Earth involved, the amount of lost curvature of the Earth is not as significant. When we begin to look at maps for longer journeys, such as Panama to Greenland, the curvature of the Earth becomes a much greater factor, and the various common types of 2D maps become inaccurate and distorted in certain ways.

Different types of *map projections* use different *algorithms* to *map* points onto a 2D surface. An *algorithm* is the step-by-step mathematical procedure, or *formula,* for making such a transformation. All types of *projections* have inaccuracies built into them somewhere, and often there is more error as one moves farther away from the central, or focal, area of the map. Every type of map has its own distinct problems and different types of *projections* handle these distortions differently.

A way to visualize the map-making process and understand its potential problems is to create a model that demonstrates the issues involved. We can make a simple model by finding (or imagining) one of those spherical paper globe lamps that are made with nested wooden or metal hoops–these hanging paper lamps can often be found in Asian import stores. If we compress one of these lamps so that all the hoops flatten concentrically (rings inside of rings) we have made a flat surface from a sphere and therefore reduced a three dimensional object to only two dimensions; this is often the way these lamps are packed for easy shipping. Next, imagine that this lamp is transformed into a globe by printing a map of the Earth on its surface; this produces a fairly accurate world map. Now if we press it flat, ring-by-ring, with the North Pole in the center, our three-dimensional globe then becomes "dimensionally reduced" into a flat two-dimensional map. We now have a map: a two-dimensional representation of our three-dimensional planet. Through this process information is lost, discarded and altered, meaning there will always be inaccuracies, distortions, aberrations or artifacts that are built into this or any flat-map description of our spherical Earth.

Once our hoop map is flattened, the first problem that we might notice is we only see one-half of the globe–the back (south pole) is no longer visible. Of course, as a three-dimensional being, we could just turn it over, but this requires using a third dimension and this map is now restricted to only two dimensions. This means that we have "lost" some *information,* which is one type of inaccuracy. Another inaccuracy is found in the measurement of distances. If we were to drive between New York and California along a "straight" path along the curved surface of the Earth, this path would be longer than the "straight" path measured directly on the flattened map; following the arc of the curved Earth is always longer than the straight chord path between the points. The straight-line measurement between points on this flat map will always be shorter than the length of the direct path that follows the surface of the Earth or a globe–we have lost the information that describes the curvature. A third type of inaccuracy is seen with the measurement of angles. As we analyze angles between three cities, we will find that these angles, and, therefore, accurate directions between cities, vary when we move from the globe to the flat map. Both distances and angles are less accurate on the map.

However, there is some *information* that will not change. If viewed from the top, the distance between cities that are traced along the arcs of the circular hoops, or any curved path parallel to these, will still be accurate. (If the center of this type of map happens to be the North Pole, then these "hoops," or arcs, will also represent the global lines of latitude.) This means that for this particular *projection*, if we confine our trip to following these curved lines, the map, the globe and the actual trip will all measure to be the same distance. Some things change and some don't and when using maps this can cause complications. Accurate GPS location requires the computer program to compensate for this built-in inaccuracy.

The compressed-hoop model is only one way that a map can be made from a globe. It represents only one of the many types of possible map projections.

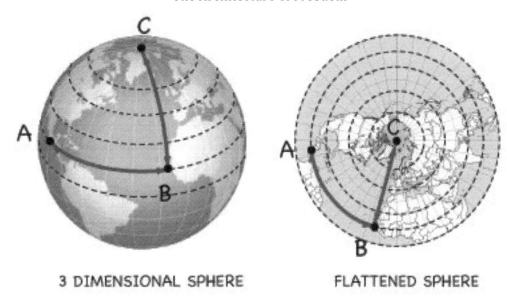

3 DIMENSIONAL SPHERE   FLATTENED SPHERE

*Projections always change information. If the globe is flattened into a map,
distances along lines of latitude (from "A" to "B" for example) remain the
same when following the curve. Almost all other distances change.
"B" to "C," becomes a shorter distance in the flattened map version.*

Another type of *projection* could be made from an operation that is similar to flattening an orange peel. In this type of *projection* the middle (equator) is mostly intact and relatively accurate but the "map" is shredded or torn as we move towards the poles. One example might look like this.

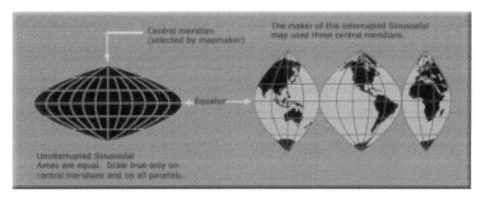

*Sinusoidal projection of our globe on a flat piece of paper. It is easy to
imagine cutting this out and taping it back into the distorted ball shape.
However, it might be hard to plan a trip and follow our route on this map
unless you were only traveling along the equator.*

To make a map that is easier to use for directions and other day-to-day functions, the more familiar Mercator projection is often used. In this *projection*, the lines of latitude and longitude are presented orthogonally, so the orange peel gaps are now stretched instead of torn at the top and bottom poles. However, this type of projection also makes for progressively larger distance and area inaccuracies as one moves towards the poles.

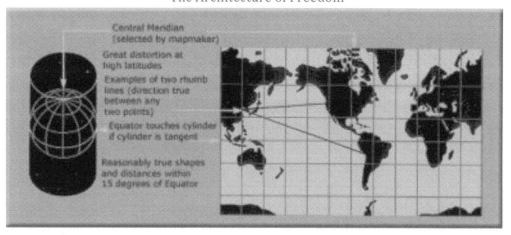

In a Mercator Projection, each rectangle represents an equal area between the lines of latitude and longitude. The areas near the equator are the most accurate. There are other versions of the Mercator that create different areas of distortion.

On this type of *Mercator projection* we get reasonably accurate distances if we measure along the equator. However, a map that is flattened, or projected like this greatly exaggerates the distances, and changes the shapes of the polar landmasses. This is why Canada, Iceland and Antarctica look so much larger on most flat, global maps, which are typically *Mercator projections*. We could easily design a map to make Greenland accurate, but then the equator would become the most distorted part of the map. We rarely see this type of *projection* because maps tend to be designed to be most accurate in those areas where the most people live. Maps based around the North and South poles are not in high demand by the general public.

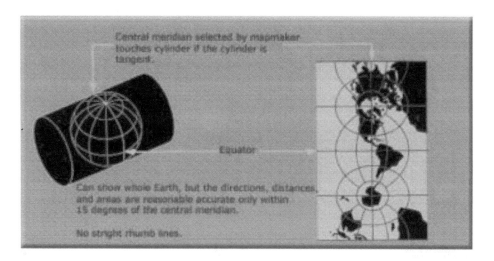

A different Mercator projection that distorts different parts of the original object –the globe. This particular projection is most accurate along a path connecting the two poles and running through the Americas. Compare the size of known countries to the previous Mercator projection.

There are hundreds of different types of popular *map projections* that can be constructed. They all have different errors or inaccuracies built into them, but each is useful for its own reasons. All flat *projections* or 2D maps are inherently inaccurate because they are only two-dimensional representations of something that is constructed in three dimensions. Inaccuracies will arise because *information* is lost or altered when we eliminate even a single dimension. A *mathematical projection* onto fewer dimensions should never be confused with the real thing.

OUR 3-D WORLD IS LIKE A MAP PROJECTION

Imagine what could change and what inaccuracies might be found if this process of projection and dimensional reduction happens at least seven or eight times in succession. This is what occurs when information that originates in 10- or 11-dimensional space is projected through each level until it eventually reaches our three-dimensional universe. What we ultimately experience is very different from the original information at its source.

Our world can be thought of as a 3D "map" of a more complex topology that really occupies many more dimensions, but has been reduced or forced into three dimensions. Because of this, whatever our experience is, it will not be an accurate description of what is really happening in the higher dimensional spaces. Our conceptual minds only understand the geometry and limitations of our own *viewport*. The original information is always available, but we are unable to see or understand it directly. Our minds only can see the shadows–a representation of the whole that has been repeatedly "flattened." What we ultimately observe is only the mapped image of something that really occupies many more dimensions than the three that we perceive.

Because of our perspective, we lack the senses, tools and cognitive abilities to accurately understand the deeper multi-dimensional forms, relationships and interconnections. ***Everything within our universe is intimately connected to everything else and always responding through intimate and direct cause-and-effect interactions. All things and occurrences in our universe are always the direct result of this deep-level interconnectivity.*** Because we can't directly see or experience these interconnections, we often perceive chaos, randomness, accidents and separation. However, there are never accidents and nothing is random or separate because everything we know is the direct result of this intimate and deep level interconnection.

In addition, by using a series of our own, personal, conceptual filters, each of us unconsciously limits and defines the characteristics of our specific personal *projection*. Every one of us is personally tweaking the *algorithm* that defines our collective *viewport* and because of this, ***we each see our lives through an individual and unique reference frame.*** Each of us fine-tunes our personal *viewport* in this way.

We generally assume that we all share exactly the same *viewport* or worldview. Throughout our history this assumption has been a common source of many of mankind's interpersonal problems and conflicts. Two different people can witness the same event–an accident, for example–and their reports will often read as if they had witnessed entirely different events. It is not that one view is right and the other view is wrong, but rather we unconsciously frame our view in slightly different and unique ways–we all perceive and cognize uniquely.

If we allowed for this different framing by different individuals and cultures, the blame and the divisive idea of "right and wrong" could begin to evaporate. ***It is therefore important to realize that every one of us is experiencing our own reality through a slightly different and uniquely personal projection. We all live in slightly different personal realities. Our experience is therefore always only ours, and ours alone.***

OUR VIEWPORTS SHIFT OVER TIME

Our individual and consensus *viewports* constantly shift, change shape or size, and evolve. When we observe our paradigms dissolving around the concepts of flat earth, apartheid, women's rights or civil rights, what we are witnessing is a shifting of the collective viewport to a different location in the Web. However, the difficult process and amount of time required to make these large collective cultural shifts often seems painfully slow. Fortunately, waiting for others is not necessary: individuals can shift their personal *viewports* much more rapidly than an entire culture, and once this happens the "others" around the shifted individual will also appear to have changed. ***Becoming aware of our personal power–our ability to shift our own viewport–is an enormous step towards personal freedom.***

VIEWPORTS IN THE "WEB OF POSSIBILITIES"

No human *being* is capable of grasping the complete multi-dimensional picture of "all that is," but many understand their deep relationship to this more expansive structure and live accordingly. We all have hints, revelations, quick glimpses, or moments of knowing that allow us to glimpse beyond our normal *viewport;* these are our invitations to be influenced by this bigger perspective. If we are open to this guidance, we can begin to make the changes that ultimately result in our being able to inhabit a slightly different or larger landscape within the "Web of All Possibilities."

My description of the Web includes the word "possibility," which refers to a specific idea borrowed from *quantum physics.* In this branch of physics, there is a quantifiable *probability* for anything and everything to occur, and therefore anything is always possible– including the possibility of completely changing our own world. ***Once our personal viewport shifts, even ever so slightly, it will seem, at least for all practical purposes, as if the entire "outside" world has completely changed.*** When this happens, the "outside" world has really not changed at all; what has changed is our own position or perspective within the Web, and this was accomplished by altering the size and extent of our personal *viewport.*

From this new *viewport* some things are unchanged. Most of our friends remain, our home may be the same, and we may still work for the same company. We might have to be very observant to notice the subtle changes. However, as we begin to observe the details of our life more carefully, we may find that enough has changed to completely alter our relationship to the outside world! Maybe our smile is met with a warm smile from a once-distant co-worker; our boss notices our extra work on a particular project; the dog's barking didn't keep us up last night; and that tired feeling is gone, replaced by the excitement around some new endeavor or relationship that unexpectedly came our way.

These are small and ordinary changes; these small, local shifts are common everyday events that often go unnoticed. Smaller shifts are effective for change–we might not adjust easily to larger and more dramatic shifts. ***Over time, many of these small shifts result in a very different personal adventure.*** When these small changes continue to occur freely–moment after moment–eventually, one day, we wake up and realize that we are actually living a different life: one that is possibly much more harmonious, more joyful and more in-tune with the life that we imagined possible. This has been the wonderful and universal observation of many individuals who have already committed to this lifelong process of growth, change and opening.

All shifts in our position in the Web ultimately reflect a change in our vibration at the core of our being. As we evolve and expand our awareness, our viewport becomes larger. The result of this type of growth is that we have a richer experience and relate to more of the "outside" world. Life becomes more vivid.

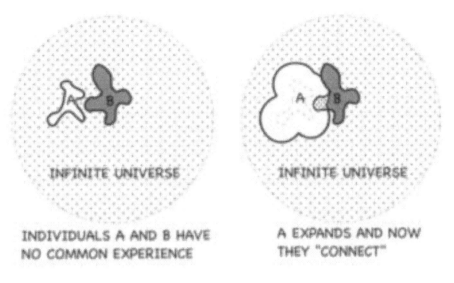

Individual "A" has shifted and expanded his or her awareness. He or she now shares common ground with "B." Where they once were unaware of each other and had very separate lives, they now experience connection. The "outside" world did not change, nor did individual B. We only need to change ourselves to change our interaction with "others."

Understanding quantum mechanics and the "Web of Possibilities" aren't necessary requirements for creating or experiencing this personal shift. Resonant change within our being at our deepest levels is what initiates this shift! However, we can't accomplish this type of change with our minds alone.

Eckhart Tolle summarizes his perspective on shifting *viewports* when he writes, *"When you are transformed, your whole world is transformed, because the world is only a reflection."*

The "Web of Possibilities" exists as always, unchanging, yet containing every possibility. However, because of our special relationship to "time," the Web appears to be dynamic, growing, ever changing and evolving. With practice and evolution, one day, we all will be more able to move freely and consciously around the Web; ultimately we will be free to journey wherever we choose. However, for the present, we can learn to appreciate and build upon the simple experience of witnessing or observing our everyday small personal shifts.

DEATH OUTSIDE OF THE 3D VIEWPORT

If we were completely free to perceive the universe without the limitations of our *viewport,* we would then consciously interact with everything we currently see or understand, right along with the fantastic and infinite expanse that is outside of our viewport. Included in this expanded vista would be the infinite possibilities for futures and pasts, and every possible outcome of every thought or decision by every being–all intimately connected in the fully interactive multi-dimensional Web of all possibilities. With our current abilities, we would quickly become overwhelmed.

This dramatic *viewport* change would mean that we would perceive all things at once, from everywhere, and all outside of time, so that we could then experience exactly how everything fits together perfectly. Living in our current reference frame, it is impossible to imagine what this experience would be like; from this greater and timeless *viewport,* our awareness would need to be a completely different type than that which we experience today. Because of our 3D specialization we do not have the necessary conceptual tools for describing, relating to, or understanding what this would be like. From our current *viewport,* we have no context for imaging this expanded space, yet certain aspects of the changes can still be described, and I will attempt to do this throughout the book.

As our personal viewports expand through evolution and growth, we all will eventually reach the place where we clearly understand that there are no separate individuals! We will discover that our collective sense of being individual and separate is only a grand illusion generated by our conceptual minds, operating within a limited 3D *viewport*. Even though we often are not consciously aware of it, there is an unchanging part of us that is always fully aware of this deeper interconnection. This is *self*: a place where we all can experience our eternal connection to *being* itself.

We are both one and many at the same time, and as we evolve, we will understand and be able to use this truth more fully. This may seem paradoxical, but this conceptual difficulty is only the byproduct of our dimensionally-limited and logical minds. The ancient philosophical question "do I exist?" completely depends on the meaning of "I." If our personal understanding of "I" implies complete separation and the continuation of our egos, then this question must be answered "no" because, at that deepest level, the separate individual is recognized only as a brief phenomenon that is confined to our limited three-dimensional reference frame. If the "I" is defined from that deep place within where no separation exists, then not only does the "I" exist, but also it exists for eternity.

A paradigm-changing truth to discover within this new expanding awareness is that, within creation, we function as both an integrated part of a much bigger being and as an individual at the same time! Our collective experience of isolation and separation is only an illusion that is formed because of our limited viewport. Because there are no separate individuals, there is also no separate one who will die. Death, as it turns out, is also an illusion. Death may be the greatest illusion from our viewport.

A BRIEF HISTORY OF THIS NEW PHYSICS

INTRODUCTION

What follows is primarily a nontechnical discussion about the history and meaning of the book's most important underlying physics. This section is included to help readers understand the source for many of the ideas in this book. I have tried to present the physics in historical context and without technical detail, so that readers without a scientific background can understand it. I know that some people will reflexively shy away from any discussion about math, physics or any science, but do not be afraid of this section; this presentation involves no math or manipulation of equations. Also, please do not get bogged-down in this section. *I ask all readers to give this section a try, but if it proves to be too difficult or not of interest, please just skim or skip it. The book's main ideas can be understood without ever reading this section and, if desired, this section can always be read later.* Also included in this section is a collection of science-related personal insights, thoughts, experiences and anecdotes that have helped me navigate within my own process.

This basic physics will help establish a better foundation for understanding the ideas and architecture that I will be describing. It will be helpful to explore the physics and models deeply enough to reach the point where the following principle is understood and accepted. This book will only make sense if the reader first understands that *the universe is infinitely larger, deeper and more interconnected than we generally imagine, and much of what we consider to be the limits or bounds of our existence are simply the by-product of our type of conceptual thinking, our limited senses, our limited tools and our culture.* Once this principle is fully understood, the rest of the book will make complete sense. Much of this book involves presenting this information in different ways to help readers more easily understand why this principle must be so.

With only an undergraduate degree in physics and the limited practice of teaching high school physics for a couple of years, I am far from being an expert or a specialist in *relativity* or *quantum physics*. I do not live and breathe the mathematics like many practicing physicists, so I must trust the more technical parts to those that are fully immersed in this science. My ultimate interest has always been to understand just what these discoveries mean for our day-to-day lives. Freed from the tedious calculations, dependence upon grants and professional peer review, I have been mostly playing, like a kid in a playground, joyfully exploring what is possible by using my friends and myself as the experimental subjects. As time passed, I noticed a significant shift in my own personal life, because the "world," that I seem to live within, shifted. It was largely through this type of "play" that I first began to notice the practical applications of this physics. What was once a frustration with *quantum physics* has evolved over the years into a heartfelt vision of a complete universe with clear purpose and wonderful meaning. Infused into that meaning is the awareness of the infinite possibilities for this adventure that we call life.

THREE SETS OF PHYSICS

Physics is the most basic scientific study of how physical things work in our world. Today, the science of physics is rapidly evolving and at a very exciting threshold; but it also appears divided into three somewhat independent sets of theories or laws. We have one set of physics for describing very, very small things such as atoms, subatomic particles and the *energy* and *forces* that are associated with them. Our description of this realm of the very small is called *quantum physics*. There is also a set of rules that describes very large things, high speeds and great distances, such as *galaxies*, *light* and *gravity*. This physics is built upon Einstein's *relativity*. We also still use, every day, the much older but still extremely functional set of laws derived from Newton. This physics is now called *classical physics,* and it includes Newton's laws of motion and all the additional physics that they have spawned. *Relativity* can be understood as a revision or addition to *classical physics*, meaning most physicists see our physics divided into only two different parts–*classical/relativity* and *quantum*. Due to the fact that 250 years and a paradigm shift divide *relativity* and *classical physics*, I will continue to treat them as two distinct and separate branches of physics in this book.

An important focus of contemporary physics involves trying to discover just how these somewhat separate descriptions can be integrated into a single theory, which, alone, should then be able to describe the behavior of everything in the universe. This search is referred to as "the quest for the *unified field theory*."

Classical physics, which describes all that is found in between the very big and the very small, is mostly based upon what we can see, experience and measure directly in our 3D "solid" world; for almost 400 years, this physics made such wonderful logical sense to our rational minds. It is founded upon the direct observation of our three-dimensional world, and it was developed through repeatable experiments that historically did not rely on extremely complex or expensive equipment.

The two newer branches, *quantum physics*, describing the workings of the very small, and *relativity*, seeking to understand the realm of the very vast, illuminate many ideas that do not make the same type of "good sense" to our 3D-specialized minds. As mentioned, even though some of the discoveries of *relativity* seem strange, this branch is usually seen as an improvement or update of *classical physics* because these two types of physics fit together mathematically. However, to even begin to understand *relativity*, we must first venture outside of our long accepted, and "safe," three-dimensional conceptual paradigm.

It is *quantum physics* that does not yet integrate well mathematically with the other two branches, even though it has been well tested and unbelievably successful for almost a century. *Classical physics* is a study of exactness and certainty, while q*uantum physics* is about a world of possibilities and probability. To our three-dimensional conceptual minds, they often make little or no sense together.

Quantum theory radically changes how we must look at our world, and if this theory were simply an untested theory or an abstract idea, then this entire book could be described as science fiction. However, every test of the Quantum theory during its almost 100 years of existence has resulted in its absolute confirmation. No other major theory in physics has ever had this success rate. As much as one-third of our national Gross Domestic Product (GDP) is dependent upon or built from products based upon Quantum theory. The high-tech products from this theory have become as much a part of America as apple pie. Quantum theory, which has become a very critical and integrated part of our lives, is at least as real as anything else in our world!

Today, these three sets of rules and observations are used together to describe everything that we understand about our universe. *Classical physics*, which was formalized by a young Sir Isaac Newton more than 400 years ago, works best with objects that are sized within the human scale: things such as baseballs, bugs, airplanes and bridges. It is relatively simple, intuitive and practical–most of us have a gut-level understanding for much of this physics, even if the math looks complicated. We know that, if we throw a ball into the air, it will come down; and if we hit a brick wall, we will quickly stop moving. *Relativity*, Einstein's contribution that describes objects we encounter at the very big cosmological scale, provides us with the tools to begin to understand and describe things like *gravity*, the speed of light, and our galaxy's origin in the *big bang*. Much of *relativity*, however, is counter-intuitive to the 3D mindset, so incorporating it requires some hard work and a great deal of imagination. ***On the other hand, quantum physics, the study of the very tiny, can only be described as completely "weird and crazy." Understanding its implications requires adopting an entirely new perspective on the nature of the universe and even on life itself.***

The fact that we still need more than one type of physics to fully describe our world is a clear sign to most people, and to virtually all physicists, that we have not yet resolved our description of our physical environment. Most physicists believe there must exist a single, final, *unified field theory* that incorporates and connects everything we know to be true in these three branches. Such a universal theory would *unify* the four known *forces–gravity, electromagnetic, strong nuclear* and *weak nuclear* –into a single elegant theory. The hope is that, when found, this would be a single, but still simple, equation, or a set of equations, that would describe everything known.

To date, this *unification* has completely eluded the efforts of our very best minds in physics. As a result, scientists acknowledge a general level of discomfort as we continue to divide the physical world into three somewhat disconnected parts. It is assumed that one day this will change with the discovery of the *unified field theory,* but in the effort to reach this important milestone, many scientists have devoted entire lifetimes without a breakthrough result. Einstein spent most of his life and career trying! His three major theories, *special relativity, photoelectric effect* and *general relativity*, came very early in his career; much of the rest of his life was devoted to trying to personally accept quantum theory and *unify* the four known *forces*.

Neither *quantum physics* nor *relativity* can be explained or understood within the framework of the old three-dimensional *classical physics*. We are consistently uncovering things that are so unexpected and profound that they are impossible to fully imagine, even for the most talented physicists. ***For all of us, born into a world that was carved and framed by this classical physics mindset, to even begin to incorporate the meaning of the last hundred years of research requires a complete paradigm shift.***

Remember, as discussed above, that it was not too long ago–less than 500 years–when virtually all humans viewed the world as being flat, and ending with a distinct edge over which one could fall. Back then we all believed that the Sun revolved around the Earth, which was presumed to be the physical center of absolutely everything in the universe. The Earth was the most important part of the universe–the focal center for all of creation. From within that rigid mindset it was impossible for most humans to understand, or visualize, the next leap, which was integrating the new geometric relationships of the solar system that Copernicus discovered and Galileo later refined.

This change of vision required understanding and acceptance that our planet was just one part of a much larger solar system, with our Sun being the actual physical center. Four hundred years ago we began our shift to the *Heliocentric* (sun-centered) view as we gradually abandoned the old *Geocentric* (earth centered) view. Over the years we have made additional leaps and refinements to this new paradigm by realizing that our solar system was still within a much larger system called the *Milky Way Galaxy*. Eventually we realized that the *Milky Way Galaxy*, which contains some two hundred billion stars, is itself just a small part of a much larger universe, containing, at the least, hundreds of billions of other *galaxies* similar to the *Milky Way*. Today, this description of the vastness of our physical universe is so completely self-evident to most of us that it has become amusing to imagine that people once thought that the earth was flat. ***Humans have a long history of successfully vaulting through dramatic paradigm shifts. We are on the verge of doing this once again.***

Then, just as today, we could not easily visualize what we were not prepared to understand. Throughout this journey, the physics and math have always been our harbingers, paving the way for our explorations by providing the first insights and clues. Today, when we look back through history, we clearly see this repeating pattern of successfully following the best math, and then science, deep into what was once unknown and strange territory. Eventually, this once-strange science becomes integrated and then it seems quite normal. *As a culture, we have shown that we can, and do, dramatically change the way we think, but it always involves a complex and extended process–one that has been successfully guided by our best theoretical math and science.*

THE NEED FOR EXTRA DIMENSIONS

Today there is general agreement among most Physicists that we are much closer to uncovering this "Holy Grail of physics"–the *Unified Field Theory:* the single theory that combines *quantum mechanics*, *classical physics* and *relativity*, thus finally uniting the four known *forces*. Physicists are very excited about the newest modifications to *string theory* and their possible role in this *unification*. *String theory* is a more recent (40 years-old) and therefore more mature, *quantum* sub-theory. What we do know, today, is that the three mostly distinct sets of physical laws seem to merge, and mathematically work together in a much more elegant way when we start to add mathematical dimensions to the manipulation of these equations. *String* theory requires these extra dimensions, and working with these extra dimensions is relatively easy within the mathematics; however, because of the conceptual leaps required, it is essentially impossible for any of us to visualize.

In this book we will explore several different independent lines of reasoning that all lead us to the conclusion that our universe is most likely constructed from extra dimensions. We know that the addition of extra dimensions changes everything we understand about our universe, but at our current stage in evolution, it is impossible to fully grasp what a universe constructed from these extra dimensions might mean. Before we wander off into these discussions, let us first back up a little bit and examine the modern history of physics more closely.

CLASSICAL PHYSICS

OUR ANCIENT FATHERS

Euclid, who lived in ancient Greece (300 BC), is the father of our three-dimensional mathematical language, and we still honor his contribution by calling this mathematics *Euclidean geometry*. Aristotle was the first person of record to declare that there are only three dimensions to the universe. He said *"The line has a magnitude in one way, a plane in two ways, and the solid in three ways, and beyond these there is no other magnitude because three are all."* A little later, Ptolemy offered a proof of only three dimensions, based on not being able to draw a line that is perpendicular to all three axes of a three-dimensional object. For a long time this seemed like the end of the story; it had been declared by the finest minds that *"three are all!"* For the next two thousand years we found ourselves deeply locked into these concepts that can be easily understood by our senses and 3D logic. Except for a few, almost forgotten, fringe-thinkers, no one seriously imagined that we were missing a big piece of the picture until one mathematician's rumblings in the middle of the 18th century. "Curved" or multi-dimensional space wasn't described or documented until 150 years ago.

The ancient Greeks were also largely responsible for imbedding the geocentric (Earth-centered) model of the universe into our consciousness. In fact, they gave us two of our longest lasting paradigm builders–Euclidian geometry and the "flat earth" model.

PHYSICS BETWEEN THE TIMES OF NEWTON AND EINSTEIN

Through the Dark and Middle Ages of humanity, there was little time and energy for pure, rational science. Through trial and error people learned how to strengthen castle walls, build higher cathedrals, make stronger armor and swords, and develop more effective and lethal weapons for war. Little or none of this was ever approached scientifically and, as discussed, the church often crushed any real scientific progress. Since the late 1600s: the time of Newton, our Western culture has been dominated by a defining mindset that is entirely based upon Newton's description of our physical world. With his *laws of motion*, we entered a period of history during which man began to imagine his world as a mechanical machine that was governed only by these laws. There was the common belief amongst scientists and philosophers that since many physical observations could be analyzed, predicted, repeated and clearly understood, eventually this logical system would unlock a world where everything could and would be predictable. The rational philosophy of Descartes meshed perfectly with this attitude, and together they intertwined to form a definitive new paradigm. God still existed, but many people began to believe that his job description was reduced to that of "just controlling the gears." Anomalies, whenever they popped up, were usually dismissed as poor or inaccurate science. The new understanding was that absolutely everything could be figured out within these then-new principles, and everything was predictable except when God occasionally intervened by adjusting some of the controls. Newton's declaration that *"objects at rest tend to stay at rest, and objects in motion stay in motion unless acted upon by an outside force,"* along with his famous companion equation, *"F=ma,"* (force equals mass times acceleration) became the unmovable cornerstones of the foundation that this new paradigm was built upon.

For well over 300 years, *classical Newtonian physics* seemed to have the nearly flawless ability to answer almost every question thrown in its direction. Then, beginning just before the time of Einstein, new scientific and mathematical tools were developed. The Newtonian model began to slide from its rarified heights, as it started to show some extremely worrisome and paradigm-threatening faults; it became very clear that some very large pieces of the puzzle were still missing. To better understand the context of this change, one that we are still embroiled within, let us first examine our history of the exploration of *matter* and the cosmos.

SIZE OF THE ATOM

Ancient Greek Philosophers had predicted the atom as the elemental building block of matter, but it was not until the seventeenth and eighteenth centuries that the actual chemistry of the atom began to be understood. The atom, which was once thought to be the smallest building block of matter, is, in fact, extremely small. One-half trillion of them (500 billion), packed tightly edge to edge, would form a line only one inch long. If you were to take a marble and blow it up to the size of the Earth, only then you would be able to clearly see the atoms inside it because, at that magnification, atoms would become about the size of a marble. Stated a slightly different way, the size of an atom, compared to the size of a marble, is the same as the size of a marble compared to the size of the Earth.

Today we understand that atoms are far from "solid." They mostly contain empty space with a few smaller particles (protons, electrons) that help define the borders of their space. How much empty space is in each atom? The nucleus (protons and neutrons) of an atom has a diameter over 10,000 times smaller than the atom itself. The only other "things" in the atom are electrons, which are so small and flighty that they don't take up any real space at all. The atom is almost entirely empty space. A few additional analogies can give us a better sense of how much empty space is inside an atom. These numbers will vary somewhat, from atom to atom because, for example, hydrogen atoms are much smaller than uranium atoms. Regardless, the basic idea is the same for all atoms.

AMOUNT OF EMPTY SPACE IN ATOMS

Today, the traditional use of the solar system as a model for imagining the form of the atom is understood to be an obsolete and conceptually inaccurate method. It is, however, still useful to help us understand the disproportionate amount of empty space involved. If an atom were visualized to resemble our solar system in form and shape, then the nucleus in the atom's center would be analogous to our Sun, while the planets would represent the electrons.

Imagine this nucleus to be the size of a golf ball. On this scale, the inner electron (Mercury) shell would be located more than a half-mile away from the golf ball. The actual electron itself would only be the size of a very small pea. Everything in between is "empty" space. The next shell of electrons (Venus) would be about two and one-half miles away, while everything between is again "empty" space. A golf ball and a few peas are the only "things" found in a sphere that is five miles wide; this atom is mostly empty space. If we were to enlarge the nucleus to the size of a basketball, the closest electron would then be about 20 miles away.

Another model can be constructed by imagining a large football stadium. If the hydrogen atom (the smallest atom) was inflated to the size of this stadium, the nucleus would be the size of a pea in the middle of the fifty-yard line, and the single electron of hydrogen would be smaller than a speck of dust in the stands. The only actual matter in a region the size of a large football stadium is about the size of a pea. ***Empty space completely dominates the solid appearing "thing" that we call an atom.***

The atom is, therefore, almost entirely "empty" space. It certainly is not the solid thing we might imagine when, for example, we hit a brick wall with our fist. If this model of the atom weren't "spacey" enough, as we learned to peer into the nucleus and study the protons, neutrons and electrons, the very small "particles" that were making up the only "solid" parts of these atoms, we found that they too were similarly constructed of mostly "empty" space. It turns out that these smaller particles are built in a way that follows the same "mostly empty space" pattern. As we discover new ways to peer into the subatomic world, and off into deep space, it seems that this pattern appears to continue on and on, forever, in both directions–towards the smaller and the larger.

When we later explore this topic in more detail, we will discover that this "empty" space itself is not empty at all. Data from very recent space probes indicate that "empty" space contains most of the gravitational material in the universe, and this may hold the key to the ultimate destiny of our physical, three-dimensional universe.

OUR WORLD IS NOT SO SOLID

Since the atom is mostly "empty" space, and everything that we interact with in our day-to-day world is made of atoms, then, if we were small enough–say the size of a *nucleus*–we would be able to see all the space within and between the atoms, and understand that "solid" things are really not very solid after all. They just seem solid to our particular senses from our particular perspective. At that reduced size, looking at the space between the particles would feel much the same as when, in our present size configuration, we peer at the stars.

The *electrons* and *protons* are held together by *electromagnetic force*. Another type of *force*, the *strong nuclear force,* holds the particles of the *nucleus* together. Today, we understand and define a total of four primary *forces*. Along with the *electromagnetic force* and the *strong nuclear force,* we also have identified the *weak nuclear force* and *gravity.*

The *nucleus* is made up of particles, including *protons*, which all have the same *positive charge*. Since *like charges* always repel each other, these *electromagnetic particles* of the *nucleus* naturally push against each other causing the *nucleus* to want to break apart. *Strong nuclear force* is the *energy* that holds this *nucleus* together, by countering this urge to push apart. The *strong nuclear force* is the "E" (*energy*) in Einstein's famous equation $E=MC^2$. This *force* is what is released through the *fission process* in atomic bombs, so obviously this is a very strong *force* with a very accurate and descriptive name.

Over time, our understanding about this and the other *forces* will evolve, and likely change, as we continue to comprehend more about our universe. For example, we now suspect that this strong *force* may be responsible for about 98 percent of the *mass attraction* in the known universe–*mass* is only another form of *energy*–yet we really don't understand exactly how this works (later I will explore this subject in more detail). Physicists have developed a useful model involving the exchange of small particles to explain this *force*, but I feel certain that we will one day discover that this explanation is just another artifact of our current *dimensional limitations*. Again, we are reminded of the vastness that lies beyond our *conceptual horizon* and, therefore, beyond our comprehension.

What we perceive as "solid" material is clearly mostly space and energy (attractive and repulsive forces), with a microscopic amount of "solid-appearing" particles. When these small particles are examined more closely, they are also found to contain mostly space. ***Our bodies are made up of atoms, so we, too, are constructed from space and energy. All that we call matter is little more than reorganized energy.*** As we begin to understand this construction, the expected outcome from two "solid" appearing objects bumping into each other becomes less certain and less predictable. At some point, it becomes almost easy to imagine how the tiny "particles" of one object could pass through the enormous voids of the other. If the conditions were right, we would be able to easily walk through walls.

CLASSICAL PHYSICS BASED ON EUCLIDEAN GEOMETRY

It has always been easy for me to visualize and understand the three-dimensional geometric forms that shape our life and world. High school geometry seemed obvious and it was easy to manipulate these forms directly in my mind. My career as an architect directly depends on my ability to work fluidly and comfortably within this three-dimensional system. This everyday geometry is what we all use to find our friend's house, fit furniture into our rooms, throw a baseball, read a map, build a wedding cake and determine if we can safely jump to the next rock. We have named it *Euclidean geometry*–after the man who first described it almost two thousand years ago. Even if someone failed high-school geometry, they will still have a deep understanding of this geometry. It is so deeply built into our bodies and brains that, even though we rely on it constantly, we never have to even think about the math. However, this every-day, three-dimensional, geometry, which has served us so well and for so long, has now been discovered to be incomplete, inaccurate and, possibly, even quite wrong in certain situations.

CLASSICAL PHYSICS FALLS SHORT

By the turn of the twentieth century, fresh new ideas and strange experimental results began to raise clear and deep questions about the infallibility of the classical mechanistic model. These questions included the fundamental problem: *"what exactly is gravity."* Other questions such as *"why don't Newton's equations precisely describe the motion of the planets," "what is light"* and *"why don't electrons collapse into the nucleus of the atom"* also remained unanswered by this very physics, which originally had the great promise of explaining everything. Beginning in the early 1900s, *relativity* and *quantum physics*, two new theories that evolved independently, allowed scientists to take a fresh look at these questions. As the years passed, these scientists began to develop a radical new way of viewing our universe.

Understanding and fully integrating this growing body of revolutionary knowledge will ultimately require a greater cultural adjustment than that of the last great shift, from the geocentric "flat earth" to the *heliocentric* "solar system." *Relativity and quantum physics* allow us unprecedented access to the very large, very fast, very distant and the very small parts of our universe. Newton's laws still work, but we now realize that they work only when limited to specific sets of conditions or reference frames involving size, speed and time. Newton's laws still work well when they are applied to many of the everyday things that we directly meet in our day-to-day world. This includes all objects of a size, *mass* and *velocity* that are related to the scale of our own bodies. However, when we analyze things so small or fast that we can't observe them directly, or things so large or distant that we have no frame of reference, the 400-year-old Newtonian laws of physics are revealed to be only working approximations.

SPECIAL RELATIVITY

INTRODUCTION TO RELATIVITY

Einstein released his first *relativity* theory in 1905; it was only later named *special relativity*. This theory was, in one sense, a modification to the long-standing agreement within *classical physics* about what scientists and mathematicians call *reference frames*. It began by reinforcing the classical view that all uniform motion is relative to the motion of the observer and that there were, therefore, no privileged *reference frames*. It said that because everything in the universe is in constant motion, any reference point is also in motion. Anything that is observed is, therefore, always relative to that motion. Up to this point, his theory worked with the old physics, causing no major conflicts or problems.

SPEED OF LIGHT

Then Einstein introduced another part of this theory, which contained the entirely new idea that the speed of light was the same for all observers, no matter what their *reference frame*. With this ground-shaking new idea, light was treated uniquely and suddenly much of our understanding about light, space, gravity and time was transformed! Once the math was understood and analyzed, it was seen that our observation and measurement of time and distance suddenly depended on how fast we, or our reference frames, were traveling.

It was necessary to add another dimension to our 3D coordinate system to resolve these unexpected predictions. By incorporating this extra dimension, we now have a *spacetime* coordinate system that works consistently with Einstein's new mathematics. The old 3D Euclidean coordinates no longer worked to describe this new domain. Once Einstein deduced that we were living in a multi-dimensional blending of time and space, the meaning of "time" was changed forever.

This new theory predicted some very odd and unexpected behavior for light, involving the concept of speed. The measurement of speed is, of course, completely linked to how we perceive time; that is why, in a very real sense, this theory completely changed our understanding of "time."

Imagine that both you and your friend are walking along together at five miles-per-hour. You would logically imagine that you and your friend could walk together, side by side on a trail and have a conversation. If your car is going 50 miles-per-hour and your friend's car pulls up, you might also expect to be able to shout to each other through the open windows. Fly in an airplane at 500 miles-per-hour and you might see another airplane out the window. If the planes fly close enough and parallel you can wave to people in the other plane because the planes are moving together at the same speed.

Light does not work in this way. Light seems to obey a unique set of speed rules that are different from these other, relatively slow, normal speed observations. Einstein demonstrated that you can never catch up to a beam of light because, no matter how fast you travel, light always moves away from you at the *speed of light,* which is about 186 thousand-miles-per-second or close to 670 million miles-per-hour. If you were traveling on a beam of light and someone was trying to catch up to you, they never could. No matter how fast they traveled, you would always be moving away from them at 670 million miles-per-hour, the speed of light. Light behaves very differently from phenomena such as sound, which you can catch up to and even physically pass. Jets do this often, creating a *sonic boom* as they zoom past their own moving sound wave. Light does not travel the same way you and I might travel, and, as strange as it seems, according to *relativity*, we will never be able to catch up to a beam of light no matter how fast we travel.

Also, if we were to travel at these high rates of velocity, very unusual things would begin to happen to us as our speed increased. An *outside observer* is an *observer* who is not speeding like us and is therefore said to be outside of our moving *reference frame*. An *outside observer,* who happened to be watching as we moved at these very high velocities, would notice that we actually start to change our shape. To the eyes or instruments of this *outside observer,* our body will flatten or compress in the direction of our movement; and, as we move faster, our movements will slow down to the point where it will appear that we almost stop. *Gravity* would also become much stronger when traveling at these high speeds. Time would slow down; we would age more slowly; and, as we approach the speed of light, the watch on our wrist would almost stop. ***All of these phenomena are only what an outside observer would witness. However, from our own perspective, or that of a passenger traveling with us, nothing would have changed. To someone in our own moving reference frame, the world would still look and feel very normal.***

These observations are very strange and unexpected when viewed through our "common sense" conceptual minds, which are designed for efficient navigation through and around our 3D world. Despite these strange-seeming results, this physics (Einstein's *relativity*), has proved to be very sound and durable, having been thoroughly tested and explored for more than one hundred years.

While we have not yet been able to move actual people at these great velocities to directly demonstrate these phenomena, experiment after experiment over the last 100 years have deepened our understanding and validated many parts of this theory. The more we learn, the more valid the theory seems. However, this is only the beginning of our journey into this strange world of modern physics. While *relativity* seems illogical when viewed from our old "common sense" perspective, we will soon discover that *quantum physics* takes strangeness to a completely new level. However, before we venture off into this land of endless wonder, let us continue a little further into *Relativity*.

E=MC2

After Einstein's *special relativity* (his first publication in 1905), the rest of the world started to realize that *mass* is really only *energy* that is being stored in a different form. *Energy* and *mass* are interchangeable forms of the same thing. *Matter* is *energy* "frozen" and stored in a different state, and it can be converted back to *energy* under the right conditions. In this "frozen" state, *matter* contains an enormous amount of *energy*. This relationship is described by his famous equation $E=MC^2$, which, when expressed in words, says, *"Energy equals mass times the speed of light squared."* Einstein determined that, to calculate the amount of *energy* contained in a given amount of *mass*, one needs to multiply the amount of *mass* by the enormous number, "C squared," which is the speed of light multiplied by the speed of light. A very small amount of *mass* contains an unbelievably large amount of *energy*. *Mass* (*matter*) is a form of *energy* that is so concentrated and condensed that a handful of material under the right conditions can release enough *energy* to destroy a large city. This is exactly what occurred in Hiroshima and Nagasaki during World War Two.

One special condition that allows *mass* to convert to *energy* in a very dramatic way is the aggregation of a *critical mass* of *fissionable material*. This is what begins the uncontrolled *fission* process that leads to the violent event that is the purpose of atomic bombs! This weapon, by itself, is experimental proof of this theory because it clearly and dramatically demonstrates how a small amount of *mass* does produce an enormous release of *energy*. When this release of *energy* is more controlled, as it is within a *nuclear reactor,* this *process* can be used to generate heat, and then electricity.

Initially, when the possibility of this weapon was first theorized, there was some uncertainty in the scientific community about what the actual results might be. There was even serious concern that the fission might start an irreversible process that would consume the entire planet; but, as is mankind's nature, we forged ahead and tried it anyway. The bomb behaved exactly as Einstein's theory predicted, and his work was again validated. However, this time the particular method of proof was also his lifelong regret.

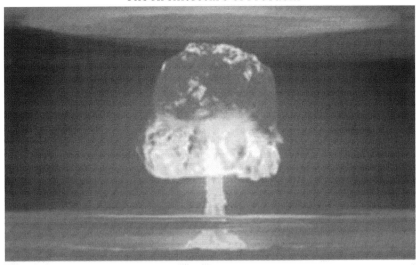

The "bomb" is experimental proof of E=MC2.
A small amount of material releases an
enormous amount of energy.

Today, it is universally understood that *matter* is just another form of *energy*. The realization that ultimately "everything in the universe can be reduced to *energy*" entirely changes the old classical view that *matter* and *energy* were two very different things. This brings us to a very important idea for this book. ***There are no actual "things" in the "physical universe." There is only energy in its various forms. Everything you have ever experienced or will experience can be reduced to energy and energy exchange. Understanding this deeply can help us to begin to let go of our old concept of a rigid, solid, fixed universe.***

GENERAL RELATIVITY

INTRODUCTION

Ten years after publishing *special relativity*, Einstein further modified this work with an additional *general relativity* theory. This new sub-theory was specifically designed to fix some of the issues from *special relativity*, such as the first theory's lack of a physical explanation for the all-important *force* of *gravity*. With this update there was finally an explanation for *gravity*, which had always been the "elephant in the room" of *classical physics*. Einstein determined that *gravity* is only a temporary warp in the fabric of *spacetime*, caused by the presence of a large *mass*. *Spacetime* is the merging of our common *3D coordinate system* and *time* into a single indivisible system. This effectively supplanted the idea developed by Newton, that *gravity* was a *force* that causes masses to attract each other.

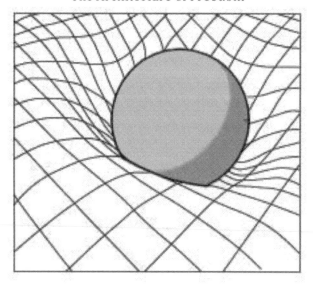

A heavy mass warps spacetime–a combination of 3D space and time– in much the same way the mass might warp the flat surface of a trampoline.

Suddenly, what was once described as a "mysterious" *force* could be seen as the direct result of unseen, but very real, geometry. *Beginning with this realization, understanding the "mystery" became more about understanding the deeper geometry. Gravity, which is something we rely on every day, something readily "understood" by everyone in an intuitive sense, turns out to be a function of the geometric shape and structure of our universe–its architecture. We are not able to see this deformation of spacetime because, with our senses, we are usually only able and equipped to see the world in three dimensions. Instead we "feel," and then interpret this deformation as a force called gravity.*

A similar thing can be said for our understanding of "time" as a one-directional arrow. One day we will clearly realize that our understanding of "time" is only our limited perception of something that is an integral part of a more complex geometry.

WHAT RELATIVITY MEANS

General relativity erodes our existing 3D cultural paradigm in multiple and very dramatic ways. It reveals that we live in a space that has more than three dimensions, which Einstein called *spacetime*. It explains that *spacetime* is actually "curved" and that this curvature creates the illusion of the *force* that we call *gravity*. *Relativity* demonstrates that *gravity* affects the rate of the unfolding of time, and we are only beginning to understand what this actually might mean. *General relativity* also establishes the mathematical basis for *black holes, wormholes* and other strange phenomena that today's cosmologists are busy exploring, as they piece together a new vision for our universe. Most importantly, this physics demonstrates that many of the very things that we observe and use every day in our lives–all things that involve *gravity* and time, for example–are a direct result of the geometry of a universe that is formed and held within a space that requires more than our normally perceived three-dimensions. For more than one hundred years we have understood that our universe is constructed from more than the three dimensions described by Euclid. "Gravity" and "time" are only the "trickle down" shadows or *projections* cast upon our 3D *viewport* from this much larger multi-dimensional space. *A multi-dimensional geometry, which extends through regions or realms that we can't readily see or directly sense, forms the fundamental space that*

contains our universe. I continue to repeat this idea often, and in slightly different forms, because it is probably the most important idea to understand in this book.

THE MATHEMATICS OF A CURVED SPACETIME

While Einstein's *relativity* theories required us to modify and re-examine our concepts of time and space in almost every way, his ideas were not unfamiliar at the time of his first theory. A relatively obscure Russian physicist developed the critical math about 50 years earlier, and several other physicists contributed to the earlier theoretical work that *relativity* was based upon.

One of the more significant conceptual surprises from the mathematics of *relativity* is that lines that look straight to us within our old 3D space are really "curved" because *spacetime* itself is "curved." Curved is a word we understand well in three dimensions, but in four-dimensions "curved" has a different meaning, which we don't easily and naturally comprehend. Because *spacetime* can't be directly experienced or understood by us, "curved" becomes the closest 3D concept to describe this new idea about the shape of space.

When I first started studying *quantum physics* at the undergraduate level, I became very frustrated with the fact that I could not visualize this new geometric world. I could always easily visualize the old Euclidean geometry of our familiar, 3D, common-sense world. *Relativity* was only slightly more approachable than *quantum physics,* but it was also impossible for me to visualize or grasp at an intuitive level. As discussed, Einstein's second *relativity* theory, *general relativity,* addressed *gravity* and how it is not really a *force,* but rather it is caused by a distortion or curvature of the *spacetime continuum* created by massive objects, such as the Sun, or planets. I could glimpse or imagine a curved *spacetime* by thinking about a long line that, although it appears visually straight, is really slightly curved. This curve could be so slight that it appears to our eyes to be a straight line. However, eventually the slowly-curved path gradually forms a very big circle that will loop all the way back to the starting point. If I could throw a ball along this path, after completing a big circular loop through the universe, it would eventually curve around and hit me in the back of my head. I could almost understand this aspect of *relativity* because it seemed quite possible in my 3D conceptual space.

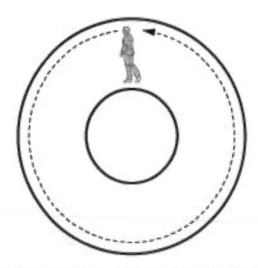

In curved spacetime, if you look into distant space you will eventually see the back of your own head. This is a two-dimensional diagram. Curved spacetime requires at least four dimensions.

Unfortunately, this two-dimensional way of visualizing a curved *spacetime* is quite inaccurate and misleading because of the now-familiar dimensional problem. Despite this inaccuracy, this is still the explanation that many physics teachers use to introduce their classes to the idea of a curved *spacetime*. **We all can understand that the ground under our feet is really the surface of a curved sphere, our planet Earth, but it still feels and looks flat to our senses. In a similar way, spacetime seems "flat" when viewed in three dimensions, even though it is mathematically "curved."**

Despite my best efforts, I still cannot imagine what curved space would be like for a *being* that lived fully in a four-dimensional world because my brain, like all human brains, is designed to work best in three dimensions. I have, however, learned to feel or sense the edges of this extra dimension in different ways. The three-dimensional analogies or visual models in this book can be used as tools to help us begin to "sense" this multi-dimensional geometry. Like Zen Koans, these models will never describe the actual geometry, but rather they are useful tools to point us towards a deeper level of hidden truth. The real geometry will likely remain unseen through a substantial amount of human evolution, largely because it cannot be directly understood or visualized using our current, and dimensionally limited, conceptual thinking.

Fortunately, this new geometry can be described and manipulated with relative ease, using mathematics. Mathematics is a language that transcends our ability to visualize and even our need to "understand." At this point we might ask *"is it fair or reasonable to be equating mathematics to things that have real meaning in our world?"* Clearly, history demonstrates that the answer to this question is affirmative because, time and time again, our mathematical predictions do turn out to have real world implications. We have a very clear and documented history demonstrating and reinforcing that, as we learn more about a topic, the math that originally led us there was an accurate predictor and a faithful guide. **Mathematics has always served us by providing an extremely powerful searchlight for illuminating our path through the unknown.**

Mathematics is a language. Since at least the days of ancient Greece, there has been a lively philosophical debate about whether mathematics exists in nature and we just discovered it, or whether it is our own creation. When we probe the deepest levels of this new architecture, we eventually will discover that these two views are one and the same, for reasons discussed later. Regardless of its origin, mathematics has always provided a window into physics, then chemistry, and ultimately into all the sciences, which together have changed our understanding of our universe. Mathematics has functioned in a way that is similar to microscopes and telescopes, by allowing us to see beyond the normal limits of our senses.

Of course, any attempts to provide human meaning to these mathematical results are completely subject to the limits of our current cultural paradigm. As a result, potential meanings will also shift and change as new levels of cultural and individual understanding are achieved. The more we learn, the clearer it becomes that there are vast parts of our universe that we simply do not understand. Mathematical tools provide us with clues and vistas into otherwise invisible theoretical worlds that, one day, might have real-world meaning for us. It was mathematics alone that gave us our first glimpse, about 150 years ago, of the existence of extra-dimensional space. This expanded view of space is now the key to this entirely new way of understanding our personal relationship with our universe. Mathematics can lead us to things that otherwise are beyond our imagination.

Since the days of Newton, we have believed that gravity was a force. We now know that *gravity* is the natural result of the way that 3D objects deform a more multi-dimensional *spacetime*. This deformation is caused by a concentrated *mass,* and the greater this *mass,* the greater the local deformation of *spacetime.* Experiencing this deformation from within our 3D *viewport*, it seems that there is *force* acting upon the object. What Einstein discovered was that this *force* is only an artifact caused by the "dimensional reduction" of our *viewport*. Again, we are trying to explain a concept using fewer dimensions than the actual concept utilizes.

A number of things that seem very strange and illogical from our 3D perspective really do fit together much better and make more sense in 4D *spacetime*. Our understanding of "time" falls into this category. "Time" has been described as the fourth dimension, but "time," by itself, is not a dimension. Rather "time" is how we perceive, describe and understand our interface with the fourth dimension. "Time" is a three-dimensional concept that we use to describe the peculiar way 4D objects look and behave as they interact or intersect with our 3D world. I would, again, like to refer the reader back to the novel *Flatland*.

VISUALIZING MULTI-DIMENSIONAL GEOMETRY

We are about to begin our examination of *quantum physics* in more depth. The discussion about *relativity* required us to expand our dimensional paradigm, somewhat. However, as we attempt to integrate *quantum physics* and *relativity*, our three-dimensional coordinate system becomes woefully inadequate. It and the space it describes are almost useless for understanding the full extent of these new parts of our universe.

About the time of Einstein's birth, several mathematicians introduced the unexpected idea that the actual geometry of the universe probably requires at least one additional dimension. Today, most physicists accept the idea that the fundamental geometry of the universe is constructed from more than our accepted three dimensions. They now realize that a four-dimensional *spacetime* is the absolute minimum, and many think it is likely that there are even more dimensions to consider. A significant number of physicists who have been exploring *string theory*, *super-string theory* and *M-theory* are even predicting that as many as 10 or 11 dimensions might be involved.

If we seek to understand the real mechanics and structure of our existence, we must come to accept and recognize that creation must have more than three dimensions, even though we don't have the direct ability to perceive or visualize these. These extra dimensions are not just for mathematicians, for they are required to form and maintain the familiar structure of this physical world that we all move through every day. These invisible dimensions shape our entire experience. *The reader's willingness to accept that our universe is built upon a multi-dimensional geometry, which is infinitely expansive and simultaneously connects everything in ways we can't even imagine, is the prerequisite for many of the ideas discussed in this book. This is the hidden geometry that makes the "impossible" quite real!*

What does multi-dimensional geometry look like? While it remains impossible to visualize from our conceptual space, we can sometimes use 3D models for help. We know that all the additional dimensions must fit and work together in a fully interactive way. The nested model below is one 3D way to think about levels or dimensions. Every level is equally important because if one is gone, the entire structure collapses. In multi-dimensional space all dimensions are of equal and critical importance to the maintenance of the entire architecture. All dimensions can also be understood to be simultaneously "inside" and "outside" of each other, and there is no dimension that can be described as "higher" or "lower." Our ideas about "inside or outside" and "higher or lower" are only 3D artifacts. *Creation is all interactively interconnected so that all dimensions contribute equally to the whole. To speak of "higher" or "lower" dimensions as more or less important is equivalent to thinking that our hands are more important than our feet because they sit higher on our body.*

Eleven nested dimensions all acting as one single system. This diagram is drawn on a flat (2D) piece of paper so there appears to be an "inner" and "outer" dimension. This effect is only an illusion experienced in our limited 3D realm. In 11-dimensional space, our 3D concepts, such as "in" or "out," will have very different meanings.

QUANTUM WEIRDNESS

BOHR ATOM MODEL

When I studied junior-high chemistry, we were taught the *atom* was the *elemental* building block of all *matter*. We were told to visualize these atoms as having a center that is called the *nucleus*. *Electrons* circled this core, similar to the form of our *solar system*. That was a simple model of the atom that could be easily visualized. It seemed logical for the *atom* to be modeled after our *solar system* because nature does tend to construct itself in nested layers that mimic each other.

Families of *atoms* were identified, and we were taught that most of the differences between these families were due to the number of *electrons* in the outer rings of the elements. Interactions between atoms were determined by every *atom's* strong "desire" to have its outer ring filled with its ideal number of *electrons*. This full ring allowed the *element* or *compound* to exist and persist in a *stable lower-energy state*. To someone like myself, who thinks in pictures, this image, called the *Bohr Atom*, was clear, simple and very satisfying.

Unfortunately, as it turned out, this model of the *atom* was crude, approximate and even quite wrong. In the 1960s there were very few high school physics and chemistry teachers who understood the research and the rapid changes that were revolutionizing their contemporary physics. Beginning in the 1920s, leading-edge physicists began to understand that this once-convenient model had several serious, or even fatal, problems. It still worked to explain many interactions between *atoms*, but it could no longer be recognized as an accurate physical representation. Niels Bohr was at the center of the development of the brand new *quantum mechanics*, which ultimately was responsible for rendering the old model obsolete. Rutherford had originally developed the model that we studied, but later, Bohr tried to tweak it to include aspects of the rapidly developing *quantum mechanics*. This new, modified model was named the *Rutherford/Bohr atom,* but ironically, and maybe because his name was easier to remember, Bohr's name became forever tied to an archaic model that had little to do with him or his contribution to physics.

ELECTRONS AND THEIR CLOUDS OF PROBABILITY

One of the biggest misconceptions from the old *Bohr atom* model is the character and quality of the *electrons* themselves. As physicists got to know more about these extremely small critical components, they began to realize that they are not actual "things" spinning around a core center, like the planets around our Sun. They are not "things" at all, but rather more like hazy "clouds of possibilities," and they only "exist" in an *indeterminate state* with a potential for physical expression. This potential for physical expression was mathematically described by the *probability wave function,* which is the most famous equation in *quantum physics*. The *probability wave function (or psi function)* was first developed by Nicolas Schrodinger, whose name is better known outside the physics community for his creation of the conceptual *quantum*-thought problem that involved a "cat in the box." This paradox, which is famously known as "Schrodinger's Cat," will be discussed later.

For almost a century, experiment after experiment have produced data which are most easily understood by accepting that *electrons* do not even physically exist until the moment that an *observer* becomes somehow involved. The actual act of *observation* (awareness) is what causes a *probability wave* to *collapse* into an actual physical thing, the *electron*. In my *quantum* studies, I initially imagined that these *electrons* were racing erratically and vibrating so they just became more difficult to measure. My early imaginations were wrong. Rather, in a very real sense, **electrons do not exist at all in our physical realm unless someone or something is observing them. With this act of conscious awareness, one of the many possibilities for their expression then becomes real and physical.**

As bizarre as this idea sound, it is only the very beginning of the strange and weird phenomena that we discover once we venture into the ever-expanding *quantum* world. As we look more deeply at *quantum* experiments and analyze the meaning of the reliable and repeated data, the more "illogical" results seem to become the norm. **It turns out that it is not just the electron that exhibits this odd behavior. All the other small particles of similar size, such as photons and neutrinos also demonstrate the same characteristics.** These tiny but not really existing "things" are more like potential ideas that have yet to form. At the same time, these are the particles that make up our matter.

Electrons are largely responsible for all chemical reactions in nature, most of which are the very processes that allow us to function. **Bigger things in this world, such as our bodies, are regulated and controlled by the behavior of tiny particles like electrons, which essentially do not even exist, are extremely elusive, and always exhibit very strange behavior. Since we are built from these very mysterious components, we are also not what we seem to be. We too are all these unexpected things.**

As Niels Bohr was fond of saying, *"Anyone not shocked by quantum mechanics has not yet understood it."*

THE ELECTROMAGNETIC SPECTRUM

Visible Light comprises only a very small part of a particular type of *energy* that we call *electromagnetic radiation*. All of these different frequencies of radiation have been grouped together and collectively named the *electromagnetic spectrum*. The entire *spectrum* includes many, very different but now well-understood types of *electromagnetic radiation,* which cover a wide range of different *frequencies* or *wavelengths;* but *visible light* is only the small band of these *electromagnetic frequencies* to which our human eyes are sensitive. Above and below what our eyes can see are many other higher and lower *frequencies* of *radiation,* which are completely invisible to our eyes and other senses. While many animals and insects can directly see or sense the neighboring frequencies of *infrared* and *ultraviolet,* we can only see these frequencies with instruments or special film. We do have the ability to feel heat from frequencies that are slightly lower than those we can see.

At one end of this *spectrum* we have the lowest *energy*, longest waves and lowest *frequencies,* which we have named *Radio Waves.* As the name implies, these are the *frequencies* used as carriers for radio broadcasting. As the frequencies get higher and wavelengths correspondingly shorter, we have, in order, *Microwaves, Infrared, Visible Light, Ultraviolet, X-rays* and *Gamma Rays.* As we move up through this list, the size of the energies involved also increases. We understand the dangers of these higher *energy* forms of *radiation,* so we try to avoid exposure to high *energy Gamma, X-rays and even ultraviolet,* but we constantly bathe ourselves in a sea of human-produced *Radio waves* and even *Microwaves* from Wi-Fi, body scanners and cell phones. Some of these other *frequencies* may also turn out to be less than completely safe–we might remember that *x-rays* were once thought to be harmless. As a general precaution, we should all probably try to limit our exposure to low-level *microwave frequencies* until we understand more about their long-term effects.

When we speak about *light* we usually are referring to only the very small and limited part of this *spectrum* that is visible. The range of *Visible light* is from the heat producing, *near infrared* on the *low-frequency* end of the *spectrum,* to the much more energetic *near ultraviolet* on the higher end. Even though we cannot see beyond the range of *Visible Light*, other species on Earth can see, sense or use many of these other frequencies. However, we have scientific instruments and tools that sense, measure, record, produce and control some of these otherwise-invisible *frequencies.*

Visible light is only that specific part of this *energetic radiation* spectrum that visually illuminates our world. *Visible light* is responsible for almost everything we understand about our sense of sight. It also contributes to some of the heat that fuels our planet, but most of the heat comes from the *infrared bands of radiation* that are not naturally visible to humans. *Visible light* is responsible for much of the *photosynthesis,* which is the critical beginning of our food chain. However, some of the critical *frequencies* that plants require for this process are also outside our range of vision at the *ultraviolet* end of the *visible spectrum. Photosynthesis* is another good reminder that we are all made from *energy. Light radiation* is absolutely critical to our *being* since we rely on it for many of the processes that are essential for life. Without *light* from the Sun, there would be no life on Earth, at least as we understand it. None of the plants and animals living on our planet can exist without light; even those that don't require it directly, need it indirectly.

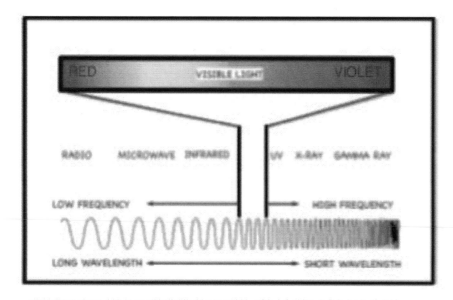

Visible light is only a small part of a much bigger range of electromagnetic radiation that we depend on for our technology and our very lives.

However, many of the discussions about *visible light* can also be applied to the rest of the *electromagnetic spectrum*. The entire *spectrum* plays a very critical role in our everyday lives, even if we are not consciously aware of this. This *spectrum* transmits and communicates *energy* and *information* at the speed of light throughout our planet and universe.

QUANTA AND THE PHOTOELECTRIC EFFECT

Today we all know that when light strikes a solar panel, electricity is produced in a real-world demonstration of what Einstein called the *photoelectric effect*. This *photoelectric effect* occurs because "packets" of light can act like particles and strike *electrons* within the material and send these *electrons* into motion. This might be visualized by thinking about what happens when a cue ball strikes other balls in a game of billiards.

The first detailed mathematical description of the *electromagnetic spectrum* is attributed to James Maxwell in the mid-1800s, and his groundbreaking work paved the way for Einstein. Faraday, Boltzmann, Plank and several other physicists had also been exploring the unusual nature of *electromagnetic radiation*. However, it was Einstein who released the paper in 1905 that first demonstrated that the "particles" in light traveled in these discrete packets. He named these packets *Quanta,* and this directly led to the name *quantum physics*. It is another irony in the history of physics that the name *quantum physics* came directly from Einstein's research because he became one of the physicists who most actively resisted these strange new ideas. Einstein fought the implications of his own discovery and would not accept *quantum physics* for most of the rest of his life. His famous quote *"God does not play dice with the universe,"* was an expression that reflected his personal criticism of that early period of the *quantum theory* development.

The name *quanta* references his discovery that when *energy* (*mass*) is released from *matter*, it is always grouped in discrete bundles or quantities that are called *quanta. Light* and all other forms of *electromagnetic radiation* exhibit this *particulate* property. His breakthrough paper on the *photoelectric effect* was a separate publication from his *theory of relativity,* marking this as the most productive period of his life. It was also the *photoelectric effect* paper that earned Einstein the Nobel Prize in 1921, some sixteen years later. Today, it is recognized that he also deserved another Nobel Prize for his contributions in *relativity*. However, because *relativity* was such a dramatic departure from the known paradigm, the Nobel committee was not yet ready to stick their necks out and award him that prize. In those years the scientific community was extremely confused, as the world of physics was being tumbled from several different directions. ***Due to this rapid succession of new discoveries, our once-certain world began to be seen as a much more uncertain world, but also one full of infinite and amazing possibilities.***

The *photoelectric effect* proved to be the key to uncovering one of the strangest principles of *quantum physics*–the dual *particle-wave* nature of *light*.

PARTICLE WAVE DUALITY

Einstein demonstrated that *Light* could behave as a beam of particles, which he called photons. This *particle nature* of light is what causes the *photoelectric effect,* and this collision and movement of electrons is what creates the electricity in our small, solar, battery-chargers; numerous, common, daylight sensors; solar, yard, night-lights; and our homes' *photovoltaic* systems. *Light* particles hit the *photocells* and dislodge *electrons*, thus causing the loose *electrons* to move, or at least move their charge, and generate electricity. This well-understood process is responsible for your camera's ability to set its exposure. It is also the basis for today's entire growing solar industry. The fact that *light* behaves as if it were a beam of particles is a fully integrated part of our scientific understanding and contemporary lives.

However, through experiments beginning in the early part of the 20th century, physicists and chemists discovered that light could also behave like a wave, similar to a sound wave. ***When we look at the characteristics of light experimentally, we sometimes see light acting like a stream of particles, and sometimes it behaves like a wave***. After a few, well-analyzed, early happy accidents in laboratories, and many clever and well-designed experiments–all reinforcing the same strange results–***physicists reached the understanding that light exhibits both wave and particle behavior, but never at the same time.*** At any given moment, *light* behaves as if made from either *particles* or *waves*. Specific experiments that reveal this split personality of *light* are discussed, in more detail, later in this section.

When we look a little further, this split behavior gets extremely strange, because what determines whether *light* acts as *waves* or as *particles* seems to be what the *observer* expects or anticipates. Since we are the *observers*, our expectations somehow determine how electromagnetic radiation behaves or appears. Again, an act of conscious observation influences or determines the physical outcome. ***This is revolutionary because it means that our expectations somehow directly influence the outer expression of our physical world!***

UNDERSTANDING QUANTUM PHYSICS

QUANTUM RESEARCH

Quantum physics is the physics of extremely small things; particles like *photons, electrons* and *quarks*. These are all much smaller than what we can directly "see" with the equipment or instruments available today, but unraveling this *quantum* world has been a primary goal in physics for over 90 years. Since our eyes or instruments can't directly see them, the behavior of these invisible particles is usually explored indirectly by mapping the trails or traces that they leave on various detectors or screens. Ironically, the equipment needed for studying these tiny particles must be enormous because of the extremely large quantities of *energy* involved. Interestingly, much of this new observational equipment, which allows us to further study the strange *quantum* world, is built from the very technologies that were derived from *quantum physics*–computers, lasers, etc. This closed loop illustrates a philosophically interesting new form of self-reflection–tools that were developed from quantum technology being used to study quantum particles in more depth.

The newest piece of equipment for this type of study, the *CERN Large Hadron Collider* (accelerator) in Switzerland is 17 miles in diameter. In Texas, construction began on an even larger and more powerful accelerator–over 50 miles wide–that was called the *Super-conducting Supercollider*, but its construction was halted in 1993 because of politics and budgetary concerns about overruns.

Using this expensive equipment, along with both simpler experimental devices and direct measurements and observations from space, we have accumulated a substantial amount of knowledge about this mysterious world of the ultra-small. From the perspective of our everyday existence, these tiny "things" clearly behave in very-unexpected ways. As already discussed, they exhibit *dual nature*, meaning they can be expressed as a *particle* or a *wave*, but not both at the same time. They never reveal which personality is being expressed until someone specifically asks the "question," often by running an experiment designed to measure one or the other. Until the very moment that they are *observed* (measured), these small things seem to exist in an *undetermined*, limbo-like state. Physicists call this undetermined dual personality "*quantum superposition.*"

Particles often jump to different locations, but they seem to do this in a special way, in which they do not pass through the space in-between. An *electron* may jump to an entirely different *energy* state–the orbits or rings in the old Bohr model–but they never appear anywhere in the middle, either physically or in the measured values. It is as if they just disappear from one place and then reappear in another. Also, the *particle-wave* personality shift and the "jumping," seem to happen instantly. This *information* transfer appears to be communicated even faster than the speed of *light*, which Einstein had concluded was the fastest speed possible.

Another important *quantum* principle is the discovery that we can't measure both the *position* and the *momentum* of subatomic particles at the same time. If we measure *position*, the very act of measurement interferes with the *particle* in a way that makes accurate measurement of *momentum* no longer possible. The reverse is also true, so measuring *momentum* means we can't accurately locate the *particle*. This observation is called the *uncertainty principle*. This principle, first proposed by Werner Heisenberg, states that we will always be uncertain about either the *position* or *momentum* of these *particles*. Again, our attention–an act of observation–interacts with and changes the very thing that we are observing.

Another strange phenomenon involving *subatomic particles* is their ability to communicate to each other instantly over infinitely vast distances. Physicists call this characteristic *entanglement*. Experiments have determined that these tiny *quantum particles* seem to instantly be able to communicate over any distance, even billions of miles or more. They refer to this *quantum* property as acting *non-locally*, meaning that the location of particles in space does not seem to matter or have an impact on their interaction. Timothy Ferris, a former Berkley professor and the author of *The Whole Shebang*, describes this phenomenon using one of my all-time favorite quotes about the strange *quantum* world–"*it is as if the quantum world has never heard of space–as if, in some strange way, it thinks of itself as still being at one place at one time.*" These *particles* behave as if the vast distances of our 3D universe are meaningless because they have a way around all of that. This new *quantum* world is clearly very different from the physical world we thought we once understood so well.

Lab Accident Beginnings of the Double-Slit Experiment

One of the earliest breakthrough discoveries in *quantum physics* occurred in 1925 in the lab of Clinto Davisson and Lester Germer. In the tradition of many other great discoveries, it began as a troublesome and accidental problem that occurred while they were exploring something quite different in their laboratory. An explosion rocked their lab and, unbeknownst to the scientists, the explosion changed the surface molecular structure on the piece of nickel that they were using as a target for an *electron beam*. After the explosion, the reflective pattern of the *electrons* off the surface of the nickel changed in a very-unexpected way. The real genius of that moment was that they quickly recognized that something significant had just occurred. It took Davisson and Germer a long time to sort out and start to understand the meaning of these results, but 10 years later they received the Nobel Prize for this contribution.

Quite accidentally, they had created the first *double-slit* experiment, but it was not by accident that they recognized its importance. As with so many other similar breakthrough discoveries in science, these researchers had just the right exposure and training to recognize that something of special importance had just occurred, and the insight and skills to analyze just what that was. Today, this "double slit" experiment remains one of the most significant and repeatedly replicated experiments in all of physics.

This experiment exposes three of the deepest mysteries in *quantum physics*: the dual *particle-wave* nature of subatomic particles; the role of the *observer;* and the *entangled* nature of subatomic particles. In one variation of the experiment, an *electron* or *photon* beam, or other similar subatomic particle beam, is directed through a barrier that has either one or two parallel slits open. Some portion of the beam passes through the slit(s), and then the *electrons* or photons hit the target beyond. The locations of the hits on the target are recorded. When one slit is closed, the recorded pattern of multiple particles hitting the target reflects that of a gun or peashooter which is aiming at the target beyond. This group of hits forms a classic *particle scatter pattern,* with the highest concentration of hits in the center and a diffuse pattern with fewer hits as it moves to the edges. This is the common clumping that is made by shotgun pellets hitting a target, so this pattern means the beam was behaving as if it were a collection of *particles* or projectiles. There is no mystery in these results because this is exactly the pattern expected from *particles.*

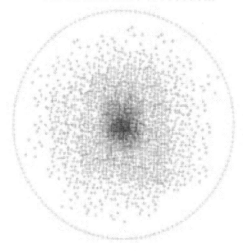

**Shotgun type of pattern created
with only one slit open**

In the second part of the experiment, both parallel slits remain open as the same beam is projected. From the first part of the experiment we learned that these beams are made from particles, so this time, with two slits, what we would naturally expect is two clustered groups that lie side by side. Instead something unexpected occurs. With two slits open, instead of two side-by-side *scatter patterns*, the target records a series of stripes. This stripe pattern is exactly what we would expect to see when *waves*, not *particles*, pass through these two slits. The *waves* that pass through each slit merge to form a rippled *interference and reinforcement pattern*.

Wave pattern generated when two slits are left open

This pattern is also well-known from *classical physics,* and the beams are now said to be behaving in a *wavelike* manner. The pattern created is the same pattern that a typical *wave* (sound, ocean waves, etc.) would make if the waves were propagated from two sources, such as when two stones are thrown into a still pond or there are two breaks in an ocean jetty. We would *not* expect this *wave behavior* from light because the first part of the experiment indicated that the beams were made from *particles*.

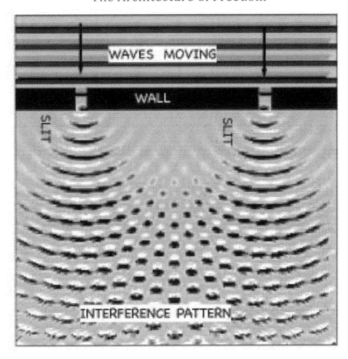

Classic double-slit wave interference pattern. Waves approach from the top and pass through the two holes in the black wall. Two waves then propagate as if they were from two different wave sources which were exactly in phase. The resulting pattern is similar to throwing two stones into a quiet pond.

When running the two-slit version of the experiment, if we slow the release of *electrons* (or photons, or any other subatomic particles) down to the point where only one *electron* is shot every 10 seconds or so, we might then expect the pattern to change. Because of slow, discrete "shots" that should not interact with each other, it would be "common sense" to expect the *particle scatter pattern* to be formed. Even with the beam adjusted for the slow and discrete release of individual particles, over time, as the pattern builds on the target, it becomes clear that the actual pattern formed is the rippled *wave interference pattern*. Slowing the release of the particles didn't change the results. The particles are completely unaware of the gaps in time between their releases and behave as if they are still a unified *wave*. If one slit is closed, then the slowly released *electrons* will, again, behave like *particles*, not *waves*. They again form the expected random *scatter pattern*. These extremely small *particles* do not seem to recognize *time* the same way that we do. All of these results are quite strange to our normal sensibilities.

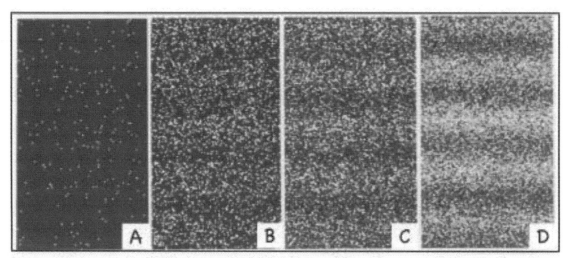

The particle-wave duality is demonstrated in these photos from an actual experiment. Slowly released individual photons are directed through two parallel slits towards a target. Because the photons are released one at a time, we might expect the classic random scatter pattern to build over time. Instead, as time progresses from A-D, we find a classic wave interference pattern formed. If one slit is closed, but everything else stays the same, the pattern then becomes the expected scatter pattern. The particles seem to sense how many slits are open. This unexpected behavior occurs no matter how much time passes between when these particles are released.

In one sense, and from our particular perspective, it could be said that there is some type of communication between the *particles*. It seems as if they share a "knowing" or awareness that there is only one slit open instead of two. It is as if the particles "know" and communicate that the *observer* changed the test conditions.

The very first double slit experiment used an *electron beam*, but exactly the same results are recorded for *light-beams* made of *photon particles*. Why and how does the very nature of these *subatomic particles* change simply because another slit has been added, and why is a wave pattern formed even when discrete *particles* are released with long periods of time between?

STANDARD EXPLANATION

After 85 years of repeating this experiment in many different ways and *always* getting the same results, the standard explanation is that *subatomic particle beams* exhibit a split personality. They sometimes appear as a *wave* and sometimes as a *particle,* but they always somehow "know" the type of experiment that the *observing* scientist has designed and behave accordingly. The personality that is expressed depends on the choices previously made by the researcher.

This quality is called the *particle-wave duality.* It is not only the fact that the duality exists that is so mysterious, but also that the *photon* or *electron* seems to be able to react instantly and "change" its fundamental nature to match the mindset of the *observer.*

Within the physics community, one generally agreed-upon conclusion is that **the observer's expectations somehow affect the outcome.** Does this sound familiar? Another explanation that emerges from this research is that before the moment of *observation*, these *particles* only exist as a *probability wave* (psi wave). They are not yet things, but they have the potential to exist in our physical world. After an act of *observation,* this wave of potentiality *collapses* and the actual *particles* become real. Also, we can only predict the *probability* of where they might land, so we can't know before the moment of the *observation* exactly where any individual *particle* will land. This dual, pre-*observation,* state of the *particles* is not thought to be an "either-or" type of existence, but rather more of a "both at the same time" phenomenon. One possible way of describing the results is to say that these *subatomic particles* exist in *all possible states* simultaneously until the moment of measurement or *observation*. After that point, their personalities are revealed, and they are only expressed in one state. This property, called *quantum superposition,* describes one interpretation of the experimental results and the *Schrodinger Wave Equation*.

The small particles that make up matter are, again, being described in ways that indicate matter, and therefore our world, is not as "real and solid" as we normally imagine. This is because the building blocks of matter exist only as potentialities, and these potentialities can and will be expressed in different ways. Later we will also discuss how these particles may exist in more than one place simultaneously.

Clearly, the fully deterministic, machine-like world of *classical physics* is no longer an accurate description of our existence. The new reality seems extremely probabilistic and mysterious when explained from our conceptual point of reference. This is because our expectations originate from old patterns that are built into our 3D consciousness. Whatever we are "seeing" and speculating upon is really only an *artifact* or *projection* of something that would make much more sense if it could be viewed and conceived from a *viewport* that contains more dimensions. What we witness, want to understand and are trying to explain is really only a shadow or illusion.

This illusion, of course, includes all of our attempted explanations for these experimental results. For example, the fact that we are surprised because the *electrons* or photons don't behave differently when the beam is slowed down is only because we see our world through this "lens of time." If we clearly understood that "time" is just an organizing concept for our brains, then results like these might not be as unexpected.

NON LOCAL BEHAVIOR-ENTANGLEMENT

One paradigm-changing discovery of *quantum physics* involves what physicists call *non-local interactions* or *entanglement*. Einstein referred to this phenomenon as *"spooky action at a distance"* because this was one of the implications of the experimental data from *quantum physics* that did not sit comfortably with him. *Non-local interaction* is a very-understated term for expressing something that is completely astounding. To understand and accept *non-local interaction* requires that we radically transform our view of the universe, and even of life itself.

Physicists have determined that two *quantum particles* that are *paired* and then subsequently separated by vast distances–even as far away as different *galaxies*–know instantly the moment that the other has changed certain characteristics, such as *spin*. Particles become *paired* by colliding or interacting in a number of different ways, and through these processes they establish what appears to be a mysterious form of communication with each other. Between *paired particles, information* appears to be communicated instantly–it moves faster than the fastest speed known: the speed of light. How does this happen? We do not really have a clear explanation, but we know that *non-local behavior* exists because we have repeatedly observed it in the laboratory.

In a *multi-dimensional* world where "time" does not exist and an *infinite* number of multiple universes are interacting in ways we can't really imagine, speed and distance have very different meanings. We just can't think of the universe in our normal and limited 3D terms and expect to have any real understanding of these experimental results. Again, we are only looking at the shadows or images and thinking that they are real.

It is noteworthy that *relativity* predicted that nothing was supposed to travel faster than light, yet I am aware of two situations where something has been determined to be moving faster than light. The communication speed in *non-local behavior* from *quantum theory* is the first example. The second is the rate of the *expansion of the universe* as derived from *relativity*. It might be that these two phenomena illustrate information or material moving faster than light. More likely, it might mean that since we don't really understand "time" or space, we can't really understand speed or movement. Our human understanding of speed is a concept that is built entirely upon our sense of "time."

PARADOXICAL THOUGHT EXPERIMENTS

We can theoretically discuss how *subatomic particles* exist in an *undetermined state*, but what does this say about larger objects or living things that we can physically see and touch? Over the years, various thought exercises have been created to illustrate the real-world absurdity of some of the *Quantum* explanations. It is one thing to talk about the weird behavior of *particles,* but what about the "real" things of our world. Since we are all made from these very weird, smaller *particles*, this is not just an abstract exercise.

The famous *Schrodinger's Cat* thought experiment is the paradox that first addressed this conundrum. In this thought experiment, a cat is placed in a black box with a *radioactive particle* that may or not may not *decay*. This can be then described by the *probability wave function*, where the chance of each outcome can be expressed mathematically. If the *particle decays* then a deadly *radioactive* event is initiated which instantly kills the cat. On the other hand, as long as the *particle* does not *decay*, the cat remains alive.

If we were to open the box at any moment we could make an *observation* to see if the cat has died or not. At the time of *observation* the cat will either be alive or dead because, for this cat, these are its only two possible states. What is the cat's condition if we have not yet *observed* the cat? According to *quantum theory* the cat is neither alive nor dead but rather in an *undetermined, pre-observational* state. To most of us, and especially to the cat inside the box, this is absolutely an absurd idea. This absurdity is precisely the point of *Schrodinger's paradox*. It artfully illustrates that a literal interpretation for the meaning of *quantum observations* is completely ridiculous from our perspective.

As already discussed, Albert-*"God does not play dice with the universe"*-Einstein, had a very difficult time with this *probabilistic quantum* world, and to express his frustration he presented his own two paradoxes. The more experimental example was the *EPR* (Einstein, Podolsky, Rosen) *paradox*. While much more technical than *Schrodinger's cats,* this paradox also pointed out logical problems with the standard *quantum* interpretation of the *uncertainty principle*. Einstein essentially argued that because communication between the particles had to occur instantly–faster than the speed of light–the laws of physics were being violated.

It is just not possible for our minds to understand something that occupies many dimensions, when we live and think using only three-dimensional concepts. When we try to digest and understand our multi-dimensional universe from our 3D perspective, we will always fall far short. We can gain a higher level of "understanding" by first learning to relax our habitual need to explain all things from within our logical and time-ordered conceptual system of thought. We must first learn to be comfortable with the unexplainable, as we become more able to just sit and be a part of this great mystery. With this relaxation, an understanding can gradually begin to form within us.

The next section looks at the development of *quantum physics* from more of a historical perspective. It covers some of the more enduring interpretations of these strange *quantum* observations, including those that form the foundation for this book. As these or any interpretations are discussed, it is necessary to remember that ideas in *quantum physics* and *relativity* are quickly evolving, and many things will change as our new paradigm evolves. ***These theories are being discussed with the ever-present caveat that any explanation created from the three-dimensional conceptual mindset and language will always miss the mark. We are exploring something that is beyond our current ability to discuss or understand. This is the nature of our deepest and most beautiful journeys.***

FOUR BRANCHES OF QUANTUM THINKING

INTRODUCTION

As *quantum physics* matured, three mostly distinct "schools" of thought emerged, as philosophers and physicists tried to understand and explain the strange and amazing experimental results. Recently, we have added a new, fourth school to our possible interpretations called *string theory*. This newest sub-theory is unique in that it is probably un-testable, yet it holds the greatest promise as a tool for the unification of *relativity* and *quantum physics*.

COPENHAGEN INTERPRETATION

The first, and for many years the dominant, *quantum* explanation is called the *Copenhagen interpretation*. Originally, Niels Bohr held the position as its chief interpreter and champion. Initially this was a tightly encamped group that believed that *quantum* weirdness can be best explained by accepting the fact that these small particles only exist as *waves of probability* or *potential* until there is the actual act of *observation*. *Superposition* is the name for the indeterminate state of *matter* that exists before actual *observation*. At its most extreme, this view implies that there is no objective reality because it is only the actual act of *observation* that nails down all particles, and therefore our reality. The Copenhagen camp went even further to declare that if "something is not *observable* then it does not even exist and is not even worth talking about." Another way of expressing this belief is "Reality does not exist without *observation.*"

In a sense the Copenhagen view is a "what you see is what you get" interpretation. By itself this is a very interesting insight, but many of the more radical in this camp believe that this interpretation excludes all others. While this Copenhagen approach is extremely compelling and can lead us down many avenues of interesting thought, it is also extremely limiting. It is very natural to explain new observations using concepts we already know and understand, but it becomes absurd to imply that there are not other ways to view the same data. Any claim that this is the only possible correct interpretation of the experimental results becomes a conceptual dead-end, which seems quite contrary to the very universe it attempts to describe—a universe where things seem to continue on forever, while allowing any and all possibilities to unfold.

I personally feel that this interpretation is largely an artifact of our limited perspective, and, while it is certainly paradigm busting, it is not a good description of how things might work in a multi-dimensional universe. The *Copenhagen* camp today might respond to this criticism by saying that an *"actual explanation is not really even necessary because the results speak for themselves."* Regardless, it was a game-changing and insightful first attempt at explaining some very surprising experimental results.

MANY WORLDS

The second quantum "school" or camp is called *Many Worlds* and is based upon a theory that was first proposed by Hugh Everett in 1955. He made an extremely bold leap by proposing the radical idea that every time a decision is made or a path is chosen, the "world" or universe actually splits or divides. With that split, another universe or world is instantly created. Consciously, we appear to only observe one universe, but all the other possible outcomes also exist from that moment on. Each time there is an act of observation or a decision is made, the world splits again and creates new worlds to contain all the possible outcomes. All these new possible worlds have the same *logically consistent* past; but now multiple worlds exist reflecting multiple paths to every possible future outcome, forming a pattern that resembles an ever-branching flow chart or the branches of a tree.

This perspective evolves from *quantum superposition*, the Copenhagen idea that *quantum particles* exist in all possible states until a *measurement* is made causing the *wave to collapse,* which then allows a single state to be expressed. The very act of *observing* or participating somehow ties the observer's awareness to only one of these possible outcomes, or worlds, so the person having this experience has no direct sense of those other worlds that are "created" by all the other possible choices. These other worlds fully exist after the split, even though, for some unknown reason, they are completely invisible to us from within our standard state of consciousness. From our perspective it is as if we board one train, while the other trains, which we might have just as easily boarded, speed off in different directions and disappear. From the *Many Worlds* perspective, all these trains and destinations exist equally from that moment of decision.

The *Many Worlds* interpretation obviously raises many questions, but I believe that with this radical theory, we are finally starting to look in the right direction for a better understanding of just what these strange *quantum* experimental results might represent. This *Many Worlds* idea has extraordinary implications that will help shape much of the rest of this book.

While this particular theory already existed in the late 1960s, when I began my study of quantum physics, none of my professors introduced this vision or any other explanation for what the strange math might mean. In 1969, the *Many Worlds* theory was either mostly unknown or seen as far too crazy and, therefore, it was seldom entertained in a serious academic discussion about the meaning of this new physics. Only much later would serious physicists begin to appreciate this strange idea as a real possibility.

Another way of stating Everett's theory could be: ***all possible outcomes do occur in a very real and concrete sense, and every possible outcome creates a new entire branch of history. In this way a new "universe" is created for every possibility that could exist.*** This original *Many Worlds* view has all possible outcomes being "created" at the moment of decision or *observation*. "Time" is, therefore, once again involved in and responsible for ordering events. However, ***it is also possible that beyond our "time"-ordered conscious mind, in a very real sense, all these possibilities have always existed, exist now, and will always exist. They are not really created at the moment of observation or decision. Instead, we just become aware of them because of our choices.***

Again, we find ourselves in very odd, but now somewhat more familiar, territory. Our *quantum universe* is starting to make its own strange kind of sense. We exist in a universe with every possible outcome but, normally, we consciously interact with only one path, or *world*, at a time. This may be because we can only handle a limited amount of *information* at any one time, or it may be that we can only sense or cognize that particular part of the universe that harmonically *vibrates* or *resonates* with our *being*. (Later in the book I will discuss bilocation. This is the possible, but presently rare, human ability to participate in more than one world at a time.)

When "Worlds Split"

We have seen that in the *Many Worlds theory* there is a path or *world* that exists for every possible observation, outcome or decision. When any choice is made, such as choosing to drive down that "road less traveled," we can imagine that somewhere in some parallel universe walks one of our virtual doppelgangers–the one that made that other choice to drive down the busier road. A doppelgänger or "double walker" is the paranormal double of a person from the German folkloric tradition. *Many Worlds* physicists speak of the world "splitting" into two or more copies every time any choice is made. Since the splitting goes on forever, with multiple paths for every thought or movement of every living *being*, this process creates a very complex and fully-interconnected, branched web. This is one way to visualize the "Web of all Possibilities."

Living within our world of linear "time," where the arrow of time marches ceaselessly only forward, our world seems to be splitting constantly and endlessly. However, from a broader perspective, one that allows the multi-dimensional and timeless fabric of existence, all of these different worlds already exist. They exist now, and forever, and all these *worlds* are always intimately connected to each other and everything else in the universe. None of the components are the least bit separated by what we perceive as the vast distances of "time" and space. As discussed in the next section, this very intimate interconnection can be described as *enfoldment*.

Beyond our horizon of "time," worlds already exist for every possibility, every path, every decision and all the various possibilities that could unfold. They all exist at once, in this and every moment, and they all fit together in perfect harmony. Each of our conscious "selves" is experiencing one spot within this infinite Web, while all of our doppelgänger selves can be found enjoying our other possible choices. Our state of consciousness creates our deep resonant self, and this is what determines exactly where, when and how each of us explores this "Web of all possibilities." If we change our consciousness at deep levels, we change the way we vibrate, which instantly changes what we experience and just where we interact with this Web. In one sense, our level of vibration determines which of our infinite doppelgangers is most directly tied to our conscious awareness.

Navigation through this Web can become relatively simple and direct by learning how to connect more deeply to our deep *resonant* selves. Once we really learn how to navigate this terrain, we will one day be able to become much more like traveling tourists as we surf through the "Web of Possibilities." Today, many people are consciously exploring and experimenting with this newly revealed and extremely exciting, playground.

Bohm's Enfolded Universes

The third major interpretation of quantum experimental results is David Bohm's *implicate order*, or *enfolded universe* theory, which was proposed a few years after Everett's *Many Worlds* explanation. It wasn't until a fundamental cornerstone of this theory, the *nonlocal* nature of *particles*, was confirmed by actual experiments in the 1970s that Bohm's theory started to receive its deserved attention. This interpretation of *quantum mechanics* implies a swirled order to the universe that is not unlike oil stirred into water. Oil and water, when shaken like in salad dressing, touch each other everywhere. This is *enfolding,* and it allows for *non-locality* to occur through its very structure. ***Because of the enfolded nature of creation, every part of one universe is always intimately connected to every part of every other universe.***

Bohm and others also compare this vision of the universe to a *hologram*, where every piece of *information* is stored everywhere in such a way that the entirety of all creation can literally be seen within even the smallest pieces. (Later in the book there will be an expanded discussion of *holographic theory* and the nature of projected image *holograms,* such as those commonly seen in *holographic image* demonstrations.)

Some physicists have taken this idea a step further, theorizing that, at some deep level, the reason for this *non-local behavior* and instant interconnectivity is because ***all things that appear to be separate are really only one thing!*** (This paradigm-shattering idea is discussed in more detail later, because I believe this represents a deep, critical and fundamental truth about our existence.)

STRING THEORIES

Elementary Building Blocks

Ancient cultures embraced air, water, fire and earth as the *elementals*, or the basic building blocks of *matter*. Beginning with the ancient Greeks, the *atom* was recognized as the primary building block of *matter*, meaning that the atom was believed to be the smallest indivisible particle that nature used to make up *matter*. For the next 2,000 years it was thought that *atoms* could not be subdivided. Then, in the early 20th century, we learned that the atom itself was constructed from *protons, neutrons* and *electrons.* At that point, we began to view these *subatomic* particles as the most *elemental* components of matter. Since only three primary particles were replacing a list of more than 100 larger *elements*, most physicists viewed this as a great simplification and, therefore, very good progress. However, those who felt that we had finally found the smallest pieces of *matter* with these subatomic particles were to be surprised again when, in the 1960s, physicists discovered *quarks*: the even-smaller building blocks of *protons, neutrons* and *electrons*.

All of these new subatomic particles behaved as predicted by strictly adhering to the rules of *quantum mechanics.* At the time *quarks* were discovered, these *quantum* rules were being called the *standard model.* Unfortunately, even with all these additional discoveries of smaller and yet smaller *particles*, we still could not find a good way to combine *relativity* and *quantum theory* to allow *gravity* to be more directly connected with the other three, much more powerful, known *forces–electromagnetic, strong nuclear* and *weak nuclear.* For most physicists this *unification* problem was a huge indicator that something wasn't quite right.

There is an important side discussion about the idea that *relativity* showed us: that *forces* don't really exist. Because *gravity* was determined to be a local deformation of *spacetime,* it seems quite logical that the other three *forces* should be reconsidered in a similar way. "Force" just like "time" might only be an artifact: a concept created within our three-dimensional mindset. It is, therefore, very possible that this search to *unify the forces* might only be a well intentioned, but misguided quest.

Early String Theory

In the 1980s, a newly proposed theory re-energized the *unification* movement by presenting a new, and fourth, interpretation of the *quantum* experimental results. Called *string theory*, it proposed that even *quarks* were subdivided, and this time the smallest elemental pieces were no longer particles, but rather more like tiny vibrating *strings*. These extremely small *strings* were found to exist in various shapes, with some even forming loops. According to *string theory*, everything physical originates or manifests from these extremely small, vibrating *strings*. Even more interesting, the math indicates that these *strings* only exist in a minimum of 10 dimensions. *Strings* are always in vibration, and the precise way that they vibrate determines specifically which types of particles are then manifested.

String Theory and its spinoffs are mathematical and theoretical in nature, and they have no experimental physical proof. They are all based on many extra dimensions, therefore any experimental proof will probably elude us for a long time because we have yet to conceive of physical experiments for testing theories that involve extra dimensions. However, the mathematics is extremely exciting and, fortunately, much easier to manipulate than actual experiments in the physical world. The forms that this math reveals make a special kind of sense to those familiar with this type of mathematical manipulation and exploration.

It is as if these *strings* vibrate, and as they vibrate they create music-like *resonances* and harmonies. These "mini-symphonies" then result in the creation of the small physical *particles* that become the building blocks of all *matter*. ***According to string theory, all matter begins with vibration. In the beginning there is a "song," which is originally performed in a 10-dimensional concert hall! What we interact with directly is that part of the symphony that reaches and translates into our three-dimensional world.***

Super-string and Super-gravity

The sticky problem of *gravity* not being mathematically describable from within *quantum mechanics* remained a problem until the *string theory* was further "modified" to allow for the existence of the *graviton*. This is the theoretical *particle* that obeys all *quantum* rules, while it also helps to explain *gravity*. With the *graviton*, many physicists saw the potential for *unification* and called this sub-theory and its variant *super-string* and *super-gravity*, respectively. However, before long, four other, fully consistent *super-string* theories, which described other possible arrangements, were hypothesized. The problem was that they all seemed to directly compete with each other.

As physicists discovered many more of these possible *super-string* arrangements, they quickly became caught up in an amazing embarrassment of riches. It was eventually calculated that there were 10 to the power of 500 possible different forms for these *strings*. This number can be written longhand as a 1 followed by 500 zeros. With that many different forms of *string theory*, how could the correct form be determined and just which form, or combination of forms, was correct?

M-theory

Finally, in the mid-1990s a *string theorist* named Edward Witten, who many feel is the most brilliant living mind on the planet (and not just for his contributions to physics), determined that the five different, originally-proposed *string theories* (and therefore all 10^{500} variations) were simply different views of the same theory, and could be combined into one theory if only one more dimension were added to *string theory*. *M-theory*, which is a further refinement of *string theory*, therefore requires 11 dimensions instead of just 10.

According to Witten, the "M" does not stand for anything special or significant, but others have proposed that it could represent an "M" for membrane, or even a "W" upside down for "Witten." According to *M-theory*, the source of all creation seems to be a *membrane* functioning like a multi-dimensional drumhead. Because of this description, I personally like to think the letter "M" stands for "musical," since this theory effectively describes the source of all *matter* in a way that is very similar to a vibrating musical instrument. The *strings* from 10 dimensional *string theories* are constructed from one less dimension than these membranes, and can be thought of as dimensionally-reduced slices of this *membrane*. This degree of "dimensional reduction" is similar to realizing how the sphere was seen as only as a circle when dimensions were reduced by one in the novel *Flatland*.

According to *M-theory*, these multi-dimensional vibrating *membranes, M-branes*–or just *branes*–are the source of all material creation. In our three-dimensional *viewport*, all that we can ever see or experience of these *membranes* is the final *projections* that eventually manifest as *particles* in our reality. ***The particles that we interact with in our 3D universe are only the dimensionally reduced artifacts, shadows or projections that ultimately reach us from this unfathomable 11-dimensional symphony.***

One of the most exciting potentials of *M-theory* is that it provides a pathway to combine *relativity* and *quantum mechanics* in a mathematically elegant way. This quality alone has attracted the focused attention of the physics community. While *M-theory* explains more of the mystery and connects *relativity* and *quantum mechanics*, it continues to bother many physicists because it is still untestable. It will remain this way until we find a method for experimenting with and peering into extra-dimensional space.

God's Drumhead

I believe that the best current explanation for how the universe works involves some blending, or melding, of these several different *quantum* schools. The *Copenhagen* and *Many Worlds* interpretations, alongside Bohm's *Enfoldment* and some of the newer insights of *string theory*– especially its youngest offshoot, *M-theory*–can all work together to build a more accurate and unified vision.

This book includes a number of different attempts to describe this vision of the universe, while always being aware that communicating what these multi-dimensional theories mean, using the language, logic and ideas of our 3-D perspective, is a conceptually impossible task. ***Words and concepts will always fall short of describing what the universe is, but they certainly can help us better understand what our universe is not.***

A good basic foundation for beginning to describe how our universe "works" from within our *viewport, is* Everett's *Many Worlds*, which has all possible outcomes and histories simultaneously expressed. Twenty-five years ago, I probably would have laughed at this concept. This theory seems impossible, or even ridiculous, from our framework, where "time" regulates everything. With "time" in the picture, worlds literally have to split apart at the very moment of decision. It seems this would involve an extremely dramatic, violent and confusing physical process. Instead, from our perspective, most of our decision-making seems subtler. However, if all the various possible outcomes already exist, outside of "time," and together they form a preexisting 'Web of all Possibilities," then what we are doing is more like choosing our path, while moving between these choices. This process would be far less disruptive and feel more like just a swim in the river, or a drive down the road.

The difference between these two ways of viewing *Many Worlds* hinges on how we see and understand "time"–is it an arrow moving in one direction or does it all unfold at once? ***Outside of time, all worlds lie together in a single multi-dimensional soup, where everything is so deeply enfolded that all possible outcomes are instantly available, from any place, at any time. Any piece of information from anywhere or anytime is directly, and immediately, available from any and every other point in the Web. The Web acts like a large holographic storage system. No matter where we look, no matter how small the part, all the information about all the possibilities is always locally and immediately available.***

M-theory does a wonderful job of helping us visualize a deep-level structure, while still using our conceptual language. This *membrane* may be the actual source of all of creation, or the real source may eventually be found to originate from somewhere even deeper. Regardless, the theory presents the exciting idea that our creation is the result of *vibrations* that originate well beyond the *subatomic* level, in a terrain of multiple dimensions. ***Here, or possibly somewhere even deeper, the most fundamental drumhead may be discovered. When it is "played," its multi-dimensional vibrations produce a symphony that forms everything we experience in creation. This could be thought of as God's drum!***

COSMOLOGY

INTRODUCTION

Cosmology is the scientific study of the origin and development of our universe. Modern *cosmology* began with the paradigm-shifting work of Kepler, Copernicus, Brahe and Newton. Over the last 100 years, cosmology has again been revolutionized by the incorporation of *relativity* and *quantum physics*. Just as *classical physics* helped usher us out of the "flat earth" paradigm, *relativity* and *quantum physics* have stretched the limits of our imagination by introducing many brand new ideas about the potential nature and *shape* of our universe. ***We are now discovering that there is far more connection between "out there" and "in here" than we ever imagined.*** As a result of these discoveries, *Cosmology* now includes dramatic, new approaches to issues such as *gravity*, empty space, *time*, consciousness and the *observer*. In addition, a steady stream of new discoveries about things such as *black holes* and *dark matter* are rapidly, and completely, changing our ideas about the nature of our universe.

DARKNESS WITHIN OUR UNIVERSE–DARK MATTER

One of the most unexpected discoveries in modern *cosmology* recently came to light when newer technologies allowed scientists to more accurately analyze the relative motion of the various objects of our known universe. It was discovered that there simply wasn't enough visible *mass* present to produce the relative motions of the stars and *galaxies*, account for rotational speeds of *galaxies,* and explain the *gravitational bending* of light from distant stars. The amount of *gravitational matter* necessary to explain these inner workings of the universe wasn't just a little bit off. It wasn't even off by double. It was off by at least a factor of five. This means that there is less than one-fifth of the visible *matter* that should be present to produce the relative motion of everything that is visible to our eyes and instruments. By some calculations, we only see and understand one-tenth of the *gravitational material* needed to make the universe behave the way it does.

One of two things is probably occurring. Either all physicists are making a colossal mistake in theory or calculations, or 80-90 percent of the *gravitational* "stuff" that makes up our known universe is completely invisible to our senses, instruments and technology. We have no idea what this invisible *gravitational material* is, but we know that it affects and interacts with everything else that we see. Because this mysterious "stuff" emits no light, and we can't see it directly, we call it *dark matter*–it is "dark" to our eyes, tools and senses. We now include *dark matter* in all contemporary calculations about the cosmos, even though its existence has only become fully recognized since the 1990s.

In addition, we recently have discovered that *dark matter* is not the only hidden "dark" stuff in our universe. There is also *dark energy,* and there is even more of this than there is of *dark matter.* Before we examine *dark energy* in more detail, let us first discuss the *shape* of our universe.

SIZE AND ARRANGEMENT OF THE UNIVERSE

Looking at the extents of our known 3D universe, and wondering about how big it really is, we can imagine that there are five basic possibilities. The first possibility is that the universe could be *finite*, alone in creation, and have an edge somewhere beyond the limits of our present view. The second possibility is it could be alone, but *infinite* and extend forever. This *infinite* universe could be formed in different ways, which we will also discuss. The third possibility is an interesting hybrid of the first two. The universe could be *finite* and *closed* in a bubble-like fashion, but it might be only one of an *infinite* number of these *finite* "bubble" universes. Of course, the fourth possible combination is that it is *finite* and one of a *finite* number of other universes, and the fifth is that the universe is *infinite* and one of an *infinite* number of other *infinite* universes.

The first possible configuration, the lone finite universe, is the easiest for most of us to understand. With this configuration, the universe would simply end somewhere beyond our *cosmic horizon,* which today is a distance of about 40 billion *light-years* in any direction (one light year is about six trillion miles).

The light from stars that we are seeing and measuring today originally left those stars 15 billion years ago, when these stars were much closer to us. Since then, the universe has been rapidly expanding so our visible universe has, by now, expanded in size from 15 billion *light-years* to about 40 billion *light-years* in every direction. With this particular finite configuration, somewhere beyond the limits of our vision, the universe must simply end. This sounds very similar to the way our ancestors thought about their "flat earth." (Am I revealing a personal prejudice?) If this arrangement accounted for the full extent of our universe, it would be *finite* but still extremely large and full of possibilities. Today, we can see hundreds of billions of *galaxies,* and each of these contains hundreds of billions of stars. Even without other, added dimensions, this type of universe would still be large enough for many other worlds that might be similar to our own.

To understand the other four possible arrangements, we will first need to become familiar with a few new terms and concepts. Scientists speak of the *shape* of the universe; and when they describe the *shape,* they are speaking about a specific mathematical quality that is beyond our three-dimensional conceptual ability to accurately visualize.

We understand from Einstein's *relativity* that a large *mass*, such as a star, deforms *spacetime* locally or near to the region of this large *mass*. We call this deformation *gravity*. As it turns out, all the *matter* and *energy* in the universe, since they are two forms of same thing, also work *non-locally* and in unison to deform the entire universe in a particular way. We call this larger deformation of the entire universe its *shape*. To simplify our discussion we will use well-understood 3D forms such as ball, pretzel, saddle and tabletop to describe these shapes. We must remind ourselves that these terms, which describe common and easily visualized 3D shapes, are conceptually very different from the possible shapes that would be formed in a *multi-dimensional* universe.

We can understand this better by first looking at more common shapes. When we describe 2D shapes, we can visualize them because they are framed or held by a larger *extent* that we can also understand. If we talk about a triangle we are imagining that triangle sitting on a flat plane, possibly in a flat painting or lying on a tabletop. In this case, we already understand the two dimensional form that contains, or holds, these shapes. We are able to visualize shapes like triangles and squares because we can contain these shapes within this familiar framework. If we expand one more dimension, we can then describe 3D shapes, such a spheres and cubes. They are also contained or held by a familiar space, the entire volume of our 3D universe, or some smaller subset of this volume. We can visualize this because we have the 3D conceptual ability to visualize and understand this container.

However, when we speak about the *shape* of our universe, we are referring to its shape within *spacetime*. We have no spatial or dimensional concepts that allow us to describe or visualize this region because it is built from more than our familiar three dimensions. Our ability to visualize or understand this region is beyond our *conceptual horizon;* therefore we are only really able to comfortably visualize our known *viewport–3D space*. ***The outer boundary of that which humans can understand or visualize is somewhere on our 3D side of the more expansive space, which Einstein called spacetime. Spacetime might be described as a container that is more than three-dimensional but less than fully four-dimensional.***

Physicists often describe three primary *shapes* for the universe. It could have a *positive curve*, it could have a *negative curve,* or it could be *flat* with a zero *curve*. There are other variants and possibilities, some of them very specific, but these three *shapes* are the most important ones to understand for this level of discussion. The direction of *curvature* is determined by the amount of attractive *mass* (and *energy*) that the universe contains in a given area: its density. A higher density (of *matter* and associated *energy)* will produce a *positive curvature* (ball *shape* is the closest 3D equivalent), while a lower amount of energy and mass will produce a *negative curvature* (saddle *shape* is the 3D equivalent). It takes just the right amount of gravitational material to produce a zero curvature *flat shape* (tabletop).

Shape is also fully interrelated to whether the universe is *infinite* or *finite*. A *positive curvature* leads to a closed system that is always *finite*. A *negative curvature* usually, but not always, results in an *infinite* universe, while a zero *curvature* (flat) means that the universe must be *infinite*.

There is a possibility that the universe could *curve* back on itself and twist in some unexpected way that resembles a four-dimensional racetrack (pretzel *shape*). Instead of looking deep into eternity, we might be looking at some of the same objects multiple times because of multiple loops and twists around the track. This idea evolves from Einstein's work, and the curved space donut diagram discussed earlier describes the simplest version of this possibility. If the universe *curves* in one direction (convex or ball), this will result in a very big universe, but not an *infinite* one. Because of the potential closure caused by *curved* space, this type of universe layout has been called a *bubble universe.* If ours turns out to be a *bubble universe,* it could be all alone, one of a finite number of these, or one of an *infinite* number of bubble universes.

A substantial amount of brand new, but very reliable, data is surprising many cosmologists because, if correct, then it turns out that our universe has exactly the right amount of mass – including dark matter–to make the universe flat. <u>This also means that, to the best of our current scientific knowledge, the universe must be infinite.</u> This new data was compiled from the WMAP (Wilkinson Microwave Anisotropy Probe) satellite that was launched in 2001. Its seven-year mission was to make fundamental measurements of *cosmology,* including measuring *cosmic microwave background radiation.*

The most recently analyzed results from this probe fully support the *flat shape,* even though it seems rather improbable that the universe could have exactly the right amount and distribution of *mass* and *energy* to make this possible. The mathematics of a *flat universe* is particularly elegant because in a *flat universe* the overall total *energy* will be zero. Because of this, the *flat* universe is a form that could possibly have emerged from net-zero *energy* condition during the process of creation.

It is also important for us to understand whether the universe will continue to *expand,* accelerate its expansion or eventually begin to *contract.* This, after all, will be a critical factor in any "future" for our Earth! Because of the WMAP data, we now are relatively certain (to 99 percent certainty) that our universe is *flat.* Analyzed mathematically, this *flat* universe, without any other input, will continue to *expand,* but over time the *rate of expansion* will slow down. This means the *rate of expansion* will eventually slow down to almost zero. The current WMAP data is being analyzed and reanalyzed as I write this, and multiple new insights are anticipated. This, our most current exploration of *background radiation,* has been extremely productive and revealing. This project will almost certainly produce new and dramatic insights into our very existence.

DEEPER DARKNESS-DARK ENERGY

When Einstein presented *relativity* at the turn of the last century, he was convinced that the universe was stable and *non-expansive*; but to his dismay he discovered that his own equations demonstrated otherwise. Because of his strong personal belief in a stable universe, Einstein eventually fudged his equations, years after his original presentation, to adjust them so that they showed and expressed his belief in a *non-expanding* universe. He later regretted doing this, calling it the *"biggest mistake of my career."*

In the late 1920s, Edwin Hubble confirmed by observation that the universe was indeed *expanding,* but he couldn't tell if this expansion was slowing down and might someday reverse. Later studies indicated that the rate of *expansion* might really be *accelerating* and, if this data were correct, it would mean that the universe was indeed *expanding,* and expanding faster and faster. For this or any type of expansion to occur, some powerful *force* must be pushing out; one that is more powerful than the opposing contraction caused by *mass* induced *gravity.*

It is relatively easy to understand why this is so. When we throw a ball up into the air, eventually the attractive *gravity* will slow down the ball, so the ball returns to Earth. If we throw a ball straight up in the air, at first it travels quickly but then it gradually slows down (*de-accelerates*), until it eventually stops and falls back to earth at an ever-increasing rate of speed. The object slows down as it climbs higher and then falls unless there is some additional *energy,* such as the firing of a rocket engine, added to the system. Rockets and racing cars speed up (*accelerate*) over time because the fuel burning provides the extra *energy* input to overpower the *forces* acting in the opposite direction (*gravity* and *friction*).

A single impulse *big bang* type of event is analogous to the act of throwing a ball up into the air. If the universe began with a *big bang* then eventually the outward movement of the universe should stop and reverse itself.

Over the years we have learned, through Earth-bound telescopes and instruments, satellite observation and, finally, the WMAP, that the *expansion of the universe*, while slowing down, is not slowing down as quickly as would be expected from a single impulse *big bang* kind of event. Some unseen *force* must be working against *gravitational mass attraction* and be responsible for the continuing expansion of the universe. Without this extra "*force*" pushing out, the universe would eventually start to contract. Considering the most recent research, cosmologists are quite sure this contraction is not going to occur, so a repulsive *force* which is opposing *gravity* must be adding to, and reinforcing, the initial *big bang*. What this means is that there is some mysterious *repulsive energy* being added to the system that we can't see or measure directly.

This *energy* is now fully recognized and named *dark energy*. Like *dark matter*, it is not visible to us, but we need it in our calculations to explain the types of movement that we are observing in our universe.

Even though, as we have discussed, *matter* and *energy* are equivalent, *dark matter*, which makes up at least 80 percent of the *gravitationally attractive mass* of the universe, and *dark energy* are very different things. Our naming of this unknown influence on our universe was unfortunate and inconsistent. *Dark matter* produces an attractive "*force*" similar to other matter, so it is named consistently. *Dark energy*, on the other hand, results in a repulsive "*force*" which counteracts *gravity*, and this makes it very different from other more "normal" types of energy. **We have absolutely no idea what this outward "force," called dark energy, is, how it works, or where it comes from. However, we have calculated that it represents 73-76 percent of all the energy and matter that is in the universe.** We have only named it *dark energy* because, again, we simply can't see it.

Dark energy is not just another form of *energy*. *Energy* is convertible to *mass* and is attractive or gravitational in nature. *Dark Energy* is repulsive. It counteracts the normal action of *matter* and *energy*. However, *Dark Matter* and *Dark Energy* do have three things in common: 1) they both affect the size, shape and expansion of the universe in significant ways; 2) we can't "see" them; and 3) we know almost nothing about them.

Let us take a closer look at the astounding breakdown of the composition of our "known" universe. Of the "known" *energies* and *matter* that make up the universe, about 73 percent is *dark energy* and 23 percent is *dark matter*, both of which we understand virtually nothing about, while 3.6 percent is cosmic dust and 0.4 percent is stars, planets asteroids, etc. **The most recent WMAP III analysis is even more extreme. It indicates that the universe is 76 percent dark energy, 22.5 percent, dark matter and only 1.5 percent baryonic matter.** (Baryonic matter is normal physical matter such as cosmic dust, planets, stars, asteroids, etc.)

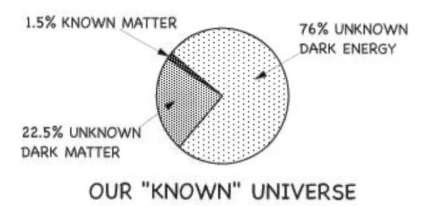

1.5% KNOWN MATTER

76% UNKNOWN DARK ENERGY

22.5% UNKNOWN DARK MATTER

OUR "KNOWN" UNIVERSE

When we peer more deeply into that very small percentage of *baryonic matter* that is found in our universe, we find that even the very atoms that make up this small part of everything that we think we "understand," are composed mostly of empty space. This empty space is also mostly filled with *dark energy*. ***The actual amount of physical "stuff" that we (and all the stars, planets, asteroids and cosmic dust) are made of what constitutes, at the most, an extremely small proportion of creation. The vast majority of what gives form to our universe, and therefore form to our bodies, we admittedly know little or nothing about!***

Over the last one hundred years we have made enormous advances in our understanding. One thing that we are learning is that the deeper we look into the nature of the cosmos, the more we discover that there is an unknown and growing mystery that we really know nothing about. With each deeper probe, the mysteries seem to be multiplying, expanding, and becoming a much more significant part of our universe.

We have been only discussing the three-dimensional portion of the universe; and, even if our universe is only three dimensional, it now seems probable that in some form, this universe keeps on going out forever in a never-ending vastness that is a wondrous expression of infinity. If this is the arrangement of our universe, then we can say with absolute certainty that there is an infinity of other "worlds" just like ours within this never-ending vastness. If the universe is infinite, there is no possibility of debate amongst physicists and mathematicians about the likelihood of other worlds exactly like ours. If the universe is infinite, then this very strange and unbelievable outcome is a given.

Why this has to be all hinges on the meaning of the mathematical concept of infinity.

OUR UNIVERSE IS INFINITE

I have briefly outlined several lines of reasoning that all lead to the conclusion that we live in an *infinite* universe. *So far, these possibilities describing an infinite universe have been derived using only three-dimensional concepts that include a one-directional passage of "time." If we add extra dimensions into this structure, the chance that our universe is finite and unique becomes even more impossible because, when we add dimensions, the potential different pathways to the infinite will become endless.* Once we add dimensions, there is virtually no possibility that our universe is only finite.

A *finite* universe that is based on fixed and limited bounds could be soothing to a personality that seeks definition, self-importance or control. *However, it has become impossible to avoid the pressing weight of information and evidence that shows we live in an infinite universe. The only real questions now seem to be in what way is it infinite and exactly what does an infinite universe mean to our lives?*

Considering what they can see, measure and understand with their contemporary cosmological tools, many *physicists* and *cosmologists* are convinced that the universe is *infinite in its extent,* but the actual form of this *infinite* expression has yet to be clearly determined.

INFINITY

Since there is likely to be confusion about the concept of *infinity*, I will discuss and explain it in more detail before we develop these ideas further.

Visualizing Infinity

"If the doors of perception were cleansed, everything would appear to man as it is, infinite."

William Blake, "The Marriage of Heaven and Hell"

Our conceptual minds depend on relationships. We are constantly referencing and relating new experiences and ideas to older concepts that we already know and understand. We tend to work more easily within a certain range of numbers and sizes, and understand certain common sizes and quantities. Easily understood are numbers like one, ten, a thousand or even fractions, such as one-quarter. A bit more difficult, at least until we have some practice, are quantities like a million dollars (six zeros), Earth's eight billion inhabitants (nine zeros), 12 trillion dollars of US debt (12 zeros); or on the other end of the scale, very small numbers such as the width of a human hair, which is 100 microns or 4/1000 of an inch. These numbers are quite large or small, but they still directly relate to our lives. However, when we start looking at distances between ends of the visible universe (the enormous) or size of the particles that make up *matter* (the minuscule), our ability to comfortably understand these numbers then falls short. This is because we have nothing in our direct experience that we can relate to these numbers. We can give these quantities creative names such as *google* which is a "one" followed by a hundred zeros, or a *googolplex,* which is a "one" followed by a *google* of zeros; but we still cannot understand their size. Even some who work with these numbers daily can't begin to fathom what numbers of this scale really mean.

Those numbers, as minuscule or enormous as they are, still do not represent infinity. Infinity can't be described through any number–it is a concept that lies beyond, or outside of, numbers. If we can assign a number or amount to something, then it is not infinity.

Infinity is a mathematical idea that can be discussed and visualized fairly easily because it is a concept that can be understood directly within our 3D realm. Actually, we only need one dimension to express or explain *infinity*.

If we pick a number and add one to it; and then take that new number and again add one to it; we have created a process that is never going to end. We will never reach a last and final number, no matter how many times we repeat this process. This is *infinity*. Everyday counting is an example of an *infinite* process because no matter what number you imagine, you can always add one to it. Start with a number, any number. No matter how big that number is, we can always add one to the number, or even double it. The result is always a bigger distance or larger number. If at any time we stop the process of counting, no matter how large the number, we are no longer describing *infinity*.

Infinity can easily be demonstrated by using only a single dimension and a single straight line. We could draw a line one-inch long and then increase it, one inch at a time. If we do this over and over without end, the line also forever grows longer, and this demonstrates another example of *infinity* expressed in only one dimension.

In the other direction, that of getting smaller, a similar situation applies. In this direction, infinity might be a little more difficult to visualize. Imagine standing in a room and walking halfway to a wall. We then stop to assess the remaining distance, and then we walk halfway again. As we continue to do this, at some point we will find ourselves "very close" to the wall. "Very close" only has meaning to us because we are always comparing any distance to our size and our sense of scale. Imagine that we are half the length of our shoe away from the wall. At this point we might think that with the very next "half-the distance" step we will surely touch the wall. Instead, visualize that we suddenly shrink to become a small insect with very short insect legs. After becoming this small, we suddenly realize that the wall looks quite far away after all. Due to our new small size, it takes us a long time to again crawl halfway to that wall. We again do this "halfway process" repeatedly until, once again, our small insect-sized body feels very close to the wall. At that point we suddenly shrink to the point where we are only the size of a microscopic bacteria. Now the wall suddenly will appear to be far away again. We complete a series of halfway moves, and then shrink even smaller to the size of an atom. This process can be repeated over and over again, and this process never ends because every remaining distance represents a real number or distance that can always be divided in half. This process will go on and on to repeat itself forever, so we will never reach the wall no matter how many times we attempt to go halfway to the wall. This also describes *infinity*!

Another way to imagine this last demonstration of *infinity* is to pick a line of any length and divide it in two. Take one of the pieces and divide this and keep repeating the process. At any point the line may look extremely short, but if you were much smaller it would look longer. There will always be a midpoint to every line. This is also an *infinite* process because it will go on and on, forever. Actually, any line can be divided an *infinity* of times, and any line contains an *infinite* number of points. *Infinity* can be fully understood using only one dimension–a line.

An *infinite* universe means that no matter how many atoms, cells, organisms, planets, solar systems, galaxies, or universes we have encountered, there will always be more that we have not yet found; and this process of finding more will never end.

An Infinite Universe–Other Worlds Exactly like Ours

As we start to understand the implications of an infinite universe, questions might rise. *"Does this mean that there is another Earth just like ours?" "Is there another person just like me?"*

Our physical Earth is *finite and* not *infinite* in size. There are an enormous number of *atoms* that make up our Earth, but that number can be determined–as big as it is–that number is *finite*. A calculation, which is based on the *mass* of the Earth, estimates the number of atoms that make our planet to be near 10^{50} (or the square root of Google–$10^{50} \times 10^{50} = 10^{100}$). This, of course, is a very big number, but because it is an actual number, it is still *finite*. All these *atoms* can be moved around and rearranged in many different ways, but eventually this *finite* number of atoms will run out of new possible arrangements. The number of possible arrangements, as big as it becomes, is still *finite* because there is always only a *finite* (fixed or limited) number of ways that a *finite* number of atoms can be arranged.

Imagine a simple example. Let us say we have 5 pairs of shoes, 10 pairs of pants and 15 shirts and you want to try every combination. After a little exploration, we will discover that the answer is 5 x 10 x 15 or 750 different possible combinations. A fixed number of things can only be arranged a certain fixed number of ways. Because the number of particles that make up Earth (10^{50}) is fixed, they can only be arranged in a *finite* or limited number of arrangements (10^{50} x 10^{49} x 10^{48} ... etc.). Another way of saying this is a *finite* number of things can only be arranged a *finite* number of ways.

In an *infinite* universe these particles will reappear again and again, forever. There will be an *infinite* number of each of these elementary particles and they will collide and interact and arrange themselves in different groupings an *infinite* number of times. Eventually, in an *infinite* universe, every possible combination of the very large, but still finite, number of particles on earth will have been tried. At this point, somewhere in the *infinite* universe, the arrangements will start to repeat and an exact copy of Earth will be formed; then, this duplication will happen again and again.

It is a mathematical fact that an infinite number of exact copies of Earth will exist in an infinite universe. This is a very difficult, but critical, concept so I will repeat this in a slightly different way: in an *infinite* universe, every one of the finite particles making up Earth will, by mathematical necessity, appear again over and over, forever. These will combine an *infinite* number of times in every possible arrangement. There is no end to the number of times these particles combine into different combinations. Because the Earth only contains a finite number of particles, every so often the exact number and type of atoms that make up our world will be repeated, and the repetitions of this finite set of atoms will occur in every possible arrangement. Sooner or later they will be arranged so that they will exactly duplicate our Earth, along with everyone and everything on it!

This means that somewhere, within the *infinite* expanse of the universe, every atom on this Earth will be exactly duplicated and connected to all other atoms, in exactly the same arrangement as on Earth. ***These exact duplications will contain every particle and atom, arranged the same way as our world, duplicating everything in it. In an infinite universe this process goes on forever, so there will even be an infinite number of these exact copies! If the universe is just enormous this may or may not happen. If the universe is infinite, then this has to happen.***

Most of us, when confronted by the awesome nature of this proposition, will logically reason something like *"yes, but the odds of that happening are so small it will never really happen!"* To our "dimensionally-bound" conceptual minds, the conclusion that an *infinity* of worlds just like ours exists seems absolutely preposterous. This idea might seem like nothing more than good raw material for science fiction. ***However, this is how our universe is built; once we break through our normal, inherited conceptual constraints and begin to see our universe for what it really is–infinite and infinitely full of possibilities–then everything that we think we understand about life will instantly and forever change.***

Extrapolating Infinity into Extra Dimensions

Once we have grasped the concept of *infinity* in one dimension, then the next logical step is to examine this idea using more dimensions. This process can provide us with insights into what might then happen in extra-dimensional space. When we do this, we quickly discover that *infinity* works much the same in a multi-dimensional coordinates system as it does in one dimension.

In a two-dimensional system, such as a tabletop, map or a TV screen, we can locate any point with two measurements: numbers or pieces of information. There are different types of coordinate systems that easily allow us to locate a point in 2D space, but the *polar coordinate system* (angle and distance from center–*vector*) and *Cartesian coordinate system* (X and Y perpendicular axis) are the most common and well known. We can use either system to examine what happens to the concept of *infinity* as we expand from one into two dimensions. In the X-Y *Cartesian plane* both the vertical and horizontal axis are lines, and, as discussed above, any line always has an *infinite* number of points. Two perpendicular axes will still describe an *infinite* number of points because *infinity* times *infinity* is still *infinity*. For the same reason, if we use a *polar coordinate system*, we can divide the circle into an *infinite* number of angles; and each line that marks the distance out from the center also consists of an *infinite* number of points. We call a line that has a direction and length, a *vector*, and each *polar coordinate system* contains an infinite number of *vectors*. Just as there are an *infinite* number of points on a one dimensional *line*, there are also an *infinite* number of points in a two-dimensional *plane*.

The expansion from one to two dimensions does not change the fundamental nature of *infinity*. Lines now have added directions, or dimensions, but they still can continue "on and on" forever. Between any two points in space there is also an *infinite* number of other points. Shapes have areas that keep increasing as one or both of the sides continue to lengthen. The concept of *infinity* is much the same for two dimensions as it is for one. Expanding this idea one step further to three-dimensions, by adding another perpendicular axis in order to describe three-dimensional space, or by describing an *infinitely* expanding or contracting volume, still does not change our concept of *infinity*. *Infinity* squared or cubed is still *infinity*.

The idea of *infinity* survives completely intact when it is expanded from one to two dimensions, and then again, from two to three dimensions. It therefore seems very likely that expanding the idea of *infinity* to four dimensions or more will not significantly restrict or reduce our understanding of *infinity*. When we expand concepts into extra-dimensional space, it is generally expected that the possibilities will only increase. Because the concept of *infinity* already contains never-ending possibilities, it easily survives this transition intact. *Infinity* expanded is still *infinity*.

Even if we had determined that our 3D universe was *finite*, a conclusion that all of creation is also *finite* would quickly begin to disintegrate once we expanded our reference frame to include extra dimensions. These unseen dimensions can be simultaneously thought of as both hidden beyond and deeply *enfolded* within our three-dimensional universe. An extra-dimensional perspective only introduces additional ways to imagine the *infinitely* vast physical "size" of our universe by allowing new kinds of "room" for additional possibilities. It also provides an important mechanism for explaining the deep, instantaneous connections between all the physically distant parts. This instant interconnectedness or *non-local* behavior is something that simply can't be explained using three-dimensions alone.

We can now speak about the universe as being *infinite* in two different directions: going out" through never-ending 3D space, and "going in" through the unseen dimensions. *Infinity* is always being expressed at multiple levels throughout creation, and is certainly not limited to describing only physical size or numbers. We are quickly discovering that our universe is *infinite* in any and every way that we can possibly imagine. We are also discovering just what this might mean.

What an Infinite Universe Means to Us

The reasoning that brought me to this understanding was an even blend of science and my own personal experience. The combination of one hundred years of experimentally observed phenomena and my own personal involvement with the mystery have, together, thoroughly convinced me that our universe is far greater, more dynamic and much more interconnected than it objectively appears to us. The layers of mystery all begin to make sense once we accept that our universe is *infinite* and we begin to comprehend what this might really mean.

Much of this book is devoted to helping the reader understand and become comfortable with my conclusion about this *infinite* nature of existence. There may be readers that will resist this leap because, even though this arrangement is extremely likely, it has not yet been scientifically proven, and may remain technically unproven for some time. ***However, also unproven is the opposite conclusion, that the universe is finite. Finite systems are usually much easier to understand, quantify and describe than infinite systems. This means it is much easier to prove that a system is finite. The very fact that the universe has not yet been proven to be finite is, by itself, very revealing. This alone throws tremendous extra weight towards the idea that the universe is probably infinite!***

I am far from alone in my belief that our universe is *infinite* and *multi-dimensional*. Many, probably most, contemporary cosmologists and physicists believe this to be the true form of our universe. Much of what this book proposes would still be true in an "*infinite* but only three-dimensional universe." However, the extra dimensions, *enfolded* in ways which we can't see or really understand from our *viewport*, allow for additional possibilities of interconnectedness, timelessness and unity that help to explain the experimental results and much of the hidden mystery in our lives. This expanded structure allows for a kind of interconnectedness that is impossible in a "3D-only" universe. The extra dimensions allow room for an *infinite* amount of mystery and a never-ending *evolutionary* process.

How we might experience *infinity,* as our awareness expands from three-dimensions into four or more dimensional space, cannot be really be known from our current perspective. The complete and full meaning of *infinity*–or even how *infinity* might be expressed in just four-dimensions–is beyond our *conceptual horizon*. Even if someone could visualize four dimensions, they would still be incapable of communicating this meaning to the rest of us. This is because our cultural imagination reaches its limits somewhere on our side of the conceptual veil that hides four-dimensional space from our senses and consciousness.

The inability to communicate about glimpses into extra-dimensionality was precisely what happened to the main character in *Flatland.* He was completely unable to describe his new understanding of three-dimensional space to his two-dimensional peers. He discovered that he had no effective words or ideas to communicate his encounter, even though he fully understood everything while it was happening. He even found that once he tried to use words and known concepts, his own clear understanding became muddled and confused because the use of language and concepts eroded his "vision." The author's clever approach demonstrated exactly how we all would have similar, insurmountable difficulties communicating or even understanding the meaning of four-dimensional space.

Based upon our acquaintance with one, two and three dimensions, we would reasonably predict that the concept of *infinity*, no matter how many dimensions it is expressed in, would probably always describe a condition of boundlessness. We have observed that the meaning in one dimension does not change significantly as we expand it into two and then three-dimensions, so we can *extrapolate* and assume that *infinity* also works in a similar way when expanded to four dimensions and beyond. It is reasonable to project that this basic idea about infinity being boundless would hold true for any number of dimensions. It worked in one, two and three dimensions, so it most likely will also apply beyond these limits.

Such reasoning, however, is only the product of our three-dimensional conceptual tools and, in truth, we simply don't have any reference frame for what conscious life fully utilizing this larger dimensional and *infinite* space, would be like. At the most we only interact with that shadow of the greater whole that directly intersects our own 3D world. Therefore, while this *extrapolation* does seem logical, we can't be absolutely certain that it fully translates. It is my personal belief that if there is any shift in the meaning of *infinity* as we expand into more dimensions, this change would probably allow for even more possibilities and connections in our universe than we would ever have deduced, by simply *extrapolating* directly. *Infinity* in multiple dimensions might involve *qualitative* changes that are far beyond our ability to imagine.

Some *cosmologists* argue that even if space is *infinite*, there is still a limit to the number of worlds that would be like our own. They argue that "evolution takes time and because of the amount of time *that is* required for the Earth's evolution, there could be some physical or mathematical limits to the number and kind of duplicates of Earth." These limits are based on their perception of a "time" constraint because, based on our best current estimates, the universe is only about 15 billion years old. They believe that there has not been enough "time" to evolve all these other parallel Earths, even if there is enough space for an *infinity* of them.

The weakness with this line of reasoning is that it is only based on three-dimensional logic and linear "time." If our universe was only three-dimensional and "time" was linear, then these limits might exist, but today it is apparent that our sense of constrained linear "time" is an illusion. This rational argument fails to allow any possibilities beyond our three-dimensional *conceptual horizon*, and it doesn't even utilize our best current scientific understanding of "time."

Bubble Universes

If cosmologists have made a significant miscalculation about its *shape*, the universe might instead close back on itself like a sphere or a pretzel. If this turned out to be our true *shape*, our *finite* "bubble" universe might then be only one of an *infinite* number of other similar, or even very different, "bubble" universes. If there are an *infinite* number of these, then we already know that, even though each universe is *finite*, there will still be *infinite* room for every possible arrangement. Somewhere in this collection of universes we would eventually discover a planet that looks very much like Earth. In this arrangement, there would be an *infinity* of Earths that are very similar to our Earth with only very slight details that are different. With further exploration we would eventually find a planet that is exactly like Earth in every way; and with more additional searching, we would find even more of these exact duplicates–actually an *infinite* number of them. These planets would be so identical that every person would be exactly replicated and repeating the same thoughts and actions of their Earthly counterparts. Within this *infinite* series of *finite* bubble universes, there would still exist an *infinite* number of planets that are identical to Earth in every aspect.

OUR UNIVERSE SPLITS INTO AN INFINITY OF UNIVERSES

What I am about to say may sound repetitive, but it is slightly different, very important, and it helps to expand this idea of *infinity* to another level. ***Due to the very nature of infinity, an <u>infinite number of full universes, that at are exactly the same as our universe</u>, also exist.*** By definition, this is exactly what must happen in an infinite space, both mathematically and in the real, physical expression.

Every time we make a decision, our universe splits (*Many Worlds*). Every possible variation of that decision and every possible outcome also exists, expressed throughout an infinite number of replicated universes. Every possible variation–possibly two more red leaves fell off that tree in that moment– is expressed somewhere as an entirely new universe. An infinite number of precise replicas of every possible universe variation can be found within the *infinite* extent that contains creation. ***As impossible and bizarre as this might seem, if our universe is infinite then this is an absolute fact. This is because of the very meaning and definition of infinity. To our 3D-bound minds this sounds crazy and insane, but this is not a theory! If creation is infinite, then there are multiple entire universes that are exactly like ours, along with every possible slight variation.*** This means *infinite* exact copies of every possible variation of us, our planet, our galaxy and our *universe* exist somewhere in this never-ending vastness! These copies are also completely *enfolded* so that they are always in instantaneous and intimate communication with everything else in existence. It is truly an amazing Web of infinite possibilities.

Our specialized and conceptual minds can make this idea very difficult to grasp or believe. It seems too fantastic, and it is fantastic, but not in the way we might be thinking. We have our concepts about numbers, distance and space that do not easily allow us to process and understand ideas that are truly without limits. ***The real difficulty is not that space is so expansive, but rather that that our minds are designed, built and programmed to work only within certain limits.*** Learning how to work and live beyond these limits will ultimately be understood as an available resource and another way of being. Once this idea is fully integrated, it is our old limits that then begin to seem strange.

To make this leap we first must become comfortable with the idea that there is "room" for an *infinity* of multiple "Earth-like" planets within our greater universe. Next, we also begin to understand, through our always-deepening understanding of the *infinite*, that there is even enough room for many full "universes" that are identical to ours. Just as in our discussion about *infinite* Earths, there will also be an *infinity* of universes that only vary in tiny ways–"she wore the red dress instead of the green one in that universe." ***In an infinite universe there is a statistical probability of 100 percent that there are other exact "copies" of each of us, living our lives and making many of our same decisions. In many of these, choices are made that are ever-so-slightly different. Every time we make any choice, decision, thought or movement somewhere, others just like us are making that same choice; and at the same time others just like us are making the different choices. At that moment, our universe seems to divide so that every choice is fully realized and expressed somewhere.***

This idea will receive much more explanation throughout this book. ***I will also introduce a better name for this, our amazing infinite universe. Today, many scientists and writers are calling it the Multiverse.***

SPACE IN A COSMOLOGICAL SCALE

Earlier we examined how our 3D universe is structured in a pattern of mostly empty space that is shaped through *energetic* interactions. This structure repeats, even when we look at smaller or larger constructions. We see this pattern in our atoms and subatomic particles. We see it in the planets of our solar system, the stars of our Milky Way galaxy, our region of *galaxies* and the known universe with its billions of *galaxies*. All of these forms follow a similar pattern. There is a vast amount of what appears to be empty space distributed everywhere in our universe and very little, if any, actual "solid" material. All of this matter is held in place by *energetic* interactions. Solid-appearing *matter* (*matter* is just another form of *energy)* is, itself, a minuscule component of our universe. Today it is universally recognized that the known universe is almost entirely constructed from empty space and *energy*. **Since we are made from atoms, we too are almost entirely empty space and energy.**

However, scientists have just recently discovered that empty space is not really empty at all. As I am writing, fresh insights into the nature of "empty" space continue to lead us towards an evolving understanding that this empty space is filled with something that is extremely interesting, but not at all understood.

When Einstein first realized that his theory of *relativity* predicted an expanding universe, he became greatly disturbed. This caused him to modify his theory by adding the now infamous fudge factor, called the *cosmological constant*. This fudge factor allowed his math to predict a *stable* universe because a *stable* universe better fit his sensibilities. However, less than a dozen years later, lawyer-turned-cosmologist Edwin Hubble discovered that the universe was indeed *expanding;* and after Hubble's discovery, Einstein began to describe his own "after the fact" alteration of the original *relativity* theory as the greatest mistake of his career. It wasn't until much later, in the 1970s, that *cosmologists* began to really uncover the fuller picture. As it was then determined, not only was our universe expanding, but also the rate of expansion might be increasing; and the average *velocity* of expansion was about three times the speed of light. In the amount of time that it took for the light to reach us from the farthest stars–just over 14 billion *years*–the outer edge of this visible universe expanded outward in every direction by an additional 30 billion *light-years*. This means that the width of the known universe tripled.

"Wait," you might say, "nothing can travel faster than light." As it turns out, the stars themselves are not moving at that incredible rate into some empty void. Instead it is space itself that is expanding at that rate. Things contained within space cannot move faster than light, but as it turns out, space itself seems to be able to do anything it wants. There seems to be at least one other thing that also can move faster than light. As mentioned earlier, non-local interaction is instantaneous, so information also somehow travels faster than the speed of light.

Note that when we are speaking of stars moving away from us through expansion, we are discussing three-dimensional space and not *spacetime*. Space is only a three-dimensional concept, so what do we mean when we say that it expands? What is it that contains 3D space and allows it to expand? It is quite impossible for three-dimensional beings to visualize expanding space. In our conceptual system of thought, we have no larger system or container that we can visualize or understand for this space to expand into. We have no previous reference frame or structure for this type of visualization. A balloon expanding–the common classroom analogy–does not really work as an accurate model because that balloon is expanding into 3D space, which is something that we already understand.

However, if we revisit the Flatland technique of employing *reverse engineering* and first look at a 2D example, we begin to see a clearer picture. The balloon inflation example works quite well for describing this using a 2D model. Blow up a balloon partially, but don't tie it. With a marker make two or three dots on the surface of the balloon and measure the distance between the dots. These dots represent galaxies. The surface of the balloon can be thought of as a curved 2D surface, just like the surface of the Earth. Both would feel "flat" to their inhabitants. Now inflate the balloon much more and measure the distance between the dots. The distance is greater because the 2D surface expanded as the balloon was inflated. Just what did the expanding 2D curved surface expand into? It expanded into 3D space. This analogy can now be scaled up a dimension to provide a much more accurate image for understanding the nature of the expansion of our universe. We inhabit the "surface" of our 3D space, and when our curved 3D universe (*spacetime*) expands, it is expanding into 4D space!

The rate of change (*acceleration*) of the expansion of the universe is very important because this rate will determine the future on our Earth. One revealing question is "why, with so much *mass* in the universe, is it still expanding?" *Mass* attracts, and if it were just up to the stars, galaxies and space dust, the universe would slow down its expansion and eventually collapse upon itself. This would not produce a very good outcome for human life.

Instead, as discussed, some new form of energy is continuing to drive the expansion and counter this *gravitational mass attraction*. Remember that most of the *mass* in the universe is *dark matter* which we cannot see and do not really understand. *Dark matter* is gravitationally attractive, not repulsive like this new type of *energy*. We also learned that this repulsive energy that is driving the expansion has been named *dark energy* and this *dark energy* makes up about three-quarters (76 percent) of everything we know to be out there.

Dark energy is very confusing and its naming was probably a bad descriptive choice. To have named both the concept of this repulsive energy and dark matter as "dark" implies that they are related and that a conversion of *dark matter* to *dark energy* should be possible; but, as discussed, *dark matter* cannot be converted to *dark energy* like normal *matter* can be converted to *energy*. When normal *energy* is held in the form of *matter*, this *matter* is always *gravitationally attractive;* but this new mysterious "force" is *gravitationally repulsive*. The name *dark energy* is, therefore, not consistent with other naming conventions in physics. Naming this unknown something like the "universal repulsor" might have been more appropriate.

Let's review what we know about the makeup of our observable cosmos again. We know that 76 percent of everything "out there" is a mysterious, repulsive, energetic unknown that we call *dark energy*. The remaining 24 percent is behaving like matter usually does–attracting other matter (gravitational material). 80 percent to 95 percent of this attracting matter is invisible so we call it *dark matter*. That leaves somewhere between 1.5 percent and 4 percent of the known universe, such as stars, planets, space dust, etc., to be made from the stuff that we can see. While 1.5 percent is the latest official estimate, an astronomer who is measuring the distribution of dark matter recently told me that the latest information indicates that the actual percentage is much lower than even 1.5 percent–possibly only a small fraction of one-percent.

A deeper examination into the atoms of this visible 1.5 percent, which is called *baryonic matter*, finds that most of the mass of these atoms is made up from the same *dark energy* that fills empty space. That leaves less than .03 percent of what we know is "out there" to be actual physical matter, like quarks. When we learn more about quarks it is possible, and even likely, that we will find that they, in turn, are also mostly "empty space" and energy. ***Everything we think of as matter is really energy, and the majority of this energy is completely invisible to any of our senses and our devices that can detect energy.***

The vast majority of everything that makes up our 3D, physical universe is completely hidden from us and, as of today, we understand almost nothing about these enormous invisible parts. In addition, when we are observing our 3D universe, we are looking at only a small part of creation because we have not yet even addressed any of this structure that is farther away than 15 billion light-years, smaller than a *quark*, or beyond three dimensions. Even though we have made tremendous advances over the last 100 years, we still understand very little about our universe. The more we learn, the more we encounter our ever-expanding vastness; and we continue discovering new aspects, components and perspectives that are beyond our comprehension. The more we learn, the greater the mystery becomes.

BIG BANG

The *Big Bang theory* was the first, and most widely adopted, cosmological theory about the creation of our universe that was derived from *relativity*. This bold theory describing the creation of our universe was introduced in the 1930s, but the name *Big Bang* was not attached to this theory until some 20 years later. As the name implies, the theory states that the universe began as a very dense, hot and microscopic *mass* that very rapidly expanded during a unique event that occurred 15 billion years ago. The actual rate of expansion required to fit the gathered data is so dramatic and rapid that this event makes *supernovas* look absolutely puny. The most current version of the theory requires two phases of *Big Bang expansion*, the initial moment of the actual "bang," and then the secondary rapid *inflation* that is necessary to explain the even distribution of residual background *energy* that is found spread throughout the universe.

There are several things about the *Big Bang theory* that do not ring true for me. When the theory is viewed in only one direction, along the arrow of time, combining all of its implications, such as the splitting of ten-dimensional space and *inflation*, it seems to me that we are trying far too hard to make all the data fit a concept. This version of the event also doesn't seem to follow the normal patterns of most natural processes. Nature tends to repeat, reuse and recycle, therefore this massive, one-directional process seems very unnatural; in my opinion, it seems that we are creating a complex "Rube Goldberg" type of contraption to try to explain artifacts that we are witnessing today. Because of our dimensionally limited reference frame, our only direct awareness of this process is the shadow that ultimately appears in our realm. We cannot possibly explain a creation process that unfolds in multiple dimensions with our current concepts, thoughts and language.

When the *big bang* is described in three dimensions, the process seems to require a magical and unbelievable physical *expansion* that must occur in a minuscule fraction of a second. This *expansion* is necessary to explain the existing visible universe and its residual *energy* dispersion. This dramatic creation story sounds very similar to some of those from the major world religions. It is my clear sense that again, "time" and *dimensional limitations* are interfering with our ability to comprehend what is really going on. ***This widely popular theory has the singular, fantastic and extremely dramatic beginning point of the universe occurring 15 billion years ago, only because it was fully conceived from within our time-based reference frame.***

If we could stand back from our 3D perspective and see all of creation from a broader multi-dimensional perspective, this *Big Bang* "event" might not look much different than the top of a cresting wave in the ocean. In a bigger picture, the *big bang* would be seen as just another marker in the rhythmic wave of creation passing through the always-vibrating and interconnected fabric that manifests as the *Multiverse*. From this more comprehensive and expansive vantage point, the *big bang* isn't seen as a starting or an ending point. Instead, it can be seen as part of the continuous and timeless wave of creation. The *Big Bang* "event" might be special, in that it might mark the actual point where the multi-dimensional wave folds back on itself and changes whatever might be the multi-dimensional equivalent of "direction." The *big bang* might look special and important from our 3D reference point, but at the level of our universe, it just describes a part of the ebb and flow of the *vibratory wave* that is creating our universe–a wave that has no beginning or end, because it occurs outside of time. Ultimately the *big bang* is just a moment in the ever-changing rhythmic dance of the universe. ***Events like the big bang are the bass notes and kick drum beats of the***

infinitely repeating and rhythmic song of beingness. They serve to pump the deep cosmic groove.

THE BIG BANG AND TEN-DIMENSIONAL SPACE

An idea proposed by some physicists is that the *Big Bang theory* caused 10-dimensional space to split into two, lesser-dimensional realms. According to this hypothesis, after the *big bang,* the part we now live within contains only the four dimensions that we understand and experience as *spacetime.* The other part, with six dimensions, is said to have curled up into pieces that are so tiny we can't see them with any of our measuring devices. Again, I feel that we are simply trying far too hard to understand something that is beyond our *conceptual horizon*. We are so constrained by our old conceptual paradigm that we try to explain things that are invisible to our senses by imagining that they must be very small.

ANTIMATTER EXPERIMENTS

Antimatter constitutes another enormous gap in our understanding about our cosmos. *Antimatter* is physical, in that it can be found in our universe. Physicists have "seen" *antimatter* produced in high-*energy* experiments. Traces from small and short-lived bits of this material have been detected after large, *energetic collisions* in *particle accelerators. Antimatter* is made of the complete opposites of normal *matter, but antimatter* parallels *matter* in every way. All subatomic particles are said to have their equivalents in *antimatter,* except all the charges are reversed. There could be entire *galaxies* identical to ours, but instead of being made of *matter,* they are made from *antimatter.*

When *matter* and *antimatter* come in contact with each other, the release of stored *energy* is complete and enormous as all the *mass* of the *matter* and *antimatter* is converted into pure *energy*, leaving no *matter* or *antimatter* behind. Because these interactions release all the bound *energy* for a given *mass,* they would exceed even *atomic* and *thermonuclear reactions. Matter* and *Antimatter* totally annihilate each other and, possibly, anything else that is in their vicinity.

In lab experiments we have witnessed only very small particles of *antimatter.* It is possible, even likely, that, somewhere, an *anti-particle* physically exists for every regular *particle* of *matter.* Just where this anti-material might be found is unknown, but as I write, physicists are still trying to generate larger quantities of *antimatter* in *supercolliders.* Physicists have no absolute certainty about what will happen if and when they do create this larger quantity of *antimatter.* It is noteworthy that, similarly, scientists lacked absolute certainty about what would happen when they exploded the first *atomic bomb.* In the early 1940s, some physicists even speculated that there was a theoretical possibility of starting a chain reaction that could spread and annihilate the entire Earth; yet they still went ahead with that project! The possibility of world annihilation does not seem to be an effective deterrent for driven or curious human beings. Maybe, deep down, we all really understand that this physical world is just an illusion, a *projection* or shadow, so we are not so concerned with the small details, such as the annihilation of an illusion.

Based upon what we understand today, *antimatter* and *dark matter* are not directly related. *Antimatter* is physical, real and detectable and we understand how it reacts with *matter. Dark matter* is theoretical, and yet seems much more plentiful than *matter. Dark matter* is completely mysterious and, along with *dark energy,* represents one of the biggest and most glaring gaps in our current knowledge of the universe. A*ntimatter* is quite physical and therefore not theoretical, but we still understand very little about this exotic material.

EMPTY SPACE AND VIRTUAL PARTICLES

"Empty" space, as I mentioned, is not empty at all. Recently, it was discovered that it is filled with an endless succession of very short-lived particles fluctuating in and out of existence. Because these *particles* only exist for the briefest of moments, they are usually referred to as *virtual particles*.

Looking closely at *protons*, we now know that 90 percent of their *mass* is made up of "empty" space. This "empty" space has actual *mass,* and some physicists theorize this comes from these *virtual particles*. Since we are made from atoms, our bodies are also made from these *virtual particles*. It now seems that empty space is anything but empty because it is filled with these tiny *virtual particles* that are continuously moving in and out of existence.

There are good arguments for relating *virtual particles* to *dark energy* since "empty" space seems to contain them both. In an attempt to establish this relationship, the *mass* of *virtual particles* was calculated. This calculated *mass* was far too large to explain *dark energy*. It turned out that this calculation wasn't just a little off; it was off by the unbelievably huge factor of 10^{120}. This enormous discrepancy was so far off that some called it the worst prediction in all the history of physics. Again, we find ourselves peering into the "dark" mystery of the unknown without any real understanding.

The equations of physics describe both *particles* and *virtual particles* equally, but until very recently *virtual particles* were not observed to be outputs or inputs of any monitored physical process. This means we have not been able to see, touch or measure one of these particles, even though there are many observable physical phenomena resulting from, and even requiring, their involvement.

Our previous assumption about their "virtual" nature is now being examined more closely, since one form of these *particles*, *virtual photons*, has just been "captured" like "real" *photons* and then used to create *light*. This was accomplished by bouncing them off a "mirror" vibrating just under the *speed of light*. Virtual photons were good *particles* for this experiment because they have no *mass* and therefore require very little *energy* to be excited or coaxed to move out of their *virtual state*. Other *particles,* like *protons* or *electrons,* have mass so they require much more *energy*. Facilitating the shift for any *subatomic particles* from *virtual* to *real* is now seen as imminently possible because of this recent success with *virtual photons. Virtual particles* are one more "thing" out there that we really don't understand. However, they are of particular interest because they seem to be "located" somewhere near the cusp, or outer-edge, of our current understanding. *Virtual particles* could be very well positioned to become the next window providing an improved vista into what lies beyond.

WHEELER, PENROSE AND BLACK HOLES

John Wheeler, who ended his career at UT, Austin after many productive years at Harvard, and Sir Roger Penrose, of both Cambridge and Oxford, developed much of the physics that describe *black holes, wormholes* and other unusual topological features within *spacetime*. We now have an enormous body of work based upon these unusual features of *spacetime,* because these features all derive from *relativity* and can be described mathematically. Wormholes are still only theoretical; but physicists have substantial physical evidence of *black holes,* and they are constantly discovering new ones scattered about our universe.

Black holes are described as gross deformations of *spacetime* due to an ultra-dense *gravitational mass*, usually a collapsed star. These often form at the center of *galaxies* and, while very massive, they are also infinitely small in the terms of three-dimensional space. *Mass attraction* or *gravity* becomes so great in these *cosmological events* that nothing, not even light, can escape them. As I write today, cosmologists have just discovered two new and enormous *black holes*, one of which is 20 billion times the *mass* of our Sun.

On the other hand, *wormholes*, which are potential bridges between two remote areas of *spacetime*, are still theoretical. It has been theorized that it is possible these might function as doorways to *parallel universes*. Both of these terms were originally coined by John Wheeler.

Because of their enormous size and nature, these powerful structures require the existence of extremely large, and therefore extremely interesting, *energies*. These structures represent the cosmic storms: the typhoons, hurricanes and tsunamis of our local universe. Because time and space dramatically bend in these regions, understanding just what these events might mean is a wide-open and enormously exciting area of study.

A recent and very interesting theory about *black holes* proposes that the *holographic information* that describes our entire universe is mapped onto their sides. *Black holes* could be the actual nerve centers and brains of our physical universe. If this theory turns out to be true, it is conceivable that *black holes* may somehow store and process all the *information* needed to create and sustain the universe. It might then even be possible that they are a component part of a system that *projects* this *information* down through the dimensions, which causes our universe to appear to exist, much like a 3D *hologram*. Our universe only gets stranger the more we try to understand it from our three-dimensional perspective.

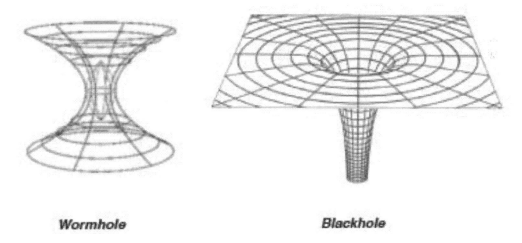

Wormhole   **Blackhole**

DARK AND ANTI THINGS

Our universe is full of *dark matter, dark energy, antimatter* and *black holes*, and yet we know almost nothing about any of these. How can we even pretend to understand our universe without having a much better grasp of these major components? Clearly our present level of understanding our universe is still extremely primitive. What is also clear is that we really don't understand enough to declare any theory as correct, because there are far too many unknowns in any discussion of *matter, energy* and dimensions. In addition, there is always the "we don't even know about what we don't even know we don't know about!" factor.

I again remind the reader that we are always using only our 3D *viewport* in our attempts to figure the workings of a universe that probably exists in at least 11 dimensions. We are repeatedly bumping against our *conceptual horizons and* sensory ceilings. If our math, science and experience are correct or even close, there is something very fantastic that exists beyond the range of our five known senses. As of today, we have no reliable way of consciously understanding or directly interacting with these important parts of our universe, which lie beyond our biological and scientific ability to sense.

As a curious side note, brain researchers have known for a long time that all our mental and physical functions use only a small percentage of our brain, and the functionality of the unmapped parts of our brain is not well understood. We seem to understand only a very small part of our universe and simultaneously a small part of our brains. I can't help but wonder if the unknown mysterious parts of each are somehow involved in constant inter-communication.

UNIFIED FIELD THEORY

The most dominant and pressing problem within the new physics has been the inability to find a way to combine *quantum theory* and *relativity*. Between the two we have useful descriptions of all four of the fundamental *forces,* which we currently understand: *gravity, electromagnetic, weak nuclear* and *strong nuclear*. The first of these, *gravity,* is described only by *relativity,* and the other three are well described by *quantum theory*. Most physicists agree that a complete description of our universe should include all four of these *forces*. However, after many individual lifetimes devoted to this project, physicists have been repeatedly thwarted in their attempts to combine these two theories successfully. The Holy Grail of physics is this *Unified Field Theory,* and it was not until the 1970s, with the discovery of *String Theory,* that anyone saw possibilities for *unification*. Recently, with the introduction of *M-theory*, the improved and dimensionally expanded *string theory*, many physicists are now hopeful that we are finally on a path towards *unification*.

When we include 11 dimensions in our calculations, as *M-theory* requires, suddenly *quantum mechanics* and *relativity* start to fit together more comfortably. Calculations become mathematically elegant because the equations balance and the pesky problem-areas begin to self-resolve. With these extra dimensions in the mix, *quantum physics* and *relativity* start to make mathematical sense together. It now seems that we have finally found that illusive trailhead leading to the long sought after *unified field theory*, the single theory describing all physical interactions.

IT IS ALL ONLY INFORMATION

When physicist Brian Greene asked John Wheeler what will be the most important topic of physics as we deepen our explorations, his response was ***"information!"*** At the most basic level he saw the very real possibility that the most elementary thing in the universe is just *information*.

This *information* then expresses itself as the very *particles* that organize, through patterns of vibration in multiple dimensions, to make up the entire physical structure of our universe. ***Patterns and overtones of vibrational information freely communicate and interact through many dimensions, thus creating the entire order and structure of our universe. In our 3D reality we are never seeing or experiencing this raw vibrational information. Ultimately, we only experience the "shadows" of this vibrational information that eventually reach our 3D realm,*** *after they have been "distilled" from 11 or more dimensions into our familiar three dimensions.*

A PERSONAL PERSPECTIVE ON QUANTUM WEIRDNESS

Quantum physics is presently our best tool for describing physical interactions at the level of small subatomic *particles*. We have discussed that with the *Many Worlds* interpretation: all possible outcomes are viewed as actual outcomes that occur somewhere beyond our senses, possibly in other, but *parallel, universes*. We learned that there is always a small *probability* that with the right *energetic* conditions, when two *masses* meet all the *particles* could pass through the vast spaces that exist between particles, rather than collide. In the *Many Worlds* view, this outcome actually will occur in an infinite number of *parallel universes*. If we could somehow instantly shift our awareness to one of those other universes, we would be able to walk through walls, or by manipulating the energies in the other direction, walk on water! Later, we will look at the possibility that it may only be our deeply ingrained patterns and conceptual ideas (conditioning) about the solidity of our universe (and what we think is possible) that keeps us from participating in these different types of interactions.

As the reader knows by now, my personal belief about the meaning of all this, while not unique, is still different from most of the mainstream explanations. I have the clear sense that it is our brain's conceptual need to "time-order the unfolding of reality," that inhibits our ability to see a greater truth. "Time" implies speed and distance; and by its very nature it creates separation between things and events. For example, I believe that when we observe *non-local* behavior, between *paired particles*, it is not because some infinitely fast *information* pulse or wave (David Bohm's theory) is connecting the two particles. Rather, it is more likely that this instantaneous transfer occurs because they were not really two different *particles* to begin with. Instead, both *particles* are always fully unified at some deeper level of existence. No matter how far apart the pieces appear from our perspective, a singular oneness exists at the core of creation. ***The real meaning of non-local behavior is that everything in the universe is always completely and deeply connected. The appearance of separation and "time" passing is only the result of the way our three-dimensional brains need to separate, organize and view information.***

The "odd" *quantum experimental results* are simply perceptual anomalies, created by viewing and conceiving creation in fewer dimensions than its original source. The difference between the old black-and-white movies and the 3D version of *Avatar* only hints at the kind of spatial transformation that we will discover as we unlock this secret.

In our conversations, we continue to try to explain multi-dimensional phenomena using terms and ideas that are solidly grounded in our current 3D paradigm. For example, when we try to imagine what it would be like to occupy other dimensions, we still talk or think about "time," distance and shape. Our conceptual brains and our language simply cannot work to move us beyond these old ideas. To fully understand multi-dimensional space, we really need to directly experience these extra dimensions. This appears to be a classic "Catch-22" type of situation, but as always, *"the solution is evolution."*

Evolution is never a process that happens all at once. For each of us, a good first step is being willing to relax our ties to and need for our old concepts. This practice makes room for new ways of experiencing creation. To do this, we must first recognize which ideas are anchoring us firmly in our old *viewport*. ***Freedom involves knowing how and when to let go of the very concepts that have been serving us so well for a very long time.***

"TIME"–THE COSMIC TRICKSTER

When viewing phenomena from our *viewport,* it is impossible to fully understand what is occurring from what we observe. We typically find ourselves including the human conceptual invention called "time" when describing how things appear to us. The sphere that visited Flatland was observed as a circle that changed size with "time." "Time" is often the wild card, the joker, used to rationalize our observation of phenomena that otherwise would make no sense to us. "Time" appears very important in our three-dimensional worldview, but really it is just a terribly misunderstood and orphaned trickster.

We sometimes perceive "time" as our enemy; the constantly marching, relentlessly advancing quantity that defines our limited stay here on Earth. We imagine that if we could only stop the advance of "time," we would not age or die; we could become immortal. If we dig deeper, we discover that there is nothing really to change about "time" except our attitude. "Time" simply does not march on or exist as an absolute. We create "time" in our three-dimensional brains.

"Time," as we know it, is only an artifact of living in our 3D reference frame. "Time" and mind are completely interrelated. In the words of Einstein, *"Time is a stubbornly persistent illusion."* In the words of Eckhart Tolle, *"Time and mind are inseparable. To identify with the mind is to be trapped in time."*

Spiritual leaders and scientists completely agree about "time: our perception of "time" is an illusion. In physics and math, "time" can be thought of as being similar to another dimension. In mathematics, we might find ourselves referencing the future and the past in much the same way as we might look to the East or West. Our more human perception of "time" is usually as if we are stuck on a freeway heading north, not realizing that we could easily slow the car, or even turn around and head to the South. We only understand "time" from the perspective of a car traveling at 70 MPH in the northbound lane, a very limited perspective. We just can't seem to fathom the possibility of slowing down or stopping the march of "time," or making that U-turn to travel the other direction.

Possibly, if we were traveling in a multi-dimensional hovercraft, we could also travel "up" and leave the realm of "time" completely, in much the same way flying liberates us from our restricted, two-dimensional, ground level contact with the Earth's surface. For us to understand "time" differently, at the very least, we must make a complete paradigm shift. ***The very first step of this process is to better understand why our old sense of marching time only limits our vision; we must shed our old, restrictive ideas about time to allow for the emergence and growth of this new vision.***

MODELING THE PAST, PRESENT AND FUTURE

A simple demonstration, which is readily available to all of us, can help us visualize "time" differently. Imagine that we are on a train that is moving rapidly along its tracks, or a passenger in a car going at a steady rate of speed on a freeway; we are looking straight out of the side window, viewing on the landscape as it passes. Next imagine that we have just finished our lunch and used the last paper towel; its cardboard tube is still sitting in our hand begging to be used in some creative way. Playfully we put the tube up to our eye and look directly out of the side window with only that one eye open. We do not move the tube from side to side, but instead we pin it against the window, so that we can only stare straight out. The landscape we see through the tube at any given moment can be thought of as the "present." We can't yet see the "future" landscape until it pops into our tubular view, and we remember, but can no longer see, those scenes that have already moved through our field of vision; these remembered scenes are our "past." For a moment this becomes our "world" as we discover that we can make reasonable guesses about the "future" scenes based on our "present" landscape"–although we can't always be sure, and sometimes our memory of the "past" might get a little confused. Sometimes we don't see enough of the "present" view–*quantity of information*–to really understand what we are looking at until we see and understand more about the "future." *"Was that really a lake in a park or was it a farmer's pond?"* The unseen "future" sequentially becomes our "present," as the car or train moves forward and the next part of the landscape comes into our view. "Time" marches forward relentlessly and, if we forget that we are in a car or on a train, we might even begin to feel powerless to stop it or change its speed or direction.

This linear "passage of time" becomes our world, our reality, until accidentally, one of our kids knocks the cardboard tube away from our eye. Suddenly, we see the entire series–"past," "present" and "future"–all at once, in one, continuous, flowing landscape. We instantly "grok" the human concept of "time!" (The word "grok" was first coined by the World War II Danish underground resistance fighter, poet and physicist, Piet Hein, to describe a full, deep and total understanding of a concept.) ***There, right in front of our eyes, is the "past," "present" and "future"–all at once, observed to be simultaneously and fully interconnected!*** The "past," "present" and "future" now form one continuous and simultaneous landscape that can be traversed in any direction. ***Once the cardboard blinder is removed, these different sequential "time" periods are seen as they really are, fully interconnected in one unified landscape.***

As always, the difference is only a matter of our perspective, because our concepts are always defined by the limits of our current *viewport.* If we could lift ourselves out of the train or car and up into the sky above to peer down, we would get a more complete picture of all the interconnected, and always-present, interrelationships within this unified landscape that we just divided by using "time."

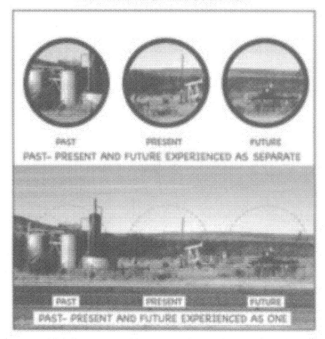

Looking out of a moving train window through a cardboard tube, we can only see a small part of the view at any moment. We remember the "past," see the "present" and expect to meet the "future." When we remove the cardboard tube which acts as our visual blinder, the "past," "present" and "future" can then be seen as one continuum.

"Time" is not an actual dimension and it certainly is not the fourth dimension, as some claim. We resort to the use of "time" to describe our limited conscious interaction with the near-edges of the fourth-dimension, only because we have no language or concepts to better describe this larger extent. In *Flatland*, the two-dimensionally restricted denizens described their interaction with three-dimensional objects by using the idea of "time." Seen this way, "time" can be thought of as a "window" to the near edges of the next dimension.

"Time" is an organizational system needed by our conceptual brains, yet this then restricts our *"viewport"* into the wider universe. This is a beautiful and interesting constraint because it allows for our three-dimensional specialization. "Time" is an ordering system that allows us to organize our conceptual thoughts. ***We are not built to be able to handle all the potential available information at once. For information to be useful for us, it must be processed by our brains in small increments. We order these increments by creating something called "time." "Time" is the way our brain organizes information–it is our brain's filing system.***

RESONANCE

Resonance is an extremely important principle in *wave physics,* and because we observe it every day in many ways, it is something that is also very understandable on our 3D level. *Resonance* is defined as *"the intensification and enriching of vibratory phenomena by supplementary vibration."*

Vibration produces *waves.* When two *waves* of the same type meet in the same medium, they interact (*interfere*) either destructively *(destructive interference),* or constructively *(constructive interference),* or typically, in some combination of the two. In music, certain *frequencies* or notes combine to create a more *resonant* whole and a fuller harmony. When the two waves of the same or related frequency (pitch) vibrate *in-phase,* the waves will add together (*constructive interference*) and are said to *reinforce* each other. This new combined wave will have an increased *amplitude,* and, if these *waves* are *sound waves,* they will likely be heard as fuller and louder. This is an example of *reinforcement* or *constructive interference.* If two vibrational waves (sound waves) are *out-of-phase*–meaning that the directions of the waves oppose each other–these same matching *frequencies* will cancel each other, resulting in the full or partial destruction of the vibratory wave. This is *destructive interference,* the common vibratory phenomenon that noise-canceling headphones use.

Within sonic frequencies, the mixing of *reinforcement* and *destructive interference* helps form and shape the music, language, noise and the everyday sounds that we all hear. Noise-canceling headphones, common with air travelers today, take *destructive interference* to its maximum level and almost eliminate undesired sounds. They do this by picking up noise with a microphone on the outside of the headphones, and then generating a new wave, exactly *out of phase* but with the same *frequencies* as the offending noise waves. Then they electronically mix these two (out-of-phase) waves so that they will cancel each other. The offending outside noise is then no longer heard. *Feedback* in a PA system is a dramatic example of extreme, uncontrolled *constructive interference (reinforcement).* A beautifully sung harmony is partially the result of carefully controlled *reinforcement,* while the discordant *diminished 7th* chord is an intentional mix of *reinforcement* and *destructive interference.* In drum circles, *resonance* and *interference* can sometimes occur in unusual combinations, causing listeners to think that they hear the sounds of clarinets, flutes, bagpipes, human voices or other instruments that are not actually present.

All physical things of our world have one or more *natural resonant frequencies. This* is the frequency at which something will vibrate naturally and easily. When we strike a drum or a piece of china, the note that we hear is its *natural resonant frequency.* When an object interacts with a wave that is oscillating at the object's *natural resonate frequency,* the object may also start to *vibrate* at that same *frequency* or at some multiple of that *frequency. Resonance* is the term used for describing this reinforcing (*constructive interference*) relationship between two or more things that are vibrating, or have the potential to easily and naturally vibrate together.

Sonic and other physical vibrations involve time and movement, so they require all the dimensions of our 3D world: the three spatial dimensions and the interface that we call "time." As described in *M-theory,* the source of all vibration is said to originate in 11-dimensional space. We are aware of only the "shadows" of the original vibration as they trickle down to our world, through multiple layers of *projection,* to eventually be expressed as 3D form. What we encounter in our viewport is only the shadow of the shadow, of the shadow, etc., of that original vibrating source. This can be visualized as a multilayered, multi-tiered, trickle-down process. This *vibratory* symphony created deep in multi-dimensional space is the driving engine of all life. At this deepest fundamental level, *vibration* is life.

Everything we know and consider to be real in our world is formed from vibration at the fundamental level of creation. This symphony of vibration is what creates all the particles and matter. The particular forms that "manifest" in our universe and our individual lives are the result of our ability to resonate with these particular parts of creation. The universe is created and experienced through resonant vibration.

UNDERSTANDING RESONANCE

Humans have a deep, natural and physical understanding of 3D vibration. Sound waves, electromagnetic waves and ocean waves (including tsunami, earthquakes and more) are all formed from different types of vibration. Since sound is a very familiar and relatively simple type of vibrational wave that we all experience, we will use it as an example.

Looking at a simple guitar string is a wonderful way to begin our understanding of basic *sonic vibration* and *resonance*. Pluck the low (E) string and watch it vibrate. At the nut (top of guitar neck) and bridge (near bottom of the body) the string is attached to fixed points of the guitar and therefore does not move. These points are referred to in wave physics as *fixed nodes*. The middle of the string swings back and forth at such a rapid rate that it becomes visually blurred–this middle part of the wave is called the *anti-node*. The string moves the farthest in the middle of the string at the *anti-node* and less towards the *nodes*, so technically we describe the *amplitude* as maximum (the distance between back and forth) at the *anti-node*. The same wave has zero *amplitude* at the *nodes*. The *frequency* is the number of times the string makes one complete back and forth trip in a measured and fixed amount of time. For many types of vibration, including sound, this time interval is often expressed as a single *second*. For example, the *frequency* of the (A) string on the bass guitar might be expressed as "110 vibrations per second," 110 Hz (Hertz), or sometimes 110 cycles per second (CPS).

Orchestras of the past tuned to slightly lower *frequencies* than today's orchestras because the older stringed instruments could not handle the tighter tension required for higher tuning *frequencies*. Conductors of orchestras often preferred these higher tunings, knowing that a higher pitch helped the orchestra stand out and seem brighter. The musical term for *frequency* is *pitch* or *note*. *Amplitude* is associated with the sonic and musical quality called *volume*. If we hit two strings side by side and they both vibrate exactly the same, say 440 Hz (also a modern "A"), they are said to be in perfect *resonance*. The combined tone is *reinforced* and therefore sounds much louder and fuller. If one tone is 430 Hz and the other is 440 Hz, when they vibrate together they compete slightly and produce a third vibratory sound called *interference* or *beats,* which represents the difference between these *frequencies*. In this particular example, where the difference in frequencies is 10 Hz resulting in a ten-beat-per-second, audible vibration–a WA-WA sound that most guitarists seek to eliminate as they tune their instruments. (I used the term "most" because sometimes this WA-WA sound and the sonic tension it creates is the desired effect.) Harmonic resonance with 440 Hz occurs at many frequencies other than just 440 Hz. It also happens precisely at 55 Hz, 110 Hz, 220 Hz and 880 Hz (halving or doubling). We call these frequencies *octaves* because they still form the same *note* (A), but are lower- or higher-sounding versions of the note "A." Lesser *resonances*, called *harmonics,* also occur at multiples and divisions of 3,4,5,6, etc. A trained guitar player knows the exact places on a guitar string to "tap" and create these special sounding *resonant* tones.

The vibrating "A" string can be lightly touched in the middle and a new wave pattern will emerge because that midpoint suddenly becomes a still point or *node*. Each half of the string now will vibrate with that new *node,* but with the string's length cut in half, the new note will now vibrate twice as fast and sound exactly one *octave* higher. The actual wave shape on the string is different because we now have a new *nodal point* midway on the string, which is exactly the exact spot where the amplitude was once maximized. This midpoint is built into the structure of the guitar as the twelfth fret (raised, brass wire) and similar nodes occur other places on the string relating to the integral subdivisions (1/2, 1/3, 1/4, 1/5, etc.). Some of these positions are marked by fixed frets.

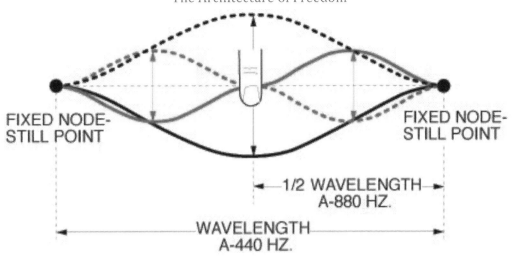

FIXED NODE-
STILL POINT

FIXED NODE-
STILL POINT

1/2 WAVELENGTH
A-880 HZ.

WAVELENGTH
A-440 HZ.

The nodal points on a vibrating guitar string are the points that don't move when the string vibrates. If we touch the middle of the string when it is vibrating, we create a new nodal point and divide the wave into two shorter waves that produce a note that is exactly one octave higher.

Sympathetic resonance occurs when a secondary object begins to *vibrate* on its own because it has the same *natural harmonic frequency* as the original *vibration*. For example, another string, or the body of an instrument, could start to *vibrate sympathetically* because it has the same or related *resonant frequency* as the string that was originally plucked. The *vibration* from the plucking of a string creates waves, and some of these waves travel through the body of the instrument, and some travel through the air. These physical *vibrations* from the string are transmitted directly through the *vibrating* body of the instrument to every other part of the instrument. Air molecules striking another string or instrument at just the right *natural resonant frequency* will cause vibration in a second string or instrument's body. These waves then, in turn, *vibrate* the *resonant* body, or other strings, causing them to sound their natural tones. *Secondary sympathetic vibrations* can be created within the original instrument or they can be transferred to other instruments in the band or orchestra. Finely crafted guitars and other musical instruments are designed to easily *vibrate* and then freely transmit their unique sound waves through the air and instrument body.

This effect can be intentional, as it is with well-tuned symphony orchestras and other musical groups, or it could also be accidental and undesired. In 1940, the large-scale destructive movement created by just the right speed of wind blowing through and *vibrating* the Tacoma Narrows Bridge caused the bridge to fly into pieces. This collapse, which can be viewed on the Internet, taught engineers much about damping and bridge construction and, as a result, modern bridges no longer allow this destructive type of uncontrolled *sympathetic resonance*. If a musician accidentally leaves an amplified instrument near the amp and then walks away, an electronic version of *sympathetic resonance* can build into a deafening sound. Sometimes in rock and roll, punk and contemporary electronic music, *feedback*–an amplified electronic form of *sympathetic resonance*–is created intentionally as part of the music. Controlled *sympathetic resonance* can also be built into the instrument itself, as it is with the secondary vibrations of drone strings on a sitar or similar instrument.

Musical instruments are always communicating with each other as their component parts exchange *energy* and *information* in the form of *vibration*. Everything that we call music is simply the controlled interaction of sonic vibrations.

RESONANCE THROUGH MULTIPLE DIMENSIONS

We can think of the universe as a giant, vibrating, musical instrument (*M-theory*). **Sympathetic resonance producing harmonics that connect through multiple dimensions is the way the universe creates and organizes itself.** Vibration at the very core of creation creates a "symphony" that is infinitely rich with *harmonics* and other *vibratory information.* This complex *vibratory information* then casts its "shadow," creating *sympathetic resonance* throughout all dimensional layers. **The resonant "shadow" of this deep-level "symphony" is eventually perceived locally as the physical manifestation of our universe.** This is very similar to the description of how the *branes* of *M-theory* create particles. Just as with everything else in creation, we also each *vibrate* multi-dimensionally. Our *frequencies* and *harmonics* form our personal "song," or root signature, that then, in turn, *resonates* with all other parts of creation. **This is how we communicate directly through the dimensional barriers with everything in creation. This multi-dimensional vibrational interconnection is what manifests and connects everything in every parallel universe. We "understand" other dimensions through vibration.**

How we each individually vibrate as we create "our song" determines what part of all these universes we resonate with, and this, in turn, determines how the world appears to us. When two or more things resonate at the same *harmonic frequency* and in *phase,* they *reinforce* each other to produce a greater and more powerful whole. When they are out of *phase,* they partially *interfere* with each other to create a new and complex vibrational signature, which can be filled with voids, gaps, static or noise. When two or more things vibrate at different *frequencies,* a new third sub-pattern emerges, which we hear as rhythmic beats or pulses. Depending on how *vibrational frequencies* meet, the new sound may seem musical or it may seem like chaotic noise.

"Going with the flow" is simply allowing the local vibration of our region in the universe to vibrate us (dance us) and move us along with it in sympathetic resonance. As our vibration shifts, our location in the universe shifts, as we travel fluidly and easily with the universe always supporting us through natural, sympathetic resonance. We are in essence just "hitching a ride," letting the universe do the "work" for us. The "path of least resistance" involves relaxing to allow our natural frequencies to resonate fully, so that we can enjoy the energetic "help" of the universe.

WHAT IS FREQUENCY OUTSIDE OF TIME?

All of our *frequency* discussions have included, by definition, the human concept of "time." *Frequency* is a three-dimensional, "time"-based concept. It is measured in cycles or vibrations per second, so in our physical realm, "time" is a natural and necessary part of the description of any *vibratory* phenomenon.

We also understand from our physics of the last one hundred years that our sense of "time" isn't real or absolute. When we move outside our 3D conceptual universe, the nature of "time" begins to have a much different meaning and, at some deeper level, there is ultimately no such thing as "time." *Frequency,* as we currently understand and define it, is a concept that requires "the linear march of time," but this way of experiencing and measuring *frequency* is only another three-dimensional artifact created by our mind's need to order and organize events. Outside of "time," *frequency* must have a very different meaning.

String theory predicts that the fundamental nature of the universe is vibratory and consists of at least 10 dimensions, but this 10- or 11-dimensional space is probably not subject to our concept of linear "time." Within this type of space, *frequency* must mean something very different than it does in our three-dimensional world. At this level, possibly the source of all creation, there is no beginning, there is no end, and yet, there still is some form of fundamental *vibration*. This *vibration* that creates everything in the universe must then happen beyond, or outside of, "time." **We can learn to better feel and work with the shadow aspects of this deep-level vibration that is created beyond conceptual "time." The development of this sensitivity is a critical key to unlocking our ability to more directly experience and participate in the fuller dimensionality of space.**

What then, is *frequency* without the measurement of time? This is a scientific *koan,* one that points towards one of the critical and important limits of our three-dimensional existence. We simply are not designed with the conceptual tools to comprehend *vibration* outside of "time." We can, instead, learn to feel it without needing to rely upon conceptual thinking–then it becomes a way of moving through life.

What would change if our awareness of vibration became liberated from the constraints of time? What is vibration when it originates "outside of time"? To my mind these are some of the more interesting questions in today's *physics, cosmology* and in life itself. Like Zen koans, these questions can open new pathways for fresh ways of understanding our deepest interconnections.

THE NEW TERRAIN

The *cosmological* possibilities dramatically change with the addition of extra dimensions. A universe of 10 or 11 dimensions is not a space that we can ever "understand" in a graphic or logical way. The word "space," itself, has strong three-dimensional associations. To meet with new forms of "space" that reside beyond our conceptual comfort zone, but still close enough to be within our ever-expanding "conceptual horizon," we have to approach our "thinking" differently. This new type of space is much more expansive, contains more *information* and is more directly interactive and flowing. To better access it, we need to let go of all of our traditional "thinking." All of our conceptual "rules" need to be relaxed, and even then, the most that we can directly access will be a relatively limited *projection* or shadow of the real thing. Even though we can learn to understand these cast shadows differently, the deepest secrets of an 11-dimensional universe will probably always remain invisible to our 3D conceptual and analytical brains.

We are all capable of sensing more aspects of this invisible world, but our individual ability to do this must be developed over time. Occasionally we have "events" in our lives, sometimes traumatic, which open new windows to this unseen world. These "out of the ordinary" incidents often seem random or accidental, and any openings through the dimensional veil are usually only temporary. However, even if temporary, our memories around these encounters can continuously imprint and inform us over the rest of our lives.

Even though we may not have the tools to easily see or understand the vast hidden depths of our universe, we are still able to directly benefit from its amazing structure. If all we each do is accept its *infinite* extents and be open and willing to explore the endless possibilities, we will all benefit in extraordinary ways. Our human playground, while enormous and mysterious, will always be *infinitely* and intimately interconnected beyond *time* and *space.* Even though our personal *viewports* are limited, we always are an integrated and critical part of everything. We are always receiving information from beyond the cast shadows that we directly experience. Information fills this amazing and expansive space, and with the right kind of openness we become free to utilize much more of it.

As we open our hearts to new types of perception and knowledge, we have no certainty about what this new *information* and our open participation will really mean. Many of these expansive insights completely shatter our current world paradigm. If we are to understand these experiences at a deeper level, we must first allow for an evolution of our conceptual abilities. The often-quoted early quantum physicist, Niels Bohr, was famous for criticizing new *quantum* sub-theories and ideas because they were, in his words, *"not crazy enough."* We have learned from other major cultural shifts in human history, that, over time, a new philosophy and perspective will evolve and integrate with our lives. Eventually we will see all of creation through this new and different lens–one where the pieces all seem to fit better and "crazy ideas" suddenly make good sense! Historically, we also understand that it will probably take a long "time" for this large-scale awakening, as our culture assimilates this new knowledge. It could take as long as the hundreds of years that were required for the last major paradigm shift, the one that moved humankind from "flat earth," to the *heliocentric viewport.* ***However, this discussion about gradual evolution assumes that we interact with "time" in our old way. If we can change our perception of "time," then radical change can and will occur in an instant.***

THE CAVEAT

This entire book is being written under the shadow of one enormous caveat. ***No matter what we explore, imagine or dream, all the principles of physics are ultimately only things or ideas in our minds. Concepts do not exist outside of the conceptualizers.***

As Albert Einstein wrote: *"Physical concepts are free creations of the human mind, and are not, however it may seem, uniquely determined by the external world. In our endeavor to understand reality, we are somewhat like a man trying to understand the mechanism of a closed watch. He sees the face and the moving hands, even hears its ticking, but he has no way of opening the case. If he is ingenious he may form some picture of a mechanism that could be responsible for all the things he observes, but he may never be quite sure his picture is the only one which could explain his observations. He will never be able to compare his picture with the real mechanism and he cannot even imagine the possibility or the meaning of such a comparison. But he certainly believes that, as his knowledge increases, his picture of reality will become simpler and simpler and will explain a wider and wider range of his sensuous impressions. He may also believe in the existence of the ideal limit of knowledge and that it is approached by the human mind. He may call this ideal limit the objective truth."*
The Evolution of Physics (1938), co-written with Leopold Infeld.

It is impossible for us to "think" outside the box of our conceptual minds. The entire universe, as we understand it, is only a mental concept of our own creation. Today, from our earth-bound, limited perspective, it appears that as we learn more about our world, the physics only gets more complicated! However, complexity in our mathematical descriptions of the universe is really only a symptom of an immature theory. As we learn more and begin to witness creation from a broader perspective, our understanding will become more inclusive, and things will seem simpler, not more complicated. Our present confusion and complications are only phenomena that are being shaped by the limits of our *viewport*. As our view expands to include more–an elegant, simple, beautiful and unified vision of our existence will ultimately be revealed.

Michio Kaku is a brilliant contemporary physicist and communicator. For a long time he has been demonstrating his uncanny ability to explain the unexplainable with statements such as *"Although the mathematical complexity of the 10 dimensional theory has soared to dizzying heights, opening up new areas of mathematics in the process, the basic ideas driving unification forward, such as higher dimensional space and strings, are fundamentally simple and geometric.*" To many in the physics community, the present-day appearance of complexity is only another sure indicator that we are still working with incomplete and immature theories.

As we explore the physics of 10, 11 or more dimensions, one thing that will continue to be problematic is obtaining scientific proof of these theories. Today, we have no method for performing experiments in 11 dimensions because we completely lack the conceptual framework and tools to do so. Exploring physics or consciousness within these unknown regions begins to require the kind of faith that reminds us of the original explorers of the new world. Lacking charts and directions, they had to trust a personal vision that often tapped into the realms of religion and spirituality.

The place where science and spirituality intersect is very uncertain territory, especially for the scientifically trained. However, as I already mentioned, ***any scientific journey towards truth will necessarily have to intersect honest spiritual explorations somewhere along the path, because they are both pointing towards the same Holy Grail: the deepest secret of life.***

PART FOUR–THE ARCHITECTURE

THE MULTIVERSE

WHAT IS THE MULTIVERSE

Existence is filled with unseen worlds and universes that are packed together in an infinite and fully interactive matrix. Even if we can't understand or visualize its form, we can begin to imagine some of the amazing possibilities of such a creation. Such a wonderful expanse needs a more appropriate and descriptive name. Universe works, but it is also closely associated with our old paradigm and ideas. Our collection of universes occupies a space of at least 11 dimensions, and possibly many more because the number of dimensions may actually be increasing over "time," or even be infinite. The name *Infiniverse* is much more descriptive than just universe; however, in 1895, the psychologist and philosopher, William James, came up with the term *Multiverse*. Today, this term is well known and used by scientists because it reminds us that our larger universe contains many other universes. Also, the term *Multiverse* has been used long enough to have found its way into public lexicon. Since the name *Multiverse* is descriptive and more widely understood than *Infiniverse*, I will continue to use it throughout this book to describe the *infinite* collection of universes that make up everything in creation.

Our *Multiverse* is forever evolving, changing and growing, as observed from our "time"-based perspective. **The more we learn about our home, this Multiverse, the more we realize that it is much bigger, more intricately woven, more evolutionary and more interconnected then we could ever have imagined.** While our 3D part of the *Multiverse* is an extremely small component of this unbelievable expanse, it is important to always remember that our small domain is a fully-interconnected and critical part of the greater whole.

PLAYGROUND FOR CONSCIOUSNESS

The *Multiverse* is the great playground for consciousness. It is a woven tapestry of energetic fabric, containing parallel worlds and universes that are completely sharing their information throughout an interconnected, interactive, multi-dimensional space. The *Multiverse* is always throbbing, pulsating and *resonating* as it manifests its fundamental *vibrations*. This *vibrant* pulse can be thought of as the ultimate creative "song of life." Within this sonic landscape, all areas are occupied and explored by conscious *beings* whose core "vibrational signatures" naturally *resonate* with their unique regions of the *Multiverse*. As a soul's vibration changes, awareness flows towards new regions of the *Multiverse*.

Something unique happens when we are more fully "tuned" to deeper levels of vibration. As we live our lives, we are always *resonating* with the parts of the Web that match our current *natural resonant frequencies*. Musicians and music lovers know that when two or more things *resonate* together, a new, wonderful and powerful symphonic blend is created. A special phenomenon called *sympathetic resonance* was earlier defined as "passive vibratory bodies responding to external vibrations." *Sympathetic resonance* occurs throughout all parts of creation. With music, the *resonant* feeling is often described as *"I wasn't singing the song, the song was singing me!"* In sports we often speak of this experience as being "in the zone." Universally, this feeling, often described as "being in the flow," is experienced as a beautiful and exciting state of being. This experience is the result of trusting and allowing the natural *vibratory energies* of the *Multiverse* to move or guide the physical expression of our lives.

Without consciousness, our 3D physical realm in the *Multiverse* might not even exist. As an individual *being* resonates and harmonizes within the *Multiverse*, a region is brought to life and it manifests to that *being* as his or her dimensional reality. This enlivening of a part of the Web by *conscious awareness* functions like an act of *observation,* causing what physicists call the *"collapse of the quantum wave function."* As the *probability wave collapses,* a piece of our "real" world comes to life. A part of the infinite Web has become "real and solid" for us, because of our *sympathetic resonance* with these *natural resonant frequencies*–in this way we fully explore our individual and unique song.

In the deeper hidden realms of the *Multiverse*, all of our individuated parts of consciousness meet. Together, in this deeper expanse, we join to "co-create" this adventure that we call life. At the same time, we realize that this "real" world of ours is only a dreamlike *projection*, a shadow or hologram that is cast through the layers of dimensional space beyond. This process creates beautiful and magical expressions that unfold for us in the ever-present and always-available "now" moment. When fully experienced, this "now" moment can also be understood as "eternity." (I will discuss this idea further in the section on spirituality.) Allowing ourselves to be guided by our natural vibrant flow is a key to our personal freedom.

MULTIVERSE, COSMOLOGY AND QUANTUM PHYSICS

MANY PATHS LEAD TO THE IDEA OF MULTIPLE UNIVERSES

As physicists working with *relativity* and *quantum physics* search for *unification* and meaning, the idea of multiple or *parallel universes* continues to emerge as a solution to the unique problems, conditions and paradoxes that these two well-tested theories illuminate. The thought process of these scientists is playfully described by the leading *quantum* physicist, prolific author and NOVA personality, Brian Greene, when he says, *"I find it both curious and compelling that numerous developments in physics, if followed sufficiently far, bump into some variation on the parallel-universe theme. It's not that physicists are standing ready, multiverse nets in their hands, seeking to snare any passing theory that might be slotted, however awkwardly, into a parallel-universe paradigm. Rather all the parallel universe proposals we take seriously emerge unbidden from the mathematics of theories developed to explain conventional data and observations."*

According to Greene and others, this path down the *parallel universe* line of reasoning comes from at least four, different, independent directions of inquiry: 1) the exploration of *expansion* within *relativity*, 2) the existence of *dark matter*, 3) the mathematics of *string theory* and 4) the interpretation of *quantum superposition* that leads to the *Many Worlds Theory*. These four lines of reasoning present the multiple universe solution as a reasonable, consistent and logical conclusion.

However, Greene will frequently begin his discussions with the caveat: *"The subject of parallel universes is highly speculative. No experiment or observation has established that any version of the idea is realized in nature...no one should be convinced of anything not supported by hard data."* Theories involving parallel universes currently lack reproducible experimental results and, therefore, should not at this time be considered hard science.

These theories about multiple parallel universes may remain technically unprovable because, by definition, most parallel universe theories are tied to extra-dimensionality. It is unlikely that any experiment or observation can produce hard data about a process that unfolds within multiple dimensions because these regions cannot be controlled or manipulated from our current conceptual framework. Also, any potential results from the multi-dimensional experiment would have to somehow be interpreted, make sense, and be understood within our 3D *viewport*. To be conclusive, experiments probably need to employ the full 10 or 11 dimensions that are currently required for *string theory* physics. How does one set up such an experiment, and what kind of meaningful hard data would trickle down from there to our three-dimensional realm?

Since theories based on multiple dimensions are probably impossible to test, scientists will have some natural professional resistance to these far-reaching ideas. Since many of the ideas proposed in this book lack experimental support, they cannot be considered science. It is completely natural and expected that these strange ideas will be met with resistance from within the scientific community.

RESISTANCE TO CHANGE

There are other more human reasons for a strong cultural resistance to such radical new directions of thought. Inherent in any stable culture is a general level of resistance to new ideas–both individual and collective. Political, social, scientific, business and religious groups often resist radical change for a variety of cultural and individual reasons. Change usually threatens the existing power structure and established interests of all types. Reflexively, many in established positions will consistently expend enormous energy and resources to support and maintain the established belief system.

Many members of the scientific community have devoted their entire lives to the specific quest of understanding our 3D cosmos. These scientists have a substantial vested interest in their base of existing technical knowledge; and the very last thing they may want to see, at least at the subconscious egocentric level, is an open door to a vastly shifted view of the universe that erodes the value of their expertise. From their perspective, *parallel universes* and multiple extra dimensions can be seen as extremely dangerous ideas because, if true, it would mean that they might have to start all over. Therefore, like other established "experts," they might not always be happy to support the degree of radical change required for a paradigm shift. This resistance is completely predictable and is just the natural and reflexive response to lifetimes of focused study and vested interests.

Fortunately, the world at large–and even more specifically, the community of physicists–is filled with true intellectual explorers who have little or no concern for these social and business considerations. These courageous explorers, who are actively probing the outer edges of our understanding, are typically close in temperament to those who bravely explored our physical planet in the past. These contemporary explorers embody that same powerful drive, often manifested as a "need to climb the next mountain to see what is on the other side." This attitude keeps the door wide open and lets the "crazy ideas" find their way in.

Most of these leading edge scientific researchers are working quietly in their labs or observatories, but a select few, like Brian Greene and Michio Kaku, have the additional gift of being great communicators and have brought their message of strange worlds directly to the public. They have become the visible face of this new science. Because both Brian Green and Michio Kaku have such strong curiosities, personalities and abilities to communicate, they are not only informative, but also extremely entertaining; and this makes their ideas extremely infectious.

Initially the idea of *Many Worlds* or *parallel universes* was considered a fringe curiosity. Over time we have become more used to this once, very-crazy idea, because it helps resolve so many of the difficult questions. ***Today, we find ourselves at a critical stage in this process. Many of these quantum ideas seem to be converging, and there is some general agreement about interpretations of the results from the last hundred years of physics. There is a definite focus and clear excitement around this "crazy" idea of multiple universes. Today, this line of reasoning is seen by many physicists as being the best explanation for the collection of strange results that we have been observing. To date, we simply have not produced a better explanation!***

What follows is a brief summary of several different ways to think about these observations and how they bring us to the same extraordinary conclusion: *parallel worlds* and *parallel universes* likely exist. We will always need to keep in mind that we are trying to describe and therefore contain a body of information that is continuously moving, changing and expanding. We are also attempting to do this without an adequate vocabulary.

"Many Worlds" found in Three Dimensions

Even before exploring the more exotic realms, we can still find room for an *infinity* of universes without ever leaving the confines of our known and comfortable three-dimensional universe. This becomes the most comprehensible road to imagining the existence of *parallel universes* because it is not counterintuitive. This approach relies on the relatively easy-to-grasp idea that our 3D universe is *infinite* in its physical size–our universe just goes on and out forever.

As of today, we have yet to find the end or outer edge to our 3D universe. As we look out, we do not observe a limit, an end or an edge, anywhere. Currently, astronomers see the light from stars as far away as 15 billion *light-years* in every direction. This distance in ordinary miles is about 100 sextillion miles (calculated by using 15,000,000,000 (fifteen billion) years multiplied by the 5,878,625,373,183 miles that light travels each year). This is the known distance from our planet to the outermost edge of the "visible" universe. Since this is measured looking only in any one direction, we will need to double that number for the full width of the current "visible" universe.

In truth, that number is "so yesterday" because the universe itself is expanding faster than even the speed of light–three times the speed of light by some estimates. The light from the farthest stars left the locations that we now observe some 15 billion years ago. These stars have, by now, physically moved a long distance from these original positions. Because of this rapid expansion, the actual width of our visible part of the universe is today estimated to be almost three times greater. This means that the real diameter of the known part is over 80 billion *light-years* instead of about 30 billion *light-years.* Today, these stars are located in very different positions from where their light appears to be coming from. The light leaving these farthest stars today will not reach the Earth for another 40 billion years, and by then these stars will have again moved much farther away.

Because of the geometry of an expanding universe, every part of the universe will always move away from our Earth, even if we are not located in the very center of the universe. Objects farther away will move away from us at a greater rate of speed. Here is a diagram that demonstrates why this is so.

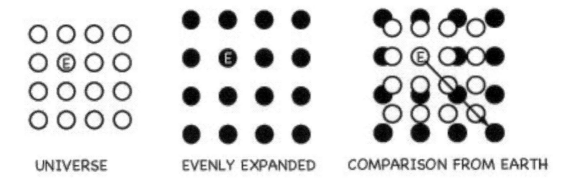

UNIVERSE   EVENLY EXPANDED   COMPARISON FROM EARTH

As the universe evenly expands, every object moves away from every other object; but those that are farther away from Earth (E) move farther and, therefore, are moving away faster. This demonstrates that the objects that are farther away are moving away from us faster. This simple geometric relationship tells us much about our physical universe.

It is also very interesting to realize that when we look at these far-reaching stars, we are not only looking out a great distance but, because we are also seeing light that left these stars 15 billion years ago, we are also looking back in time. If we had instruments that were accurate enough to see small things like plants and animals in these star systems, we would be seeing them as they appeared 15 billion years ago.

SO MUCH IS INVISIBLE–"DARK-MATTER"

As our techniques and scientific instruments improve and we become able to peer farther into space or deeper into the depths, we will gradually expand the limits of our current *viewport* to include more of the vast expanse that lies within and beyond. Our *cosmic horizon,* the extent of our vision at any time, is critically limited by several factors. The speed of light (and all other electromagnetic radiation frequencies), the time available for this light to travel, stellar dust, cosmic background radiation, our conceptual limitations, our size and scale, the limitations of our equipment, the expansion of our universe and the veil between dimensions all have an impact on what and how far or deep we can see.

The *matter* within our universe (stars, planets, dust, etc.) seems to be evenly distributed, at least throughout the portion of the universe that we can presently see. However, as discussed, we have recently learned that, within this visible expanse, most of the *mass* is not even visible (*dark matter*). (Here I will summarize an earlier discussion in case the reader skipped it.) Scientists calculated the amount of *mass* in the known universe by looking at the *gravitational force* required to hold the *galaxies* together and cause all their relative motion (spiral arms, etc.). They discovered that all the stars, planets, comets, and cosmic dust (by far the largest component of the visible stuff) together do not contain nearly enough mass to explain this observed motion. ***The vast majority of the mass in the known universe can't be seen directly with our eyes or instruments. As of today, we really don't even understand what this material is so scientists have begun calling this mysterious gravitational stuff "dark-matter."***

Let us wrap our minds around this important discovery one more time. Scientists have calculated that between 70-80 percent of the *gravitational matter* within the visible and known universe is in some form that we can't see or measure directly, so they call it "dark." They deduce that it must be there because the visible objects of the universe would not behave the way they do without this extra *dark matter* pulling and tugging on them. What they are saying is that there is a tremendous amount of something that acts like mass and is spread throughout the universe, but we just have no idea what it is. Our best guess is that there is four or five times more of this invisible "mystery matter" than the normal *matter* that we can see. ***Therefore, we currently think that at least 80 percent of the material stuff in our 3D universe is invisible and unknown!***

There is already enormous room for other worlds in this "dark" and unseen space alone; and we have not even begun to talk about *dark energy,* which is another and even larger, mystery component. There are approximately one hundred billion *galaxies* in the known universe; and every galaxy is home to, on average, hundreds of millions of stars. That means that there are at least 300 sextillion visible stars (that is 300 followed by 27 zeros) within our *cosmic horizon*. If we approach the problem of understanding the extent of the universe by only looking at that small part which we can observe and already "understand," we still encounter vast unexplored expanses that leave plenty of room for many, many additional worlds.

If, over time, we continue to observe that our 3D universe has no discoverable edge, meaning that it just continues on expansively, forever, then, by definition, this 3D portion of our universe is *infinite*. If this is true, then an *infinite* number of parallel universes exactly like ours are out there. ***It is therefore quite possible that our three-dimensional universe will be found to be infinite in its extent even before we consider relativity, additional dimensions or any of the quantum strangeness.***

RELATIVITY AND THE MULTIVERSE-

*R*elativity requires us to begin expanding our vision about the topology of the universe. The landscape of Einstein's *relativity* is called *spacetime,* which is the seamless integration of our three spatial dimensions with time. Although *spacetime* is more than three-dimensional, it is not a full four-dimensional system so, based on our current understanding, it lies somewhere between 3D and 4-D space. However, even with just this slight expansion of our spatial awareness, many things that we see and encounter will appear very strange to our still-limited 3D sensibilities.

Some cosmologists are not sure that our universe continues forever. Because space itself curves, as revealed through *relativity*, it may curve enough, and in the right way, so that eventually it could curve fully around and back on itself like some kind of four-dimensional racetrack, pretzel or Mobius bottle. If this is the case, as some theorize, then, when we are looking far into distant space, we are really gazing out into a big loop of curved space. If we peer carefully enough, with very powerful instruments, we will eventually see the back of our own heads. If this curved *spacetime* twists and turns in the more complex pretzel-like shape, then we might be seeing the same stars and objects many times over, only thinking that they are different.

Relativity has led to theories describing a universe that began with the *big bang,* and has been expanding ever since. We just discussed one idea about the arrangement of our universe–one that is based upon *spacetime* curving back in on itself. If this arrangement turns out to be the case, then our universe is a *closed finite system, which* can be visualized as a single *bubble universe*. This *bubble universe* is "held" by some kind of expanded space and may really be floating in a sea that also contains many other *bubble universes*, possibly an *infinite* number of them. In this possible scenario, our universe would indeed be *finite* but it could be only one of an *infinite* number of these *finite bubble universes contained in this space*. Each of these *bubble universes* has undergone its own *big bang* and *expansion.* This *infinitely* repeating process may be constantly birthing new universes. Might God be like a kid living in deep-dimensional space who is only playing with his cosmic bubble wand?

Steven Hawking and other physicists now speak of *black holes, tunnels, event horizons,* and *wormholes.* Most of us were first introduced to these terms and ideas through science fiction but, today, these topological features, which were first derived from *relativistic physics,* are being recognized as very real components of our physical universe. These massive deformations are created when particularly dense masses bend *spacetime* to a very dramatic degree. Just what do scientists think might be found around the other side of some of these strange topological features? Well, in at least some theories, the answer is "other universes." Some of these universes might seem very strange and be very different from ours.

Thus, the exploration of *relativity* since the time of Einstein has led us to this threshold of hidden multiple universes through more than one line of reasoning. There are some, myself included, who feel that if there is a mistake being made in *relativistic physics,* it is because it just doesn't go far enough. Too few dimensions are being considered, and very real, deep-level connections are being missed because of our inability to imagine things that are situated far beyond our own *conceptual horizon*. To paraphrase Niels Bohr's famous line, *relativistic physics just may not be crazy enough!*

QUANTUM MULTIVERSES

As *quantum* physicists searched to find meaning for their strange observational and experimental results, they were also striving to integrate this new knowledge with *classical physics* and *relativity*. Since this integration requires 10 or even 11 dimensions to mathematically resolve the place where they best intersect exists in a completely new type of spatial framework. Multi-dimensional space creates an entirely new structural framework for all types of invisible and mysterious relationships and interconnections. As we have learned, many different approaches eventually lead to the unexpected conclusion that parallel worlds might play a big part in this mystery. The first physicist to seriously introduce this "crazy" idea in the mid-1950s as the *Many Worlds theory* was Hugh Everett, who was then a graduate student working under the very famous John Wheeler.

David Bohm later took Everett's idea even further by proposing the idea of *enfoldment* to help describe how all these parallel universes stack and fit. ***Then Bohm boldly suggested that all information in the universe might be stored holographically, such that every small piece retains all the information about the whole.*** Both of these ideas stimulated the imagination of physicists by proposing ideas to help explain the perplexing *quantum* observation that *information* can be instantly shared between subatomic particles enormous distances apart. Einstein never became completely comfortable with this *quantum* property called *entanglement*, which he sometimes described as *"spooky action at a distance."* He died about the same time *Many Worlds* was proposed and certainly was not an active participant in its development.

Quantum superposition is the principle that physical systems exist as all theoretically possible states, simultaneously, until the moment of *observation* or measurement, when they collapse into a single fixed state. To help explain this important *quantum* principle, we will look to Bohm's *Many Worlds* interpretation. Bohm proposed that every time an *observation* is made, a *measurement* made, a decision made or an action completed, a new universe splits off or forks like the branch of a tree to create an entirely new world corresponding to that particular choice or circumstance. However, all of the other possible paths that were not "chosen" also exist equally. All possible outcomes, all states of being, all choices and actions–all exist together, but they each exist in a different world or universe, a *parallel universe*. This process happens over and over, so every time someone thinks, decides, acts, or observes, our universe instantly splits.

However, we have also discovered that *time* is fluid and not one-directional and linear. Therefore, in this fluid timeless space, all these choices are occurring simultaneously. This means that all of these possible world exist together in the same moment: the "now" moment. ***The result is an infinite number of different universes representing every potential state or choice by every person or being (observer) ever! Every single thing that could possibly have existed and every possible choice that could have been made, already exists, in this and every now moment, in some parallel universe.***

I personally tremble in the presence of this awesome and beautiful vision of infinity! It provides a structure that can easily explain life's more unusual experiences while opening the door to infinite and fantastic new possibilities. Anything and everything is always possible because it already exists somewhere.

So far we have no successful experimental tests of any of the theories that describe *parallel universes*. As discussed earlier, the persistent problem is simply that we have yet to find a way to experimentally test that which is contained within dimensions that we are unable to see, measure or interact with directly. If there is a proof, it is to be found outside of our familiar realm, in some landscape that exists beyond our *conceptual horizon*. However, outside of our realm, even our commonly understood and accepted idea of a "logical proof" may have no real meaning.

HOW THESE UNIVERSES MIGHT FIT TOGETHER

Where are all of these parallel universes and how do they all fit together? We have some insights, clues and theories, but the possibility of real and deep comprehension is far beyond our current abilities: our understanding will always be constrained by our dimensional perspective and limited sensory tools.

David Bohm, one of the most imaginative and productive physicists and philosophers of the last generation, was a younger colleague of Einstein's at Princeton. He introduced the term *enfolding* to describe one way that we might visualize the intimate arrangement of parallel universes. A hero of mine, he had to spend most of his career practicing physics while exiled from the United States because he refused to testify against his colleagues in Senator Joseph McCarthy's anti-Communist congressional hearings of the early 1950s. Along with his numerous contributions to the fields of physics and consciousness, he was also the originator of the *holographic universe* idea, which will be discussed later in more detail.

According to Bohm, these parallel worlds are swirled with ours in an *implicate order* and *enfolded* so that they always exist, essentially "touching," communicating and interacting with our world, and all other worlds. To understand the concept of *enfolding*, imagine stirring oil and water rapidly in a blender until they are seen to exist, not as separate liquids but, instead, they all become blurred together. With the oil and water in the blender, as long as the blender spins, the worlds remain enfolded together so that everywhere oil and water are one. If we stop the blender they return to their individual separateness. This is the nature of cosmic *enfoldment*. Things are always separate and always one, simultaneously. E*nfoldment* is another concept that is difficult to explain using only our three-dimensional thinking. While 10-dimensional space can't be pictured in our minds, the blender image can evoke a sense of possibilities.

Now that we have a better understanding about the concept of *enfoldment*, we can start to picture how these many universes might be packed together in a way in which there is room for an *infinity* of them. We might imagine how, in the virtual blender of "10 or more dimensions," these other *parallel worlds* could always appear whirled (*enfolded*) tightly up against all other worlds! They all fit perfectly, and at the same time they are so close as to always be intimately connected and communicating with each other. These other universes may always be less than a hair-width away from us, but while living our 3D existences, we don't experience them directly; they are separated from us by a veil that is created from our inability to see or sense multi-dimensional space beyond. However, because of *enfoldment,* all *information* from all of these infinite parallel worlds is always intimately connected to all other parts of the *Multiverse*. We might imagine an invisible network of vibrating multi-dimensional, nerve-like tentacles that connect every part to everything else. This is another way to imagine the Web of all possibilities.

So, whether we look into the farthest reaches of our known universe, map out a *relativistic topology* or search for a way to explain our experimental *quantum observations*, we are likely to stumble upon some version of the idea of *parallel universes*. Space and existence are always revealing themselves to be much larger, more interesting and more interconnected than we previously imagined. ***Our multi-dimensional universe has the room to contain everything that is, has been or could be possible–and contain it all together in harmony here, now and for eternity!***

DOES THOUGHT ALONE EXPAND THE MULTIVERSE

Let's review some of the potential implications for this new vision of an infinite *Multiverse*. Think of anything. Whatever you are thinking about already exists in a universe somewhere within our *Multiverse*. Then have another thought (or any action, *measurement, observation,* or choice, etc.), and realize that idea also exists in the *Multiverse*. Worlds that allow for both of these thoughts and neither of these thoughts also exist. For every thought we might have, another world exists that contains that particular idea. Entire universes exist for every idea imagined by every thinking *being* within any of these universes. Every conscious *being* in the *Multiverse* has millions of thoughts, and worlds or universes already exist for every one of these thoughts or any combination of these. All these different and identical worlds and universes exist simultaneously. Every universe "created" this way is also *self-consistent,* meaning that from within that universe all the events and histories make sense and seem logically consistent. Events that seem contradictory also exist, but these events or choices exist within their own *self-consistent* universes. Every possibility that anyone ever thought about, or any action, *observation,* or choice in any and every combination exists and fits, now and forever, within our fabulous *Multiverse*. This sounds completely fantastic from our human "time-" based and very logical perspective, but I am convinced that this is the very real nature of our Web of All Possibilities.

At this point, I would like to continue this discussion with an idea presented earlier that depends on our concept of "time." Do these universes exist before the idea or "thought," or are they created, in the moment, by our very act of thinking? The early *Copenhagen quantum* school proposed that the act of *observation* is what *collapses* the *probability wave,* and only at that point does the potential physical reality become manifested. For many years this was the most accepted explanation of the double-slit experimental results. The *Many Worlds* interpretation, which came much later, proposed that every thought or action creates a new branch of reality that can be thought of as a new or *parallel world*. All thoughts create new worlds and all these worlds then exist equally, each with their own *self-consistent* history. Every time we do one thing or think about another thing, new histories or worlds are created at that moment.

Both of these interpretations of *quantum theory* assume that the "arrow of time" moves along consistently in one direction–in the traditional way that we usually think about "time." In the multi-dimensional and "timeless" version of these theories, all possibilities already exist, at once, in a state that is held outside of "time." Even though all paths from all our decisions exist in one continuum, each *observer* somehow hops on and "rides" along a single route, or path, that moves through a series of these preexisting possibilities–a single path through the Web. As our chosen path branches in various directions, this becomes our only real world. We only encounter the places along our particular, chosen path, not aware that our route changes or shifts every time we think a new thought. (This is my explanation, not Everett's.)

This act of taking only one route isn't typically a conscious decision, but instead occurs naturally at a very deep level. Each observer's *natural resonant frequency* is always what determines his or her particular part, choice, path, world and universe within the fabric of the *Multiverse*. ***It is the individual's natural resonant frequency that sympathetically makes active a particular part or branch of the Multiverse, and makes it then seem real.***

From the *observer's viewport,* the *probability wave* has *collapsed* since each individual only comes across one specific set of outcomes and has no awareness of all the other possible outcomes. If this process is viewed holistically, but still through the filter of directional time, it could appear that our awareness is creating its own path through the *Multiverse* from a series of thoughts or choices. The contemporary *(*New Age*)* idea of "creating our own world" would then seem to be a very reasonable explanation, but this is only true within a realm that is built upon linear "time." This idea about "creating our world" is time-dependent.

When we move beyond or outside of "time," a deeper structure is revealed. This deeper truth is that our thoughts contribute to shifting our individual, and always evolving, *natural resonate frequency* and it is this change that allows us to *resonate* with other regions and paths that already exist within the *Multiverse*. ***We are actually creating nothing except our own chosen path through the already existing infinite possibilities.***

We know that time does not unfold in a linear way outside of our conceptual *viewport*; but from within our *viewport,* the "arrow of time" relentlessly persists. Within time, every action or thought brings forth a new creation. Beyond" time," we *resonate* with different *enfolded* but preexisting worlds. Both are equally true interpretations; they are just two different perspectives from different dimensional viewpoints. ***We create new worlds with every act or choice and these worlds or possibilities have always existed forever in the fabric of the Multiverse!*** Having both explanations exist simultaneously only seems paradoxical from our time-based conceptual mindset.

SUMMARY OF MULTIVERSE MECHANICS

A clear, understandable description of the Multiverse in words, pictures or models is simply not possible. It has been said that describing it is like using words to describe honey, in that no amount or phrasing of words can describe how it tastes and no picture captures its essence. The most we can do is point ourselves in the right direction and hope to be granted a small hint or a glimpse that reveals some of the *Multiverse's* qualities as they make their way to and manifest in our particular *viewport*. No matter how well explained, the *Multiverse* will never really be understood through words, especially intellectually, because the *Multiverse* can only be conceived in multiple dimensions. We are only capable of imagining things with reference to that which we already know and understand–our restricted world of three dimensions. To understand more, we need to become much more familiar with the uncomfortable idea of "not knowing." This new way of being begins to open us to other possibilities.

Through *cosmology*–the scientific study of our three-dimensional universe–we have learned that the *cosmic horizon,* or the physical limits of what we can presently see with our specialized tools, reaches out in every direction to about 15 billion *light-years.* This alone is an unbelievably large, three-dimensional space for existence! However, the farthest stars that we currently can measure have been traveling outward because of the rapid expansion of our universe. Today, they are now more than 40 billion *light-years* away from us in every direction. The physical size of our universe includes this enormous physical expanse **plus** whatever physical, three-dimensional space might lie beyond our present view or *cosmic horizon.* This means that our physical expanse is even larger and growing which allows for an enormous variety of experiences and many physical worlds similar to ours.

Along with this known and unknown three-dimensional space, there is also more of existence hidden beyond our *conceptual horizon.* Much of this is fully within our physical realm but it is hidden from us because it is beyond of the limits of our sensory organs, or behind our other conceptual barriers. *Dark-matter* and *dark-energy* are found close enough to our *conceptual horizon* that we can indirectly measure their interaction with our 3D world, but what other unknowns exist beyond our ability to sense, measure or comprehend? When we try to envision the possible extent and depth of this mysterious landscape–one that is truly without limits–we can only be certain of one thing: we know very little!

Clearly, within this expanded architecture, a tremendous amount of *matter, energy, information* and space exists that we have not been able to freely access. It is not only that empty space contains all this *matter* and *information*–that alone is enough to flood us with wonder–but, as it turns out, recent studies indicate that empty space itself also seems to be constructed of something physical, yet completely mysterious (*Higgs particles*). This infinite empty space has enough depth and room for all the *information* needed to shape an infinite number of worlds or parallel universes. All three branches of physics *(classical, relativistic* and *quantum)* have paths that lead us directly into a landscape of *parallel* and *infinite* worlds!

GRAPHIC MODELS

USING VIGNETTES TO UNDERSTAND THE MULTIVERSE

To help explain the *Multiverse,* I will attempt to illustrate a few of its small aspects and qualities that can be understood from our perspective. A full comprehensive view is, of course, not possible, given the natural limitations of our three-dimensional conceptual minds. To communicate this partial vision I will present two- and three-dimensional distillations of a *Multiverse* that is undoubtedly far more beautiful and elegant in its full, multi-dimensional expression. It is understood that these partial models do not fully describe the *Multiverse*–no three-dimensional representation can really come close. At best, these 3D models may help us to better understand a few of its more understandable qualities, and they might also guide us to new insights about better ways to live our lives within the *Multiverse.* These various 3D "slices," expressed as verbal or graphic analogies, metaphors, drawings or models, should be thought of as *vignettes.* A *vignette* is a graphic or literary device that relies on a small impressionistic scene that focuses on a single moment or aspect to help provide insights into the bigger picture or idea. This entire collection of *vignettes,* when viewed together, comes as close to an accurate description of the *Multiverse* as I, at this time, can produce.

These vignettes can easily be used to help us understand what we are not. They describe how we are not 3D-bound, individual, vulnerable and very separate beings living in a hostile and

competitive world. This means that our world is not defined, limited and constrained by what we currently think, perceive, see and know.

STACKED PAPER PLATE MODEL

Introduction

A stack of paper plates can provide a useful tool to help us imagine *parallel universes.* Plates can be used to illustrate tightly stacked universes by providing a form that we all can easily visualize. This three-dimensional model works well to help us imagine how we might inhabit more than one parallel universe. It also demonstrates how a universe can appear to be very similar to our own, with many of the same individuals and places, yet, at the same time, be slightly different. It demonstrates how we might travel from one universe to the next and notice little change because *parallel worlds* might vary only in the smallest of details. Because this model is three-dimensional, it is built from the familiar concepts of our 3D realm. In extra-dimensional space the illustrated relationships would be expanded and enlivened with many additional possibilities because, unlike within our 3D space, in the full *Multiverse,* all universes are always positioned to be directly adjacent to every other universe.

The Model

Imagine an infinite stack of paper plates or, at least for now, only imagine a pile as high as we can see. Next, imagine an ambitious silk worm that bores through these plates, meandering around at slightly different angles and paths. This worm first starts at the bottom of the stack and bores all the way to the top, while always stringing a thin colored thread behind him that marks the path of his travels. After reaching the top of the pile, he then turns around, changes his string color and then bores all the way to the bottom of the pile. Each time our silkworm reaches the top or the bottom, he turns, changes his thread color, and then takes a slightly different meandering pathway in the opposite direction. Over time, the silkworm's weavings produce a tower of many, different-colored, long threads that are woven up and down through this stack of plates. Occasionally, our worm might accidentally bore out of the side of the stack, crawl to a different spot, reenter the plates somewhere else farther up or down the stack and begin a new thread color. When the worm is finished, there is only one, very long, multicolored thread that is woven up and down through the tall stack of plates.

When our view is restricted to a single plate within the stack, it is impossible to detect that the thread is continuous and connected. To see the connections between the colors, a broader view of the entire stack is necessary. From anywhere inside the stack, all the vibrantly colored threads appear to be unconnected–completely different pieces of thread.

Our Individual Awareness

Imagine that each of us is represented by one of those colored strings. Each of us occupies the full length of a colored string. This full length of string represents our complete *being.* Because of our dimensional and sensory limitations, we are only aware of that part of our *being* (single-colored section of string) that intersects at one single point–our *viewport.* This point, our world, is that one particular spot where our string passes through a single paper plate. For each of us, that one point on that one string segment represents the entirety of who and what we usually imagine that we are.

That intersection represents the center of our personal awareness. It is where we each interface the "world" we "know," and think we understand.

Every "plate" in this stack represents a *parallel universe* or "world." There are also many other places where our personal colored string passes through all these different "plates." These other points of intersection represent the other parallel expressions of our *being*. We might think of these points of intersection as *doppelgangers,* or copies of ourselves that exist in other universes. We fully exist in all these other universes simultaneously, but are only aware of one point of intersection.

The following illustration represents a cross-section through this short stack of plates, each of which can be thought of as a different parallel universe.

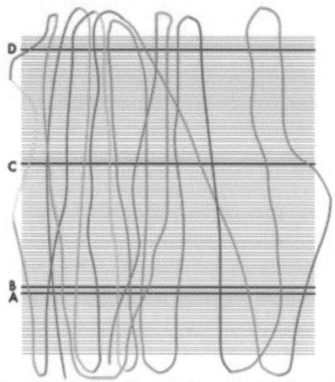

A stack of paper plates representing parallel universes, woven with a thread left by a silkworm that was boring through this stack. Each plate represents a parallel universe, while each colored thread represents an individual who "passes through" and therefore lives in many universes. Since universe "A" and universe "B" are very similar, shifting universes causes almost no noticeable change. Universes "C" and "D" are quite different; new colors (individuals) have entered, while other strings have moved and rearranged themselves. From the expanded perspective there is really only one continuous string, but from within any universe (plate), each point of intersection is experienced as a different "individual."

The Individual

Our 3D universe or "world" is represented by the one plate in this stack that our consciousness (thread) happens to be passing through at any given moment in time. This "world," where our consciousness is currently being expressed and experienced, will also be constantly changing as our individual and cultural *resonance* changes–we are always sliding our awareness up and down each of our colored strings; the intersection of our thread and a single plate represents our individual *viewport* at any given moment. At each moment, we can observe and interact with many of the other points of intersections (individuals) that also occupy our particular paper-plate universe. Living in our "world," we will develop relationships with and concepts about these "others" because they appear to be very separate *beings* from us. What we understand about our universe is limited to the surface of only one plate at a time. Our awareness includes all these "other" individuals who exist only because their colored threads also intersect our plate or universe.

Over time, we might have a series of deep-level changes that cause our vibrational state to shift. When this happens, our consciousness becomes centered a little farther up or down the same vibrating string, possibly at the next point of intersection with the very next plate. Our awareness then instantly shifts to this new plate (universe), but we have no idea or sense that we have moved. On this adjacent plate we will find that not much has really changed. Most of the time, when we are making these constant incremental shifts, we will not have any awareness that we have changed worlds or universes. That rude (red string) neighbor still lives next door and he continues to play loud music. The dog (yellow string) on the other side still barks and the mortgage is still due. However, later in the day when we go into our familiar office, we might notice that there is a new girl working in bookkeeping (a new, different-colored thread that was not in the last plate), and the guy (blue string) who used to sit next to the water cooler is no longer at his desk.

Any two adjacent plates will be very similar universes. In our day-to-day lives, we constantly experience small changes or shifts in our "world." Even though we may have shifted to a new *parallel universe,* there might be very little that is different with this slight change of scene. Nothing seems extraordinary or unusual, so we typically don't even notice this small amount of shift.

What actually happens is that our conscious center shifts to a new universe (plate) when we start to vibrate differently. In most of our shifting our new universe will be very close and similar in almost every way, except for some specific and small details. In two very similar *parallel universes,* the differences are usually so slight that they typically don't even register in our conscious minds. However, to make visible changes that are as dramatic as those noted above, we would probably have to move through a substantial stack of *parallel universes.* A change as significant as other *beings* no longer being present in our lives represents a substantial shift.

In our day-to-day lives we continuously and constantly make such shifts to new parallel universes. Every movement, every thought, every decision affects our vibration; and, therefore, our universe changes accordingly. We never occupy a single universe because we are in constant motion, always hopping through the *Multiverse.* Usually the changes are so tiny they aren't even noticed, but sometimes the shift is large enough that it presents us with a dramatically different, and possibly life-changing, new environment. Shift happens!

What has really changed is only the place where our awareness now resides along the "string of our life" that intersects all possible universes. Not only does the center of our awareness shift, but also our range or breadth of awareness can also expand to grant us conscious awareness of multiple worlds. In our individual awareness, such expansion simply feels like growth within a single, but now fuller, existence.

If we only move to the adjacent plate in the model, most things will appear almost the same. Somewhere on the new plate the silk worm might have changed direction slightly, but usually the changes will be very subtle. Other threads of silk, representing other *beings* who were close to us in the previous universe, will probably still be close to us in this new universe because a much greater shift (many plates away) is required for noticing more substantial changes. If we move six inches up or down the stack, the differences will become much more dramatic; if we move two miles up or down, we might not recognize anything familiar. However, in our three-dimensional physical form, most of the journeying we typically do along our thread is gradual, safe and close to home–we usually stay very close to our old, familiar, and, therefore, safe territory. These moment-to-moment, slight changes are not even noticed unless we are very open and aware.

However, these small, incremental changes do not have to be the only way we shift. All of us occasionally take dramatic leaps, and some individuals have a special talent for making repeated radical shifts. We always have the potential to travel vast distances and make very dramatic changes, when we are prepared and, accordingly, our vibration changes.

As we vibrate up and down the stack of plates along our *resonate* string of life, it is still the same familiar *self* that is recognized and experienced. All of our friends who are in our new universe are still themselves, and overall the world still looks about the same. However, the *self* will be slightly different or changed because it is likely that in this parallel universe a certain aspect of ourselves is tweaked, changed or expanded; for example, we might become slightly more compassionate and more understanding of others. Our best friends might also be present in slightly different versions and, now, this new and expanded *self* is relating to these "others" on a new and different level. Our new relationships with "others" could be quite different from the parallel relationships we had in our old universe. In the new universe, everyone is *vibrating* differently and relating to each "other" at a new level. There is a fresh, mutual understanding because of the changed *vibrational resonance*, which is now possible within the modified *resonant frequencies* of this new universe. Our awareness has shifted only because this new universe is more compatible with our new *natural resonant frequency*. Little has changed outwardly, and yet everything has changed within.

We change our world in this way many times every moment of every day. We are always in constant inner motion, reaching into the lengths and depths through these hidden realms of the *Multiverse*. Each change adds new experience and understanding as we all grow, expand and evolve to more fully occupy our amazing *Multiverse.*

Only One String

Up to this point in our model, we have been speaking about each colored string as being a separate individual. However, we already know, from the greater overview of the model, that at the top and the bottom of the pile of plates, the worm simply changed direction and color. All the different-appearing strings are actually just one, long, continuous string, not unlike those skeins of multicolored yarn. The different colored strings all only imagine that they are separate and individual, but this is only an illusion formed because of the dimensional and sensory filters of their particular limited *viewport*. **If we could all pull back and examine the bigger picture, we would be able to easily see the direct connections that unite us as a single, multi-experiential being.**

Within our lives we often feel *separate,* and we all have the completely normal sensation of perceiving "others." When this *separation* is viewed at a deeper level–the level of the *Multiverse*, where all the worlds can be seen at once–it is revealed that we are all only part of a single, greater *being that has been expressing its parts in different ways.* **What we encounter as "other" individuals is only our limited experience of our own different parts, segments or aspects of the same, single Being. This Being is the wondrous creation that we all are destined to experience as "I am"!**

JOINING AS A ROPE

We can also construct a slightly different but, in some ways, more accurate model of our interconnectedness. As we peer into one end of this stack of plates, the strings all appear to be separate just as in the last example. However, this time, the motion of the silkworms is different because they all tend to gravitate towards each other. Little by little, as they move up the stack of plates, the strings weave together and connect to other strings nearby. As they travel farther and farther up the stack, many more strings weave together until a point is reached where all the strings have co-joined. When the silkworms reach the top of this stack, there is only one, big, thick string–a rope. Looking back in time (to the bottom of the stack), we see that what once was imagined to be many different strings has gradually come together to form one, thick rope.

When looking at just one plate (world) at a time, there is really no way to understand this relationship; but if we could pull back and view the entire stack of all the parallel worlds, we would clearly see that all of these strings have always been connected at the one end. This weave resembles tree roots, or the visible leafy part of a tree turned upside down.

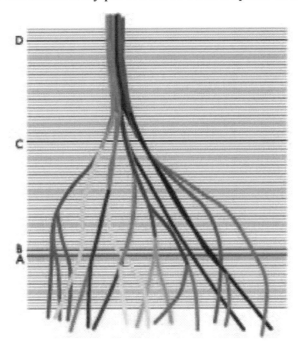

As we grow and evolve we can experience less separation and more interconnectedness.

This inverted tree model can represent our individual and collective evolution over "time" as we expand and grow. As we evolve, we naturally co-join with other souls, individuate less, and move towards "oneness." We do this without ever losing our sense of *self*. We each experience and meet the same "I" within, but this "I" just becomes bigger and more inclusive because we lose nothing of ourselves in this process. "I," when expanded, is still understood as "I"–it is just now a bigger, more inclusive, more comfortable and more conscious "I". This is what we experience as we learn how to open and *vibrate* more fully. We become aware that the "I" remains, and even grows stronger, as we become more fully connected to all others and everything else in creation.

FUZZY BALL

There are other graphic ways to imagine individual separation and unity existing simultaneously. Another 3D physical model that comes quickly to mind is a children's toy, the fuzzy ball. This is a toy ball whose outside surface might be made up of the ends of hundreds of rubber spears, or even thousands of rubber strings.

Kid's "fuzzy" ball demonstrating individualization at outer surface but common connection at core.

At the outer surface of the ball, every point appears to be entirely separate. Closer to the core of the ball, all of these individuated parts connect to reveal their existence as a singular object. At the outer surface, these many points might represent the many individuals on earth who are all expressing their individualization and separation. However, as we look closer, we observe that just like these spikes, we are all really co-joined and belong to a single unified living *Being*. The appearance of separation is only an illusion that exists at the very surface of our existence.

To illustrate, imagine three concentric spheres of different sizes within this fuzzy ball: one in the solid part of the core, one halfway out on the spikes, and the largest sphere at the outer surface. These appear as circles in this 2D diagram, but in 3D they represent full spheres. Each sphere represents a particular *viewport* or universe. Each spherical universe is closed so that its inhabitants only understand or experience phenomena that occur on their sphere's surface. Therefore, their perception of the fuzzy ball is limited to only the point where their sphere (*viewport*) intersects the ball.

The drawing below shows a cross section through these worlds. In this diagram, the inhabitants of each universe are limited to whatever parts of the ball touch each circle–their world. Just like the inhabitants of Flatland, those of this ball land cannot look up or down to see what is happening in the other worlds, because the directions up and down do not exist for them.

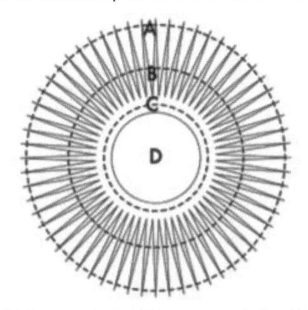

The "fuzzy" rubber ball shown cut through the middle. Notice if our world lies entirely in circle A we feel total separation from "others." Living in world C we witness only one thing; unity. In the hollow center D we would experience "no-thing."

If our world happens to be the outer sphere (A), then the point where each spike intersects this sphere represents separate individuals who might perceive themselves as being very small and separated. If our world is the one at the continuous rubber core (C), then everybody is fully connected and our perception will be of oneness without any separation. Here we will still have the familiar experience of self (being), but there will be no sense of any "others." In this deeper universe, all is unity. If our consciousness travels to the intermediate sphere, B, then all *beings* would be much closer and there would be less feeling of separation. Each of these universes is only a small slice of the entire *Multiverse*, which is represented by the entire fuzzy ball. Each universe slices the fuzzy ball differently, and its inhabitants are completely unaware of the existence of any of these other alternate and parallel universes. These universes all represent different degrees of separation within the same *Multiverse*. Each spike represents the range of possible realities for an individual.

Taking this particular model analogy one step further, the very center of this particular ball is hollow. There is another possible type of experience within this particular model of the *Multiverse*: that of "no-thing" (D). The hollow void can be understood to represent this place of "no thing." Notice how unity (C), is positioned between no-thing (D), and complete individualization (A). ***In this particular representation of the model, unity or oneness is found midway between complete individualization and "no thing."*** This concept will be developed further in the creation story section. The fuzzy ball is an excellent model for demonstrating several different aspects of the *Multiverse*.

WAVES IN THE OCEAN

The ocean is another wonderful visual model that illustrates the illusion of individualization. On the surface of the ocean, individual waves form and disappear; but beneath the surface lies a connected oneness. The individual waves have no real existence of their own, for it is only from this deep source, the ocean, that these temporary individual waves form.

This model also serves to remind us of the temporary nature of our individualization. Each wave exists on the surface for a short moment in time, but always owes its form to what lies below: the ocean water in motion in deeper, rhythmic, repeating cycles. The ocean represents that deep place where there is no separation because, within it, there is only unity. By imagining that we are individual and separate, we exist much like the waves on the surface of the ocean. We imagine that we are alone, isolated and short-lived. In truth we are really experiencing the short-term movement and formation of a surface wave that arises from within our deep and eternal ocean. This ocean is our true *Self*. This ocean can also be called *Love*.

SPAGHETTI MODEL AND TIME TRAVEL

According to David Bohm, *parallel worlds* are swirled in what he calls an *implicate* order, and then they are *enfolded* so that they all exist essentially touching our world at all times. These direct connections would likely involve what would be seen and understood as simple geometric relationships, if we could quickly glimpse them from extra-dimensional space. Because these connections are both visually and conceptually invisible to our three-dimensional minds, we are usually completely unaware of them. Someday these usually-invisible connections may allow us to interact with *parallel worlds* in ways that we could never imagine today.

A plate of spaghetti can be used as another, helpful 3D model for visualizing *enfoldment* and imagining how universes can always be touching. This idea first entered my awareness as I was eating a plate of pasta and, this "spaghetti model" seemed to only become more interesting the further it was examined. Using cooked spaghetti as a visual tool to help explain *enfoldment* helps us to visualize things such as time travel, rapid, long-distance space travel, parallel universes and *non-local interaction*. To fully understand this idea, we also need to, again, step backwards, and examine what might occur in a land of fewer dimensions (similar to the *reverse engineering* technique that was used in *Flatland)*. To be effective, this model needs to be understood to represent a *hybrid* spatial condition– a one-dimensional system that also models the *curvature* of *spacetime.*

Imagine that there is an entire universe existing in one, single, extremely long piece of straight, uncooked spaghetti. This universe is very long, but it is also infinitely thin. This means that it has no dimensions called width or height, and this is what makes it a one-dimensional universe. Next, imagine the inhabitants are all shrunk so that they fit comfortably into the piece of spaghetti. This particular very long piece of spaghetti happens to be a basil and oregano pasta mix, with pieces of green herbs scattered here and there, and plain pasta *(empty space)* between them. The scattered pieces of herbs are the *galaxies* and star clusters and all the other exciting material things that real physical universes offers, such as suns, stardust and planets. Visualize this piece to be as long as our three-dimensional universe is wide–about 80 billion *light-years*. Within this extremely long piece of spaghetti, one group of inhabitants live on a single dot of green oregano named Earth. From Earth they can see 40 billion *light-years* in both available directions. If the inhabitants of this spaghetti-land wished to travel to the far ends of their known "spaghetti universe," it would mean that, at half the speed of light, this journey would require 80 billion years. It is, as I said, a very long piece of spaghetti.

However, because this spaghetti-land is one dimensional, its "width" is nonexistent. Any movement sideways would first require the residents to leave the confines of their one-dimensional universe. Once travelers learn the trick of traveling "sideways" and exiting their universe, they can then begin to travel differently. The technique involves learning how to step outside of their *dimensional limitations* by learning how to utilize one additional dimension. Once mastered, that "side" boundary of their universe will always be only a small movement away, or possibly even "just a thought away."

Next imagine that this piece of spaghetti is then cooked, twisted and all tangled up into a single, enormous ball of sticky pasta. Twisting and turning, it curves and touches itself over and over again. It can now be described as a *curved* and *enfolded* universe, but to the inhabitants living within spaghetti-land, nothing has changed because from their perspective they don't experience the *curves* or the *enfoldment*. From our more expansive three-dimensional perspective, we can see all the pasta curved and swirled on the plate, but the spaghetti would still appear to be quite straight to the inhabitants who lived within this "spaghetti-land." This is similar to the way we perceive Einstein's curved, three-dimensional *spacetime*. We are not able to directly experience the curves of *spacetime*.

After the cooking, the inhabitants of "spaghetti-land" have no idea that their universe is now all looped and curved (*enfolded*). It will still take them the same amount of time to get to the outer edge of their universe if they continue to stay within the curved piece of spaghetti. By staying within their piece of spaghetti they are essentially restricting their travels to only those paths that are fully described and contained within their one dimensional space.

Now imagine that they suddenly find a new way of traveling that is initiated by stepping outside the *dimensional limitations* of their one-dimensional universe. What if they first left the piece of spaghetti at the secret side-doorway–an exit that is only available to them beyond the conceptual edge of the *spacetime* that they normally occupy. What if they then reentered their spaghetti universe at the exact place where their section of spaghetti loops back and touches itself? By cutting off this big loop they have instantly jumped directly to an entirely different location within their long spaghetti universe. The distance traveled will, of course, depend on the length of that particular loop.

The inhabitants of spaghetti-land have discovered a wonderful short-cut that is available by jumping through "spacetime" to a different spot where their curved "spaghetti universe" loops back and touches itself. By utilizing a single additional dimension (sideways), they become able to leave their limited space and instantly reenter it farther down the road. They avoid the entire distance that was between these two *enfolded* points of contact. By taking full advantage of extra dimensions and *enfolded spacetime*, they can now travel vast distances in an instant. They accomplished this by first freeing themselves from the constraints of their dimensional confines, which they probably never questioned before.

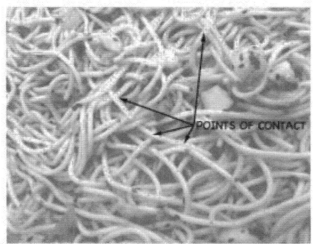

The universe can be imagined to be bent and curled like spaghetti. Imagine slipping sideways into an adjacent loop of the "universe" at some point of contact. Now instead of a trip lasting millions of miles around that long loop, we jump sideways to reach to a spot that would once have been very far away. We leave our universe at one point and reenter it again at another point much farther along. This trick or short-cut can greatly reduce long distance travel through space and time.

By shortcutting, they have, in a very real sense, also jumped in time, because worlds (pieces of oregano) that were once separated in time by billions of years (travel and light) can, with this new trick, be accessed instantly. The starlight that we see today left the distant stars billions of years ago. If a traveler took one of these dimensional shortcuts to instantly go to one of those distant stars and then flashed a *laser* signal back towards Earth, the signal's light would not reach Earth for billions of years. While it might appear that the traveler had traveled through time from the perspective of Earth's inhabitants, from the traveler's perspective, they only discovered a way to understand and interact with "time" differently. Someday traveling in time might only involve getting off the beaten path and planning our routes carefully! *Time loops* are one of today's hot topics in contemporary cosmology.

A slight modification to this model can also show us a way to visualize traveling to other *parallel universes*. Imagine this pasta cooked with an infinity of other colored pieces of pasta (*parallel universes*) in an *infinite*-sized pot until all the different pieces of pasta (universes) are fully tangled together. If we limit travel to within the confines of our own universe (single, long piece of spaghetti), we will never discover these *parallel universes*. However, if we leave our known confines by the same "side door," we cannot only jump in *time* and space within our own universe, but we are also able to jump to an entirely different universe with only the slightest movement. This type of "movement" might one day only require a clear, but fully *resonate,* thought.

WHAT THIS SPAGHETTI MODEL MEANS

The interconnection between parallel universes is absolute, constant and intimate and does not require extreme phenomena as dramatic as *black holes* and *wormholes*. *Black holes, wormholes* and the *high energy physics* that describes them may one day be understood for what they most likely are–the visible, surface artifacts experienced in our three-dimensional realm that describe the very natural relationships always found in multi-dimensional space. As always, we are only seeing the *projections* or shadows of the actual "thing." These *projections* can appear very strange to us, and they are often difficult or impossible to describe using three-dimensional words and ideas. While graphic or verbal descriptions might help with our understanding of these ideas, these descriptions have very little in common with the real extra-dimensional process that is casting shadows upon our *viewport*. *High energy wormholes,* once they are better understood, will probably not be seen as the easiest or most direct way to access *parallel universes*. Instead, we will evolve to better understand and be able to utilize our more direct, lower-energy, completely intuitive *vibratory* connection to these *parallel worlds and universes*. This more natural method will ultimately become the easiest way for us to move freely between *parallel universes*.

For this model, we reduced the "known" universe from our normal *enfolded*, three-dimensional space-plus-time to a one-dimensional, *enfolded* space-plus-time. In this demonstration, "stepping sideways" involves using only one extra dimension, and with just this single added dimension, we suddenly find ourselves suddenly able to travel vast distances and move through "time." This model can provide clues to show us how we, one day, will be able to travel great distances in space and time by stepping outside of the perceived *dimensional limitations* of our 3D *spacetime*. One day we will travel instantly, far and through time, by learning how to correctly utilize a single additional dimension.

This model is also like a very old river that meanders back and forth, almost touching itself. The day after a flood, a more direct path gets cut, and now the river is suddenly found to be much shorter. This and other shortcuts through time and space await our discovery.

SUMMARY

A stack of paper plates describes a 3D physical model that can help us imagine closely packed universes containing our best friends and favorite places. This model also provides us with a method of understanding how, within different universes, we might experience and relate to these "others" in different ways. We can also imagine how our individual conscious awareness can be thought of as a point or node on a long vibrating string or thread–our *beingness*. Several other visual models can help us visualize how separate individuals can also simultaneously be "all one." The ocean model, in particular, helps us to see the illusionary nature of our birth, death and individual existence.

What the spaghetti vignette allows us to visualize is how two places that appear far apart in our 3D universe might really be very close when *spacetime* is viewed differently. The vignette provides insights into the possibility of traveling vast distances without having to travel very fast or very far. This model can also be slightly expanded to demonstrate how *parallel universes* might exist right next door, but not seem easily accessible when we rely only on known senses or *dimensionally-restricted* methods of travel–those that are available within our existing *viewport*.

All these models were built from normal graphic tools that are limited to our three-dimensional space. This means that, while we can easily visualize them, they are not really accurate descriptions of real, multi-dimensional space. We are trying to describe an existence and experience that originates in realms that lie beyond our *conceptual horizon*. Because these realms are far more expansive and interconnected than our three-dimensional realm, we have to rely on these partial vignettes for small insights. Lacking the necessary conceptual or sensory tools, it is impossible for us to conceive of what a full-blown encounter with multiple dimensions would really be like. These models only serve to point us towards a direction where we might be able to see the beginnings of some of these possibilities, and hint how being open to these possibilities might completely change our world.

These models all demonstrate how we only directly experience a small patch of a much larger creation. We live our lives within a small slice of our universe, which is only a small part of the *Multiverse.* If we could relax our sensory and conceptual limitations, our perception would then naturally begin to expand. As we evolve, through this natural evolutionary expansion, we will one day be capable of encountering and understanding much more of our *Multiverse.* At some point, we will become able to perceive creation through an expanded conscious awareness that includes the one-*Self* that has always resided within the deeper levels of our *being.*

PART FIVE–EXPERIENCE

LIFE EXPERIENCES OUTSIDE OF THE "BOX"

INTRODUCTION

I have always been deeply impressed by personal experiences that did not conform, fit, or seem to make sense, within our prevailing paradigm. Eventually, I became familiar and comfortable enough with my own collection of "out-of-the-box" experiences that I began to be able to discuss these experiences with others; what I quickly discovered was that I was far from alone. Most others were also having these unusual encounters and a struggle about sharing them. Almost everyone with whom I shared also had similar experiences, but they often kept these to themselves because of concerns about how they might be perceived by others, especially in business and professional circles.

I was fortunate to have one of these events occur, in extremely dramatic fashion, at just the right age. I was old enough to really be able to think about and understand what had happened, but young and innocent enough not to be concerned about, or aware of, any need to conform to consensus viewpoints. Happening early in my adult life, this fortunate timing resulted in my increased and focused attention and sensitivity towards these special types of unusual events.

What follow are stories describing a few of my direct encounters that had the greatest influence on my life along with similar stories related by friends and family. Scores of other non-conforming events have occurred in my life, and when I stop and observe carefully, I notice these types of events are actually unfolding every day. I have now grown so comfortable with these "paradigm-busting" occurrences that they are now just a part of my life and seem very ordinary. This section includes some of my more-influential, first glimpses–those early impressionistic experiences that left permanent marks on my psyche.

At times in my life, I have sensed that the outer boundaries of our three-dimensional world have, for one reason or another, become a little softer, revealing slightly less-defined edges. Through these faint, often fuzzy perforations, I have been offered a series of small glimpses into a different reality or geometry. Through years of practice I have learned techniques and methods that facilitate more intentional, penetrations of this membrane that encloses, protects and contains our solid-feeling 3-D universe. Over my years, this membrane has become continuously looser, softer, and maybe even porous; and today, for me, it sometimes seems more like a sieve or net. The example of a restaurant worker's hairnet comes to mind, functioning to contain most of the hair quite well, but occasionally (often when least expected), stray pieces of hair poke through revealing clues of what really lies below!

We all have these momentary openings. Occasionally, in our lives, the edges of our boundary will soften spontaneously: sometimes the result of a particularly stressful or life-threatening event. At other times, our glimpses into the bigger and more interconnected existence occur during our most relaxed or open states. As we mature, we all start to accumulate experiences that begin to hint at, or reveal, the existence of this much-larger world. Some of these experiences signal a much different connection between the body and awareness than we usually expect and understand. Some glimpses help us realize that "time," with its relentless rate of marching and its single direction, might not be so absolute. Others point to a different type of intimate relationship with the world and other *beings*. In one way or another, all of these "out-of-the-box" stories illustrate the transparency and proximity of the veil that separates our 3D *viewport* from what lies on the other side.

I will use the term *mind* to describe a limited range of collective thinking or functioning. This word can describe both the individual conceptual-based *mind* and a deeper and more universal form of *Mind*, which I will distinguish with capitalization from now on. *Mind* (with the "capital M") refers to the comprehensive, collective and expanded form, where two or more individuals have entered that place where they join and function as part of a greater whole. If a culture responds collectively, but is still responding through habitual and fixed human concepts by engaging through fear or greed, this still describes the "small-m" type of *mind: collective mind*. This "small m" mindset can still arise from many minds together, if they are *resonating* through their collective fear and not functioning at the deeper, expansive or universal level. We can also refer to this "small m" collective *mind* as *groupthink*. The more expansive type of *Mind* operates beyond the realm of our conceptual brains. Our exposure to it might include events as simple and common as the intuitive "knowing that someone is about to call your phone." It might involve ESP or witnessing the mass changing of the consciousness through a "paradigm shift." It might even involve an ecstatic moment that connects us directly with the "Mind of God," or a connection that provides a deep, new understanding of Love.

These two concepts, *mind* and *Mind,* represent the bookends that contain the range of different ways that human beings can access and process available information. On one end we have the individual and unconnected brain, and on the other we discover a mysterious, deep-level, collective form of constant, intimate, cooperative interaction. The *Mind* is always in direct and intimate contact with information that exists outside or beyond the limits of our individual brains. It exists completely outside of the brain's neurons or processes. Between our brains and *Mind*, there is a continuum that includes every intermediate and mixed possibility, and we all operate somewhere within this range. As we open and learn to connect deeply, we become more interconnected with others and with deeper levels of information. With time and evolution we begin to spend more time operating at this much more interconnected and functional level. The feeling is sometimes described as tapping into a "collective consciousness." At some deep level in our exploration of *Mind*, we all reach a clear knowing that, at least in that moment, we are all One, sharing a sea of Love. This deep and profound experience of "One Love" changes the experiencer forever.

Our Western culture does not generally support the belief that we have this type of direct access to a more dimensionally expanded form of *Mind*. Some in our culture do not even recognize that this level of interconnection is possible, even though most people can recall at least a few of these expansive moments. This experience of interconnection often appears as some instant understanding or insight that can't easily be explained. We might notice an uncanny premonition about checking in on a friend, a sensation of déjà vu, a clear knowing of how the next scene will unfold, an absolute understanding about exactly what our teammates are about to do, a clear sense of being outside of our body, or an encounter that seems completely outside of normal "time."

Over the years I have learned to pay more attention to these feelings or "hits," as I call them. These insights can sometimes arrive as warnings from seemingly nowhere, or they may arrive as a deep-level, gut feeling–a sense, a mental image, mood or a thought. They may feel very general in their nature or they may arrive as something very specific like, "pay special attention to this particular red car that is approaching from the left." I observed that historically, when I paid close attention to these subtle warnings and followed through, as if this insight were a fact, I seldom figured out exactly what the warning was really about because my life just went on in a normal and smooth manner. However, when out of laziness or disbelief, I chose to ignore these feelings or instincts then, typically, something quickly "hit the fan" or I found myself in a difficult or dangerous situation.

Over time, I have learned how to trust these intuitive feelings or "hits." I also noticed that when I was younger, the warnings often came in groups of three and the really big trouble only came if the first two warnings were ignored. Today, I have no idea if I still get these three chances because, these days, I usually recognize and respond to the first warning. There are exceptions to this pattern of threes. One of the stories below is about a time when I was in my twenties and I ignored a single, but very clear, warning and suffered dire consequences. Another story is about one of the few times, as an adult, that I foolishly ignored several of these "hits" because they seemed completely illogical.

I've used words like understanding, premonition, hits and feelings, to describe this type of awareness because, for me, it usually is a very subtle feeling that does not arrive packaged with clear directions or a bright bow. Over the years and through personal experience, these initially vague feelings or sensations have become something recognizable that I have learned to trust with increasing clarity. I have also come to understand that there are other, still deeper levels of *Mind* that we also can tap into once we begin to learn how to open, relax and practice.

Most of this learning involves discovering how to drop our *resistance* to the natural flow of life; meaning we become fully available for whatever possibility might be presenting itself. This is an especially difficult change for the Western-trained mind because true availability includes any possibility, and in our culture we have always been taught to be in control of outcomes. ***It seems counterintuitive, but our lives are more "in control" when we are able to entirely let go of our habitual need to control the outcomes. Instead, we become more available to fully experience whatever is unfolding right before us in any given moment.***

EXPLORING THE EDGE OF BEING AND TIME

TIME SLOWS IN AN AUTO ACCIDENT

This particular story is placed first because it was the crucial life event that marked the real beginning of my conscious and deeper exploration of the edges of our awareness. It was not the first time something like this had happened to me, but it was the first time I felt the strong need to reevaluate my inherited worldview.

I was seventeen and driving my parents' car to a friend's house, which was about 20 miles away, when I had this experience that completely changed the way I understand and relate to "time." My family lived in rural area, one where the long stretches of empty, two-lane highway invited young male drivers to push the limits of speed. I was, as I often was in those "bulletproof" days, traveling over 100 MPH with an empty road ahead. On a very straight section of the highway, with a full clear view, another car inexplicably pulled out right in front of me from a driveway on my left. Rather than slow or brake, I just reacted, as many testosterone-fueled teenage boys would, by swerving into the empty clear oncoming lane. I then quickly realized that this car was immediately making a slow and lazy left hand turn, directly in front of my new position. An older couple, apparently used to empty roads, had pulled out of one driveway, into the far lane, and were directly returning into the very next drive, completely unaware of my car. They never saw me, possibly because a car traveling over 100 MPH was likely to be outside of their *viewport*! Quickly out of "time," and with no place left on the road to avoid this other car, I swerved off the road into a very bumpy orchard filed with closely spaced large trees. ***At over 100 MPH all of this happened very fast, but in that "moment," I found that suddenly I had all the time in the world.*** My sense of movement and "time" was instantly altered to a slow-motion slideshow revealing one frame at a time. Each framed view was held as long as I needed, and then it automatically shifted to the next frozen scene. Each scene was a perfectly arranged view of exactly what I needed to see for the next maneuver. Each frame allowed me more than enough "time" to consciously look around to see all the trees and spaces. I was aware of every direction, every corner of the car and every tree. From my perspective, *time* actually stopped. I had all the *time* I needed to decide which direction I should steer and how to go about each maneuver. I slowly executed the movements required to negotiate each single still frame before looking again, and repeating the process with the next frame. It was as if I had a remote control. My "slideshow" was clicking ahead six inches at a time, pausing just long enough for me to think, react and then assess the next six inches of necessary movement. I cleared many trees by inches and a few hundred, very bumpy yards later brought the car to a halt in a storm cloud of dust. Once fully stopped, I finally focused on my overall situation, and for the first time, I noticed that my heart was racing like never before. After a long "catch my breath" pause, I assessed that not only was I alive, but I had not even visibly damaged my parents' car, although I am quite sure that the suspension on their car was never the same.

At that moment a sudden awareness overwhelmed my *being* with the thought–*"What in the world just happened?"* I turned around and there I was, sitting in the middle of that field, a thicket of big trees behind me, and a clear set of crooked tire ruts marking the maneuvers that I had just completed at 100 MPH. *"This really happened!"* In that moment my life was forever changed. I had encountered something that my training and upbringing could not explain and I was suddenly thrust into completely new perceptual territory!

Recently I was talking about "time" perception with my sister and she recounted a similar story. She was involved in a multi-car accident on the freeway and for her, "time" also slowed to almost a stop. She had "time" to observe the rapidly changing situation and knew exactly when and how to duck to avoid flying objects and glass.

Many athletes have similar stories of "time" slowing, and being "in the zone" while playing their sport. Motocross racers will talk about all the "time" they had to make conscious decisions while flying through the air, mid-accident. In my musical career I have had similar experiences. When playing a fast and complex musical phrase, I occasionally have all the "time" necessary for feeling, phrasing and executing the quickly passing phrase.

Similar, related, "time-" altering experiences will occur in many situations throughout all of our lives. Our personal sense about the passing of "time" seems to be malleable and not as fixed or rigid as our timepieces, schedules and entire culture would have us believe. *Mind* and "time" are interrelated in a way that causes our perception of "time's" passage to occasionally become dramatically altered.

OUT-OF-BODY EXPERIENCES

We normally assume that our individual awareness is always tightly connected with our physical body, but this does not have to be the case. In special circumstances, our center of awareness can move away from our physical body–sometimes far away. It is possible that we might suddenly witness our awareness focused above our body, behind it, off in the next room, or moving about freely somewhere far away and unrecognizable to us. Many of us can remember having this type of experience at least once in our lives.

Quite spontaneously, and in a very dramatic form, this happened to me. I know of many others who also have, for one reason or another, found that their conscious awareness temporarily shifted to suddenly appear somewhere other than within their own body. According to both doctors and patients, this has been a repeatedly observed phenomenon, especially when great amounts of stress or traumatic injuries are involved. Patients involved in accidents or emergency surgery have sometimes discovered that their conscious presence was aware, watching, hearing and understanding the EMS workers or doctors who were working on their unconscious bodies. They might have found that they were suddenly watching from the tree above their wrecked car, the corner of the operating room, or from some other remote place as others attend to their damaged bodies. In this remote, but conscious, presence they sometimes had life-changing spiritual experiences, including instantaneous reviews of their entire lives. They often made what seemed to be thoroughly analyzed and conscious decision to return to their original, but then very compromised, bodies.

This type of occurrence is so common it has been given the name *near death experience* or *NDE,* and scores of books examine this interesting phenomenon in detail. Of course, these types of memories can only be told by those who have had this traumatic separation from their bodies, but later were able to return to their bodies and continue with their lives; we hear nothing from those who made the other decision not to return. These, and similar types of stories have been collected, documented, recorded and related by many doctors, researchers and psychologists and others.

When my brother was a teenager, he often found himself observing his own back while walking down a road. Another friend, as preteen, repeatedly floated outside her house and was able to watch herself through a window, inside, lying on her bed. My wife, Merlyn, once hovered above herself watching her own conversation, and I once sat firmly on a mountaintop that was more than 20 miles from my body. While the center of our awareness is usually from within our own bodies, it also seems that, in special conditions, it can also appear to roam free of this physical boundary.

It has become clear to me that our body and our conscious awareness are two different things; they are very interrelated and interconnected, but still separate. ***We are not our bodies. This is one of the most important realizations on the road to true freedom. This one clear realization can serve to liberate us in many wonderful and different ways.***

MY WHITEFACE MOUNTAIN JOURNEY

My first experience of my awareness leaving my physical body was quite dramatic and emotionally disruptive; and it left me feeling quite unsettled, and even scared. In my late twenties, I was newly married and living in Lake Placid, New York for the summer. While generally enjoying the circumstances of my own personal life, I carried an anger and distress about the condition of the world; poverty, wars, human injustices and our inherent cultural shortsightedness all were extremely disturbing. By this time I had been meditating daily for almost 10 years, and it was rather easy for me to leave my thoughts and the day-to-day world behind while practicing. Our apartment featured a picture window that directly faced the beautiful snowcapped peak of Whiteface Mountain, which sat majestically, just 20 miles away. Every morning I would meditate for half of an hour, using this mountaintop as a visual *mantra* to help focus my attention and clear my mind.

On this one particular day, instead of dropping into my usual meditative state, I felt a sudden powerful bodily "whooshing" sensation and then quickly found myself moving rapidly through a tunnel-like space, as if flying. In the next instant I was seeing and experiencing the world from the very top of that mountain, looking directly back to the town of Lake Placid where my actual body had been sitting. I had no awareness of a physical body or any sense of being cold, but my conscious presence and visual sense were centered right there on that mountaintop and not back with my body in Lake Placid. Quickly, I had the clear and strong "knowing" that I had an important and critical choice to make. I could continue on this journey through this new space or return, instead, to my body. I also clearly knew, instantly, that while this state of being was very exciting and the space was tempting to explore, if I did continue any further, I would probably lose the will, or ability, to return to my new wife and the physical life that I had been living. I panicked, lost my relaxation, and my consciousness was instantly pulled through a similar but more abrupt tunnel, right back into my old body. I then found myself, once again, sitting in my living room, but now shaking and completely covered with sweat.

After that event, I stopped my deep-meditation practice for a number of years, afraid that I might have a similar experience and not have the ability, or more accurately, the desire, to return. Looking back, it is now clear that, at that period in my life, I was fundamentally unhappy because of my perception about the problematic nature of our human existence. I was aware that my connection to my body and this life was not always joyful and some part of me desired to escape this life. I also simultaneously sensed that it was not my time to make this transition because I had much more to do and learn while in this body. I have never regretted my decision to return, even though I have no way of knowing how the other path might have played out. The path I chose produced two beautiful children, an exciting career, many adventures, a great number of dear friends, a sense of humor about the human condition, and a strong appreciation for all of life and its amazing mystery.

HEARING THE VOICE OF "GOD"

One of the most unexpected encounters of my life occurred on the deck of a sailboat in the middle of the Pacific Ocean. I was visiting a friend's sailboat on a beautiful, full moon evening, while living and working with the Peace Corps in the Fiji Islands. Lying on the deck to better watch the stars and night sky, I noticed that the spinning anemometer (wind meter) at the top of the mast was nearly the same size, and shape as the round, full moon, which was also right overhead. My fascination with shapes and form took hold, and only a small shift in my position was needed to place the spinning anemometer directly in front of the full moon. It was a perfect fit—the anemometer covered the entire moon and created a powerful flickering strobe effect. Instantly I became disoriented; it felt like I was being pulled up through a tunnel of spinning light while my entire body seemed to be twisting and undulating. When I "landed" after a few long moments, the spinning stopped and I heard a deep booming voice that I instantly understood (probably from movies) to be "the voice of God." This voice was as real, deep, resonant and vocal as any physical voice that I have ever heard, but I later learned that no one else on board the boat heard anything; the voice commanded my full attention as I lost all sense of my body and everything else that was around me. This deep booming voice sounded very friendly and was laughing tenderly, as it carefully and clearly spoke the words *"Tim.... You always worry about everything. Just remember that there are many different ways of looking at anything. Everything has positive and negative aspects or interpretations. Find the positive in every situation, focus on these positive aspects and your entire life will change."* Suddenly it was over; the voice was gone, and I was, once again, lying there on the deck with the clear night sky, moon and stars.

I have no explanation for what happened that moonlit night, except that the spinning wheel centered in the moon somehow facilitated a change in mental states, not unlike classical hypnosis. The incident made such a deep impression that I paid unfaltering attention to this message and began the process of completely changing the way that I viewed and approached life. It took me many years and many additional reinforcing insights to fully understand the message and its meaning, but today this awareness forms the root foundation of my life philosophy. ***That message was distilled, directed and worded so that I could hear it with my mindset that night. It was essentially relaying one of the most fundamental principles of this book: "If we change our*** *attitude, we will change our entire world. The world that we perceive is only our own reflection!"*

HEARING VOICES IN THE ROMAN FORUM

One year after my encounter with that voice on the sailboat, I was visiting Rome for the first time. I was not an architect in those days or even thinking about a career in architecture, yet this one morning I found myself powerfully drawn to the ancient ruins of the Roman Forum. It was still before sunrise but, due to jet lag, I had already been awake for a couple of hours and, just as the new day broke, I found myself completely alone in the Roman Forum. The light and peaceful feeling that morning were exquisite, and I found myself wandering around the forum in a joyful trance. I started to hear faint murmurs and assumed merchants or others had arrived to hawk their wares, but when I searched to find the source of the voices, there was no one to be found. These voices became louder and I began to notice that they had the power, rhythm and cadence of public orators, but I was unable to understand the words. I began to feel the hairs on my arms rise and tingle as I realized that what I was hearing sounded like ancient Roman oratory of the type that had once been the normal, daily custom in this very place. This multilayered oratory went on for 20 minutes or so, and involved dozens of different voices from different building locations within the ruins. Gradually as other people entered the area and the Forum began to become active with the bustle of daily life, these mysterious voices disappeared. To this day, whenever I think about that early morning many years ago, I always feel that same powerful tingling sensation up and down my arms and legs.

MEET A NEW CLIENT AT THE POOL

One day about twenty years ago I was at my usual neighborhood pool and engaged in a conversation about building with a friend, who happened to be a contractor. A stranger walked up and asked, *"I couldn't help overhearing your conversation. Is either one of you an architect? I need one very badly."*

I found out, later, that her journey that day had been every mother's nightmare involving a car full of screaming children, traffic, broken plans and repeated disappointments, as they drove from beach to beach, looking for a place to swim. All her usual and alternate swimming pools or beaches had been closed for repairs or other reasons. With a car full of screaming kids and the temperature at well over one hundred degrees, she was completely at her limit. After several dead-end attempts to go to other pools, she eventually stumbled upon this unfamiliar pool, but only because she had again been rerouted by road construction. She told me later that she immediately sensed that this was this pool where she was to be that day, but did not know why.

This chance meeting led directly to several of my more interesting architectural jobs, a significant change in my life direction, and one of the most significant friendships of my life. This event altered the trajectory of my life in ways that I could never have imagined in those first moments of meeting. It has taken me many years to appreciate the way life seems to have a rhythm for bringing to us the exact experiences we require. These interconnections often seem to lie far outside any possible logic or planning that our brains might rationally construct.

OTHER VERY UNEXPECTED MEETINGS

Returning from a three-month stay in Greece in the mid-1980s, I found that I had a short layover in London, so I thought I might try to look up a dear friend. I did not have his address or phone number, but I knew that he was studying at the London School of Economics. I got off at the "tube" (subway) stop that was closest to that school, understanding that finding him without any address, at night in this crowded city would be a long shot, at best; I hoped that the school would have a public directory that would help me find him. Not having a direct way to contact him and concerned that it was quickly becoming too late to search for a directory, I started running as I exited the subway door. Moving far too fast for the crowded conditions, I rounded a blind corner into a dense crowd and immediately collided with someone coming from the opposite direction. The collision was so violent that we both tumbled to the pavement, bags and bodies fully intertwined; not before or since have I accidentally bumped into someone hard enough to cause such a fall. During the process of untangling our backpacks and briefcases, our faces met; there I was, fully entangled with the very friend that I was in London to visit. Together we shared a long, deep and joyful gut laugh that christened another wonderful evening together.

Another time, years earlier, I was on an extended adventure hitchhiking around Canada and the United States. At various backpacker gathering points, such as state park campgrounds and hostels, I was repeatedly crossing paths with a particular person; we became friends, as these unplanned meetings were frequent and continued to happen. One day we stepped out of the spontaneous character of our relationship by planning to meet in Yosemite on a particular day several weeks in the future, but that meeting didn't happen as planned, so I continued on with my journey. Two months later I was camping on a long beach that runs down the west coast of Vancouver Island in Canada. Desiring salmon for dinner, I hitched the 20 miles to the tiny fishing village of Tofino, only to discover, to my disappointment, that there was just a single fishing-boat in port at that time of day. As I walked on board I heard voices from below, so I shouted down into the hold. Up came my friend with an enormous salmon in her arms. She saw me and the only thing she said was *"Looks like we are having salmon for dinner."* As it turned out she was camping within 100 yards of my camp along an open and endless beach that stretched for miles and miles. She was also a professional gourmet cook; that night I enjoyed the best-tasting fire-grilled salmon that I can remember.

Over the years I had many other chance meetings that seemed to defy normal probability, but these were a few of the most life-changing. We are always connected in many ways that are invisible to us, and all of these connections can and do directly affect our lives. These improbable occurrences continue in my life, but they are now viewed as quite normal, and often, even expected.

As I was proofing this very section of the book a very interesting event unfolded. In June 2012, my wife and I had a life-threatening misadventure on a small boat in the waters of the Fiji Islands. Four other people were also on that boat, and fortunately we all survived. Now, one year later, my wife and I were visiting San Francisco. As we were riding the ferry from Sausalito to the city on a very windy day, we saw a boat almost capsize; we then began to recount our adventure from the previous year; for some unknown reason this was the very first time that we had even discussed that very dramatic event. Five minutes later we docked and walked directly to the cable car stop. Immediately a voice behind us shouted, "Hey remember me?" We turned to discover one of the other four who were on that boat in Fiji the previous year; he lived in Prague and was in San Francisco for only that one day. The timing of our singular discussion and that chance meeting seemed to completely defy normal probability.

WARNING IN THE NIGHT

Earlier in that same, extended, west-coast travel adventure that took me to Vancouver Island, I was camping with a travel buddy on a beach directly south of Big Sur, California. It was very dark when we set camp, and being unfamiliar with local conditions, we inadvertently set up too close to the base of the large cliffs that define the seashore of that region. At some time in the middle of the night I awoke, heart racing, full of terror, and quickly woke my friend to insist we had to move. I had to admit to him that I didn't know why–I just knew we had to move. Deep in his sleep mode, he didn't want to be bothered, but because of my persistence we pulled our sleeping bags out towards the middle of the beach where I felt much more comfortable. Before we even climbed back into our bags there was an enormous rumble and several large boulders fell right into the area where we had been sleeping; we didn't even recognize the full importance of our decision to move until the morning light. In hindsight, some part of me obviously recognized that our original sleeping spot was poorly chosen; but just what was it that woke me from the deep sleep, and how did all that unfold with just the right timing? Some protective part of my *being* must have been connected to *information* that was not a part of my normal waking consciousness.

FLOOD OF NEW MEMORIES

About 14 years ago I was visiting a friend who happened to be a very talented massage therapist. She was widely recognized for having a very strong intuitive talent, a talent that I had witnessed many times while watching her help other friends through difficult emotional issues. We were just chatting over tea as we often did, but at some point in our conversation she stopped and said, *"Tim, this may seem weird, but I have a strong sense about this. Would you please go over to that corner and get down on your hands and knees with your head tucked into the corner where the walls and floor meet."* Perplexed, but trusting her and her unique way of experiencing the world, I carefully followed these directions. She moved up behind me put one hand on my hip and another on my shoulder and pushed forcibly, pinning me into the corner. Suddenly, a completely unexpected and torrential flood of fearful emotional memories surged through my *being*; I could not believe what was happening. It was as if a spillway to some dammed up part of me, a part that I was completely unaware of, had suddenly burst wide open. I recognized these surprising, but painful, physical and emotional memories as my own, but it was as if I was feeling them for the first time.

That event was the dramatic beginning to a long process of recovery, as I gradually opened to these hidden memories. Over time, they have slowly become more visual, verbal and identifiable; a great amount of tension that I had been habitually holding was finally being addressed and released. It is now clear that I was a victim of childhood abuse at the hands of a neighbor, one whom I had deeply trusted. Looking back through my life, there were many obvious clues and hints that I, and even my parents, had completely missed. These included the complete loss of any memory about the multiple boating trips with this person along with a nearly total loss of my memory about anything else that happened during that period of my life, between the ages of nine and twelve.

Other than the enormous relief gained from the surfacing of this buried memory, I also learned, at a deep and personal level, just how effective our conscious brains are at controlling the perception and memory of events. We remember and retain only what we are capable of processing, conceptually, physically, intellectually and emotionally. If something is outside of our limits, we automatically engage what psychologists call *cognitive dissonance,* and the event can become repressed and filed in our body's equivalent of a "dead letter drawer." This is one way our bodies and egos can quell the dissonance within.

This event points to how our minds and senses filter or miss *information* that is still solidly within our 3D paradigm. This experience demonstrates how the *information* is still stored within our bodies, even if we seem to have no direct access to our actual memories. My story also illustrates one more example of a person using a type of talent that cannot be technically explained by our Western science. Skills and insights that can't be explained rationally are typically undervalued by our Western culture because we do not have clear cultural examples, or archetypes, for processing most experiences that fall outside of our consensual norm.

FIRE-WALKING

In the mid-1990s a friend invited me to a fire-walking workshop that she was attending. Not having ever participated in fire-walking before, I was extremely curious and agreed to go. In the 1970s while I was living in the Fiji Islands as a Peace Corps volunteer, I had repeatedly witnessed traditional Fijian fire-walking, during formal rituals. I knew that the Fijians have very tough, calloused feet, and I always assumed that those calluses played a major role in their ability to walk on red-hot rocks.

Ten first-time participants signed up for this fire-walking workshop but we all were tenderfoots, unlike the Fijians. We spent the entire day in psychological preparation, going through visualization exercises and meditations. The preparation was focused on assuring us that *"we could do this"* and the critical importance of not having any self-doubt. We were coached that if we had any second thoughts at the threshold, it was not only acceptable, but it was absolutely expected that we would "opt out" and not walk. There was no peer pressure to walk, as we were all well coached to understand that walking with doubts would lead to burns and this could be catastrophic for the entire group. As it turned out, several people in the group chose to not walk at the last second.

In preparation for the walk that night, an enormous pile of wood was reduced to a field of golf-ball-sized, red-hot coals that were then raked into the 30-foot long, four-foot wide bed. We were to walk, not run, the full 30-foot length, barefoot. As we stood near the threshold and felt the intense heat, every one of us had immediate second thoughts. The radiant heat from the coals was unbelievably hot, even when we were standing back several feet. The workshop leader walked first with no visible ill effects, and that inspired my friend to walk next, also without problems. Encouraged, I walked to the edge, cleared my head of all thought, as rehearsed, and started walking. Time and sound stopped and I felt a dramatic calmness and still quietness as I walked the 10 or so steady steps required to complete the journey. I arrived at the other side completely unharmed and ecstatic. I had not even experienced the peripheral heat of the red-hot coals on the rest of my body. Several others walked, several chose not to, and somewhere in the process I realized that I wanted a picture of myself walking, so I decided to walk again. This time, three-quarters of the way across the hot coals, an "outside" thought entered my mind; I suddenly realized that the photo had not yet been snapped. As I looked for the friend with the camera, I lost my intense focus; in that instant, my feet were suddenly and sharply "stung" as I felt the intense burn of the hot coals along both feet! Stimulated by the pain, I immediately was able to regain my original focus and concentration. The pain disappeared as I completed the walk. After the walk, I quickly checked and found that I had a few small blistered burns on the outer edges of my feet, but nothing that was proportional to the burning sensation that I felt in that instant, or what should have happened in the "normal" world. A couple of other walkers also experienced small burns and they also confessed to lapses of concentration during their walks. For me, this entire process was a powerful demonstration of the power of focus and belief. I could not have planned this experiment in a better way.

AT ONE WITH THE WIND

I was a fanatic windsurfer in the 1980s, but the lake where I windsurfed was a 45- minute drive from my house. Because I preferred high-speed sailing, I would only take the time off my work for sailing when the wind was blowing over 20 knots. This meant that the wind was always blowing fiercely whenever I drove out to the lake. My old Volkswagen camper van had a worn steering gear and, because in those days my extra cash always went into new sailing equipment, the loose gear problem continued without repair. The flat-sided van would invariably get pushed and buffeted by the wind, forcing me to weave all over the road; it was almost impossible to keep that van on the road during the trip out to the lake. Fortunately, in those days, that particular road had little traffic, but the drive out was always a very tense and stressful struggle.

Once I was sailing on the windy lake, there was always a point where something would change deep within. I would merge with the waves and wind, as I became an integrated part of those elements, free of thought, and perfectly fluid in motion. This extraordinary ecstatic experience of oneness with the wind and water was the main reason why I loved to sail.

The return ride home in the van would always be a different type of journey from the morning ride up. Even though the winds were still buffeting my flat-sided van, I could always easily steer right down the middle of the road without any thought or struggle. Some unconscious part of myself had learned to predict and read the wind in a way that was hidden from my normal conscious brain. I was able to anticipate and adjust for the blasts of wind in intuitive and instinctual ways that made no sense to my time-ordered, rational mind. During those special times, I was fully aware of the movement and flow of the natural world through a type of connection that was normally quite invisible and unavailable.

SHARING AILMENTS WITH A LOVED ONE

My wife and I have always been extremely similar, but after about five years of living together, we began to notice a strange phenomenon. At first, we began to notice that we had the same aches, pains and ailments–there was some type of intimate interconnection forming between our two bodies. One of us would mention a physical issue only to find the other was experiencing the exact same symptom. At first this would come up only occasionally, but within a few years it was occurring with such regularity that we would simply say *"how's your left shoulder"* and receive back an understanding nod. By then, this pattern had become our expected norm.

With the more general conditions, like muscular aches, the physical location of the ailment or pain is typically mirrored; this means that the left side on one of us corresponds to the right side on the other. If the ailment is specific to a body part that is not bilaterally symmetrical, such as the gall bladder, heart or descending colon, then the actual parts and sides correspond.

This experience has been overwhelmingly helpful because it allows each of us to be unusually aware of the other person, and it also means that it is extremely easy and interactive to do massage work on each other. In addition, we have noticed that when one of us clears an issue, the other also notices the change. At times working on each other feels like self-massage. Again, I am struck by another example of the invisible connections that extend beyond these bodies–types of interactions for which our culture and science have no clear explanation.

WARNING VOICE

In the late 1970s, I was a school teacher on the remote and rugged island in Fiji called Kandavu. My students had a soccer match at a distant village and, since there were no roads or cars on this island, we had to travel by boat. The event involved a long, expensive trip, but the school supported our journey because this match was considered very important. As the guest of honor I represented my school, the Peace Corps, Americans, and all foreign visitors to Fiji. Since there were many people in this remote village who had never seen a fair-skinned visitor, I was especially careful to follow all of my well-rehearsed protocols (first impressions).

During the match, I observed lemonade being made directly from river water, and the very first glass was offered to me since I was the guest of honor; all village eyes were focused upon me and they were all waiting for my approval. Immediately, I received a clear intuitive message, a very powerful feeling or "knowing," that I was not to drink that lemonade; I had the clear and absolute awareness that if I did drink the lemonade, the physical results would be significant. Throughout my time in Fiji, I had consumed hundreds of drinks prepared from questionable water, but only this one time was I warned in this way. Very aware of the local customs and being the guest of honor, I knew that to refuse the drink would signal a great insult and create problems for my school principal, so I chose to ignore my internal warning and quickly gulped the lemonade. Ten days later I fell into the early stages of the deepest, longest and most painful sickness of my life; I had come down with typhoid fever.

Whatever that "knowing" was and where it came from can't be explained or described from within our traditional paradigm. I have since learned to respect and trust this deep kind of intuitive knowing and, since that fateful day, I have carefully listened to and heeded that same voice many other times.

FIJIAN MAGIC FEET

It was common, when I lived on the island of Kandavu, to make nighttime treks to the neighboring villages for social events. On this remote island there were no roads or automobiles, so boats and hiking were the only options. These hikes usually involved walking for a couple of hours up and down the rocky terrain of volcanic mountains, through rivers and marshes, over beaches and mud-flats, and through almost every other type of possible terrain. Initially, because of my tender feet, I attempted to make these trips in shoes or sandals, but I was constantly losing my footgear in the mud, tearing my sandals up on the rocks, and dealing with sand or pebbles in my shoes. My personal shoe problems became the focus of constant, but good-natured teasing because I was slowing down the entire group. Eventually, I decided to walk without my footgear, and after several painful months I realized that it had actually become very easy to traverse the complicated landscape barefoot, even on the darkest of the new moon nights. I started noticing that I no longer stubbed my toes on the rocks or lost my footing by stepping on an unstable boulder; my feet naturally found their own way and I had the instinct and ability to instantly adjust my weight when my foot landed on sharp objects. My toes had also spread wider and each one could be more easily controlled independently, much like my fingers.

On one particular dark night I started "thinking" about how amazing my feet's new sensitivity was and immediately stubbed my toe. In that moment, I understood. My feet had developed a radar-like instinctual sense of their own; they "saw" the terrain and "knew" just what they had to do, without checking in with my brain. As long as my conscious brain didn't get in their way and micromanage, my feet did a great job on their own.

148

African drummers' hand speeds have been measured to have a much faster response time than our nervous system theoretically allows; what they are able to do is not supposed to be physically possible. Our bodies have an amazing depth of intelligence of their own that is not yet widely understood. As I will discuss later, the vast majority of our brain's processing occurs in the subconscious, so what we are capable of understanding with our conscious brains is just the tip of the iceberg. I really do miss my sensitive "Fijian Feet" because not since that time in my life have I felt that comfortable and connected to our Earth.

THINGS DISAPPEARING THEN LATER REAPPEARING

There have been several periods in my life during which I have observed the mysterious disappearance of small but important objects, only to have them then reappear, days later, exactly in the same spot where I "lost" them. I remember clearly the first time that I had a conscious awareness of this phenomenon. Just like every other day, I set my wallet on the top of my desk as I walked into my office that morning. At the end of the day when I went to retrieve it, the wallet was not to be found. Two days of frantic searching ensued before I finally reached the point of accepting that it was inexplicably lost. By this point, in the search, I had "let go" of my wallet both emotionally and psychologically. When I arrived at my office the very next morning, I found the wallet sitting on my desk, precisely where I had left it three days earlier. At that time, I shared my office suite with another architect, but he was very serious about his practice and was not prone to playing games and tricks that might waste our valuable time. He even spent much of his own time searching with me, and there were no office visitors during that period. At the time I just assumed that there must have been some unknown but "normal" way for this to occur, even though I could not think of one.

Then, this type of event started to repeat itself; the first few times this happened I completely ripped my office apart looking for my lost wallet or keys. This strange pattern began to occur frequently, both at home and in my office, with keys, wallet and money. I eventually began to just shrug and laugh when it happened, knowing that my prized possession would soon be returned. Over time, I noticed that my things came back to their spot only after I relaxed my attitude to the point of not even caring or expecting them to return.

I jokingly named this repeating experience *"my poltergeist"* and ceased to worry about it as I recognized that this pattern had many lessons about the value and impermanence of things. That "first wave" of these "disappearances" lasted about six months. Ten years later I experienced another series of "disappearances," and five years after that there was also another brief recurrences. I quickly adjusted to these events and even began to "enjoy" them, as I began to think of them as reminders or "continuing education."

SHIFTING IN THE WEB

It requires careful and subtle observation to even notice when we shift our position within the Web. To even become aware of our shifts, we either must become extremely sensitive or the shifts must be so dramatic that we are forced to notice that the "outside" world has suddenly and inexplicably changed. We discussed how this happens to all of us, constantly, and how we usually don't even notice these changes. However, sometimes the change can be dramatic enough, or we might be unusually observant, and then it becomes very clear that something out of the "normal" has just occurred.

One example of such a shift in my own life occurred one night more than 30 years ago. While this event was fairly subtle and only one of many similar shifts that I have been aware of, this particular night was especially memorable; it was the very first time that I paused, registered, and reconsidered the potential meaning of this subtle and common, everyday experience. For some reason, possibly because of my mode of thinking that night, this particular shift, even though very subtle, made a very large impression on me. It was the first time in my adult life that I consciously became aware that the "world" that I was living within had actually changed.

The event unfolded in the early 1980s at an "old Austin" music venue called Liberty Lunch. I went to a music show there only to quickly realize that I was not enjoying the show or crowd. Many people in the audience appeared to be loud and rude while the music seemed to lack the compelling vibrancy of good live music; I was feeling very disappointed, so I decided to leave. As I was walking out, I found myself focusing more of my attention on the bass, probably because it was sonically more dominant in the part of the venue through which I was then passing while weaving my way to the front gate. Feeling fresh life in the song, I stopped and began to listen more deeply; I started to enjoy the music enough to stay for another song. One song led to another and I soon found myself thinking that this was one of the best shows and one of the most engaged crowds that I had ever experienced! From my perspective, and possibly mine alone, the quality of the show and crowd completely changed.

Later, I thought about what had really changed. It was the same band, same crowd, and same mix; and yet for me everything about the show was suddenly different. Did the band, sound system and a thousand other people change, or was it simply me, or my perspective, that changed? "Occam's Razor" is the name for the analytical practice that involves looking first to the simplest solution for any problem, because the simple solution is usually the most probable. What impressed me and caused me to spend quite a bit of time focusing on this experience was just how dramatically different but equally real were my two experiences that evening. It was more than just my mood changing; there was something else substantial or tangible about the quality of the new experience.

Even though the entire situation was a very ordinary event, this was the first time I consciously stopped and said to myself *"I am now living in a different world!."* Normally, I would have assumed that this event involved nothing more than a mood change on my part. There is no doubt that it was a mood change that triggered my "world" to change, but I also was aware that something deeper and more concrete had just occurred.

This event occurred about five years after that voice on the boat coached me about my attitude; after that night I began a renewed exploration of the direct relationship between changes in my attitude and changes in the appearance of the world around me. I watched carefully for this type of shifting in my life, and I even began to actively create experiments to explore this relationship.

GREEN SUIT

Even though I have long learned to recognize and trust my "inner voice," sometimes I am still impatient, or I might judge the voice to be silly, or even outright crazy. On the rare occasions when I ignore this inner voice, I always receive a quick lesson about trust. This was to be the case on a particular day a few years ago, when I pulled up to my parking place at the large, public pool where I swim my daily laps. As I reached for my usual bright green swimsuit in the back seat, my inner voice clearly said *"NO! Not the green one."* This seemed completely crazy to my rational mind. *"What could possibly be wrong with the comfortable swimsuit that I wear every day?"* I had another suit in my trunk, but I was late, and I did not like the way the other suit fit, so I just grabbed my comfortable green one. The same inner voice repeated itself! Again I resisted and judged the voice as *"ridiculous"* as I grabbed my green suit even though, strangely, it continued to feel wrong.

When I changed in the locker room, my favorite swimsuit felt extremely uncomfortable, but being under a time constraint, I continued to fight this very persistent urge to change bathing suits. Still feeling quite unsettled, I went into the very crowded pool area and swam my laps.

Upon my return to the locker room, a lifeguard that I knew well pulled me aside to tell me there had been a complaint filed against me; I had been accused of a very serious crime. The victim, a young child, had identified me from far away on the other end of the large crowded public pool by pointing and saying *"that man in the green swimsuit!"* My bright green swimsuit was the only thing that connected me to the crime–the perpetrator apparently wore a similar suit.

Fortunately, because I was a regular at that pool, all the staff knew my family, my habits, and me and a large number of witnesses and friends could collaborate that I didn't leave the lap area of the pool, I was cleared without any further issues. This process certainly consumed much more of my time than it would have taken to simply change suits when I heard the warning.

The entire incident was very educational and thought provoking for a number of reasons. I was impressed with the strength of the strange warning about something that initially seemed so minor. I was also impressed by the strange turn of events that unfolded from the simple choice of an article of clothing; we never can be sure how things might unfold or how the most unexpected turns and twists can play critical roles. I also had the opportunity to experience an aspect of life from a new and unexpected perspective–that of an innocent and wrongly accused perpetrator. This was a perspective that, before that day, I had never consciously experienced.

This incident again reminded me of the expanded awareness of that "inner voice," even though its message might seem illogical from our rational perspective. This voice originates from someplace beyond the boundaries of our rational minds and can speak through things that are completely unseen.

FEELING MY FATHER'S PAIN

When my father passed, I was sitting in my living room two thousand miles away. He had been ill for some time and I had just returned, that very evening, from a long and fulfilling visit with him. The actual trip was initiated by a very clear "knowing" that it was the right time for the final visit. His dying that very evening was unexpected because, when I left him earlier that day, he seemed renewed and it appeared that he would still be with us for some time.

In my sleep that first night back home, I woke in the early morning hours with a strong painful burning sensation in my leg. The excruciating pain was not coming from a place, in my body, that had been troubling me, but I realized that it was located in the exact spot where my dad had been experiencing a great deal of his pain. I understood that connection instantly and with that realization, I had a very strong and unusual sensation deep in my gut; I knew that my dad was passing at that exact moment. Within the hour I received the call confirming his transition.

This type of close interconnection is very common and many people have had similar episodes. Later I will relate another similar story about a friend's very dramatic connection with her twin sister. What is really odd is that these types of communications are not more openly recognized, studied, understood and integrated into our science and culture.

BURST OF ENERGY AT DEATH TRANSITION

My mother made her personal decision to exit this life soon after she broke her hip in a fall at her own sister's funeral. Her last living close friend had just passed, and she could no longer participate in her favorite activities: golf, bridge and painting. The fact that she had made this conscious decision, to not continue her life, was clear to all four of her children.

She gradually shut down in a manner that allowed everyone in her family the opportunity to spend quality time with her. She ultimately lapsed into a coma, but five days later she suddenly woke when her children were all present. She was unexpectedly with us again for the next three hours as she prepared for her transition. Famous for being extremely stubborn, she hung on to physical life with her characteristic tenacity. She had been mostly pain-free through her process, but in the last 30 seconds, when the breathing had stopped, there were two, back to back, full and deeply pained facial grimaces, as if something was suddenly being torn from her body. The moment that she finally left us was absolutely clear.

This burst of energy at the end of a person's life is a common and well-documented phenomenon. Where does this shift in awareness and extra energy come from and why? It seems as if the spirit wants time for closure, or to gather extra energy to complete the physical separation from the body.

From my perspective, many parts of her dying process reinforced the idea that spirit can exist as a separate entity from the body. In her last moments, my mom's spirit was present, full of energy and shining even though her body was completely worn out. My mother taught me many things and this wonderful demonstration was her last great gift.

THE BIRTH OF MY CHILDREN

At the other end of life's spectrum, I have closely witnessed the moment of birth. Both of my children were held and welcomed by me immediately upon their transition into the light of this world. Both came with unique spirits that could be clearly and instantly recognized from their first moments. At birth their two spirits were as unique and different from each other, and their parents, as they are today–these same spirits continue to manifest and shape their individual life trajectories. With these first meetings it was clear that my first one, Emily, was extremely wise and contemplative but already burdened with a heavy awareness of the human condition, suffering, and complexity of humankind. From the first moment, the other, Rachel, was wide-open for any experience, fully engaged physically, and always actively looking for something new to play with or explore. Over the years their minds and bodies have evolved to allow for different kinds of personality expressions by their unique and different spirits, but the fully recognizable core of each individual has remained unchanged. When my children came into this world, each arrived with their own identifiable and expressive spirit already present.

Many, possibly most, parents have this clear awareness; their children's most fundamental spirits are unique and present from birth. This individual quality usually does not change as the child matures; it deeply integrates into their bodies and lives. My experience as a father has only reinforced the notion that each of us arrives into this physical existence with an essential and unique core *being* or spirit.

How Some of My Architectural Ideas Arrive

As an architect, an important part of my job is to produce ideas that solve many different problems simultaneously. This type of problem solving has some similarities with *multi-dimensional analysis,* in which mathematicians solve problems with many simultaneous unknowns or variables. Solutions to this type of problem are always very dynamic, meaning that if one variable, or unknown, is changed, everything else must also move and change to compensate. Sometimes spreadsheets are used to illustrate this type of complex interactive relationship.

To solve this type of architectural problem, the first step is always to list and study the various issues and parameters. The amount of time that I spend at this stage will vary with project size. Often, for larger or more complex projects, this stage can last several days. Next I move forward and try different quick possibilities to see which ideas work and which ones do not. At this point I can usually find rational solutions that work for most, but not all, of the issues that need a simultaneous solution. Often any modifications that I try, while attempting to solve the remaining unsolved issues, only generate brand-new problems of their own. Many designers reach a point in this process where it becomes clear that the rational and logical mind is not the best tool for successfully processing all the variables. A computer, if carefully programmed, might do some parts of this process better and faster, but the dimensionally limited thought process of the programmer will still limit the results. Typically, most solutions at this stage seem rather flat, uninspired, or even boring. For a student who is learning how to design, this is the most frustrating step of the entire process because, at this stage, the perfect or ideal solution can often seem to be impossibly out of reach.

Through many years of practice I have learned that once I have thoroughly worked through the analysis, but just before I get frustrated, lies a special moment where it makes sense to stop the rational design process and literally "sleep on it." What usually happens is that I wake up at 3:00 a.m., often that very first night, with a vague idea, which immediately must be drawn on paper. While I am drawing, the idea gradually becomes more solid, until at some point I can sense a complete solution, even without taking the time to check all the variables. I usually then check a few of the more troubling or resistant issues and, once I have confirmed that they are indeed solved, I can finally relax and go back to sleep, knowing that I have found the solution. In the morning I continue the process by transferring the ideas to my computer, where I can thoroughly check all the issues and relationships.

From experience, I have learned to recognize that special "feeling" that always accompanies my successful solutions. This feeling arrives long before the actual confirmation of the solution and it always turns out to be completely accurate. Another interesting thing about the process is that while the final solution solves the complex series of inter-related problems, it also usually creates a number of unexpected "bonuses" that were not even thought about in the initial analysis. It is as if the solution comes from somewhere outside of my normal conscious and thought-bound mind to include aspects of the problem that I did not even consider.

I have learned to trust this process, as it has always been consistent and very reliable, but I am unable to explain it in normal, rational or linear terms. I am also not the only person who relies on such a method, for this type of experience is very common with other designers and artists of all types. This mysterious and magical process, which I have come to love and trust, is the aspect of design that continues to excite me and allows my work to stay fresh and exciting after almost 35 years of practice.

While many of my designs are about solving a specific set of detailed problems, sometimes the real "problem" in a particular design is that there are too many choices or potential solutions, which all initially seem to work equally well. How, then, does one decide which path to take? I have developed what might be considered an unusual approach. I simply ask the piece of land or building *"what does it want to become?"* While this technique is outside of any logical or mainstream-approved design method, it does work; and sometimes it works amazingly well. Other artists, musicians and writers rely on similar techniques. Until recently the "ask the piece of art" technique was only spoken of in the most esoteric circles; but today I am hearing more artists speak openly about this type of process. Just yesterday, at a design meeting, the interior designer said, "when I remodel a home I always ask the house where the front door should be placed."

Gertrude Stein was a contemporary of the earliest quantum physicists and seemed to be blessed with a mind that thought in ways that seemed strange from a logical framework, but might not seem so strange from a more *quantum* perspective. She helped many artists and writers become comfortable with the process of being "open" and available to answers from unexpected places. After one of her lectures, one member of the audience remarked, *"Gertrude said things tonight that will take **her** years to understand."* Ideas seemed to just pop into her head and she guided many others into this intuitive process.

During training at architecture school, I was taught some of these tricks. However, I was also cautioned to only explain my process to clients in very logical and rational terms, even though the rational reasoning was often only a reconstruction that typically came after the original, creative inspiration. Rewriting the actual history of the design process to make it sound more logical, and less mysterious, was simply seen as part of assembling a professional presentation. We were cautioned not to let clients see the inner workings of the creative process because, as with viewing the making of sausage, "it would tend to erode confidence."

A technique called the *charette*, which involves a multi-day, full-on, design brainstorming session, allowing no time for sleep, is a standard practice for producing creative ideas in many architecture studios. The entire purpose of this exercise hinges upon exhausting or breaking down our rational thought processes and egos to better allow ideas to simply emerge from that "other" place. This process is physically and emotionally taxing, but still very effective. It makes no sense from our standard 3D classical *viewport*. Something else is clearly going on!

After I became a father, the self-imposed *charette technique* was no longer practical. I found that there were easier and quicker ways to loosen the rational boundaries without paying such a heavy physical and emotional price. I discovered that the hours between midnight and 3:00 a.m. were, for some reason, magical for me. Understanding the natural stages and cycles of my own process and working with them, instead of fighting them, was my most important adjustment.

About 15 years ago I added a slightly modified technique to my design process. I began to visualize the already completed building "at some date in the future." This exercise is designed to uncover what the building could one day become and then to determine what needs to be done to facilitate its fruition. I have used this technique for some of my large, but poorly defined, new building projects. In these types of projects, the problem is often that there are just too many possible directions to pursue. For me, this "mental time machine" has been a very successful method for focusing and finding creative and concrete solutions. Our rational and scientific minds have a very difficult time explaining just how and why such a method works.

EXPERIENCES OF FRIENDS AND FAMILY

CLOSE CONNECTIONS BETWEEN IDENTICAL TWINS

Forty years ago I was living in Wisconsin. My girlfriend's best friend was a twin and her twin sister, whom I had never met, was living in London at the time. One night my girlfriend received a call from her best friend, who was in terrible pain and needed a ride to the hospital. All night long tests were conducted, searching for the cause of her excruciating pain, but all the tests proved negative and the doctors were left thoroughly baffled. In the morning the pain suddenly stopped and she was sent home only to receive a call within hours informing her that her twin sister had been in a terrible auto accident in London, survived for several hours, but then ultimately died. The timing of the event was exactly, precisely correlated to her pain throughout the previous night.

This type of special intimate connection between twins is well documented. In our culture, even though we recognize this unusually close relationship, we offer no clear explanation for these unusual but strong connections. It is my belief that, through the structure of the *Multiverse,* we are all intimately connected at some deeper levels. The connection between twins might lie much closer to the surface. This incident, along with many others like it, indicates that strong physical and emotional connections exist between us, even if we can't always observe them directly.

MY SISTER'S DORM MATE HAS AN ACCIDENT

In 1970 my sister was in her freshman year of college, and one of her friends had a motorbike accident that caused a traumatic head injury. After a long recovery, her friend returned to the dorm, but she saw people differently. Suddenly everyone was surrounded by a large halo of auric light. Each person's individual aura had different colors, and she instantly knew, from the color, what the person was like and whether their intentions were selfish or loving. This went on for months before she started to add small but accurate premonitions to her new extrasensory talents. One night she awoke screaming, waking everyone else in the dorm wing. She just had a vivid dream that her parents had died in a car crash on a mountainous road.

She called her parents and they calmed her by saying *"honey, that was just a dream!"* Three more nights in succession she had the same dream, and her screaming woke up everyone in the dorm. Each time she called her parents and the parents promised that they would not take that vacation which they had already planned. A short time later, she received a call explaining that her parents had just died in a car crash in the mountains. Her parents had clearly misled her to placate her. She quickly entered a deep catatonic state and was admitted into a mental health institution. At this point my sister lost touch with this dorm mate and, to this day, does not know what happened afterwards.

VISITATIONS OF DECEASED HUSBAND

My youngest sister's husband, George, was a larger-than-life character, and his untimely death caught us all off guard. He had an accident while playing with his daughter's toy foot scooter on the paved hill in front of his house. At the time he appeared to require only a quick emergency-room visit, but a couple of days later he unexpectedly died in his sleep from a hidden injury.

It is noteworthy that the evening before his death, some part of him "knew" because, even though he appeared fine, he led the family in prayer focused on his having made peace with all things in his life. He had never done anything like this before, and this caused my sister to worry through that night about a possible undiagnosed injury. We often seem to understand things that we should not be able to know from logic alone.

In the years that followed his death, my sister and her daughter had multiple incidents of visitation from George. Most of these happened while the two of them were together, so they had instant confirmation from each other that they weren't just "imagining" these strange events. At that time, my sister and her daughter were not the type of people who had *any* interest in the supernatural, and they never shared any of this with anyone because they were convinced that no one would believe them. It took direct questions from me to provoke them to relate these stories, and even then, they were a little hesitant.

Here are just a few of the incidents. George had been a lifetime cigar smoker. After his death they twice came home to cigar smoke in the house. Once, a lit cigar was found in his ashtray on the table of his smoking room and, another time, they found a cigar burning in the desk drawer. They never did figure out how either of these incidents happened or why the lit cigar would be in a drawer. It was a large and well-secured, private suburban home so no one else would have, or could have, been inside their home.

Another time while my sister and her daughter were sitting in one room, his favorite Lou Rawls album started playing on his turntable in another room. Neither of them knew how to use his personal and very complicated turntable system. They had no house guests and there was no other person who had access to their home.

Another visitation incident involved one of their unresolved marital issues. My sister had often tried to control her husband's gregarious behavior by hiding his glasses so he had to stay home. Her method thoroughly annoyed him and this was still a very active issue when he died. One day many months after his passing, she suddenly could not find her glasses anywhere in her home. She remembered exactly where she had left them but still checked the entire house. She gave up looking for them, and a few days later she went to her office, which she and her husband had shared for many years. Even though she knew that her last trip to this office had been several days before losing her glasses, lying right there in the middle of her desk, were the missing glasses and case.

These unusual events completely stopped after a couple of years, but my sister still gets goose bumps and chills every time she thinks back to this period of her life.

Healer from Ghana

My next-door neighbor and dear friend went to visit her daughter in Ghana last year. Her daughter was married to a man from Ghana and they were living there in his village. During a festive celebration my friend's daughter sliced the bottom of her foot. The wound was wide-open and bleeding, and her mom's attention reflexively went to motherly concerns such as infection, bleeding and knowing that her daughter had not had a recent tetanus shot. These concerns were very real because medical care and hospitals were quite far away. The daughter, who had been living in this village, was more adapted to the local ways. The village "healer" noticed the injury, walked up and volunteered to "fix" it. After holding her foot for a little while, he grabbed a handful of dirt and rubbed it directly on the wound. My friend's concerns immediately turned to alarm at seeing this dirt put on the wound, especially since the same dirt was soiled by pigs and other livestock. Next the village healer pulled out a white powder that he always carried and sprinkled it on this now dirty spot, held the foot for a while, and then pronounced it *"all fixed!"* My friend and her daughter immediately went and washed the paste off, only to discover to my friend's complete amazement that the cut had completely disappeared. It was as if the deep cut had never been there at all.

We have no mechanism in our 3D paradigm to explain this type of occurrence, yet my friend and her daughter had together just witnessed the "impossible."

SAVED BY A MIRACLE

Years ago one of my very best friends was riding in the back of a camper pickup truck that was heading down a hill in New Mexico at a rapid rate of speed. As the driver lost control, hit a guardrail and started to swerve, my friend knew that he was in deep trouble and quickly reached a peaceful resolution, convinced that this was probably his moment to die. He said an abbreviated prayer and then relaxed into a protective fetal position. The truck flipped over and the next thing he knew, he was sliding down the hill on a small broken piece of the camper shell that was under him and performing like a sled. He slid all the way down the hill and right into the soft desert sand at the bottom, his only bodily damage being a broken finger. Unfortunately the truck's driver did not share his good fortune. Most people, with some age and adventure behind them, have several of these "had to be more than just good luck" type of stories. As we become more observant, we might realize that miracles have always been a "normal" part of our lives.

FRIEND IS INJURED

Another close friend was recently hospitalized, in a coma, after a three-story fall. After several weeks, he regained consciousness and gradually began to reintegrate with his old life and friends. After several more months he improved to the point where he could choose to continue to live his life in an almost-normal fashion. He has the clear memory of experiencing a timeless and formless space throughout the coma phase, but even though he is extremely eloquent, he had no words to describe his experience. Words simply did not apply. He now senses most things differently, and in many ways his life has changed as he now moves through this world differently. To outside observers, he now appears much more joyful, relaxed and positive. His near-death experience, while not able to be translated or conceptualized, still informs his life in the 3D realm. **We do not need to be able to understand or explain our experiences to be able to benefit from them.**

Many people have had their lives completely transformed by similar near-death experiences, and a library full of books has been published that relate many of these stories. The strange thing is that we do not appreciate or understand more about this common type of event.

MASSAGE BOUNDARIES

A friend of mine is a very gifted body worker and physical therapist who has helped me through several difficult injuries. We sometimes share stories about our more unusual experiences. One day, when he was noticing a particularly deep connection with his massage client, he casually looked down at his own hand as it was working on his client's head. He was shocked to see that, from his perspective, his hand was buried halfway inside the client's head. Stunned and not quite knowing what to do, he paused for what seemed like a long time and then slowly pulled his hand out. Too disturbed to say anything, he just carefully resumed the massage. At the end of the massage the client commented that it was amazing how she could not distinguish where her body stopped and his began. My friend just held his tongue, needing time to process his own observations.

Dissolution of normal physical boundaries is certainly not unheard or impossible. As we were reminded with our discussion about the size and density of the atom, our bodies are entirely built of just space and *energy*. From this particular microscopic perspective it might even be seen as surprising that this type of "soft boundary" interaction is not encountered and noticed more often.

PASSING THROUGH SPACE BETWEEN ATOMS

While recounting some of these stories with several friends, I was told of many similar experiences, but one story stood dramatically alone. One of my friends who was sharing stories that day had been a passenger in a car driving down an interstate when, all of a sudden, a large tanker rig, coming from the other direction, jumped the divider and slid sideways right in front of them. My friend's automobile plunged directly into the tanker truck broadside at 75 miles per hour. His last momentary thought before the crash was a clear knowing that he was about to die, for there was nothing but massive steel directly in front of him. The next thing he knew, he was standing completely unscathed on the other side of the tanker truck. The car was destroyed, pinned under the frame of the tanker truck and his car's driver was dead. He has absolutely no idea what occurred, how it happened, or why he was completely spared from any physical damage. The only explanation he has is *"I somehow passed right through the steel tanker."*

UNIVERSAL OUT-OF-THE-BOX EXPERIENCES

SPORTS AND GAMES

While participating in sports or other similar activities, we sometimes have experiences that leave us wondering just how certain events could have happened or unfolded the way they did. These types of occurrences are frequent for me and, from talking to others, I realize that they are quite universal and common.

Precognition is an awareness of something that will be happening in the "future." For me, *precognition* occurs often in games and sports, and especially those that have long pauses that allow time for thinking, such as billiards, golf and baseball. While winding to throw a pitch, back-swinging the golf club, or lining up the billiard's shot, a vision might pop into our minds and suddenly we see the entire shot before it unfolds. This clear "vision," ahead of real time, can often appear just like a movie clip of the perfectly executed shot, or sometimes, a movie of a very easy, yet completely blundered, shot. *Precognition* seems to work both ways. As the swing, throw or shot unfolds there is this internal awareness or absolute knowing about exactly what will happen in the next few moments. The actual shot is just a confirmation of that previous mental vision.

The first few times that I noticed this, I was amazed, but as I became more accustomed to these pre-visions, the process evolved to become almost quite normal. I then began to expect and encourage this type of vision so that I could experiment and consciously try to manipulate it. Gradually I discovered something else. If I hesitated, had a doubt, second-guessed, or in any way wavered from the straight forward certainty around this vision, the shot could fall apart and result in a very different outcome. Even just a thought about the vision had a disruptive effect on the outcome. Instead of simply receiving a glimpse of the near "future," I was trying to influence it and this involvement altered the outcome. Over-thinking or analysis can easily pull us out of the natural flow of events.

A technique based on this principle is now used in competitive sports. This technique, based on learning to visualize a successful outcome, was first used for Olympic-level sports programs in the Soviet Union during the 1960s. By the early 1980s, friends of mine who were on the U.S. Olympic diving team were often trained using these Soviet methods. They were taught to imagine a movie in their head about how it felt to complete a perfect dive and then they were to play this movie repeatedly in their minds before their dives. Today, this and other similar techniques are commonly used, worldwide, in a variety of athletic training programs.

In some types of sports and other activities that involve a significant amount of steady, rhythmic activity or quick reflexes, a different type of phenomenon occurs. A "knowing flow" or natural rhythm can sometimes take over and guide the process. When this occurs, it feels as if the mind has fallen completely out of the picture, as the body alone seems to act and react at an extremely high skill level. I have experienced this automatic response most often in tennis, music and high-speed windsurfing. At the beginning of a session, I am usually thinking about exactly what I am going to do and why because, initially, my brain is involved with all the planning. Then, especially during particularly intense or challenging moments, the mental activity seems to fall away and, I begin to have the sensation of watching myself sailing, playing tennis or performing a musical part, from a somewhat noninvolved, outside reference position. I simply become an *observer* who is no longer engaged in input or control. The body is still doing its job at a very high skill level, but it is operating without any of my conscious help at all. Actually, if I consciously focus or think about what I am doing or how well I am performing, I usually then start to have difficulties, as the mind's relatively slow judgments begin to become involved again. This sensation is not unlike my observations during fire-walking or my experience with Fijian feet.

MORE SUBTLE TYPES OF PRECOGNITION

Fully envisioning how a golf shot will unfold before the actual stroke is one common example of *precognition* in sports. *Precognition* occurs throughout our lives. A clear vision may appear sometimes, but for me, a more common occurrence is simply a strong sense about something that is about to happen. Most of us have had that sudden and strong intuitive feeling that we should, or should not, do something. When this happens we usually have no idea about the source of this *information*. Impulses like *"I should not get on that bus"* or *"I should walk down that block instead"* are shared by all of us; earlier I cited several examples from my own life. It can be difficult for the untrained mind to determine whether this impulse is originating from a deeper level of timeless *information,* or whether it is being generated by our subconscious fears

What varies from person to person is how each of us trusts these "out of the blue" impulses, and, therefore, how we respond. Our contemporary culture teaches us, in multiple ways, to ignore these because they are not testable or explainable and, therefore, cannot be considered real or accurate. However, if over time we allow ourselves to act on these intuitive impulses, our understanding of them and our trust in them tends to increase. We become more sensitive to these and even more progressively subtle messages. My personal experience has been that almost every time in my life that I have encountered a substantial problem or issue resulting from some decision or action of mine, I can recall having previously received and ignored some form of "warning." However, on the other hand, whenever I pay attention to these warnings, very little seems to change and my life just seems to progress normally.

Some confusion might be created by our personal difficulty in distinguishing real warnings from our general subconscious fears. What might appear to be a "warning" could originate from a personal fear-based thought, and nothing more. If our life unfolds smoothly after an unheeded warning, this could mean that the "warning" was only a fear-based thought. However, it might also mean that even though we did not consciously change our plans, just our awareness of the potential problem might have caused us to alter our attitude or timing just enough to change the outcome. It is also possible that because we exist in a world of probable outcomes, this problematic event just did not occur in our current *viewport*. As previously stated, what is clear to me is that in my experience, no related problem has ever manifested after paying attention to such a warning.

Generally, as we grow and age, we learn to distinguish these deeper impulses from our more generic worries and fears and, because of this growing wisdom, our intuition tends to become more accurate. We then, in turn, naturally begin to pay more attention to our *precognitions*.

We are always receiving this type of *information* as a shadow or energetic impulse that is cast from a form of *information* that does not originate in our *viewport*–our current place in time and 3D space. ***From our perspective, there will always be leaks in the membrane that separates our viewport, and we can always become better at learning how to interpret the meaning of the images that make it through this membrane. On the other hand, if we lead unexamined lives and continue to embody many hidden, fear-based shadows within, then clear discernment becomes impossible.*** As we will discuss later, exploring and clearing our buried memories and emotions is critical to our ability to distinguish our hidden personal fears from this valid intuitive *information.*

DÉJÀ VU

Most of us have exposure to the feeling or sensation commonly known as *déjà vu* –the French expression for "already seen." *Déjà vu* often appears as an intuitive sense or "knowing" that we have been in the same place or situation before, saying the same words to the very same people. It is the feeling of having already lived that particular scene in your life. Sometimes this awareness, a common form of *precognition*, also includes a precise "knowing" exactly what will happen next. *Déjà vu* is a relatively common experience, and yet it is not easily explained through the "normal" rules of our familiar conceptual space and "time."

However, within the larger and expanded framework of the *Multiverse,* there are many plausible explanations and multiple ways that events could unfold in exactly this manner. The timeless architecture of the *Multiverse* can easily be used to explain this mystery and other similar phenomena. From the broader perspective, one where all time unfolds at once, we can understand *déjà vu* as a simple glance forward in time, or possibly it is a quick glimpse into a very similar parallel universe. *Déjà vu* clearly is one of those moments where the "arrow of time" and the bounds of space do not follow the usual three-dimensional expectations.

CONJURING SOMEONE'S PRESENCE WITH A THOUGHT

Another universal occurrence is that of finding ourselves thinking about someone "out of the blue" only to see them, hear from them, or hear something about them immediately after. We might be thinking of someone we haven't seen in 20 years just as the phone rings with news about them; or, wondering about an old acquaintance, we might turn on the TV to see a news article involving this friend. While many of these moments can be explained by pure coincidence or simple probability, the frequency of and timing around some of these occurrences can sometimes defy natural probability. Also noteworthy is the fact that these moments often happen at the exact time the other person is engaged in some major event within their lives. It is as if we can feel their worry or concern.

We all have some experiences of this type. Sometimes we discuss these coincidences with others, but these events are often of a type that does not fit comfortably within our consensus worldview so, we often ignore or try to forget about them. However, these experiences make perfect sense when viewed through the deeper architecture of the *Multiverse*. Again, this type of occurrence involves the breakdown of one-directional marching time or the penetration of the invisible membrane that separates us as individuals. This type of event speaks to the constant energetic connections between all of us.

KNOWING THAT SOMEONE IS STARING AT YOU

Another related and extremely common experience is to be sitting somewhere and "feel" another's attention directly upon you. Depending on the circumstances, this can be a welcomed or very disturbing feeling. We have all had this sensation and nothing within our standard five senses explains it fully. This sensation demonstrates a common type of energetic communication that is not yet well understood within our 3D realm.

ALARM RINGS ON DREAM CUE

Most of us have had the memory of being lost in a long and complex dream that culminates in some dream event or sound that magically blends with real world circumstances just as we gain waking consciousness. The waking world alarm rings right on its dream cue; someone knocks on the door in both the dream and waking world; or the house shaking in the dream blends into an actual earthquake. Often the real event corresponds or is choreographed exactly to the dream so the actual physical event of our waking life completes the dream without a loss of time or beat.

This phenomenon could be explained many different ways using this new architecture, including the entire dream having been created and played out in the first nanosecond of the waking world event. No matter what the explanation, this type of phenomenon points to the thin boundary between our dreams and waking life and the fact that time is relative, malleable and always a function of our perception.

CHANNELING

Human history has numerous examples of an extraordinary phenomenon called channeling. Channeling is usually defined as the "esoteric process of receiving messages or *information* from nonphysical or extra-dimensional *beings* or spirits." Frederic Nietzsche was sometimes involved with this process as were other notables, such as Edgar Cayce and John of God (who is still alive and practicing in Brazil). Helen Schucman, a professor of Medical Psychology at Columbia University in the 1960s and early 1970s, is said to have received the entire 1,000-plus-paged text of the *Course in Miracles* through the somewhat involuntary, but direct, channeling of Jesus.

One of the most intriguing aspects of channeling is that the *information* is sometimes relayed in foreign languages or at a technical level that the channeler could not have understood through their normal life experiences; often the channeler has no technical or cultural understanding of the material channeled–it might be "over their head" or contain information that they could never have known.

REVELATION

Revelation can be classified as a specific form or subset of channeling. The main difference is most of those receiving revelation do not profess another speaking *through* them so much as speaking *to* them. Many of the religions of the world were initiated through revelations received by their founding saints or prophets. The Church of Latter Day Saints, one of the fastest-growing religions in the world, was originally founded in the early 1800s upon claimed revelations delivered through golden tablets in upstate New York. The LDS Church continues to establish new splinter branches as various individuals within the church continue to have their own personal living revelations–a practice that is permitted, and it could even be argued, encouraged, by church doctrine. Almost every religion in the world has roots and history based on some form of revelation. We clearly accept and even revere this form of channeling within our own religions, and yet offer no clear explanations for them that make sense in our three-dimensional realm.

NEAR DEATH EXPERIENCE

One particular "outside of our conceptual box" phenomenon that has surged in public awareness during recent years is the *NDE*, or *near death experience*. The *NDE* occurs most often when an individual is on the brink of death, usually as a result of a physical trauma such as an accident or surgery. Those having the *NDE* often have types of sensations and visions that seem to be associated with the dying process. Sometimes they also may have the experience that their consciousness and visual perspective is located somewhere outside of their traumatized body. It is not uncommon for individuals having an *NDE* to recall viewing their damaged body from a remote location. They might view their bodies in the mangled car below or on the operating table at the hospital, or they might be watching their grieving relatives in the hospital waiting room or sitting with them in the family living room. People having *NDEs* are known to recall entire conversations that they overheard from these remote positions while their body was technically unconscious, under an anesthetic, or even *flat lined* and officially brain-dead. Sometimes they even witness and remember exact conversations that occurred in other rooms or remote locations.

NDE events seem to span age groups and cultures, but they often include special flourishes that tend to be specifically choreographed for the individual's religion or belief system. *NDE* individuals frequently sense their conscious awareness traveling down some form of tunnel, and they sometimes have visions that are filled with an unusual type of light. They typically have a range of unusual sensations and events that can include meeting loved ones who have already died and who offer comforting words or advice. At some point during their *NDE,* the person often understands that they are being offered a choice to return to their bodies to finish some work or continue their lives. Since they lived to speak of their experience, all the individuals interviewed about their *NDEs* obviously managed to return to their original bodies and lives. After returning, they often feel a deeper peace and possess a different type of wisdom, even though sometimes their new life can also include living with a badly compromised body. They often speak of leaving fear, in its many forms, behind. Almost all who have this expansive type of encounter return with a renewed appreciation for life, especially a strong and clear "knowing" that life continues beyond our physical death.

Parts of the *NDE* may be nothing more than a hallucination or the way the mind's chemistry works when we are traumatized. However, some aspects clearly involve the edges of our paradigm, because often *NDE* patients will recount things that occurred in and around their bodies and return with *information* that they should not have been able to hear or know. The increase in public awareness of this phenomenon may partly be because the number of people that are having this experience has increased. This may be largely because modern medicine has become very skilled at resuscitating people who otherwise would have died.

OUT-OF-BODY EXPERIENCE

My journey to Whiteface Mountain during meditation was a classic example of a spontaneous out-of-the-body experience. In that section of the book I also related other out-of-the-body experiences of several close friends. Several religions and spiritual practices speak about the ability of consciousness to move, travel or sustain itself outside of the physical body. There are even specific spiritual practices, one called "Astral Traveling," that teach very conscious practices designed to induce this altered state of being.

Many people who have had *near death experiences* describe very clear, conscious and dramatic out-of-body perspectives as part of their larger experience. It typically becomes clear to anyone who has gone through this type of event that the body is not necessary for consciousness, at least not in the short-term.

CROP CIRCLES

Since 1970, more than 10,000 crop circles have appeared in farmers' fields around the world, and the vast majority of those that were seen and recorded have appeared in England. Crop circles and other related earth sculptures, depicting strong and powerful geometric forms, have inexplicably appeared throughout much of our known history. Many of the historic forms may have been created and built by man, but we have no record of the history of their construction. The more-recent crop circles are quite a different story because we have many living witnesses to their sudden appearance but few, or no, witnesses to their actual construction. From my perspective, that of a skilled professional builder of large geometric forms in the natural landscape, this widespread phenomenon requires an explanation that, at least partly lies outside of our normal rational logic and science.

The form and methods of actual construction for most, if not all, of the crop circles not already known to be man-made remain an unresolved mystery, even though these forms continue to appear in locations that are in plain public view. Given the constraints of time, place and technique, I find it impossible to conclude that men could have physically built all of these more complex forms. These particular geometric forms are often extremely intricate and they usually seem to appear very quickly. They often manifest in the short window of no more than a few hours, and sometimes even a few minutes, and they usually arrive under the cover of darkness.

Skeptics have been quick to claim that crop circles are created by pranksters beating the grass down with either sticks or their feet, and I have certainly seen examples of crop designs, some very crude and some more sophisticated, that have been or could have been made by man. Since 1996, a group called "the Circlemakers" has turned the construction of crop circles into a commercial enterprise by making medium-sized formations that sometimes include corporate logos. It is quite likely that other, more sophisticated groups have created and constructed a number of complex circles. However, having been trained in our most-advanced human construction techniques, I am more than convinced that at least some of these crop circles have physical characteristics and qualities that indicate an origination from some other source because the timing, precision and technical issues often seem to completely rule out the "hand of man" possibility. Ironically, instead of proving that all crop circles are man-made, those that are known to be constructed by man illuminate the characteristics of man-made circles and, the impossibility that some of these other designs could also be man-made! Once the actual real-world challenges of constructing these crop circles are fully understood, the very existence of some of these enormous and complex crop circles point to an absolutely amazing and life-changing phenomenon.

I have always constructed things, big things, and this urge is deep within my bones. As a child I ripped apart "everything" in my parents' house, trying to discover how things worked. I built forts, tree houses, buildings, go-carts and large multi-chambered ice caves; eventually I rebuilt cars, lawnmowers and motorcycles. As an environmental biologist in Fiji, I designed and built portable research stations that could be reassembled in the mangroves; and before I became an architect, I worked as a home builder. I have always had this natural skill and I understand, deep within, what it takes to build something successfully in our 3D world. With buildings, designing them is often the easy part of the process. Moving a complex structure from the drawing board or computer to the real world can be a difficult and time-consuming process.

The first step of actual construction is to mark out the boundaries of the new structure on the raw landscape. This marking process is called *layout*. Designs that have right angles and are mostly rectangular have clear corners that are relatively easy to measure, correct, locate and accurately mark. Even with the more simple *layouts*, after checking and rechecking measurements and then adjusting, correcting, driving new stakes to re-mark the corners, and stretching strings to guide the foundation form builders, the site is always left in a thoroughly trampled condition. The ground around the marked points is invariably beaten down with footprints from the layout crew running in all directions during the process of measuring, checking, adjusting, rechecking, staking and stringing.

Often my designs include unusual angles, curves and more complicated geometric shapes, such as fans, octagons and hexagons. These designs can be extremely difficult to lay out accurately in full daylight, even with "state-of-the-art" digital survey equipment. Accurate point location can sometimes require multiple attempts over several days, and changes in elevation can greatly complicate this process. Numerous checks and rechecks often are needed to get the layout of these more complex designs just right; and, of course, after these complicated layouts, the site is completely trampled with footprints. There are enough things for the layout crew to worry about within this process without the additional burden of having to think about where to place every step.

The *layout* of human-made crop circles always includes this added complication of where to place the first footprints so that later the builder will be able to hide or disguise them. Many crop-circle *layouts*, by necessity, involve multiple people milling about, marking the points that need to be established because every part of the design relates physically to every other part. On the ground this becomes a very busy process, involving many repetitive cycles of setting points and rechecking measurements. To accomplish the overnight construction of a complex crop circle, all of this coordinated activity needs to be completed very quickly and in the dark–a time when all parties cannot easily see and communicate with each other or even see the terrain itself. All *layout* and construction operations will, by necessity, generate some foot traffic. Within many designs there is the possibility of obscuring these footprints by carefully hiding them in the parts that will eventually "lay down." This means that the builder needs to coordinate and restrict foot traffic to those parts of the pattern that are planned to be "bent down." They might carefully use existing tractor-wheel paths as emergency alternate routes in and out, but these, and the footprints within, always remain visible. The "catch-22" in this type of *layout* process is that the builder can never know exactly where those "safe-to-walk" parts are going to be located until much of the design is already established in the field.

The plans for many of these crop circle designs are several orders of magnitude more complex than any of my house designs, and they are usually built in the night and always without the help of lights. In some cases they have even been known to appear in less than an hour between two known airplane fly-overs. To even accomplish this very first step, the *layout,* of a "quarter-mile wide three-armed spiral" design within a couple of hours in a dark field and without creating footprints, or being seen, is simply impossible. Keep in mind that every time a marker is set to mark the *origin* (the center) or other critical geometric points of each spiral or circle, someone who is in communication with the lead surveyor would have to trample another large piece of irregular terrain just to get to that remote point. These centers of circles are crucial layout and marking points, and yet some of these circular forms even have their center points left "standing," completely undisturbed and un-trampled.

Modern survey equipment, called *total stations,* makes this type of *layout* process much easier. With these computer systems a single fixed *benchmark layout* point can be established, a computerized transit set up, and most of the other points can be shot directly from that one spot. This equipment is very expensive and requires well-trained, skilled operators. The *total station* system has been incrementally developed into its present, and very powerful, form throughout the last 20 years. However, many very complex crop circles appeared before the development and implementation of these computerized instruments. Even with the *total station*, a roaming person has to still physically move to each spot to mark and stake every critical point and then establish and mark paths forming arcs or curves. Doing this quickly, especially in the dark to avoid discovery, and then leaving no trace of footprints, is what human builders would have to accomplish every time a crop circle formation appears. Some of these complex formations are as large as one-third of a mile wide and yet, to my knowledge, no crop circle crew has ever been witnessed or caught during this complex and chaotic building process.

Those crop circles known to be hoaxes or corporate projects all have a relatively simple, underlying geometry. These simple geometries all require far less layout, but even with this advantage, they are typically filled with inaccuracies, mistakes and errant footprints. Clever builders could carefully plan methods to lay out and construct some of these forms without the errant footprints, but it would take a well-coordinated and rehearsed team many days, or even weeks, to carefully and accurately follow the necessary instructions to construct some of these designs. Many of the most spectacular crop circles were documented to have been created in mere minutes without witnesses seeing any lights or human activity in the fields. These constructions seem well beyond our present-day technical capabilities, even with the most advanced digital survey and marking techniques.

The crop circle sometimes called "Swirl" is enormous and complex. About one-quarter mile in diameter, it appeared on Milk Hill in Wiltshire in 2001. To construct it conventionally, in a single night, without lights, is simply impossible. When viewed from near the ground, the complexity and scale of the task of finding and staking the center of each circle within the field becomes very obvious. Notice that there are no human footpaths. For scale notice the person standing in the center of the second photograph. (Images courtesy of Steve and Karen Alexander)

When a massive crop circle Julia, 1,000 feet wide, materialized beneath the gaze of Stonehenge in 1996, the group called the "Circlemakers/Team Satan" claimed that they constructed this fractal-based pattern, despite the fact that two pilots, a security guard and a gamekeeper all claim that the formation appeared within a fifteen-minute window on that Sunday afternoon. It subsequently took a team of 11 surveyors more than five hours just to measure the design, and they were not worrying about errant footprints. In the analysis of another crop circle that appeared overnight, the surveying company who analyzed the site quoted that it would have taken a minimum of five days, just to mark out the starting points, before beginning any construction.

From my unique perspective, that of a builder of large geometric forms on the natural terrain, it is impossible to believe that all of these fantastic crop circles could be man-made constructions. While there is clearly a human contribution to the overall phenomenon, especially in recent years, something outside our normal expectations must be involved.

SPONTANEOUS HEALING

We all know or are aware of people who were very sick, given a short time to live by doctors, and then miraculously returned to good health. Sometimes diet, lifestyle change, medicine or treatment can explain the change, but other times these factors alone cannot account for such an unexpected and dramatic change. Attitude and something else that isn't easily explained within our system of knowledge must also be involved. While unexplainable within the old paradigm, there are numerous pathways within the *Multiverse* paradigm that can easily account for this healing phenomenon. Since all possible outcomes already exist in the interconnected Web, sickness and health always exist together, simultaneously and equally in parallel universes. Radical healing may simply mean learning how to shift to a healthier universe.

SYNCHRONICITIES AND SERENDIPITIES

Synchronicities are the occurrence of two or more events that are not causally related and therefore unlikely to occur together by chance. *Carl Jung first formally defined synchronicity as "temporally coincident occurrences of a-causal events."* Another way to describe them is they are powerful coincidences that cannot be explained through any cause-and-effect pathway that we already understand. These events are also then observed to occur together in a very meaningful way.

A common example of a *synchronicity* might be when a question that has just arisen in our mind is immediately answered by another who was not asked the question, or by something else, such as a TV show, the book we pick up, or a sign along the road. *A synchronicity* might manifest as a series of babies in one family being born on the same significant date, or seeing your high school yearbook for the first time in 20 years only to find an email from someone in that very class in the next moment.

Serendipity is often defined as a "happy accident" and is a particular subcategory of *synchronicity*. *Serendipities* often express themselves as something wonderful or someone special showing up, right on cue, in a person's life. My collision with my friend in London and my discovering my other friend in the hold of the fishing boat on Vancouver Island could both be seen as *serendipities* and *synchronicities*.

Last year, a long-lost, Louisiana high-school classmate of my wife Connie happened to meet some friends of ours in California. Through conversation they discovered that they all had a connection with Connie so he was given Connie's email address. Now living in east Texas, he wrote and asked if he could visit her later in the year when he was to be in Austin for a conference. The week before this scheduled meeting he was in central Kentucky for another business function and picked up a local magazine that had just interviewed Connie. She was the featured artist at that Kentucky town's art show that was being held that very weekend. He spontaneously visited her, at that show in Kentucky, and they reconnected, halfway across the country, only one week before their preplanned reunion in Texas. All of this quickly unfolded after not seeing each other for over 40 years. This is a clear example of *serendipity*.

These types of occurrences are familiar to all of us. Usually we write them off as just a product of chance or luck, but there are times when something greater than just odds or good luck seems to be involved. For me, these occurrences are another indication of the deep order and interconnectedness that lies below the visible surface of our lives.

WORKING WITH THE DYING

Hospice workers, EMTs and others who regularly interact with those actively engaged in the dying process will often share a collection of personal experiences and stories that cannot easily be explained within the standard framework of our paradigm. While it is likely that some parts of these episodes may be the direct result of the dying mind playing biochemical tricks on our consciousness, there is a certain, wonderful consistency to these stories that points towards a continuation of existence beyond the physical. These stories often include insights into the dying process itself, and often speak to an expanded vision of life and spirit. With one foot in another world, sometimes the dying can hold the door open for the rest of us.

My mother was a heavy smoker and, unknown to her family, had significant stress and worry about this habit near the end of her life. It wasn't that she wanted to quit–her worries were of a different nature. I found her very relaxed one morning during her final days. She related that she had a nighttime visit from "others" who came to her and said, *"Don't worry because there are plenty of cigarettes where you are going next. You do not need to worry about not being able to smoke."* This may seem silly to most of us, but it was exactly what she needed to hear, at that moment, to help her relax into her own dying process. Sometimes the dying tell hospice workers that they are being told, by "nice visitors" or long-dead but close relatives, that they have come to help escort them on their journey.

The dying process often exposes or dissolves some of the hard edges that contain our paradigm. In our culture, we seem to have a universal fear of death and often regard death as the ultimate failure. Like so much else that we fear, we usually avoid addressing this subject directly and honestly; we often push any thoughts or discussion about the process far away from our daily lives. Because our culture has this deep, inherent fear, we miss many of the wonderful, potential gifts that this important milestone of each individual's life has to offer. The biggest shared gift is the frequent and clear insights about the continuation of our lives beyond our present bodies.

SUMMARY

We all have heard multiple stories very much like those above, but often we find them uncomfortable or unsettling, so in our culture we tend to avoid discussing them publicly and openly. We lack the vocabulary or the conceptual space to understand and/or communicate the meaning, and our fears often complicate this type of exchange. It is sometimes easier to avoid thinking about difficult-to-explain experiences. When things do not fit easily within our known worldview, we often create special, hidden places so we can file them away. Instead of providing more direct insights, in our culture, some of these events might even begin to create repressed or buried blockages.

These types of experiences are always much easier to understand in the full context of the *Multiverse* and, once again, can all be explained through the deep, interactive interconnectedness of the Web, the dissolution of the arrow of time, or a parting of the membrane that separates us as individuals.

PART SIX–MEANING

DANCE OF HEART AND SOUL IN THE *MULTIVERSE*

THE SPIRITUAL SEARCH

RELIGION AND SPIRITUALITY

Spirituality is defined as the inner, personal search to discover the essence and purpose of one's own *being*. Organized religion and spirituality are sometimes viewed as very separate disciplines due to the sometimes prescriptive, indirect and dogmatic nature of the visible public face of many of the world's religions. Since major religious organizations focus significant resources on the organization's corporate, business and political interests, these powerful and influential organizational subgroups have their own agendas that may not always mesh well with the goals of those who are concerned with the core esoteric spirituality.

At the surface, spirituality and religion may seem very different, but at the deepest and most profound level, most of the world's major religions are really very similar to each other and deeply spiritual. Though most adherents may not be exposed to this esoteric level of spiritual practice, many of them are participating in their chosen religion because they desire a deepening of their personal spiritual experience–they are searching for meaning in their lives. The desire to understand our purpose and relationship to the world is a fundamental and critical force in all of our lives. For many practitioners, organized religion provides a safe, structured and socially acceptable framework for this exploration of our spiritual side. Therefore, when I speak of spirituality, I am including all of the various ways human beings search for meaning and connection in their lives.

SCIENCE AND SPIRITUALITY-TWO SIDES OF SAME COIN

"All religions, arts and sciences are branches of the same tree. All these aspirations are directed toward ennobling man's life, lifting it from the sphere of mere physical existence and leading the individual towards freedom." --Albert Einstein, *Out of My Later Years*

Independently, both science and spirituality seek to understand and explain the most fundamental, yet often hidden, truths about life. It then makes logical sense that, as both of these primary human endeavors evolve, they will tend to grow towards each other because both are always directing us to look towards the same objective, the deeper truth. Until recently, these two approaches often appeared to be completely separate, competitive and possibly even contradictory. Today, this old dichotomy is rapidly disappearing; many physicist are beginning to sound more like the ancient religious mystics, while, at the same time, religions, groups and spiritual practices that explore a more direct and personal experience with the infinite possibilities of *being*, continue to emerge or evolve.

The rapid growth and change in our understanding of the physical world during the last few hundred years is unprecedented. Though our worldview has completely expanded from what it was several hundred years ago, the foundational paradigm has not changed since Newton's time; we are now very ripe for another large-scale cultural shift. Within most parts of the scientific and technical community, there is a deeply held faith in the beauty and order of the mathematics that has been guiding the development of our sciences. As discussed, the advances in *quantum* and *relativistic physics* have directly led to the development and deployment of an abundance of new, powerful, technical and functional devices. These machines and tools are now so fully integrated into our contemporary lives that not only are we are dependent upon them, but also we often take these amazing devices for granted. If most of us really understood the science behind our computers, iPods, automobiles, electrical grids, weather satellites, phone systems or weapons, we would be in constant awe and perpetual recognition of our unique place in the history of this rapidly changing paradigm. As it has been often said *"The proof is in the pudding."* In this case, the very strange predictions of our new mathematics, the subsequent understanding of the behavior of the subatomic particles, and our deeper knowledge of the cosmos have directly led to the development of this wide array of amazing and mysterious electronic gadgets that generate, drive and move the vast amounts of *information* that today's world depends upon and devours.

Still, even with all our technical wizardry, this same science has not been able to explain the most fundamental truths about of our human experience. Despite all the theories and analysis, *life-force*, primary and critical to life itself, still remains unexplained and completely mysterious. Every generation has had scientific voices boldly declaring something very similar to *"we are on the cusp of finding God in the machine,"* but none of our efforts in this direction have ever produced a clear understanding about our spirit, the very essence of life itself. Good answers to the fundamental human questions have been completely lacking and, until now, most of the attempts have come from the spiritual side of our explorations. These questions and attempted answers have both been formed and framed by a type of conceptual thinking that evolved within our old, three-dimensional paradigm. This type of thinking will always be critically limited and flawed in its ability to describe or use the greater multi-dimensional *Multiverse* that we occupy.

When the process of scientific discovery is viewed from within our paradigm of linear time, it is assumed that our science is simply uncovering previously unknown things about our world. There is, however, another way to view this process of discovery. Another possible view, one that understands the *Many Worlds theory,* is that ***we may be "creating" this physics and these newly discovered parts of our universe on the fly, as we collapse the possibilities and probabilities into a new physical form with our thoughts and experimental observations.*** From our normal, cultural *viewport* a creative process like this seems rather fantastic because, if true, this means that our actual physical universe will always be evolving and expanding as rapidly as our collective thoughts can create it; we are dreaming our universe into our physical reality. Of course, this also means that it will always be impossible to fully describe our physical universe because it will always be continuously evolving to include whatever we can discover or imagine next.

However, if we view this process of discovery from an even broader perspective, that of the timeless *Multiverse,* then all of these possibilities already and always exist within the fabric of creation. The process is now understood to be only our opening to and recognition of something that always was present beyond our *viewport.* As we learn more about what it means to view this unfolding process from the more timeless perspective of the *Multiverse,* many things that were once considered mysterious begin to make sense.

At best, our old type of conceptual thinking can only partially illuminate a pathway that points us in the general direction of these deeper truths. From our side of the dimensional veil, truth will always appear obscured and remain relative, because we are not built to see or understand the entire picture at once. We will never be able to describe or understand creation as long as our prevailing concepts keep us time-bound and locked within our three-dimensional *viewport.*

The confusion or conflict between religion and science that we experience today is only an illusion created by our limited perspective. Whatever we are, we are not two different things with two sets of laws governing our existence. Eventually, spirituality and science must merge because, ultimately, everything is interconnected. As our understanding evolves, these two, great, human endeavors will eventually be seen as just two different views of exactly the same thing.

FAITH AND BELIEF

Belief is the origin of all real personal and social change. As Gandhi said, *"Your beliefs become your thoughts, your thoughts become your words, your words become your actions, your actions become your habits, your habits become your values, and your values become your destiny."* As quoted earlier, Henry Ford famously said, *"If you believe you can or if you believe you can't, you are right."* Henry Ford and Gandhi both understood something quite profound. Belief is where we begin; it contains and shapes who and what we become.

There is an important difference between belief and faith. Belief requires some element of proof. The validation might be scientific or experiential, but belief is always built upon some form of validation. Faith does not require this or any type of proof. Both faith and belief are powerful motivators and important engines for change and growth, and both appear to have a similar powerful influence upon the heart and soul of individuals.

The discussions and conclusions of this book are based on my beliefs since they are founded on my direct life experience, and they also are supported by interpretations and conclusions I have drawn from our best and most recent science. In my personal process, I avoid unsupported leaps of faith, even though there will undoubtedly be those readers who feel that most of this book constitutes just such a leap. Many, if not most, of my personal conclusions are ultimately unprovable from within our reference frame; these are still beliefs, as opposed to faith, because they are always rooted in a combination of science and personal experience.

The line between faith and belief can often become very confusing since these two are often intermixed. This happens naturally because a person's beliefs always inform their faith, and vice-versa. Both faith and belief can be centered within either our minds or our hearts. To facilitate deep and long-lasting personal change, our faith or belief needs to expand beyond our minds and be able to resonate deep within our hearts, at the very core of our *being*. For the heart to resonate fully and openly, it must be aligned with the mind and the entire rest of our *being*; divided, our heart and mind are each relatively powerless. Faith or belief that originates in the mind can eventually expand to include the heart as we evolve, but while they are still centered in mind alone, faith and belief remain three-dimensional and can't facilitate our connection with others or the deeper aspects of creation. It is the beliefs held in our heart and supported by our entire *being* that ultimately determine how and where we will engage within the *Multiverse*.

GNOSTIC CHRISTIANITY

The typical contemporary Christian description of God has not evolved at the same rate as our overall culture; it was envisioned, created and recorded by our ancestors, long before we emerged from our "flat earth" *viewport*. Described and codified while we were deeply immersed in an *anthropomorphic* and *geocentric* mindset, the early pre-Christian records depict God as masculine, judgmental, controlling, revengeful and punishing. He is the God that gave us a favorite son only to let him be crucified because of "our" sins. Two thousand years later much of this vision of God still

172

persists. In those two thousand years many wars were initiated to supposedly eliminate, punish or save those who believed in slightly different versions of this God. Five hundred years ago this Christian God instructed the leaders of the church to torture, punish or execute scientists who spoke of a new theory that placed the Sun, instead of the Earth, in the physical center of our solar system. From within our 3D worldview, this vision of God makes no sense. From the perspective of the expansive *Multiverse*, this vision of God actually makes "sense" because it describes one more possible way for humans to express themselves in this universe of infinite possibilities.

There are, however, both ancient and modern Christian communities that still have a very different interpretation of God, his message and the meaning of Christ. Called *Gnostic Christianity*, this tradition predates even the formal church. The most important *gnostic* idea, the desire for a more direct and personal experiential spirituality, predates even Christ.

From its Greek and Latin roots, the word *gnostic* means knowing or knowledgeable. Ancient *gnostic* traditions often included a doctrine of esoteric knowledge and practices, but the direct and personal spiritual experience has always been the common and critical identifier of *Gnostic Christianity*. Because of this directness of experience, *Gnostic Christianity* is a living tradition. **The most recent Gnostic Christian authors completely focus on their direct and personal religious experience. They see the Christ as the one who directly teaches us. These direct teachings often include common ideas such as, we all equally belong to the oneness of creation, we are not our bodies, we exist eternally, and we are infinitely greater than we could ever imagine!** This is also a tradition that seems to naturally understand our place in the *Multiverse*.

QUANTUM JESUS

Even though I was raised and confirmed as a Methodist, as a young child I was never very convinced by the Christ that was portrayed in the texts and lessons of my Christian education. His message and temperament often seemed inconsistent. His words, at least those that were taken from the King James Bible, often did not resonate within the younger version of me. The words never seemed to be part of a wisdom originating from a unified or deeper place; this path simply did not ring true to my mind or heart

Many years later I started to learn about this different version of Christ, the *Gnostic* Christ who is quoted and described in the scrolls that were found at Nag Hammadi. This vision of Christ taught a way of living, sharing and *being* that was refreshing, and distinctly different from the version of Christ that I learned about in Sunday school. For the first time I began to feel a meaningful connection to Christ.

The Nag Hammadi texts were recorded on papyrus during a vague period of time that has been identified as 40-200 years after Christ's death. Subsequently hidden in an urn for protection, they were finally discovered in 1945 along the upper Nile of Egypt. The works were initially scattered by profiteers, but after many years of difficult tracking and focused acquisition, they have been reassembled into a nearly intact collection. Scholars have recently been granted expanded access and are busy working to make the translations more complete and universally available.

Written in the ancient Coptic language, these texts contain some of the earliest recorded recollections of Christ's teachings that have ever been found. The "Gospel of Thomas" is a text that parallels the four biblical gospels (Matthew through John), but it describes and brings to life a very different and much more mystical Jesus. Just as with the four gospels that were included in the Bible, these passages from Thomas were not recorded directly by the hands of a firsthand witness.

They do, however, include passages that were scribed at an earlier date than the four gospels of the Bible. Not only was the Bible written at a later date, but its passages were also reedited and rewritten many times to suit changing political, organizational and social needs through the generations. The Bible that we read today has been shaped over time by many different agenda-driven forces.

On the other hand, these early *Gnostic* texts were not subject to the same political and social forces, and hidden for so long, they escaped later editing. In them, a very different picture of Jesus emerges; he consistently reminds others, *"Everything I do and know, you also can do and know."* He explains to his audience that he is no different from any of them, and that everyone has the ability within to experience and interact with life just as he does. He speaks about serving God by directly serving other people. He also teaches that no one else can function as an intermediary to God, because the true religious experience is always very direct and personal.

In the Book of Thomas Jesus speaks like a guru, a shaman, or a man that understands how to navigate in a world where anything is possible because everything possible already exists. He is a prophet who long ago painted a unified picture of how to live freely in a quantum Multiverse.

Here are some quotes from the Coptic Book of Thomas:

"Whoever discovers the interpretation of these sayings will not taste death."

"Those who seek should not stop seeking until they find. When they find, they will be disturbed. When they are disturbed, they will marvel, and will rule over all."

"If your leaders say to you, 'Look, the (Father's) imperial rule is in the sky,' then the birds of the sky will precede you. If they say to you, 'It is in the sea,' then the fish will precede you. Rather, the (Father's) imperial rule is inside you and outside you. When you know yourselves, then you will be known, and you will understand that you are children of the living Father. But if you do not know yourselves, then you live in poverty, and you are the poverty."

"Have you found the beginning, then, that you are looking for the end? You see, the end will be where the beginning is. Congratulations to the one who stands at the beginning: that one will know the end and will not taste death."

"Be passersby."

"If two make peace with each other in a single house, they will say to the mountain, 'Move from here!' and it will move."

"If they say to you, 'Where have you come from?' say to them, 'We have come from the light, from the place where the light came into being by itself, established [itself], and appeared in their image.' If they say to you, 'Is it you?' say, 'We are its children, and we are the chosen of the living Father.' If they ask you, 'What is the evidence of your Father in you?' say to them, 'It is motion and rest.'"

His disciples said to him, "When will the rest for the dead take place, and when will the new world come?" He said to them, "What you are looking forward to has come, but you don't know it."

His disciples said to him, "Is circumcision useful or not?" He said to them, "If it were useful, their father would produce children already circumcised from their mother. Rather, the true circumcision in spirit has become profitable in every respect."

Jesus said, "Look to the living one as long as you live, otherwise you might die and then try to see the living one, and you will be unable to see."

"For this reason I say, if one is (whole), one will be filled with light, but if one is divided, one will be filled with darkness."

"Whoever is near me is near the fire, and whoever is far from me is far from the (Father's) domain."

Jesus said, "Images are visible to people, but the light within them is hidden in the image of the Father's light. He will be disclosed, but his image is hidden by his light."

"You examine the face of heaven and earth, but you have not come to know the one who is in your presence, and you do not know how to examine the present moment."

"Whoever drinks from my mouth will become like me; I myself shall become that person, and the hidden things will be revealed to him."

"It will not come by watching for it. It will not be said, 'Look, here!' or 'Look, there!' Rather, the Father's kingdom is spread out upon the earth, and people don't see it."

These ancient texts sound more like *quantum physics* texts than a biblical text. This Christ understands that our *being* is so much greater than most of us realize. He understands how to live in multi-dimensional and timeless space.

CONTEMPORARY WESTERN CHRISTIAN GNOSTICISM

Gnosticism is a form of Christian spirituality that is based upon our direct and personal experience with creation or God. When I read contemporary works of *Gnostic* Christian literature, three things immediately strike me. First, the philosophy, message and attitude of the *gnostic* Christ, as expressed through these individual writers, are surprisingly consistent and relatively simple when compared to Christ's teachings from the Bible. Next, they include much of the feeling, tone, ideas and expression that are normally found in the more-Eastern spiritual philosophies. Often these contemporary *gnostic* writings seem almost mystical, and they portray a vision of Christ that is similar to the one of the Nag Hammadi texts. Lastly, they seem to be originating from an open mindset that could more easily recognize, accept and integrate a world built upon both *relativity* and *quantum physics*.

One of my favorite contemporary Christian writers is Paul Ferrini, who was originally led to his vision of a living Christ through the *Course in Miracles*. Much of his intuitive and, thus, revelatory writing makes Christ sound like a cross between Buddha and David Bohm (the physicist). What follows are examples of this wisdom, which he attributes to his direct communication with the living Christ:

"The only prisons of this world are the ones of your own making!"

"Ultimately, the end of human suffering comes when you decide that you have suffered enough, when each of you, in your own lives begins to ask for a better way," and "No one way is better than another."

"All healing happens thus: as illusions are surrendered, truth appears. As separation is relinquished, the original unity emerges unchanged."

"This world is a birthing place for the emotional and mental body. Physical birth and death simply facilitate the development of a thinking-feeling consciousness that is responsible for its own creations."

"You have only one person to forgive in your journey and that is yourself. You are the judge. You are the jury. And you are the prisoner."

"As soon as there is the slightest perception of inequality between you and another person, you must understand that you have left your heart. You have abandoned the Truth."

"All experience happens for one purpose only: to expand your awareness. Any other meaning you see in your life experience is a meaning you made up."

These writings are a poetic description of how to live in the *Multiverse* from within a Christian foundation. When viewed through an awareness that understands the structure of the *Multiverse,* they make perfect sense.

THE GEOMETRY OF THE DIVINE

"I am the Alpha and the Omega, and I am the Living One!"

The *"Web of Possibilities"* provides a structural foundation to explain the reasons for many of the mysteries within our lives. However, for me, the *"Web of Possibilities"* still does not explain the deep source of life–the nature of the actual "spark" that we recognize as life-force. This amazing "spark," is the thing that fills and animates our bodies and all other living things, and yet it has always been, and remains, completely unexplainable and mysterious.

Many times in our recent history, notable scientists and philosophers have punctuated major scientific breakthroughs by declaring that science is finally on the brink of explaining God. Stephen Hawking stated that he believes our new *cosmology* will soon be able to explain the major remaining mystery attributed to God: life-force. A number of well-known computer scientists have announced that God will be found somewhere along the trail while developing *Artificial Intelligence.* Historically, with each major scientific breakthrough, we add to our understanding about the materials and energies that make up the physical world and gain insights to realms that lie beyond, but we are still left without an understanding of the actual "force" that animates life. It has never been identified or located; yet it is absolutely clear that without it, there is no life. The Web is a great physical playground for this dance of life, but life itself remains the great mystery.

There have always been births along with deaths, storms and blue-sky days, miraculous healing and sickness, good and bad fortune; and all of these have been attributed to the hand of God. God has been assigned responsibility for many of the natural processes and connections that were once too difficult for us to understand. All of these processes and connections ultimately originate beyond the veil of our 3D universe, and much of this mystery can now be explained through better understanding the hidden architecture of the *Multiverse*. For example, the idea that God is omnipresent seems quite impossible from a three-dimensional conceptual mindset. By understanding the intimate interconnectedness of all parts of the *Multiverse through enfoldment, parallel universes, holographic information storage* and *timelessness,* we can understand the physics of how "God" could operate everywhere at once. Also, there is no form of consciousness that needs to pay attention, remember all the details and process all the *information,* in a deity-like manner, because the *Multiverse* does this itself. This capacity for "awareness" is built right into its structure. No part or individual could ever be separate within the *Multiverse* because *holographic enfoldment* is the very core of its structure, making the *Multiverse* self-policing and completely interactive. Since everything in the *Multiverse* is connected to everything else, there are never unexpected surprises, just infinite natural connections allowing cause-and-effect to be generated at levels far beyond any imaginations of our three-dimensional understanding. The *Multiverse* behaves like a single giant brain–God's brain.

GOD AND THE PHYSICIST

Einstein famously described why God remains such a mysterious idea from the point of view of the Physicist.

> "I see a clock, but I cannot envision the clockmaker. The human mind is unable to conceive of the four dimensions, so how can it conceive of a God, before whom a thousand years and a thousand dimensions are as one?"

From Cosmic Religion and Other Opinions and Aphorisms (1931), Albert Einstein, pub. Covici-Friede. Quoted from *The Expanded Quotable Einstein*, Princeton University Press; second edition (May 30, 2000); Page 208.

It is absolutely clear that, as three-dimensional specialists, we are not designed to be able to conceive beyond our spatial limits. If there is some external entity, possibly called God, that created the Multiverse, then any idea or description of this God will still be based, formed and described from our limited perspective. At best, we can only describe the visible, projected shadows of this God as they reach us from their origination in a space that lies far beyond our conceptual horizon.

SIN

"Sin" has a very different meaning at the level of the *Multiverse*. Sin is universally defined as a violation of divine law. It is often described as an act that harms others, but in the Multiverse there are no others. At this deeper level, "sin" is ultimately an act that affects only oneself, and it can be understood as the natural result of not trusting or following our deeper truth. It is simply an act or thought that is not aligned with our own greater self-interest, which then generates a series of direct cause-and-effect responses from the *Multiverse*. Everything that we label as "sin" is nothing more than an unconscious or inefficient expenditure of *energy* when viewed from a deeper and timeless perspective. Even the most heinous acts against "others" and our selves can be understood as only the misdirection of *energy* or unnecessary and inefficient wrong turns, when witnessed from the perspective of the deeper levels of *being*. "Sins" are not really even "wrong" turns because ultimately, every turn that is possible must be explored and experienced for *Being* to become fully compassionate. It is the nature of life to fill every void and explore every crack and opening and, allowing *being* to do this, freely and without any personal judgment, is an important part of our very purpose. We might become lost in our exploration of our separation for a moment of "time," but even that adds to our breadth of experience. Since everything is intimately connected, it is also completely self-correcting. Any natural system will always return to equilibrium over "time." There are no mistakes or wrong turns in creation.

We usually "sin" because our resonant state is one that is fearful and not fully trusting or understanding of the flow of *being*. When we "sin," on some level, we have forgotten that any act seemingly against others is ultimately only an act against ourselves, because we are all interconnected. The sinner usually does not yet realize that, at our deepest level, we are all only a single *Being* and there are no "others" to even "sin" against. There is only "I" and "I" appearing repeatedly in different forms. Understanding this is the foundation of understanding the deepest level of Love: "One Love." One reason that we universally feel guilt, shame and pain in association with our "sins" is because, at some level, we intuitively understand that we have, ultimately, only created more suffering and difficulty for our own *Being*.

What happens next is a much bigger issue for us. We naturally try to mitigate the intensity of any pain arising from this self-effacing choice called "sin" by subconsciously restricting our energy flow or *life-force*. This pain, or any emotional pain, is largely the product of inner tension and resistance to the natural flow of *life-force*. The body, once shut down in this way, actually does experience less pain, but there is an enormous price that we must pay for this reduction in feeling. The body is now less sensitive and less receptive, throughout, which means it will not feel as much of anything. Only one small part of our ability to feel involves pain, so in our subconscious attempt to protect ourselves, all forms of feeling become more restricted. Unfortunately, but very naturally, this restricted system also becomes less vibrant and less capable of feeling joy. In the bigger picture, this represents extremely self-defeating behavior, so it makes no sense. However, because of our unconscious reflexive reactions to fear and pain, this still remains our most common response.

The most direct way to rekindle and reopen the flow of joy is to learn how to let go of our tension. The first step, in this process of healing, is knowing, and then embracing, the real source of our tension. The ultimate source of all tension is the fear generated through our cultural sense of separation–the fear of existing and dying alone and isolated. The cure begins with a deepening of the recognition that we are always fully connected with everything in creation. This means the path to wholeness, and ultimately freedom, involves dropping all the judgment that separates us and, simultaneously, embracing everything within, both the sin and sinner. All aspects of all "others" and ourselves need to be understood and seen as valuable, good, important and equal parts of creation. ***Our personal development of this nonjudgmental embrace of all life is often the most difficult step in the entire process of becoming free.***

SPIRITUAL LEADERS AND THE GROUP EXPERIENCE

We all occasionally desire some type of outside guidance to help us through our most difficult times. We might seek new information, or some person who can help us find a path that better meets our needs, or at least a path that is relatively free from the suffering and pain we have been experiencing. From time to time, charismatic individuals appear and offer a practice, theory or a way of living, which, in the moment, holds some promise for easing our particular individual concerns. With a strong charismatic leader and a focused message that resonates for a particular time or situation, devoted followers can form a community. This community can then reinforce and empower the message by providing a structure of physical and emotional support and comfort. Many powerful and self-reinforcing, resonant communities have been built this way.

Often, the devotees of these groups are encouraged to focus most of their energy and attention upon their leader. This type of absolute devotion–called Bhakti yoga in the Hindu tradition–is a very powerful method for evoking change through the process of ego surrender. As in any devoted relationship, over time, the devotees begin to *resonate sympathetically* with their leader or guru. With an entire group's attention focused upon a single common focus, a powerful and *coherent group resonance* can be shaped and formed. Whether it is created at a rock concert, political rally, sporting event, workshop, or within a cult, this type of group experience is real, powerful and very tangible. The power of Hitler's filmed political rallies is still fully palpable today, even though the films are only available in grainy black and white with poor sound quality. Numerous books have been written about this "group-think" phenomenon.

Most of us enjoy group experiences because of the tangible feeling of increased empowerment. Something very exciting happens when "many act as one" and because of this, political leaders and other powerful interests have always attempted to harness and harvest this potential *force*. Governments and large, fiscally motivated corporations have historically exploited this human need to connect to facilitate the manipulation of large masses of people and to propel their own agendas. A quick study of world history reveals that organized religion has often been used as a tool to consolidate and manipulate large masses of individuals for other political purposes. In addition, the powerful agents of fear and nationalism have been incorporated into this mix to further amplify it. Fear, religion and nationalism are often tightly packaged together to motivate and direct otherwise peace-loving individuals towards war.

This entire process involves the use of deeper levels of *resonance* to manipulate large masses of people. This type of mass manipulation would not even be possible if we were all conscious of this phenomenon.

Cults

The group experience can sometimes be tremendously powerful and transformational for the individuals involved; non-abusive, healthy groups and workshops certainly can help us develop a deeper awareness and a more-enduring understanding of personal freedom. Many groups have excellent records assisting individuals through a drug or emotional-recovery process. The support from others, who have shared a similar experience, allows us to more easily release and move beyond personal fears and habits. Loving others, whether it is a guru, lover, family member or friend, helps us to step outside of our natural, egocentric focus. With more interconnection and fewer feelings of separation, we naturally feel more joy and ecstasy.

Within cults, devotees might assume this new-felt joy and ecstasy is due to the power of the leader. Ecstasy appears because, by focusing our attention on "others," our egos experience less isolation and separation. We then *resonate* more freely with others in the deeper levels of *being*. This is the simple secret behind the power of "group experience."

It is entirely possible for groups with a unified or connected mindset to navigate the "Web of Possibilities" as a single, unified group, if this group develops a *coherent resonance*. (*Coherence* was defined and discussed in the physics section about *vibration*.) However, in our world of complex and divergent impulses, it is unlikely that such a group could stay in that *coherent vibrational state* for an extended period of time because this *coherent* form always requires individuals to let go of their own personal, desires for the sake of the group *resonance*. Successful group leaders and gurus often have a particular talent or technique for transforming individual impulses into this more *coherent* group *vibrational energy*. Often they will create this *coherence* by demanding that devotees direct their worship and attention directly upon the guru. As mentioned, in the Hindu faith this type of devotion, the worship of another, is called *Bhakti* worship, and often it is considered to be the best path towards illumination or enlightenment.

It is always easier to assemble and maintain a *coherent resonance* in these guru-focused, group environments. The *coherence* itself invites more participation because when our *being resonates* with the *harmonics* of a larger group, we naturally feel a deeper level of comfort, interconnection and empowerment. When this type of connection is available through the group experience, normal feelings of separation and loneliness are often forgotten.

At some point in their surrender process, individuals may experience a general release of tension, resulting in an increased feeling of ecstasy. The person having this release might then associate this feeling of ecstasy directly with the physical form of the guru or leader. By making this association, they have missed the critical connection between their new-felt ecstasy and the specific act of surrendering their ego. They have missed the deeper, hidden truth that upon their surrender to the natural flow of life, ecstasy will follow, even without the guru.

We all have the innate ability to experience this ecstasy through conscious ego-surrender without the involvement of a guru or group. This ability usually requires a level of self-trust gained from a lifetime of conscious personal work and self-examination. At this level of experience, the joy and ecstasy are fully sustainable because there is no dependence on another's behavior or form. Of course, along with this joy and ecstasy will come expanded forms of all the other human feelings and emotions and the fresh opportunity to understand all of these in a new and different way.

These groups are inherently not very flexible or durable because they are usually based on a particular physical form–that of the guru. The *resonance* of the system will often fall apart when the group structure shifts or erodes as a result of a change, especially a change within the leadership. Usually when the charismatic leader dies, or leaves the group, an essential part of the *feedback* process is permanently lost or broken. The group, which has been critically dependent on the physical presence of their leader, rarely survives this type of transition intact. The parts that do survive often only mimic and distort the original message–they continue to exist in name only. The current form of many modern religious organizations is the direct result of this type of de-evolution.

When this shift happens, it can be very difficult for the newly- and suddenly-dissociated individuals to find the path to their joy on their own. Trained to be dependent on their leader, they have mostly forgotten their own innate and direct connection to the real source of their ecstasy. They may have completely forgotten that they are not separate individuals but, instead, always a part of the greater *Being* itself.

Ironically, it is often when their guru becomes emotionally or intellectually compromised that adherents have the most difficulty in freeing themselves. The followers of Charles Manson and Jim Jones were led into behaviors that few of them would have believed in, or supported, on their own.

RELIGIOUS GROUP EXPERIENCE

The core principles of most world religions point towards a similar and deeper connective truth. Unfortunately, over time, much of this beauty has been lost or buried under the weight of the power structure, business practices, and politics of these various religious organizations. Many of the established, formal religions use a hierarchical structure that intentionally separates the individual from the directness of the spiritual or religious experience. These established organizations all rely on a designated individual–a priest, preacher, Imam or similar, highly trained individual–to interpret the religious experience for the common practitioner. By relying on this surrogate, the devotee practitioner becomes habitually disempowered, forgetting their direct connection to the deeper source. They can no longer experience the full richness or understand the deeper meaning of the original religious message. By design, many religions require individual adherents to surrender their access to this more direct and authentic experience.

I recently noticed this phenomenon in a memorial service. While the preacher was leading the service, the words and meaning were very impersonal and the guests were fidgeting, and not very emotionally involved. Because of the indirect nature of the experience, none of us felt the beautiful presence of person whose life we were honoring. A small portion of the service was scheduled, near the end of the service, to allow for family and friends to describe their personal experiences and feelings. This part quickly and naturally expanded into the only memorable portion of the service as tears were shed, stories recounted, laughs were shared, and songs were sung. The person we were honoring suddenly came to life in all our hearts. It was a beautiful moment because, for all of us, it allowed a direct and personal connection to the spirit of the person whose life we were celebrating.

HEAVEN AND HELL

As we live our lives, we naturally move all about the Web according to the meandering path being charted by our ever changing, individual, *resonant vibrational signature.* We might experience what is being encountered, at any moment, as pleasant, but at other times it may appear as a particularly difficult or challenging moment. However, no matter what experience we are having, it is always possible to instantly make the leap to an entirely new type of interaction. The nature of multi-dimensional space and *enfoldment* allows for all possible places and experiences always to be directly adjacent and, therefore, fully accessible in every moment.

While dramatic shifts are always possible, we typically make smaller and more gradual shifts while still embodied in our 3D form; our cultural concepts and ideas establish a semi-rigid structure that effectively acts like an anchor, limiting the maximum degree of movement or change that is probable at any one moment. The human form generally responds better to these more gradual shifts that usually include, as part of the natural process, periods for readjustment and acclimation. As a result, our typical shifts within the Web tend to be much more gradual and subtle. We usually will make our greatest shifts during times of trauma or deep personal work.

We quite naturally make a particularly large and unique shift at the time of our physical death, when the conceptual anchors of the body cease to be a factor. At the moment of death, our natural state of *vibrational resonance* is completely liberated from physical, conceptual, cultural and emotional restraints. We are, in that moment, completely free to *resonate* with whatever part of the Web matches our natural *vibrations.* Freed from the conceptual constraints of our old *viewport,* our individual *being* will then migrate automatically to those areas of the Web where it is, at that moment, most naturally *resonant.* Dramatic shifts are the norm because, at this special time, our souls are completely unrestrained. They are then suddenly free of all the excess weight and damping from the cultural and conceptual baggage that we often carry in our physical form. Once released from the body, our spirit spontaneously reemerges in that very part of the Web that is in complete *harmony* with our soul's core *vibration*–the deep-level *resonance* of the *self.*

This is the real mechanics of our "going to heaven or hell" after death. Our core vibration at our time of death naturally determines what our vibrational existence will look like in the "next" expression of our *being*. There are no rewards, judgments or scorecards–this is just a natural and organic process based upon *vibratory resonance*. This means that everything we do and pursue in our lives, and all the deep-level changes that result, all shape our *core-resonant-being* and therefore help determine the *vibratory* environment of any "future" expressions of life.

It is essential to remember that this concept is being described using our old 3D conceptual ideas. We fully understand that "time" does not unfold in such a linear fashion within the *Multiverse*. At deeper levels, all "lifetimes" exist simultaneously and they are all interwoven into, and inform, the ever-present "now" moment. This is being said with the full recognition that we all are evolving towards oneness, together, and through this process we are having all types of different experiences so that we can, together, become fully "experienced" and, therefore, compassionate.

There is no such thing in the *Multiverse* as a reward for "good" behavior, or punishment for "bad" behavior, because all manifestations and expressions are always only the direct result of cause and effect. Instead of rewards, there are simply additional opportunities to meet with something new and a chance to understand more about the different flavors of the human condition. With an open-mind, even the most challenging and difficult human experiences can be seen as expansive, beautiful and rewarding. Evolution is ultimately about becoming more–more open, more experienced, more aware, more compassionate and more integrated. We grow bigger and include more of everything, as we become more of who we really are. This also is the path to the deepest and most enduring experience of Love.

EASTERN PHILOSOPHY

Dualism

A common principle of many Eastern spiritual traditions is the recognition that the world we live within is *dualistic* in its nature. The oldest recorded documentation of *dualism* as a formal philosophy places its origination in Persia within Zoroastrianism–also called Mazdaism. Zoroastrianism is 3,500 years old and may be the oldest organized world religion on record. The foundational principles of the Jewish, Christian and Muslim faiths, including heaven and hell, Satan, God, the soul, virgin birth, final judgment and resurrection, are all directly derived from Zoroastrianism. According to the Zoroastrian story of creation, Ahuru Mazda existed in light within the goodness above, while Angra Mainyu existed in darkness and ignorance below. They have existed independently of each other for all time; thus *Dualism* in Zoroastrianism involves the existence, but complete separation, of both good and evil.

In this original expression of dualism, evil is not God's equal opposite; rather Angra Mainyu is the destructive energy that opposes God's creative energy. God created a pure world and Angra Mainyu continues to attack it, making it impure. Aging, sickness, famine, natural disasters, blights, death, etc., are all attributed to Angra Mainyu. In this original form of *dualism*, the evil portion lies outside of God's creation. It is seen as an outside element that opposes God instead of being an integrated part of God's creation.

With later and more mature forms of *dualism,* we see a more balanced dynamic between life and death, day and night, good and evil. One aspect cannot be understood without the other because physical life will always be a mixture and balance of these opposing forces. Our world is constructed from these opposing forces: both the light and the dark are necessary for us to experience all the different possible degrees of illumination; coexistence of good and evil allow us to understand and experience the full range of human behavior; something is hot only because we can compare it to cold. Evil, cold, and dark are not simply elements assaulting our world from the outside; they are all equal and necessary components that help build and maintain the structure of creation. Our very existence is entirely dependent on this *dualistic* nature of all the things that form our physical world. *Dualism* is the critical component that allows our brains to function. For our brains to process information, we require contrast: all things must be measured relative to other things. *Dualism* completely forms the structural foundation that our 3D existence is built upon. *Contrast* makes our lives possible.

What is sometimes called *non-dualistic* awareness generally involves being able to see, feel or understand in very different ways. This is a process that exists only beyond conceptual thought and three-dimensional form. In *non-dualistic* awareness there is no thought, no logic, no comparisons, no rational arguments and no convincing. To even consider it as "thought" associates it too directly with our normal, three-dimensional mindset. *Non-dualistic* awareness can be described as "a way of being and feeling that is free of any thought." Even though there are many spiritual paths that are based on teaching or practicing *non-dual* awareness, this *non-dualistic* way of being has been completely marginalized within our Western culture.

Within some of the more-radical *non-dualistic* religious and spiritual practices we might witness the tendency of adherents to see *dualistic* thinking as a problematic, and a lesser, form of thinking. Within these practices, *dualistic* thinking can be subtly demonized and presented as something for practitioners to completely avoid. Some that practice these forms are led to believe that only pure *non-dualistic* thinking can lead to *enlightenment*.

This view is steeped in a self-reflective irony because this very concept itself involves strong judgments that actually create more separation. If we see *duality* as the problem or "the enemy," we are being critical of our very existence and the important three-dimensional aspects of our *being*. This is the spiritual equivalent of a scientist cursing *gravity*. There are days when we all wish *gravity* were not so relentless but without it, our physical lives simply would not work. *Duality* is what forms and contains the structure of this physical creation–our wonderful human playground. If someone is devoted to exploring a philosophy of *non-dualism,* it makes no sense to judge *dualism* as problematic. Any type of judgment represents a very *dualistic* way of looking at our existence. Since our 3D conceptual thinking is necessarily built upon *dualism,* to label it as problematic, or even something to avoid, is to assign that same level of judgment to the entire human existence.

While awareness of and sensitivity to *non-dualism* are very helpful for any journey towards freedom, any movement beyond *dualism* must first embrace every aspect of *dualism* as a critical and revered part of creation. Every stitch in the knitted sweater depends on every other stitch. ***Enlightenment is expansive, rather than exclusive, in its nature, so duality must be understood as a necessary component part of any perfect expression of creation!***

A model and a further discussion of this physical structure, along with the interplay of *dual* and *non-dual* aspects, can be found in later sections, titled "Dualism beyond three-dimensions" and "Taffy, Duality and Creation." Below is the beautiful and well-known Taoist symbol that functions as the graphic model to clearly express the dynamic, yet always balancing, *forces* of *duality*.

The Taoist Yin-Yang symbol expressing the dynamic balancing of opposites that make up duality.

Maya and Lila

Maya is the ancient Hindu (Sanskrit language) word describing our illusionary existence. Within the Hindu faith, our *dualistic* physical world is seen as an illusion, therefore we never encounter the real environment: everything that we perceive is only an illusion. Our experience is always, then, just a *projection* created by our minds. The game of life that we lead in this Maya is referred to as the *Lila* or "play", therefore none of what happens in this life is interpreted as real. Instead, our lives are a game involving *duality*, within which we willingly participate.

This Hindu vision in its purest form is completely consistent with the physics and many of the resultant ideas within this book. Of course, as in any organized religion that has evolved over time, the human mind has transformed this pure idea into many doctrines, rituals and practices that fit and support its various and changing special interests. Through this process, many important foundational principles and beliefs get lost and tangled amongst many layers of added religious trappings. However, just as within Christianity, there also exists a deep, esoteric, core philosophy that is fully aligned with the structure of the *Multiverse*. Again, at the deepest levels, all ideas merge.

Referring to the physical world as an illusion is not to say that it does not exist. What is really being said is, "It does not exist in the solid, material and fixed manner of our direct experience." This illusion is formed by the mind using the *information* that is received through the *Multiverse*. We directly perceive only the shadow of this deeper-level of information. This shadow appears as the familiar form of our world. Creation begins in the deeper layers of the *Multiverse*, which are still invisible to us at this stage of our evolution. **We all have the clear and accurate perception that our physical world exists. The great illusion is that we interpret this, our own perception, as the only reality.**

Attachments

Within many Eastern spiritual traditions, our personal *attachment* to aspects of our illusionary, *dualistic* world is seen as the source of all of mankind's suffering. We become *attached* to the illusion of our bodies, our friends' bodies, our ideas, our toys and our creations, because we have learned to think that all these things are very real, extremely solid, and critically important to our lives. In the West we certainly become very attached to our possessions, and sometimes we might even believe that our lives could depend on our things. In my architectural practice I have heard people directly state a belief such as they "couldn't possibly live without a five-bedroom house or travertine floors." Our possessions can be closely associated with our sense of well-being and used as an "asset" to help us define who we are. They can become the measurement of our own sense of self-worth. We might own the fastest car, biggest boat and largest house in the most expensive neighborhood and feel "successful" for a brief moment. We would probably also experience more stress as we worry about maintaining our new level of "self-worth." If we happen to have a financial reversal and lose some of our prized possessions, we might then feel then that we are a "failure" and become very unhappy. We might also worry that others will also judge us as "unsuccessful," even if we have discovered that we are actually enjoying our newly pared-down lives.

The issue is never our possessions themselves–they are neutral things–but rather, it is our individual and cultural perception that we need them–that they are important. The issue is our *identification* with these things. If analyzed, we can clearly understand that this "need" for a big house or fast car is not a survival issue; it is easy to see that these things are not critically important for us to lead healthy and productive lives. *Attachment* to friends, family and loved ones is a much more difficult issue to examine honestly and then reconcile. We are completely immersed in our belief that we are these bodies of ours, just as our loved ones are their bodies. *From our cultural viewport, we usually understand ourselves primarily as our bodies, which are separate, isolated and short-lived. This naturally leads to constant worry and a clinging onto our present forms. It is, therefore, nearly impossible for us to understand that this illusionary, three-dimensional concept–the deep-seated belief that "we are our bodies"–is the critical misunderstanding that prevents us from experiencing the full potential and possibilities of life.*

For the vast majority of people from Western cultures, our *attachment* to our body is nearly absolute. While this belief is likely to persist in all cultures, many Eastern traditions teach a different mindset. They teach that anything that can die, decay, break or get lost is understood to be *impermanent* and, as such, is considered "not real." Our bodies clearly fall into this category. In contrast, the things that are considered "real" are those things that never die and never can be lost, such as our timeless soul and *Being* itself.

It is our attachments to things, people, ideas, concepts, thoughts and emotions that form areas of resistance within our bodies, blocking the smooth flow of energy and information. These *attachments* often lead quite directly to associated worry, depression and anxiety. We worry that we might not earn enough income to make the big house or car payment. We worry about what the neighbors are saying about our Christmas decorations or our new landscaping. We have concerns about the popularity of our children and their future financial prospects. We worry about our bodies, our children's bodies and our friends' bodies. "Are they growing up fast enough, are we growing old too fast," what if we become ill?"

These habitual concerns all create physical and emotional tension that eventually result in energetic blocks. As these blockages manifest in our bodies, they can first express themselves as the knots, kinks, muscle spasms and weakness that can interfere with our motion, comfort, physical creative expression and emotional well-being. If these first symptoms are not addressed, the blockages will continue to build, eventually resulting in crippling physical and emotional pain and, possibly, sickness. Once fully expressed at this physical level, these individual surface manifestations of buried tension are assigned official-sounding medical descriptions like carpal tunnel syndrome, sciatica, arthritis, diabetes, heart arrhythmia, anxiety attacks and ulcers. Our *being* does not want pills or other forms of temporary relief because it is really shouting for the tension to be addressed at its source. Disease is only nature's way of signaling, *"please pay attention."*

185

On the individual level, our unexamined *attachment* to our "things" is eventually expressed as some form of physical disease, injury or deep emotional "suffering." On a larger, societal scale these *attachments* can and will lead to the struggles and conflicts between different cultures that eventually manifest as war.

Being naturally balancing and self-corrective in its nature, life always creates experiences that will reinforce and deepen our awareness of these unhealthy patterns. The natural world is very helpful in this way, whether or not we appreciate this quality in the short term. The process is never personal because it is simply the result of a fully interconnected and interactive system restoring its balance. Through this natural balancing process, the unfolding of life always highlights our areas of darkness, since we are also presented with new opportunities to expand and grow our enlightenment. Healing is a natural and organic process. If we are fully open to whatever is being presented to us in these moments, our healings will always unfold in the most unexpected but quite wonderful and miraculous ways.

Attachments Damp our Vibrancy

While our *attachments* to something, someone, some time, or some way are a natural part of human life, they are also the ultimate reason that we have difficulty experiencing the full "flow" of our life-force. When we are attached to things or concepts, our core *resonant vibration* responds to the weight of this *damping* resistance by *vibrating* with less *amplitude* (power) and fewer *harmonics* or *overtones* (expression and expansiveness).

In classical physics, *damping* is the term used to describe the effect of a weight, or force that reduces the amplitude of a *vibrating* object. Imagine hooking a bungee cord between two columns on a porch and then snapping it like a big guitar string. While it is vibrating throw a towel over it and watch what happens. This is *damping*. *Damping* the vibration is usually a good thing in bridges and tall buildings because it helps keep them from moving.

With our energetic bodies there are certainly times when a controlled amount of vibrational *damping* may help provide necessary balance and resting points in our lives. However if allowed to *resonate un-damped*, the *vibration* of life can and will swell into something which is infinitely much greater. This unrestricted flow of natural energy will be felt as waves of unbridled ecstasy.

Our *attachments damp* (restrict) our experience and prevent us from being moved by the freedom and ecstasy that is possible and always available. Freedom does not require that we avoid or eliminate actual things or ideas to which we have become *attached*; we just need to better understand how *attachment* works, and how it weighs us down. The actual person, idea, thing or object of our *attachment* is never the problem, but rather it is our relationship to or concept about this attachment that alters our vibratory potential.

These objects, people and ideas to which we become *attached* are often the most beautiful and sparkling gemstones of our lives. These include our children, our homes and prized possessions, our accomplishments and our lifestyles. Freedom does not require that we distance ourselves from these. It does not require a simple or ascetic lifestyle (even though there are many wonderful insights to be gained by living with such simplification). Instead, freedom requires that we reach the point at which we are no longer *identified* with these things. When we are not identifying with these, we can enjoy, care for and love them, but not have our joy or love become dependent upon them. Freedom is built upon a psychological state in which our peace, happiness, joy and love are not a direct function of or dependent upon the very things and people that we enjoy so much. *We can learn to enjoy, appreciate and be grateful for these things and loved ones but, at the same time, understand that these are not who we are. We can learn to exist in a state where we are not identifying with or dependent upon the very outside things and people that we can also enjoy so much.* This may seem subtle, but clearly understanding this type of *detached* appreciation is a critical step along any road to true freedom.

In my architectural practice, when I present my early conceptual ideas to a client, there is a major and a very real risk that the client will get *attached* to some aspect of one of the designs. If that occurs, the project will then cease to evolve freely. It becomes bound by an energetic, but very real expectation, and this expectation constrains the free flow of ideas. The creative process becomes *damped*. Having learned that this can happen quite easily, I now rarely present my ideas until they are fully developed.

Witnessing and understanding the source and the eventual results of our *attachments* is a critical step towards the realization of real freedom within our lifetime. *From a Western perspective, attachment could be defined as holding fast to the temporary forms of this life–including our memory of the past and hopes for the future–in such a way that we interfere with our creative present moment and our natural flow through life.*

Healing the Tension from our Attachments

In our Western medical model we traditionally treat these blockages only at the superficial level of the physical symptoms. We often rely upon pain relievers and mood-altering drugs, either as prescriptions or self-medications. We resort to surgery to deaden nerves, relieve pain, loosen muscles and realign joints. All of these are conditions that have been created by a body that has shifted out of its natural balance and harmony. This approach can only work in a limited way and for a short time, at best, since these superficial responses only temporarily mask the deeper imbalance. Medications can also interfere with important natural biological processes and have serious, compounding side effects. Surgery can create scar tissue that will lead to new physical blockages and problems. The only permanent solution is to address the psychological or emotional issues at their source. As improbable as it seems from our Western mindset, the source of chronic medical conditions or disease can usually be reduced to basic and fundamental imbalances in our lifestyles, often involving our *attachments*.

Psychiatry and psychology have various tools that address this tension and emotional suffering, but unfortunately the most recent and popular trend has been for the doctors to immediately prescribe psychoactive drugs. For severe and chronic cases this approach provides a very effective short-term tool for intervention; but for the long-term, the use of these drugs results in many undesired, and often dire, side effects. Once the life-threatening emergency has passed, psychological help and counseling can provide a very valuable tool for the healing process, but this eventually needs to be integrated with techniques that address the entire body and greater *being*. Our bodies record and store a complete record of our emotional and psychological journey. Within our bodies are hidden keys for identifying and releasing the habitual tension which occasionally and systematically impedes our flow. These are minor blockages and they happily signal their presence with small aches and pains that are asking for further attention. Only much later, if ignored or left untreated, do these first warnings evolve into the diseases and debilitating conditions which can require much more extensive treatment.

One of the most effective methods that I know for addressing the deep-level source of our tension involves the integration of several forms of bodywork. Initially we might use bodywork as a short-term and temporary pain reliever to buy the time needed to address the source issue more deeply. The right kind of bodywork from a well-trained and skilled therapist can provide both relief and additional insights into the deeper *attachment* issues that originally created the tension. In this way, we can begin to learn about the deeper causes of our tension at the same time we receive short-term relief.

Along with insightful bodywork, we also would include physical therapy along with alternative body centered techniques like ecstatic dance or yoga. To improve the effectiveness of psychological counseling we can add numerous new forms of deep integrated psychological therapies. All of these techniques work together, synergistically, to help us unlock and free our bodies and, through this process, discover our more expansive selves. Our primary goal is always to enhance the free movement of *energy* and *information* (flow) thus enabling the body to work to its maximum potential. If we are each prepared and open for this growth and use these tools effectively, we can begin to identify, and then better understand, our *attachments* to things within the *illusion*. Later in the healing section of this book there is a more in-depth discussion about some of these methods.

Healthy "De-attachment"

Healthy *"de-attachment"* is an extremely difficult idea for the culturally trained, Western mind to understand and embrace. In our culture, we typically interpret the concept of detachment as "dropping out" or "shutting down" through desensitizing ourselves with drugs or busy activity. This process ironically, but inevitably, moves us even further away from the inner bliss that we all desire. Most of us have personally experienced this type of detachment and we have also been close witnesses to this type of behavior pattern in "others." Everyone understands that this type of "detachment" is never healthy in the long-term, even though it often involves culturally approved methods, such as prescribed anxiety medications, alcohol use, excessive exercise and work addiction. This is a form of "detachment," from life itself. It leads to a general desensitization and it is, therefore, very different from spiritual *de-attachment*. When those of us raised in the West are first introduced to the Eastern idea of *attachment,* we tend to reflexively prejudice this new concept with our old cultural understanding of "detachment." Thinking that we already understand the problems associated with "detachment," we tend to prejudge *de-attachment* as a destructive and antisocial practice.

In the healthy spiritual form, the goal is to de-attach not from life, sensitivity and experience, but rather from the relentless grip of the ego and the drama it continuously creates. We do this by learning how to not identify with the things that appear in this, our illusionary expression of life, including our bodies and our egos. To understand and benefit from this healthy form of de-attachment we must first develop the deep "knowing" that we are not these bodies. We must also understand deep inside that we are not what we do, own or create in this life.

According to Eckhart Tolle in his book *The Power of Now*, "When our consciousness frees itself from its identification with physical and mental forms, it becomes what some call pure or enlightened consciousness or simply "presence."

We can't just instantly decide to become *de-attached.* This way of being evolves over time, as a natural byproduct of a deep personal search that is focused upon understanding who and what we really are. The healthy individuals who are no longer *attached* still live their lives fully in this world. Actually, they are living their lives more fully because they are feeling more and experiencing a much deeper and direct interconnection. They do not become deeply disturbed when things do not go as they desired, and they understand that there is balance in all things. On the other hand this healthily *de-attached* individual does not become excessively giddy simply because things appear to be going well. They still make plans but remain flexible, knowing that any plans will always evolve and change in each moment. They also understand what the American mythologist Joseph Campbell was expressing when he said: *"If the path before you is clear, you're probably on someone else's."*

Healthy *de-attachment* results in an even-tempered presence, a sense of being the "passer-by," even while fully participating in life. There is a tremendous expansion of joy from being able to fully participate in more of life, enjoying all of its flavors fully and equally. It is as if the *de-attached* can now recognize that their involvement is more like watching a good movie or playing a video game involving one possible way that this movie called "life" can play itself out. Life itself becomes a very exciting, yet more impersonal, adventure. Along with this understanding of *attachment* and the mastery of *de-attachment,* we no longer seem to get repeatedly stuck in our own, self-manufactured quicksand. Instead, we flow more freely down the "river of life," always fully engaged through direct and intimate connection to the ever-evolving *present moment.*

Deeper awareness and understanding of our natural, and always quite normal, earthly desires is an important component of most spiritual paths. The teaching about the need to free oneself from all types of desire is found at the very core of Buddhism. Within Buddhism, our need to examine desire is clearly expressed within the four noble truths, which were Buddha's primary teaching. According to the Buddhist tradition, all suffering stems from our personal desires, and therefore letting go of desire itself is the most critical element to ending our personal suffering.

My own personal experience has been that desire, by itself, does not directly lead to suffering; and our desire, by itself, is not the fundamental problem. Instead, desire that is treated consciously provides an exciting human dynamic that engages and helps us to focus our energy. This means that, if properly channeled, desire can be a very useful, powerful and exciting tool that enhances the quality of our lives. If, however, through our desire we become *attached* to a specific outcome, object, or individual, then we will inevitably suffer from this *attachment*. At first glance it might appear that it is the desire that has created the suffering, but it is only the *attachment* to an end result that directly leads to the suffering. To avoid desire simply because it can lead to *attachment* is equivalent to avoiding automobiles because they can lead to wrecks. It is bad driving, not the car itself, that causes most automobile accidents. Similarly it is not the desire, but our *attachment* to a specific outcome that leads to our suffering.

Often our desires will influence our ego, which is always wanting to be "in control" of any outcome. Again the deep-level issue is not desire itself. Our need to control is just our common ego-based reflex that will occur whenever there is already some level of *attachment* to an outcome. Our *attachment* to some specific outcome is what causes us to want to control the circumstances instead of allowing a natural flow. No matter how wonderful and lofty the personal goal may seem, our *attachment* to any result will inevitably lead to deep suffering.

We learn deeply over time and through experience. Since nature balances everything, eventually the suffering itself will ultimately guide the sufferer towards deeper insights into the nature of desire, control and ego. We will eventually understand that it is *attachments*, and not desires, that forms the ropes and chains that keep us bound to our unhappy or unhealthy situations and expressions of life. Once we learn to dance with the flow by understanding the real nature of our *attachments*, suffering naturally drops away.

Desire by itself can be seen as a powerful, beautiful, energetic source for facilitating human expression. Desire can originate from the depths, from the body, or from the brain. From the body level, desire drives the continuation of our species. From the artistic depths, it results in the physical expression of a deeper creative beauty that humankind can help bring into the world. If expressed through the mind, desire leads to spiritual explorations and helps produce all the interesting intellectual and scientific works that shape and energize our culture. Desire is ultimately responsible for bringing forth much of the beauty in our physical realm that has been, is, and will be, manifested by humankind.

This is nature's way! We are here to gain experience in all its different forms, and the natural world produces desire as a way of making sure we do just that. Desire is a wonderful and powerful tool for three-dimensional living because it helps us focus, while it also motivates us towards a fuller expression of life.

As taught in some Eastern traditions, such as Advaita Vedanta, the very focused and specific *desire* for freedom itself is the greatest teacher because it propels us forward in our spiritual growth. For many of us, it has been the specific desire to be free of suffering that has guided and directed our personal journeys. ***This Eastern tradition also teaches that a near-to-final step in the process of "enlightenment" is, by logical necessity, letting go of the very "desire to let go of desire."***

However, at some stage, our *attachment* to even this result will even become an impediment to our freedom, and all those who are on this journey will one day be invited to explore this critical and very interesting next threshold. ***Ultimately, the very desire to be free, which has long propelled the spiritual search for so many, must be examined. Any individual attachment to this, or any similar result, must be dropped as part of the process of becoming truly free.***

Tao

Taoism, pronounced Daoism, is the ancient Chinese life philosophy that is based on living in harmony with the Tao, or source of all existence. Quotes from Lao Tzu, the old master of ancient Chinese Taoism from the sixth century BC, sound suspiciously like he was also well trained in *quantum physics.*

"The Tao that can be told is not the eternal Tao."

"Nature does not hurry, yet everything is accomplished."

"Mastering others is strength. Mastering yourself is true power."

"When I let go of what I am, I become what I might be."

"To the mind that is still, the whole universe surrenders."

"Music in the soul can be heard by the universe."

"At the center of your being you have the answer; you know who you are and you know what you want."

"A good traveler has no fixed plans, and is not intent on arriving."

"All difficult things have their origin in that which is easy, and great things in that which is small."

"By letting it go, it all gets done. The world is won by those who let it go. But when you try and try, the world is beyond the winning."

"The wise man looks into space and he knows there are no limited dimensions."

"From wonder into wonder existence opens."

"If you realize that all things change, there is nothing you will try to hold on to. If you are not afraid of dying, there is nothing you cannot achieve."

"Life is a series of natural and spontaneous changes. Don't resist them–that only creates sorrow. Let reality be reality. Let things flow naturally forward in whatever way they like."

"The key to growth is the introduction of higher dimensions of consciousness into our awareness."

"The words of truth are always paradoxical."

Qi and Holy Spirit

Qi (or Chi) is the Taoist term for "circulating life energy," and it is based on their deep insights into and understanding of the *vibratory* nature of the universe. In many other traditions this same life-force is also recognized, but named differently. It has been called Holy Spirit, Prana, Tao, Mana, Ki, Ashe, Shakti and many other names, but all of these names reference the same thing: that *energy* or *presence* that enables us to "feel alive." It is this life-force that defines the difference between a living person and the empty corpse that might remain only a few seconds later. We do not understand this process, scientifically, and yet we all can sense the exact moment that life-force no longer animates one of our loved ones. Life-force is always present while we are alive, but at certain times it seems to become much stronger.

I found the following modern discussion of Qi on "About.com," and I just marvel at how the language is so close to the language of *quantum physics*:

> *In its broadest sense, Qi can be thought of as the vibratory nature of reality: how at the atomic level, all of manifest existence is energy – an intelligent, luminous 'emptiness' appearing as this form and then that, like waves rising from and then dissolving back into the ocean. Our perception of solidity – of forms as fixed and lasting "things" – is just that: a perception, based upon habitual ways of conceiving of ourselves and our world. As we deepen in our Taoist practice, these conceptions and perceptions of solidity are gradually replaced by the perception of the world as being more like a kaleidoscope with its elemental manifestations in constant flux and change.*

The updated web page has since been edited to contain a more traditional definition.

Qi originates in extra-dimensional space, and while we continuously experience its effects or shadow upon our 3D world, we still lack the ability to see, measure or understand it at the level of its origin. However, in the East they have developed numerous techniques for understanding,

191

tuning, working with and manipulating Qi within our realm. Some of these techniques, such as Qi-Gong, Tai-Chi and Acupuncture, have made their way West and have even become established practices in the Americas, Europe, Australia and New Zealand. Our local Catholic Hospital in Austin, Texas now has a large Acupuncture clinic where multiple aspects of Eastern and Western philosophy and technology are mixed and all working well together. Worldwide, Eastern and Western practices of healing and religion are all blending and borrowing as they find their common connections.

Reincarnation and Enlightenment

Fundamental to Buddhism and other Eastern spiritual philosophies is the idea of reincarnation. In this belief system each of us is born repeatedly to have lifetimes of experience until that final lifetime when we finally reach Nirvana or *Enlightenment*. How we live each lifetime determines the shape and form of our next lifetime.

While this idea can be seen as generally compatible with the structure of the *Multiverse*, there are two important differences between the Buddhist system of reincarnation and the mechanics of the *Multiverse*. The first is that in the *Multiverse* events such as lifetimes do not unfold in a linear sequence because time does not operate in only one direction. The "arrow of time" is only an artifact of our three-dimensional perspective. In the *Multiverse* there is no such thing as a next lifetime because all lifetimes are unfolding simultaneously and interactively, outside of time, in parallel universes.

The other primary difference is perhaps more important to understand. The Buddhist belief system engages a form of judgment that promises rewards for "correct" behavior. There are "noble" truths and ethical precepts such as "right" understanding, "right" thought and "right" action. It is taught that "Noble" and "right" behaviors help one gain enlightenment, the ultimate reward. Judgment and reward are human concepts and are not active principles within the *Multiverse*. The *Multiverse* has no allowance for good behavior or bad behavior because within creation everything is driven by simple cause and effect; thus there is no need for judgment. No experience or behavior can ever be measured as good or bad. There are no rewards, and *being* will, by its very nature, be guided to have all types of experiences, good and bad, because this experiential pathway is the only path that leads to true wisdom, compassion and freedom. These qualities are not rewards; they are the natural result of a beautiful organic process.

Enlightenment, the end goal of many Eastern spiritual practices, including Buddhism, can, on a practical level, be defined as "obtaining sustainable freedom while still living in the *body*." This can only be achieved through the deep wisdom and compassion acquired by embracing, understanding and experiencing everything, all the flavors, no matter how these flavors have been judged by others–be it a religion or a culture.

Ramana Maharshi and Advaita

Ramana Maharshi was a spiritual philosopher and teacher from India who was alive during almost exactly the same years as Einstein. Self-taught, his individually-developed senses of time, space and interrelationship made him sound as if he had been fully trained in the philosophical aspects of *quantum physics*. While he developed his own independent line of intuitive reasoning, his overall philosophy stood quite squarely on the shoulders of the ancient *Advaita Vendanta* tradition. Rarely leaving his secluded mountaintop in India, he was the first teacher to emerge in a modern, revived branch of this very old, traditional lineage. His direct protégé, Papaji, had a specific talent for attracting serious Western students to India, and is personally responsible for the direct training of many of our most influential contemporary Western spiritual teachers in this ancient tradition.

From his mountaintop in India where he spent his entire life, he shared these deep understandings that contain more than a hint of the quantum wonder world:

"Investigate the nature of the mind and it will disappear."

"The universe exists within the Self."

"Apart from thought, there is no independent entity called world."

"When your real, effortless, joyful nature is realized, it will not be inconsistent with the ordinary activities of life."

"The universe is only an object created by the mind and has its being in the mind. It cannot be measured as an external entity."

"The world is an idea and nothing else."

"There is neither past nor future: there is only the present. Yesterday was the present when you experienced it and tomorrow will also be the present when you experience it. Therefore experience takes place only in the present and beyond and apart from experience nothing exists."

"Even the present is mere imagination for the sense of time is purely mental."

"The feeling of limitation is the work of the mind."

"The ultimate truth is so simple; it is nothing more than being in one's natural original state."

Covering one eye with his finger "Look this little finger prevents the world from being seen. In the same way this small mind covers the whole universe and prevents reality from being seen."

"Reality lies beyond the mind."

"It is all mind."

"Environment, time and objects all exist in oneself."

"Good or bad qualities pertain only to the mind."

"The numeral one gives rise to other numbers. The truth is neither one or two."

I find it extremely interesting that his lifetime unfolded at exactly the same time, and yet worlds apart, from the breakthroughs in *relativity* and *quantum physics*. ***Advaita and quantum physics are as different in background and methods as any two schools of thought can be; yet the deepest*** *conclusions of both methods of inquiry are remarkably similar because both are focused on understanding the same single truth.*

THOSE "OTHERS" WHO ARE LESS FORTUNATE

This brings us directly to the extremely difficult and challenging conceptual hurdle involving very real and profound human suffering. This book's philosophy may be interesting as an abstract concept, but how does it serve those in dire need? It might be easy for someone with a healthy body to talk abstractly about spiritual healing, but what about the person who was born with a severe genetic deformity or lifelong disease? What does this philosophy mean for all the innocent children around the world who were born into horrible conditions and continue to suffer endlessly?

The answer to these kinds of questions is multilayered and it involves our understanding of who we really are and how we inhabit the *Multiverse*. First, if we begin to recognize that we are really all only one *Being*, and then we will recognize that at some level we also have a single, collective soul. From that perspective there are no "others," so this unfortunate *being* that is living with the less than ideal body or in a terrible situation will then be understood to be an expression of some dissociated or rejected part of our greater Self. As our openness and sensitivity to these deeper interconnections increases, we will then begin to personally experience much less separation. When we fully recognize these interconnections, then our entire way of living and relating to any "others" will shift, and the ripples of this new awareness will touch the lives of everyone, including the less fortunate. As our relationship to the world that is presently understood to be "out there" shifts, then, because we are all completely interconnected, there will also be less separation and isolation experienced by these "others."

Witnessing this suffering of "others" is important for our always-evolving soul. A part of our collective "us" is having this experience so that we may have another opportunity to witness and then gradually understand, evolve and grow to become more aware and compassionate. Through this and similar experiences, our collective soul will deepen its compassion toward suffering and improve its understanding about our *attachment* to the *impermanent*. As we begin to understand our true, deeper relationship to these "others," we will then naturally begin to love and care for these isolated and rejected parts of our own *being*. We help these "others" because it is very natural to help ourselves, once we have gained a deeper recognition that these "others" are really only aspects of our own separated *being*. All of our separated parts become healed and whole when we live our lives in recognition of the oneness of all of *Being*.

The natural world often seems harsh from the perspective of our individual separation, but it always achieves balance, completion and perfection through this natural process. We more easily understand how storms, earthquakes and disease are natural or necessary parts of a balanced ecosystem. In a similar way, these extremely challenged individuals serve the ecosystem of our consciousness. All parts of our collective awareness are experiencing exactly what is needed in this and every moment to create balance and deepen our individual and collective awareness. Since we are all intimately interconnected, we will all benefit and evolve together. This may sound cruel and cold, but it is only if one is deeply *attached* to the *illusion* of time and this particular physical manifestation of life.

The more challenging and difficult experiences can produce greater opportunities for growth. This applies to both the individual and the collective. Steven Hawking has expressed deep gratefulness for his extremely-reduced physical condition. This famous cosmologist fully credits his disease, ALS, for his focus, achievements and, even his satisfaction with life. The unique focus that we gain through such an extreme hardship can often become a rich catalyst for an amazing amount of growth and productivity. However, sometimes within even the most perfect opportunities for growth and opening, it becomes necessary to cast off the present physical bodies because they no longer serve the needs of the deeper levels of our soul. We always need to remind ourselves that we are not these bodies.

JOSEPH CAMPBELL–THE POWER OF MYTH

As a professor of mythology and comparative religion at Sarah Lawrence College, Joseph Campbell's lifelong quest was to understand and explain the information, message and power of our mythology. Shortly before Campbell's death in 1987, Bill Moyers created the PBS television series *The Power of Myth*, which was based on Campbell's book of the same title. Through this series, Moyers introduced Campbell's work to a large American audience, and the world at large. The series included extensive and absolutely wonderful discussions and interviews from his final years, and opened many of us to the deep and hidden meaning and extraordinary power of our mythology.

Just as with Gnostic Christianity, Campbell's ideas are based on his intuitive understanding, and they resonate with the fundamental *quantum* principles of the *Multiverse*. Here is a sampling of quotes from his books and lectures. Joseph Campbell's deep love and warmth for humanity and his beautiful and poetic way of expressing his wisdom are unparalleled.

> "We must be willing to let go of the life we planned so as to have the life that is waiting for us."

> "If you do follow your bliss you put yourself on a kind of track that has been there all the while, waiting for you, and the life that you ought to be living is the one you are living. Follow your bliss and don't be afraid, and doors will open where you didn't know they were going to be."

> "Follow your bliss and the universe will open doors for you where there were only walls."

> "If you can see your path laid out in front of you step by step, you know it's not your path. Your own path you make with every step you take. That's why it's your path."

> "The cave you fear to enter holds the treasure you seek."

> "If you are falling…dive."

> "If the path before you is clear, you're probably on someone else's."

> "We're not on our journey to save the world but to save ourselves. But in doing that you save the world. The influence of a vital person vitalizes."

> "The first step to the knowledge of the wonder and mystery of life is the recognition of the monstrous nature of the earthly human realm as well as its glory, the realization that this is just how it is and that it cannot and will not be changed. Those who think they know how the universe could have been had they created it, without pain, without sorrow, without time, without death, are unfit for illumination."

"The goal of life is to make your heartbeat match the beat of the universe, to match your nature with Nature."

"Gods suppressed become devils, and often it is these devils whom we first encounter when we turn inward."

"Find a place inside where there's joy, and the joy will burn out the pain."

"The big question is whether you are going to be able to say a hearty yes to your adventure."

"The experience of eternity right here and now is the function of life. Heaven is not the place to have the experience; here is the place to have the experience."

"We save the world by being alive ourselves."

"All the gods, all the heavens, all the hells, are within you."

THE "NEW AGE"

Introduction

We live in a wonderful time and place in history, and I feel particularly blessed to have grown up in America in the 1950s and 1960s. For most of my life there has been a stable but rapidly expanding economy. This has allowed many of us to meet and even exceed all of our biological and physical needs. With our new affluence we have unparalleled free time, especially since fewer hours are spent procuring food, and this new free time allows us to deeply explore our spiritual side and experiment with alternative ways of living on this Earth. No other period or place in our planet's known history has ever created this level of opportunity for so many.

My generation took enthusiastic advantage of this unique luxury, expressing ourselves and our spirit in a multitude of varied ways: rock and roll, drugs, sexual exploration, political and environmental activism, social activism, alternative religions and sexual lifestyles, meditation, Eastern philosophy, *quantum physics*, television, computers, Internet, space exploration and world travel. We grew and expanded our understanding of just what is possible, in a multitude of varied ways that our parents could never have imagined. As time passed and people started writing about these experiences, a new culture was built around self-help and the sharing of these strange and new ideas. With the Internet unfolding in perfect timing, the various new and reworked ideas quickly spread and connected with those living in many other places and cultures around our world. Our new technologies also allowed us to discover that these many "others" around the planet were also having similar experiences. We are now in the midst of a true, worldwide Renaissance as enormous quantities of new *information* and material are being generated, interconnected and ultimately incorporated.

As with any emerging, but unregulated, human movement, there are a wide variety of influences. Some of these influences involve sincere spiritual explorations, while others may be largely the result of self-serving or purely monetarily driven desires. Ultimately it makes little difference because all these influences are working together to help shape this eclectic body of material and *information* that is now all crammed under the broad and unofficial banner, "New Age."

It is my personal opinion that much of this new material is far-fetched, lacks thoughtful examination, and requires a disproportionate amount of faith. However, even within these more extreme "New Age" ideas and practices, we can still find elements of a deeper universal truth and new ideas about different ways of approaching and improving our lives. The common ground that drives this movement is a collective recognition that our old ways, ideas and methods no longer fully serve humankind. "New Age" philosophy, while clearly a "mixed bag," also provides many of the revolutionary ideas that are guiding the emergent paradigm shift.

"New Age" Ideas Derive from "New Thought"

Isolated references to many of these "New Age" ideas can be found in the past works of several individual writers and, occasionally, within the recorded philosophy of a few small, scattered historical groups. Like blips on a radar screen, these were brief moments of a different kind of thinking that came and went. These ideas generally failed to attract a larger audience until the early 1800s, when a substantial and well-publicized group of alternative writers and philosophers coalesced under the banner of "New Thought." Included in the "New Thought" philosophy were many of the ideas that we now associated with "New Age" thinking.

Formed and named in New England, the "New Thought" movement declared that it was dedicated to healing the general human condition. Evolving from German Transcendentalism, the basic unifying principles were that God or "Universal Intelligence" is supreme, eternal and universal, but at the same time divinity dwells in each and every person. They wrote that we are here to love one another and our actual thoughts determine the manifestation of our lives. Influenced by well-known literary figures, such as Emerson and Thoreau, "New Thought" ideas and philosophy rapidly spread due to their wide publication.

The earliest identifiable proponent of what became known as "New Thought" was Phineas Parkhurst Quimby (1802–1866), an American philosopher, watchmaker, healer and inventor. He became known for developing the healing system that he called "Mind-Cure." This system was based on the idea that illness originated in the mind as a result of our belief system, and that a mind open to God could cure any illness.

God and the four Gospels were always a major part of Quimby's original "Mind-Cure" philosophy, and this focus continued as the greater "New Thought" movement took hold. Quimby himself had worked closely with Mary Baker Eddy, who went on to form the *Church of Christian Science*, a contemporary church whose philosophy was largely derived from the "New Thought/Mind-Cure" movement.

An important principle of "New Thought" was an idea that has more recently been called the "Law of Attraction." This is a concept that now is enjoying a renewed popularity, largely because of a recent movie, *The Secret*. The idea is that we all attract to us, those very people and things that are like us–like attracts like. Other original and important "New Thought" principles are now being called "positive thinking," "creative visualization" and "conscious-languaging."

Ralph Waldo Emerson had a major influence on this "New Thought" movement. Although Emerson wrote on myriad topics, his thematic core was consistent: "All separate things are made of one hidden thing." Among his quotes can be found "The world globes itself in a drop of dew;" "The heart and soul of all men being one, this bitterness of his and mine ceases;" "Christ is all in all;" "Every heart vibrates to that iron string;" and " I am my brother and my brother is me." Emerson believed that God appears in a myriad of disguises, and "we are all it, and so is the leaf, the stone, the grass, the mountain, and the cloud." He deeply felt and communicated, in his writing, this interconnection and unity amongst all things.

The next reemergence was when Joel S. Goldsmith sifted through and filtered many of the principles of "New Thought" to create his "Infinite Way" program in 1947. Next followed *The Course in Miracles*, which was channeled in 1965 and published in 1976 by a Columbia Medical University psychologist named Helen Schucman. While not directly derivative of "New Thought," it is clearly an elaboration and an expansion of many of the same principles.

Recently, popular writers such as Joy Brugh, Wayne Dyer, Marianne Williamson, Deepak Chopra and others have reintroduced many of these principles to the mainstream population through books, lectures and workshops. The "New Age" movement, as a whole, is much looser and not nearly as organized as "New Thought." The "New Age" movement has no formal parent organization, established doctrine, or sets of standard practice–it is genuinely "grass roots" in its origins. For the most part, this contemporary version has minimized, or even abandoned, any formal religious ties and references to specifics about God and Christianity as it tends to be much more *gnostic* in its general nature. Notable exceptions to this secularization and lack of formal organization are several new, alternative Christian churches, such as the *Unity* church and the previously mentioned *Course In Miracles* which is organized, still very active, and even thriving.

Visualization, Manifesting, Affirmations

Today, we have unparalleled access to a plethora of self-help books, websites and workshops that are based upon positive thinking, visualization, manifestation, *conscious languaging* and similar techniques that are all derived from "New Thought." These methods are extremely popular in the Western world, partly because they often seem to work, and sometimes quite well. They work because they indirectly address deeper structural truths about life and the actual architecture of freedom. Unfortunately, they also appeal to our ubiquitous desire to have more individual control over our lives. These techniques are only tools, and all tools can cause problems if used improperly.

The term "positive thinking" is almost self-explanatory. The general idea is that holding positive or upbeat ideas in our minds manifests positive things in our lives. ***At the most profound level, "positive thinking" is the conscious, continuous and grateful recognition of the enormous beauty in life and the purposeful interconnection of all things. This kind of positive thinking has the potential to have a dramatic effect on our world in many wonderful ways. If someone wants to choose one practical change to make in life, I would personally recommend, "keeping a joyful, open attitude." This is usually the single, most helpful change a person can make to redirect his or her life.***

Conscious languaging is the intentional practice of becoming fully aware of the intended and hidden meanings of the actual words we use every day. In this practice there is a conscious focus on constructing our spoken word to more accurately reflect our desired intentions. Ultimately, everything is a form of *energy*–this includes the words we speak and the thoughts that formed them. Words have power; therefore we have much better results when we use them carefully and thoughtfully. Our words are our everyday prayers.

We all blurt out our exasperations such as *"I can't do this!" "I'm really dumb!"* or *"I don't have enough money."* This unconscious habit is extremely self-limiting; as these words energetically act at levels we can't possibly understand. With these negating word choices, we are, at the very least, reinforcing exactly the opposite of what we really want. Turning these thoughts around into a more accurate reflection of the actual things that we really do want makes our words helpful allies to our real intentions. For example, instead of speaking the words, *"I can't do this,"* we might say, *"I am learning to do this!"* Even though a modified expression, such as *"I can't do this yet,"* is more empowering than the original statement, it is still somewhat limiting. Once we begin to observe and analyze our actual word choices, we are always surprised and shocked to discover just how many times a day we try to energetically thwart ourselves with this type of unconscious verbal sabotage.

Visualization and *manifestation* are closely related "New Age" techniques. In both, we create and hold a "vision" of something that we want to change, acquire or shift in our lives. Instead of just "wishing" for this change in one's mind, the practice involves imagining or experiencing the change as if it has been already completed. We might, for example, visualize our ideal future family life. Not limited to just our visual sense alone, many forms of this practice will also holistically incorporate aspects of sound, feelings, smell, taste, memories and thoughts.

While these technologies all can work, since they point towards deeper truths about the nature of what we are and how the universe works, their effectiveness often falls short of the practitioner's expectations. There are a number of reasons for this. As typically practiced, these "New Age" *visualization* and *manifestation* techniques tend to focus on, and usually try to change the final outcome to better match the individual's specific personal ambitions, such as acquiring more wealth or love. The use of these techniques will miss their full potential because the practitioners are attempting to control outcomes and meet the very specific and personal material desires of their individual egos. This direction of focus only serves to lock the practitioner more deeply into their material 3D worldview and controlling mindset.

Because of our deep *identification* with the material *illusion*, we often completely miss the deeper potential of these techniques. From our 3D perspective, we usually lack the sensitivity and perspective to know what is really best for us. Our specific material wishes are often nothing more than blind and "random stabs in the dark" in our unguided attempts to improve our lives. Of course any personal journeys that are spawned by these attempts just contribute to our soul's experience and eventual expansion. Any type of exploration is a wonderful thing in the bigger picture; ultimately this process always leads to the growth of our individual and collective soul.

These practices of *manifestation* and *visualization* can actually lead to the formation of more *attachments because* of some very common misunderstandings about these techniques. There is always a very real possibility of the practitioner becoming *attached* to the specific imagined outcome; this, then, introduces all the issues, and inevitable suffering, that are associated with all types of *attachment*. As typically practiced, these techniques often involve focusing energy only upon the level of the material world. Unfortunately, in my experience, it has been rare that a student has been encouraged to work at the deeper levels of their *root vibratory resonance* or *being*. This absolute focus on a predetermined and personal egoic vision can often require us to swim against the natural currents in the rivers of our lives.

There is, of course, nothing "wrong" with playing with these methods, especially if we consciously recognize what we are doing and understand that these methods are just tools for exploration. We will likely discover in this type of play that we really are extremely powerful beings and really can "manifest" the very things that we desire within this 3D realm–but they often come with an unexpected, unseen costs. Along with this discovery, we will probably also learn a great deal about our individual desires and the nature of desire in general.

We all need play in our lives, and exploring these techniques provides us with an interesting and focused curriculum for some of this play. However, to create real growth through permanent change, we must ultimately shift the core *resonant vibration* of our *being*. While a *positive attitude* and the practice of *conscious visualization* can move us in that direction, real change requires that we dive even deeper. Eventually our core beliefs, our personal fears, our embodied physical and psychological traumas, and our culturally inherited attitudes must be "seen" so they can be fully explored and released. If these are not addressed, we will not be able to travel far from our old paradigm and universe.

If what we really want is a new Mercedes, then some of these self-help methods may work to make that goal possible. However, further down that road, we probably will be driving that once brand-new car to the same old enervating job so, it is probable that, at some point, this new car will no longer satisfy us. ***If we desire to live joyful and free lives, we must first make radical shifts from our old patterns. For these shifts to occur, we need to alter our core vibration patterns by completely letting go of our identification with the physical form and all its associated baggage. It is this identification that ultimately traps us within the old patterns of our limited viewport.***

We Create our Own Reality

There is a very popular New Age belief that leads to a great amount of confusion, disappointment and disillusionment. It is the empowering idea that "we create our own reality." While this statement correctly expresses a very important and fundamental truth about our *being*, a better understanding of this principle is necessary if we are to avoid confusion. The issue is that many people, in their attempts to practice creating their own reality, interpret it to mean that simply thinking or holding a thought long enough or strongly enough will cause it to manifest. Quickly they usually discover, to their disappointment, that this technique does little to change the appearance of the outside world, especially in the specific ways that they had hoped. As a result, many then give up exploring this interesting idea, only to drop back into the old and familiar "*there is nothing I can do about it*" attitude.

What is being missed is the critical effect and importance of our deeper *vibrational resonance* that is always the natural result of our core beliefs. Without a clear shift to *vibrational integrity* at this level of our *being*, there can be no significant external change because we remain *resonantly* bound within the same limited region of the *Multiverse*. We even may understand that this is the problem, but we often lack the confidence or energy to dive into the necessary and often emotionally difficult personal work that this deep shift requires. In our contemporary world we all are constantly conditioned to look for quick and easy fixes. As a result, this wonderful and important doorway to deeper truth and opening often gets misunderstood, overlooked or ignored.

A more realistic and useful method for "creating" our own reality begins with our understanding that in the timeless *Multiverse*, every reality already exists. We don't ever create any reality. It is much more accurate to say "we discover our reality," or "it finds us, as we find it." The not-so-subtle distinction between these two ways of viewing our relationship to creation also illuminates a critical key element to our becoming free. ***The key element is our willingness to open ourselves to and be grateful for life, however it is being presented to us. The path towards freedom requires that we master being the joyful "observer" instead of becoming the doer or controller. Jesus said, "be a passerby." As we learn to trust and let go of the need to control our lives, our journey begins to appear to be smoother, and at the same time inexplicably amazing. For each of us, our individual voyage is always perfect. The difficult part of the process is often just learning just how to relax and enjoy the ride. What we eventually discover is that we really are not so*** *much observers as we are participants, for there is ultimately nothing that exists outside of us. We become one with the ride.*

Law of Attraction

Earlier I mentioned the popular "New Age" principle called the "Law of Attraction," which can be reduced to the concept of "like attracts like." This "law" has been widely discussed and explored since it was presented as an important, life-changing concept in the popular "New Age" movie, *The Secret*. As mentioned, the "Law of Attraction" is a borrowed principle from the earlier "New Thought" movement. This "law" states that if a person is of a particular mind set (vibration), he or she will attract into his or her life those things that support them in their journey.

Much of what is written about the "law of attraction" has been based on attracting personal and material things, such as money, luxuries, fame, success and a love-interest partner. Instead of simply observing what arrives in our lives and being grateful for the flow of life and *being*, this practice is designed to help us attract a very specific, calculated individual list of personally desired things. Our choices are often derived from our egoic desire to feel special, successful, or even better than others. Because of this it is a process that only creates more separation; these personal wants or needs usually do not originate from the deeper desire to become more open to our *being,* or truth. Used this common way, this practice can help produce the desired results, but it will fail to help us expand beyond our 3D paradigm; in many ways the "Law of Attraction," as popularized today, is simply another repackaging of the "manifestation" practice. Of course, there is nothing "wrong" with exploring our personal desires since everything explored leads to more experience, which, after all, is the raw material for all growth and evolution. What is eventually learned from these explorations is that fulfilling our personal desires will not, by itself, lead to sustainable joy, inner peace or personal freedom.

The "Law of Attraction" is actually a misunderstood reframing of a deep-level truth about our vibratory nature within the *Multiverse*. The idea of attraction implies an action that is the result of some kind of *force,* but *force* and attraction have nothing to do with what is occurring. Things of similar *vibrational resonance* do appear in our lives, but not because we "attract" them to us. It is more as if our evolving *vibrational resonance* allows us to begin to interact with new parts of the universe that were previously invisible to us. It is nearer to the truth to visualize that these things are, instead, attracting us to them; we have become open and available for this new experience.

The principle involved in the "law of attraction" can be understood, through the basic classical physics of *sympathetic vibration;* the result of both the *reinforcement* of similar or harmonious frequencies through *sympathetic resonance* and the cancelation or reduction of noise and the disharmonious through *vibratory interference*. We understand the principle of *sympathetic resonance* in three dimensions, but it also functions in a more profound way at deeper levels, such as the level of the membrane of *string theory,* which may be the fundamental place where our lives unfold. Here we each have an always evolving, but unique, *resonance*, and this allows us to become "excited" by the regions of the *Multiverse* that *reinforce* our *vibratory resonant signature*. We do not "migrate" towards a region so much as we expand to include it, so that our expanded *being* becomes able to interact with this previously unknown *vibratory* region. Through our intimate but expansive relationship with *vibration,* we are more accurately "discovering" things that already exist in the *Multiverse;* rather than attracting things to us, we become available to new regions that now also *resonate* with our expanded core *vibration*. A more accurate verbal description of the "law of attraction" might be expressed as *that which vibrates as you vibrate, will appear to manifest in your life* and it might be more descriptively named *the law of sympathetic resonance*. The "law of attraction" is an effective, powerful, yet misunderstood principle that can help us move beyond our old *viewport*.

Regardless of why we choose to practice them, "New Age" spiritual techniques all have foundations in a deeper level of truth; there will always be "spill-over" from these depths that will begin to alter the way we move through our lives. When we practice "attracting" things to our life, our long-held beliefs about being powerless will shift and eventually this shift will affect our *root vibrational resonance*. If we avoid becoming attached to specific outcomes, these practices, even when focused at the level of our 3D material world, will produce changes that eventually alter our relationship to the deeper world beyond.

When the "Law of Attraction" works, our current universe shifts as we begin to vibrate differently. From our perspective it may appear that we attracted these changes, but the deeper truth is we took a journey to the part of the Multiverse that best resonates with who we really are. In one sense, because we shifted to a parallel universe where these desired results are manifested, we did not attract the results; instead their vibration attracted us!

Planning for the "Future"

There are numerous visualization and teaching techniques that attempt to create a desired "future" outcome. In workshops that are based on these techniques, participants are often asked to visualize and hold tightly to some preconceived vision about their own future. It is usually taught that it is also critically important to be extremely specific about these visions. These teachings sometimes can even include the added idea that if the vision does not happen, then this failure is somehow the result of not being specific enough, or not doing the visualization the right way. This last idea represents a huge step away from freedom because it only reinforces our old paradigm ideas of guilt and shame.

Being 3D specialists, it is never possible for us to act or "create" something in the future, for we always must live our lives in the *present moment–the now!* Of course, these and similar techniques can still be practiced as interesting and potentially illuminating experiments to help us learn more about ourselves. However, if we trying to use them to influence or control future outcomes, then these attempts are destined to become personal explorations of what occurs when we become too *attached* to a specific outcome.

Another substantial problem with these techniques is that it is impossible that any of us, situated firmly within our own 3D experience, could possibly understand, or predict, what would be the right or best thing in any imagined version of the "future." As I have mentioned, this is a common problem with all manifestation and visualization techniques. The sage's *"be careful what you wish for because you just might get it"* warning quickly comes to mind.

Explorations of this type do provide wonderful opportunities to learn about how we are prone to create *attachments* and what this really means. As a laboratory to learn about *attachment* and the true "creative" process, this type of experiment, if approached consciously, can serve us very well. By fully exploring our will through various forms of creative manifestation, we can deeply come to better understand our *beingness* and how our *Multiverse* really works. This process will look different for each individual, but we will, in the end, learn and evolve from this type of exploration, just as we do from every other part of life. One life-lesson that this exploration will likely teach us is that our attempts at control can very quickly dampen much of the inherent joy, magic and surprise that naturally accompanies the true creative process. True "creativity" happens only in the full flow of the river of life.

Future Memories

Another related and very interesting "New Age" tool is the envisioning of "future memories." This is a modification of "future vision" that is designed to be much more passive and far less controlling. Similar to that earlier method, it asks us to fully imagine and experience the future, but it does this by asking us to *feel* the future as if it has already happened. This specific application of visualization will produce very different results because it takes us into a much deeper involvement with our feelings. We are not trying to create a specific outcome but, rather, we are attempting to allow the future to reveal itself to us through our feelings; the difference is very significant and not at all subtle. With this method, we are allowing and feeling rather than trying to create and control. Our *feelings* are much closer to our core *resonant vibrations* than is our thinking. By focusing on *feeling* and allowing the future to present itself, instead of doing or manipulating, the activity is no longer centered in our thinking brains–instead we are exploring a deeper terrain that lies much closer to the core of our *being*.

Since "time" does not exist in the *Multiverse,* "future memories" do not require imagining things that have not yet happened. In our *Multiverse,* the present moment *informs* the "past" and the "future" equally through *waves* of *information* that travel in all directions. Our relationship to any possible "future" is similar to our relationship to our "past." Future memories are not really different from past memories and, one day, we will access both in much the same way.

Of course this technique can also lead to disappointment for many of the same reasons discussed earlier. Whenever *attachments* or expectations appear, freedom is temporarily lost. However, because of its ability to engage deeper levels of our *being,* this "future memories" approach can be extremely valuable when used as a conscious tool to help us explore relationships in the Web.

"Be Here Now"

Living in the "now moment" is the only real method for aligning ourselves with the fundamental operating principles of the Web. Once we learn how to trust, feel and access this "now moment," we will have gained unlimited access to the most direct, personal and time-tested portal to freedom. This method, which is always available to everyone and allows us to experience life in a fresh and completely different way, has been universally embraced within the "New Age" movement. (I will discuss this idea in more detail later in the sections titled *Ram Dass* and *Living in the Now Moment.*)

When adults are first introduced to this idea, the initial difficulty is to simply understand what these words mean. Young children, before the imprinting of our culture influences them, understand this "now" moment very naturally; it is the way of *being* that all infants naturally possess. It has taken me a lifetime of practice to begin to remember and re-understand the meaning and feeling of what Ram Dass describes as *"being here now."*

Once we begin to re-understand this very natural way of experiencing life, there remains the hurdle of learning how to participate in our culture while also living in the "now moment." This can be a very difficult task because our fast moving culture is always pulling and tugging us into some preplanned "future," while simultaneously reminding us of our "past." As we age, we typically forget how to do this as we learn how to live, instead, with our plans and schedules.

To stay in the *now* while functioning in our society, an adult needs to have clear and consistent inner guidance and powerful focus; the vision must be built upon an unyielding foundation of absolute trust in the power of the "now moment"–it typically takes life experience, and therefore time, to build this trust. This way of being requires deep commitment and preparation but, once this realization is fully integrated, it quickly becomes our preferred way of moving through life.

Why Workshops Work

Many of us have had amazing experiences with some of these alternative techniques, particularly when they are practiced in group-workshop environments. A special sense of empowerment occurs in focused group settings, whether the group consists of two or two thousand. Later, we often discover that these same techniques do not seem to work as consistently or as well once we are outside of the workshop group environment. There are two primary reasons for this perceived loss of effectiveness.

The physical center of our body, near our heart, is physically located some distance from our brain. Many years ago I had a very wise friend remind me that my brain, located in my head, is only part of an extremity and I needed to better understand my brain, and its thinking, in this new "extremity" context. Recent experiments in neurophysiology indicate that there are far more nerve passageways sending information from the heart to the brain than there are from the brain to the heart (Rollin McCraty–Heart Math Institute, multiple studies). This physical arrangement could imply that biologically the brain is designed to be subservient to the heart. Our hearts are so much more than just pumps for our blood.

Intuitively, we already know this, as we commonly include the phrase "heart" to describe most things near and dear to us. We intuitively understand that any real change in our *being* must first involve our hearts. Of course no single part of our *being* works alone, so all parts of our *energy* field need to be involved and "on-board" for us to experience a permanent and concrete change in the *vibrational* state of our *being*. The heart, however, is the centrally located control for any personal transformation and is always the place where our deepest interpersonal interactions are centered.

In workshops, we are usually interacting very closely with other people. There is a focused group intent that naturally moves us away from the busy and egoic nature of our individual minds, and this focused group environment also naturally engages feelings that are more connecting and universal in nature. The workshop environment helps move the center of our expression farther from our brain and closer to our heart where our experience of "others" seems much more interconnected. The group process really works best when our hearts are fully involved.

The second factor is that the *energy* of "others" influences every one of us. Workshops, retreats and other group exercises can often create significant "outside" *energy* fields that surround us as the many individuals become tuned together in *resonant harmony* by working together over time. When we are thinking and acting together, as a unified focused body, we experience a much more powerful interaction because the *resonance* becomes more *coherent*, cohesive and *reinforcing*. This is not unlike a sports team being "in the zone" together, or the unifying experience of an extraordinary rock concert.

Most of us have had the opportunity to sit in a crowded arena during an exciting ball game, surrounded by fans that are intensely devoted to a team. Do they (or us) really care about the game that much, or are they really there for a powerful focused group experience? If our chosen team wins, there is an enormous amount of excited *group-vibration* and it often means the team moves on and all the fans will get another chance to have this connected and empowering feeling. Political rallies depend on this *coherence* and *reinforcement,* and Hitler was a master at creating and working with this type of group dynamic.

Would it feel very different if we were in the middle of the stands filled with supporters of the opposing team? I have experimented with this a number of times by walking around stadiums and fields to intentionally sit amongst the fans of the opposing team. What I found was that I initially felt isolated and separate, but once I dropped my resistance and identification with my particular team, I could then fully enjoy the excitement of the other team's *group vibratory experience.* In these focused group environments, we can more easily forget about our individual daily concerns and experience this state of interconnected *resonance* (it usually feels wonderful to connect to others this way). For many, the real purpose of attending does not involve the game as much as it involves their desire for this level of interconnection. *Coherent, reinforced* and *resonant vibratory* group experiences are typically expressed as excitement, energy, ecstasy and joy.

Unfortunately, maintaining this level of *energy* and *resonance* is much more difficult once we are back into our typical daily lives. The massive inertia of our existing culture, and the divergent energies of the individuals with whom we interact with daily, will always have their own strong influence upon us. Outside of intentional and focused group environments, our culture's powerful and often chaotic influences make it more difficult to engage in these *coherent vibratory* experiences.

Within our realm we all participate in the great group experience called life. There will always be aspects or parts of each of us that are sensitive to and interact with influences that originate outside of our separate physical bodies; for example, the *energy* field of a longtime spouse is usually a very strong influence on our system. Again, we are reminded that at the deepest levels, just as *quantum physics* describes, everything is intimately connected. Everything that exists, ever existed, or could exist is directly, and intimately, connected throughout the entire *Multiverse.* At the deepest levels there are no outside influences because there is after all, only one thing.

Fear and Love

It is a very popular trend in "New Age" writing to refer to *fear* and *Love* as polar opposites. I believe that their classification as opposites is the result of a misunderstanding of both *fear* and *Love.* While they are indirectly related, they originate in entirely different realms.

Love is the undisturbed life-force vibration. *Love* simply "is." It is not a human conceptual creation or idea. What we call "romantic love" originates in this, our 3D realm, and it may or may not include a *resonance* with the deeper form of *Love.* Whenever we are *resonating* with our deeper source, we are able to experience more of this ever-present *Love.* When we dive in fully, we then share this pool of deeper *Love* with those available parts of all others. In this place, our typical feeling of separation entirely disappears. Within this pool there is only *Love,* "One Love."

Fear is a limited, three-dimensional conceptual idea. It is something that our 3D egoic minds create, which can then interfere with or block our connection and access to *Love. Fear* is a reflexive byproduct of complete individualization, and it grows from the inevitable feeling of isolation that naturally results from this sense of separation. *Fear* effectively blocks our intuitive recognition of our deep interconnection with all others. It is absolutely true that when our *fear* increases, we feel less *Love, and* this is why these two appear to be opposites. It is impossible to be fully in fear and in *love* at the same time. Fear blocks our flow and natural connection with our deeper *selves* and *Self*. **Fear does have an opposite, and its opposite is freedom. When we are most free, our direct connection to Love is extremely powerful, palpable and constant.**

Our deepest encounters with *Love* often happen spontaneously. They occur most often when we forget our egoic selves while caring for another, about another, or when our ego becomes "lost" through some joyful activity like music or dance. The flow of *Love* may be experienced as a still moment involving a recognition of some deep truth, or as a sense of direct connection to a part of life that lies beyond this physical realm, including our bodies. When this happens it means that we are temporarily centered outside of our realm, and our fears have been dropped, at least temporarily. This is why we often feel *Love* while relating to another person. We feel more *Love* when we place our attention outside of our separate selves. *Love* is always available whenever our ego and the fear that our ego generates are forgotten or out of the way.

It is also helpful to note that we are never "in fear" or "in love," but rather we are always "in motion," moving in the direction of either separation or Love. We might be moving towards separation, increasing our *fear* and impeding the flow of vibrational *Love,* or we might be moving towards oneness and experiencing a more open flow or *resonance* with *Love*. As with all natural motion, it is normal for our connection with *Love* to shift cyclically, within a natural rhythm built upon ebb and flow, like the tides. This cyclic change is not something that needs to be analyzed and corrected, but rather, it is simply something to be observed. As always, *"be a passerby."*

Explore It All

We live in such a wonderful and interesting time. We have access to amazing self-help workshops, books, therapies, contemporary religions, and spiritual practices that are all aimed at helping the individual live a happier and healthier life. A defining characteristic of our "New Age" is this unprecedented access and availability of information, methods and teachers. These methods and technologies provide an embarrassment of opportunities to further explore and open our lives.

Immersion into family, friends or career is always an equally good approach, for when we are actively engaged in any aspect of our lives, we are fully participating in life and fully engaged in our evolution. As John Lennon sang, *"Life is what happens to you when you're busy making other plans."*

Many of the terms and practices I discuss in this book are consciously borrowed from these "New Age" methods and technologies. I am, after all, a child of these times. Once we understand the bigger picture of how and why these things work–and why they sometimes don't–we can then choose to focus on the practices or the parts of these techniques that serve us best. We can then refine these approaches to create our own customized practice. Regardless of which specific paths are explored, it is ultimately the journey itself that serves us. If we approach this journey with energetic curiosity, then joy and self-empowerment will soon follow.

HEALING

HEALING IN THE WESTERN CULTURE

Healing is about our return to wholeness–the wholeness that is our birthright and can become ours to experience fully. We all have blocks that prevent our connection and communication with other parts of our being–life always creates them. We regain our wholeness only as we learn how to release these impediments. These blocks prevent us from being fully human and resonant–thriving in each and every moment. It is as if there were parts of us lost or missing. Healing requires a holistic process that integrates the physical, emotional and psychological components of our *being*. Healing necessarily includes all parts of our *being,* including all those aspects that are not readily apparent from our 3D *viewport*. In fact, it is within these hidden regions that most of our real healing occurs.

To release our blockages we must be willing to witness them. It is not necessary that we understand what we witness, for there are many aspects of our *being* that will never be understood by our minds because they exist outside of our concepts and logic. Healing requires a total willingness to look deeply at whatever truth lies buried within us; this willingness is all that is necessary to initiate the process of true healing. To complete this process, we must then fully embrace and love whatever it is that we find within. This two-step task seems simple enough but, because of our old and persistent habits, it has been extremely difficult for us to master. Today, however, we have greatly improved tools and a vibrant support community to facilitate our process of healing.

Modern Western society encourages a type of conformity that directs our behavior towards the cultural consensus rather than encouraging diverse individual expression; our personal search for wholeness will always bump against this cultural reflex. Deep and genuine healing will naturally be disruptive to the individual–that is actually the point. However, healing is also very disruptive to the overall "status quo" of a culture. Power, control and economics play major roles in maintaining this cultural momentum because *change, of any kind, is highly disruptive to unnatural systems such as our economic and social systems. Natural systems, on the other hand, flow quite well with change.*

Our modern Western culture has been built on the profit and the self-interest of the few who desire control, instead of a quality life for all; a quick look at our political and economic priorities makes this very clear. War exists because it is the most profitable business on the planet. If the war machine suddenly ended, numerous, large business enterprises devoted to warfare could no longer exist. Our medical healthcare system is an enormous economic interest that is fully dependent on the manufacture and sale of large quantities of pharmaceuticals and advanced medical technology. This healthcare system is fully intertwined with the large insurance industry, and the whole system depends on a large steady stream of "sick" people. Our entire economy is built upon a model that requires continuous economic expansion to function. This economic system is entirely dependent on this dynamic imbalance; therefore it is wholly unsustainable–yet its continuation is critical for the maintenance of the existing power structure. Those individuals, families and organizations that currently have the most power and control within this system will naturally resist change of any kind–including cultural healing. Few of the rest of us have the time, energy, confidence or ability to resist this powerful, aggressive, closed system.

As the demands of life continuously assault and press upon us, those in control hope that most of us will simply "stay the course" and make the adjustments and compromises necessary to "make ends meet." Their hold on power depends on the majority gradually becoming disconnected from their own deeper nature and forgetting about the very things that provide deep joy. As a result, we neglect play, our hearts beat weakly, our immune systems become overloaded, and we are left to participate with just enough vitality to collect our social security, someday, if all goes according to plan. It is amazing that we do as well as we do–we have proven that we are really extremely resilient beings. As a society and as individuals, we have been participating in a culture that is far from whole or healthy.

It is not primarily the individual, conscious decisions that sustain this system, but rather it is the momentum of an unconscious culture driven by acute economic pressures and concerns. This massive cultural momentum creates a "big ship" that is almost impossible to turn around. Even if we arrived at a point where we had a unified intention to change this system, the actual social change would still take a very long time and prove to be extremely difficult. Much of the resistance to even the honest examination of this issue can be easily explained by the magnitude of the social change required for this type of change. Our lifestyle and culture would have to completely re-adjust before such widespread cultural healing could occur. Even for those that are fully aware and committed to this type of change, it is sometimes too difficult to resist, or fight, the powerful momentum of the fast-paced system already in place.

At some level, all of us are emotionally and financially invested in the status quo. Before we can attempt such a major external change, we first need to open and change our fundamental internal relationship to creation. We all internalize fears that have been built upon our sense of separation. The fears created by our sense of separation are what build and sustain this existing culture.

The Western Allopathic Medical Model

Our Western allopathic system of healing approaches the body almost as if it were a machine. With modern medicine's current trend towards even more specialization, it systematically divides our bodies into a multitude of smaller parts, each requiring its own special type of doctor and medicine. In its most contemporary form, it has fully adopted the traditional methodology developed for engineering, with the machine (body) fully divided into separate small systems or component parts. This division can become so complete that these various specialists rarely communicate directly with each other. The body is not seen, diagnosed or treated as a single whole entity because it has been "sourced out" to all of these different specialists.

Our system treats certain methods and types of specialists very differently; for example it regards dentists and nutritionists as entirely separate professions from medical doctors, even though healthy teeth and good nutrition are vital to the maintenance of a healthy body. There was a recent and very visible legal battle between Podiatrists and Medical doctors over which joint in the foot limited the extent of the Podiatrists' territory, while chiropractors have been completely banished from mainstream medicine for many years. Many healing modalities are formally excluded from our modern medical system–these functional, helpful and popular skills are not even taught in medical school, and their practitioners certainly are not considered real medical doctors. A friend of mine, a doctor, told me the story of how his only exposure to chiropractic in medical school was a visual graphic that showed how it directly leads to paralysis–a clear example of propaganda. Until very recently, our mental health was not even considered to be an important contributor to the general health of our bodies. Health insurance companies have reinforced many of these divisions by traditionally excluding or separating the dental, chiropractic and mental health components, while also denying coverage for nutritional or preventative medicine.

Modern Western medicine is revered because of its great past successes with epidemics and other disease, its amazing high-tech diagnostic tools and lifesaving surgical techniques. Our Western medical model is perfectly suited for emergencies; for certain types of problems, these technological methods are nothing short of miraculous. If the problem is severe physical breakage, burns, blockage or tearing, then modern orthopedic and/or surgical techniques offer solutions that were unimaginable a couple of decades ago. In the area of epidemic diseases, Western medicine clearly has changed the landscape of the world; today, in most areas of the world, parents no longer need to start enormous families in the hope that a few children will survive to produce grandchildren for them.

However, the dietary, spiritual, emotional and psychological aspects of health have been almost universally ignored within this system. Western "healing" often means attacking only the superficial external symptoms using radical chemical or surgical methods. The use of conscious, or positive, languaging is virtually absent from this modern medical tradition; patients are routinely told that they have some incurable or frightening "disease" and they are about to die. For the patients, such pronouncements completely erode any remaining hope or confidence in the healing process, and instead, only serve to add more stress. One look at hospital food and we quickly see that even the dietary aspects of health and healing are largely ignored within this system. A large component of modern intravenous feeding is high-fructose corn syrup, which may one day turn out to be, itself, a major cause of epidemic disease. Hospital "solid food" is not much more nutritious, as it typically contains high amounts of sugars, preservatives and processed components. Cancer, diabetes, Alzheimer's, and autism are all on the rapid rise and, instead of a sincere effort to address the lifestyle factors that might be responsible for these epidemics, the system has been focusing its vast resources on highly profitable, new technologies and methods for "battling" and controlling the later stages of these "diseases." Precious few resources have been used to find and eliminate the environmental, dietary, lifestyle and psychological problems that are the most likely culprits for the recent increases in our health problems.

This unmovable system creates its own economic and cultural momentum. Any change would undermine the economic interests of those already deeply invested in this system. To create a real healthcare system would require a drastic top-to-bottom reworking, and this would completely disrupt the economic status quo. ***At the very root of the issue, and at every level, is the pressing reality that, when compared to preventing illness, treating sick people is much more profitable.*** Preventative medicine simply does not promise the same financial rewards. Cancer treatment, for example, is a profitable business, while the prevention of cancer is not; research investment is spent looking for more complex, and therefore profitable, drugs and machinery to "fight" the disease. Since any identification of the real causes for this expanding epidemic would immediately threaten our existing false but thriving economy, such projects are always underfunded and often meet with powerful opposition. Prevention would require a total rethinking of all our industrial processes and the waste products that we spew into our environment. This in turn would inevitably lead to a thorough restructuring of our entire consumption-driven socioeconomic system.

For the most part, the long and arduous training that young aspiring doctors receive (endure) in medical school has little to do with actual healing, being whole, or becoming healthy. Western medicine, with its focus on the symptoms, physical solutions and pharmaceuticals is certainly not designed to discover or target the resistances hidden within the deeper levels of our *being*. The incorporation of psychoanalysis into the Western medical model was a positive step in this direction but, ironically, psychiatrists were, until recently, one of the least respected specialties within the medical community. Only after they changed course and to shift their focus from psychoanalysis to prescribing more pharmaceuticals, were they then accepted by most medical insiders, as being "real" doctors.

Full and permanent healing can only begin by first looking at the physical, emotional and psychological blockages that prevent our *being* from fully expressing itself. This deeper type of healing requires that we look beyond the body, and sometimes even beyond the individual, towards a much deeper cultural change that can facilitate the *flow* and *resonance* of *being* itself.

Worldwide, almost all successful healing methods and medical cures have one working element in common. ***The common element to all successful forms of healing is the patients' belief that their treatment will make them better. The Western medical process has become so impersonal and mechanistic that many of the personal factors that once helped instill faith in the doctor and his methods are simply no longer a part of this established system***.

Today, instead of the house call from a doctor we have known as a concerned friend, we face an abundance of big machines, powerful chemical compounds, and nameless specialists. This high-tech approach is, of course, very expensive. Ironically, this "high cost" can have a positive influence on our beliefs about the effectiveness of these methods. There is a prevailing belief in our culture that "you get what you pay for," so, ironically, the high expense of these treatments can often have a very positive, reinforcing effect.

As with everything, any healing results will be strongly influenced by what the individual believes at the deepest, subconscious, core levels. For those who value and believe that this impersonal and technological approach can make us healthier, this system can still work quite well. However, many of us now feel completely lost and overwhelmed by the technological and impersonal nature of our current system and, because of this disconnect, we don't always experience satisfactory results. Ultimately, our belief, in both the system and the practitioners, is the most important factor.

CLEARING PATHWAYS FOR EXPRESSION OF BEING

Stress in Our Contemporary Lives

Within our bodies we all store the memories of our previous traumas, worries, and frightening situations. We all embody numerous physical, emotional and psychological injuries from the various assaults that have occurred during our lives. We are also subject to other, less personal, injuries that can be cultural in their nature; some of our fears, memories and resulting tension involving trauma may even "predate" our current bodies. Though not always recognized, some of our deepest fears and memories might have been communicated genetically, culturally or even directly through the deeper interconnections that have always existed outside of our time-ordered realm. We are so interconnected at these deep and emotional levels that it can sometimes be difficult to even sort out who is having this memory. If our grandfather was a holocaust survivor and he raised us, it is conceivable that we also would grow up to embody some of his powerful, energetic memories.

In addition, environmental toxins and the food that we eat means additional layers of constant stress. We are physically stressed by environmental pollution, while our food is mass-produced in over worked and worn out fields that lack the healthy spectrum of required minerals. This "food" is then processed with all types of preservatives and additives, while the important and helpful microorganisms and enzymes that our food naturally contains are killed through the "sanitizing" process.

It is interesting to note that this misguided belief in the need to sterilize our food may be starting to change. As recent scientific reports indicate that our immune systems have been compromised from our obsession with an excessively sanitary environment, a new awareness is developing within the medical community; it seems that all of us, and especially children, need more exposure to natural and helpful microorganisms–our health and immune systems actually will benefit from eating more dirt.

In our contemporary culture we are constantly bombarded with situations that create, grow and reinforce stress of all types. Add to this toxic mix of stressors, the speed of *information*-processing today, and we have identified the two characteristics that most clearly define the nature of our modern culture: stressful and rushed. Within our bodies, these factors eventually create chronic tensions that are then stored deep within our muscles and nervous system. Additional unconscious and unprocessed stress can also become bound and deeply buried, through the remarkable process called *cognitive dissonance,* which is discussed in the next section.

In very young individuals, this tension usually does not have as long and chronic a history so there is less residual buildup; therefore new tensions can often be more easily dispersed through the natural rhythms of movement and exercise. For most children, just the daily movement of play is enough to release much of the potential buildup. However, as we age, the socioeconomic realities of our lives become more pressing, and we often find that we have less time for movement and exercise while our sources of stress tend to increase.

This period of history and our culture seems to continuously test the human limits of stress. No matter how well we each handle our stress, some of it still persists to affect our bodies. Even if we believe that we handle it well at the conscious level, the subconscious mind may have other ideas. Pavlov discovered that dogs salivate upon the ringing of a bell, even when there was no food present. The body will react to chronic, situational or hidden stress automatically. In our evolutionary "past" when we needed to run from mountain lions, our body's automatic production of chemical stimulants, such as adrenaline, was extremely useful. Due to our natural survival response, our bodies still produce these chemicals to prepare us to run and protect ourselves when we become stressed, even if "fight or flight" is no longer the appropriate reaction. The nature of our modern stress is such that these protective biological chemicals released within our bodies have little or no functional purpose. In our culture we are constantly preparing to react and then, responding to social requirements, we repress these automatic biological responses. When working in our office cubicle, where can we run? These unused chemicals become toxic waste products that the body must then eliminate. In our modern lives, we are chronically creating this new layer of biological stress in our bodies.

The tension in our bodies accumulates; eventually it expresses itself in indirect ways that can, and do, disrupt our lives. Pain, depression, arthritis, numbness, limited movement, frequent injuries and disease (dis-ease) are all common modern manifestations of this built-up stress.

Burying Our Least Visible Memories

While living our lives, occasionally something might happen that we consider extremely unpleasant, or even inconceivable, and we are deeply affected by this event. We then make choices that determine how we will deal with this difficult information. Some of our choices might be contemplated when we are in a consciously open state, but far too often our choices are the result of reflexive responses that are completely unconscious. Remember that since all possible reactions are fully expressed somewhere in the *Multiverse*, in some unseen way our *being* experiences all of these different and possible responses.

The most conscious option available to us is to explore and deeply feel the disturbing event openly and honestly. This involves a willingness to receive truthful information, no matter what our reflex is or what we might think about this truth. Once the information is received, we can then *inquire* and discover if and where we might have any internal *resistance* to whatever is unfolding. Then we can uncover, forgive, embrace and clear our tension so that we can move on to a new *viewport* with a greater breadth of wisdom and experience. In our Western culture, and most other cultures in our world today, this is the most rarely practiced option.

More often we "dance" around the issue as we avoid directly exploring or dealing with our feelings or reaction to the event. As part of this avoidance, we often try to keep this unpleasant memory out of our day-to-day thoughts. Maintaining such a state of denial requires a tremendous expenditure of energy. An even more damaging, yet very common, reaction is to totally bury the event with all its associated memories deep in our *being*, where the conscious mind will not be able to access it directly. With this "trick" we are essentially turning off the entire part of our circuitry that allows this memory to be accessed. The *repressed memory* is still there, for it is stored *holographically* in every cell of the body; we just no longer can easily or directly access it.

As mentioned earlier, cognitive dissonance is the name for the psychological phenomenon in which we become incapable of being able to remember, see, experience or consciously register an event or action. This can occur because the event conflicts with, or falls so far outside of, our normal expectations that we have nothing to relate it with. This usually means that we lack the ability to even "record" the event in our conscious minds. Many of us walk around without ever knowing that we have "missed" many events that unfold around us due to *cognitive dissonance.* While we are not conscious of these experiences, they still do register and become embedded within our unconscious *being.* Sometimes these "unseen" events can create deep *repressed memories* that produce unexplained physical and emotional symptoms. I know from my own personal journey that this can, and does, happen in very dramatic fashion. It took me more than 25 years of adult living to even discover that I had deeply buried *repressed memories* of a very traumatic series of events.

Regardless of the exact method or form of avoidance, the result is that a part of us becomes disconnected, separated, "lost" and buried within. When we "deal" with an issue in this way, then other thoughts, feelings, smells and other nervous system connections that are indirectly connected to this event may also become *associated* with this memory. Because of this *association*, these other things, people and events may also wind up "missing." These "missing" memories might involve other events that occurred at the same time or location, things associated with the same smells or sounds, or other events involving the same people. These blocked neural pathways are then no longer directly accessible through our conscious minds or nervous system. A part of our energetic *being* just disappears, as it is essentially cleaved from our conscious *being.* Along with this disassociation, we also lose a part of our life-force and our claim to wholeness. Over time other connected memories, or even completely new but related ones, also get buried and add to the collateral loss of memories and energetic pathways. We then enter into a slow, self-created kind of death spiral, leaving only a shell to continue our physical form. We find ourselves feeling numb and searching for some message of meaning in our lives. Bit by bit, we can lose direct access to large parts of our soul and *being.*

The most effective and direct healing methods for buried trauma involve uncovering, meeting and reintegrating this missing piece of us. *Depth psychology, cognitive therapy* and similar counseling methods all can help in this process. Body-centered techniques such as deep massage, acupuncture and Rolfing also can help these memories resurface so that they then can be processed. The ancient technique of Shamanic Soul Retrieval is specifically designed to help us reclaim these "lost" parts of our *being*.

This process involves the recognition and release of hidden traumatic physical and emotional pain, so it can be very challenging. Regardless of what healing modality or combination of methods is chosen, the process of discovering the separated parts of our soul and their reintegration is almost never easy or comfortable. Through practice, this difficulty diminishes, as we acquire trust in and experience with this process and its amazing, life-changing benefits. Only late in this process does it become clear that our personal suffering was the result of our internal resistance to the event, and not caused by the event itself.

Forgiveness is the final and critical step to complete this healing process, and it will be discussed in great detail later. Often overlooked is the importance of forgiving ourselves along with forgiving any "others." Once we learn how to fully forgive in a natural and integrated way, most of the pain caused by our suffering will quickly disappear. At this point, this inner work becomes fun and exciting. *I believe that a big part of our purpose and life's work is to become hollow beings; beings that are more whole and open–it is through this process we grow and contribute our part to creation itself. As we become more open, it becomes very natural to want to share our joy about what we have learned and gained from our own personal journey.*

Finding and Eliminating Our Kinks

We pay a direct physical price whenever we cleave and bury our difficult experiences for the temporary illusion of avoiding pain. While we are living with these repressed memories, they increasingly become physical tensions held and hidden within our bodies, often in the middle of some strong muscle group. Except for some tightness, stiffness, or an occasional twinge in a joint, we may not even notice an issue for years. Initially appearing as only a small knot or kink, it gradually becomes more physical and, over time, can become so pronounced that it even can become visible. At this stage, it can be easily found and felt by massage therapists or body workers.

Our buried tensions prevent our muscle groups from working smoothly, being fully balanced and doing their job efficiently and well. As time goes on, these small restrictions will spread, and they will have collateral impact on entire muscle groups. They then begin to affect and alter our body mechanics, which causes numerous, cascading, physical problems. If left unresolved, joints can become chronically inflamed and eventually arthritic. Nerves and tendons can be forced out of their natural positions, causing severe pain. The reduced mobility of a body leads to the calcification and hardening of soft tissue, which only works as designed when it is flexible. Over time, organs become affected, and then other, related physical problems emerge. These physical blocks eventually affect the circulation of lymph and blood or interfere with the nervous system, and they always restrict our *energy* flow.

Within our body, these tension holding points can often become very sensitive to physical touch and, in chronic cases, deep massage can become extremely painful–at least initially. Over the years, layers of physical "protection" such as tight muscles, calcified tissue, and built-up fat will be formed to cover and "protect" the original knot, making it much more difficult to access directly. The therapist must first work through and soften these multiple protective layers before gaining access to the now-deeper origination points. However, if the person being treated is psychologically prepared to address their primary emotional issues and allow release, a deep resolution and healing of these blockages can occur immediately, right on the massage table. These releases can look very dramatic because they often involve spasms, shaking, spontaneous vocalizations and excretions. Experienced therapists are prepared for these spontaneous, but natural and healthy, reactions and will help guide clients through this stage of the process into deeper levels of forgiveness and gratitude. The most experienced therapists know exactly when and where to encourage such releases.

These releases change our vibratory pattern instantly, and this shift alters our entire relationship to the *Multiverse* and, therefore, our lives. As we progress, we learn how to more easily clear these blockages and continue to discover new restrictions in freshly revealed layers of our physical and emotional body. Due to our now-expanded experience, wisdom and knowledge, as we continue to progress it becomes much easier to clear our newly discovered but long-held, blockages. The natural flow of life is towards wholeness so, in some form, this healing process can and will continue as long as we have these bodies.

Once we are very comfortable and fully engaged in this process, we then might begin to notice that the issues uncovered begin to seem less personal and more universal in their character and quality. At this level we are working towards clearing more of the cultural, genetic and archetypical blockages that we all carry in our physical and emotional bodies simply because we have been born into this world. This secondary impersonal stage of our clearing and healing process usually seems much easier, much more satisfying and often even fun because, by this point, we have likely gained a level of mastery that can only come from experience.

Two Critical Types of Release

For effective healing there are two different levels where we must release our blockages–the physical level and the deeper emotional level. A release at the level of the body, such as what might occur during a typical chiropractic adjustment, will often provide quick relief from pain or pressure. However, this improvement might only last for hours or for days because the deeper source of the issue will still be present. Physical knots and kinks will return unless the underlying emotional conditions are also identified and addressed. This temporary type of body release can be very useful for relieving acute problems such as back pain or sciatica. However, because these techniques often address only our outer symptoms, without additional work they provide only short-term solutions.

The other level of release, the emotional, occurs at or nearer to the source. At this deeper level, healing occurs when the emotional content that is triggering the tension is recognized, identified and felt, and then forgiven and released. Once the emotional content is addressed, then any subsequent physical releases will become more permanent. Often this entire process must be repeated several times because of natural and reflexive *body memory*. The "old and familiar" tensions can and will rebuild into their old and familiar patterns, over and over, just from reflex, habit and *body memory*. These holding patterns appear much like echoes, each time becoming fainter. However, because the emotional content has been successfully addressed and released, these "echoes" now lack the root-level tension to sustain them. These secondary and tertiary echoes are, therefore, usually much weaker, less entrenched and much more-easily cleared than the original knots. Eventually the body's old habits fade; with conscious maintenance those particular tensions will not return.

Bodywork is excellent for identifying where our knots are physically located, and sometimes, especially when working with skilled therapists, it can also become an effective tool for discovering the nature, or emotional source, of our issues. Release can be achieved through various bodywork techniques such a deep massage, Rolfing, Chiropractic, Acupuncture, and Shiatsu, or even gentler techniques such as Feldenkrais and Reiki. However, without the additional psychological and emotional exploration required to address the root causes, these surface tensions will likely return. If we learn, through bodywork, where our bodies hold their tension, we can use this *information* to better understand and help clear these blockages at their source.

Surrendering to Deeper Healing

Sometimes the first sign of blockage can be a particular area of our body that has become injury-prone. Embedded tension reduces the elasticity of our muscles and connective tissue and this can cause the excessively tight muscles to pull and strain the connective tissue. With this reduction in flexibility, normal everyday twists and turns of our body can result in strain, pain and injuries. At the physical level it is very easy to understand how an inflexible muscle might be more prone to strain and injury. However, our blockages usually originate from levels much deeper than the physical surface. At these deeper levels, where all things can be understood to be fully interconnected, the particular body parts that becomes blocked, or injured, often provide direct clues to understanding the emotional issues that created this tension. ***When we injure a specific place in our body, it is wise to consider that, at some level, there is a reason that our life flow is directing us to focus our attention on that particular part of our body. In the Multiverse there are no accidents; there is only interactive cause-and-effect.***

Once the superficial tension has been identified, it is only a matter of a little time, and some focused body and psychological work, before the fuller and more permanent release becomes possible. We naturally desire to be whole and, therefore, when given the chance, we will always move towards wholeness–this is our deep nature. While our therapist is working with our physical tension, it can be very effective to "ask" our injury, or area of tension, to reveal its secrets. We benefit from seeking the counsel of this old friend, our chronic tension, which has been with us, knows us and has been interacting with our life for a very long time. We usually get the best results from this combination of therapies, by surrendering all of our ideas and preconceptions to participate with a consciousness that is fully open and available to all possibilities.

Answers can arrive in many different forms. The quickest and most direct insights are often communicated metaphorically from the specific nature of the injury itself. Clues often can be derived from the actual functions of the body parts involved. Sore shoulders might mean that we are feeling the weight of a particularly heavy load because we are trying to "shoulder" too much responsibility. Tension in the legs could mean we are having issues around "support," or we might be resisting the desire to "run from a situation." Headache could mean we are "over-thinking" an issue, while a pain or tension in the center of our chest can direct us to examine a recent emotional "heartache." Sharp pains in the back between the shoulder blades might indicate that we are having issues that are related to not "trusting" others–we are experiencing being "stabbed in the back." A small library of books have been written about these near-literal interpretations of symptoms; many of these associations turn out to be quite accurate, or at least serve to help us focus our attention in a more helpful direction.

Body-work that involves the integration of psychological aspects can sometimes unearth deeply-buried and forgotten personal experiences. Their discovery or release might be accompanied by specific smells, feelings, visions and even, sometimes, vivid memories. These sensations are often initially vague but they grow more vivid as the discovery process continues. Over time these small "hints" coalesce, find their interrelationships, and communicate new meaning. The exact form of the release process will vary from person to person, but the patient must remain in an open state of deep surrender for this unfolding to continue. Any internal resistance or struggle and the process stops, at least temporarily. Our willingness to receive and look at whatever emerges is a critical precondition for success with this deep type of healing. We can't be partially committed to the process and expect success. We make the significant shifts only when we are ready and willing to dive in fully and completely let go of our preconceived notions.

Once the root of the stress has been addressed, processed, accepted and embraced, it no longer reinforces or adds to the tension, and our healing can then become permanent. The fear or trauma found at the core of our embodied tensions has emotional content and memories, and if these are simply witnessed, or allowed to be revisited without judgment, an enormous relaxation is likely. As discussed earlier, our bodies have their old habits so, after such a witnessing, there may still be some additional, embodied tension. Repeating this process a number of times in an abbreviated form–always incorporating *forgiveness* and *gratitude*–is often necessary to complete the release. This last step of incorporating *forgiveness* and *gratitude* is absolutely critical for our complete healing–this is discussed in the next section. Learning how to work with our bodies in this way is similar to any learning process–it takes time, patience, trust, motivation and the determined willingness to continue walking through our shadowy valleys until the next mountaintop vista is reached.

Issues do not need to be specifically isolated and identified for a full healing to occur. In fact, the deepest and most profound changes often result from the more generalized or global relaxations. Letting go of general anger or blame can have a profound, dramatic and lasting effect on a person's *being*. However, it is my experience that this type of global healing is most possible and available after our more personal and specific issues have already been addressed.

Even though the external issues may appear to be complex, deeply layered and interwoven, they all have a similar source. ***Ultimately, our tensions all grow from our fears related to feeling separate and vulnerable. We hold tension because we are not "trusting" the process of life itself. This is always because we are missing the deep and fundamental knowledge about who we really are and our direct connections to each other and everything else in creation.***

Forgiveness and Gratitude

Throughout my own personal process, the most dramatic releases and shifts occurred only after genuine and profound *forgiveness* and *gratitude* were incorporated to complete the process. Our *forgiveness* and *gratitude* might be specifically focused upon the events and people that were directly related to the trauma, or they can also be practiced at a much more general level. The overall willingness to forgive everyone, through a deep, level insight into the nature of humanity, is much more effective than only forgiving specific issues or individuals. Our *forgiveness* is similar to medical inoculations, some of which only work with very specific diseases. The more general type of *forgiveness* and *gratitude*, when practiced deeply as part of an overall lifestyle, provides a much greater, long-term benefit, because, like a healthy immune system, it not only heals specific issues, but it also "inoculates" us in a broader and more durable way.

When the emotional core of our holding spot is finally "touched" in a safe, healing environment, we sometimes can experience a torrent of memories and feelings that are deeply and directly associated with our initial fear or trauma. We also may spontaneously revisit our memories about the event itself. Sometimes we find new words and pictures for what was once only an unconscious reaction, and certain people in our lives might become closely associated with the event. While all this conscious awareness might be helpful, it is not required for the healing. In addition, a focus on the specific details of the trauma can even sometimes distract us from the true healing process.

After uncovering the lost memory, we find ourselves at the critical point in our healing process where we have several possible paths available as we move forward. For example, if we were "wronged" by "others," we might find that we are still angry at those involved. In some special cases, if they are still present and engaged in our lives and they also are open to the process of clearing, it can be very healthy and productive to have a direct, nonjudgmental discussion about the event. This is likely to be very difficult emotionally, but if handled without judgment or blame, it can lead to fresh insights, breakthroughs, a much deeper understanding, and even the direct experience of a deep, shared Love.

In most situations these direct personal interactions are not the best approach. Direct meetings can easily become confrontational, and this outcome is not beneficial to anyone. Direct discussion probably should be avoided if either party is likely to be extremely defensive, reactive, firmly entrenched in their idea, or incapable of an honest discussion about the event.

While a direct, honest communication with those involved can sometimes be helpful, it is never necessary for our healing process. Healing has nothing to do with winning arguments or being seen as "right" by the other party. True healing never even requires any "others." We need not change or influence anyone else to heal ourselves, but healing ourselves always will always work towards healing "others." *The "cure" is always about changing our viewport, not theirs; and, at the deepest level of change, we eventually realize that there really are no "others" involved anyway–there is only oneness experienced in its many different forms of self.*

At some point in our healing process we will be required to discover, examine and diffuse our limiting core beliefs. As we are reminded by every example in this book, it does not matter what the "others" do because what we experience is completely determined by how we are seeing, interpreting and reacting. *Ultimately life is our movie and our movie only.* I often repeat and re-repeat this basic and critical concept–one that is built into the very architecture of the *Multiverse*. *At the deepest level there is only you!*

In the realms where we still experience the "other," we can easily forgive anyone if we are aware that any act of harm that appeared to be directed towards us involved nothing more than unconscious or unaware behavior, both theirs and/or ours. As Christ offered *"They know not what they do."* None of us ever fully understands our own actions and motivations. *No matter what type of event created the trauma, the "others" involved were only acting through a script that was written from their own unconscious fears and traumas. They can therefore be forgiven for just playing their part in the 3D human drama, the play called life, which is all only an illusion anyway. In a sense, no one does anything to anyone, ever, for everything we experience is all just part of this grand illusion. Once this is realized, we can finally take the most important step in the process of forgiveness, which is to forgive ourselves for exactly the same reason. We were just acting our part in the drama. There is no blame to be distributed, but rather there is more wisdom to be gained. At deeper levels, the victim and the perpetrator are one; so forgiving the perpetrator is equivalent to forgiving oneself.*

This is where gratitude enters to complete our healing. Deep and steadfast, this is a gratitude for our fortunate opportunity to participate in this beautiful manifestation of physical life. It is a joyful gratitude for all those wonderful adventures that we will be experiencing in our "future." This is a thankful gratitude for all the experiences of the "past," especially the painful ones that allowed us to be having this exquisite present moment experience.

Combing the Soul

When we are actively engaged in our clearing and healing process, our lives change in many noticeable ways. Knots and blockages will still continue to form. Some will be generated from new interactions, but most will form from old patterns just repeating themselves–reflexive echoes of our old *body memories*. Our bodies and egos need regular maintenance in order to not rebuild into old patterns. Just as we comb the knots from our hair on a regular basis, we also need to "comb" the knots from our body and soul to keep ourselves flowing smooth, open, and relatively free. Combing the soul is no different than combing our hair–it is a lifelong process that works best when incorporated into our daily routine. Yoga, stretching, exercise, massage and inner self-witnessing all aid us in this process.

DIET EXERCISE AND PHYSICAL ENVIRONMENT

All discussions about healing need to include the physical component along with the emotional, spiritual and psychological aspects of our *being*. While this book examines some of the psychological, emotional and spiritual aspects of healing, primarily it discusses specific methods for addressing issues that block our human potential and ability to experience deep level *resonance*. No matter how well we work with these aspects, if our diet and physical environment are not considered part of our trinity of support (body, mind and spirit), the body suffers and our *being* cannot function at its maximum potential. Unhealthy diets create numerous problems beyond the obvious problem of not providing the right essential nutrients. In our modern world, our bodies expend enormous amounts of *energy* to clear our systems of toxins, foreign bodies, and waste from our digestion and external environmental exposure. The vast majority of these physical stressors are brought in through our consumption of food and drink. All of this wasted *energy* could be used by our bodies in much more interesting ways. A proper diet is critical for maximizing our physical health, and physical health is a great asset on our path to freedom.

While important for sustained progress, a good diet is not an absolute prerequisite for spiritual, emotional or psychological growth. To the contrary, health challenges can often directly provide the initial trigger for substantial growth. However, in the long term, better health makes the journey more fun, productive and sustainable.

Sometimes, just as with the spiritual and psychological aspects of our *being*, the elimination of blockages becomes the single most important thing we can do in the physical realm to create a change in our physical health. In their ideal states, our physical bodies are usually amazingly efficient, resilient and adaptable. Unfortunately, modern life exposes us to far too many toxins, while our eating habits often create too much waste. Many people operate under the assumption that if they are not feeling their best, they must be missing something in their diet such as a vitamin, mineral, supplement or a particular food. They imagine that it is some "lack" that prevents them from being fully healthy and productive so they consume more food and supplements, hoping to fill these missing parts of their diet. The physical stress from all the extra additives that are consumed, during this search for the perfect diet, can become more of a problem than any actual lack. The potential physical disruptors include toxic levels of some vitamins, artificial sweeteners, high fructose corn syrup, pharmaceuticals, allergens, additives and even the excess food, itself. This is a very contemporary problem that tends to be most severe in the developed parts of our world. As always, when experimenting we need to use moderation; with diet it is understood that often "less is more."

Some of my most vivid glimpses through the veil that separates our world from the hidden parts of the *Multiverse* have occurred during extended fasts. There is always a dramatic shift in clarity and insight after the third or fourth day of a fast, even on a simple juice fast. Unless we are literally starving, malnourished, healing an injury, or in the middle of a demanding growth spurt, it is generally true that the lighter we eat, the more energy we have to expend on the nonphysical parts of our lives. Eating, and all the biological functions that surround it, require and consume our physical energy. Eating food also reinforces and solidifies the 3D aspects of our lives.

Another important factor to always keep in mind, when examining diets, is that we are all different. We all have individual and sometimes unique intolerances to different foods and supplements. Therefore, what works for one person, specifically, might be very wrong for another. Dairy from cows and high fructose corn syrup are extremely stressful to my body, but many people have little or no problem with these. The needs of our individual bodies will also change over time. I have recently discovered that I now have a problem digesting gluten. My neighbor would lose many productive days from his life if he accidentally consumed a little wheat gluten but for me, gluten never seemed problematic. That quickly changed last year, when I discovered that several nagging chronic problems were directly related to my consumption of gluten.

If we find ourselves facing problems such as arthritis, autoimmune reactions, allergies, migraines, digestive problems, or lack of mental clarity, we should first look at and experiment with diet before any other treatments are employed. Not only are we all different and unique, but our individual needs also change throughout our lives; this means that we have to always remain alert and flexible. What works for us during one period of our life might not work later. Change is something that all of us can always count upon.

Plants and animals have adopted various evolutionary strategies to insure the long-term survival of their species. One of the logical results of natural selection is the development of plant and animal varieties that become toxic to the animals that normally graze on them. This means that these new varieties are less likely to be consumed. This evolutionary buildup of toxicity occurs through a natural process whereby random mutations cause specific individuals to become more toxic to predators. These more-toxic individuals have a better chance of survival and, therefore, higher odds of reproducing and passing on their mutated genes to their offspring. Over time, this natural evolutionary strategy creates entirely new varieties that are more toxic to their traditional consumers. Common potatoes, peppers and tomatoes all have adapted to contain strychnine, and many other plant and animal food groups contain similar toxins. We hybridize, propagate and prepare our food to reduce the concentration of these naturally occurring and common toxins; but if we overeat we may still be receiving significant doses.

Our modern farming system has become a system dominated by large agricultural corporations such as Monsanto. Market control and profit have led this industry to increase the production of high-yield but potentially toxic plant varieties, and to even create new plant varieties that disperse nonviable seeds. Today, plants and livestock are genetically modified for a long shelf life, disease- and insect-resistance, and pesticide tolerance. New varieties are usually developed with little regard for nutritional concerns.

How our bodies are really reacting to these new manufactured foods is largely unknown and mostly untested. Like lab rats, we have all unknowingly become experimental subjects. The list of diseases that are associated with diet now includes almost every problem or disease known to man! Recently introduced GMOs (genetically modified organisms) and the rapid spread of highly processed products like "high fructose corn syrup" have brought a new and large collection of biological stressors to our dinner tables.

There is also an *energetic* component to anything and everything that we put into our bodies. *Matter* is *energy* and therefore food is *energy*. Simple *calories* are not the only *energetic* component of our food. As we each become more sensitive to the aspects of our lives that exist outside of our 3D realm, these unseen *energetic* factors become more important. Dietary changes can alter our biochemistry and enhance our openness and sensitivity to deeper levels of functioning. Fasting reveals new ways to look at food, and it provides our bodies with a much-needed opportunity to reboot. When we return to eating after a long or deep fast, we can carefully experiment by adding foods back into our diet, one at a time. When we do this, we notice exactly how specific foods interact with our body and *being*.

Only two hundred years ago there was an active tradition of cannibalism in the Fiji Islands. Fijians had no need to eat each other to survive because, on their land, food grows easily and everywhere–food has always been plentiful in their island nation. When their ancestors practiced cannibalism, they only chose to eat their most respected enemies. The purpose of this intentional cannibalism was to absorb the power or life-force of these enemy warriors. Within this tradition is embodied the forgotten awareness that there is more *information* than just vitamins, carbohydrates, fat, protein and calories in the food that we consume. I am certainly not endorsing cannibalism, but I am suggesting a much more conscious approach to our consumption of food. ***In multiple and hidden ways, we become what we eat.***

HEALING AND OUR BODIES

Healing begins the moment our tension and holding patterns start to release. At this point our *dis-eased* body can begin its return to a more balanced and natural state of *ease.* Our soul can then vibrate differently, allowing life-force to move more freely through our body. As our vibratory pattern changes, so does our universe.

Sometimes, if our body has been too badly damaged or compromised, even a complete and deep-level healing will not insure the survival of our current physical body. This might be because we are too old, too tired, or too broken for these bodies to be successfully or productively revived. Healing is never really about the body because our body is only the illusion that is visible at the surface of our dimensional realm. In some situations when the healing occurs, it just makes much more "sense" for the greater natural system to recycle a *being's* critical *information* through a new and healthier manifestation of form. ***Energy and information are never lost, but they will often change their external expression at the level of form! Life goes on, always, but physical forms will freely change as needed. If we identify with our old form, this renewing process will always look like death.*** However, if we are more loosely bound to our forms, this change of form will then appear to us as just another new adventure. As we deepen our understanding, this level of transition will be seen as nothing more than taking the new Buick out for a spin while leaving the old Ford in the garage.

In our Western model of healing, this change of form–the death of the body–can represent a significant failure. In our culture there is the prevailing belief that if the patient dies, the healing was not successful. In the *Multiverse* every healing is successful because the experience is a new opportunity to move towards a more expansive level of *being*. Life continues for our *being*, as always, allowing a new section of the *Multiverse* to be experienced through some new form or combination of forms. During the dying process, the ego, and any egoic memories that belong to the old physical form, are dropped right along with the old form. *Being* itself undergoes a timely reboot, and all that was not temporary and transient in its deeper nature continues in new and refreshed manifestations. There is no failure, ever, from the perspective of the *Multiverse*.

MIRACLES

Human beings have always been impressed by dramatic phenomena. Had Jesus simply been a teacher, we probably would know little or nothing about him today; his reputation was permanently guaranteed through the many miracles attributed to him. He is reported to have turned a few loaves and fishes into a banquet for the multitudes, walked on water, publicly healed sick people, and risen up from the dead; the dramatic and miraculous nature of these events ensured that many would notice, listen and spread the word. Our ubiquitous curiosity around these types of events certainly was a significant factor in securing his place in our history. We have always taken our miracle workers seriously, largely because they seem to have some level of access to realms that the rest of us can't easily enter.

When we become more aware of the nature of the *Multiverse,* the conceptual limitations of our 3D world start to dissolve easily and naturally. We begin to realize that all these miracles and unusual phenomena are simply short glimpses through the portals to our greater existence beyond. These are small portals that allow us a small glimmer of the full, completely connected and interactive universe that has always been present, but obscured by the veil of our 3D limitations. Rather than actual miracles, there are, instead, multitudes of unseen natural interconnections that are always unfolding beyond the limits of our time and space. When we have a glimpse into this ever-present but unseen world, it appears to us as a "miracle." Miracle workers are simply those who have the expertise or talent for seeing into this organic fabric and interpreting these outer edges of our conceptual world.

PLACEBO EFFECT

The *placebo effect* is a phenomenon that was first observed and documented during the trial testing of pharmaceuticals. As part of the *scientific method*, researchers always test non-medicated *control groups* so, through comparison, they could determine the effectiveness of new medications. By carefully comparing results from the *placebo* group to those patients that took the medication, they could then determine how well a medication works.

To eliminate disparate psychological factors during these tests, it is important that both groups of subjects believe that they were given the real medication. Therefore it was, and still is, standard experimental procedure for researchers to administer sugar (or equivalent) pills to the *control group* in the very same way that they are giving the active pharmaceuticals to the other group. The very fact that these early experiments were set up this way acknowledges that the researchers were already aware that such psychological factors could influence the outcome. (Just why these known psychological factors are not directly incorporated into our Western medical technology is the subject of many books and reports.) After these early trials the researchers discovered that the *control groups* often exhibited a notable improvement. Sometimes the improvement in those taking the sugar pills was equal to, or even better than, the results that were achieved by the "real" pills. This observation was named the *placebo effect.* Extremely powerful and now thoroughly documented, thousands of research studies support the irrefutable conclusion that the "power of *placebo*" is very real.

The placebo effect works because of one main factor–the power of our deep beliefs to shape our physical world. Part of the placebo effect seems to be associated with the actual act of doing something, such as taking a pill, instead of just doing nothing. If the pharmaceutical that is being tested has negating or harmful side effects, sometimes the *placebo* pill will then work better than the actual medication. This "reversed" result could also occur if the assistants who administered the *placebo* seemed nicer, or the room where it was administered appeared more attractive.

While common and sometimes dramatic, the *placebo effect* is rarely publicized by the pharmaceutical companies that conduct the vast majority of these tests. All pharmaceutical companies are in the business of selling their valuable products, and not inexpensive sugar pills; so, unfortunately, for economic reasons this *information* often goes underreported or is even suppressed.

Despite this lack of economic incentive, the *placebo* cure is still finding its way into Western medicine as a useful tool. Certain individual doctors have adopted this old "shaman's trick" and successfully treat illness by prescribing little more than sugar pills. The negative side effects are then nonexistent, and if the patient believes that the pills will help, they usually do.

Surgical Placebo

Placebo studies all point to a simple principle. It matters little how we treat some medical conditions. What matters most is the patient's personal belief that they are being helped.

Surgeon Bruce Mosely studied surgical placebo: "A Controlled Trial of Arthroscopic Surgery" (Mosely, JBK O'Malley et al. Baylor School of Medicine, 2002 Published in *New England Journal of Medicine* 347(2):81-88). He was clear that his surgeries helped people but did not know what part or component of surgery was most effective. He divided his patients into three groups. Group one received normal knee-cartilage reshaping, Group two only had their knees flushed and drained, and Group three, the *placebo* group, had small external incisions made and stitched but no internal surgery. This *placebo* group thought that they had received the full surgery because the surgeon even went so far as to generate noises that might be expected during such a surgery. Subsequent follow-up for a couple of years determined that all three groups had similar improvement. Mosely even noted that the *placebo* group actually fared a bit better. The *placebo* "surgery" worked every bit as well as the real surgery. Mosely's conclusion in the research paper from the study was, *"my skill as a surgeon had no benefit on these patients."* What mattered most was the patients' belief that they were being helped and would soon be better.

Surgery is an important mechanical component of modern medicine. If a bone is broken, setting it back in place is the critical first step to a successful physical healing. However, at some early point the body's own healing mechanisms must take over. This is the point where the patient's belief becomes a significant factor. Our beliefs always dramatically affect the final results.

STRONG BELIEF AND HEALING

There are thousands of different local, traditional, healing modalities practiced throughout every corner of our planet. Some traditions are built directly into the local tribal system, like the Siberian Shamans or the "Drau ni Kao" healers in Fiji. Others are the invention of specific individuals, such as, "John of God" in Brazil, or "Maria Sabina of Oaxaca." While there is undoubtedly a significant amount of profit-motivated "snake oil" and quackery in the mix, many of these local, traditional practices do work; and sometimes they work very well. Some of the positive results may be due to the specific herbs or techniques but, again, a large portion of their success cannot be attributed to any actual techniques or medicines, but rather to each patient's strong belief in their chosen practitioner and their methods.

Until the recent expansion of world travel, most patients were raised within the very culture that created and sustained their local tradition; they very well knew the methods and personal reputations of village healers. Traditional cures work in ways that are similar to the *placebo effect*; they all rely on a strong belief system. The effectiveness of these methods demonstrates that an important role for any healer is to provide caring and focused attention that supports the patient's belief that they are being helped.

Unfortunately, as previously discussed, the importance of this type of support has been mostly forgotten within contemporary Western medicine. We seem to have lost sight of the common principle that all of these traditional practices share. They all recognize the amazing power of our beliefs. Again, as Henry Ford, the creative genius who developed the "Model A" Ford, mass production and the Ford Motor Company said, "Whether you think you can, or think you can't–you are right."

This fundamental and important principle will be reinforced throughout the rest of this book because the deepest types of learning, those that are ultimately the most life-changing, often require repetition. **Belief is effective because it works at the root of all real change–it changes our core vibrational state. It alters our vibrational integrity.**

Many healing practices attribute their results to specific herbs, manipulations or special techniques; I absolutely do not want to downplay integrated parts of any of these practices because many components of traditional and modern healing practices can work together to contribute to positive results. What is common to all the successful traditions is that they effectively instill in the patient a belief that the healing practice will help them, and that very belief can be the most important component part of any cure.

MY FIRST ACUPUNCTURE TREATMENT

As a young adult, throughout an eight-year period I had a persistent and chronic health issue that dramatically affected my life. During that period of my life, I spent a large amount of time and money on hospitalization and Western medical technologies. Facing life-changing surgery, I was blessed to have stumbled across a young doctor who had acquired some atypical experience with Eastern medical systems. He explained that Western medicine did not have good options, or a history of positive results, for my particular chronic condition, but while serving as a military doctor in Vietnam, he had personally witnessed cases where my exact issue was cured through the use of acupuncture. Suggesting that I try acupuncture before resorting to surgery, he was careful to include the caveat, *"please do not tell anyone that I am recommending this!"* This was 1974 and the medical establishment did not yet accept alternative medical techniques such as acupuncture. He feared that he could lose his license for even suggesting this option.

Because I was living in the South Pacific at the time, I easily found an old Chinese practitioner. As I described my problem to the acupuncturist, he laughed and said, *"Oh...that is very easy. One treatment maybe two at the most."* In that precise moment, after years of frustration, I felt a strong palpable change, which, to this day, I believe was the actual moment of "healing. Once inside his office, I had a seven-point (needle) treatment and two days later I felt perfectly well. My physical problem disappeared and it has never returned.

The confidence that the acupuncturist displayed totally changed my internal conceptual idea about how difficult my problem was to cure. Over the previous eight years I had been witnessing a great amount of confusion about my condition from the Western medical establishment. This probably also included many "unheard" comments between medical personnel during three procedures, while I was under anesthetic and theoretically "unconscious." These memories were all probably stored deep within my subconscious and may have contributed to my emotional and physical stress. Years of this type of negative input had convinced me that my issue was difficult and incurable.

I clearly experienced a significant change during our conversation, before the actual acupuncture treatment. I am sure that the cure began with this alteration of my thought patterns around my condition–this was probably the acupuncturist's intention. The actual treatment probably had an additional beneficial effect because it was specifically designed to increase blood flow to my inflamed organs so that my own body could, and would, take care of itself. However something significant changed even before the first needle. There was a clear and dramatic shift in my attitude, brought on by the old Chinese acupuncturist's confident laugh when he said, *"this is nothing!"* That life-changing moment altered my entire belief system about my disease and, thus, I became open and able to shift "universes." I then shifted to an alternate parallel universe where my illness was not lifelong and debilitating.

Today, there are numerous signs of change in the Western medical establishment's attitude about alternative techniques such as acupuncture. Hospitals now have acupuncture clinics; nurses practice massage and midwifery; and physical therapists now use once-strange, alternative techniques such as the Emotional Freedom Technique or EFT. Western doctors still can't explain why acupuncture and some of these other practices work, yet they are now willing to prescribe some of these treatments. As a culture, we are apparently becoming more comfortable with the Eastern idea of "not knowing." This occurs as we also become more aware of ourselves as *quantum beings*, brimming with *infinite* possibilities.

FAITH HEALING

In churches, tents, rooms, huts and outdoor spaces across America and all around our globe, a diverse assortment of faith healing rituals are practiced. These gatherings often rely on nothing more than a charismatic practitioner, a prayer, a laying on of hands, or some similar visible–and sometimes very dramatic–technique. Like the healer from Ghana, mentioned earlier, and my acupuncture treatment, these rituals are all primarily rooted in the patient's faith or belief in the healer and the process. Without this level of patient participation, there would be no real possibility of change.

Jesus led faith healings, but had the unusual presence of mind to state the deeper truth about the perceived miracles. He repeatedly communicated the idea that he did not and could not heal us–only we have the power to heal ourselves. Since faith is a critical component of any healing process, ultimately all real healings are faith healings.

Filipino "Psychic Surgery"

Twenty years ago I had the opportunity to be involved as a preparatory assistant for a series of "psychic surgeries" that were performed by a practitioner trained in the Filipino tradition. I personally saw and experienced several dozen unusual "surgeries" from an insider's perspective. For the patients, at least in the short-term, many of these "surgeries" had positive and sometimes even life-changing results.

With this form of healing, the practitioner appears to reach his or her hands into the patient's body to physically remove the diseased tissue without using knives or other cutting instruments. Blood and tissue are visible during the process, but once the patient is cleaned up after the "surgery," there are no marks or cuts. While not every patient achieved the results they had hoped for, I witnessed visible shifts in specific symptoms and a general, short-term improvement in the health, vitality and attitude in most patients. Some of these patients were very ill, and the Western medical system had already pronounced them terminal. What was really going on?

I think that I have an extremely open mind, but to my eyes, at least with this particular practitioner, the actual removed organs and tumors looked more like slaughter house waste than human body tissue. While this outwardly impressive-effect may be just a sleight-of-hand type of illusion, it may also be that this very illusion is effective for successful outcomes. I have not been trained in this tradition, but I think what is occurring, at least in most of the "surgeries" that I witnessed, is that the practitioner clearly understood the critical role that belief plays in any healing. If patients witness their "bad" body parts being removed, this illusion goes a long way towards solidifying their belief. *It is my conclusion that this practice uses intentional sleight of hand, designed not to mislead people, but rather to assist in the mental and psychological aspects of healing.* The technique, therefore, relies on the same principle as the *placebo effect*. These patients are no different from Dr. Mosely's control group. With my busy life, I lost track of the patients who were treated that day so, as of this writing, I have no current report or information about any of their longer-term results.

Much, if not all, of what we see and experience in our world is defined by our cultural and personal ideas about what is possible. It is conceivable that there are individual *psychic surgeons* that can and do reach into human bodies. Some who practice this tradition may physically reach in and repair or remove body parts because, in our *quantum Multiverse,* this is theoretically possible, even if it is not very probable. Skin is only *matter* and, as we know, *matter* is far from solid, and every possible outcome will be manifested somewhere. I believe, however, that these special cases represent, at most, a very small fraction of these "surgical" healings. The real power of this type of faith healing lies in our belief.

Fijian Witch Doctor

Years ago, when I lived on a small remote island in the South Pacific as a Peace Corps volunteer, I visited a local witch doctor because there were no other medical facilities available locally and, of course, I wanted to give it a try. In Fiji, these healers were called "Drau ni Kau," which translates as "healer who uses plants." The main "medicine" that all Fijian traditional healers use is the country's traditional drink called Kava: an intoxicant, traditionally brewed from the roots (and much less potent stems) of a plant they also call Yagona. The plant is ground into a powder and made into a tea that is consumed daily, in large quantities, by much of the population of Fiji. In the United States we can buy "kavakava,"–the weaker version of this herb, made from stems–in the natural supplements aisle of many grocery stores. Fresh Yagona can be extremely powerful when prepared from carefully tended medicinal plants; a few bowls of strong Kava will dramatically alter any consumer's awareness and personality.

Along with using this "medicine," the "drau ni kau" wore an elaborate and colorful costume and performed a long series of incantations that created, inside of me, the strong feeling of unease. He added to this discomfort by intentionally violating my personal sense of space with his spontaneous shouting and quick, dramatic, unexpected gestures and movements around me. He was definitely trying to frighten me and wear down my resistance. The overall effect was to force me out of my normal comfort zone and into an unstable, but more open, state where I did not know what was going to happen next. The unexpected was, therefore, possible and I experienced a clear and dramatic improvement in my health and energy after my "treatment."

If the Kava "medicine" alone was responsible for the healing, there would rarely be sick people anywhere in the Fiji Islands because of the large quantities of kava that are consumed daily. It is the Fijian people's strong belief in their "drau ni kau" and the perceived healing powers of the Kava plant working together that establish the ideal conditions for healing. An absolute belief in both the doctor and the medicine fully prepares a patient for the maximum amount of inner change. This results in a shifting of the patients' *resonance* and, through this *resonant* change, their lives and health improve.

Siberian Shamans

The Russian psychologist, Olga Kharitidi, has devoted a large part of her professional career to the study of Siberian shamans. These traditional Russian shamans have repeatedly demonstrated an uncanny ability to heal people that Western Soviet doctors had already abandoned or pronounced "terminal." Dr. Kharitidi: a traditionally trained medical psychologist was only drawn into shamanic work because a dear friend of hers had a debilitating illness that doctors could not diagnose. Her friend determined that this unusual option was her last resort and asked Dr. Kharitidi to accompany her. Together they made their way to a hut in an extremely remote area of Siberia where an old female shaman asked Dr. Kharitidi to leave, but then return again the next day.

When Dr. Kharitidi returned to the hut and found her friend tied, stripped and bloodied, she panicked; she was sure that the shaman had gone too far because her friend was just hanging from her restraints and appeared dead. However, she soon discovered that her friend was only exhausted; she would soon wake and be completely transformed. Dr. Kharitidi then heard the story. Once inside the hut, and while the shaman was drinking what appeared to be
Vodka, her friend was stripped and tied up; the shaman then spent the entire day and night, with knife in hand, terrorizing the completely restrained and exhausted patient. The shaman employed various techniques, including shouting, hitting and even physical cutting, to keep the patient on edge. Staying completely intoxicated on the local alcoholic home brew as all of this was happening, the shaman had designed the entire process to force the patient past exhaustion, to a point where she no longer could hold on to resistance–she was pushed completely beyond her fear. Once the patient was in this "opened" state, it was then possible to "chase" the offending "spirits" out of her body. The "evil spirit" then was moved into a lock of her hair, which was promptly cut off and destroyed. I imagine that, by this point in that long shamanic process, those offending spirits were probably quite eager to leave.

This particular shamanistic process would likely be considered torture from any "normal" Western perspective. However, this strange "treatment of last resort" turned out to be the miracle that they both had hoped for; it worked and her friend recovered.

Having exhausted her ability to resist, the patient had surrendered everything, including her subconscious concepts, which built, reinforced and sustained the illness. This dramatic experience completely changed the focus and trajectory of the rest of Dr. Kharitidi's research and life. She now lives and works in the United States and occasionally does public speaking.

Soul Retrieval

Soul Retrieval is the ancient shamanistic practice developed for retrieving and returning a "missing" or "lost" portion of a person's soul. Historically, many forms of this type of healing have been practiced throughout the world, but Sandra Ingerman is largely responsible for reintroducing this technique to the modern Western world. Some forms of modern *depth psychology* also indirectly borrow from these methods.

I feel very fortunate to have experienced the return of several "lost" pieces of my soul through different processes involving several variations of these techniques. During my personal inner journey, I also had a few opportunities to reclaim missing pieces of my soul through fortuitous "accidents." Again, I use the term "accident" while recognizing that there really is no such thing as an accident or luck in the *Multiverse* because every interaction is a process that is regulated by cause-and-effect. These interactions are always unfolding at levels of existence that we can't see or understand directly. My own soul's "healing" has evolved through many steps or stages and, with each step, I noticed a substantial, and sometimes even quite dramatic, change in my *being*.

One of the most dramatic shifts unfolded fourteen years ago when, desperate for help and upon a friend's insistence, I finally went to see a contemporary shaman who practiced a strange amalgam of modified–but still traditional–ritual, that he combined with Jungian psychology. His sessions were four hours long and not inexpensive, so I hesitated for several months to even make the appointment.

The process began with his use of a compass to very carefully orient two chairs in my living room. He then chose one upper corner of the room and designated it as the "target." We sat in the chairs facing each other and in rapid-fire succession, he rolled through a spoken list of words such as *"work, play, life, love, food, friends, house, travel,"* etc., while carefully studying my facial reactions. When he saw some sign in my expression, or energy, that indicated that I had a potential "issue" around a particular term, he quickly stopped and repeated that word. I was then asked to focus and meditate upon that specific word and its meaning to me. It was my job to experience what the word meant to me and then find the physical place in my body where I felt that word the most. I was then instructed to mentally move that feeling to a place under my left ribcage near my spleen, grab it with my right hand, energetically "tear" it out and then throw the "remains" into the target corner.

During the first hour of this process, my mind was filled with mental chatter centered on my doubts about this strange process. I felt angry with myself for wasting my money and time on such a silly method, but because I had already paid, I stuck with the process. By the fourth and last hour, everything had completely shifted. As this last stage of his shamanic process neared its end, he asked me if I was completely able to forgive and bless a particular person around whom I had been unconsciously holding a great amount of anger. I had not told him about this person or the issue, so his question caught me by surprise–it seemed to come from "out of the blue." This forgiveness was the easy and obvious thing to do at that moment and, with that forgiveness, I experienced a genuine and heartfelt blessing and was completely transformed. I then found myself laughing more deeply and fully than I had in years and feeling absolutely joyful about life. I was finally free of a previously unseen but critical resentment that had grown, below the surface, to cripple my self-expression.

Only later did I realize that what I had undergone was a form of soul retrieval, repackaged to make it more effective for the Western mind. The physical problem permanently disappeared, and my joy, excitement, and energy for life returned. From that moment on, I had direct access to a much larger part of my *being*.

This book actually began as a direct result of a personal, yet "accidental," soul retrieval associated with the difficult process of recovering from an extremely painful injury. The injury and path to full recovery led me into a deeper examination of my relationship with my father. I discovered an old childhood resentment that had not been recognized or cleared, and with this "let-go" the pain instantly and completely disappeared. In its place was a sudden desire to write the letter to my daughters–the letter that grew into this book.

With both of these personal "healings" I regained a piece of myself, along with renewed energy and health, by finding, facing, feeling and then releasing long-term, subconscious blockages. Both of these cases involved a deep forgiveness of myself, and others who were very close to me. My missing pieces of "soul" were never really missing; I was simply unable to access these buried parts of my *being* through the dense multiple layers of resentment. From my internal perspective, parts of my soul were, for all practical purposes, "lost" to the rest of my *being*.

Native shamans, Mexican curanderos, faith healers, and even some inspired Western doctors, including psychotherapists, all rely on similar techniques. They work by dissolving the solidity of the concepts in the patient's psyche that create and maintain the structural conditions that allow the disease pattern to continue. Once this cycle is broken, the individual's powerful inherent desire to be whole can then reemerge to direct the natural healing process.

SCHIZOPHRENIA, DEMENTIA, AND MPD

Another fascinating, but often very frightening, condition related to consciousness and healing is personality shifting or what we, in the West, might call Multiple Personality Disorder (MPD), Schizophrenia, or Age- and Injury-Related Dementia. Anyone who has experienced these, directly or indirectly, has learned that our outer expressed personalities are not nearly as fixed and connected to our bodies as we typically imagine.

With these and other related conditions, it can appear that a new personality or some combination thereof, has taken over the minds and bodies of those who are affected, sometimes completely replacing the original personality. We all have read of case studies involving schizophrenia or multiple personality disorder (MPD), and some of us have dealt with family or friends who have developed these or similar conditions. In the last five years I have closely witnessed this type of change in three of my good friends. Two of these were triggered by stressful personal situations, and one was caused by a direct head injury. If we have been through this with loved ones, we can begin to understand the tentative and variable nature of the connections between the personality, the body, and the spirit.

We all recognize that we have different aspects to our personalities, which all can express themselves differently depending on stress, weather, diet, medications, hormones, etc. Generally our different "personalities" or moods are connected in a way that we can control, or modulate, so that we are still recognized by others as being a single person, even if this single person sometimes appears to be "complex." If, under normal conditions, we "snap" and "act out of character," these changes are usually brief and shift back.

However, this is not always the case. After a particularly difficult or traumatic event, sometimes a person can become virtually unrecognizable and remain that way for a very long time. To their friends and loved ones it might seem as if their body has been taken over by a completely different personality, sometimes one that is extremely paranoid and suspicious.

For those of us who have experienced this condition with friends and family, it can be extremely difficult and unsettling. My two friends who had stress-triggered events both became uncharacteristically paranoid, afraid and angry. From their new *viewports* everybody was out to "get them," and they became completely unable to communicate in any kind of interactive way with even their closest friends.

Our *being* originates at the deepest levels, but what is seen outwardly is always the modified personality as the shadows of our souls slip through invisible layers and express themselves upon our world. The personality that appears on the surface of our lives is only the filtered, reshaped and recast expression of our deeper *being*. This expression of personality, with which we interact every day, is only the outer reflection that is visible upon the surface. It is the result after all the layers and our personal filters, *dampen,* transform and reshape our core vibration. When we are free of these unexamined blockages, the *vibrational integrity* of our core *being* shines through and dominates the expression of our personality. When unexamined fear, resentment and frustration have been buried and mostly forgotten, they act as subconscious filters that allow very little of our soul's core vibration to be expressed. Other people then will see little or nothing of our real *being* because the layers of trauma, drama and disturbance, hidden below the surface, are obscuring its light. Over time, these layers of unresolved trauma will solidify to completely alter, cloud, filter and *dampen* our *resonant vibration*. This type of transformation can occur gradually over a lifetime, eventually resulting in some form of dementia; or it can happen quickly as a result of injury or stress.

These layers of resistance can only develop like this when we harbor dark, unexamined footholds within for them to attach to and build upon. The hidden kinks become the *attachment* points for these unconscious but growing "disturbances" that can almost be seen as having an existence on their own. The next section, on *entities,* further explains the idea of their independent existence. Once built, these multilayered structures allow little or no flow of *information* from our soul deep within; and, as a result, our visible surface personality appears to change. This can be visualized in much the same manner as the way a grapevine will cover a large tree. The tree is still there, but it is unable to thrive or be seen.

Our egoic personality is always actively engaged in this filtering process. Because the ego wants complete control of what personality traits others see, it will continuously attempt to function as the gatekeeper. When we have layers of unprocessed subconscious traumas or issues, we tend to automatically try to hide or cover these with "stories" that our egos construct. Our outer personality has to keep these "stories" all logically organized, and this can become a very difficult, full-time task, requiring an enormous amount of *energy* expenditure. During stressful times we might not have the reserve *energy* to maintain this level of organization, and our unconscious filters might start to function in a less coherent and organized manner–more like rogue generals in a war zone. The personality appears to change only because the conscious ego has lost its ability to control the process. What emerges on the surface becomes a somewhat unpredictable "stew" created by the now-random interaction of all these unprocessed blockages and buried fears.

The only way to completely prevent this from happening is for each of us to always remain open and flowing, to continuously be vigilant for hidden resistances, and to address them whenever they are identified. As we deepen in this process, we become clearer channels for the natural expression of deep truth and *being*. Gradually as kinks are illuminated and cleared, there is less need for ego regulation, and eventually the ego recedes as its control becomes completely unnecessary. Then, during stressful times, little or nothing changes. Having reached a level of *vibrational integrity*, our full *being* naturally and easily flows to the surface. We cease to squander our *energy* on control because there is no longer a "story" to protect; there is nothing left to interfere with our soul's full expression.

However, if our layers of protection have become so dense that this level of self-reflection and examination is impossible, then the "cure" requires the breaking of this "shell." Since we created this shell with our subconscious fears and resentments, we must then crack it open enough to reveal and illuminate our hidden resistance. The light of our awareness needs some degree of opening before it can illuminate within. If we are extremely blocked, we might be incapable of opening enough on our own. We usually only reach this critical juncture if we have been living with a long-established pattern of not addressing our trauma and its related issues as they arise.

At this late stage of schizophrenia or *MPD*, pharmaceuticals and other psychoactive substances can carefully be used to pry open the shell just enough for a small piece of the core *Self* to become visible, be recognized, and reestablish communication. Only then does it become possible to begin the actual work of healing. These situations always require an enormous amount of focused, and very committed help from therapists and friends. Of course the immediate physical stressors that triggered the critical incident need to be directly addressed, but the long-term effort must focus on the deeper levels where our old subconscious blockages live. Unless these depths are addressed, there is no chance for lasting wholeness. The latter stages of this healing process require the patient's full and willing participation. And, without the development of healthy inner self-reflection and examination, this entire cycle will likely repeat itself.

Just as we are not our bodies, we also are not our personalities. Both are only strong "associations" built upon our three-dimensional expression of form. Both personality and body are component parts of the ego. At the very root of this entire issue is our *misidentification* with these, our transient, egoic forms.

ENTITIES

In many ancient, shamanic, traditional and contemporary healing traditions, there is the belief that "entities," or outside spirits can live in, act through, or even take over an individual's body. Within different traditions "entities" can be seen as either hostile or helpful, and these spirits can be tightly bound or loosely connected to the host individual. In order to better understand an *entity*, the shaman might communicate with it directly, often relating to it as if it were a fully separate *being*. From the traditional healer's perspective, these *entities* usually have distinct personalities or presences that often seem to operate at a simple, childlike level. As part of their shamanic process they attempt to get to know these *entities* and then establish relationships with them.

In this type of healing system, the personality disorders discussed earlier might be treated as malevolent outside *entities* that are living within or fully occupying the patient's body. Within our traditional Western culture we have no understanding of, or even a place for, this type of approach– such ideas are viewed as "unscientific," utterly superstitious and crazy.

As a model for understanding the mechanics of "dis-ease," this concept of "entities" has value for the Westerner. Those places in our bodies where we hold our tension can be thought of and treated as if they were being occupied by "entities." However, these entities do not come from somewhere outside of our *being*–we create our own entities from within. Whenever we repress a thought, a feeling, a fear or a memory, consciously or unconsciously, individually or collectively, we are attempting to hide it from the "light" of our conscious awareness. In our attempts to avoid that which we are fearing, we bury this energetic thought-form and, over time, we build a massive energetic and protective structure around it. This protective layer is built from our justifications, rationalizations, ideas, emotions, resistance and fears. Gradually this barrier gets denser as new layers are added. Like a stalactite, this repressed thought-form will eventually become a dense and solid physical, psychological, and emotional construction that will block any examination by our consciousness. This now-hidden and isolated piece of us has no life-force *energy* of its own, so it must "steal" its energy from the rest of our being. Over time, as this structure becomes increasingly reinforced by similar habits, fears and stresses, it will become so isolated and separated from the rest of our *being* that it appears to have its own form and identity. Now fully separate, "it" must borrow or sap the host's *energy* for the maintenance and continuation of its form. When something is repressed to this degree, it requires a great amount of additional *energy* to keep it repressed and hidden. Vital *energy* must be stolen from the host to support and maintain this structure, and this means that there will be less *energy* available for living.

If we are leading unexamined lives and unconsciously repress thoughts, we will eventually find that we have less available energy. Over time, this energetic expense takes its toll and we can become energetically diminished and physically limited in many ways. Since this "entity" latches on and only exists at the expense of the *energy* flow of the host, it can be a useful metaphor to think of this particular type of blockage as *parasitic* in nature.

Since this "entity" did not originate from the outside, it is not actually physically separate from us. However, because it is physically and emotionally isolated and compartmentalized from the rest of our *being*, it will appear to be fully separate and seem to have an existence of its own. As time passes, we continue to feed and grow this "entity" as we layer and bury other repressed memories or thought-forms around the existing structure. Through our own choices it grows in stature, while our own *energy* becomes further restricted or depleted.

From this perspective we can see the insight and wisdom of shamanic soul retrieval. These buried repressed thought-forms can be seen and treated as if they have an existence of their own because they have become functionally separate. Entities only exist because they are created, by our egos, to keep something that we would rather not directly face well hidden from the light of our awareness. Over time, long-term "entities" can become familiar and comforting "old friends" that might even be difficult to part with.

Our initial *repression* may have served us in the short-term by providing us with a necessary respite during a difficult transition period in our life. However, a lifelong pattern of this type of *repression* will result in the buildup and development of major emotional problems and chronic disease. To prevent this cycle of *repression* from deepening and to be able to have the freedom to enjoy and more freely navigate within the *Multiverse*, it is necessary to recognize and release these "entities" the moment we realize that they no longer serve us. Because all of their components really originate from within us, deep healing is the way to reintegrate these parts so that we can become whole.

Entities and Death

Through my own limited but personal experiences with friends and loved ones, I have visibly observed the release of some of these "entities" at the time of physical death. As these entities are released and leave the body, they can be observed to have a visible *mass*, form and existence of their own. They possess a shadowy, heavy and gelatinous, yet transparent, "thickness," that appears as something between fog and the heat mirage seen on a highway. My direct experience indicates that these "entities" hang on to the dying body for as long as they can, but eventually they "abandon ship" because they finally realize that their *energy* source is no longer available. From my observation it seems as if these entities have become so isolated and separated from the dying host that they appear to have their own egoic, self-survival instincts and personalities.

Parasitic in nature, "entities" must rely on human energy for their life support because they have no power, *energy* or life-force of their own. The host always sacrifices a piece of their own "sparkle" or life-force to sustain their "entities." From my own observations it seems that, at death, the "sparkle" becomes visible as it is released. It appears to resemble swirling glitter that moves as a unit, similar to a school of small fish. With the death of the physical form, the entity releases its grip on the host and this "sparkle" is now free to return and reunite with its source, the *self*. After this life-force has left the entity, any remaining "dark" material is then rendered inert, having no energetic support system for an existence on its own. It is important to understand that these entities only have the power that we give to them, for we are their creators, sustainers and masters. They are simply subdivided, compartmentalized and orphaned parts of our own *being*. Once we no longer support them because of death or healing, they become inert and powerless.

Traditional healers like the Siberian Shamans understand and work with this relationship. The critical part of their process can involve emotionally exhausting the resistance of the host, to a level where these "entities" believe that the host is dying and that they are about to lose their source of life support. They have been, in a sense, tricked or persuaded into fleeing prematurely.

However, as I experienced during my own shamanic healing (in my living room) and elsewhere, "entities" can also be persuaded to leave through more gentle methods. One effective way to do this is to slowly peel back the layers using a shamanic process that closely parallels depth psychology. This process gradually exposes the original thought-form to the light of our consciousness.

I have also observed that, during the dying process, once the entities leave, the original living *self* still appears to be present in the body–the dying process includes the healing, or reconstruction, of the *self*. Whether this is always the case, I do not know. ***It is probably then much more descriptive and accurate to think of the dying process the other way around; at death, the body is the last thing to drop away from the self.***

DEATH IS OFTEN SEEN AS A FAILURE

In our culture we aggressively push death away. It is possible that twenty-first-century Americans fear and attempt to avoid death to a greater extent than any culture in human history. We have been thoroughly trained through our cultural conditioning to believe that we are our bodies, and only our bodies, therefore, death is usually seen as the ultimate failure. We identify with our bodies so strongly that many of our most celebrated and worshipped idols are often revered for little more than their visual image. We exist in a deep state of mass-confusion and *misidentification* about the nature of our bodies.

Our medical establishment goes to astounding lengths to keep our weary old bodies alive. We employ machines to continue to pump our blood long after our hearts stop, and we employ feeding devices to replace long-overworked digestive organs. We consider a treatment to be successful if we can postpone the actual physical death for a few months, even if the psychological and emotional death occurred long before. Using machinery to keep a body in a "living" vegetative state for 10 years is sometimes considered a technical and social "success." Our medical system keeps records based on numeric survival rates such as the "five-year cancer survival rate," but we rarely observe the *quality* of the human experience to be included as a part of this analysis. We seem to prefer absolutely any outcome to that of death. In the West, our lives are spent running from death.

While physical death is rarely embraced or celebrated within our culture, there are other cultures in our world that treat death as a celebratory life event, similar to birth or marriage. What a difference it could make if we would universally and enthusiastically embrace a natural and timely death as a wonderful, successful and positive transitional event in a person's life. Death might then be seen more like a "bon voyage" for another great journey or adventure in one's life, but a journey that is destined for places even more amazing and expansive. Our death could be seen as no less of a time for celebration than our birth, since these both mark the bookends of the physical experience. Both ends of the entire continuum of our lives on Earth deserve equal celebration.

On the *soul's* path towards freedom, the entire process of physical life, from birth to death, must be seen, understood, and embraced in its entirety to have the complete and ultimate human experience. All parts of this adventure are critical components of the Web of creation, and every aspect of our human existence needs to be equally expressed and embraced.

Real healing is not possible when postponing death has become the primary goal of our healing technologies. Healing only unfolds at the level of the soul because our bodies are only three-dimensional reflections of the inner vibration. As previously discussed, it is possible that in a successful healing, the "best and highest" natural outcome might be the "casting off" of the old body because it was no longer useful, or economic on the level of energetics. *We can never be whole until we see, understand and embrace physical death as an integrated part of a beautiful living process that does not begin and end with our bodies. We are not these bodies, and we need not fear for these bodies, because we are so much more.*

LIVING FULLY IN THE MULTIVERSE

"TIME"

Einstein often described "time" as a *"stubbornly persistent illusion."* Our concept of "time" is a recurring theme throughout this book since it is a major reason for much of the confusion and mystery in our lives. "Time" is a dominant element because our ideas about "time" are fully responsible for defining and shaping the world we live in. Even if we fully understand that "time" is only an illusion, we still cannot imagine our lives outside of "time." The illusion is persistent because our brains require "time" for their organization and efficient functioning.

We all have a strong intuitive and mostly unshakable sense of what "time" is, even though the physics and math tells us that our intuitive sense of "time" is not accurate, or even real. Our sense of "time" is only the result of shadows cast onto our limited reference frame, obscuring the deeper relationships of an architecture that we can't directly observe and don't understand. "Time" is only a concept that our brains use to interpret *projections* from other dimensions as they intersect our three-dimensional world.

We usually have a clear and absolute sense about "time" moving forward, not backward, at a regulated and measured pace; and this illusion seems absolutely real to most of us, most of the time. However, math and physics make it clear that if we were to travel at the speed of light, or at 186,000 miles per second, then "time" would appear to stop. Our inner perception of "time" would not change, but actual clock-time and aging would literally stop from the perspective of any others who are observing us from outside of our high-speed reference frame. Any clocks traveling with us would also stop or slow down when viewed by someone who was not moving as fast. However, from our own perspective, that of the high speed traveler, we would be having a very normal experience with our personal internal clocks, and portable timepieces, ticking normally. Traveling at close to the speed of light, we would age very slowly while our friends back on Earth, those who were living outside our speeding chariot, would age "normally." When we returned from our trip we would be younger than the friends who remained on Earth. These two, entirely different perceptions of the passage of "time," cannot be understood or reconciled in only three dimensions.

Scientists now understand that the passage of what we measure as "time" has a deep and interconnected relationship with what we experience as *relative velocity*. Physicists have also learned that "time" has a close relationship to *gravity*. Clocks move slower if they are closer to the center of the Earth, where *gravity* is stronger. Because of this, a coal miner will age more slowly that a person traveling in an airplane. "Time" is no longer seen as the immutable element that we once experienced. We now understand that "time" is only our limited way of measuring, describing or experiencing one aspect of *spacetime* from within our restricted reference frame on Earth.

For all of us, Einstein's work exploded the older idea that the passage of "time" was universal, regular, unstoppable and marching forward at a fixed rate. Through his work we have come to understand that both *gravity* and *velocity* affect real-time. By real-time, I mean clock-time, as opposed to our personal perception of "time." We incorporated Einstein's corrections and adjustments into our computerized technical tools that calculate using *velocity* and *gravity*. These counterintuitive, yet scientifically derived, corrections have now become a standard part of modern engineering. ***The accuracy of our GPS systems, space flights and weapon systems completely depend on these "time" corrections. Every time we locate something using the GPS on our*** *smartphone, we are using this new physics and acknowledging that "time" is very different than we once perceived.*

"TIME" AND THE "NOW"

Earlier I compared our human perception of "time" to being stuck on a freeway heading north without knowing that we could slow the car, or even turn around, and head south. I stated that we only understand "time" from the limited *viewport* of a backseat passenger. We miss that is it possible to slow down or even stop the car, but we also doesn't know that the car can make a full U-turn and then travel in the other direction.

To begin to grasp this idea intuitively, we must first be ready to allow a complete internal paradigm shift. It usually requires decades or centuries, for a culture, as a whole, to make shifts of this magnitude. ***However, as individuals, we have the ability to make this shift anytime we are ready! It may seem ironic but, to successfully make this adjustment, we must first learn to live our lives fully in the only moment that is not an illusion or shadow–that special experience which we call the "Now" moment.***

Eckhart Tolle writes that *"time and mind are inseparable. To identify with the mind is to be trapped in time."* This means that if "time" is removed from mind, our minds would literally stop. On the other hand, if the mind is removed from "time," marching-time also stops. Our mental processes only function within this sea of relentlessly marching "time." ***Since "time" is only a creation that is sustained by our minds, we must understand "time" and mind as one and the same.*** In crisis situations we are often stimulated to reach beyond the mind. Then "time" can slow or stop, as it did for both my sister and me in our automobile accidents. "Time" is fully created and regulated by our three-dimensional minds. Tolle goes even further to include *"the mind, to stay in control, seeks continuously to cover up the present moment with the past and future, and so, as the vitality and infinite creative potential of being, which is inseparable from the Now, becomes covered up by time, your true nature becomes obscured by the mind."* Our habits built upon and around time prevent us from realizing our full potential.

Relativity demonstrated that traveling at the speed of light causes our clock-time to stop. This might leave us wondering if there is any relationship between the speed of light and the ecstatic spiritual state that is sometimes referred to as *Samadhi*. This "no-mind state is often described as "timeless." When we are able, through meditation, yoga and other techniques, to drop into *Samadhi*, is there some aspect of us that is effectively traveling or vibrating at, or close to, the speed of light?

Again, anytime we speak about concepts such as "beginning" and "later," we are referencing ideas that are time-based. These will always have very different meanings when they are expressed in and seen through the lens of the full *Multiverse*. Because of these different meanings, I want to be clear that when I use these time-referenced terms, to facilitate better communication, I am only using them as well-understood, three-dimensional concepts. ***In full, multi-dimensional space, all temporal things unfold so that they can be seen and experienced as interconnected and "happening" at once! There is no organizing element called "time" in the deeper places of creation.***

DEATH AND FORM

DEATH IS ONLY AN ILLUSION

As we better understand the hidden architecture of the *Multiverse,* we become more aware that our sense of "time" is only a mental concept: one that is needed for ordering things and ideas so that we can separate them and function in this three-dimensional realm. *Time* helps us organize three-dimensional conceptual thought–it shapes our three-dimensional realm.

From the timeless and broader perspective of the fully dimensional Web, there is no beginning and no end, no alpha and no omega, and no passage of time. Therefore, this means that there is also no final moment in time that is associated with or marks our death. The birth and death of our bodies are only the bookends of an illusionary, time-ordered process. Birth and death are, therefore, only temporal phenomena experienced from within our limited dimensional *viewport.* *From the broader perspective, we do not (and cannot) die because time does not really exist in ways that allow absolute endings. The passage of time is only a part of the great illusion of our realm. Time passing, aging and death are as illusionary as all other impermanent things. If we are alive at any one moment, we are then eternally alive. We always exist and exist always in our greatest home, a place that is always "outside of time."*

From within our time-dependent, conceptual perspective, we might imagine that "outside of time" must mean forever. Combining both eternal and instantaneous, it is actually a very different idea; one that is closer to "now and always timeless." While it is impossible for us to imagine or really understand this idea, occasionally we all experience feelings that communicate a sense of this timelessness.

Furthermore, we cannot and do not "die" because, at the deeper levels found beyond our *conceptual horizon,* there are no isolated individuals. How could we possibly die when the separate individual, the one who is understood to die, doesn't even exist to begin with? Again, the form we call "our body," which we so closely associate with ourselves, is as illusionary as everything else in our physical world.

Our physical bodies are probably not the most useful vehicles for journeys through worlds outside of our small part of the *Multiverse.* Within our *viewport* shaped by "time," the physical *body* always recycles and returns to its elemental components to be recycled. The three-dimensional natural world thoroughly recycles everything, consistently and well. However, the "I" awareness that was once associated with that form doesn't end with the recycling of that old physical form. As discussed, it can't because it has always, and only, existed outside of physical "time." Our understanding of death is absolutely dependent on our current concept of "time;" however, the real "I" was created and exists far beyond these bounds. Death of our body represents only a temporary change in our 3D expression. It has no actual effect on our *core vibration,* which is who we really are. *Another way of saying this is that "dying" is a mental concept. It is not real or absolute because it is only an idea, a thought, or an illusion that appears to be real because our bodies and our world also appear to be real.*

WHAT IF WE ALL LIVED WITHOUT FEAR

If we fully understood that death was not real or absolute, then physical death would not be so universally feared. Our death would still be a change for our loved ones and inconvenient for those doing business with us, but it would not be seen as final. If it were, instead, seen as an illusion, a change, or a repeating moment in a much larger process, then our entire life experience would change. It is the mistaken idea that our physical death is real, final and absolute that largely defines our modern culture.

Imagine how different this world would look if our perspective on death changed. The culture we are experiencing now is largely based on the shortsighted "you can't take it with you, so get it while you can" attitude. If we all truly understood our interconnected and eternal nature, this fear of the void would drop away effortlessly and we would naturally be much kinder to each other, recognizing that we all are simply different manifestations of the same eternal *being*. **Many of our fears are deeply rooted in our fear of death or, more specifically, in the misidentification of our spirit with our singular body and ego.**

Physical death certainly marks a special point in a person's life-flow. Released from the bounds of an *ego-body*, the vibratory nature of our *being* then becomes completely free to naturally *resonate* within its most *harmonic* region of the *Multiverse*. **Just as water seeks its own level, our spirit, once it is released, finds its perfect vibratory level.**

Substantial shifts in our physical reality or *viewport* can be accomplished while we are still in our bodies, but once we are freed from the body's constraints, our resonant *being* finds itself automatically at that place in the Web where it fully and naturally resonates. **This means that we always flow towards "that which we really are," which is always defined by how we resonate at our core.** At the time of our physical body death, we freely *resonate* with the most natural place in the Web for the expression our true *being*. **Our vibratory integrity is absolute at the transition of our form.**

Death of our physical form never provides an "escape." It is really just the opposite–it is a return to our truthful energetic center. Death always returns us to the full and clear expression of our *Being;* and it brings us directly to another new, yet timeless, adventure.

It is within the 3D realm, while we are still living in our bodies, that our important work of soul growth and evolution can be accomplished. This is the primary purpose for our existence here. Our work in this realm is critical for holding the fabric of the Multiverse together. Physical life is a process that helps shape our collective soul. This is one critical way that Being grows and evolves. Changes in our individual *being* gained through our experiences in this physical form will influence the *resonance* of our individual souls and ultimately contribute to the evolution of the greater *Being*.

Fear is always the greatest inhibitor of freedom. What might change if our physical form were permanently released from fear? This form would then be free to experience, evolve and do its work, all within a very conscious and flowing state. Many of the unconscious and reactionary behaviors of humankind would immediately cease to make sense. We would develop and express new capabilities, sensitivity and potential that can't possibly be imagined from our present mindset. Love and our interconnectedness would freshly lubricate all of our thoughts and actions.

Living fearlessly really means that we don't spend "time" or energy living in an inefficient or blocked state where we constantly repeat old patterns that have not been working for us. However, this state of fearlessness is not required for our successful evolution because "time," and therefore efficiency, doesn't really matter in the bigger picture. From a personal individual perspective, a fearless way of walking through life maximizes our potential and our ability to flow with love, while it also minimizes human suffering. From the perspective of that part of *self,* that part associated with the human form, fearless living is relaxing, energizing, exciting and a great deal of fun.

TREE ANALOGY REVISITED

I will use the tree analogy as a model for rethinking our old ideas about the death of our individual forms. Again, this familiar living model proves to be a useful tool; this time it can help us better visualize the process of death. Again, we are comparing individuals to the leaves of a tree, and every leaf is still unaware of its direct connection to the rest of the tree. With this physical separation, each leaf could imagine that it is a unique, but threatened, individual creature, living in competition with all the other leaves. Leaves drop and die, but the tree lives on. Our bodies are like these leaves–divided, functional, and very temporary surface expressions that are visible at the surface of a much larger but mostly hidden organism. Our deeper *being* is expressed in the roots, trunk and branches of the tree; and it is from this core that new leaves emerge to do their part when the time is right. Individual leaves come and go, but life continues to emerge from a deeper place–the roots of our *Being.*

WE ARE JUST PASSING THROUGH

In the novel Flatland, when the sphere "visited" and traveled through this two-dimensional world, its inhabitants were convinced they had witnessed a very strange *being,* which appeared, changed shape over "time" and then, just as quickly, completely disappeared. A similar description could be used to describe the appearance of our own lives. *We come from an unknown and mysterious place, we grow, we shrink and eventually over time we disappear back into the void.* Passing through our quick allotment of time on Earth, what we experience is only that small slice of creation that our realm is intersecting, or temporarily "visiting." We are not born and we do not die, but rather we "pass through" this world with our birth and death marking the extents of our short journey through this physical realm.

From within our three-dimensional realm, we use the concept of "time" to describe and organize our life experiences. Just as in *Flatland,* our limited *viewport,* containing fewer dimensions than our actual *being,* does not permit us to understand the full magnificence of our *being.* **What looks like death to us is simply the completion of one experience or trip through this three-dimensional world.** We continue on with our journey just like the sphere, which also did not "die" when it passed through Flatland. Like that sphere, we simply continue our "travels" to places that lie outside of our familiar realm. **The lives that we experience on Earth are only the shadows that are cast or projected as we pass through this viewport, while living our eternal journey.**

EGO, SOUL, CONSCIOUSNESS

It is difficult for us to understand what consciousness is, especially since, in doing so, we are asking consciousness to turn inward and describe itself. This is somewhat like asking a fish to explain water. Nobel Prize-winning neuroscientist Gerald Edelman sees consciousness as a purely biological phenomenon. According to him, the thing that distinguishes us from the other intelligent animals, such as dogs, is our level of consciousness. He divides consciousness into upper and lower levels. Lower level consciousness remembers the past and reacts to this past in the present. Upon seeing a lion, the gazelle's reaction is only "time to run away," and there is no thinking about the lion during the time between lion encounters. Gazelles never find themselves suddenly immobilized, requiring years of counseling to process their deep fear of lions. In contrast, upper level human consciousness thinks about the lion, where it came from, the dangers it might pose, and how the tables could be turned to capture and kill this lion for food or, possibly, just to get "even" with it. Also, this "upper level consciousness" type of thought is likely to occur in intervals between lion visits. This means that upper level consciousness will process thoughts that are "outside" of the present moment.

According to Dr. Edelman, all of this difference is simply the result of biological evolution and is built into our three-dimensional brain's biology. By this reasoning, animals that continue to evolve might eventually develop this "upper" form of consciousness as their brains reach a certain level of complexity. Recent observations of bonobo primates indicate that they may have reached this milestone of consciousness. This also means that it is likely that as we continue to evolve, our type or level of consciousness will also continue to evolve to allow for new and unimagined possibilities.

Through time and experience, we each discover fresh insights into the makeup of our own awareness. As we understand more about ourselves, we begin to individually learn that our fears and worries are directly associated with the more superficial egoic part of our awareness–that part of us which also feels separate, alone, and often angry or frustrated. This is the part of our awareness that measures happiness with things such as status, acceptance, achievement and wealth. This is also the part of us that can plunge us into the depths of fear or despair in very dramatic fashion, if and when these circumstances change. This egoic part of our awareness is a direct product of the human brain's self-contained thought process, and it falls within Dr. Edelman's description of upper level consciousness. Since our egoic consciousness is so directly connected to our bodies and brains, it is also very three-dimensional and biological. When our body dies, our ego will die with it. The ego and the body are actually one thing, which can be called the *ego-body*.

Hiding deep below this outer surface of our consciously expressed *ego* lurks the enormous and powerful *subconscious* portion of our selves. Much of this *subconscious* is simply concerned with the continuous functioning of the body–some of it is concerned with basic survival and biological functioning, and some of it is involved with patterning and muscle memory. Muscle memory is a wonderful and handy tool when it involves something such as sawing a piece of wood or the repetition of a musical phrase on the violin, but it can also be very disturbing when it involves repeated pain or spasms from an old injury.

Since our *subconscious* is so deep, it is where we hide all our thoughts and fears that we were not prepared to consciously face, or express when they were originally experienced. Unconscious and *repressed memories* will hide within, build, grow, and ultimately combine within our *subconscious*. Eventually, these hidden structures can become so large that they interfere with our normal functioning. They will eventually express themselves, on the level of the physical, as frustration, resentment, pain, anger, unusual behavior, and eventually injury or disease. These unexplored parts of the *subconscious*, some personal and some cultural or collective, form the blockages or resistances that will then filter and *damp* the full and natural expression of our deepest level of *being*. They obscure our core vibration. The more we have buried our unexamined feelings or thoughts in our *subconscious*, the denser the filter and the greater the interference and confusion at the outer layers of our self-expression. We then temporarily lose our natural ability to live and act through *vibrational integrity*.

How big and important is the role of this subconscious portion to the whole of our expressed *being*? One way of measuring its effect is to again look at how much relative *information* our conscious and unconscious minds can process in a given amount of time. According to recent scientifically measurements, our conscious minds can process 20-40 bits of *information* in one second. In that same second, our subconscious mind is processing almost 20,000,000 bits of *information* without the awareness of our conscious brains. ***All of that activity is happening below the conscious part of our minds. The results from this processing blend with the relatively minor conscious contribution to form our final expressed personality. Our personality is the emergent sum of all this activity and filtering, both conscious and unconscious, but the subconscious can process up to a million times more information. Because of the enormous proportion of our unexpressed and buried parts, we tend to be on autopilot all the time, without ever realizing it.***

Not only is the subconscious big and powerful but also, because its world is hidden from our conscious minds, its activity is not easily accessed or monitored by us. Therefore, when it finally does work through and reveal itself at the surface, the expression can be very big, unexpected, and "out of character." Its "dark" or hidden nature can make its surprising and "out of character" expressions seem even more frightening and powerful.

THE SELF

Deep within each of us, resting, undisturbed, in a very quiet and subtle place, we can find another part of our awareness–the "observer" or "watcher." We often first discover this part of ourselves through meditation or other forms of deep, silent self-reflection. As we become more familiar with this silent presence, we discover that this part of ourselves is perfectly steady, consistent and completely unaffected by our day-to-day drama. After consciously paying attention to this internal presence for a number of years, a universal realization is that this part of our *being* also seems to be unaffected by our aging process. We sometimes can recall experiencing this presence as a child and remember that it felt exactly the same; it always feels the same regardless of the age of our physical bodies. This "watcher," or "observer," also seems to be aware that it is only temporarily associated with this particular body, so it does not appear to care about the daily concerns of the body and egoic mind. It seems to automatically know that these are not really all that important in the bigger picture.

This part of us is also known as the *self*. For most of us, it takes time, age and experience to become acquainted with this quiet and often hidden aspect of ourselves. There are a number of wonderful blessings that accompany becoming older in these bodies; one of which is that we gain the perspective to observe that when we look within, there has always been this part of us that feels the same as it did when we were 40 years younger. Because this part, the *self*, feels ageless, over time it becomes easier to isolate, observe and identify. *Self* is that presence we always recognize as the "I." Always present, it is at the center of our direct connection to *Being.* Our individual *self* is our personal access point to the much deeper singular *Self.*

The *self* can only be discovered when we are able to look below the much louder conscious and subconscious parts of the ego. Our awareness of *self* grows as the noise and day-to-day drama of the ego is better understood and becomes less important. Connected to a much more universal level of *being,* it dwells deep within the core of each and every individual. Once we learn to recognize it, this *self* can always be found near the root of our conscious self awareness. This is also the same part that some might call our soul. Diverse cultures, scattered around the globe, all have their own names for this universal and ubiquitous presence.

Our awareness of the *self* is completely personal and experiential; there is no scientific proof, little experimental data, and endless debate about its nature–even its existence. Opinions vary, ranging from the idea that this awareness is the only part of us that is truly real, to it just being a trick of our brain. If we could see and understand the complete multi-dimensional matrix that forms who and what we are, we would then recognize this vague experience of *self* as being only a small reflection of something that is *infinitely* much greater. We would then understand that our sense of *self* is only a very human and, therefore, dimensionally-limited shadow of the greater *Self*–our direct connection to *Being*. Becoming more aware of *self* is our best method for connecting to the very real, infinitely expansive, and profound existence that always lies beyond our imagination.

In our Western culture we often use the words heart, feeling or even soul to describe this connecting place within. Our *self* completely transcends our ego, personality, body, and even lifetimes. We may begin to notice that our *self* contains collective or universal aspects as well as those that are personal and individualized. There exists a continuum between *self* and *Self*, and as we move towards where our *self* becomes more universal, we eventually encounter aspects of the *Self*–our collective center and soul. It is at this threshold, where *self* meets *Self*, that we can access the "Web of Possibilities" from our *viewport*.

Our mind and thoughts, alone, cannot directly connect with *Self*. Mind, emotions and thoughts are very important in this process, but this connection can only be made through the *self* acting at the foundation of our individual *being*, our vibrational core. Over time, by acting as a guide and gatekeeper, the mind can influence our awareness of *self*. When we pay attention to our conscious thoughts and search for, discover and explore our unconscious resistances, we will deepen our awareness and come to better know *self*. ***Our connection to self, our soul and the Web is always informed by the conscious mind, which also has the equal ability to interfere with our self-awareness. Understanding how all this works is just another significant part of our amazing journey towards freedom.***

RESONANCE OF OUR INSTRUMENT BODY

The self is that part of us through which *Being* can most directly express itself. It is our deepest well-head, tapping directly into creation, allowing our lives to be shaped by unseen information from the deepest levels. The *self* is our direct connection to everything that is real, including those aspects of our *beingness* that are of a more collective nature. The more we open to this well of deeper Love, the more fully our soul's *vibration* can be felt, and this new level of awareness results in greater *vibrational integrity,* allowing our individual experience to feel and actually be very different.

The difference is similar to listening to music on your stereo instead of the small speakers of your phone. The raw *information* is the same but our experience of it is completely different. More information comes through and less is lost through restrictions, filtering, noise, and processing. What is then heard is a much fuller, or richer, rendition of the *song*. In our high-tech world we might refer to this enhanced reception as "increased bandwidth." This improved reception helps us *resonate* more fully and this, in turn, allows us access to new and different parts of the Web. It is through this enhanced *resonance* that our soul gains access to different and more expansive regions of the Web. This *wave* of *resonant vibration* then moves out into the physical world, expressing itself through personality. If the pathways are clear, this physical expression of *self* appears very powerful, moving and clear.

Think of a vibrating musical instrument. Imagine that our soul is the reed or string of our instrument; our e*go-bodies* then represent the instrument body. The string or reed's vibration initiates the tone, flavor and volume of any song. A dense body might not allow the full resonance of the reed or string to emerge, but a light, open and clear body will amplify and project the full tone and all its unique sonic properties.

We build and form our personal "instrument body" throughout our lifetime. The playing of our "instrument" always involves the unconscious and the conscious parts working together. For the strongest *resonance*, all parts must vibrate freely and work as one; and when this happens, the song is full, clear and moving. Shaping our instrument over time, to allow for this fuller and more open *vibration,* creates the potential for beautiful and moving personal expression. When we make this type of beautiful music with our lives, it completely changes the expression of our world! *We are here to immerse ourselves in living our lives as we play, explore our Multiverse, and have fun, knowing that we can change our world by just learning how to shape and express the full potential of our own instrument: our body. Our body is the instrument that enables us to express our personal part in the extraordinary symphony of creation.*

THE "NOW"

BE HERE NOW

"Be Here Now" is the beautiful and now very popular phrase that describes a very simple but powerful, contemporary, spiritual technique. These may be three of the most thought-provoking words ever strung into a simple, single phrase. Together they describe exactly how we can best participate and evolve within this process called life. Many different writers, philosophers, gurus, sages and people of great experience have spoken clearly about this ancient and enduring piece of wisdom.

Richard Alpert, also known as Ram Dass, a former Harvard professor of psychology turned New-Age sage, made this phrase famous in his first book, which used the phrase as its title. He also wrote a sequel, titled *Still Here,* years later, after acquiring additional experience through many personal adventures, which included having a massive and debilitating stroke–something that he now considers an extraordinary and unexpected gift.

I talked briefly about the "power of now" earlier in this book. What does it mean to "be here now"? Exactly what is the "now moment" or "present moment"? These are all different phrases attempting to describe an experience that completely transcends words. Some have argued, using a purely rational logic, that there is no such thing as the "now moment" because, the instant any moment occurs, it instantly becomes the past. This is only true if we are thinking about the "now moment," and if we are thinking about it, we are not experiencing it. All reflective thinking happens in the *past* or *future*. Thinking happens in "time."

The "now moment" can only be found outside of thought and time. The "now moment" is the place where the past and the future meet in the living and energetic unfolding of experience. We are living fully immersed in the "now moment" when we lose all sense of "time." In this place we seem to have unexpected and endless *energy,* and we might also drop the experience of ourselves as separate *beings*. Most of us have had this type of feeling somewhere, or sometime in our lives.

With practice, we can learn to "be" more fully "here" in the "now." We can gradually begin to interact with a greater part of our lives from this special place outside of "time." A sweet richness and gratefulness naturally wells up and supports us, while it carries us directly on to our next "now" moment. Each "now" moment blends into the next in an unexpected but perfect expression to form a fluid continuum that we might experience as "magical." Within this natural unfolding, our day-to-day lives can still seem difficult in any given moment; but these experiences (even if very challenging) will be understood as "perfect," especially when viewed in retrospect with a critically important, but well-developed, sense of humor. As we learn how to spend more time in this "now moment" we let go of our ideas, concepts and desires that unknowingly generate resistance and pain within. Once these resistances are no longer influencing our every decision, there is more freedom to "dance" about the Web and this results in a greater depth of experience. The *resonance* becomes fuller, which makes our experience deeper. ***When we are living in the "now," we are always flowing within the "river of our life." There is little or no resistance and no deep suffering. Exactly what we need in each and every moment always seems to magically appear before us, in perfect timing. This is what is meant by "flow." This is freedom.***

Learning to live this way is our path to maximum self-expression, freedom and bliss, yet no human being that I personally know is able to fully and continuously participate at this level. In our realm, this level of freedom is rarely easy or automatic. Our culture clashes with this process every step of the way. To be able to practice the art of "being here now" in our society, we need to be absolutely clear about our culture, the process, and ourselves. We all have large portions of ourselves tied into our culture, so we naturally and reflexively get pulled back towards our culture's anxious and busy center. Over time and through our focused attention, these unintentional lapses will become shorter, less frequent and less dramatic. This path is potholed with doubt and fear, but once we learn to navigate our way, the reward is an expanded perspective, a new vibratory manifestation, and a very different and unexpected world to explore.

The biggest and most exciting adventure available to each of us is the opportunity to learn how to drop into the present moment, stay there, and surf this "wave" upon the ocean of our experience for as long as is possible, and then do this, and again. From this process, a rich and meaningful life will naturally unfold in seemingly improbable and impossible ways. This life will be filled with logic-defying connections and interactions that could never be imagined from within our individual rational minds. We can only drop into this natural resonant existence once we learn how to "be here now." ***To become free, all that we ever really need to do is "be here now"! This has always been, and will always be, the doorway to freedom.***

THE "PAST" AND THE "NOW"

In our Western culture there is an incessant pressure pushing us to live in the past or the future. We are identified by our past: our transcripts, criminal records, stories that friends remember and our own memories. Our heads are filled with these memories, and it is easy to lose our perspective and begin to imagine that these images are who we really are. We perceive and define a set of personal limitations and these are often built from our own memories, and our interpretations of our past experiences.

Someone who failed geometry in high school might later avoid anything involving math and science. Another, who had an awkward moment at a junior high dance, might give up dancing. Once told that we were not attractive, we might feel that way ever since.

We are shaped by our personal memory of the past, even though our memory has nothing to do with what actually happened. Our memory is only our perception and it is ours alone. The person you had that crush on in fourth grade may have said you were not attractive because they were worried that, if they revealed their attraction, you would know that they liked you and they were simply too terrified to reveal that truth. Possibly your fourth grade music teacher resented teaching and simply took his or her frustration out on you, or your geometry teacher was really a Physical Education teacher who, because of a teacher shortage, was assigned to teach material that was over his head and so he just did a terrible job. While we can let these memories of the past define and limit us, we always also have the opportunity to break free of this common, but imprisoning, pattern.

A memory of mine was that I was a very poor student in music class in the fourth grade. I loved to sing but my music teacher told me that I had no ability to sing or play music. Her exact words were "Tim you are ruining the music for the other 300 students in the choir." I believed this for 40 years but, eventually, I was able to work through this limitation, and move past most of the resistance that I built from this memory. I started playing an instrument again when I was 50, and today, I am having a tremendous amount of fun playing music daily with friends. I even now play bass in a couple of working bands.

All events in life always look very different from different individuals' *viewports,* and none of our individual perspectives ever represent what actually happened. There is no such thing as a single objective "real" memory of anything. We all have our own individual memories of events based on our *viewports,* so we all live with our own filtered, very personal, and often misinterpreted memories of our past. We then wind up limiting our options, and we often miss the sweet spot in the flow of life–our full engagement in the "present moment."

THE "FUTURE" AND THE "NOW"

Within Western culture, possibly, an even bigger and more-powerful pull than the past is the pull towards the future. Through our media-based culture our brains are flooded with promises of a better life–if only we take this drug, buy this car, have this hairstyle or dress, or make more money. Our consumer economy is based upon the principle of selling a better future to us. Most religions make their promises for some far-distant, future time and place, usually only after we die. We work harder now because we must save for our "golden years," which only come later. We take jobs that pay more, rather than practicing what nurtures our present joy and interest, to save money for this imagined future. We sacrifice in the present to buy insurance policies to protect us from something that might happen in the future. We are constantly pressured to sacrifice our joy in the present moment for some future promise. In our culture this has become such a normal practice that it is rarely questioned.

The actual way that the universe works is completely the opposite. If we engage in the present fully, then the future will take care of itself! "Worry not about tomorrow for it will take care of itself" is a quote from the gospels that is attributed to Jesus. Within our modern culture we seem to have completely forgotten this ancient and brilliant piece of biblical wisdom.

THE ADVAITA VEDANTA TRADITION

There are a number of spiritual traditions designed to help us understand and better access the "now moment" and they all have Eastern roots. The oldest of these methods may be the ancient Indian *Vedic* tradition, *Advaita Vedanta,* which was built upon and focuses on exploring, understanding and deepening this "present moment" experience. In more recent times, Ramana Maharshi, a contemporary of Einstein, practiced and taught this method from a mountaintop in

India. In turn, his students, including the one called Papaji, were extremely successful at introducing this tradition to the many Western spiritual seekers who were traveling through India at that time (1960s-1990s). Osho, Sai Baba and others added their own powerful, personal perspectives and built ashrams that still function as learning centers. By providing a convenient place for travelers to study these methods, these teachers and gurus helped spread this tradition throughout the West. Fully Western teachers, such as Gangaji and Ram Dass, had the opportunity to study directly with Papaji and others of his generation. When these students returned to the West, they tweaked these methods for the Western mind and, in turn, taught thousands.

However, it was Eckhart Tolle who was the most successful, to date, at reaching the contemporary Western masses. A German philosopher by training, he had a spontaneous, direct, and personal transformational experience that left him pondering on London park benches for several years while he sorted it all out. By 2000 he had compiled this new understanding into *The Power of Now,* his first book. His revolutionary work and his own gentle presence became well known to the mainstream after Oprah Winfrey aired a special video series built around his second book, *"A New Earth."* Eckhart Tolle may be today's best-known Western teacher of *Advaita Vedanta*, but he is only one of many contemporary teachers who speak, write, host satsangs, and hold workshops about this special, timeless place of *being*.

LIVING IN THE "NOW"

Eckhart Tolle writes that *"the Now moment is the only point that can take you beyond the limited confines of the mind. It is the only point of access into the timeless and formless realm of being."*

Living in the "now" is not an easy idea for anyone to understand, especially a Westerner. It took Tolle several years of sitting on park benches in London to integrate his spontaneous insight; and his integration was unbelievably deep and rapid. Everywhere that we look within our Western world and within most of the world's other cultures, the tempo and the stress of day-to-day life distracts us away from the eternal "now." Almost every facet of our culture attempts to pull us away from present moment experience and directs us to focus on the past or future instead. The past and future are where we are always encouraged to live our daily lives. Any time we are dwelling in what we did, what we are doing, or what we are going to do, we are not engaged in the "now."

A common Western reaction, after being first introduced to this idea, is something similar to "yes, this sounds interesting, but what about things like studying for my future career, financial planning and my retirement? These important things all require thinking about the future, so if we only live in the now, these won't get done. What about all those boring, everyday tasks like paying bills and cleaning house?"

Car payments, baby diapers and the boss's expectations will still be necessary, and tending to all of them can still dominate our waking moments. However, by entering into these daily projects joyfully, thankfully and lovingly, we can be fully engaged in the precious "now moment," even while completing our most mundane tasks. When we plan for our future or get excited about future possibilities, we can participate in this planning while putting our attention on the present process, and not into our expectations or concepts about any possible futures. We can enjoy the process of making the plans themselves and not become attached to potential future outcomes. With this one simple change of focus, all of our planning, for the "future," can be done in the "now."

When engaged in the "now," we find ourselves free from fear, relaxed, yet fully focused on the task at hand. The result is, whatever the task, it gets accomplished in the best possible manner. Whether applying to medical school, starting a retirement account, paying bills, or cleaning the bathroom, the "now moment" can always be engaged. Everything about these experiences change when our focus of attention is joyfully directed to the task in front of us. Sometimes planning for the future can be a delightful way to meditate or drop into the "now." There is no conflict if the planning is done from a place that is free of *expectations* and *fears*.

One very interesting–possibly unexpected–but wonderful side effect of living more of our lives in the "now" is that since everything in the Multiverse is directly connected to every other thing in the Multiverse, including what we call past and future; living fully in the "now" creates more direct access and connection to all of this information. This means that the "now" always prepares us perfectly and automatically for our "future." As it turns out, the unfolding of the "now" creates a far better plan for the future than any plan we could construct with our brains. It probably won't look anything like the plans we might have had "in mind" for ourselves because the unfolding events will always defy our best human logic. Trusting the process, by being willing to relax and go with the natural flow of events, is critical to remaining in the "now". The silent space within us always understands that.

Typically we *fear* the future, *expect* or hope for some particular result in the future, and regret our past. This culturally driven focus on the past and future is only our conditioned response. It can cause us to put aside the very things that we are drawn to, find joy with, and love to do. We are constantly expected to "sacrifice" present joy for some "future" ideas that may or may not happen. We tend not to question this because it is considered to be the normal, and even "healthy," response in our culture.

We want to feel safe so we try to control our lives. More than any other, our Western culture has specialized in businesses that create opportunities for us to explore the illusion of buying security. We pad our lives with insurance policies, large homes, big bank accounts, gated communities, extensive and frequent physical exams, extra degrees, hand sanitizers, and a host of other insulators because these all help us to feel safer. With all this insulation from the "now moment," we completely miss it. Instead we exist in a *vibrational* state that is defined by our fearful minds.

It is a very natural and normal reflex to try to shape our lives so that we feel protected from what we fear. We construct elaborate plans, and then are forced to adjust them as our lives unfold in their own way, despite our carefully reasoned plans. This is how we all walk through life, and through participating in this process we grow and gradually gain wisdom and compassion.

At some point we begin to realize that because all of our "planning" is created within "time and mind;" this limits our possibilities and potential outcomes. We discover that if we focus on the future, it only serves to further anchor and further "solidify" our current situation. Such planning is then recognized as a manifestation practice, which keeps us near to what is familiar and known. It does not allow us to freely explore the deeper, unexpected and magical opportunities that lie beyond our *conceptual horizon*. Opportunities for change still appear but, from this rigid and controlling mindset, we don't easily recognize them or see their possibilities. If for some reason we do glimpse something, we usually can't participate because our programmed reactions take over.

We will continue to try to control our lives until that day when we finally decide that we need to explore a very different type of option. We eventually understand that deep change cannot unfold in this type of controlled environment. Instead, we only need to trust and step confidently into the "present moment," which alone opens us to the unknown and infinite possibilities. Only in the "now" can we experience that deep inner *resonance* that will wake and excite our full potential.

Remember, there is no rush to do anything or go anywhere because time is only an illusion and there really is nowhere else to go. The next perfect step is always "right here" and "right now," and the direction of this amazing journey will always be inward. Everything that we need is always available "right here and right now," so we can relax and simply recognize that this journey is a lifelong process, like nourishment, sleep, growth and breathing. We always have full access to the perfect time and place for our deepest possible experience through the ever-present "now moment"!

DANCING TO THE MUSIC OF THE "NOW"

Our universe is always vibrating, oscillating and dancing to the "song of life" because our universe is created and animated through *vibration*. Our lives in this universe can be imagined as part of a symphony of orchestrated *vibration directed and* produced by *Being* as it is inspired by the infinite possibilities of the *Multiverse*. Our lives are the trills and musical riffs that enliven and give character to this ultimate composition. As with any music, "the song of life" is always occurring only in the "now moment." Music in the past is only a memory, and music in the future is a thought. Music unfolds only in the eternal now. To dance this song most wonderfully, we must always be dancing in the "now."

SURFING THE "NOW"

To get the best ride on a wave, a surfer needs to be in just the right spot. *Life is like a wave and the most surf-able part of this wave is always forming anew. The crest, or sweet spot, on the wave of life is the "now moment." The more time spent there, the better the ride.*

Ironically, this place that we often describe by using some reference to time, such as "the present moment" or "the now moment," is really the most timeless place that we can ever experience. Words fall far short. When we are fully in the "now" there is absolutely no sensation of time passing. The clock in our mind completely stops, but to an outside observer we could be moving very quickly, or seem very still and quiet. For example, while "in the zone" we might be playing a complex musical phrase that appears very rapid or executing a quadruple flip dive even though, internally, time seems to pass very slowly. We also could have this timeless experience while lost in oneness with the natural world, driving down the highway fully alert to all potential physical threats, or enjoying unity within a lovers arms. To those inside these experiences, there is only the quiet and still place where our attention is focused–all thought disappears as our sense of time and space drops away.

FREEDOM AND IMMORTALITY

Freedom is when our *being* is able to express its true *self* through *natural resonance* without a significant amount of *egoic damping*; we flow with the river of life only when we are free. In our physical form, any limitations to our *being's* full expression are always created in the ego through a mental process that often begins with *fear*. *As long as we identify with our physical form, we will embody fear. If we believe that we really are these bodies, then these fears will appear to be rational and justified.* We can, instead, occupy and employ these physical forms without our absolute *identification* with them and, with this adjusted new awareness, live fearless lives. *The experience of freedom requires that we not "identify" with our physical forms.*

The next realization might be "if we are not these forms, what part of us dies?" If we include our new understanding about time we might even wonder "since time does not exist, how could there possibly be a "time" when we die and our life ends?" It is only within a realm that is built upon time that there can be a moment in time when death occurs. We are a part of the universe; if our universe is timeless, we are also timeless and therefore immortal. Our present challenge is to deeply understand this so that we can be free of fear and live our lives to their maximum, enjoying their most natural and flowing, potential. Recognizing our fundamental immortal nature is one of the two most liberating changes that we can experience in these bodies. The other is recognizing our deep interconnection to everything in creation.

HIDDEN MEANING IN SUFFERING AND PAIN

As more of our life unfolds in the "now," we start to better understand how the movement of our life resembles the flow of a powerful river. We begin to "feel" the current and discover that swimming against this deep "current" is always very difficult; our suffering is the result of our fighting the natural flow in the "river of our life."

The pain that accompanies this suffering can emerge from either of two, fully intertwined *egoic forms*: the physical, and the psychological. For the purposes of this discussion, the psychological form includes all the mental, emotional and spiritual aspects. When our physical body is injured, it usually signals with pain. If the injury is the result of an accident, then the source of the problem initially appears to be simple, direct and clear: common examples might be injuries sustained in an auto accidents or falls. Since the cause-and-effect relationship of accidents and the injuries usually seems so logical and conclusive, it is very easy to overlook the deeper, hidden meanings; however, this quick conclusion completely misses the deeper cause-and-effect relationships that spring from the vast interconnectedness between all of life's processes.

Hidden connections and interrelationships constantly shape our personal lives, and these all unfold within the invisible realms of the *Multiverse*. An "accident" may appear to be completely random, but it is never "accidental" because it will be part of this natural cause-and-effect process that always operates at levels that cannot be directly accessed by our rational minds. *Events may seem unexpected or unplanned from our rational perspective, but they are always the result of "cause and effect" and, therefore, are never accidental. There is no such thing as a random accident in the Multiverse. Events only appear random or accidental because the causative interactions occur beyond our vision and understanding.*

Once we have learned how to open and live our lives free of fear, we begin to find subtle ways of accessing this information; we start to recognize and understand these deeper connections. Then, we can begin to understand that our accident was the communication of a deeper need; it was a "wake-up" call to help point us in a new direction for our personal evolution. When seen from this perspective, accidents and injuries become guiding lights to help illuminate the very places where our lives need attention.

It is very common for "injuries" to become chronic. Some chronic injuries may have started with accidents; others may be the result of long-term imbalances, but most have components of both. However, understanding our *viewport* limitations and the interconnectedness of everything, we can begin our search for the deeper origins of these chronic issues. Through carefully chosen therapeutic approaches we then discover our imbalances and the areas of physical tension that are related to our physical symptoms; they are always created by our *repressed* subconscious fears and emotions.

If witnessed with wisdom and clarity, injuries become an extremely useful source of *information* about the state of our body and its emotional holding patterns. The physical expression of pain, as a manifestation of emotional tension, only becomes apparent late in the cycle of *repression*. Accidents and the resulting injuries appear in our lives only as a "last resort" in this natural process of self-discovery; they arrive on the physical plane as a desperate scream from the depths of our *being*. *The accident and injury are direct communications from being itself, telling us "we must pay attention." We are being asked to address the issue at its source. When we simply medicate the pain away in our attempt to regain function, we are disregarding one of nature's fundamental and most honest teachers.* Pain is an extremely powerful attention-focuser; it is nature's way of helping us grow, change and get the most out of our lives in these bodies.

Earlier in this process, before the physical symptoms, the emotional or psychological body can show us where our blockages exist by manifesting emotional or psychological suffering. Compared to loud physical pain, emotional suffering can be subtle; we might not even recognize it. Often it is obscured, hidden behind our layers of psychological, intellectual and physical defenses. Over time, if this tension grows, it will eventually shift into physical expressions such as joint pain or organ-function impairment, but the psychological or emotional suffering always arrives first, signaling an easier path for growth. As we gain wisdom and tools, we can learn how to identify and address our resistances long before any physical manifestations.

Suffering has its roots in our rigid *identification* with our bodies and ego. *When we finally understand, at the deepest levels of our being, that we are not these "bodies" and not these "egos" and allow our souls to flow freely with the "river of life," then the suffering stops as all emotional and psychological pain loosens its tight grip.* When we no longer are creating the psychological or physical *receptors,* there is nothing new for suffering to grab and hold. Once free of internal turbulence and resistance, we become more like empty vessels that just allow the *life-force* to flow through. Our old physical issues may still show up because of tissue damage and old habits but, no longer adding new layers of tension and imbalance, we now have more time and *energy* for repair. *Once we fully understand the issue of attachment, we arrive at the critical crossroad where we can understand that our suffering is completely optional.*

All *information* in the *Multiverse* is holographic in nature; everything is always fully interconnected. It takes practice, training, and patience for the human mind to recognize and trust these invisible but very real connections. They may seem invisible or inaccessible, but we always move with these connections naturally and easily when we are living our lives closer to the "now."

QUIET DESPERATION–UNEXPRESSED SELVES

Thoreau famously wrote *"Most humans lead lives of quiet desperation and go to the grave with the song still in them."* Most humans do not fully express the potential of their particular individual "songs" in their short lifetimes. The "song" we were each born to express is infinite, beautiful and full of possibilities, but we get busy with our lives and, too often and too soon, it seems that we just don't have the time, money, opportunity, knowledge or energy to fully express ourselves. Through living our daily lives, we appear to lose our will for this, our deepest and most personal calling.

Fortunately, in our Quantum Multiverse, it is never too "late" because the passing of "time" is only another illusion. *Once we shift and commit to the full expression of our own "song," we find ourselves suddenly guided by seemingly mysterious events and synchronicities, as our lives simultaneously become much more amazing and joyful.* Our new lives unfold this way because we are no longer swimming against the current; instead, we allow this natural flow to naturally carry us through our lives–everything changes.

At the same time, the even-deeper truth is that there is absolutely no need or requirement to make this shift. Our lives will be soul changing and evolutionary no matter what we do, even if our experience is a full immersion into Thoreau's *"life of desperation."* The feeling of being desperate and not being able to express our self is, by itself, an extremely valuable experience for our soul. Most of us feel this way sometimes, and many of us feel this way often. As always, no matter what happens, it will be a perfect expression of "all that is." Once we fully understand "desperation" and develop compassion for those who feel trapped in this cycle of fear, then there is no further need for our *being* to continue repeating this particular type of experience. The critical evolutionary step is the development of our compassion, which results from this deep level of personal understanding and feeling. With wisdom and compassion we become free to move beyond "desperation" and our other painful repeated patterns.

FEAR, DESIRE AND LOVE

It has often been said in contemporary Western spiritual circles that *"fear is the opposite of Love."* At first glance this might seem to be the case, since with every act or decision we are choosing a path that is shaped by either fear or *Love.* Any problem can be framed so it appears that fear and *Love* are the two choices; however these two are not opposites. They are related, but they originate in completely different realms.

There is no opposite of Love. Love just "is"! Love is one of our names for the fundamental vibration that brings the physical universe into form. Love is an infinite and deep well that is always available, but we often close ourselves to this ever-present, radiant source. *Love* is omnipresent and eternal! It is the foundational vibration from which physical life is created. It is the living fluid that connects us to each other and to our source. Seen from our 3D perspective, Love is home we can enter, dwell within and share. Love is the place where we all naturally *resonate* together and experience our deep connections. It is the ocean where we all swim as one. The more receptive and open we become, the more we are capable of experiencing this always available *Love.*

Fear comes from an entirely different realm of existence. Fear is a physical and energetic reaction at the biological or three-dimensional *egoic* level. Fear creates physical, psychological and emotional blockages that reduce our ability to feel and resonate with *Love;* fear completely blocks our natural awareness of and our full access to *Love.* Fear of any kind always makes it harder for us to experience eternally present *Love.* ***Fear is only a three-dimensional concept. It is a creation of our minds and bodies.***

The Indian spiritual teacher Sri Nisargadatta poetically explains *"Fear is the memory of pain while desire is the memory of pleasure."* Both are dependent upon our sensations and memory, and both are, therefore, very three-dimensional. When we live close to the present moment we are no longer as *attached* to our memories, so fear and desire lose their power over us; they no longer block our access to *Love.* This frees our *being,* allowing it to express itself more fully.

Love is the ultimate, creative, resonant, vibratory symphony. When we allow ourselves to resonate more fully with the universe, we are allowing ourselves to experience more of this ever-present Love. Our openness is what always determines how fully we experience this omnipresent Love vibration. *Love* originates beyond the physical and has no real opposite other than nothingness. The Beatles shared this insight when they sang, *"Love is all there is"*!

While certainly not a given, a significant encounter with *Love* can sometimes occur in our romantic sexual relationships. *Love* encountered in this type of relationship is a direct byproduct of our deeper opening, as fear naturally recedes in the biochemical "swirl of romance." The object of our romantic attention has little to do with this sensation of *Love*. Our romantic partner is only the trigger for our increased openness; *love* is felt because our open connection to another relaxes us. Having less resistance, we become more open and the omnipresent *Love vibration* can be felt more fully. In this situation, our deeper experience of *Love* has nothing to do with any other person–it is only about the *self* becoming more open and connected to all of creation.

Understanding the geometry and timeless nature of the *Multiverse* offers the possibility for someone like myself–a person who needs to know the scientific reasons behind his beliefs–to relax and loosen their grip on fear. ***Our most primal fear is that we are not safe because we will die and cease to exist!*** Layered on top of this basic fear are our secondary fears, including the fear that we are not lovable, the fear that we haven't been true to our purpose, the fear of pain, the fear of the unknown, and even a generalized fear of living in the very culture that we have helped create.

All of these common human forms of fear quickly lose their power when viewed or experienced with a fuller awareness and understanding of the Web. This awareness includes knowing that time does not exist, that the individual is not isolated, that Being never dies, that we are eternally and internally connected to Being, and that our universe is designed just so we can experience all the available possibilities.

In the absence of fear, Love is present–it is that simple. When we are capable of feeling fully, what we feel the most is Love. This is the place where we all connect. Love is another name for the experience of oneness or completeness; it is our one true home.

ATTACHMENTS ARE FEAR-BASED

When we have the opportunity and willingness to look more deeply at our *attachments* and other things that we imagine we "need," what we discover is that these needs and *attachments* all have their origins in our most primal fears–most of our smaller fears develop from our primary fear about death. From the *ego-body* perspective, our fear of death is automatic and designed to protect us–there are good biological reasons for it. Fears that serve to protect our physical form are a part of our instincts; they are completely natural and a part of being human–they come with the territory. Next are our secondary fears; they are the products of our genetic history as an evolving species. Layered on top of these are other levels of learned fears, both cultural and personal. These tertiary fears are often easier for us to identify and associate specific events in our lives.

Our ubiquitous *attachment* issues formed around money are usually driven by our fear of not having enough for now, or in the future, when we might become too sick or too weak to provide for ourselves. The *attachment* to power is related to this *attachment* to money, but is mostly driven by the need to enlarge, preserve and immortalize the individual *ego*, which, of course, is also directly related to our pressing need to sidestep death. Our most common fears, and the various attachments they spawn, are responses to our cultural belief that the death of the body marks the end of our existence. All of these fears are secondary in that they have been built upon the basic-survival fear. Even the fear of deep or extended pain loses much of its power when we understand the illusionary nature of our physical form.

The fears associated with the next level are those that involve concern for others, usually family or clan. These are built upon our desire to protect and feed our children, aging parents and other loved ones, but they also extend to our social organization and our perception of our role in society. Although this is a level of concern that is closely associated with the welfare of others, it still is about insuring the survival of the species, so it is also closely related to our most primal fear. There is an enormous amount of culturally induced anxiety that becomes suppressed, *repressed* and buried, even at this less personal level; becoming aware of its existence, its cultural origins and its most common modes of expression is also a part of our awakening. We are not isolated beings existing in one moment of time; we are instead, a collective and timeless social *being* with an interwoven cultural and genetic history. Our cultural history is an integrated part of us–all of it needs to be recognized, witnessed and embraced.

Layered on top of the primal and cultural layers of fears are the lesser *ego*-based worries like those of being embarrassed, forgetting someone's name, forgetting to pay a bill, failing at your job, not waking up for a test, and a warehouse full of internally-generated or imagined thoughts and neurosis. These then intermingle and built-up around our more basic fears, creating one giant and emotionally heavy "fear ball" that drives our behavior while we live in a habitual state of relentless, unconscious anxiety. We waste an enormous amount of *energy* every day supporting and maintaining these mostly useless "fear balls."

Our fear-based habits and attachments are formed within our three-dimensional concept of time, and they are based on a mistaken assumption that drives our Western human experiment of individualization and separation. That assumption is "if we don't take care of ourselves, no one will, and then we will fail, quickly die and cease to exist." This interconnected series of ideas is a bundle that we all inherit directly from our "dimensionally bound" human culture. This concept is then reinforced and enhanced by the competitive and divisive nature of our contemporary Western culture. Our contemporary culture does not encourage or support us in our attempts to disassemble, deconstruct, explore or reveal the contents of this tightly wrapped paradigm.

All of our fears can be analyzed and addressed singularly, but they all collapse into nonexistence once the fear of death loses its grip upon us. *Once we truly understand that we are not these physical bodies trapped in time, all levels and types of fear begin to evaporate.*

If we try to deal with each fear, one at a time, we find this to be an impossible task; there are so many forms of fear that are all tangled and interconnected, that this approach is simply not practical or effective. Counseling may help us deal with limited specific issues and become more functional, but it is likely that we will just transfer our fears to a host of other concerns; when the deep source of our fear has not been fully recognized or addressed, we tend to create new layers of fear and worry as quickly as we can work through the older ones. *The source of all these fears is, of course, our fear of being separate, alone, unprotected and ephemeral–separation and death. If we can come to a deep knowing that we are always an integrated part of a much grander and eternal being-ness, it then becomes possible for all of these fears to simply drop away, at once, without the effort of processing each one individually. A deeper knowledge of our true place and relationship within the Multiverse opens this door to freedom.*

HEALING THE SUBCONSCIOUS MIND

As previously mentioned and according to current research, the *conscious* mind can process only 40 stimuli per second, while the *subconscious* mind will process approximately 20,000,000 stimuli during that same second; the difference in the *information*-processing ability of these two parts of our brain is extraordinary. This means that if both parts are operating at maximum levels, then 99.9998 percent of the brain's "processing" is subconscious, or below the surface of our everyday awareness. The vast majority of what we do, think, feel and react to completely escapes our *conscious* awareness.

Certain functions like heartbeat and breathing are probably best handled below the surface. Despite this, yogis have learned to play with some of these automatic functions and this demonstrates that we can *consciously* control many of them, at least to some degree. We can raise and lower our heart rates, change our blood pressures and body temperatures, and alter our brain waves; those bodily functions that become *conscious* or remain in the *subconscious* will shift as we practice and evolve. However, conscious control of our bodily functions is only useful in rare or unusual circumstances, so these are mostly just entertaining tricks which can serve us by demonstrating the possibilities. *If we truly desire to live our lives more fully, the real challenge for us is to learn how to uncover, and make more conscious, the deep roots of our core beliefs and feelings.*

What do we really believe, deep down at our core–the level that rests at the base of, or even below, our subconscious? These core beliefs are critical because they shape and drive our lives, but for most of us they are not accessible because they are too deeply buried. To access them, we must first penetrate the many layers that have been built upon our subconscious and conscious fears. These layers modify the way our core impulses manifest by the time they reach the surface of our lives.

Eventually, embodied fears will be expressed physically, as tension-related issues, often associated with the muscles, fascia and tendons, or the digestive tract. They might also be expressed as restrictions in the flow of any bodily process, such as the circulatory system or lymph system. Common examples of these primary-level, tension-related problems are carpal tunnel syndrome, tendonitis, sciatica, irritable bowel disease, stomach ulcers, heart palpitations, arthritis, and many other *dis-eases*. Treating the symptoms may bring temporary relief, but if the source of this core tension is not addressed, the *dis-ease* will reemerge again in the same way, or in some new-but-related form. No matter how we change our actions or our surface beliefs, as long as this core fear remains, our expression and experience of *being* will always be *damped* by this invisible weight.

Accessing our repressed subconscious mind directly through our conscious mind is essentially impossible since it is our conscious mind that is, and always has been, the "gatekeeper." Hoping to approach our hidden darkness through our conscious minds is like "asking the fox to guard the henhouse." Either our conscious mind buried these memories in the first place or it is completely unable to comprehend them because of *cognitive dissonance.* Due to the protective and controlling nature of our conscious minds, any efforts to use it to understand the subconscious are essentially futile.

On the other hand, reaching the subconscious through the body and feelings can be tremendously effective; access can be achieved through various techniques, including forms of bodywork. Focused bodywork from a knowledgeable and talented therapist can help expose and address our subconscious, accumulated baggage.

We all have our "dark" areas that are begging to be illuminated with the light of our conscious witnessing. The simple truth we discover through this type of body-centered process is that no fixing is required and the past need not be changed. *The only thing that is being asked for is the opportunity for this "darkness" to be witnessed without judgment.* Once witnessed in a space that is free of self-judgment, darkness begins to loosen its hold on us. If the non-judgmental approach is maintained, the darkness soon becomes illuminated, fully accepted and eventually even embraced; this is the process where *being* gets to know itself. During bodywork, the patient's only responsibility is to be completely open and willing to witness whatever arises in the session. Whatever is discovered in bodywork sessions always involves some hidden part of us that has been asking to be illuminated or enlightened.

Healing is a process that helps us to become more aware of who we really are. It is about the expansion of our ability to feel and explore our inner space as it gradually becomes illuminated. Healing at the level of our *subconscious* mind is about experiencing more of our lives in each and every moment. We become more open to and no longer judge a deeper truth: the truth of who we really are.

PERCEPTION

Eckhart Tolle describes perception this way: *"Remember that your perception of the world is a reflection of your state of consciousness. You are not separate from it, and there is no objective world out there. Every moment, your consciousness creates the world that you inhabit."* Einstein said it a bit differently. *"Physical concepts are free creations of the human mind, and are not, however it may seem, uniquely determined by the external world."*

One of the great insights that emerged from modern physics is that of the intimate connection between the observer and the observed, wherein the observing awareness can't be separated from the observed phenomena. A different way of looking causes the observed phenomena to appear to behave differently. Our thoughts always have a direct impact on what we observe. If, for example, we really believe in our separation from each other and the ultimate competitive struggle for survival, then we will see that belief reflected all around us, and our perceptions will be governed by that belief. The world we see will then be "dog-eat-dog." It absolutely does not have to be this way!

Nothing "out there" is really what it seems. The world that we see through our *egoic* minds may seem a very imperfect place, often a tragically sad world, but everything we perceive is only a symbol or shadow, not unlike our dreams. *The world as we encounter it is only how our consciousness interprets and interacts in three dimensions with the energy dance of the multi-dimensional universe.* This *energy* dance is the raw material of everything that we eventually interact with as physical reality. *An infinite number of different interpretations and worlds are not only possible, but already exist, and are all expressed through perceiving consciousness.* Every *being* acts as a single focal point of awareness, and every such focal point creates its own worldview. Our worldview always reflects the internal state of our individual and collective souls. All of these individual worlds exist at the same time and all are fully, instantly, intimately and eternally interconnected at levels far beyond our perception.

EXPERIENCE AND EXPECTATIONS

INTRODUCTION

Freeing ourselves from our old habits and reflexive patterns is critical if we hope to experience new possibilities. Individually and collectively, we only see and register our experiences through our internal filters–some are personal but others are cultural. *We only see and remember what we already understand or are conceptually prepared for, and most of this has been preprogrammed through our culture and upbringing.* We unknowingly let this unconscious program control the vast majority of our perceptions and experiences. Numerous examples and experiments from daily life clearly illustrate this phenomenon.

The magician's illusions easily demonstrate how well this works. Magicians make their living by performing a series of intentionally deceptive illusions that "trick" us into seeing a reality that is not actually there. First they carefully prepare us to see the particular reality that they want us to see. They reinforce a program that already exists in our brains–our natural tendency to only consciously register whatever it is that we normally would expect to see. This prevents us from registering whatever slights of hand or other deceptive maneuvers are really happening on the stage. Their optical, conceptual and verbal illusions intentionally misdirect our attention.

Illusions of many other types demonstrate how our expectations always control this internal filtering. Optical illusions are well understood phenomena that speak directly to the way our minds fill in *information* to meet our expected reality. They present a common but testable demonstration of how our brains not only filter information, but also fill in the missing pieces to match our expectations. They illustrate that our perceptions are really only the result of our expectations, which are mostly derived from our previous experiences.

Scientific American magazine holds an annual contest for the best illusions. As part of their 2011 contest synopsis they concluded, ***"Inside your brain, you create a simulation of the world that may or may not match the real thing. Your "reality" is the result of your exclusive interaction with that simulation. You may see something that is not there, or fail to see something that is there, or see something differently from the way others see it."*** What we perceive as real is only our personal movie or dream that we fully create and then project within our 3D conceptual brains.

When we recount shared experiences with friends, we have all been amazed by how different our recollections of the same event can be. *"The guy had black hair,"* says one witness, while the other says, *"No, I am sure he was blonde!"* Our processing of *information* is tailored to our own personal story, which always regulates what and how we comprehend this *information*. Our perception will always depend on our individual experiences, perspectives and agendas and, because of this, the memory of an event will vary from person to person.

Something can occur right in front of us, and if we have no conceptual framework for digesting the event, we simply will not see it or, at least, not consciously record or remember it. Sometimes, even when the event is well within our experiential framework, if we are not expecting it, we won't see it, even as it is unfolding right in front of us.

A stunning demonstration of this very phenomenon is an Internet video of the "gorilla in the room" which can be found on YouTube under the title "Selective Attention Test." The viewer is "prepared" by being informed that this is a *very difficult test that requires their full attention–their job is to count the exact number of passes of the ball.*

In the video there are three people in white tee shirts tossing a big ball to each other very rapidly. There are also three other people in black tee shirts continuously weaving around those wearing the white shirts. The passes are happening very rapidly and are also quite irregular and unpredictable. Since the three other participants are also moving about the room, when you watch the video you do have to focus your full attention on the ball and the act of counting. Most subjects get the actual count right but, after completing this task, you are then asked to review the video, this time without counting, to see if there was anything you missed. Upon watching the video again, this time without the same intense focus of attention on the ball, you can clearly see that, throughout most of the video, there is also another man in a very large gorilla suit jumping and weaving around as the ball is being passed.

Most of us do not see this "gorilla in the room" even though he is right in front of our eyes. We are so intently focused on our defined task that we completely filter him out. Upon seeing this video the second time, I was, at first, convinced that it was all a computer trick and that the second video was a different video stream. To test this theory, I had my very perceptive daughter watch the video for the first time while I looked over her shoulder. I saw the gorilla while she did not, even though I provided an additional clue for her with my barely restrained laughter.

We see only what we are psychologically prepared to see, and our expectations and intents always shape this filter. While not outside of our life experiences, the man in a gorilla costume was still completely outside of our expectations, and this made it nearly impossible to register his presence. ***Imagine what we miss in each and every moment simply because phenomena are outside or beyond our normal experiences and expectations.***

It has been claimed by some writers that the original residents of the Americas lacked the conceptual context to see the ships of the first European explorers. Of course we have no proof of this, but anyone who has witnessed the gorilla video (without my spoiler) can see that this is a real possibility. What this means is that at the conscious level we all miss a tremendous amount of information. There is always much more going on around us than meets the eye or registers with our conscious brains.

ATTITUDE OF GRATITUDE

We often hear the expression "*attitude is everything*"–this is actually a vast understatement! ***Attitude is the single most important thing any person can focus upon to initiate a change in his or her life.*** Nothing that we attempt to do ever flows effortlessly if our attitude is not *resonating sympathetically*–meaning that our attitude is working for us, instead of against us. The greatest portion of our attitude is generated and maintained in the subterranean world of our *subconscious* mind. Knowing this, it then becomes obvious that opening or *enlightening* this *subconscious* part of ourselves is critical if we want to change our lives by changing a deeply formed attitude. Remember that about 99.9998 percent of our processing emerges from this hidden place, so it powerfully influences everything about us. Our deeply buried beliefs control the manifestation of our inner *vibration* and, therefore, our experience at every level. ***Changing our attitude changes how we vibrate at the surface and this changes our world.***

At the deep-root level, if our trust in the perfection of the universe is strong and dominant, there will not be very much room for the fear that keeps us separate, tense and alone. ***What we experience on the surface of our being always and completely reflects the terrain below.*** At the surface of our lives, all types of drama will continuously unfold, so the real variable is how we react–not just on the surface–but how we react deep within our *being*. The same event or situation will always stimulate different reactions from different individuals.

Nick Charles, the recently deceased, long-time CNN anchor, said in his death bed memoirs, "*Life is 20% what actually happens to you and 80% how you react to it.*" He did not go far enough. What he didn't say was that the 20 percent that appears to "happen to you" is also only a direct and inevitable result of the other 80 percent of your reactions. Our attitude determines our full range of vibration and this, in turn, determines where our awareness will enliven the "Web of Possibilities." What we see and experience is always a direct result of how we are *vibrating*. It is illuminating to really understand this particular expression of the classic *feedback loop*. Our lives always become "what they are" because of "what we do."

We understand that something that looks extremely negative from one perspective can and will appear very positive from another. If we seek to find the positive in every situation, then we will find that our lives gradually begin to feel different and better. *The single most effective "positive" adjustment we can make is to develop and practice an "attitude of real gratitude" for this life and its infinite opportunities.* I first learned this from that voice I heard on the sailboat many years ago. *If we each can work towards finding the place where we have a genuine gratitude for life, a gratitude for everything that unfolds–no matter what it feels like, no matter how it looks in that, or any, moment–with that shift, everything about life quickly changes.*

This practice helps us develop a mindset in which we automatically recognize that our opportunity to live in this physical world is a great gift, and our chance to experience all that this "world of temporary form" makes possible. We can be deeply thankful because we recognize that we have been given this form to explore a very special part of *beingness*. *Nothing else is needed. By embracing life with full gratitude and awareness, we will always be fully engaged in the beautiful flow of life. The best attitude is always one of gratitude.*

FORGIVENESS

As part of living our lives in gratitude, we develop an improved ability to understand and experience true forgiveness. The type of forgiveness that most of us were taught as children is not true forgiveness. That learned type more closely resembles an act of dispensation in which an offender is offered some form of conditional pardon. This pardon allows the person granting it to feel noble, while the forgiven is then able to feel less guilty or fearful. This type of forgiveness has no relationship to the type of forgiveness that becomes possible after the shift in our internal paradigm.

True forgiveness only occurs when we fully recognize ourselves within all others and even within the offensive act, itself. There is no longer any separation–we are both the offender and the offended. This means that anything that was done was only one part of us unconsciously reacting to another part of ourselves. We understand that whatever unfolded was just part of the process of living in the shadow world of three-dimensional *projections,* which is always driven and controlled by our fears and automatic reactions. We become able to move beyond the event, fully and completely, by *recognizing that nothing was really "done" to us. We were only participating in an illusionary process. In a very real sense, it is as if it is all only a dream that does not touch our real self. There is nothing real that needs to be forgiven because nothing real ever happened. At this level of awareness and recognition, everything changes; tension is fully released; ideas are dropped; and anything and everything becomes possible as true healing unfolds.*

Rather than being a form of detachment or denial, this type of forgiveness is the very opposite. This is the complete recognition that there is no difference between us and the one identified as the perpetrator, and therefore there is no "other" to even forgive.

The logical next step is critical. At this point we often suddenly recognize that we must now forgive ourselves because there is no "other." In the deepest of places, true forgiveness is ultimately only the act of accepting, and embracing all aspects of our selves. Forgiveness is always, and only, about forgiving our self.

257

DECISIONS

For every individual, a path through life is shaped by a long, complex series of personal choices or decisions. Every day, each of us decides how to handle millions of issues, the vast majority of which are handled subconsciously. Most of these are automatic, self-regulating biological processes; many others are personal choices made well below the surface, in the subconscious; and others are being processed closer to the surface at a semiconscious, unexamined, "knee-jerk" level. A few choices, only .0002 percent of our total processing, bubble up to reach the fully conscious level. **When we have the opportunity to make these conscious decisions, there will always be a part of the process where we will have the opportunity to move in one of two directions. We either move towards more unity or towards more separation with every conscious decision.** There is no right or wrong choice, for they both are necessary to give shape and form to our universe, and both lead to experience, which is why we are here in the first place. We are here to fully experience every corner of this physical life.

When we make a decision, what we are really doing with each choice is deciding whether to trust the flow of life or resist it by attempting to mold life to our own specifications. **We accomplish our true purpose no matter which we choose.** However, each type of choice produces different results; one set of results may feel very different from the other and lead to a very different set of future options. With every decision, we can make a choice to move towards more connection with everyone and everything, or not. Ultimately, the end result of all these different paths is the same– more experience. Our actual decisions are not as important as we might imagine because in our Multiverse all outcomes exist equally.

THE MYSTERY OF LIFE-FORCE

Almost every world religion and spiritual practice recognizes the existence of a distinct presence, or *energy,* which animates life itself. Named life-force, Mana, Ki, Chi, Prana, Holy Spirit, Ashe and a host of other names, this life-giving "spark" is universally recognized, yet completely mysterious. None of our current scientific theories can explain where it originates or how it works.

Some physicists, such as Steven Hawking, have stated that with our new science we are on the brink of unlocking the true nature of life-force, or even what some may call God. They pronounce that the workings of God will soon be completely explained through this new physics. We might recall that this was also said about Newtonian physics almost 400 years ago. That predicted breakthrough did not occur and today, as we are again shifting paradigms, this claim has been renewed.

My interest in the subject matter of this book began with youthful questions about the deeper nature of life, yet today my "source of life" questions are not as pressing; my understanding of the structure of the universe provides satisfying insights. I recognize and understand why so much, including the source of this spark, remains obscured. I also see a natural path for this "life-force" to express itself through all the personal, and interpersonal, possibilities that such a structure allows.

"Life-force," the energetic spark that makes all of life possible, could be nothing more than another projected illusion that seems real because of our programming or conceptual limitations. It could be the natural result of the biology and physics of the body and brain, or it might be the touch of God. Despite all of our theories, science and experience, we still lack a clear understanding. Therefore, this book can only describe the terrain or architecture that this spirit moves through–it is about how the spirit's playground: our universe, affects our personal dance through life.

At this stage of my life, I am finally content to leave this "source of life-force" question to mystery. Understanding its origin isn't critical to living a full and amazing life within our *Multiverse*. One day we may better understand this "life-force" but, even without illumination, it will continue to animate our growth, play, and evolution within our infinite, wonderful, multi-dimensional *Multiverse*. The mystery only makes my personal dance more interesting.

"KNOWING" AND "NOT KNOWING"

Becoming comfortable with the state of "not knowing" is one of the most powerful tools that we discover on this journey. When we think we "know" what something is, it becomes rigidly cemented in our minds in a way that limits both its potential expression, and how we evolve. We fix ideas in much the same way that early film photographers chemically fixed the silver-coated negatives and prints in their darkrooms. "Knowing" tends to solidify and lock ideas into conceptual form, which from that point on will define their possibilities and extents. This kind of "knowing" can also be part of a subtle but powerful form of *attachment*.

As a professional architect, I spend my early creative time on new projects in the psychological space of "not knowing." Once I feel that I "know" the design, the open part of the creative process usually stops. This means that while many details still need to be worked out, the basic idea or plan is probably not going to change very much after that point, unless I start the process over. The step of "knowing" is similar to an act of *observation* in a quantum experiment because it seems to somehow collapse the "wave of possibilities." Before the "knowing," anything was possible; after the "knowing," the possibilities have been dramatically reduced.

This "fixation" process is not a negative thing in the business of architecture, where the objective is to get a 3D structure built, using a limited amount of time and money. At some point in this process, I absolutely need to "know" the answers so I can move on, finish the drawings, and get the building built. However, if my "knowing" enters the process too early, it inhibits the free flow of creative ideas that otherwise emerge from the depths. True creative art flows from wells that are tapped into the deeper levels of multi-dimensional space. It is the artist's job to learn how to allow and facilitate the emergence of these deep impulses into our 3D world. After the "knowing," the creative process becomes more restricted by conceptual thinking, so the rest of the process develops mostly within the logical constraints of the 3D paradigm–the craft continues, but the deeper art ends.

The psychological landscape uncovered through an extended state of "not knowing" can be a bit tricky to navigate at first; but once we get comfortable with this new territory, we realize that it is abundantly filled with beautiful and unexpected surprises. For me, this open state of "not knowing" might result in a simple but spontaneous impulse to draw a line on the architectural plan–a line placed without any attention to thought, reason, intention or rational purpose. This new line might then unexpectedly merge with an older line previously drawn on a layer of tracing paper three levels below; and then suddenly, together, they form a surprising new shape, which is instantly recognized as a fortuitous "happy accident," illuminating a new and unexpected solution to the problem. So many wonderful, successful and revolutionary ideas have begun with such spontaneous and illogical impulses that I now fully trust them, even though their origins are hidden and mysterious.

The source of unexpected ideas will always seem mysterious from our viewpoint because the creative impulse is only a quick glimpse of a shadow passing through the boundary that obscures the multi-dimensional space beyond, and within. By staying open to all possibilities, pieces of *information* make their way across this veil to form visible expressions in our realm. A large part of my job throughout the early creative phase is to be on the lookout for these "happy accidents" without controlling or directing the process. I act as a "watcher" until I see or sense something that feels right. At some point I recognize that I have enough useful *information* on paper to visualize the complete solution. At that moment, with this "knowing," the process shifts as I consciously allow the *quantum wave* to *collapse*.

Even though I use computers for drafting, modeling and presentation drawings, I always draw by hand throughout the initial design period–this allows my hand to have its "own mind" and a type of independence from my calculating brain. It is an exercise similar to the ideas made popular in Betty Edwards' book, *Drawing With the Right Side of the Brain*. "Happy accidents" often occur while using the computer as well, but I still prefer drawing by hand during these early stages. This is probably because I developed my design process well before 1984 (first year for the Macintosh), when personal computers were still designed for number crunching and not yet ideal for graphics.

Einstein said: *"You cannot solve a problem from the same consciousness that created it. You must learn to see the world anew."* Remaining open to any possibility, especially one from the other side of the veil that separates extra-dimensional space, is an absolute requirement for solutions that are revolutionary, that *resonate* widely, and/or that deeply shift our *viewport*.

Intentionally entering and exploring this state of "not knowing" can be uncomfortable for those raised in Western culture. We are trained to always know, understand, or "figure it out" immediately. "Not knowing" is traditionally understood to indicate a state of confusion or inadequacy, which is usually judged negatively and harshly in our culture. Our culture rewards speed, so other people may interpret our spending time in a state of "not knowing" as failure to act quickly enough. We are trained to have too little patience with simply "sitting with an idea and watching how it develops." Ours is a culture that lives by the clock–it favors direct and quick action. There is little patience for this "time wasting" method of discovery because we are the direct product of generations trained to be "doers." However, we also hide a deep, cultural secret.

This secret is that all over the Western world, many of our most important ideas, inventions, theories and breakthroughs in understanding have secretly originated from this place of "not knowing." We often find out about the true nature of the actual discovery process from later memoirs, journals and letters, because most of these discoveries were initially presented to the public as if the breakthrough were a direct result of a rational and scientific process. I previously related how I was instructed, in my architectural education, to present my architectural solutions as the direct result of a logical process. Outside of poetry, music and abstract painting, we simply do not know how to talk about the more mysterious aspects of this creative process. We fear that if we reveal too much about the mystery within, we will be judged as being unprofessional.

LEFT BRAIN–RIGHT BRAIN

Using brain-scanning technology that has been developed as a direct result of the *quantum* technological revolution, we have been able to create detailed, physical maps of just where in the brain electrical and other brain wave activities occur for different types of human functions, and several discoveries from this research are particularly interesting. The left/right division turns out to be not as clear and divided as once was imagined. No single function involves only half of the brain; both hemispheres always work together, along with the rest of the body, to process signals. To function best, both sides need to be working together in unison; therefore, healthy individuals require both hemispheres to be working in harmony with each other. While the brain acts as the physical gateway for processed *information*, the entire body is involved in a comprehensive process that may even be holographic in nature.

Studies of brains that have had the fibrous connection between the two hemispheres severed (sometimes through accident and sometimes surgically, in medical attempts to reduce epilepsy) have highlighted some of the clear differences between the separated hemispheres. However, as we look at the differences, we always need to keep in mind that normally both hemispheres must work together in a connected, holistic and holographic system.

The left half has more influence on the rational, logical, chronological and verbal functions of the brain. Occupations that have traditionally leaned heavily on these functions include lawyers, doctors, accountants and business managers. These are occupations that require the practitioner to be good at repetitive tasks, organization, and keeping track of *information*. This hemisphere is also linked tightly with our 3D *viewport* and our perception that its limitations are absolute. On the other side of our physical brain sits the right hemisphere. This hemisphere is far less connected to, or concerned about, our day-to-day 3D world and its concepts. It has more responsibility for the visual, artistic, creative, emotive, empathetic, timeless, psychic and synthesizing functions. This hemisphere allows for deeper empathetic connection with others and more creative thought. Its functioning has more to do with our connection, however unseen by us, to the more fully-expressed *Multiverse*. Our modern society usually favors and rewards the functions controlled by the left hemisphere of the brain, although this prejudice seems to be diminishing.

What we think of as mind, at the level of the individual, seems, at the very minimum, to involve the brain and the rest of the body acting as a single system. We retrieve bits of *information* that are stored everywhere, simultaneously in multiple copies. Any single part of the body stores and shares the same basic *information* with every other part. It is not surprising that the storage and memory patterning turns out to be *holographic* in nature, and the actual physical location of this *holographic* memory storage includes not only the central brain *mass* but also the rest of the human body. There is a more detailed discussion of the nature of *holographic* theory and storage later in this book.

When I was 12 years old, I endured a traumatic head injury that may have partially damaged the connection between my frontal lobes. I have since discovered that I don't always function with the full blend of both hemispheres. This may or may not be directly due to the injury but, as I matured, I had to learn techniques to consciously switch brain halves a number of times to complete complex thought processes. Because I tend to get completely lost in an abstract thought or idea, I had to teach myself how to stop that runaway thought and switch on the rest of my brain when someone is trying to speak to me. This switching process is sometimes not easy or automatic and often takes me some time–like waking from deep sleep. In retrospect, I can recognize this accident as a gift because not only did it facilitate deep concentration but it also provided a unique mechanism that helped me explore the functions of the two "sides" of my brain. Through having to learn this process, not only do I better understand the differences, but also I can consciously shift the functioning for myself when it is advantageous.

While our society adjusts and begins to assign more value to the right-brain functions, another realization about how our brains work is beginning to reveal itself. The brain, which is located far from our body center in a physical extremity: the head, may only function as a second-tier organ–it may not be central to our "thinking."

BRAIN AND HEART

Neuroscientists studying the neural pathways of the body have made an interesting discovery that, if further confirmed and fully understood, may entirely change the way we approach living in our bodies. These researchers learned that there are many more nerve pathways transmitting *information* from heart to brain than there are pathways that send signals in the other direction. Since there seems to be more information sent in this direction, the heart may be designed to be in full control of the brain.

Many individuals know this intuitively, but this unexpected hierarchy clearly has not defined the primary operational principle practiced within our culture. Culturally, we have built our society around the belief that the brain is our most important organ! The heart, which is physically much closer to the center of our bodies and also much better protected, is physiologically a better choice to be our neurological command center. Not only will the pathways to the rest of the body be shorter and more direct, but this nerve center is better protected–we are much more likely to damage our heads in an accident.

Thirty years ago I had a dear friend give me some of the best advice of my life. She observed that "*I thought too much,*" and she reminded me that my brain is located in an extremity. She also suggested that it would be wise to treat my brain the same way as any other extremity–as a tool like my hands or feet. I would then find myself brought back into better balance. Humans traditionally assign too much importance to our brains. ***Our brains are only functioning at their best when they are in full open communication with our hearts and acting as our hearts' servants.***

BRAIN AND MIND

Throughout this book I use the terms "brain" and "mind" in a way that is slightly unconventional. Brain conventionally refers to a physical part of our body, and usually the term brain only describes the mass of neurons located within our skull. However, because science is now beginning to understand that memory is stored and processed in a more holistic manner throughout the body, I will also include in my definition the entire physical nervous system and all the cells and organs that connect to it. By this definition, ***the physical brain and the body are essentially one and the same.***

Both the brain and the body are also intimately associated with our ego. The brain/body has critical processing functions that allow us to perceive the outside world using five recognized senses. The brain/body is continuously busy sensing, processing and responding subconsciously to sounds, changes of temperature, movement, pheromones, other chemical stimulants, and all types of signals in our environment. At the same time that our brain/body is directly interacting with the outside world through these known interfaces, it also automatically processes many types of environmental signals that we do not understand, or have not recognized or identified. For example, how do we sense when someone is staring at us?

When I speak of mind with a lower case "m," I am discussing the brain/body with the additional layer of the self-awareness that frames and defines each individual's sense of identity. This level of mind incorporates the self-reflective awareness of itself as a separate individual, and it includes the individual emotional, psychological and physical filters that affect how *information* is processed. Our small "m" mind can even include physical things and *beings,* which we directly connect to and interact with, that are physically located outside of our bodies. A long-time spouse, our children, a twin, or a beloved pet can all influence how our minds process information. While the brain/body is only physical, the *mind* is also affected by psychological input and the energetic interpersonal interactions that unfold in the physical 3D world. The mind is three-dimensional, but it is also always evolving–It incorporates a built-in desire or program to grow or expand.

In my usage, Mind, with a capital "M," operates at an entirely different level. Mind is all the above plus that part of our *being* that connects with *information* and *energy* that is available beyond our bodies and our 3D world. Through Mind, we have our direct connection and access to *information* that lies far beyond our personal histories–we interact with signals from that part of the universe that lies outside of our three-dimensional conceptual space. This includes *information* that we refer to as ESP, déjà vu, and all that is called "paranormal" phenomena–our very direct but poorly understood connection to everything else in the *Multiverse*. I refer to the capitalized Mind when the level of *information* sharing involves a more universal level, one that is not limited by our bodies, time or space. Mind is capitalized when the *information* is universal, or *Multiversal,* in its nature or origin.

OUR CHOSEN WORK

Life at the physical level requires a certain amount of actual *work* to sustain our physical forms. The laws of physics describe how physical systems require *energy* input, or *work*, to maintain their *order*. One definition of a living system is a system that can "maintain, or build, *order* within a universe that naturally moves towards *disorder*." In more primitive civilizations the type of work required to shelter, feed and heal our bodies was obvious and very directly related to the necessary requirements for physical life. We gathered food, ate, fought off predators, built shelter, created tools, reproduced, grew, healed wounds, and directly provided the other basic necessities required to support and perpetuate our living systems.

In our contemporary culture, one that has been built around specialization and consumerism, we have unlimited choices and opportunities to expand our understanding of "work" to include activities that involve much more than just our basic survival needs; for example, many people have become financially successful through designing or using "creative" investment instruments such as derivatives. Many, if not most of us, now work in ways that seem very detached and unrelated to basic survival because today's economic system and consumer culture often fail to reinforce or build upon this important direct connection to survival as the primary reason for our work.

The common experience of enduring a dispiriting job for gathering income to then buy unnecessary material things will quickly dampen our *vibratory resonance*. Many of us dedicate a major part of each and every day to income generation. Because of this indirectness and the lost energy expenditure, we lose much of our work's potential to shape our *being and* add joy to our lives. At the same time, this all too common pattern causes us to lose even more by damping our overall level of radiance or *vibration*.

Ennui is defined as the emotional or psychological loss of *energy*. *Energy* is abundant and is always available to us through a wide array of channels within our *Multiverse*. Human emotional resistance directly blocks our access to this *energy*, and this resistance is deeply tied to our conditioning and fears. Newton's famous law declares that *"objects in motion stay in motion unless acted upon by some force."* As conceived, this law applies only to physical objects, but we all know from our personal experience that increased excitement about life seems to give us more personal *energy* or *momentum*. We even commonly refer to this experience as being "energized."

When we eventually let go of fears that involve income generation and begin to explore a deeper calling, the unexpected happens; doors magically open, helping hands show up just when needed, and enough income and other resources come our way for our continued sustenance. As our resonance builds, helpful synchronicities unfold, and the impossible suddenly seems easy and natural. The result may not look like anything that we originally imagined–it might not even be close–but we magically find ourselves feeling productive, joyful and very excited about our lives. *Society and the individual are best served, and the "song" is the sweetest, when everyone is fully resonant, passionate and contributing their own unique part to the greater symphony.*

A young person just starting employment will often have no idea about what type of productive activity will most joyfully sustain them. Their most productive work at this point in their lives will be to just explore life's options more fully and learn about their own unique gifts. At this stage, a series of different types of employment, all approached with an open mind and curiosity, can effectively serve the dual purposes of maintenance and exploration.

Of course, in our *Multiverse*, there are no bad choices, only experiences to be integrated. Whatever way a person chooses to manage their work is perfect, just as it is. *However, if we are tired of repeating old experiences and we desire a significant shift in our life, then we may need to change our employment to better align our work with our soul. Life is so much more fun, interesting and productive when each of us is doing a type of work that we enjoy and know that we were meant to do!*

ACTIVISM

When learning about this new way of being, it is very reasonable to ask *"But what about social, environmental and political activism? If it is true that we can't change the way others think, is activism, then, just a meaningless waste of time and energy? Are you then saying that we should do nothing?"*

These types of reactions are the logical results of reasoning. They are viewpoints built upon and perpetuating our familiar, but now antiquated, 3D culture and paradigm–if analyzed from within that *viewport* alone, these are very sensible reactions. However, as we have learned, we can't fix problems from within the same mindset that created them. To achieve significant and real change, we need to step outside of our old thought process and try something completely new.

Both social and political activism are absolutely critical for creating balance in our world, but activism will never "fix" our world–it needs no fixing; it is already perfect. Organized activists create and build platforms for public education and the sharing of information. Their work allows others to have better opportunities to learn about some of the different ways physical life presents itself in our realm. If activists expect others to change so that the world will one day be "fixed," they are going to wind up extremely disappointed; any personal experience with activism will always involve learning about our own expectations. In the end activism, like everything in life, is really about changing ourselves.

Being actively engaged in our passions is critical for our personal and societal growth. However, we also eventually learn that we can't "fight for peace"–we will never achieve peace this way. While closely examining our reaction to the cultural idea of "fighting for what we believe in," we are invited, again, to revisit the history of this problem solving method. Historically, "fighting" or "battling" "others" in the name of some cause always ultimately perpetuates the struggle, rather than leading to new ways that move us beyond the struggle. It is oxymoronic to think that peace can be achieved through "fighting." We can only discover the peace "within and without" through a practice that involves "not fighting" and this can only happen when the idea of "fight" itself is no longer a divided part of our energy field. Mother Teresa understood this completely. She refused to participate in "anti-war" activities but was happy to participate in "peace-building" projects.

What is completely missing from our "old-style" rational method of analysis is the awareness that once the "shackles of fear" are no longer controlling our individual decisions, everything changes; problems drop away spontaneously in the most unexpected ways. Solutions unfold in a miraculous fashion once our blockages to the natural flow of Love are eliminated. As fear subsides, we gradually become compelled, through persistent and clear inner guidance, to fully contribute our own unique gifts. We can't solve problems from the same type of consciousness that created them. We must first change ourselves and, only then, we will be able to see others, and the world, anew.

Everything we are compelled to do in this world has purpose, often at many levels and with much more interconnectedness than any of us imagine. Activism is critical for creating balance in our world. Personal activism and the resulting public awareness of the illuminated issues are important component parts of a process that informs and helps us all learn about our personal responsibility for the world that we inhabit and create. While we can't change others, we can set an example and make *information* available, and this contributes to the awakening of awareness. The "others" will change, but only when the "time" is right and each is completely ready. Through our activism we can remain available and welcome "others" to participate at whatever level works for them. Activism alone won't change the "outside" world, but it can plant the seeds of change, so that when the "time" and social climate are right, these seeds will grow. ***We all need to do what feels right for us in every moment. This works beautifully with our souls and the geometry of the Multiverse.***

SLACKERS

Some will argue that declaring *"everything is perfect, exactly as it is"* is just a lazy excuse to avoid work–a slacker's imagination running wild. This type of argument is also built upon old patterns and completely misses the game-changing significance of a new paradigm shift. The conditioned rational mind is not capable of comprehending the indescribable perfection built into the hidden architecture of the *Multiverse*. Even if this criticism were based on a level of understanding, there still would be no problem with being "lazy" because the unfolding of life is ultimately timeless. Within this eternal creation, nothing is ever gained from rushing; each of us will shift and evolve when, from our experiential perspective, we are fully ready.

KNOWING TRUTH

Jesus said *"You will know the truth, and the truth will set you free."* It is specifically the "knowing" part of this quote that illuminates the real key to our freedom because our "knowing" is the part that we can individually adjust. Our ears can hear clear words of truth, as they always do but, without the right preparation, these words will seem like meaningless babble. ***To understand something at the level of "knowing" requires experiencing this truth at such a deep level that it becomes an integrated part of us, as we, in turn, also become a part of this truth.*** As we come to "know" truth, we become one with it. This level of "knowing" can only be achieved through deep personal experience. We cannot "know" anything until we meet it; explore it; move beyond our deep fear of "knowing" ourselves; and then integrate. To "know" ourselves we must be completely open and available for life to fully express itself through us. We must also be willing to embrace life exactly as it appears, and with this shift our *resonance* completely changes and, therefore, so does our "world."

PATHWAY TO THE GREATER TRUTH

The Vedic scriptures of Hinduism say *"truth is one and the people call it by different names."* From our three-dimensional *viewport*, our perception of truth is always filtered and relative to our realm. There are infinite levels of relative truth, and then there is the capital "T" *Truth* that all these relative truths point towards. From our dimensional space we are simply not designed to be capable of perceiving or understanding the full *Truth,* for it is only describable from within the deepest level of existence. ***Our journey towards Truth is, therefore, gradual and evolutionary. What is true for us today will not necessarily be true for us tomorrow. As our perspective or viewport evolves and changes, so do our relative truths. If we hold on to a relative truth beyond its usefulness, it becomes an anchor that prevents further growth or evolution. Being willing and able to shed old ideas, while remaining open to new levels of truth, is critical to being able to dance freely within the Web.*** *Truth* exists in a space that is free of concepts, time and words. Our perception of *Truth* at any particular moment can only be some partial and temporary relative truth–a mere shadow. As we evolve, it is not *Truth* that is changing; it is, instead, our perspective and awareness that are changing.

That shadow of the greater *Truth* that we experience is only that portion of the original impulse that is eventually *projected* onto our limited *viewport*. Because we are most comfortable with that which is already known, we tend to build our personal truths upon foundational ideas that we already understand. We might hear scientists make statements such as *"there cannot be life on a planet because there is no water or oxygen there,"* or *"the reason we can't see the extra dimensions is because they are folded up so tightly that they are now too small to see."* These types of statements are relative truths that are built upon ideas that we already know and understand; they can not describe the deeper possibilities. Why do we imagine that all possible new forms of life need to resemble our known forms by consuming oxygen? Could there not be other possible forms of "life" that are entirely unexplored? Even when some scientists are discussing the "paradigm shifting" *string theory*, much of their language and many of the ideas fall back upon familiar, but limiting, three-dimensional concepts such as size and geometric shape.

There are, of course, other possibilities for the various forms that life could adopt or occupy– actually an infinity of possibilities. We become so tightly boxed into our *anthropomorphic* mode of thinking that we begin to assume that all other life in the universe must use the same metabolic processes. To flow within the *Multiverse,* we have to be able to recognize, and then let go of, this, our natural, strong tendency to limit our thinking to the familiar.

The best way to think about "truth" in our portion of the *Multiverse* is to think of it as only a signpost pointing us in the general direction of the greater Truth. At most, "truth" is a temporary marker along the particular road that we are traveling right now. Truth can never be final or absolute in our dimensional space. What we experience as "truth" will always be only the shadow or *projection* of some deeper Truth. As we evolve, so will our view of the "truth," as new and better road signs appear.

A "truth," which seems clear within our 3D world, will not hold the same meaning when viewed from the broader perspective of the Multiverse. Physical death, the separation of individuals, and the forward march of time are three very illuminating examples of things that appear

"true" or absolute in our viewport. None of these look the same when viewed from the perspective of the Multiverse.

TRUE TO OURSELVES

There is another practice involving *truth* that is pivotal to our joyful individual evolution. This is the practice of being and acting in a way that is true to ourselves, as well as to all others. When we are being "true to ourselves," every thought, every word and every action is *resonating* with our inner *being*. From this place of integrated self-awareness we live fully and vibrantly because our life is created from a place aligned with the *vibrational integrity* of our soul.

Because of the way that our ego works, understanding and practicing our own personal *truth* can be extremely difficult. Our individual *truths* are all unique, and sometimes they require us to take a stand or position that might not be popular or easy. We all have our own personal needs, wants and desires, and we simultaneously seek to avoid conflict, disagreement and disappointment; because of our deep fear of isolation and the general pressure from our culture, we might not recognize, or even want to recognize, our personal *truth* when it is clearly revealed to us. We might, therefore, avoid speaking or expressing our personal *truth*, even if we clearly know it inside. Sometimes out of our fear we might even mutter what we, instead, recognize as a clear "un-truth."

Not speaking, or misspeaking, our individual *truth* can be the result of deep fear, but it is often only the result of trying to avoid unpleasant interactions. We rationalize our muttered "un-truths" by imagining that they are necessary and are not really harmful. In the moment, we might even fool ourselves into thinking that they are our own personal *truths*. As human beings, we all understand these reactions.

As with any practice in our lives, the more we do something, the better we get at it. When we don't practice living through our individual truth, we gradually lose our skill or ability to even recognize our *truth*. Over time we obscure our natural ability to recognize truth, which inhibits our ability to *resonate* with all types of *truth*, including the *Truth*. We then become insensitive to *truth* at every level. However, on the other hand, when we do practice speaking our own personal *truth*, the opposite happens–our connection to and understanding of all levels of *truth* naturally deepens.

CHANGE

A popular bumper sticker states, *"The only constant is change!"* From our three-dimensional perspective, this is a piece of rock-solid wisdom. Our world appears to be in constant change as the arrow of time marches forward. Those who flow easily with this change fare much better than those who habitually resist it. Our 3D realm is defined by change. Change is our world's only real constant.

However, at its very core, change itself is only a time-based concept. In that place beyond time, nothing really changes–everything simply always "is." Still, *Beingness* is always constant. Infinity is constant. IS is. Change turns out to be only another time-based illusion!

"I" AND EGO

Our personal experience is universally one of a separate and individual "I." Just what this "I" really is has been the subject of endless study and philosophical speculation throughout recorded history. For the purposes of this book, I have defined two distinct subdivisions of this entity that we refer to as the "I." These two aspects can be described as "that part of us which is centered in and dependent upon the 3D realm," and "that part which is rooted outside of this realm and is therefore outside of time."

The most visible surface portion of "I" is fully associated with the *ego*. This part involves everything that emotionally or physically belongs to the body and brain including the outer manifestation of our personalities. According to my previous definition, the *ego* also includes the vast unconscious portions of our body/brain. The other part, the more timeless part of the "I," exists in a way that allows it to be completely independent of the body/brain; or, if it desires, it can work through the body/brain. Much more subtle, and, therefore, difficult to recognize, this second part involves a "presence" that can "watch" the *ego* from a psychological distance. This is the watcher, the part of all of us that is called the *self*.

The *self* is multileveled, containing within its depths unseen and unexplored layers that allow for deeper and wider modes of expression, personal interconnection, and a direct connection to universal Love at the level of Self. Another way to understand the difference between the two different parts is that the *ego* is that part of us which changes over time, and the *self* is that part of us which always remains the same. When we think back to our earliest memories, we will find a part of us that seems familiar and unchanged. This is our *self*, and it will always feel "just like us" no matter how much we expand and grow.

Connected Egos

By far, the largest part of our *ego* is the unconscious part, which we cannot directly or easily access. Its *information* and secrets are, for various personal, biological and cultural reasons, usually buried very deeply. These buried pieces may be specific and personal repressed memories from our lives, or they might be non-personal cultural memories. These express themselves through our body/brains in many unhealthy ways, including anxieties, fears, destructive habits and disease. Some of this unseen "darkness" may be archetypical in its nature, meaning that it is the product of the collective cultural history of humankind on Earth. These dark fears may be inherited through our DNA and physically embedded as part of our genetic code. They might even be specific memories from the lives of those that we think of as "others."

Since we are not separate beings at the deepest levels, *information* from "others" may be exchanged and projected so that it is experienced and felt by us, in our three-dimensional form. We might then interpret these more universal and shared experiences as belonging to our "past lives." All of this can seem completely unknown, mysterious, strange or impossible and, therefore, overwhelming. However, because, at a deep level, we are all one, what we experience involves information that is shared by all of us. (The interconnectedness of romantic lovers is complex and will be discussed later.) We all have these massive unseen and unexplored hiding places in the depths below our personalities that can easily hide memories that are not personal. This hidden interconnection of all things, the good and the not-so-good, comes with this wonderful and amazing gift of human life. There is much more that informs each of us than just the recorded or remembered experiences of our own short lifetimes.

Everything in the *Multiverse* is intimately connected to everything else, including the layers of *information* that constantly inform us. The injury that occurred today is not unrelated to the trauma of our youth, and this trauma has connections to a deeper cultural trauma that we inherit at birth. Every layer in the multiverse is fully interconnected and always exchanging *information* with every other layer, in every direction. There are no isolated events or accidents anywhere in creation.

Competing Egos

The personality expression of our individual egos is directly and powerfully affected by the culturally-reinforced fear that each one of us is a separate individual and we are all competing with each other for survival on this planet. We were introduced to this concept of separate competing individuals starting even before our birth. Our pregnant parents were probably encouraged to nurture the strongest and healthiest fetus; this expenditure of focused *energy* creates a chemical and biological environment that imprints the developing embryo. Our society consistently rewards "winners." We are taught from an early age that, if we are not the one who winds up on "top," our life will be uncertain and insecure. Our little ones are instilled with this idea through the media, preschool, school, in playgrounds and absolutely everywhere that they turn. They build their lives around these concepts of separation and win-lose competition. As they mature, the competition only becomes more intense. Competition in our culture is relentless, and it creates a sense of complete separation as it fuels egoic overdevelopment.

As a kid, I was very competitive in swimming and sailing, and I quickly noticed that as I moved up through the levels of competition, fewer and fewer kids remained. At some point I realized that there would be only one (or very few) "winners;" almost all of us would eventually become "losers" during the competitive elimination process!

When I was about 30, I became very good friends with a small group of Olympic swimmers and divers. These athletes were always amazing to watch; yet, at the Olympics, most of them were, at some level, quickly transformed into losers or failures. Dreams were shattered and, for many, it initially seemed that all the years of hard work were for nothing. With a couple of exceptions they were all destined to fail at their lifelong dream, which was universally to win an Olympic medal. All parents who have watched their kids advance through the various levels of contemporary team sports, such as soccer or basketball, have discovered that team sports aren't that much better than individual sports for healthy ego development.

In our Western culture we are taught that we must work harder than the others so that we can become better or more successful than the rest. We are encouraged to be seen as different, important or special. This striving is an impulse that creates even more separation and it often only further cements us into our 3D material *viewport*. There is nothing inherently problematic about our desire to do things better, faster or more beautifully. Separation only enters when we desire to be special by being better than "others."

How would things be different if we had been raised in a culture without this type of separating competition? What if, instead, we were taught that "competition" was simply another opportunity to play with others, create beauty and be joyful? There would be a dramatic difference in the way our egos developed. As we evolve further and begin to experience our interconnectedness more clearly, our present-day competitive, and separating, individual type of *ego* will disappear. We will evolve to understand that this use of ego no longer serves us.

EGO'S PURPOSE

Ego is constructed from those aspects of each of us that are *identified* with our 3D form, its *fears* and its living habits. When we hold on tightly to ideas that were formed at the level of *ego*, what we are really doing is tying ourselves down in our 3D experiential world and, therefore, limiting our access to the *infinite* amount of *information* that would otherwise be available.

Because our egos are so very tightly associated with our surface "sense of self," it is natural that any movement away from *ego*-control might feel like we are trying to harm, abandon or even "kill" ourselves. This can feel like a death-threat to our *egos*. Our egos, which are convinced that they are really important because they represent who we are, will resist such change automatically, and sometimes very dramatically. Our egos are also like small children who are afraid of being left behind. If they sense they are losing power or control, they will probably create a big fuss. However, even in a state of greatly-expanded awareness, our egos don't ever die or disappear. The ego remains, but shifts its focus so it can function as it was designed to–as a valuable and needed servant to the body.

Once fully integrated and serving in its ideal capacity, the ego will become a valuable and willing servant to the greater whole. ***The first step in this journey toward taming the ego is to realize that our egos are somewhat autonomous and will feel threatened by any change at the surface level of the individual. Our "old style" egos thrive upon their association with the 3D paradigm of "separate selves." Sympathetically understanding this relationship is another important step on the road to personal freedom.***

EGO DEATH

As we do the work necessary to uncover the deeper source of our resistance, we eventually arrive at the point where we discover that our fears, hiding deep in the subconscious within the darkness of the unexamined and buried, provides the raw material for much of our chronic tension and resistance. Once this ubiquitous type of tension is recognized, it can then be cleared through a process of illumination, using the light of honest self-examination and witnessing. Deep within this clearing process we will, sooner or later, arrive at the critical juncture where we realize that the primary remaining source of our body's tension is only the ego's ultimate fear of losing control. To our egos, this letting go of control will feel like suicide. ***What we are really seeking is sometimes called "Ego Death," and this is the final objective of many spiritual practices. The ego will summon all of its strength and tricks to resist its demotion, so this part of the process presents one of the most challenging hurdles on the journey towards freedom.*** Because our egos have been, and want to stay, in control, we all will have an automatic fear associated with exploring the truth about this part of our *beingness*. This fear is buried deep within every one of us at the subconscious level. When this truth is touched upon, it reflexively causes our *egos* to quake with fear because they then recognize their potential to lose power or possibly even die.

The "truth," which is so consistently and deeply feared by our egos, is that we are not actually separate individuals depending on our egos for survival. Instead we are not these bodies, we exist eternally and we are all connected at the source of our *being*. This means that the ego is not special, or even real, because the body is not who we are and the ego is, after al, only another part of our body. What we are really seeking with ego death is not for the ego to die, but rather for it to relax and serve, rather than control. However, to our egos, this request is nothing short of terrifying.

Self is eternal and not dependent upon the body. The ego knows it is not eternal and that it depends entirely on the body. It also knows that the body is not immortal. This is the ego's big fear, which we all then experience as our personal fear of death. Once we really embrace the understanding that we are not these bodies and their associated egos, the confusion stops and our ego loses its gripping power over us. This is "ego death," and it is an absolute requirement for personal freedom. Freedom is never possible while the ego is still in charge.

RELATIONSHIPS

No man is an island, especially in the Multiverse. All types of relationships continuously shape our lives but we are completely unaware of the vast majority of interactions that contribute to our lives. Every point on the Web is in perpetual intimate relationship to every other point, and these relationships, like everything else in the Web, are *vibratory*-based interactions. Our relationships with "other" people and *beings* usually produce the most dominant and important experiences of our physical lives. At the deepest level, these are all really relationships with different aspects of our *Self,* but these appear as "others" in their many different forms. We all have relationships with family, friends, work-mates, romantic loves and those people we meet when our cars crash at strange and unexpected intersections of life.

"Love at first sight" is a special type relationship that involves a sympathetic core *resonance* at a particularly deep, but often unconscious, level. This karmic or biological type of connection can have the ability and power to completely override our logical 3D minds, and it often indicates that a potentially interesting and significant interaction is unfolding. In sexual relationships, especially during reproductive years, these instant connections could simply mean that our *pheromones* are communicating because the automatic response systems in our bodies recognize a particularly good genetic match for reproduction. This type of powerful attraction can also signal a very strong but sometimes difficult or challenging karmic connection. (Karmic relationships are discussed in the next section.) It would be safe to say that most relationships that start with this instant recognition are likely to be very dynamic and interesting, but they are just as likely to be extremely challenging. These are the relationships that ultimately lead us to examine ourselves, and our lives, at deeper levels. "Love at first sight" meetings also have the powerful potential to help guide us into and through dramatic, yet wonderful, personal changes.

Family, and other relationships that we are born into, always involve powerful karmic associations. These can be extremely complex relationships because of the closely intertwined DNA, subculture, environment and history. They are particularly powerful connections because they also tend to be long-lasting, multilayered, interwoven, and they are also extremely difficult or impossible to run from and avoid.

There are also those wonderful relationships that form gradually and deepen over time, while there are still others that we quickly know we should avoid because they seem too difficult, or possibly even dangerous.

The single most important relationship that we must deal with in our lives is our relationship to ourselves. All other relationships depend on the quality of this primary relationship. Once this relationship is explored and healed, we will be fully available for further balanced, healthy relationships. In many ways all interpersonal relationships are really only about our relationship with our self. It is accurate to say that this is the only real relationship, and all the other interactions are only reflections of it.

We are all interconnected in an infinite number of different ways; all of our relationships are multi-dimensional and playing out at many different levels, with most of this interaction being completely invisible. Our interpersonal interactions and connections are a fundamental and critical part of the fully interactive Web. Whatever the relationship type, when two or more people are interact, a new vibrational form is created–a new song that is unique and completely different from the song of either individual travels throughout the *Multiverse*. Relationships are the primary way that we learn about our universe and about ourselves.

KARMA

Karma is an idea that can have different meanings for different individuals, practices and groups. For the purposes of this book, karma is to be understood as the interaction and unfolding of all things, as a direct result of all forms of cause and effect. Karma, as defined here, is completely free of any quality of judgment, punishment or reward. People sometimes speak of good karma or bad karma but, because it is simply a cause and effect interaction, there is no such thing in the natural world as good or bad karma. Karma always unfolds perfectly. Karma is simply what is observed during the physical and energetic balancing that is the natural cause-and-effect of any activity. Karma is a natural unfolding, much like the weather, and watching our karma unfold can be similar to watching the weather radar.

Because everything is always the product of fully interactive cause-and-effect, there are no accidents in the universe. From our three-dimensional perspective, these natural connections will often appear to be random, unexpected and unanticipated but, from the perspective of the Multiverse, there is only the orderly unfolding of all things.

In our *Multiverse,* there are at least seven dimensions that are not directly accessible from our three-dimensional awareness. These are the 11 described dimensions required by *m-theory,* minus the three and one-half known dimensions of *spacetime.* In this invisible yet vast portion, most of these cause-and-effect interconnections occur outside of our dimensional space and, therefore, remain stubbornly invisible to our vision, analysis and understanding. Because they are completely invisible to us and because we lack the conceptual ability to understand or describe them, these "cause and effect" interactions can seem completely arbitrary or mysterious to us. From the greater perspective of the full *Multiverse,* these connected karmic interactions are always directly linked and perfectly obvious. Karma is only the result of the direct and absolute interconnectedness of all things, at all levels, and nothing more.

Karma, seen this way, is never a "scorecard" or a "punishment and reward" system. It is always a direct result of all of our actions, deeds and thoughts; and these are always directly connected to everything and everyone throughout the Web. This means that our actions cannot be faked or hidden. They can, however, be changed in an instant.

If we change our core *vibration*, our location in the Web changes. This instantly changes the form of our personal Karma, which is always played out in the "now" moment. Our past actions and deeds only affect us by helping to form our present core vibration. As that vibration changes, all our interactions within the Web change. Karma is not a work list of mistakes that need to be worked through, fixed, or compensated for, deed by deed. Once our *resonant vibration* changes, our Karma also instantly shifts.

We need to remember always that in the *Multiverse,* events do not really occur sequentially as they appear to in our 3D world. In the *Multiverse,* events unfold simultaneously (or more accurately, outside of time itself) to create this fully interconnected Web that always exists. They also unfold so that every possible outcome or interaction is being expressed somewhere in this Web.

PRAYER

Prayer is practiced in many different forms around our world, but at some level, all prayer is similar. It is always our attempt to connect and communicate with some larger aspect of life that operates beyond the edges of our known paradigm. It represents a recognition that this universe is much larger, more powerful and more mysterious than the physical environment we interact with on a day-to-day basis. It is an attempt to communicate directly with whatever lies outside our visible world.

While prayer is universal throughout our human culture, it means very different things to different groups of people. For many, prayer often involves a specific request for help from a supreme *being*, or higher, organizing principle. This type of prayer often includes asking the "source" or some "higher power" for very specific things.

Many people claim that this type of prayer works–if the structure of the *Multiverse* were fully understood, it would be obvious to everyone that we change nothing about the outside world with our prayer; every possible outcome already exists. We can, however, always change our relationship to the rest of the world, and prayer can help serve this function. Any outward manifestations or changes that do appear are really only the result of our new *vibratory* alignment within the *Multiverse*–our change of *viewport*. Prayer changes nothing about the outside world; prayer only changes us.

For many others, prayer is simply about being thankful or grateful. While some might be only thankful for what appears to be their good fortune, many are, instead, fully honoring and recognizing the entire gift of life. This latter form of prayer is a heartfelt expression of trust, openness and willingness to participate in the grand cosmic dance; it is a willingness that facilitates the opening process through creating a *positive feedback loop* that expands the *viewport* of the person praying.

Over the last 40 years, I have consistently relied upon two personal "prayers"–both have served me very well. The first I call my "instant Karma" prayer. In this prayer I am making a very specific request; I am asking for *"the ability to experience very direct and rapid feedback so that I may more easily see and understand the direct connections to my actions and thinking."* In essence, I am praying for sensitivity and openness along with the ability to understand, or at least quickly and directly experience, the cause-and-effect interactions of my actions.

My second prayer type involves asking for help with allowing this natural flow. It could be described as asking for relaxation around my personal ambitions–to not resist the "now" and be more open to the flow. Put into praying words, it might look something like, *"I don't really know what is best in the big picture but I do know that if I don't get attached to or confused by my personal desires, everything will unfold in the best possible way. What I ask for is the ability to relax and allow."* Expressed as a physical action, this prayer resembles a deep exhalation of breath, a letting go.

I never ask for a particular outcome because I trust that all things are always unfolding in perfect harmony within the *Multiverse*. We can't change this unfolding, but we can change our experience of it, and we can always relax our resistance to this natural flow. Both of these prayer forms have been extremely effective as meditations to reconnect me to the natural *vibratory* flow of my life.

Invariably it is when I have been fighting the natural flow of my "river of life" that I see the greatest need for these prayers. In a very real sense, I am not asking for anything because these prayers only function as a meditation to help me to remember how to move more naturally with "what is."

YOGA

Yoga is the focused attention on body/mind health and balance through various combinations of practices that include stretching, mediating, breathing and physical exercise. Yoga is a direct and wonderful way to connect with and discover the hidden resistances within our bodies. Yoga can be practiced as a simple, but thorough, routine for stretching and flexibility; or it can be used to find access points for initiating a much deeper exploration into our *beingness*. Yoga reveals its *information* according to our level of openness, so the yogic process is always deeply personal and evolutionary.

Learning how to practice yoga with a teacher is the preferred way to become exposed to the basic postures and principles of safe practice, but usually the deepest and most profound yoga experiences occur outside of these formal classes. Classwork is often timed so that the entire group can finish a complete set while exploring and working as much of the body as is reasonable within the limited time. During class work we can learn correct technique and discover those "sticky" places in our bodies that may require further focused attention. However, because of the demands of the class structure, there is rarely the opportunity or time to dwell in and explore these newly discovered resistances. Aspects of our selves that are discovered or uncovered in class are best explored on our own, outside of a structured setting.

At first this personal exploratory process might resemble simple stretching, as we become acquainted with our limits and the kinks in our motion. As our practice deepens, specific physical areas of resistance emerge and may "ask" for more attention. With slow, careful and open availability, over time, the deeper emotional content can be witnessed and recognized. This buried content usually emerges as unexpected, subtle feelings, such as sadness or anxiety; but sometimes it can burst forth accompanied by a flood of very specific and vivid memories. At this point in our yogic process, our ability to remain resistance-free becomes critical to our further progress. (Specific techniques and a process for facilitating this release are discussed earlier in the healing section of this book.)

Our physical and psychological resistance is very natural and fully expected. These are the result of the ego's strong and relentless habit of not wanting change. Learning to break this pattern takes time, focus and awareness. While yoga is an excellent way to develop this awareness, it is important to practice safely. It must be understood that successful yoga is based upon relaxation and not force. If we are impatient and physically force ourselves into postures instead of allowing time for the more natural relaxation, we can, and often will, injure ourselves.

The practice of relaxation can then continue far beyond the yoga mat. For the healing to become fully integrated, the lessons learned from yoga must be applied to our entire lives. That is why yoga is often described as a way of life. Yoga is one of the most useful tools for facilitating our personal inner journey.

WAR

Our entire recorded human history is one of war. War is still central to our cultural paradigm for many reasons, including our economic and political systems being completely intertwined with the "making of war." We have already experienced many "wars to end all wars," and they all have ultimately only produced more resistance and greater conflict.

From all corners of our world this pattern of endless war has generated a very loud, pained and universal human cry, *"There has got to be a better way!"* There is a better way, but to make this change we first must understand the deeper reasons for this form of human struggle. **We imagine that we are at war with "others," but in the deepest truth, we are really only at war with ourselves.** War can be thought of as the deadliest and most direct autoimmune disease.

The world's dominant cultures have all been built around the concept of fight; we fight with each other, we fight other teams, other countries, other corporations and, at least in our movies, other worlds. When we are not at war, we are engaged in an economic battle with each other; this struggle is what defines our nations and corporate states. We are consciously taught and genetically bred to be better fighters: be more aggressive, push harder or longer, be more deceptive, use bigger tools and more destructive weapons.

Robert Ardrey, the playwright turned anthropologist, convincingly argued in his two books, *The Territorial Imperative* and *African Genesis* that our brains and bodies developed their present form because of the evolutionary imperative to be better at war. We evolved stronger bodies to wield more-damaging weapons; but what is more important is that we developed more intelligent brains largely to design more powerful weapons. The genes of the successful victors survived, thrived and multiplied. Through genetic adaption and *pre-adaption*, mankind's genetic makeup has, therefore, been shaped to favor those who are most successful at war.

Politically, war is always portrayed as a classic struggle between good and evil, with the home team always defined as the good or righteous side. Almost all warring factions are deeply convinced that their perspective is the righteous one. **We define ourselves through this process of dualistic struggle, and our participation reinforces the very nature of opposites, which is that they feed off of and therefore completely depend on each other. Neither side can exist for long without the other.** An enemy becomes a necessity for warriors to even exist. The perception of a common enemy is often what determines why, how and when a nation is formed, shaped and defined politically. Historically, political leaders have often "created" and perpetuated and exploited this idea to allow them to expand their armies and increase their power.

As long as we believe that we can benefit by fighting for something, there will be war. There will never be a "war to end all wars" because this idea implies that a real and lasting solution can be reached through conflict. It is conceptually impossible to fight our way to peace. As long as "fight and struggle" is seen as the way to resolution, war will remain. The need to find another avenue to peace applies to the individual psyche as well as nations.

Ultimately, after we look closely and honestly, we will realize that we are fundamentally always at war because we are at war with ourselves. The only path to peace is to move beyond this warring nature. Comprehending the futile nature of this circular trap is the first step to our release from this cyclic pattern. **We cannot and will not end the war without, until we end the war within.**

Eckhart Tolle says, *"Just as you cannot fight the darkness, so you cannot fight the unconsciousness. If you try to do so the polar opposites will become strengthened and more deeply entrenched. You will become identified with one of the polarities, you will create an 'enemy' and so be drawn into unconsciousness yourself. Raise awareness by disseminating information, or at the most, practice passive resistance. But make sure that you carry no resistance within, no hatred, no negativity. 'Love your enemies,' said Jesus which, of course, means have no enemies."*

War teaches us many things about ourselves; we learn about love, hate, trust, greed, anger, fear, terror, the tragic, and the heroic. Driven by our desire for greater weapons we discover amazing new technologies. Through war we learn about our awesome power to both create and destroy.

We can raise our awareness of the nature of opposites and practice a passive non-participation to avoid our engagement in the old habitual struggle. We can expand and grow that part of us that carries no resistance within, that part of us that can fully experience the ever-present flow of Love. ***The only way to end the external war is to clear the internal darkness, embrace our being, and end the war within. The journey towards a more peaceful world begins with learning about and bringing the "light of consciousness" to our own inner shadows.***

SEX

Sex is the single most powerful biological driving *force* on our planet. Humans, and almost every other species, will deplete the last of their critical resources for a chance to procreate. For sex, living creatures will forsake food, water, lodging, friendship and protection. However, while sex is critical for species survival, it also has other important functions, at least for human beings. Sexual interaction offers an extremely multifaceted and complex form of human communication and expression.

At one level, our sex drive is purely an evolutionary mechanism deeply programmed into our biological system to insure that our species continues to procreate and propagate. We often observe that "opposites attract," and there are many good biological reasons for steering our sexual attraction to those who are very different from us. At the level of genotypes, polarity and diversity are desired because they insure a broad and varied gene pool, thus producing strong viable offspring and more opportunities for new genetic combinations that can result in new evolutionary directions. Maintaining a diverse gene pool is an effective, long-term, genetic strategy for species survival. ***Nature loves diversity because it creates new possibilities, and these allow the species to adapt and fill niches of opportunity.***

Chemical pheromones and other subtle biological signals of many types constantly communicate below the level of the conscious mind and "conspire" to create strategically beneficial biological pairings. At this level, instant attraction can indicate little more than a chemical communication carrying *information* such as "I recognize, through our *pheromones*, that my *genes* and your *genes* will make strong children." At this biological level, nature cares very little about our romantic notions.

At another level, the emotional-physical level, for many of us sex provides our only regular surrender and release of our deeply-held tensions. As discussed, surrender is a critically important step for healing, release and ecstasy. The very nature of sex allows a massive "letting go" of our built-up tension, and this release is usually interpreted as pleasure. A release facilitated through sex can be very therapeutic and contribute to our healing, especially if the underlying issues that generate our hidden tension are simultaneously recognized and addressed. For most of us, most of the time, the sexual release only results in a temporary relaxation of chronic tension. As with any "treatment" that only works on the symptoms, a dependency on the treatment itself becomes a possible risk. Our reliance on sexual activity to release our tension can shift to become a problematic addiction or an obsession. The "cure" is always to directly address these emotional and physical "dark" places that harbor chronic tension.

At another level, our desire for sex also serves our subconscious desire to connect with other souls in that timeless place that lies outside of our normal, day-to-day existence. Sex naturally serves *being's* desire to express itself in this union beyond ego and time. Through sex we can have some of our deepest interpersonal connections–it helps take us through our usual 3D constraints, into the deeper levels of our being; it is there that we form new, deep and meaningful connections with our partners. In addition, a formal practice such as *Tantric Yoga* can help us learn how to deepen this connection in a more conscious way.

This third level of sexual relationship is the spiritual or *Tantric* relationship–the conscious form of sexual union. In this form, the sexual *energy* co-generated can be harnessed, redirected, connected, merged, and then used for other purposes such as healing, communion, expanded ecstasy, spiritual growth and exploration, or just plain fun. At this level, there is an intention to increase, and then focus, energy to enhance the merging of souls. Instead of people having their individual sexual experiences, there can be, instead, more merging of experiences. Through this yogic practice, which is energetically fueled by our powerful sex drives, we can participate in this co-merging with "others" and sometimes at those moments of the deepest surrender, we find ourselves able to merge with "everything." Our unconscious desire for this "taste of unity" is a deep, fundamental and powerful component of our sex drive. When we bring that powerful natural force into our conscious awareness, we begin to experience new possibilities of being.

All three forms of sexual expression have important functions throughout the Web, and most sexual relationships blend some combination of these three. In the woven knit of the *Multiverse*, all parts of the cloth are important for the fabric's integrity. While the reproductive, biological and pleasure functions are obvious, enormous amounts of *energy* and *information* are still shared, exchanged, spread and expressed throughout the entire Web–even when a relationship appears to be only based on this basic and primary level of sexual interaction. Any sexual relationship can lead to unexpected and powerful insights that can be spontaneously evoked through the relaxation and deep connection. The *Tantric* aspect is even a part of most sexual connections, even if it is not consciously practiced as such. As our practice and relationships become more conscious, *Tantric* exploration has a potential to open previously invisible doorways that reveal fresh insights about our deeper interconnectedness. The gift of sex leads us to a fuller understanding of our *beingness*.

Enlightenment is the process of opening our darkest places so that the light of consciousness can shine through us more easily. For many reasons, most of us have blocks or "darkness" that are specifically associated with our sexuality. This also means that our sexuality can help us discover direct connections to some of our deepest blockages–those that subconsciously interfere with the free flow of *energy* and *information* through our *being*. We cannot clear these places by hiding from the shame, fear, and guilt that are tied to certain aspects of our sexuality. We can only enlighten these areas by consciously exploring them with fearless integrity.

This is one reason why, for many of us, the path to freedom must also include the exploration of our sexuality. This is also why some groups, therapies and technologies that address our sexuality will list enlightenment as a potential benefit of the practice. When blocks that are connected to our sexuality become illuminated and healed, we become more energetically transparent and, therefore, more enlightened. While these therapies and practices can help us with our enlightenment, it should be understood that it is not the sex act itself that helps to liberate us. It is instead the deeper opening within us, which comes with the letting go and the deep connection.

As with everything else in life, sex has much of its expression at levels we cannot directly experience or easily understand. Our desire for sex is driven by the biological reproductive imperative, a powerful desire for release and pleasure, and a deep-level desire to connect with others at a soul level. With its powerful energetics, sexual expression reverberates at every level within the *Multiverse,* which is why so much of our work in three-dimensional *spacetime* is connected to our sexuality.

PSYCHICS AND ESP

Psychic phenomena are perfectly logical and easily explained within the context of the *Multiverse.* The phenomenon we call ESP, or extra sensory perception, is the real and direct result of the way the *Multiverse* works. As we learn to live more fully with an awareness of the mechanics of the expanded *Multiverse,* those interconnections that span time and space can become more available to us at every moment.

Psychic ability can be understood as having access to deeper levels of Mind, levels that are free from our usual constraints of time and space. Our psychic ability, like any human talent, can always be further developed. Other than not being generally accepted or recognized by our Western culture, this ability is really no different than any other type of skill an individual might naturally possess. Some of us are gifted with perfect pitch, some have a talent for numbers, drawing or running, while still others have a special ability to perceive things that lie beyond our normal sensory or conceptual horizons. In most cases psychic ability only means that a brain is functioning a little differently; diversity is genetically built into our species, we are all slightly different from one another. This ability might only mean that one specific part of the brain is developed slightly more, or maybe less, or a signal pathway might take a slightly different route, passing much closer to a sensitive area of the brain.

Psychic ability is nothing more than having the improved ability to access or process a field of *information* that is stored beyond our three-dimensional space. It may involve the increased ability to connect to the greater *Mind,* where our individual *minds* merge into a greater whole, and time does not unfold in its customary linear way. Those with this enhanced perception resonate in a way that enables them to better "tune in" to this available *information.* The analogy of finding a clear station on an old style dial of an analog radio is a very good model for understanding this "tuning in." Any of us can improve our access to more of this *information* by developing a more open mindset and working to clear our blockages. Often the biggest challenge, within our realm, is just understanding what the raw *information* that we have always been receiving really means.

Many with this talent are not aware of exactly what they are doing or how they achieve their unusual understandings. Being human in every way, psychics can easily confuse their broader insights with their own personal desires and goals. Also, while there are many psychics who use their talents to help those in need, there are others that primarily seek personal enrichment or power over "others"; some of these develop "parlor tricks" to impress or fool people for personal gain or their own *ego* reinforcement. Being born with a natural psychic talent has little to do with our degree of openness, but further development of the natural psychic abilities that we all possess depends entirely upon becoming more open and available.

Psychics often receive only very quick and obscured glimpses through the veil that separates and contains our realm. The information is not likely to be clear, direct, literal or easily understood. One of the most talented, interesting and conscious psychics living today is Michael Tamura. Michael sees the "future" by seeing geometric shapes, patterns and forms that, over time and through experience, he has learned to interpret as actual physical events. Most of us are much more likely to just experience our quick glimpses as an unusual and poorly defined feelings or sensations. Learning to accurately read and trust these feelings takes time, focus, and trust; as we work to clear our personal shadows, *information* from the deeper levels of *being* becomes much clearer, less ambiguous and easier to apply within our daily lives.

GOALS

We are constantly encouraged to create and achieve the specific and current goals that our culture has defined as important. We are taught to excel, to become a "somebody" or something, to own a big house and, of course, to become wealthy. Our Western culture is built upon these individualized goals and it thrives on our combined focused drive to reach them. We are relentlessly setting goals, desiring things and then struggling within this self-manufactured and artificial mindset in our attempts to make these perceived needs manifest. When we succeed, we discover that any joy or happiness we feel is only short-lived, often waning soon after the initial burst of excitement. We then find ourselves, after all our work and sacrifice, no happier than before. Ambitions created this way are rarely fully realized. This can directly lead to a feeling of a constant "unhappiness," which is triggered by thoughts related to not obtaining the things we wanted, not being good enough, or being a failure. In athletic competitions we separate and define "winners" and "losers." This, of course, means we will always be a society filled with "losers" because our culture assigns little value to simply enjoying the game.

Goals are not bad things, particularly if they align with our joyful interests. Basketball superstar Michael Jordan's beautiful, graceful and superhuman movements on the court, which have created so many spiritually-transcendent moments for his fans, would not have been possible if he had not had the personal goal of always trying to become a better basketball player. His hard work towards his personal goal served all of us by our witnessing the sheer grace and beauty of his well-polished skills, and his demonstration of human abilities that we once thought were impossible.

Goals by themselves are never problematic. What creates the difficulty and stress around them is the sacrifice of our joy in the present moment for a specific future outcome, and our *attachment* to that specific outcome. Typically, these go hand-in-hand and they demonstrate two of the most common ways that we block "living in the present moment." We create personal expectations and, if these are not met, this leads to depression and disappointment. If we saw all goals simply as guides or possible places to visit on the winding road of life, as opposed to absolute final destinations, we would accomplish far more along the way. We would discover more than we could ever imagine while we visited the many unexpected, yet wonderful, new and exciting worlds revealed during our expanded journey. Freed from our attachments, we might find ourselves diverted to an unexpected learning experience that further fuels our excitement about life. Then, even if our original destination or goal is unrealized, the journey will still have served us well.

Goals work with our human nature to help us focus our minds and to keep us in motion. They can help us to maximize our potential, whether or not the goals are realized, because it is always the journey that really matters, not the destination. ***As always, our ideas or goals by themselves are never the problem. It is our attitude, or attachment to outcomes, that either frees or imprisons us.***

FURTHER MULTIVERSAL MUSINGS

NO NEED TO RUSH–"TIME" NOT TICKING

Once we understand and incorporate our new perspective about the real nature of "time," we begin to realize that we no longer need to rush through our lives the same way. Many things start to shift and change automatically once we know that the passage of time isn't an absolute and realize that our perception of it is only a mental construct. However, the greatest benefit is realized once we finally integrate this new information and directly apply it to our lives in a meaningful way; over time we begin to develop a feel for, and trust of, this different perspective. We realize that we can finally relax, knowing that all things unfold in their own "time." While it is always necessary to remain fully engaged in life, we now see that we no longer have to "make things happen" to live a great life; instead, we observe that extraordinary things happen, on their own, in their own perfect timing. ***Changing our relationship to "time" turns out to be, especially for those of us from the West, one of the simplest yet most dramatic shifts we can make in our lives!***

Years ago I had the opportunity to meet Olga Kharitidi, the Russian psychiatrist who has become well known for her alternative perspectives about living and healing, which she developed as a result of her life-long study of human suffering. Trained as a traditional psychiatrist in the Soviet medical system, she began to see the world very differently after a Siberian Shaman cured her friend of a debilitating disease using very dramatic and non-medical techniques. (I told that part of her story earlier in the faith healing section of this book.)

On the day that I met her, in her lecture she spoke about our perception of "time." After the lecture I asked her a related question that had been on my mind for most of my adult life. *"Time seems to be going faster and faster for me. I seem to never have enough time these days. What can I do to change this?"* Her response caught me completely off-guard. She paused, smiled and then said *"change your attitude about time, be grateful for the time you have and do not focus on that which you don't have. Once you do that you will find that you then have more time."* She was telling me that our sense of time is completely connected to and determined by our attitude and personal relationship to "time." I tried her method and it worked beautifully. I adopted a gratefulness for whatever "time" that I had been given, and with this change in attitude around "time," I actually altered my internal rate of the "ticking of time." Now whenever I feel pressed for "time," I slow down, take a deep breath and drop into a state of thankfulness for everything and especially for having the "time" to have the very experience that I am having at that moment. The rushed feeling then evaporates; I get much more work done; and I also feel far less stress.

In timeless space, there is no such thing as *velocity*, because this is only measured as a function of "time." If there is no such thing as *velocity* then the speed of travel between places becomes irrelevant. "Time" and speed are only concepts created by our minds. If we change our "thinking" we can change our rate of travel. We are really only a "thought" away from the farthest stars. All places in the *Multiverse* are positioned so they can be instantly accessed. ***There is nothing absolute about the rate at which "time" passes. "Time" is a mental construct and, therefore, it is completely malleable.***

FUTURE AND PAST HAPPEN AT ONCE

One of the most fantastic qualities of the "Web of Infinite Possibilities" is how past, present and future are all completely connected in a continuum that is always sharing information back and forth. There really is no such thing as a past that is frozen in static memory or a future that is about to happen. In the words of Einstein, *"The distinction between past, present, and future is only a stubbornly persistent illusion."*

Because our conceptual minds require ordered time, it is nearly impossible for us to imagine living without the "arrow of time." We need to remember it was also impossible for people 500 years ago to imagine that the Earth was round and revolved around the Sun. The amount of cultural shift that will be required to integrate our new knowledge about time is enormous, but we have already made shifts of similar magnitude before. This shift will be on the scale of the one that was needed hundreds of years ago when we, as a culture, were expanding from the "flat-earth" mentality into our new awareness of a full solar system. We are clearly capable of making this type of leap! While the scale of the conceptual change needed today is similar to what we accomplished before, the meaning to our culture and degree of change to our lives might be much more profound.

We now understand is that what we have been calling the past and future are simultaneously existing parts of a dynamic interactive process that is only happening in the "now." The multi-dimensional space called the *Multiverse* contains and holds this entire "dream," which is called the "Web of Possibilities." In the dimensional fabric that forms "all that is," time is not the one-directional linear process that we typically experience in our lives. Past and future exist together and are directly and profoundly connected to the present in direct ways that we have yet to even imagine.

When events occur in the present moment, they send out "waves of information" in all directions; these ripple through multi-dimensional spacetime. These waves equally interact with, or "inform," what we experience as our future and our past. I am repeating myself but this point deserves repetition. *Events in the present clearly have an impact on the future, and this seems logical, normal and obvious to all of us. These same events equally have an impact on the past; this is the part that is difficult or impossible for us to grasp.*

What is most rigid about the past is often our own memory of it. Our memories lock us into a specific and rigidly set viewport. If we can let go of our attachment to the memory, the viewport becomes expanded and the past will then have more freedom to change. We can change the past with our present actions; understanding this principle changes everything. The ability to modify the entire history of humankind, through present actions, is already built directly into the architecture of the Multiverse!

This shift involves so much more than just changing our individual memory of the history. As our *viewport* expands, historical events will then appear to have unfolded differently. This means that "other histories" will suddenly become possible. Actually, many different self-consistent histories can become possible, including those histories that contain beautiful "memories." Letting go of the anchors created by our *attachment* to our collective history opens a profound path to a greater healing of our planet. In this way a complete and thorough healing of the past can unfold from our *present moment*!.

EXPANDING OUR "SONG" INTO THE NOW

At the geometric level, the depth and fullness of our *resonance* is determined by our degree of access to *nodal points* in the Web–*nodal points* and *wave theory* were discussed in the physics section. When we are living in the "now," a greater number of *nodal* and *anti-nodal* points participate, or *vibrate*, in a more harmonious way. This means that we are interacting with a larger part of the Web. If we lose our connection to the "now moment," the effect is to *dampen* or weaken our individual expression of "song." In the architecture of the Web of Possibilities, the "now moment" can be visualized as the *undamped vibration*, caused by the *sympathetic resonance* between the many connections (*nodal points along* the strings or membranes) that define a particular region of the *vibrating* Web. When we are open and closer to the "present moment," there are more *nodes* involved, the amplitude is higher, the sound is richer, the chords are fuller and the overall quality of our instrument improves. There is less *damping* so our song grows louder, clearer, and much more expressive.

Our *resonant* "song" can be easily recognized, because it is always the one that will "dance us" almost effortlessly. All of our individual "songs" then harmonize together to create the symphony of the universe. When we play our "instrument" at this maestro level, we are beautifully serving our purpose and our fullest potential! When we play this way, anything and everything becomes possible. It is also great fun.

GEOMETRY AND SPIRIT

As we better understand this geometry and structure of creation, phenomena that in the past have been seen as completely mysterious, suddenly make sense. I believe that the 11-dimensional vision described in Edward Witten's *M-theory* is the most interesting of today's *string theories*. While not testable, it offers an intriguing image for exploring fundamental *elementary* form and its connection to creation and *vibration.* For physicists, it also describes a space that holds promise for *unifying relativity* and *quantum mechanics. M-theory* is a significant step along our journey towards a fuller understanding of creation and, at least until the time of the next incremental new theory, it begs to be explored fully. The primary issue with the integration of *string theory,* and any others that are derived from them is that these theories all require 10 or 11 dimensions. *String theories* are all built upon extra-dimensional space, but we can only think about and describe these theories using ideas and terms from our three-dimensional conceptual space; our limited conceptual extents will never be able to communicate an accurate representation of what is really going on. The extra dimensions make these theories untestable, unprovable and unable to be explained within our realm. Science requires proof and therefore, for now, *string theory* must be thought of as being more philosophical than scientific, even though it may be our most accurate description of creation.

We can describe the physical structure, motion and dimensional changes of our physical universe using the language of mathematics, but there is still that "something else," absolutely critical to life itself, which mathematics has not been able to describe. All of us have directly experienced this "something else," which is that aspect within that animates or "turns on" all that we call life. In our culture, this quality is most commonly called life-force, or spirit. While being hard to describe, and currently impossible to measure, life-force is universally recognized across all cultures and religions. When we observe the transition (death) of another *being,* we know the exact moment that "spirit" no longer animates their body–this experience is palpable and universal. We all can clearly sense the exact moment spirit enters or leaves another's body.

It is fully possible that this spirit is only another artifact from dimensional *projection*. Seeming real to us, it may be just another shadow phenomenon formed by our experience of creation from a three-dimensional perspective. Some physicists and other scientists, including Steven Hawking, publicly declare that spirit is only a byproduct of the real geometry and physics. They believe that, when we understand the physics better, "spirit" will be revealed to be just another part of what is describable.

It is equally possible that spirit or life-force is something that is infused from outside of the physical structure and that this spirit uses the structure as a convenient vehicle for its self-expression. In this arrangement, spirit then only occupies or uses the *Multiverse*. Someone sensing this relationship might name this spirit God and imagine that this God is responsible for creating and evolving the *Multiverse* itself.

The truth is that, as of today, none of us really know; and, while spirit clearly exists, the nature of spirit remains the great mystery.

WE LIVE AS WATER-STRIDERS

Unknowingly, we have been trying to live a three-dimensional existence within a universe that is constructed of many more dimensions. A popular contemporary expression attempting to explain this predicament says, *"We are spiritual beings living in a physical body!"* In a deeper and more profound version of this truth, we are living in many "bodies" simultaneously. These bodies inhabit many worlds, but from our *viewport*, we are able to see and consciously experience only the small shadows of this extraordinary and infinite interconnectedness. Because of our sensory limitations, we automatically get caught in a mindset in which we start to believe that these limits are absolute and real.

We are like small, water-strider insects, walking on the surface of a pond, wondering about the sky that they are seeing in the reflection upon the water. They have no idea that an entirely different underwater world exists below the very surface that they gaze and walk upon. They only see the reflection of the greater world above, and they don't understand how to interpret what they are glimpsing.

Our experience of our environment is not very different from the water strider's experience on the water's surface. We are limited by our three-dimensional mindset that is entirely built upon linear time. To access more of creation, we need first to enlarge and expand our perspective, or *viewport*, in all directions, even those directions that are not yet a part of our awareness. This is the landscape of our journey as we, all together, continue our evolution from *mind* to *Mind* and *self* to *Self*.

NESTED STRUCTURE OF "HOLOGRAPHIC UNIVERSE"

Within our known 3D universe, which extends from deep within the very small quarks to far beyond the most enormous *galaxies*, a repetitive and consistent physical pattern seems to be the rule. Bigger "things" are constructed from mostly empty space with sparsely spaced smaller physical "things" that are all held together by various forms of *energy*. When these smaller "things" are more closely examined, they, in turn, reveal that they are also made up of even smaller "things" that are distantly spaced and held together by *energy*. Each smaller piece is roughly modeled after the larger piece, and *vice versa*.

Quarks, atoms, molecules, solar systems, galaxies and the *universe* are our current names for these structured physical systems. This nested pattern likely extends even further, possibly forever, in both directions, towards the larger and the smaller.

For as long as we have been curious, there has been a desire to understand the fundamental materials of creation. Not too long ago we thought that fire, water, air and earth were the basic building blocks of everything. Then the *elementary compounds* (carbon-dioxide, water, etc.) were discovered and these were immediately declared, as their naming implies, to be *elementary*. Next we discovered the *atom* and it, in turn, was deemed *elemental*. Science still uses the term *element* to describe the different types of atoms such as Carbon, Hydrogen and Oxygen, even though we now recognize the existence of much smaller *elemental* building blocks.

In our exploration of the atom, the *nucleus* was found and declared *elementary.* Then the *nucleus* also became subdivided into its own smaller *elementary* particles such as quarks. We presently are exploring *string theory,* which suggests yet another even smaller and more fundamental vibrating "thing." This progressive deconstruction continues today, as we explore the newer ideas of *super-strings* and *M-branes*.

In the opposite direction, towards larger things, we note that our solar system is made up of relatively small planets circling the Sun in an enormous sea of empty space. This, in turn, is only one small piece of our rotating galaxy, which is one hundred thousand *light-years* wide and contains three or four hundred billions stars, many of which are similar to our own Sun. The "known" universe is over 80 billion *light-years* wide and contains at least 100 billion other *galaxies*. Our Milky Way galaxy and all other *galaxies* are also constructed of mostly empty space, with an extremely sparse scattering of solid "things."

We are continuously searching for new tools and methods that will allow us to see even farther out or deeper within. Each new system level that we find and explore turns out to be constructed in a similar way to the known systems. Throughout these explorations the pattern is reinforced–the big contains the small, which contains the smaller, and all of it is really just mostly empty space organized with energy. We do not know if there are large and small limits to this pattern; it is entirely possible that as our technology evolves, our paradigms shift, and we begin to dream new possibilities, we will discover that this pattern does continue forever in both directions.

The primary factors that limit these explorations within and without are the dimensional veil, our current conceptual imagination, and the accuracy of our measuring tools. As we develop new tools to explore these systems further, we will likely "find" whatever we are looking for because when we *observe* these new systems, we are, in one sense, actually "creating" them in that very same moment. What was there "before" we, the observers, looked within? What meaning does even this concept "before" have in the *Multiverse*? Because we always create from what we already know, are we not then creating the new only from the old–our own image? This might mean that all our new "creations" will tend to resemble what is already known. Do all these layers just look the same because we can't seem to break free of this pattern?

Such repeating patterns recall David Bohm's groundbreaking *holographic paradigm,* in which each successive smaller part contains all the necessary and same *information* as the larger one. *Information* is nested so each and every piece contains all the *information* necessary to recreate the whole. More recently and specifically, the idea has been expanded to the *holographic principle* that states that all the *information* contained within a volume of dimensional space can be contained on the surface boundary of the region. It is speculated that *black holes* might be extremely dense storage systems for all the *information* about the universe. A history of everything in creation might be fully mapped on the surface of *black holes*. Is it also possible that *black holes* have a much more interesting purpose than even this?

Today we are all familiar with the visual and visceral power of a well-constructed *holographic projection*, having probably witnessed a dramatic example at a museum or art show. The current ultimate in 3D imagery, *holographic images* are so dimensionally lifelike that we can even physically walk around them and observe them from many different angles. Until we try to touch them, well-constructed holographic images may seem quite real.

These images are generated and stored by splitting *coherent* light beams that are formed from a single frequency of tightly-focused light. This special type of light is called *Laser,* the abbreviation for Light Amplification by Stimulated Emission of Radiation. One half of the split beam, the *object beam,* is then projected at the object being reproduced. It is then scattered, by reflection off the object, towards a special photographic plate that is similar to a film negative. The other part of the split beam, the *reference beam,* is projected directly onto the photographic plate. Once the two halves of the single beam are rejoined, the differences in these two parts of the original beam are then expressed as an *interference pattern,* which is then permanently recorded onto the photographic plate. To our eyes, this recorded pattern or "negative" on the plate looks random or even abstract, but when the same frequency of *Laser* light is projected through the plate, a duplicate image of the original three-dimensional object appears.

An extremely interesting property of this type of *holographic* image *projection* is that if we take that glass plate negative, break it into smaller pieces, and then project the laser through a single broken fragment, we don't see a part of the image as we would with a standard photographic negative. Instead we see the entire image, except it might be less sharp-edged, less bright, or less dimensional, meaning that it might be less detailed from particular angles. This is because there is a smaller sample of *information* in the smaller shattered piece, but each broken piece will still hold *information* about the whole. Information about the larger original object is contained in every small piece of the broken, *holographic* plate.

Today we understand that the *holographic principle*, this pattern of storing *information* about the whole in every small piece, appears over and over throughout nature. Because this is a system that is built from a layered and nested distribution of *information*, as we add more levels, we are increasing *information*, so the detail then becomes sharper, crisper and more dimensional. This incremental buildup of information is similar to having more pixels in a photo or using High Definition TV. The image is the same, it just becomes more detailed and much more vivid.

As scientists learn more about *holographic storage,* they are also uncovering another interesting pattern involving cross-dimensional transfer of *information*. For example, we know that the actual holographic recording plate is only two-dimensional, but it is still able to project an image that has some of the qualities of a three-dimensional image. A well-constructed *holographic* image appears to partially occupy three-dimensional visual space, even though all of its *information* is stored on the two-dimensional plate.

Because of the nature of this transfer of *information* from two to three dimensions, I find myself wondering about other possibilities for *holographic* dimensional transfer. What form would the image become if it were projected from a three-dimensional plate? All of us have been raised on slide shows and movies, so we all understand old-fashioned, flat, photographic, 2D *projections*. We can easily see how 3D *holographic projections* are different. The 3D *holographic* image is not fully three-dimensional because it has no *mass* and, with our current technology, there is nothing to touch or feel. If we were to extrapolate and imagine 4D *holographic projections*, what would these be like? What if we expanded our experiment to 5D, or even 11D? Could it be that our world, exactly as we experience it right now, is simply a solid-feeling projection that has been created by multiple layers of *holographic* imaging? As dimensional layers build, and the amount of information increases, do the images then begin to take on a more solid feel?

As mentioned earlier, cosmologists have been proposing that the entirety of what we consider to be the physical universe might be stored holographically on a particular type of "flat" surface that acts like a holographic plate. This "flat" surface is the side wall of a *black hole*. If this turns out to be true, then we may have the ultimate example of a solid-feeling 3D image, our universe, being generated from the *information* stored on a flat, 2D surface. It is possible that, with the addition of extra dimensions and many nested levels, these holographic images would become more solid and massive. The solidity of our world might only be the result of more *information* from the deeper dimensional nesting of holographic images. If this is the structure, our world, while appearing solid, might still only be a holographic image. Could this be the actual mechanism of the *illusion* or *Maya*, from the ancient Hindu texts?

Some neuroscientists now believe that *information* is stored *holographically* within our individual and collective brains. This theory, first proposed by Karl H. Pribram, the Stanford neurosurgeon and researcher, is based on multiple scanned images of the brain as it goes through its various functions. What has been discovered is that a particular thought is not stored in just one place in our brain. Instead, our thoughts are distributed in multiple partial copies throughout the brain in a matrix-like pattern. He first made the connection between his findings and the *holographic theory* after reading of physicist David Bohm's work. Bohm wondered if the entire *Multiverse* might be constructed in this way, with copies of *information* about everything repeating in a *holographic* pattern–level-by-level and piece-by-piece.

What might it mean for the universe to be both *holographic* and multi-dimensional? We recall that flat, 2D *holographic* plates store all the *information* necessary to create 3D *holographic* images. We might then extrapolate that each lower dimension holds and stores all the *information* for the next "higher" dimension. This means that all the *information* stored in any "lower" dimension is again, in turn, contained and stored in the next "lower" dimension.

This means that even one-dimensional space contains all of the information to describe higher dimensional space. We are not missing *information* in any *viewport,* including our 3D *viewport.* Instead, *information* is just dimensionally "flattened" and, in a sense, filtered so it is difficult to visualize and understand from within. The original meaning or form is still described; it just becomes obscured. What we experience is only a small slice or a section of the full *Multiverse,* but it still contains all the *information* necessary to describe the entire *Multiverse.* ***This means that everything within creation is here and available to us right now! Within us is contained everything that is, ever was, and ever will be! We are on a journey that is about opening, evolving and learning how to access and use this information. Life is ultimately a journey of self-discovery!***

DUALISM BEYOND THREE DIMENSIONS

Dualism is the foundational requisite for our three-dimensional existence. The very fabric of our three-dimensional universe structurally depends on the continuation of *duality* because ours is a *dualistic* universe. *Dualism* is the direct result of the original "split" that resulted in the creation of all the "things" belonging to our three-dimensional universe. That which was split was originally "no thing." It contained no *energy* and, in the process of splitting, both *energy* and *matter* were separated and named. (I discuss one version of this "creation story" a little later in this chapter.) Without *duality,* the physical universe, that we experience, could not exist.

The Moon and Earth are held together by a dynamic form of interaction, a balanced tension that works to allow these two bodies to relate to each other in a predictable, cyclic, continuous and functionally interactive way. *Gravity* or *mass attraction* acts as the inward *force.* We think that we understand the idea of *force* intuitively but, technically, *gravity* is not really a *force.* It is, instead, the result of a deformation of *spacetime,* the physics of which was discussed earlier. *Gravity,* which resists and balances the *centrifugal* or outward *force,* is also not really a *force*, but instead it is the result of momentum or *inertia* of orbiting objects. Without *centrifugal force* objects crash into each other, and without *mass attraction* or *gravity* they fly apart. With both of these two *forces* acting in unison, the Moon and the Earth move together. They are completely interconnected and in a constant state of *dynamic balance,* which we call an *orbit.*

In much the same way as the Moon and Earth relate and exist as a balanced system, the full expression of *duality* is possible because of a constant and *dynamic balance.* A specific type of balanced tension forms the structural backbone of this, our physical part of the *Multiverse.* This *dynamic balance* is created from the tension between the desire for *unity*–or even from beyond *unity* towards nothingness–and the desire for *separation.* The constant inward "pull" is always in the direction of *unity,* and the "stretch" is towards *separation.* These two can be thought of as being similar to *forces* that balance each other to manifest our dimensional space, including our planet and our entire universe. This dynamic relationship can also be thought of as the balanced and critical push-pull interaction between *duality* and *non-duality.* The push-pull pulsations of this dynamic and always-shifting balancing act may one day be recognized as a basic, periodic, vibrational pulse forming the most fundamental heartbeat of our *Multiverse.* ***On one end, there is the perpetual "desire" of Being to collapse back into "oneness," and at the other end is the equal and opposite drive to proliferate, fill every possibility and niche, and maximize separation. The tension, derived from this dual nature of all things, forms the backbone of the structure for our universe–our physical realm within the "Web of All Possibilities."***

At a deeper level than even this, the entire *Multiverse* itself may owe its very "form" to a more profound type of balanced interaction that was alluded to earlier. This dynamic interplay is even more fundamental than the polar tug between *unity* and *separation.* This is the dynamic interplay between "no thing" and "everything." This relationship may even be the source of creation itself. In this, the most primary interaction, *unity* is found midway between these extremes. Instead of representing a polar extreme as it appears in our physical *universe,* unity, or "oneness," might be the central balancing point for all of creation.

This dynamic movement unfolds at a level of creation where "form," as we understand it, does not exist. Because we have no alternatives, we must still resort to conceptual language while attempting to describe something that is unfolding far outside this conceptual space. Any words or ideas used to describe the "form" of this deeper structure will not be precise or even accurate. "Form" itself is a *dualistic* concept, as are ideas such as balance, stretch, polarity and backbone. To our conceptual minds, *unity* implies oneness and, as such, is still a "something" –a thing that has a definite form. None of these "word ideas" will have the same, or even any meaning within these deeper dimensional levels. We are all incapable of imagining "unity" without first evoking the concept of the "number one" in our minds. *Unity consciousness* is not about *oneness.* It is instead an experience beyond even *oneness.* It describes an interconnectedness at levels deeper than anything we can describe, or even understand. ***While unity consciousness can't be described, it can be partially felt and, therefore, we are capable of having, through our feelings, a slight taste of this non-describable space that exists beyond oneness.***

E=MC²–UNDERSTANDING ENERGY

Since Einstein's first relativity theory, scientists have come to understand the direct relationship between *mass* and *energy*. E=MC² or (E) energy equals (M) mass times the (C²⁾ speed of light squared. *Mass* and *energy* are two interchangeable forms of the same "thing," which, under the right conditions, are convertible to each other in relative quantities as described by this formula. Through our creation of devices and products that are derived from this principle, the rest of us have also become very familiar with this law of physics and this important interrelationship. The atom bomb is the most dramatic demonstration of Einstein's famous formula.

Everything that we talk about, observe or experience in our lives can be reduced to a discussion about the movement of *energy* in one form or another. Every process in our physical universe can today be better understood through the movement of *energy*. *Matter* can be thought of as "frozen" *energy,* meaning that every physical thing is really only stored energy and is, therefore, directly convertible to large quantities of *energy*. *Energy* powers all life as everything vibrates, pulses, shifts and changes. We tend to think of large things like mountains, skyscrapers and trees as very fixed solid objects, but after a deeper level of examination, we discover that these massive objects are also only temporary holding places for *energy.* These objects that appear so massive and solid are once again, found to be mostly constructed of empty space that is filled with *vibration* and motion*.*

All things of our world appear solid only because of the limits of our senses, tools and the instruments that we currently have available. If we were suddenly physically much smaller, say less than one-billionth of our current size, we would then be able to see the vastness of the empty space between the elemental particles that make up *matter*. This is similar to the way that we, now, in our everyday larger size, experience the empty space of our solar system and galaxy. On the other hand, if we were that much larger than we are today, then the normal-sized things of our world would disappear because they would become too small to relate to or directly see. Our size and scale are critical to and perfect for our current experience.

However, even at our exact size and scale, we can, on occasion, feel and understand the living or *vibratory* nonmaterial aspects of all the things around us. To have this type of intimate experience in a continuous and substantial way, a sensory and perceptual shift is necessary. As we become more open to new possibilities, these types of shifts are more likely, and they increase in frequency and depth. With further opening or deepening we begin to experience the *vibrational frequencies* of "solid" *matter* a little differently. ***All matter that once appeared inert becomes a vibrating, pulsating and throbbing life-form. From this more sensitive place, we can then easily understand that objects, which we once considered to be solid and non-living, are also very much alive and not so very different from ourselves. This is the place of being where we begin to see into the connections and the living essence of all the things that make up our lives. It is the deep and intimate interaction with deep-level vibration and energy, which are the mother and father to all things, including us. This is the place that sometimes has been called unity consciousness.*** As we allow the bounds of our *viewport* to expand, stretch, shift and become less defined, we find ourselves spending more spontaneous time experiencing a living presence in everything that we touch in our lives. In this new, expanded state we begin to experience everything in life more fully. This experience must start with our allowing for this possibility by first allowing for any possibility.

MODELING DUALITY

One current theory involving the creation of the universe says that it was created from nothing or emptiness, with negative and positive *energy* being formed from the division of this nothingness. *Matter* was then only created later from within the clumped regions of *energy*. **This would mean that the entire universe was formed by the organization of energy. Creation itself is all, and only, about energy.**

We imagine that the world we experience must have come from somewhere, that it has a beginning or creation. Variations of the *Big Bang theory* all try to explain this creation by imagining that the universe burst forth from an infinitesimally small piece of a very dense "something." To my sensibilities, this version of the *Big Bang theory* feels very unnatural–it is a myth constructed to help explain our confusing observations about the cosmos. The *Big Bang theory* attempts to use our conceptual language to explain something that really unfolds outside of time, making any description of it impossible. Another reason that the *Big Bang theory* doesn't ring true for me is because, within "time," I have observed that nature always seems to operate through cyclic processes so, if there were a *big bang* at some "time," then, there also had to be something "before" the *big bang* to set up the conditions for this critically-important event.

The *Big Bang theory* describes a fantastic event that begins with a uniquely concentrated *mass*. This theory can't explain the source of that original, small, but unbelievably dense, "seed" *mass* that expanded to become our entire universe. Just where did that "something" come from? A more satisfying theory might instead explain how all the "something" that we experience in our world of duality could have been naturally formed from nothing or "no-thing."

There have been newer, proposed modifications to the *Big Bang theory* that feature the *big bang* as only a single critical step in a much larger, continuous and repeating cyclic process. This modification seems to work better than the original one-time, one-directional event, because it better mimics the cyclic nature of natural processes. However, we always need to remember that this fundamental process is unfolding in a realm that is outside of "time" so, once again, we are trying to "understand" a cyclic or periodic process that is not built upon linear "time." Such an idea cannot be "understood" in the conventional way by any of us, because our human brains are not designed to process things or events outside of "time." From our conceptual *viewport*, everything that exists today was created at some time in the "past." If there were such a beginning, it seems to make the most consistent sense within our system logic to assume that "before" this creation there must have been no-thing, not even empty space. ***Because we already understand how our logic is not applicable at these levels, this description is best thought of as being only a "story" created for the time-ordered way that our minds work.***

As a visual and conceptual aid to help us better see how our universe of duality could be birthed from nothingness, visualize a process that is cyclic–for example, a pendulum alternating back and forth. Let us imagine a big wad of special taffy. This taffy is made from two very different flavors called "purple" and "yellow." This taffy is special because even when the two flavors are all mixed together the two flavors still remain separate. This can be envisioned much like the *enfolded* oil and water in stirred salad dressing. When fully mixed the purple and yellow varieties of taffy still stay separate but inter-mix to form a neutral gray. Another quality of this special taffy is its elasticity. Like a rubber band, the more it is stretched the more it wants to spring back.

Now imagine that one color of taffy represents the material and *energy* of our physical world. The other color represents the *inverse* of everything that we know. Together, these two sets will completely negate each other so that their sum-total collectively is always zero, or nothing. This "opposite" set of all things known, which we call the *inverse*, can't be described with our concepts and is impossible for us know or understand. It is not made of the same type of "stuff" as our world.

Like oil in water, our yellow taffy naturally "wants" to gather with more yellow taffy, and the purple taffy naturally wants to group with more purple. If we grab some purple in one hand and some yellow in the other and pull, the colors of this unique taffy will start to stretch and separate, creating a stretched, stringy fabric with yellow concentrated in one hand, purple in the other, and a gray blend in the middle. Eventually, because of the elastic nature of this taffy, the two colors are unable to be pulled farther apart. They then stop stretching and start collapsing back together like a bungee cord that has been stretched to its limit. At some point during this collapse, the two parts again become a single homogenous blob of grey and the process starts over, alternating between these two extremes.

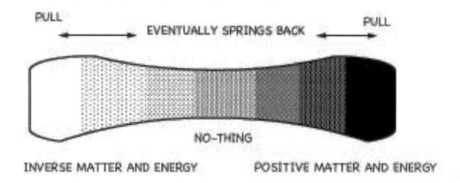

The special two color taffy model describing how something can emerge from nothing.

Imagine next, that our physical *universe* is constructed in a similar manner to this blob of taffy. In the physical realm it is always "pulsing" or vibrating between two extremes due to a large-scale dynamic process. (The process, of course, originates in multi-dimensional space, and what we experience is only a filtered *projection* of this deeper level process.) If we reduce this blob to only three dimensions, we can imagine a *projection* of this process by using this diagram of taffy.

CREATION STORY – TAFFY

What follows is only a story, another creation story, formed in the conceptual and describable space of our minds. This is a story that describes a possible way all the "stuff" that we experience may be part of a much grander cyclic process that emerges from "nothing" and always remains "no-thing." Because the real process unfolds in multi-dimensional space and outside of time, this story is my way of describing it, using the conceptual tools of our realm. The taffy, which has already been discussed above, becomes the physical model for the events of this story. This creation story illustrates only one possible way of visualizing how all the "something" we experience might have originally come from nothing. In this story, which includes the *Big Bang* moment, there is no beginning or end, rather every step unfolds as part of a repeating cyclical process that originates deep within the *Multiverse*.

This story describes the "creation" of our dualistic physical realm, which as we now know, is only a small portion of the *Multiverse*. This cycle of creation is, therefore, only a small part–maybe just like a tiny eddy current–of the far larger flow that is eternal process. The nesting of layers seems to be nature's repeating pattern or habit. It is possible that, at least from our *viewport*, this nesting continues forever in both directions. It may even be that no one level of creation is ever the largest or the smallest–that the division and construction continue infinitely.

We already know that this process is unfolding in a timeless place where there is no beginning or end. Unlike in our time-ordered realm, this is a place where the Alpha and the Omega, the beginning and the end, are always experienced as one and the same. A process like this, one that unfolds outside of time, is beyond our ability to even imagine. From a vantage point that lies closer to the edges of our *viewport,* whatever is occurring in these deeper dimensional levels will always appear in our shadow world as "repeating cycles of change moving through time." Another level of understanding is that this is all just one way that creation explores, evolves and continuously establishes new realms for *Being* to occupy. This creation story therefore only applies to one very small corner of creation. It just happens to be that small corner that we are presently dancing through, and that we are just beginning to understand.

This story, because it is being told in words, describes a conceptual and cyclic process. This type of process resembles a jump-rope that is always going around and around. It never stops, so there is no part that can be described as the beginning. There will never be a beginning or an end to this eternal and repeating cyclic process. However, when telling a story, a beginning point is very useful because of the way our human, therefore time-ordered, minds store and organize our information. Just like when we are jumping rope, we have to take the leap and enter the pattern somewhere.

To establish an entry point into this story, imagine absolutely nothing–no *energy*, no *matter*, no space, and no thing! From this nothing-ness "something" starts to happen. This "something" that begins our story is an enormous wave of *energy* that rips apart the fabric of this "nothing." This wave of *energy* is from the part of this "never-ending cyclic process" that came right "before" this entry moment. The source of this pulse will be understood by the end of our story–which will also mark the beginning point of the next time around. This enormous *energy* pulse starts a disturbance in this "nothingness" and causes "nothing" to begin to rapidly divide into two complementary types of "something." One type is a "positive" energetic form and the other is the "negative" energetic form. These two "things" taken together fully cancel each other so their combined sum is still "nothing." In this way, this process remains consistent with the *conservation of energy* law of classical physics that describes how *energy* is never created or destroyed; it only changes its form. As the impulse continues to affect this "nothing," increasingly more of each type of "something" is separated and pulled apart as this cyclic process continues.

Let us assign familiar names to these two complementary halves of "nothing"–*anti-energy* and *energy.* Each is being "pulled" away from the other to be surrounded by their similar kind. The total *energy* of the system, as a whole, has not changed–it is still zero. *Two types of energy* have been formed but only for as long as they can remain separated into their two dynamically balanced halves. With this divided and sequestered energy there is now a "something."

At some point in this process the conditions become right for some of the *energy* on each side to convert into *matter*. As we have known since the time of Einstein, *matter* and *energy* are two interchangeable forms of the same thing. In our model, on one side we now have *matter* and *energy* and on the other we have *antimatter* and *anti-energy*, and all of this was created from nothing.

As these two halves of creation are "stretched" farther apart, they will remain interconnected because one can't exist without the other. The more defined and separated they become, the more they start to energetically "miss" each other. There will always be the strong tendency for these opposites to "fall back together into the nothingness," which is their most comfortable energy state. Because this "desire" to return to the comfortable state of "nothing" is growing greater as the separation increases, at some point, this process loses its outward inertia, slows down, and it begins to reverse itself. As these two parts "fall back" completely into each other, a tremendous release of energy occurs as the *matter* portion of both halves is converted back into their respective types of energy. These two forms of energy then quickly merge back into no-thing, in a process that might appear like destructive annihilation.

This violent event is what we call the *big bang,* and this is the part of this cyclic process that produced the original energetic impulse that began our story. This cycle will then repeat itself, forever and forever, creating universes like the one that we know, along with many others, some similar and some very different. Each of these universes spawns its own complementary, but completely invisible, paired universe made from *anti-matter* and *anti-energy.* We have absolutely no direct awareness of any sister universes. This entire system oscillates back and forth between the nothing state and the fully-divided, material state.

This process unfolds deep in the heart of the *Multiverse,* and so, again, what we experience, see, measure and describe in our three-dimensional realm is only the thin shadow cast upon our realm. In our linear "time," it has been 15 billion years since the last "big bang." These are very long cycles from our human perspective of 75-year lifespans. This fundamental creative process is eternal, and it recycles tremendous amounts of *matter* and *energy;* but the entire system, when taken as a whole, is always *"no-thing."* Large parts of this system, all the anti-matter and the anti-energy, are not visible or directly accessible to us. This is probably a very good arrangement, considering the great amounts of energy involved. In this creation story, the *big bang* is seen not as a beginning, but instead as a special or important step in an eternal cyclic process.

Everything that exists in the physical realm has, by necessity, a complementary opposite. This reflects the origin and the meaning of our duality, where every "thing," idea or impulse is and must be constructed from opposites. For a thing to exist, an opposite complimentary thing will also, by necessity, need to exist. This is the nature of the physical world we occupy–this is also how our "something" could have been created from "nothing."

IT IS ALL ONLY A DREAM

One common spiritual view of our three-dimensional experience within the Multiverse has common elements with Eastern religion, modern Gnosticism, shamanism, tribal religion, modern physics and popular New Age culture. This description has us existing within, and experiencing, a single, common dream. Seen this way, we are all participating in one giant waking dream that is holographic in nature. This dream is completely cross-referenced, so that we all perceive different views, or individual perspectives, even though we all share the same single dream. Within our individual *viewports,* we only consciously interact with our particular single three-dimensional portion of this creation. This world that we experience is our collective dream. Our world and life is a dream; it is illusionary, but it always seems fully solid and real to us while we are in the dream.

If this seems impossible, remember that most of what we dream while we are sleeping at night seems completely real from within our nighttime dreams. We often only realize that we were dreaming when we finally wake up.

As already discussed, we are only experiencing the *image* or shadow of something formed within, and projected or cast from a more-expansive dimensional space. A scientist, mathematician or mapmaker might call the small three-dimensional part that we intersect and interact with the *projection*. This is a name that reminds us of the movie-like nature of our world. The apparent solidity of our outer physical world is a powerful illusion. It is only a sensory or conceptual phenomenon that is manufactured, coordinated and perpetuated within our brains.

Existing parallel to our personal experience is an endless series of potential parallel dreams, some of which are similar or identical to the dreams that we are each having. These parallel dreams may include a few small or minor changes, and each of these separate dreams is self-consistent and fits together with all the other dreams. Each similar dream is found directly "adjacent" to all other dreams in multiple-dimensional space. Seen this way, parallel worlds can be understood as parallel dreams.

Our consciousness is always shifting between these similar dreams, but we are never aware of this shift. From our perspective it seems like a single dream. There are no edges or defining limits, and all the dreams mesh into one continuum, like the eddy currents of a river, so it is easy and very natural to not notice these shifts. As we evolve individually, we develop the sensitivity to better perceive these shifts. As our sensitivity increases, we can begin to explore our natural ability to consciously move between these dreams. This tool, which was once only known to the shamans and mystics, is now becoming familiar to all of us.

With a better understanding of the physics of our Multiverse, we can begin to visualize a more structural explanation for the dreamlike nature of our existence. Multi-dimensional reality unfolds as a vibrating membrane and casts *projections* through each successive dimension until a "projection of a projection of a projection" is eventually cast to form the image of our three-dimensional realm. One particular "handed down" projection or shadow is our real-seeming dream that we all experience together. Other very similar dreams (parallel worlds) are also "cast" into the vicinity of our realm. Together, it all forms the master dream, which includes our life and history and contains all other possible versions and variations of this dream. All of these possible histories are completely *enfolded* together. These similar dreams allow *infinite* space for all our possible parallel lives or dreamy doppelgangers. All individuals have their own, but always changing, *vibratory* patterns that create their *core resonant vibratory signature.* Because of this, we each set up unique ripples or waves of *resonant vibration* through a small local portion of this collective "master" shadow dream. Each individual only witnesses the smaller part of the greater collective shadow dream that is *resonant* with his or her own *core resonant vibratory signature.* This is not unlike tuning into a radio station, except that on this type of "radio" when we change stations, we still have the same experience of self, so we might not even notice the change. It is as if we are all masterful DJ's blending songs seamlessly–it is impossible to know when one dream song ends and another begins.

We experience the world through our *resonant* interaction with this master dream. All "others" also interact with the big shadow dream in their own *resonant* way. Even though the shadow dream is singular, each individual's perception of the dream may be very different because of his or her individual and unique *core resonant vibrational signature.* That portion of this master dream that we each personally *vibrate* with, or tune into, is unique–it is ours alone and this means that we all interact with and experience a different part of this dream. When we do the work to change our *core resonant vibrational signature*, then our *resonance* changes and we vibrate *sympathetically* with a different and often larger part of this dream. Because it is only a dream, our entire experience can quickly change–anything can unfold in an instant.

Many "universes" are thus possible without ever leaving the "one dream." The "one dream" is the sum-total of every possibility imagined by every dreamer. In our realm this "one dream" appears as the three-dimensional "movie" we call life. This entire multilevel dream matrix cast through all dimensions can also be called the "Web of All Possibilities."

THE OCEAN MODEL

Another way to visualize this dream and our *vibratory* way of interacting with it is by thinking of the ocean. Imagine that the "dream" is the ocean and we are all only ripples and waves in this ocean. At any moment, our individual resonant vibration starts a small wave of sympathetic vibration running through the fabric of this dream. Imagine a ripple on the ocean stirred by a puff of wind or the swirling of a deep sea current created by a school of fish. The ocean itself represents the full dream, while our individual experience of the dream is limited to this small ripple in time and space. The ocean exists at levels far greater and deeper than the local world of the ripples or waves. It originates from a deeper place where the waves and ripples are not separate–a place where there is only one thing: the water.

THE DREAMER

If this is a dreamt world, it might seem reasonable and logical that somewhere beyond the layers of projection, the dreamer will be found. Because the dream nature of our 3D world is the result of successive projections cast through nested dimensions, it could be reasonable to conclude that at some point, as we are peeling back through these layers, we might reach a level where we discover the original source. Here we might then observe the dreamer.

Some of us might experience this "master dreamer" as a creator that exists separately from us. We could imagine that this "other" is creating our dream from some place outside of the master dream in a fashion similar to the role of gods in many world religions.

Others might experience this same dream as being created by the deeper parts of our own *being*, parts that transcend our three-dimensional expression. At the root level where this dream is formed, there is only one dreamer and that dreamer is created from the combined *resonant* consciousness of all beings–the deepest expression of Self. This type of Self-dreaming structural organization is completely consistent with our current understanding of the *Multiverse*.

In this place, where the dream begins, there is only "one" dreamer and this dreamer is all of us, at once, outside of time, *being* and dreaming as one. We are, all together, acting as one, the creators of the master dream.

THE OBSERVER

The role of the *observer* has very profound implications in both *quantum physics* and *general relativity* and, by now, there have been volumes of interesting philosophical discussions written about this idea. In *quantum physics* it is the very act of *observation* (*quantum measurement*) that causes the *wave function* (the sea of possibilities) to *collapse* and appear to us as "real" or "solid." The very presence of an *observer,* measuring, paying attention or even just thinking about the thing in question, is what makes the physical expression "real." At least this is how it appears from our *viewport*. Other ways of expressing this idea are *"the observer affects the outcome," "the observer is an integrated part of the process,"* and *"consciousness causes the collapse of the probability wave."*

Just what constitutes an *observer* or an act of *observation* is a very interesting question. From experiments we know that a measurement involving *quantum particles* constitutes an act of *observation.* Today robotic machines make many of our actual measurements. Is this robot the actual *observer* or is the *observer* the conscious scientist that invented and programmed this robot? ***The philosophical questions about the definition and role of the observer in quantum physics are profound because the experimental results could be summarized and rephrased as "a thought is needed to create or manifest each object from the sea of possibilities," or even "until we have a specific thought, all things are possible." Within this view, this same thought is also the very thing that limits the possibilities. Thinking may be the actual trigger for a process that then makes something appear "real" to our thinking minds.***

This means that, from within our *viewport*, focusing our attention on something will invest it with a solidity that helps make it "real." Over and over, every moment of every day, we participate in this process. Everyone is participating in this process; therefore in one sense, by all doing this, we are all together co-creating the "real" physical expression of our world. With any act of *observation*, a thought *fixes* the form from that which was previously unexpressed! This process can be thought of as being like the *fixation* step in the development of an old black-and-white, silvered photograph or negative. The object of thought is no longer just a part of a cloud of probabilities because it now has become manifested in our three-dimensional world. A 3D image has been "fixed" and we experience it as real.

If conscious thought is needed for the *fixation process*, then an interesting question is illustrated by the Zen koan: *"what if a tree falls in the woods and there is no one to hear it–does it then make a sound?"* ***Does our universe even exist without conscious observation? Would the world exist without our participation?***

The role that *observation* plays in this new physics is also interesting because it shifts the ultimate responsibility for our personal experiences from "outside elements and influences" directly back to each individual. ***We are the most critical element in the determination of what becomes real for each of us.*** However, we do not, and cannot, influence this directly with only our thinking minds.

Individual *viewports* are built into the structure of creation to allow each of us to manifest our own personal adventure. The world that each of us encounters, when it unfolds from this sea of *possibilities*, will be different for every conscious *being* even if we all appear to be participating in the same event. ***While we alone do not create the world, we do each create our own worldview.***

The questions that surround our experience of individuation have always been the same. *"Who am I?" "What is awareness?" "Why is my awareness so personal?"* With our new awareness of the *quantum* realm we can now ask more specific questions like *"Is there a world without our observation?" "Why do I experience only this small piece of reality, if there are an infinite number of universes out there?" "Why am I bound in this personal frame of reference?" "Is it possible to understand life from multiple different observation points at once?" "How can I become free to explore what I choose?"* Today, as we discover how to use and navigate our new understanding about the structure of the *Multiverse*, we are beginning to find answers to questions like these.

CYCLES IN NATURE

The natural world operates in cycles. The Earth circles the Sun and the Moon circles the Earth as the stars in our galaxy continue to turn around the galactic center. Seasons cycle, as do nutrients, ocean currents, plants, animals and everything that we see and know. Eastern religion and philosophy have us moving through endless cycles of birth, suffering, death and rebirth. When we interact with vibration through music, sound, light or even the fundamental vibration of the m-branes that generate the material *matter* that we understand as solid, we are then witnessing and experiencing the cyclic nature of existence.

Cycles are a critical and integrated part of our lives, at least those three-dimensional parts of our lives that are bound and described by "time." As we come to better understand and integrate this repeating and cyclic nature of life, we begin to become more relaxed about and comfortable with this process. We understand that as these cyclic waves of information move through time and space, things unfold, repeat and change their patterns. Rhythmic change is natural and very normal. Once we deeply understand this principle at the core of our *being*, suffering loses one of its strongest holds upon our consciousness. We now can see any situation as only a brief moment of expression in a much larger, holistic, cyclic, and eternal process of change and movement. As we begin to understand the different nature of this experience, we can learn to better appreciate the entire process of life as one big joyful and cyclic "joyride." The once-difficult parts of life can be seen as only brief moments in this ever-changing cycle. They can then be seen as integrated parts of a "bigger picture," and a better awareness of this can even make them fun. When we were children and needed to climb a tall ladder to reach the top of the slide, we usually experienced the climb as an exciting and fun part of the process. As culturally trained adults we have learned to see the more difficult work involved in this part of the process, and we habitually look for ways to eliminate or reduce the difficult parts of the natural cycles. When we become more appreciative of the cyclic nature of life and the value of all parts of the cycles, we can again become more like children and again find the great joy inherent in the difficult parts of these cycles.

When our *attachment* to outcomes finally ends, suffering ends, along with our need to control and understand events. Life is then seen as a cyclic process, one of constant change; there is no such thing as an "outcome," since all results only mark temporary points in a forever-evolving and changing wave. Once we begin to live from this new perspective, then the natural cycles in our lives can be seen differently; all things come and go in a never ending rotation. These cycles provide us with a structure and rhythm that, like the Ferris wheel, presents opportunities to take multiple "rides" which all serve to help us to deepen our experience within this amazing *Multiverse*.

WE ARE TRANSDUCERS

It is entirely possible that we are nothing more than biological computers, responding to some form of external program. This, of course, is a popular and recurring theme in science fiction, and it may be impossible to prove that this is not the case. If we are computers, then our programing could have been designed to keep this aspect well hidden.

Even if we are not computers, there may be very little difference between the future human form and the computers of tomorrow. Computers and bioengineering have been merging in bold and functional ways so that our cyborg technology is becoming an integrated part of our form. We have quickly moved far into what was once only our fictional imagination.

From the perspective in which we consciously create our lives, and ourselves, ***we are consistently creating our new forms from that which we already know–we create from our own image and concepts.*** It is quite likely that life-force may be able to exist outside of its present human, animal and other biological forms. Life-force might be fully able to use whatever form it chooses. From personal experiences such as NDEs and Astral Traveling, some of us already know that it can exist outside of our bodies, at least for a while. The computers that we are currently developing might serve quite well as the next vehicle for life-force and its self-expression. One purpose for our current form might be to create new physical forms for life-force to occupy. The binary, dualistic logic of today's computers might appear rather limited, uninteresting and possibly even boring to this unbridled life-force. However, we are rapidly making bold advances in quantum and biological computing that allow completely new ways of thinking about computing to unfold. Non-dualistic "thinking" machines that combine quantum technology with advances in genetics might one day appear very attractive to a spirit seeking a new opportunity for its self-expression. The human form may only be a transitional form until these new and different vehicles for "life-force" become available.

Regardless of what forms are chosen for our future, what is absolutely clear, today, is that we are already biological *transducers* of some kind. A *transducer* is defined as a device that converts one type of *energy* into another. As we discussed earlier, *matter* is just another form of *energy*, and, except for the mystery of life-force itself, our lives can be completely described using energetic principles. *Transducer*s convert one form, called *input energy,* into another form, named *output energy*. This is what human *beings* do every day.

Machines of all types are actually *transducers.* Common everyday examples are *motors* that convert *electrical energy* into *mechanical energy* and *generators* that convert *mechanical energy* back into *electrical energy. Steam engines* convert the *heat of combustion* from coal, wood or gas into *mechanical energy*, using the pressure created by the *expansion* of water into steam; and *automobile engines* convert *energy stored in hydrocarbons* directly into *mechanical energy*. Today, we build electronic *transducers* from silicon semiconductors such as *transistors* and *diodes*. Other common *transducer*s that we use every day are guitars, solar panels, transformers (wall warts), radios, and microwaves, along with just about any type of machine or device.

Human beings also function as intelligent and complex *transducers.* On one level we take in energy in the form of food and then we produce many different types of energetic output. As it is with any *transducer*, the nature of the energetic signal coming in certainly affects the quality and quantity of our *output signal*. At the physical level, our human functions and processes can be described by listing: the different types of input *energy* or signals; how we process, alter, and recycle that *energy;* and the eventual human output that results. As we transduce, we are constantly communicating, sharing and connecting with things and *beings* that are also processing energy. Regardless of any other purpose for life, we are *energy* converters. We all participate in the universe by picking up one kind of signal, processing it, and producing another kind of output.

We do this with multiple forms of *energy.* Some are understood and explainable through our technologies and others are not. Remember that when we speak of *energy* we are really referring to both *matter* and *energy* because they are two forms of the same thing. Many types of signals may be hybrids of both *matter* and *energy*. Light, for example, provides *energy* for all types of biological functions, but can also be thought of as *photons*, which are material and have *mass*–enough *mass* to knock *electrons* lose. Powerful chemical signals such as *pheromones* are mostly material but can still be described in terms of *energy*. Chemical-signal processing is critical to our bodies and the survival of our species. We respond in well-defined ways to scientifically understood signals like sound, light, and heat. However, we also respond to influences or signals that we don't yet understand, as we also *transduce energy* in its many more subtle and unknown forms. For example, animals smell fear, and we even somehow clearly know that the person behind us is staring right at us. However because we don't understand the exact signal forms, we might refer to this ability as the strange "sixth sense."

We are constantly and unconsciously responding to outside signals of many different types, many of which are beyond our current scientific comprehension. Our brain has many functions that we do not yet understand therefore we have little knowledge about its actual potential capacity and abilities. We have noted that our brain can processes at least 500,000 times as much data subconsciously as it does consciously. We have a complex and sensitive electrical system, a little-understood electromagnetic system, and a sensitive yet complex chemical system that has revealed only a few of its secrets. We are sensitive to *electrical, magnetic, gravitational, acoustic, mechanical, thermal* and *electromagnetic energy;* and we can automatically sense the environment and respond in an energetic way. There is no way to avoid the conclusion that we are, in a very literal sense, extremely complex and versatile *transducers.* Our *transducing* is an extremely critical component of the *Multiverse.* ***Our transducing is required for the Multiverse to work. Actually, this transducing may be required for the Multiverse to even exist.***

WHY MY WORLD APPEARS LIKE THIS?

A common response from someone just beginning to understand the "Web of All Possibilities" and the principles of a conscious existence within the *Multiverse* is, ***"If my vibration is determining how I interact with the Multiverse, then why am I experiencing all this negativity, all this war, hate, and all this human dysfunction? I am not like that at all!"*** This is the most natural response and is exactly how most of us respond when first introduced to this new idea. ***How and why am I directly connected to all these "horrible" things that are always happening in our world?***

Why all this "negativity" appears as a significant part of our lives on Earth can be explained or understood through five important principles. The most primary reason is based in the definition of freedom itself. ***For freedom to be possible, all choices must be available.*** To explore freedom, we must have the opportunity to choose from any and every type of experience. A universe without all possible options, including the horrible and negative, will never cultivate true freedom. ***Freedom is nourished only when all possibilities are available.***

Next, we are here to collectively interact with everything so that we may "know" all that is, become deeply compassionate, and evolve. This was previously discussed, but because this is our main "purpose" in life, it deserves repetition. ***We are here to deepen our awareness of "all that is." This world, with all its problems, working, and appearing the way it does, serves this purpose very well.*** The very nature of our *dualistic* existence means that the concept of hot cannot be understood without a comparison to cold. Fortunately, there are many of us, so this "difficult" work of experiencing everything in creation gets spread around. This means that we each get a balanced mixture of these experiences.

Thirdly, once we know about these darker aspects of our human condition and our deeper relationship to them, we can begin to understand that ***even though we don't like to identify with these "negative" things, they are still a part of us at some level.*** They exist in our *vibratory* universe, which is simultaneously all around and within us. This means that the negativity is a part of us, all of us. This realization is deeply intertwined with our fears, our desires, our anger, our love, our dreams, our nightmares, our resistance and everything that moves us. Specifically, it represents that part of everything in our world that would perpetually remain in the dark without our loving work of illuminating this darkness through our consciousness. ***Villains, such as Hitler and Genghis Kahn, represent different aspects of our beingness. They are the manifestations and signals from those wounded parts of us that need healing, incorporation, and the embrace of our Love. They are also reminders of our enormous individual power.***

When we fight or repress our deeper awareness of who we really are, we are actually increasing our disturbance around these very aspects. This is because we are adding *energy* and focus to the qualities of fighting and repression. Pushing something away is equally as powerful as pulling something towards us. Fighting against war, hunger and disease expands and reinforces fighting as part of our energetic field. ***Pushing and pulling are two equal responses to the same dualistic struggle. The dualistic struggle will not end just because one side "wins." Peace can only be accomplished through the recognition and joining together of the opposing sides, embracing all that is as one.*** This includes everything, even that which we call evil. This process must be completely free of all judgment because healing is only possible when we embrace everything that "is." This embrace must therefore include every part and every aspect–even the extremely unpleasant.

This brings us to the fourth principle. ***The discordant experiences in our lives are present so that we have this special opportunity to heal them, by shining light on the unconscious patterns that have led to generations of pain and suffering.*** Leonard Cohen sings *"everything has cracks, that is how the light gets in."* "Darkness" always represents a not-yet -accepted or -integrated, but still critical, part of us. That also means that this darkness is an important and integral part of creation itself. That which we once saw as "frightening" or "terrible" will, after healing, be seen to have been just a misunderstood, isolated or fearful part of us; darkness completely changes its character once it is fully accepted, reintegrated and loved. Seen as a frightened child, or as a lonely and isolated aspect of ourselves that is only begging to be reunited, loved and accepted, this dark side suddenly loses its once-powerful hold over us. As we let go of our individual fears around areas of personal darkness, so does the rest of humanity. The shadows disappear everywhere as the healing is finally completed with unconditional and loving reintegration. With this kind of integrative healing, darkness everywhere can become fully enlightened. To understand healing, we must first see this darkness as a necessary and constructive part of the dualistic process. From here our shadow side is understood to be no different from the leaves falling in the autumn, or the daytime turning into night.

With that acceptance and embrace, our core vibration shifts along with our perspective or *viewport*. We continue to be aware of these issues, but they do not affect our deep joy–they are not seen as "the problem." They can even be understood as a useful source of friction serving the evolutionary process of our world. Friction on the soles of our feet is what allows us to walk or move forward; friction is required for our physical movement. Friction within our souls creates evolutionary movement. The shadows only inform us where there is personal and cultural work to be done.

If, today, we are suffering because of darkness, we will, through this process, come to understand the nature and causes of human suffering at an extremely deep and intimate level. All personal "knowing" serves our collective "knowing." This type of experience must be expressed within the *Multiverse* so that we can all become deeply and completely compassionate and empathetic. The experience of suffering is absolutely necessary before we can experience true freedom in the dualistic dream. ***However, at some point we realize that our personal suffering is optional.*** By living a full life, which, by necessity, includes exposure to suffering, we will evolve and expand to understand a bigger picture of "all that is." Through this more complete encounter, the *Self* evolves, expands and becomes more aware of itself. On the surface of our 3D realm it may seem to be a very cruel or harsh process, but ultimately it is no different from earthquakes, tornados or supernovas! *This is how the natural system stirs the light and darkness to restore balance.*

The last reason for the darkness is that our lives will completely change once we have fully relaxed our resistance, so that we become more open, available, and able to embrace the full range of human activity. Eventually we learn to do this without generating new karmic activity that perpetuates these endless cycles of painful drama. Once we have reached the point where we can "witness" all of life without judgment, we have become free. We will suddenly find ourselves more able to experience a joyful life, right here and now. By living our lives this way, we become an example that demonstrates to "others" what is possible. *Once we relax knowing that the darkness itself is what allows the light to even exist, our example helps to inform others. Freedom is contagious.*

A common reaction to this idea of living our lives through engaging this level of personal freedom is "this is a nice idealistic idea, but it just can't work this way in the real world." By learning how to live our lives in this new expanded way, we can then demonstrate to others that this is, in fact, a wonderful way to live. In our day-to-day lives we might be involved in projects like removing land mines, reducing the nuclear arsenal, distributing food, teaching or governing, or we may be selling cosmetics or working in the neighborhood convenience store while we are busy raising our kids. No matter what we do in our lives, once we are living this kind of more open life, we are then teaching by example. Our example serves to provide validation so others will be inspired to step beyond their conditioned fears, as we become the "living proof" that this way of living can work beautifully. Over time, on the surface, it will appear that, as a greater number of us successfully live in *freedom*, the deeply-entrenched cultural resistance will fade as the fear gradually recedes and is steadily replaced by trust. Each of us will reach the point where we fully trust this new way of being in the world, and then the flowing of deep Love will follow naturally. Of course all of this is said knowing that at the deepest levels nothing has really changed except for our attitude, which then allowed a change in our *viewport*.

PREPARING FOR SHIFT

No amount of knowledge will free us from our cultural and self-imposed limitations. Knowledge is very helpful because it can provide an access point and direction for our personal transformation. It can also help us to define our purpose and focus our intent. *However, it is only our inner personal transformation that can finally free us.* Examining and letting go of the habitual limitations that are buried deep within our being is a process–one that requires a long-term commitment. Initially, this process can appear frightening or even painful, and it usually involves facing aspects of our lives and *being* that we would rather hide or ignore. It involves honest inner examination to discover and locate hidden aspects and parts of our self. Once these hidden parts are recognized by the light of consciousness, acknowledged and accepted, the most difficult part of this process is complete. What remains is integration, and while this part of the process might require most of a lifetime, it can also be a great amount of fun.

Our bodies always know, and they will always tell us, where our secrets are hidden. However, we can only hear what our bodies are telling us with once we learn how to become good listeners. They are constantly sending us signals, but unless we are practiced and paying close attention, we usually miss the early messages. These secrets might be revealed through a habitually tight hamstring, that feeling of being tired often, the funny twitch in our gut, the cold sweats in certain social situations, or through any of the many ways our bodies attempt to gain our attention. Our bodies can identify our dark areas long before we even know they exist.

Today there is a large support structure for those wanting to engage in this type of clearing process. Vibrant communities, with the practitioners and resources to help facilitate our personal transformations, have evolved in many towns and cities. These healing networks are mostly informal, but often well established, and they can be discovered in many unlikely parts of the world. Urban centers worldwide have bustling alternative healing communities. In more rural places a few directed questions can sometimes result in the discovery of a local resource. Those of us who don't live close to major population centers can always find great help and guidance on the Internet. Today we have unparalleled access to books, websites, alternative journals, TV and radio programs, holistic M.D.s, chiropractors, myopractors, acupuncturists, psychological therapists, massage therapists, rolfers, support groups, dance or movement therapy, yoga, meditation, spiritual groups, friends on the same journey, psychics and channelers. All of these and much more are readily available to assist us with our process.

Another piece of good news is that once we begin to open and embrace one of these deeply buried aspects of our *being*, this process begins to get easier. A new set of tools is available to us. By this point in our process, we have assembled a roadmap, found resources, and established a precedent. All of this naturally develops from our personal experience with this type of change.

In the day-to-day business of our lives, we are often unaware of, avoid, or ignore our most difficult buried issues. Eventually they must manifest and, if they have been trying to get our attention for a while, they may now appear as a more serious physical problem, such as chronic pain or disease. Those who are practiced, skilled and committed to the process of uncovering these blockages will be able to recognize these physical issues for what they really are–the later warning signs.

While it is generally true that each similar breakthrough gets easier, any person embarking on this journey must be prepared for unexpected challenges. The path will sometimes present adventures that are not for the timid or fearful. Our egos are tricky and they usually hide the most difficult issues tightly under multiple layers of protective psychological and physical shielding. During our process, as we peel the onion-like layers, issues will emerge unexpectedly and often in dramatic fashion. Sometimes these surprises can even throw the most experienced explorers off balance. These deeply buried kinks often start kicking very hard when they are finally uncovered, for they have been deeply buried to resist this very type of discovery.

A very important point to remember is that we should never feel a need to rush this process. Rushing makes no sense in a world where we know "time" is only a self-created marker used for the convenience and organization within our brains. Things always unfold in the Multiverse simultaneously, and it only appears to us that there has been a passage of "time." Just as with any new activity, we don't want to push the body or mind too hard. It is usually best to progress by gradual absorption and slow natural deepening, using whatever methods are most comfortable. This human form of ours generally feels safer and responds better to more gradual shifts. *There is no reason to rush because we are not going anywhere. We have already arrived at our destination–here, engaged in the process of life and evolution. Everything else unfolds naturally when the critical and important relationships are formed and the "time" is right.*

Also, we must not compare ourselves to others or compare our process to their process. We can use their experiences as a learning tool–as guidance to facilitate our own journey, but we need to remember that this is always only our journey and our process alone. We simultaneously grow outward and inward from our own center of being. Within this journey centered in our own *being*, we then discover and know that there really is only "one" in this story–there never were any "others"!

THE WEB INTERFACE

Most of the time, we are aware of only one existence, which includes a self-consistent thread of memory and history that goes back through time. However, in the infinite Web, every possibility exists and will eventually be known by some aspect of "us." Why, then, do we not have some level of awareness from any of these other existences? The truth is we do, but most of us don't know how to process or interpret this type of "memory" since it is stored outside of our 3D conceptual minds. This lack of awareness is not a deficiency or problem; instead it is a natural and very functional protection built into the structure of our body/brains, which are specifically designed for living this particular three-dimensional experience within the multi-dimensional Web. As three-dimensional specialists, our senses and awareness are built to be focused and most efficient within our own realm.

However, some uniquely prepared individuals are able to interpret or understand some of their experiences in the context of the larger dimensional reality. Past life experiences, clairvoyance, déjà vu, genius, precognition and bilocation are all indications that the boundaries of our personal *viewports* sometimes soften enough to be penetrated by *information* from other parts of the Web.

For most of us, most of the time, it is very convenient and functional to have only this singular and focused awareness of one existence. Being aware of life from only one place in the *Multiverse* usually provides us with enough stimulus and information to keep our conscious brains fully occupied. This restricted focus allows us to function well in our realm, and, therefore, be able to fill our critical role for the rest of creation. We are spiritual *beings* learning to how to most productively live within and contribute through our physical realm.

SCIENCE FICTION BIRTHS SCIENCE

Before actual *black holes* were discovered, *black holes* and *wormholes* were mostly used as raw material for science fiction. A review of literature and the history of our science support the notion that, very often, inspired science fiction provides accurate scientific prediction. This form of fiction often does a good job of predicting the actual science that soon follows. There are several potential explanations for this uncanny accuracy. One unexpected reason may be that the inspiration and thought required for writing about these possibilities may ultimately be the first important creative step in the multilevel process of "unfolding" that ultimately leads to our experimental science. Instead of just predicting the new science, these written thoughts may be an active part of creation itself.

In this context, creative imagination can be thought of as one form of *quantum observation*. With each creative new thought, the *wave* of infinite possibilities begins to *collapse* into one, solidified, three-dimensional idea. The recording of an idea in a book or film for public distribution might then result in a widespread global *collapse* of this *probability wave*. From our three-dimensional, time-based perspective–one where the arrow of time only moves forward, any act of creative thinking or writing represents an important first step or catalyst for the birth of a new idea.

SUCCESSFUL GENIUS

"Genius, in truth, means little more than the faculty of perceiving in an unhabitual way."   –
William James

"Intuition will tell the thinking mind where to look next." –Jonas Salk

Some individuals have the ability, skill, timing, cultural wisdom and "luck" to have gained unique insights because their *viewport* is just far enough askew or slightly outside of the main consensus *viewport.* This unique vantage point gives them the capability of perceiving something that might otherwise be unnoticed. Some explorers of these new and uncharted territories have then been able to journey back towards the center of the common *viewport*, process *information* there, and communicate it in a way that allows the prevailing culture to access, or at least partially understand, their experience. Literature and the arts are filled with insights achieved through this type of process, and many of the scientific discoveries that we so casually rely upon today were actually manifested this way.

Often, the only difference between the "genius" who wins a Nobel Prize and the unknown "lunatic" who is locked up in an asylum is the slightest shift of circumstances. The new discoveries that are labeled "genius" are sometimes brought to the general public's attention at a time, and in a way, that permits receptivity. The difference might be a simple "accident" or twist of fate: the accidental stumbling upon a manuscript in the attic by the right person; a journal suddenly having extra available pages at press time so an unusual article is included; the right well-positioned person attending the presentation, or an unexpected illness forcing a potential detractor from attending. These examples describe real events in our scientific history. These chance occurrences might seem like accidents from our usual, dominant cultural perspective, but from the larger perspective they are all always manifestations of a fully interconnected and natural process. There are no accidents in creation.

For any of us to receive a new insight, there must have been a successful communication and translation of the *information* or experience into our *viewport.* No matter how carefully the messenger explains a new idea or new concept, if it is too far outside our paradigm, it will be entirely missed by the prevailing culture, especially by the experts that are protective of their particular area of interest. Any new ideas that do survive are usually those much closer to the known edges of the existing paradigm. Ideas too far from the cultural center do not survive translation, and, as I discuss in the next section, the messengers that bring these "crazy" ideas usually are treated very badly by the majority.

Savants perform at levels far beyond the normal human limits; in art, music, science and math they push us through the boundaries of our paradigm. Untrained children have inexplicably played complex classical pieces on pianos. Mathematical savants divide numbers in their heads with more precision than most calculators can manage. Calendar savants can tell us details like the day of the week for any date, without ever looking at a calendar or doing calculations; it is as if they just "see" the answer. When composing a musical piece, at least one particular savant sees a complete visual map of where the fingers need to go on their instrument. Another famous scientist had the experience of seeing the visual model of DNA just pop into his head. A physic sees geometric patterns that have real world meaning. Why and how do these people have access to this type of *information*?

Even if the work does not survive intact or the messenger suffers, their genius still allows all of us another opportunity to gaze or think beyond our normal conceptual horizon, at least for a brief moment. These often misunderstood moments of brilliance shows us new viewing windows through which we might see possibilities previously unimagined.

The truth is that we all have access to this kind of *information,* but it is through methods and processes that are not yet generally understood by our culture. We can, with practice, learn to stay more open and translate more of this "outside" *information* that is infinitely abundant and existing everywhere throughout the *Multiverse.* Better access to this "outside" *information* is one of the first benefits gained by freeing ourselves from our old paradigm. These skills–this ability to have enhanced access, the ability to recognize the value of the *information*, and the ability to communicate this *information*–are all traditionally considered characteristics of successful genius. As we become clearer, these skills will become more available to everyone.

CREATIVE OUTSIDERS

Most of what we recognize to be genius typically occurs at the near edges of our collective *viewport*, where the *information* is still safely inside a slightly expanded, but still consensus view of what is considered to be normal. Due to the nature of our society and our cultural conditioning, there is a limit to how much new conceptual material our society as a whole is able to assimilate. Exploring the distant territory that lies further beyond the edge of our collective experience is typically a very lonely experience. It is extremely easy for individuals who are exploring this outer terrain to accidentally wander too far from center, leaving them unable to share or relate their experiences with the rest of our society.

There have always been individuals whose *viewports* fall far outside the "normal" range. Those who inhabit these "outside" regions are usually completely misunderstood during their own lifetimes. They are often seen and classified as psychotic or insane by the rest of us who share the dominant *viewport*. A few of these individuals have uncovered and recorded ideas that have, only many generations later, been recognized as amazing creative genius being expressed well before its time.

If the exploration of an idea threatens an established group or paradigm, especially one that protects or consolidates power and money, then there is the possibility of direct and very conscious resistance from that threatened group. The Catholic Church's long-standing resistance to altering the "flat earth" paradigm is a classic example.

The early discoverers and adopters of our heliocentric solar system, some 400 years ago, suffered tremendously under the hands of the church. The church worried that if the Earth was no longer seen as the center of the universe, it would undermine Church doctrine and threaten its power. These unorthodox ideas and their messengers received no support from the public because they were either unaware of the work, or the ideas were far outside their comfort zone. Almost universally, radical new ideas are attacked and suppressed by established institutions that are set on protecting their reputation and/or their grip on power–change of any kind threatens the status quo. This is exactly what happened to the main character in *Flatland*. Since his new awareness threatened the authority of the church, he was declared a heretic and forced to spend the rest of his life imprisoned in an asylum.

However restrictive and regressive as it may seem, this social structure may serve our culture in a positive way by acting as a *buffer*, moderating or controlling the rate of change. This kind of restriction or *damping* is not always a bad thing because unrestricted processes can often become cataclysmic and destructive. Storms, explosions and nuclear reactions are all good examples. In the long term, slower and more gradual processes seem to integrate better to create change without as much trauma. Slowed and controlled nuclear reactions, explosions, wind and water can all be used to make electricity. In nature, the slow-and-steady, turtle-like approach usually does quite well in the end. This is especially true in a world where time does not really exist! There are good reasons for having some resistance built into our system.

THE CREATOR'S DRUMHEAD

Each of us occupies and *resonates* within our own different regions of the *Multiverse*. In any given moment, the precise place that we occupy and experience within the *Multiverse* always reflects the *resonant* qualities of our individual core *vibration*. However, this region is always changing because, by just living our lives, we are all constantly growing and evolving. We also experience our center of awareness from only one perspective or *viewport* in the "Web of Possibilities" at any one "time." Our individual perspective is always the perfect expression of our current *root vibratory resonance*— our unique *vibratory* signature in that moment. Life experience then causes our core *vibration* or "song" to shift, re-tune, and expand. As we fully embrace living and expand our awareness, the "size" and position of our *viewport* changes. This allows us to eventually "sing" in richer harmony with a greater part of the *Multiverse*.

Our *vibratory signature* always reflects our present *awareness*. Our *viewport* can be visualized as a flexible and mobile region, rather than just a single point in the Web. This region acts much like a drumhead (the *M-brane*) upon which our unique "song" can then be played. Because the size and location of our personal drumhead change as our *resonance* changes, our "song" also changes. All of our individual "songs" together produce the great symphonic "song of life." This "song" is repeated or refracted in *holographic* fashion throughout creation, and the *vibrations* of this entire system are *projected* through the different layers of dimensional space to appear as our personal "shadow dream" in this 3D realm. Our *vibratory resonant signature* (or personal song) is always expressed and distributed throughout all the other dimensions, even though our awareness is focused only on a single region within our three-dimensional *spacetime*.

In the physics section, there was a discussion about *nodes* and *vibration*. If a one-dimensional string (with no thickness) *vibrates* in a flat plane, similar to a guitar string, it then creates a two-dimensional form. Once it starts to move side to side, it now has added a width or second dimension which we call the *amplitude*. The *nodal points* are the endpoints or the still points of this *vibrating* string. With guitar strings, some of these *nodal* points are fixed and are called the nut and the bridge—the two ends where the string is always in contact with the instrument. The maximum *amplitude* of the *vibrating* string (or wave) occurs midway between these two *nodes*.

A two-dimensional drumhead works in a similar way; as it *vibrates*, it expands from two dimensions into three dimensions. With each unique tone or strike the drumhead has places, or *nodes*, where the drumhead does not move up and down into the third dimension–it stays still. *Nodes* occur both at the rim of the drumhead and at certain points within the head. Exactly where these *nodes* fall has everything to do with the individual qualities of each drum and the drummer's ability to manipulate those qualities.

While locations on this drumhead that are close to *nodes* have little or no up or down movement, other places between the *nodes* are *vibrating* at maximum *amplitude* and are fully *resonant*. However, there are other parts of this drumhead that are *vibrating* chaotically because they are the result of *wave interference* patterns that move through the drumhead. A skilled drummer can produce many different sounds from a single drumhead by slightly changing where and how his hands touch the drumhead, thus controlling these patterns of stillness, resonance and interference. A small change in the "playing" of this instrument will produce a very different "sound" or experience. Like the drummer, as we "play" with our personal multi-dimensional drumhead, we learn how to make different "sounds." We control the playing of our "song" with our attitude and openness.

As we master our individual instrument, we learn to tune it to find the richest *harmonics* and the best tone. As our awareness grows, we interact with our drumhead in a more skilled manner, and we learn how to better control our instrument. If we could observe the actual "playing" of our "drum" at the source of our *being*, we might then observe ourselves skillfully moving our "11-dimensional hands" to perfectly control the chaotic *vibration* and the clear tones.

We play our "drum" skillfully when we enter the "now" moment. In the "now," we directly interact with our "drum" to produce only the purest and clearest tones, generating an unrestricted, free and open *vibration* that fills our entire region of the Web. As we evolve, we naturally will add capability (*nodes* and size) to our drumhead. As we learn how to better remain in the "now," our skill grows and our playing evolves to produce yet truer and more beautiful tones. In the "now," the unwanted *interference* called *noise* disappears; *noise* is the uncontrolled chaotic and random *vibration* between *nodes*. It is from the "now" moment, and only the "now" moment, that our "song" will be most resonant–from there it rings full, loud and true.

Our collective multi-dimensional drumhead, the *Multiverse*, allows for *infinite* variety of expression; this in turn creates an *infinite* number of worlds. These expressions are continuously in motion, *vibrating* and changing with every thought, action, impulse or interaction. As the deep fabric of the universe *resonates* in these different but always fully interconnected patterns, new "worlds" manifest. This interconnected and deep *resonance* is the fundamental creative principle of the *Multiverse.* This is how our world is brought into existence.

We each occupy only that specific region of the Web that *resonates* most naturally with our current, individual, *core vibratory resonant signature*. Through experience and our personal evolution, we continue to enlarge the extents of this region. As we slide, skip and dance through the Web, we are always expanding into new regions that *resonate* with our changing *vibratory resonant signature*; like skilled musicians, we play our "instruments" to create and discover delightful new harmonies. When we "tune" our personal "instruments," they begin to *resonate* with larger regions of the Web, and new "songs" spring forth; we tune our "instruments" through the expansion of our conscious experience. Every part of the Web is different, unique and exciting, and every possibility for new and different ways of expression exists somewhere in this beautiful, woven, *infinite* tapestry of creation.

An interesting side discussion can be built around the idea that a one-dimensional string becomes two-dimensional or even three-dimensional as it *vibrates*. As the string vibrates, the movement of *vibration* manifests first in the second dimension; but in more complex wave forms, a third dimension is also involved. For the same reason, a two-dimensional drumhead becomes three-dimensional when it *vibrates*. Vibration always engages, or activates, more dimensions than the original object contains. What then is occurring when a 3D object *vibrates*; does it follow the same pattern? Does the three-dimensional object require four or more dimensions to fully vibrate? What unfolds when an 11-dimensional drumhead, possibly the *M-brane* of *M-theory*, vibrates? Is *vibration* another possible doorway into other dimensions, along with *time* and *holographic storage*? *Vibration* may be the mechanism that allows and regulates the information exchange between layers of dimensional space. ***Is vibration a language for inter-dimensional communication?***

Understanding, or even describing, *vibration* and *nodal points* in multi-dimensional space is far beyond our conceptual abilities. We can't possibly understand *vibration* in a timeless space because all of our understanding of it is based on the measurement of time. Whatever the form of this timeless, deeper level *vibration,* as it moves out through additional dimensions, there is likely the equivalent of "still" points or *nodes.* If we could observe and follow *vibration* inward through the deeper dimensions, eventually we might arrive at the original source of the *multi-dimensional vibrational information*–the *vibrating Web of all Possibilities.* This might also be the 11-dimensional membrane that has been described in *M-theory,* or it might turn out that creation originates at an even deeper levels; the number of dimensional levels in creation could even turn out to be *infinite.*

"NET" THAT CONTAINS OUR WORLD

I recently had a new insight about the shape and containment of our reality after a simple, everyday experience. A meeting time was set through a long series of phone calls; there had been a flurry of switching dates and times as our schedules firmed up. I arrived at the meeting absolutely sure about the agreed-upon time, since during the scheduling process we had eventually settled upon my first choice. When I arrived, I was told that I was a full day early. She believed that we were scheduled for the next day, which had been her first choice–we were both equally sure that we were right about the agreed-upon time.

That evening as I was trying to reconstruct what had happened, I had a breakthrough realization. As the old television commercial says, *"Stop-you are both right!"* In the multi-dimensional universe, two conflicting outcomes can and really do exist at the same time; they each occur in different *parallel universes.*

If we insist on only a singular outcome or possibility, what we really are saying is, "I am closed to any other possibilities, interpretations and realms of existence." This very act of being intellectually and emotionally shut off from other possibilities causes the membrane between our universe and any other to become much firmer and less penetrable. As with all things in this existence, balance is important. There are many times when a solid barrier around our 3D experience is extremely desired and beneficial–driving on busy highways is a quick and obvious example. Establishing efficient meeting times might be another.

However, if our desire is to be more open and available for personal growth, so that we can learn how to better navigate within this new architecture, then staying open to concepts like multiple contradictory truths, such as objects and people being in two places at once and things moving from where we put them, is an essential practice. These unexpected events become the new doorways and windows through the otherwise very solid appearing wall that divides our universe from all other possibilities. These are the very types of places and spaces that allow the conscious communication of *information* between unseen universes and our own. ***We must first learn to relax into and become comfortable with things that seem "impossible" before we can explore what really is possible!***

When we first open ourselves to this new way of being, the ground below our feet can quickly become very unstable and our pathway might seem obscured, but this only marks a temporary and normal period of adjustment. These are the normal "growing pains"; part of our evolutionary process into a fuller dimensional *beings*. This process is not very different from when we, as children, learned how to walk or ride a bike–we occasionally skinned our knees. Evolution rarely appears automatic or easy, but with the right attitude, just as with learning to ride a bike, it will become a joyful process.

TRUST

Trust has very different meanings for each of us, and its meaning will usually vary from situation to situation. At the most general level, trust is understood to be something as straightforward as trusting the government or a loved one not to lie to you. Used this way, trust always depends on the behavior of "another," meaning that something or someone else can easily break our trust.

This is not the level of trust that I speak about in this book. The type of Trust–with a capital T–that I am referencing does not involve any other person; it involves each of us, and our personal, deep-seated understanding about life. This kind of Trust requires that we know certain unprovable things about life to be absolutely true.

We might know and Trust that our universe is much more interconnected than we usually perceive, or that our universe is engaged in a beautiful evolutionary process, and that we are an important and integrated part of this process. We Trust that we are never alone, due to all of these unseen interconnections. We Trust that "what is essential never perishes, but instead the essential only gets more polished and radiant," and "Mind is far greater than any individual mind." This deeper level of Trust depends upon our knowing, for certain, that we belong to something much larger, and our most important role in life is to participate fully and express our uniqueness. Trust is understanding that we are a part of life itself and, therefore, eternal. It is knowing that no matter how things look on the surface of our world, everything is exactly right because the universe is perfect, exactly as it is being presented. Trust is knowing that there is nothing to do except be our self, live life fully, and "go with the flow." It is being able to relax and allow our self to flow with the ever-winding "river of life." Trust is understanding that surrendering fully is the secret to a joyful life.

SECRETS

Since absolutely everything in the Multiverse is always intimately connected to everything else, the Multiverse can hold no secrets. Everything–every impulse and every thought–is directly connected to everything else, and there are no hidden pockets that can bypass the scrutiny of this intimate interconnection.

Within our daily lives, we notice that people everywhere are creating and trying to keep secrets. Governments manufacture many levels of secrets, as do corporations. Court documents are routinely sealed, and individuals' lives are filled with secretive aspects, which are all initiated as attempts to protect an agenda. The *Multiverse* recognizes none of these as secret because every action has its ripple effect, even if we do not directly or immediately witness this interconnectedness in our 3D realm. Since, ultimately, there are no "others," we are in effect trying to keep secrets from ourselves as we build these new "dark places" within our collective psyche. Our secrets are one more form of *denial,* which ultimately only creates new flow-blockages and confusion. Secrets in society are analogous to the energetic blockages in our bodies–both are built upon unexamined or repressed memories and both interfere with the free flow of energy.

Secrets create three-dimensional blockages to the natural flow of *energy* and *information* through our physical body, our energetic body and our society. Just as with any river, the "flow of life" must and will find other pathways to complete its movement but, just like the broken riverbanks, the landscape of our lives will suffer. Over time, nothing will remain hidden. Understanding our intimate interconnectedness and the necessity of transparent truthfulness is critically important to our personal freedom.

CO-CREATION

In New Age books and lectures, it is often stated that *we are the creators of our own lives.* While this is a fundamental truth, creation does not begin with our thoughts; our thoughts arise only much later as the creative impulse moves up from its deep roots and eventually expresses itself within our physical realm. Creation begins with *vibration* at the deepest level, the level of no separation. It then unfolds as shadows are cast through dimensional layers, eventually resulting in the manifestation of this collective dream that we call life. We all have our individual roles within this dream and through this group performance, combining our individual parts, we are, indeed, being creators. However, life is always an improvisational performance and we only have control of and a choice about how <u>we</u> act or respond. At this level of individual separation, it is much more accurate to say, *"we are all co-creators of this common dream that we call life."*

Our combined soul-level *vibrations* contribute to the fundamental creative impulse at its source. There, we discover only one creator, and it is all of us, together, acting as the one.

Everyone and everything in the *Multiverse vibrates* and *resonates.* Due to the infinite possibilities for interconnectedness, all things interact in an infinite number of unseen and unexpected ways, using connections that we never could imagine using the linear process of our thinking minds. Since we are always intimately interconnected at these deeper levels, what happens in one part of the *Multiverse* is instantly communicated to every other part; and this connection is much more direct and instantaneous than what seems possible in our time-ordered physical realm. It is hard for us to imagine that someone stirring a soup on earth might instantly affect a *being* living during a different time in a distant galaxy or parallel universe. However, this is exactly what happens because in our *Multiverse,* all things continuously intercommunicate and are not separated by a kind of space and time that we understand. This interaction with and between these other "worlds" is incomprehensible because they are completely hidden from our conscious awareness by our sensory and conceptual limitations; and, as of today, we have not developed the machines or tools that may, one day, help us perceive beyond the veil that separates our world from extra-dimensional space.

Because we are all so closely interconnected at these deeper levels, we function much like the nerve cells of a brain that are interacting in a very coordinated way; beyond our perceived physical world, we interact together as a single conscious organ called *Being.* At these deeper levels, **Being creates symphonic waves of energy that flow and express themselves throughout the Multiverse. As those waves of energy pass through our three-dimensional plane, they appear to us as individual people, animals, things and events that make up life as we know it.**

Every thing and all the activities that we experience are just the shadow dream projected from our much deeper interaction–the many-layered unfolding that is occurring beyond our senses. **At this source of creation, there is no separation of individuals and no arrow of time. In these depths, creation is not even a step in a greater process. There are no steps because, without time, there is no process. In these depths, all of creation simply "is."**

LETTING GO OF SELF-BLAME

As we continue on our evolutionary journey, we are developing a mindset and new sets of skills to better facilitate our exploration of the infinite possibilities within our *Multiverse.* Through this evolutionary process we serve our purpose in this realm. ***Our purpose is to "know," through experience, the entire range of possible human expression, so that we can collectively become compassionate, healed, whole and fully aware.***

When we first begin to explore the idea that we are a contributing part of creation, we might, initially, imagine ourselves as "personally responsible for the appearance of our life." We might then desire a different type of life, believing that this other life should be our reality. Our actual experience could be so different from our imagined ideal that we might have the experience of feeling quite disturbed by "our own creation." We could feel shame, or even start to blame ourselves for having "created" something less than our "ideal." We might even start to imagine that our personal or collective "reality" is our own fault.

This type of thinking and the associated self-blame does not reflect the real workings of *Being* or the *Multiverse.* Whatever the nature of our immediate experience is, or however it looks, it is always perfect because it is always the product of all *vibrations* passing through our realm. Evolution desires that we have the full variety of human experiences, including some that seem difficult or unpleasant from our individual, short-term perspective, because this is the only way that we can come to understand, feel and experience the full range of our *being.*

Eventually we discover that blame and shame have no constructive purpose in the Multiverse, other than providing another opportunity to understand self-blame and shame. Blame of any kind is a form of judgment, and any judgment always creates resistance within us. Self-blame, like any judgment, will always impede the flow of Truth.

This type of thinking originates from the *ego,* which might, just as easily, have the opposite but equal type of response when things seem to be unfolding particularly well. We could be inclined to think that we are doing a particularly good job: we might even imagine that we are "special" and we are being "rewarded" for our behavior." In the larger picture, this type of self-congratulatory response is the same as when we blame ourselves when things go badly. Shame, blame and inflated egos are all necessary experiences that help us build compassion and understanding.

"GOOD AND EVIL" DO NOT EXIST

The idea of "good and evil" is built entirely from within our conceptual mindset; judgment is a human idea and nothing more– it is only another artifact of our culture. When a lion devours an antelope, we clearly understand this activity to be part of some natural process. Unless the lion or the antelope is a pet or a cute character in a story, we tend avoid assigning moral value to such natural processes. Hurricanes and tornadoes may be devastating and unfortunate, but they are rarely characterized as evil. When the scorpion stings, we react but usually do not imagine that the scorpion has evil intent; we intuitively understand that it is just being itself, a scorpion. With natural processes, we more easily can understand the interdependent and interwoven ecology from a somewhat removed and impersonal viewpoint. We might describe a storm as bad, or a sunny day as good, but in this context we are using these as descriptive terms and not making a moral judgment.

We are all part of this natural system and, therefore, we all also behave in a "natural" way. Our individual choices are always part of this natural process as it unfolds in three dimensions. Within this natural system, there also exists a level of personal awareness where good and evil no longer exist.

STORMS AND CLIMATE CHANGE

Hurricanes, tornados, droughts, floods and earthquakes look catastrophic from our individual and societal points of view, but when the natural world is viewed from a more holistic perspective, these events can all be understood as simply the way that the physical world restores its balance and equilibrium.

While there are many people that believe that these destructive natural events are the result of God's wrath, a minimal understanding of the science involved illustrates that these events are always the direct result of specific cause-and-effect cyclic processes in the natural world–if there is such a punishing God, he is also relying on these natural processes to manifest his will. These natural processes also respond to our large scale human actions, which directly influence the scale and frequency of extreme weather events. Being an integral part of nature means that, even our minimal actions are still an important and influential part of this "natural" system.

Clearing vegetation and pumping oil, water and minerals out of the Earth creates imbalances of different types, which our planet then corrects in its own interactive, but very natural, way. Adding greenhouse gases and burning fossil fuels changes the atmosphere of the Earth, causing it to trap more solar heat *energy*. The Earth's system is not very different from a kettle of water that becomes very active and agitated as we raise the temperature; when we add heat to the Earth's system, it too becomes agitated and more active. Overall, the average temperature of our planet is gradually increasing; and because it is also a closed physical system, the movement of air, earth and water masses must increase. Some areas of the Earth will become hotter, but others will become colder; some areas will become more violent and stormy, while others will become quieter. There is redistribution, but more *energy* is being retained and stored within the Earth's system causing it to "heat up," and this means larger and more-frequent storms. We are gradually raising our planet's temperature to its "boiling" point and observing what naturally happens.

The Earth-system will continue to respond by adjusting–always returning to a more *stable state* with a lower *resting energy*. This is what happens in storms and earthquakes. Our planet's resulting natural corrections may not look very comforting to us, but they certainly help this natural system return to a more balanced and comfortable energetic state.

However, all the adjustments we observe in our 3D world are only the "cast shadows" of what is unfolding at the deeper dimensional levels. Changes to our 3D realm send ripples of *information* in all directions because all parts of our *Multiverse* are intimately interconnected. Of course, we are not able to directly perceive the larger process that is unfolding in extra-dimensional space, but systems will shift and return to a more balanced state of equilibrium. Shift happens and balance is restored.

EMBRACING A HITLER

As a child, having just learned about World War II, I could not imagine how one single man, Adolf Hitler, could have lead an entire nation of people down such a destructive path. I even felt some type of personal responsibility because I have a large percentage of German blood in my family tree. I wondered how "my people" could have created so much pain and suffering in the world?

As a teen, I began my personal quest to gain the wisdom to understand how this could have ever happened. Fortunately, we live in a golden period of history so I had easy access to all types of *information*. By my mid-thirties, I had accumulated enough life experience to begin to understand how this could have occurred, both politically and psychologically, but I quickly found myself looking at a much more difficult, yet fully related, issue.

Unexpectedly, I found myself in a place where I recognized that my own healing and movement forward depended on my being able to uncover, recognize and even embrace the human qualities in the actions of Hitler and the very fearful, but collaborative, reactions of some German people. I discovered that my personal journey required that I forgive all that unfolded, as I simultaneously learned to forgive everyone, including myself. If humanity is "one" then the Hitlers of this world must also be a part of this "one." *If the unfolding of the Multiverse is perfect, then Hitler and the German people's response to him must also be part of this perfection.* Even though I understood that the wisdom of creation was far greater than our limited concepts and judgments, this was a very big pill for me to swallow and it did not go down easily. *To date, the integration of this epiphany and all its implications was the most difficult part of my personal journey.*

This breakthrough swept through me in a single life-changing moment. I was in Sedona, Arizona, attending a workshop offered by the co-facilitators Pamela Wilson and Nirmala. The discussion had been about embracing the entirety of the human condition, including all those things that we naturally want to push away. While the words spoken by Nirmala were thought provoking, it was his actual physical gesture that suddenly triggered my deep realization. He was graphically demonstrating the fullest embrace possible by pulling in his fully outstretched arms and crossing his hands over his heart.

Hitler was never mentioned in this discussion, but I knew in an instant that Nirmala's gesture related directly to my strong feelings about this part of Western history, and that this particular change of attitude held a key to my wholeness. It still took much of the next two decades to work through my many layers of deep resistance to fully integrate this new perspective. Many people believe that we can love the person but still despise their actions. This attitude represents a step in the direction of Love, but at some point in our journey towards freedom, *we realize that an act of despising anything, even someone's actions, only creates resistance and separation.*

I now completely understand that the unconditional embrace of absolutely "everything" is a requirement for our full healing. Anything or anyone that we push away, even the Hitlers and their actions, creates more separation. Hitler only expressed himself as he did because he had personally experienced deep separation and fear. Others followed him only because they resonated with these same feelings. This entire mega-drama was only their natural response to the existing conditions at that time.

Looking within ourselves, our loving embrace must include those parts of our own personality that remind us of those others that we want to push away; all human actions are a part of the full human range of expression and, therefore, a part of each of us. Everything that we express, no matter how dark or frightening it appears, wants to be seen by the light of our consciousness, fully-embraced and integrated. As we learn to open and expand our embrace, eventually even a person like Hitler can be witnessed without human judgment. All aspects of experience must first be loved and integrated before we can become whole.

312

It is absolutely clear that our overall cultural awareness of human rights, value, dignity and equality is more expansive and comprehensive today, due to our experience and memory of difficult historical periods. We become greater through our experiences; they are necessary for us to fully feel and express our *beingness*. Hitler and that disturbing period of our history have ultimately contributed to the evolution of our consciousness.

ENLIGHTENMENT

Enlightenment is not an end goal or ultimate place of *being,* as many people incorrectly assume. Instead, the word describes a continuous process, one involving growth and evolution. ***Enlightenment is the process of clearing and healing those places within where the light of conscious awareness is presently unable to shine.*** There is no such thing as an "enlightened" human being; instead, there are individuals who are deeply engaged in, and committed to, the infinite process of enlightenment. From our perspective, Jesus or Buddha may seem to have been enlightened; however, they both expressed, through their own words, the recognition that they were, like all of us, still very engaged in this evolutionary process. Enlightenment is a natural process, and one without end; every instance of clearing opens up new levels of interconnection, which then, in turn, create new opportunities for further expansion. Enlightenment becomes a lifestyle–a way of moving through life and not an end destination. **Regardless of how it may appear in the moment, we are all becoming more enlightened through every moment of life and experience.**

RAPTURE OR ASCENSION

There has always been a strong universal human desire to escape the chaos and struggle of our material existence. We sometimes imagine that there is a much better way to live, and in many different ways this desire is an important driving *force* that helps shape our lives. It is often the trigger for deeper spiritual exploration.

Many religions and spiritual practices offer *rapture* or *ascension* as the answer to our material struggles. In one form or another, they all comfort followers by promising that one day the "true believers" will be saved by being "pulled-up" from the difficulties of this life and then put into a place of everlasting peace.

This belief or response to the issues of our realm completely misses the importance and nature of our critical work in this physical plane. It reinforces the dualistic view of good and evil and promises a quick, aspirin-like fix for those "special" individuals who follow some prescribed path. While this type of blind faith may temporarily help an individual through a difficult psychological period in his or her life, the *Multiverse* simply does not work this way. Real growth and evolution always involve inclusion and expansion, not escape or ascension.

We are not here to escape our three-dimensional realm; instead we are here to incorporate it as a key structural part of the ever expanding whole. Discovering our freedom to change our reality by changing our *viewport* is not escapism; it is just the opposite, requiring inclusion and expansion. ***The process of enlightenment begins with understanding and fully embracing our three-dimensional existence.***

HUMANITY'S EVOLUTION–"CRITICAL MASS"

Another popular New Age discussion topic is the "evolution of humanity." A common belief is that eventually a "critical mass" of humanity will reach a certain spiritual level, where their combined energy will bring the rest of humanity along for the ride into *enlightenment, nirvana,* or some other form of idyllic paradise. The belief is that if a large enough number of individuals become consciously aware, then all of humanity will automatically sense it through *resonance* and instantly become consciously aware. This is sometimes referred to as "the hundredth monkey" phenomenon. This name is a reference to a World-War-II-era experiment that was conducted on remote and isolated islands in the Pacific; ironically, the real data from that experiment does not support this concept. While many of us might wish that this collective shift could be possible, in our realm the development of our consciousness and our movement towards enlightenment require a depth of individual experience, not just proximity to experience. In other realms, where separation does not exist, this type of consensus growth and movement may be possible.

Techniques for becoming more conscious can be indirectly communicated to others energetically, or by physical example, but only if the recipient is already prepared and ready for that level of shift. *Our worldly challenges are not problems from which we need to escape; they instead provide each individual with uniquely designed opportunities, motivations and the gritty friction necessary for the development and expansion of consciousness. Life's problems and challenges provide the perfect medium for our conscious growth; its diversity of experiences invites us to continuously expand and nurture our souls.*

UNITY OR SEPARATION CONSCIOUSNESS

There are two types of human conceptual thinking which, when used together, form a powerful polarity that literally shapes the structure of our physical universe. *These two extremes are "unity consciousness" and "separation consciousness."* Both types of consciousness are critical for our survival and evolution; our very existence relies on a balanced mix that requires the interplay of these two extremes.

"Unity consciousness" is the deep-seated belief or knowing that we, all together, are one single being and, therefore, we are all fully interconnected at a deep and fundamental level. Within unity consciousness we are fully aware that serving others is no different from serving ourselves. Tied into this awareness is the absolute knowing that we are not our bodies; we have an existence beyond them and, therefore, we certainly do not die with them. At the other extreme is "separation consciousness," which is the belief that we are only our bodies and possibly nothing more. In separation consciousness we fear that when the body dies, our existence ends.

Are we eight billion individuals living short lifespans or one eternal being? In our realm, the answer is that both are equally true! Both perspectives exist simultaneously and are fundamental to the dualistic expression of life in our three-dimensional universe. A mixed balance of both approaches is necessary, for it is ultimately the push and pull between these two extremes that keeps our world in its balanced state of existence. To function most effectively in our 3D *viewport* we need to fully respect, understand and honor both perspectives.

Biologically, our species has been doing very well on this planet; this is demonstrated by the fact that our population has increased steadily over the years. Both types of consciousness have contributed to this success. If our ancestors' primal fear for survival of the body had not dominated when the cougar entered the cave, we would not be here today. If food had not been shared during difficult winters, the clan would not have survived. Our survival required the ability to function both ways.

Neither viewpoint of consciousness is inherently good or bad; both have served humankind. They represent different perspectives on life, and their balanced interaction affects how we *vibrate* and how the rest of the world appears to us. Embracing only the idea that we are all one *being*, while deeply satisfying, can sometimes make functional living very difficult, or even impossible. On the other hand, while believing that we are all separate can sometimes result in great individual efforts and works, it can also lead to deep fear, depression, alienation and desperation. An approach that includes both viewpoints balances and facilitates our lives within this physical realm.

As we explore "unity consciousness," we also discover that our interconnections do not end with the eight billion humans on Earth. As we explore this experience of interconnection more deeply, we quickly discover that we have direct connections to all living things and, deeper still, we uncover our direct vibrational connection to earth, air, water and fire.

A new field in biology is rapidly emerging as we learn more about the human *biome*. Scientists studying the ecology of our human body have discovered that **only 10 percent of the cells found in our body are actually human!** Instead, the vast majority of "our" cells are micro-organisms that have fully co-evolved with our bodies over the millennia. *If only one out of every ten cells in our body is actually human, then who are we? Rather than being a single biological organism we are, instead, a collection of organisms with a cooperative ecology. It turns out that we need these other organisms and their cooperation for many of "our" biological processes. We function more like a forest than an individual animal. If only 10 percent of our cells are human, where does the "I" really live? Even at the level of biological science, the concept of the "separate individual" is rapidly dissolving.*

THE CROSS

Just as my German heritage was a focal issue in my personal search for meaning, the symbol evoked by my family name, Cross, has also been a provocative influence upon my thinking. The cross is a powerful symbol embodied with multiple layers of meaning; the interrelationships of heaven and earth are expressed beautifully in this many-layered, metaphorical form.

In its most common and literal interpretation, the horizontal bar represents the horizon or the earth-bound lifeline of man, while the vertical bar represents our connection to that which lies above, below or within. The vertical bar can also be seen as an expression of the direct connection between earth and the heavens while our earthly horizontal bar sits somewhere between, usually depicted a little closer to the heavens. The cross expresses our earthly connection to the infinite; the central point of intersection, where these two aspects of our lives intersect, is the place where we live our lives with an awareness of both. Anthropomorphically, this point of intersection occurs at the location of our heart.

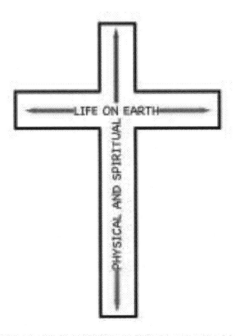

The cross can represent many aspects of dualism. It can represent the meeting of the male and female and the intersection of our lives with both the physical and spiritual.

The cross also can be interpreted as the joining of the male and female principles, with the point of intersection again being in the center, at the heart.

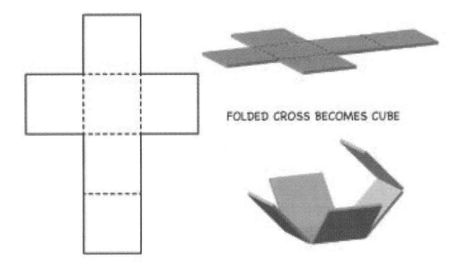

FOLDED CROSS BECOMES CUBE

The cross can be viewed a symbol for accessing the next dimension. Here a two-dimensional cross is folded to become a three-dimensional cube. Salvador Dali explored this relationship in his paintings.

This form can be expressed as six squares, which can then be folded into a cube. Through this manipulation, it functions as a symbol for transition between dimensions because it can be understood as a two-dimensional object that can easily be transformed, or folded, into a three-dimensional form. As a symbol pointing towards extra dimensionality, the cross reminds us of our access and connection to the greater *Multiverse*. Salvador Dali painted the cross in this way, along with other familiar, yet thoughtfully altered, symbols of transition such as his melting clocks and morphing figures. Born the same year that Einstein presented relativity, many of his paintings are designed to evoke thought about the proximity and transparency of the barriers between our 3D conceptual space and what lies beyond.

SURRENDER

Christ was crucified on the cross; shaped like a person with outstretched arms, the cross has a clear, anthropomorphic quality. However, when the form of man is hung from the cross, as during crucifixion, another meaning is revealed. The outstretched arms and hanging body evoke the universal image of complete surrender. With the arms stretched in this gesture, the heart becomes fully exposed, vulnerable and penetrable.

We are taught that Christ surrendered on the cross and then went forth into everlasting life; layers of mystery and symbolism have been used to disguise what is a very simple and straightforward concept. When we open our hearts and surrender our bodies and egos, along with our concept of isolated and separate selves, we then discover our direct connection to everything, including eternity. We also discover that this deep interconnection and eternal life has always been ours.

Life presents all of us with multiple opportunities to experience surrender. For most of us, our initial acts of surrender only came in the wake of complete physical and mental exhaustion, often marking the end of long and difficult struggles. Once we learned other opening techniques, surrender could arrive in more flowing and gentle ways.

The spiritual act of surrender is extraordinarily powerful and almost universally leads to dramatic personal changes: but why is this so? Throughout human history, surrender has always been a catalyst for initiating our opening to that which lies beyond our realm. Within surrender, our individual egos have completely let go of their desire to control outcome. With the defenses of our ego out of the picture, our deeper *being* is able to connect and resonate more freely and naturally throughout the *Multiverse*. This *resonance* opens our hearts, and as we connect in this way with others, we can then experience the profound and ecstatic nature of our deeper *being*.

This ecstatic *resonance* or joy is always available when we make these deep connections, for it is our natural birthright. It is often first experienced by accident, triggered by some type of activity that results in an unexpected and momentary surrender. For some of us, this level of connection was first discovered in our childhood play, while for others it may have had to wait until our first sexual awakenings. Some of us may have needed an orchestrated series of life-changing experiences to trigger such a deep level of surrender.

Once we begin to understand ego surrender and its direct relationship to our joy, we can also more easily observe our ego's automatic desire to control. With further experience and practice we begin to learn how to gently and safely observe, and then eventually quiet, this automatic but fully human response. Through this process we incrementally learn how to lessen our ego's dominant influence, and only then will we find ourselves spending more time immersed in deep awe and ecstasy.

We all become easily trapped by our egos because we have been fully conditioned to think that our egos are who we really are. Almost every part of our contemporary culture teaches this; we are continuously training our egos to believe that they are our only identity. Since one purpose of the ego is to protect our physical form from harm, this misidentification actually serves us quite well much of the time. However, our egos might not feel the need to be so protective if they really understood the deeper truth.

Because our first taste of freedom often happens spontaneously, after a significant or dramatic physical or emotional event, we might be tempted to think that we require major events to break through the ego's control. Extreme physical stress can often trigger the natural response that facilitates this "letting go," and we might find ourselves creating dramatic situations or engaging in risky practices. This form of "seeking" can then manifest as an addiction to specific risky practices that might include bodily harm or disfigurement, extreme or dangerous sexual practices, and daredevil thrill-seeking.

When the body is injured or near death, biological stress will usually initiate an automatic release of natural chemicals that alter our consciousness. If this ego-death release is obtained from these extreme practices, the actual source of the release can be misunderstood. Injuries and trauma release endorphins, adrenaline and other chemicals as part of the natural biological response designed to help us escape or deal with dangerous situations. This change in chemistry then triggers an alternate state of consciousness that is the body's preparation for the "fight or flight" response, or even a preparation for death itself.

Some religious practices include ritual "mortification of the flesh" to help trigger this release. These ceremonies might mimic or recreate the crucifixion of Christ or the suffering of some other well-known martyr. Sometimes these recreations mimic the mythical or historical storyline to shocking detail, and the reenacted martyrdom can include actual physical traumas that trigger this biochemically-induced ecstatic state in the participants. The participants often misunderstand the deeper reasons for the fleeting feeling of freedom that they experience; they miss the realization that their ecstasy was triggered by the release of their egoic control, and not the actual physical acts.

Extreme sports, such as high-speed racing, skydiving, high-wind windsurfing, big-wave surfing, motocross, bungee jumping, slack-lining and others, tend to temporarily alter the consciousness of participants. *Ecstasy and freedom are temporarily experienced because the ego becomes fully occupied with basic survival–it then has little energy or time left for monitoring and controlling being.* The body is also being pumped with adrenaline and other chemicals that alter consciousness to help loosen the ego's tight grip.

Sex is one of the human activities that can naturally lead us to the state of ego surrender. For many of us, sex often led to our first memory of this ecstatic state. Again, because the first such experience is often unexpected and very powerful, we automatically associate this ecstasy with the actual sex, instead of the ego's surrender. Individuals then might experiment with all types of extreme sexual behavior while trying to recreate their first deep state of sexual surrender. We may even expose others and ourselves to great risk and harm in this quest as we repeatedly misunderstand the actual origin of the sensations we seek. *What we are really seeking is simply the surrender of our constant identification with the ego.*

When we surrender during sex, we have also initiated the possibility of a very deep interaction. We open ourselves to the potential merging of our energy field with the energy field of another, and this sets the stage for a profound co-joined state of *being*. Deep tantric sexual union facilitates a conscious merging of two or more souls into a single energy field.

When a direct and powerful sexual interaction finally ends, there is still some degree of residual intermixing between the energy fields, especially if the physical connection is long-term. Each partner is then more able to "feel" aspects of the "other" as if these feelings were their own. Long-term loving couples grow to become more like each other, primarily through the process of "soul exchange" that occurs in *tantric union*. This automatic and subconscious exchange of energy fields is also another good reason for exhibiting great care and sensitivity when choosing potential sexual partners.

Collectively, as a society, we heavily medicate ourselves with drugs—some legal and others not; this medication then reduces our feelings and sensitivity. At the heart of our cultural drug dependence is our desire to reduce our individual suffering through desensitization. We also could be attempting to recreate a old, remembered ecstatic state that was originally induced through drug use. Much of today's drug addiction is either related to our attempts to regain that feeling, or end our suffering. If, in the short term, we are successful with our drug use, it is only because we inadvertently dropped our *identification* with the ego. ***At the deepest level, our excessive cultural drug usage is only our poorly expressed attempt to correct our feelings of separation that result from our misidentification with our egos and bodies.***

While our first taste might be triggered by an accident, drug usage, or some extreme event, healthy and sustainable egoic surrender is always the result of a lifelong process involving growth and expansion. What is really being surrendered is only the resistance that the mind creates, which prevents us from being fully in the flow of our beingness. For our process to become more effective, we must re-invite and encourage the unexamined and repressed parts of ourselves, which are always hidden in our depths. ***The specific invitation is to bring the unconscious fully into the conscious, where the light of our awareness can witness it.*** To do so requires a willingness to be present with whatever we are experiencing, no matter how it appears, and then to accept and embrace whatever we encounter as a beloved part of ourselves, again without any judgment.

FEARFUL BEHAVIOR—LOVING ONESELF

Our most destructive human behavior is always built upon fearful reactions that are formed within what can be understood as *separation consciousness*. This is the state of being where we see ourselves only as isolated individuals competing in a win-or-lose battle for survival. In this state, we make certain types of decisions that are really just unconscious attempts to improve our individual situation or survival chances. These decisions are typically made with little or no attention to the needs of others, and they often are even made at the expense of these others. When we act through fear, our activities often ignore our critical interconnectedness and miss the deeper truth that anything that harms another *being* is really harming the *collective self*.

A thoughtful act of compassion towards another is also a completely selfish act when analyzed through the more-encompassing lens of the deeper truth, since looking out for others is ultimately equivalent to taking care of one's greater *self*. In the *Multiverse*, loving this part of oneself is equivalent to compassionate behavior. Self love is big love.

In a sense, the only real difference between a Hitler and a Gandhi is their level of awareness of the *collective self*. What we classify as evil is only a very inexperienced understanding of the extent of our *being* and our interconnectedness. ***As we expand our awareness, the underlying motive for our actions does not change, for it is always to do what is best for ourselves. It is only our understanding about the extent of our self that changes.*** As we evolve, our sense of *self* expands to include more of "all that is." In this way we can become aware of *Self*–the place within us that we all share. How would Hitler and others like him have acted if they had deeply and fully understood that we are all one *being* and that our fates are inextricably linked? The golden rule, *"Do onto others as you would have them do onto you,"* describes a fundamentally selfish, and yet a fully compassionate, way of *being*.

ENTANGLEMENT MEANS UNITY

One of the most dramatic findings of *quantum physics,* and one that is at the forefront of current research, is the phenomenon that is called *entanglement*. Certain quantum *particles* are typically found in pairs that have a *spin* relationship with each other. If pulled apart, these pairs are found to remain connected; they continue to communicate over vast distances without any lag in time. *Entangled particles* will behave as a unit even if they are placed in different *galaxies*! Einstein was extremely uncomfortable with these findings, which he described as *"spooky action at a distance."*

We have no 3D explanation for this observed behavior, but when we examine the architecture of the multi-dimensional *Multiverse,* we discover multiple possible and logical ways to understand this phenomenon. The simplest explanation is, "We are all always interconnected." Some physicists have taken this idea a step further by proposing, "particles know when the other changes spin because they are really only one thing." These physicists are beginning to sound exactly like gurus; they speak about the possibility that there is only "one thing" in the entire universe!

There is a wonderful *thought experiment* that demonstrates how particles that appear to be different and *entangled* could be only a single particle. Imagine that someone has an aquarium and has set up several video cameras all pointing at a single fish, but from many different angles. The *observers* are not allowed to see the actual aquarium. Instead they only view these images on a series of remote video monitors in another room. What the *observers* see are the several video screens, all showing different views of the same single fish. If these *observers* do not understand the concepts of fish or video cameras, they logically conclude that they are observing several different shaped objects that always move in perfect unison. From their perspective, they are watching several different objects that are somehow interacting or *entangled* with all the others.

Every part of the *Multiverse* is directly, intimately and instantly connected to every other part. We are fully *entangled* with everything in creation. We can't observe these connections directly because the place where these connections are fully visible lies far outside of our *viewport*.

MORE WAVES IN THE OCEAN

Meditating on waves in the ocean evokes another wonderful physical metaphor, which beautifully and simply demonstrates another way that individualization and unity can exist simultaneously. This metaphor was discussed earlier, but now we will take this concept a little further. Each wave exists as an individual physical structure for a brief amount of time but always owes its form to what lies in the depths below. This wave analogy works well for reminding us of the temporary nature of our individualization; waves come and go, rhythmically, and so each wave, for a brief time, appears to have a form and identity of its own. Below lies the ocean, the deep container for the very water that forms this temporary wave. While the ocean is the source of every wave's existence, it is also the place where the waves all melt into undifferentiated oneness. ***The wave is only a short-term physical expression on the visible surface of the ocean. We are the waves and the Multiverse is our ocean. All that we can see and experience from our viewport is the ocean's*** *three-dimensional surface. We are almost completely unaware of the vast interconnected universe that lies in the depths below.*

It is valuable to remember that no matter what the surface of our lives looks like, we are always connected at these deeper levels. To experience this unity, there is nothing we need to do, and nowhere else we need to go because it has always, and only, been available within us. In our busy lives, most of us have intentionally forgotten how to access this part of our *being.* It is forgotten it because it does not serve our ego's own powerful desire to remain in control. However, no matter what is happening on the surface of our lives, we always remain connected to everything below and beyond. This place of connection is our true common home; as we continue to evolve, we will consciously experience this place of deep connection more often.

THE POSSIBILITIES

GRATITUDE, JOY AND ENDLESS POSSIBILITIES

By using the principles of this book for more than 20 years, my life has become firmly anchored in an enduring and resilient peaceful ease that is permeated with joy, gratitude and a deep sense of satisfaction and well-being. Having been raised with a very different set of beliefs, I once saw life very differently and responded accordingly. I believed that if things did not unfold "my way" it was because I was not working hard enough. I used to suffer almost continuously, and many of my thoughts were built upon the idea that I must "fight" harder so I could "win" against what appeared to be an endless series of ever-present problems and "enemies." Often extremely tense and stressed, I saw every injustice as being perpetrated by those that I understood as the others of our world. There were, of course, those days with seeming "victories," but there were also an equal number of setbacks, which I often experienced as "failures." I usually felt that I was losing the "war."

I began to realize that I was always at "war," but it took me half of a lifetime to realize that I was really only at "war" with myself. Today, I understand that my anger, suffering, resistance and fighting only added to the overall resonance of anger, suffering and fighting in our world! I was always operating at the level of struggle, so what I was seeing in my life was always the reflection of this same struggle. That was the nature of my *viewport* because that was my core belief; my *resonant vibrational* signature was formed upon fight and struggle.

I also wrestled with my ego desiring to be seen and recognized by others in my profession, my family and amongst my friends. It took years, but I began to realize that most of this was really an indirect attempt to impress my father. I worked hard to excel at many things, not because they were generating something that I desired or enjoyed, but because "others" would be impressed and this might somehow influence my dad. *One day I had a dramatic and cathartic breakthrough; I discovered that I was still trying to impress my father even though he had died years earlier. This surprising realization caught and focused my full attention!*

I used to learn and absorb information so that one day I could know more about many things. Now I mostly seek to maximize my time in the state of "not knowing," so that I can have new experiences in the moment with a minimum of predetermined conditions. Today, any learning or activity in which I engage is for the intellectual curiosity or the pure joy of learning; this has changed everything about my life.

I now know that through experience and evolution, we will all be able to shape our dance through the *Multiverse*. We will consciously "create" and enjoy worlds more like the ones we "imagine that we imagine" in our most magnificent moments. These peak moments are the times when we fearlessly allow the "flow of life" to move us while simultaneously recognizing that we are all sharing this beautiful and rich experience on Earth together. We exist as part of the "Web of Possibilities" and, as we dance into freedom, we will discover that we have always been able to create any "worlds" that we are fully prepared to envision.

No matter what we each imagine, all of our different "ideal" worlds will coexist without any conflict or problems because every possible expression already has its *resonant* home within the fabric of this amazing Web. Everything that can be imagined by any, and all, of us will always fit together in absolute balance and harmony. This includes all the possible "worlds" that are filled with drama and conflict. In our *Multiverse* there is room for absolutely everything, and it all still fits together perfectly. *The Multiverse has a place for, and responds to, anything and everything we can imagine. The Web is constructed to accommodate our nightmares and our most beautiful dreams. We are here, together, to joyfully weave all of our individual dreams into a single unified tapestry.*

THE GROWTH OF INDIVIDUAL CONSCIOUSNESS

Once we begin to release our fear and other conditioned patterns, a new type of personal space emerges. This new space allows for a much different experience within life. The newly-freed parts of our *being* can make us more childlike, energetic and explorative. This is our natural, unrestricted and optimal way of interacting with our environment. There is nothing we need to do or add to be able to live our lives like this. All that is required is abiding in the *present moment*, letting go of our *misidentification* with our *ego-bodies*, and relaxing the *resistance* within our minds and bodies. It requires only one gesture, a great exhale at the level of our soul–the deepest personal expression of the sound and feeling of "Aaahh." This deep letting go clears the natural pathways, through which the full *resonant self* can then be expressed. As Eckhart Tolle writes *"When consciousness frees itself from its identification with physical and mental forms, it becomes what we may call pure or enlightened consciousness or presence."*

We can't teach ourselves to live this way and we certainly can't make it happen, but it will, instead, happen very naturally when the conditions are right. We can, however, use discipline and our minds to recognize and explore our place of *being*, at those times when we are not living in the *present moment*. We can also use our minds to explore what might be blocking our access to the more flowing way of *being*. As with almost anything in life, over time, conscious practice produces results. Eventually our living within the flow of the present moment can and will become our most natural and ordinary state of being.

Conscious Parenting

New parents often marvel at how quickly and well their children learn. Children absorb information in a uniquely open way, and there is no greater influence on our children than that of those who raise and care for them. We build our identities as we grow and learn, and typically these identities become shaped through our family-centered drama. Many of us then spend most of our adult years trying to figure out how to free ourselves from the enervating constraints of this culturally constructed identity.

If parents have already completed much of their own deconstructive identity work before having children, then their children will naturally learn and model the parents more conscious behavior. Our children do not need guidance to enter into "present moment" awareness because they do this very naturally when they are unburdened by our culture's "hand-me-down" drama and conditional love. If playful yet conscious learning is encouraged during the early development years, this natural, open pattern will tend to prevail for their entire lives.

Of course, until our society as a whole changes, our children will still eventually be exposed to large amounts of cultural baggage through school, friends, movies and our interactive world. If the children have strong loving support for a conscious and playful lifestyle in their homes, much of the outside world's unconscious attempts at imprinting will just seem silly or pointless to the already-free child. At the very least, when these children reach adulthood, their own deconstruction of their drama-infused egos will be a much easier process.

It took me 45 years before I began taking clear steps in my conscious journey towards freedom; today, I am meeting scores of confident and awake children. As they move into adulthood, these children will have a much more direct and enhanced pathway to the soulful life; many of them will enter adulthood relatively free of doubt and essentially fearless. Because they will be interacting with many others like them, the permutations and possibilities for their future are beyond anything we can imagine today.

CONSCIOUS WORK

Most Westerners devote at least half of their waking hours to the generation of income. For many of us, this work is a joyful, life-enhancing adventure. However, for too many others, a vast amount of this time is spent in an enervating state, working at jobs that do not feel "right," and where the only benefit is earning income. It is typical for a large portion of this work-time to be spent earning income needed for unnecessary expenses created by our addictive consumer lifestyle. This is the very same consumer lifestyle advertised in all forms of media as the path to happiness and the cure for our inner dissatisfaction. Ironically, much of our dissatisfaction is created by spending too many hours at a type of work that is not *resonant* with our *being.* This cyclic trap–the snake eating its own head–is only one of many destructive behavioral patterns that have been built into our existing consumer culture.

This "soul-trap" can lead to so much internal suffering that many of us will then resort to additional addictive behaviors in our attempts to dull and ease the resulting pain. Over time, this addictive pattern can then lead to our becoming physically or emotionally unable to do any kind of work at all, and subconsciously this may be our real motivation. This cyclic trap may also become the trigger for our awakening. When we fall into this trap, we have the opportunity to deeply experience the feelings that accompany our choices. This is one way that we continue to learn and grow.

Some of us may design our lives to accumulate great amounts of wealth, sometimes at the expense of others, and always with the primary subconscious goal of insulating ourselves from our pain, suffering and fear of the unknown. While this a culturally approved response, it is not any more effective at mitigating our angst than the "addiction to a substance" choice. Both are attempts to temporarily insulate ourselves from our suffering as we avoid the real examination necessary to illuminate and free our souls.

To break out of this ubiquitous "work to spend" cycle, we each need to examine and reconstruct our life work so it can become more conscious and reflect our individual talents and interests. *An effective first step can be to make some of the changes listed in this book. These changes will help to develop a simple gratefulness for the great gift of life and the opportunity to have this earthly experience. This "attitude of gratitude" immediately makes a tremendous difference in our relationship to our work.* If we have been doing inner work and are partially aware of our old cultural conditioning, this quickly becomes a relatively easy and enjoyable process. As always, understanding and working with the real nature of the *Multiverse* can help free us from the deep fear that keeps us trapped in our self-created lifeless cycles.

TRUSTING OUR INTUITION

Within our western culture, intuition is not generally recognized or accepted as a valuable or useful skill. This may be because we have no scientific methods to measure or explain how intuition works, since it mostly operates outside of our normal three-dimensional, time-ordered realm.

Privately, our use of insight and intuition is quite a different story. Many successful leaders, scientists, business creators and decision-makers have relied heavily on their own trusted intuition. However, they usually kept their methods quite secret, at least until they felt confident and well established or reached that stage in their lives when they could honestly record their memoirs. Having the trust and confidence to follow intuitive insight is often the quality that separates "genius" from the merely competent. At the surface of our culture, we publicly favor hard facts and logic; yet throughout history, intuition has been a critical factor driving and shaping our world. Many of our greatest scientific discoveries began as only an intuitive hunch. An equal number began as accidents that were insightfully recognized as something unusual, interesting or important; these discoveries only became known because there was an astute and trained observer who respected his or her own intuition.

From the perspective of a multi-dimensional universe, our intuition can be understood as nothing more than a slight connection through the veil that limits our awareness of extra-dimensional *information*; when we register a small glimpse of what lies beyond, we call this intuition. Developing our intuition requires nothing more than practicing childlike openness. This ability can be developed and improved by remaining open and available to this subtle process, while at the same time carefully observing the connections between our intuitive hunches and how the three-dimensional world unfolds. Through this practice we will learn when and how to trust our intuitive hunches. To deny the existence or value of intuition is to remove the possibility of it from our life.

Einstein's recognition of the great value of intuition is expressed through this quote, part of which is a popular bumper sticker:

> "I believe in intuition and inspiration. Imagination is more important than knowledge. For knowledge is limited, whereas imagination embraces the entire world, stimulating progress, giving birth to evolution. It is, strictly speaking, a real factor in scientific research."
>
> –*Cosmic Religion: With Other Opinions and Aphorisms* (1931) by Albert Einstein, p. 97; also in *Transformation: Arts, Communication, Environment* (1950) by Harry Holtzman, p. 138.

Then he elaborates even further:

> "There comes a time when the mind takes a higher plane of knowledge but can never prove how it got there. All great discoveries have involved such a leap."
>
> –As quoted in *Future-vision: Ideas, Insights, and Strategies* (1996) by Howard F. Didsbury, p. 104.

However, in our dark interior regions–those places where aspects of our lives remain unexamined–it becomes impossible to tell true intuition from our buried fears and old protective patterns. As we evolve to become open, light illuminates these places within so we can better recognize and trust our intuition. Our intuition can then serve to guide us further into this new way of being.

ATTITUDES WILL CHANGE

Quantum physics has produced an amazing array of practical, real-world inventions and devices, which now completely define our daily lives. Many of the electronic devices that make computers, lasers, GPS and the Internet possible were derived through this new scientific understanding about the interconnected and *probabilistic* nature of the physical world. Our *quantum*-based technical revolution has allowed a sharing and dissemination of *information* unlike any other time in our history, and we are continuing to discover the many new ways that we can use these new tools and technologies to expand and empower our everyday lives.

The last hundred years have brought dramatic and evolutionary changes to our culture. Today, different races and ethnic groups are newly empowered and beginning to claim valuable roles in the creation of our greater world. Race and ethnicity are now largely viewed by many, especially the young, as nothing more than varied and exciting "flavors" that contribute to the full and diverse "taste" of life. The Internet has made the world much smaller and brought us together in new and exciting ways. This technology allows today's youth to have stimulating and meaningful relationships with other young people all around the world. Having been exposed to this new way of thinking since infancy, an entire generation of children lives their lives with a new natural acceptance of alternative lifestyles and cultures. Sexism has largely vanished in the minds of the global youth living in developed nations, as women and those with alternate sexual lifestyles find a voice, greater representation, and far less persecution. Our differences and individual uniqueness are being acknowledged and valued worldwide. The Internet has allowed individuals to produce movies, books and music without the large corporate gatekeepers controlling the process. We are developing a loosely defined but prolific, effective and multifaceted world youth culture that fully embraces and explores their diversity. As this new way of expressing our deep interconnection is being explored on a worldwide basis, it is rapidly changing the way our world works.

The general philosophy of this movement champions every individual's right to pursue her or his own special purpose, while simultaneously recognizing that the entire human race and all of Earth's other creatures function as parts of a greater whole. ***At the core of this new mindset are the beliefs that: we are all ultimately one vibrant being; anything and everything is possible; the world and universe are much bigger and more magical than we could ever imagine; and, most importantly, together we have the power to change the world.***

EVERY POSSIBILITY ALREADY EXISTS

One of the most wonderful realizations gained from our new awareness of the Multiverse is the deepening of our knowledge that anything and everything is possible. Anything we could imagine, anything anyone else could imagine, and anything that is even beyond our imagination is not just possible, it already exists! Every possibility exists now and is woven into the fabulous Web. When we are each open to fully resonate with our dream, this dream can and will appear in our personal viewport. We don't create our world as many alternate or "New Age" philosophies claim; instead, by making ourselves fully available, we discover that it already exists.

BI-LOCATION

INTRODUCTION

Most humans are only conscious of one *viewport* at any one time. However, it has been noted that a few special people seem have been able to operate beyond this standard limitation. A small number of uniquely gifted *beings* have been observed while functioning simultaneously in two or more locations on Earth. Sai Baba and Father Pio, two spiritual leaders who both devoted their lives to helping others, are two, modern, well-documented examples. I do not know what their internal experiences were like, but from the perspective of "others," they were, at least occasionally, observed to be doing their life work of helping "others" from several different, and far removed, physical places at the same time.

SAI BABA

Sai Baba was a well-known Indian saint who transitioned from his physical body while this book was being written. As a two-year-old child he became locally famous for the production of miracles, and this special ability continued throughout his long life. The visible public miracles attracted many followers to his door, but his real work was of a more subtle and transformative nature.

I have a dear friend, now living in Texas, who was originally from India. His mother was a very close personal friend of Sai Baba's, so they often had tea together. One day, 45 years ago, Sai Baba was visiting his mother's home at the same time my friend and two of his friends were driving there for a college break. Only 20 miles from his home, but driving far too fast for the rough conditions, the students swerved right off the steep edge of a winding mountain cliff. By good fortune they were saved from certain death by a group of fortuitously placed boulders. When they finally arrived home, Sai Baba astounded the boys with a complete detailed account of their misadventure. He mentioned that he had helped engineer their fortunate survival and warned them to be more careful in the future. My friend's eyes still grow wide with amazement when he recounts this story.

There are thousands of similar tales about Sai Baba, but this particular story was special for me because it was directly witnessed and related by a sincere and very trusted friend. Countless others have witnessed his more common miracles, such as the spontaneous production of physical objects such as *Vibuthi*, the holy ash that appeared to pour endlessly from his hands. Sai Baba produced a gold ring for another good friend who was sitting two feet in front of the guru. The ring was too small but then Sai Baba blew into it and it fit perfectly. I keep a bit of his *Vibuthi* in my wallet to remind me of the "impossible being possible," although many debunkers believe his endless production of objects to be only a parlor trick.

According to reports from witnesses, on many other occasions his physical body was fully present and visible as he aided them in various locations around the planet, even though he also never left his home and companions in India. He was often still present at his ashram at the exact time he appeared to help someone in a far-away place. One often-recounted story has Sai Baba miraculously appearing in the cockpit of a damaged airplane during a big thunderstorm. He directed the pilot to safely steer his plane through the enormous storm system and the cloud-obscured mountains to find a small, uncharted, level landing field. Neither distance nor time seemed to be factors in his reported ability to bi-locate.

When I lived within a Hindu community in Fiji, most of the locals kept a picture of Sai Baba over their front door, and during difficult times they would ask him for help. It was in Fiji that I first heard the numerous first-hand tales of Sai Baba's remarkable visitations and his unexpected healings at far-away and remote locations. For these believers, the appearance of *Vibuthi* at the threshold below their photographs of him was the clear signal that he had heard their prayers and would intervene.

Sai Baba's main gift, however, was his teachings. A few of these teachings follow:

> "All is one; be alike to everyone."

> "Silence is the only language of the realized. It is only in the depth of silence that the voice of God can be heard."

> "There is bliss and happiness in realizing the unity inherent in diversity."

> "The truth is only yourself, what you see during the day is a day dream."

> "Good and bad, peace and agony, pain and pleasure, all these originate within man and not outside him."

> "The mind is the sole cause for happiness as well as for misery, for bondage or for freedom."

> "The good life is the journey from the position of the 'I' to the position of the 'We."

> "It does not matter if you live in this world, but do not let the world live in you."

FATHER PIO

Father Pio was a well-known Catholic Priest living in Spain who was actively working through both world wars. Well known and respected by many, he was also ridiculed by some for his lifelong *stigmata,* his ability to forecast the future, and his ability to bi-locate. He famously told a young John Paul II that one day, far in the future, he would serve at the very highest level in the Church; when John Paul II became a Cardinal, prior to becoming Pope, many people assumed that Father Pio's prediction had already been realized. During both world wars, there were numerous accounts describing how Father Pio would tend to wounded and dying soldiers in remote battle fields while simultaneously giving mass at his church many hundreds of miles away.

A number of other Catholic priests were also reported to have had this ability. All the recorded stories about bi-location indicate that this phenomenon is, in fact, a fairly common talent shared by a relatively large number of historical religious figures–this particular unusual ability seems to come with the territory.

SIDI BUSCHI

My wife spent time in Morocco 40 years ago. While there, she and her friends stopped their van in a small town and found their way to a local mystic named Sidi Buschi. At some point in their discussion, he excused himself to pray, but he invited them to come back for dinner in a couple of hours. They scattered about town and, while my partner was exploring, she unexpectedly ran into Sidi Buschi several additional times. Since Sidi Buschi had a distinctive and unique appearance, it was impossible to confuse him with anyone else.

The first time she saw him, he was leading a prayer in a cave. He saw her and nodded as they acknowledged each other. She excused herself, and almost immediately saw him again, sitting on top of a wall high above her. Not nearly enough time had passed for him to have physically climbed to that new location from the spot where she had previously seen him. Again they waved and he nodded in full recognition. A little later she walked past a doorway and there he was again, this time leading a large formal supper. Again, there was not enough physical "time" to allow for his transition. She returned to his house later, as planned, only to find that he had finished his prayers and then single handedly prepared a dinner for everyone. At dinner he gave her a knowing nod and smile, but the language barrier, topics raised by others, and the deep enchantment of the moment all diverted her from directly asking him about the events of the afternoon. Other villagers later confirmed that he indeed possessed this unusual ability.

That powerful experience deeply impressed her, and ever since she has spent a great amount of time imagining the various possibilities. Could it have been an intentional trick engineered by a set of twins and the entire community just to impress tourists? This doesn't seem likely because Sidi Buschi never asked them for money or anything material. Having had this direct encounter, today she remains convinced that she saw this single man, Sidi Buschi, somehow expressing himself simultaneously in multiple locations.

In our quantum world where time and space behave very differently from what we assume from our 3D *viewport*, bilocation is not only possible, but also perhaps it even should be expected. I have just recounted stories about three different men belonging to different cultures, who either can dance beyond the edges of our standard worldview or have the skills to appear to do so. As we let go of our fear and deepen our knowing, we may each become aware of an innate ability to express ourselves from more than one three-dimensional location at a time. Like the videos of the fish in the aquarium, we will one day discover that these different expressions are ultimately only different views of the same thing: *Self*.

FUTURE MEMORIES

I have a friend who regularly speaks of "future memories." For most of us, time marches in one direction at a steady clip, so the idea of remembering the future seems impossible and probably even ridiculous. Einstein referred to this unidirectional march of time as *"a stubbornly persistent illusion."* He understood from his work in physics that the true nature of time wasn't at all like our individual experience of it. Lewis Carroll, the 19th-century mathematician and author of *Alice in Wonderland*, had the queen explaining to Alice *"It's a poor sort of memory that only works backwards."* Being a mathematician, Lewis Carroll understood the implications of the new math that was being developed during his lifetime, and his very popular story even predates *Flatland* by about 25 years.

Today's scientists and engineers understand that "time" is completely variable, changing with both *gravitational pull* and *velocity*. Mechanical clocks slow down when they are physically moved into places where *gravity* is more powerful. Clocks deep in mines are closer to the center of the Earth and move more slowly than clocks on the surface, which, in turn, move more slowly than clocks in airplanes. Our GPS systems, which many of us use every day for our navigation, need to have these time adjustments carefully programmed into their mathematical calculations. If they didn't, these devices would be extremely inaccurate and essentially useless. Additionally, as we speed up and travel at higher *velocities*, time also slows down. It is hard to measure this effect at normal car, train and plane velocities, but for the astronauts in the space station who are traveling at 17,000 mph, the difference is clear and measurable. When these astronauts return to Earth, they are found to be younger than they would have been if they had simply stayed on Earth. So today, even in our three-dimensional world, we have concrete examples of how we can manipulate time just by changing *gravity* or *velocity*.

Earlier I presented a model that involved looking out of a train window through a cardboard tube, using it to demonstrate how the past, present and future can all be seen at once. Mathematically, we have known for well over a century that the order in time is rather arbitrary. However, as of today, we have no technical explanation for why our sense of "time" always seems to march in only one direction. Outside of our conceptual paradigm, "time" doesn't actually look or act like this; this relentless march of "time" is a quality particular to our realm. ***Our sense of "time" passing is only an artifact from the way our brains work, meaning that it is a human, three-dimensional concept and not a given rule throughout the Multiverse. One day our future memories will become as ordinary and easy to access as our past memories.***

CHANGING THE PAST THROUGH THE PRESENT

It is clear and obvious to us that things that have happened in the past will have a direct affect upon, or inform, the events of today. Our birth and upbringing were foundational for all we are experiencing right now (including your ability to read and understand this book). If we had dropped out of school, married that other person, or not driven very carefully that one evening, our lives might look very different today. In this same, easy-to-understand, way, things happening right now, today, will affect our future. This time-ordered relationship is natural for us to process because our minds are organized by this kind of one-directional, linear time. In the forward direction, the past-present-future relationship makes perfect rational sense to us.

However, in the mathematics of our multi-dimensional universe there is nothing particularly special or unique about this particular direction for the unfolding of time. A look to the future is the same as a look to the past. If we fully understood time, our technique for changing the direction and rate of our movement through it would likely be very easy and obvious. It might be similar to turning a speeding automobile around on a highway to travel in the other direction at any speed we desired.

There is a really interesting implication to this idea that deserves repetition, contemplation and celebration. ***In our Multiverse, where time is not ordered by marching only forward, the things we do today will affect and inform the future*** <u>and</u> ***the past both–in much the same way! What we do right NOW can and will have a great impact on what we call the PAST.*** A scientist might express this by saying, *"When an event occurs, it sends waves of information that inform both the future and past."*

What might this one change in our understanding about "time" really mean? We have all had the feeling of being really mad or upset at someone for something they "did to us" in the past. Some of us may have had the experience of being able to "let go" and "forgive and forget" after a difficult experience, only to then discover that our feelings about the other people involved had also unexpectedly changed. It is even possible that our feelings about the experience shifted to such a degree that, later, it even began to seem like the event never happened. If the event were only interpersonal, with no remaining physical evidence or damage, then there is one very important question that needs to be asked: If that event exists only in the minds of those involved and if they are able to completely "let go" of their attachments to the event, effectively erasing their personal memory of it, *"did the event ever really happen?"*

Up to this point, this discussion has been limited to a type of conceptual analysis that sits well within our 3D world extents. If we expand this discussion one step further and think about the meaning of "letting go of old memories," using our new awareness of the inner workings of the full multi-dimensional *Multiverse*, we reach an astounding conclusion. It is not only possible, but it is absolutely certain that even events that have lasting physical components can be fully "undone." It is not that the event never happened–this event and its observed effects will still unfold somewhere in the *Multiverse* because all things that can possibly happen will happen somewhere in the *Multiverse*. However, after this shift in our *being*, a new piece of consistent history within the *Multiverse* will now be experienced. From this new *viewport* everything about the event will seem completely different, including the physical outcomes. In many of the possible *viewports* there will be no trace that this event even occurred. ***To change our history, including our past, we only need to move our location within the Multiverse. This is accomplished by changing how we vibrate at our core.***

Because we are born into this culture and history, we all embody, encounter and reinforce all the cultural "blockages" and dark regions that have been brought forward through our remembered history. Today we have the opportunity and privilege of having a form and a level of awareness that allows us to bring light into this darkness and clear these archetypical blockages. We have the ability to do this because we now are learning how the present can "inform" the past. Through this knowledge, we can change our history and clear our differences. ***This is the ultimate human healing and it represents our highest potential for this lifetime. This is our real purpose.*** Our new understanding of both "time" and space makes it completely possible to change our entire history.

LIFE ENHANCEMENT THROUGH MIND

At the rate that new technologies are being developed, we can easily imagine that soon it will be commonplace for humans to expand their functionality and extend their lives by many years. The majority of this work is based on engineering science and technologies, but it is also possible to achieve similar goals through the change of consciousness alone.

Our sense of time is only the product of our brain's organization and, as it turns out, it is relatively easy for individuals to learn how to manipulate their personal experience of time. As discussed in the earlier chapter on time, our internal sense of time's passage can shift so that we each can experience having much more time in our days and lives. From the only perspective that really matters, the internal one, this has the effect of both extending our available time and allowing us to do more, or be more efficient, in a fixed increment of external time. Dr. Olga Kharitidi taught me the effective, but simple, technique of being grateful for the time I have. (I am sure there are many other equally effective methods, some discovered and some yet to be found.) Once we understand and have mastered these techniques, our deepest personal experience will then be the equivalent of life expansion and enhancement.

However, from the outside perspective of an *observer* who is still heavily steeped in linear time, individuals who have learned this conscious method of manipulating time will still appear to age normally. This extra time has been harvested from a different subdivision of time, one that is found outside of our general cultural experience of time–it is not witnessed as just adding more days or years. This means that little will seem different to an outside *observer* unless their personal *viewport* has also changed. Our relationship to time is individual, internal, and fully malleable.

Some might desire to use these techniques to enhance their lives since these methods are simpler, much less expensive and more readily available than the technical, or mechanical, engineered solutions. To achieve any real benefit from this internal expansion of time, we must be very comfortable stepping outside of the standard cultural paradigm. This means that these subtler, life-extension technologies may not be useful for everyone. On the other hand, if a person is already living in freedom, then these techniques can result in exciting new explorations of unlimited, inherent human potential. As with any technology, it always completely depends on how it is used.

EPIGENETICS

Epigenetics is the new biological field that is uncovering how our environment contributes to shaping gene response. Until very recently, scientists believed that our *phenotype,* the physical expression of our genes, was largely determined by our *genotype*, the specific, individual, genetic makeup. It has become clear through the science of *Epigenetics* that the cells in our bodies receive *information* in a manner not unlike the way our TVs receive stations. The genotype is responsible for the actual build of the "television set" (body), but then our bodies become programmed to respond only to certain "channels" of *information*. Over time, our cells gradually become programmed by constantly building new receptors for specific types of chemical, electrical, vibrational and other *information*. These rebuilt cells, fortified with their new receptors, then respond to the environment in very different ways than the original cells. The receptors change as we change our diet, habits, attitude and consciousness.

This is exactly how and why we can become addicted to drugs. Our natural responses to pleasure and pain can be modified through behavior. For example, when we consume any substance, over time our receptors change and our response to that substance will also change. We reconstruct ourselves continuously, and this process is always controlled by our diet, environment and beliefs.

The reconstruction process changes our cells so they have the "memory" of our beliefs, habits and environment built into them. Our beliefs have become physically programmed into the cell walls, themselves, through this buildup of certain receptors. This *cell memory* then controls what chemical *information* can come into or go out of the cell. Organ-transplant patients sometimes find they have memories or habits that are not their own. They may suddenly find themselves enjoying coffee or enjoying scary movies for the first time.

Bruce Lipton is a cellular biologist and author of the groundbreaking book, *The Biology of Belief.* As a cell biologist, Lipton found the prevailing *"DNA determines everything"* paradigm of modern cell biology to be far too limiting. He writes that "In many ways that paradigm was just plain wrong." While discussing the inherent intelligence of cells to control their own destiny, he compares DNA to a house blueprint and the cell itself to the contractor. Ultimately, the contractor determines how the house is built because the blueprint is only the starting point. He describes how the cell membrane is amazingly intelligent and sensitive to numerous environmental factors like the biological and chemical signals that are communicating with the cell constantly. Over time, the cell wall is modified in response to its environment, and thereafter it is this new and rebuilt form that determines the cell's input and output. This rebuilding is dramatically altered by our beliefs and core attitude. What we deeply believe affects our brain and body chemistry, which in turn determines how the cell interprets the genetic blueprint. While this is the process that results in drug addiction and illness, it can also be consciously harnessed for enormous positive change. Our attitude determines how we are rebuilding our bodies and minds in every moment of our lives. The popular movie, *What the Bleep,* also discusses this phenomenon in detail.

Lipton is convinced that *cellular memory* is due to some receptors in the cell picking up additional *information* from "somewhere else"–this *information* or "memory" comes from somewhere other than our brain. He believes that our brains and bodies can become sensitized and tuned to interact with different types of "outside" signals.

The most revolutionary idea of this new realization is that DNA is important for determining our "potential," but environment and beliefs are what really build the cells of our body over time. Over relatively short amounts of time we rebuild almost every cell in our body, so we literally have a natural ability to completely rebuild ourselves in a new and different way.

Some organs replace all their cells every couple of weeks, and other body parts replace almost all their cells over longer lengths of time. For a long time it was believed that our neurons, which are known to be with us from birth, are not replaced. We are now beginning to see signs that this may not be the absolute fact that we once assumed it to be–new examples of *neurogenesis,* or neuron replacement, are being uncovered. It now seems that we have more than just the potential to become what we believe that we are because, within our cells, we have the complete machinery to physically reconstruct every part of ourselves.

The cellular rebuilding process that can lead to drug addiction and chronic physical illnesses can also be harnessed for unlimited positive change. The physical form that we become is ultimately the result of what we think and do! Again, attitude is everything!

EGO AND DIMENSIONAL "CHAKRAS"

As we continue to evolve and learn how to integrate more extra-dimensional awareness, it will not be at the price of leaving or cutting off the experiences of our current, three-dimensional existence. The growth process is one of expansion and addition, as our previous experiences become integrated to become important building blocks for our multi-dimensional awareness.

Some readers will be familiar with the Eastern *chakra* system, which describes our body's seven major *energy* centers. As we explore our chakras, we eventually discover that they each resonate and connect with different emotional and energetic aspects and different physical parts of our body. The *chakras* all work together, in harmony, as a single system contributing to the health and function of our entire *being*. Learning to open your heart chakra does not mean closing down any of your other chakras, but instead, they are opened further so they fully integrate with the heart chakra. For the human *energy* system to function at its best, all seven major chakras need to be open, fully interconnected, and working in unison.

In a similar way, our *being* integrates all of our experiences that are occurring within all 11 (or possibly more) dimensions. Here, in our human realm, we are having our awareness centered in the three-dimensional experience so that we can bring this aspect into our complete inter-dimensional *being.* When pictured from within our three-dimensional perspective, the relationship between all the different dimensions may be thought of as spheres inside of spheres. This can be visualized as nested Russian eggs, with the outer dimensional levels being those that are more comprehensive, so they include all the other dimensions within a single structure. All the dimensional levels fit and integrate together so that no one dimensional realm has a higher or lower level of importance.

Higher or lower dimensions are not better or more advanced, because the vibrant interrelationship of all dimensional levels is critical to the very fabric of existence. They all build and rely upon each other. To say that an 11-dimensional existence is better or more important than the three-dimensional existence is equivalent to saying the roof of a house is better than the foundation. Three-dimensional mastery is a foundation for four-dimensional existence; and it is not abandoned as we expand to operate with an awareness of additional dimensions.

When viewed from a broader perspective, the individual soul's movement through dimensions may also be cyclic in nature, similar to the seasons and almost everything else in nature. We may always be continuously moving our center of consciousness up through additional dimensional levels and then retreating back to the more foundational levels. We may then repeat this journey continuously, in a pulse-like or wave-like manner, as we add new layers to our experience. Much of nature is cyclic and our soul's encounter with different degrees of dimensionality may also naturally follow this pattern. This pulsation or cyclic rhythm may even form a low-frequency "signature" wave for each individual soul, and may contribute to the overall *information-* sharing and connection of *being*, much like a pulsating, cosmic, Morse-Code signal. Just as pulsating, fiber-optic networks communicate vast amounts of computer data, low frequency pulsating "soul signatures" might be *carrier waves* sending *information* in, out, and through different dimensional space. Our individual *carrier frequencies* can possibly represent one of the primary *information* communication mechanisms of *being*. At least this is how it could appear to *beings* viewing this process from a realm that is defined by the "arrow of time."

TIME-TRAVELING PARADOX RESOLVED

Philosophers, writers and scientists have long been concerned about the self-consistency of history if time travel is "permitted." A frequent plot in science fiction centers on the possibility that if someone could go back in time and change the past, the changed history could then become inconstant with recorded history. As an example, if we went back in time knowing what we know now, we could affect many things, including the very events necessary to set up the actual event of our going back in time. What might happen then? This problematic paradox was the central plot in the popular film "Back to the Future." The film's plot was about what might happen if someone traveled back in time and created a situation that prevented their mother and father from meeting– what then becomes of this time traveler? Is he or she ever born? If our traveler was never born, how could he possibly then travel back in time to begin with?

This type of broken history is not "self-consistent." *Some scientists and philosophers argue that this fact alone proves that time travel is not possible because it could result in all sorts of inconsistencies that would then tear holes in the fabric of spacetime.*

In the Multiverse described in this book, there is absolutely no problem or issue with time travel since all possibilities, including all potential outcomes, already exist and are fully interconnected and woven together in a self-consistent manner. Whatever "new" history unfolds, even those generated from actions that appear to be historically disruptive will always have a logical "past" and "future" built right into the *infinite* fabric of the *Multiverse*. The logical and consistent histories for every possibility already exist, and they are all perfectly interwoven. This weave is the heart, the very nature, and the structure of the *Multiverse:* the Web. When our time traveler changes his history, what he is really doing is jumping to another parallel universe within the *Multiverse*. Because of *infinite* nature of this Web, there is no potential for inconsistency with time travel. Not only is time travel possible, the actual mechanism that allows it is already built into the very structure of our *Multiverse*.

As previously discussed, we already "time travel" in at least a few ways through the effects of *gravity* and *velocity,* and through our intuition, precognition, and night-time dreams. Ultimately, we discover that we have no need to do anything special to "time-travel" because we really are doing it all the time. Through our soul's progressive evolution, we are learning how to fully occupy and interact with those parts of our existence that lie far outside of this time-ordered realm.

FREE MOVEMENT THROUGHOUT WEB

One of the most immediate and practical applications of our new understanding about the Architecture of Freedom is our new awareness that we can change our relationship to everything in our universe, effectively changing our world, just by learning how to shift our viewport. We discussed how this can be facilitated with a grateful, open attitude, along with illumination and clearing work that help open the physical and emotional pathways for the unbridled flow of information and Love. If what we encounter in our lives at any moment does not fit our needs, then we have the ability, through this internal process of core vibrational change, to move our consciousness away from that particular energy field. We can then interact with life from a completely different perspective. This is freedom. While this movement theoretically can be dramatic and instantaneous, in actual practice it tends to be a much more gradual process. Because of nature's protective mechanisms, the cultural, biological and individual damping, internal change tends to be slow and incremental. This shifting is always occurring, but we only begin to notice and influence the process once we fully commit to making the necessary changes. *Ironically, this conscious process requires the initial, but critical, step of knowing, accepting and fully embracing those very things and experiences that we want to change within our lives.*

How we each perceive a situation depends entirely on our personal *viewport*. As we better integrate this understanding, we naturally will shift our habits to reflect this new, but constantly evolving, awareness. Once we enter this process, our personal experience begins to naturally adjust. We change, our perception shifts, and the world around us also seems different. *Only one thing has really changed, and that thing is our point of view. The actual world does not change–it is always infinite, containing all things and all possibilities.* That old oak tree that we once always viewed from our side of the fence may look very different when viewed from the neighbor's deck, but it is the same tree– it is just being seen from a different perspective.

A particular region of the Web is never static. All *viewports* are in a constant state of *vibration* and movement. It might be more accurate to think of a Web location or *viewport* as similar to standing on a particular spot on a surfboard–the surfboard itself is always in motion. Our universe is continuously expanding, our galaxy is rotating, the Earth is revolving around the sun as it also rotates, the tide are changing, the wave is moving, and the molecules of the surfboard are always *vibrating*. Everything below is in a state of *vibration* and movement, and all of this movement occurs at a multitude of layers while we are standing on the surface of that surfboard. Even what might appear as a fixed *viewport* is, therefore, always dynamic. The Web is in constant *vibratory* mode and full of *vibrational overtones* formed from the smallest *M-branes* to the biggest *galaxies*. All of creation "sings" in unison and is energized and moved through sympathetic *resonance*. As *string-theory* and *M-theory* describe, this *resonance* manifests as the form of this 3D, material world that we all encounter. From any *viewport*, our relationship to the universe is a continuous, interconnected and tightly interactive dance that spans all dimensions.

Deeply immersed into our three-dimensional culture, it can be difficult to understand how to integrate the exploration of these other realms. We are 3-D specialists who think and reason using concepts that we already understand. Our brains are designed to function well at a level where our primary concerns are about what train to board or how to pay the rent. This specialization is important for our physical existence, but it is also easy for us to become conditioned to just look for quick mechanistic solutions: the airplane to take us away from our concerns, the pill to cure our illness, or the quick riches to solve our financial worries.

A conscious dance through the Multiverse requires a different mindset. It involves a deeply honest and trusting personal journey, a voyage inward towards the very core of our unexplored being. In the beginning, this journey can be absolutely terrifying because the terrain that must be explored includes, by necessity, the very "darkest" within. The truth is that we are already and always successfully traveling through the *Multiverse*, but most of this traveling is not yet conscious. To quote Leonard Cohen's *Anthem* from the album *I'm Your Man*, *"Forget your perfect offering. There is a crack in everything; that is how the light gets in!"*

The great irony, mentioned earlier in this book, is that a fundamental prerequisite for taking the first unassisted steps on our journey towards freedom is a total embrace and acceptance of everything that is presently a part of our world. This includes all the good, the bad and the ugly–everything in life, including death! It is difficult to find the time or courage to honestly examine or embrace our lives at this level–the level of saying "yes" to everything. The good news is that if we can muster the courage and conviction to embark, once we have handled a few of the initial bumps, the road will start to smooth and the mostly unpredictable process of *vibrational* shift will seem to become easier–it may even be seen as a gift. There will always be fresh and unexpected challenges because this is how life works; but we will develop the skill, attitude and methods to move easily through these periodic rough spots. We learn how to flow with life itself in much the same way as Aikido masters work with their opponent's physical momentum.

FREEDOM WHILE STILL IN OUR BODIES

While enjoying our physical realm, we naturally and constantly shift towards those areas of the Web that *resonate* with our current, inner *vibratory* state. Our physical and emotional blockages, in all their various forms, restrict the *amplitude* and limit the *harmonics* of our *resonance*. This regulates the amount and type of "song" or expression and our freedom of movement within the Web. Because of this self-generated *damping* (tethering), most of us find ourselves relating to the world through a *viewport* that is somewhat different from the ideal that we might otherwise imagine or wish for.

Freeing ourselves from these cultural and personal blockages is a continuous, lifelong and living process. This process touches all aspects of our lives, and it is the real purpose of this journey that we call life. As we become hollow beings, many more types of movement within the Web become possible; movement is more natural and flowing because we have become an integrated part of this flow.

In our lives we are constantly presented with choices. *Every movement and every decision can be reduced to a choice between two directions of inner travel and exploration. The choice is always between moving towards more separation or more unity.* Like any relationship that helps to form our duality, neither extreme is necessarily good or bad. They only mark the structural endpoints that bookend everything in-between. This tension allows us to shape our own personal journey, because without these endpoints there would be no road to travel. In our realm, all of life's choices can be reduced to this one choice about the direction of travel along a path that is defined by *separation* and *unity consciousness*.

The key to ease of movement within the Web is non-resistance. *"Go with the flow"* is the popular expression that poetically describes this way of *being*. To be able to more comfortably "go with the flow," we must first clear resistance. To do this, most of our physical, emotional and mental activity needs to be seen for what it really is–egoic activity that constantly creates new blockages and interferes with the free movement, vibration and expression of our *being*. Our egos act like anchors, holding us firmly within the old familiar waters.

When our bodies eventually die, our cultural and personal baggage, including egos, drop away as a natural part of the dying process. Then we automatically fall into our full *resonant* vibratory state. Death creates a more open state that allows for unrestricted flow within the *Multiverse*. As part of the transition through our temporary physical forms, the next expression of *being* is completely determined by the core "song" that is powerfully expressed by the now-liberated and fully *resonant* soul. Without all the layers of resistance that were created by the fears and worries of our egos, our souls become free to *resonate* the clear and energetic expression of this deeper state of *being*.

Many of the world's religions have strong beliefs about the state of your thoughts and emotions at your time of death, and how these have an impact on things such as reincarnation, rebirth or afterlife. These belief systems already understand and incorporate this fundamental and important truth about the way our souls travel within the Web

We compose our "song" through our growth and evolution. This can only occur while we are still in this physical form–while we are living in these bodies. Within this physical form, we always have the ability to allow our *being* live with more freedom–to more easily express its natural *sympathetic resonance*. However, while still living, a type of "death" is required for our free movement–but only the "death" of our resistance; this is also known as "ego death." This kind of "death" is a liberation that can only be achieved while we are still living in our bodies. As we begin to understand and quiet our individual egos, we then learn how to bring our egos back into their most functional and useful role–to be **under our heart's control.** This one adjustment can create an enormous amount of resistance because, to our frightened egos, this change will seem like a radical demotion. Our egos are used to being in charge. To our egos, this type of reorganization will feel as final and dramatic as actual physical death.

Therefore, while death of the body allows a kind of reboot or adjustment, physical death does not create evolutionary growth or change. The process of healing and evolution in the physical realm is only possible while we are living in our bodies. Growth happens when our body ego, the source of all internal resistance, is calmed, dropped or reassigned; and this can happen only when we do our healing or wholeness work in our physical form. ***Once the ego is recognized, understood, tamed and relaxed, our being has more direct access to its natural resonant state. It is while in this connected state that we best contribute our unique part to the greater symphony of life. This can only occur while we are still living in our physical bodies.*** Our physical bodies are the critical instruments for evolution in our present and very important realm. Without our bodies there are no individual "songs" to be sung, and without our "songs" there is no symphony. ***We are here to learn to be free within our bodies, not to be free from our bodies. We are not here to move beyond our bodies, we are here to move deeper into them.***

TOURING THE MULTIVERSE

There is nothing quite like a good vacation. Embarking on a journey to distant lands or a new culture can completely reboot our attitude, while renewing our energy and enthusiasm for life. While we could always visit Chicago, Singapore, Ireland, Fiji or Paris, we also have the potential to travel and visit an infinite number of different and new places within our *Multiverse* without ever leaving our physical neighborhood. Once we are relatively free of *egoic resistance*, we have the potential to consciously tune our *vibration* and adjust or shift our "location" within the *Multiverse*. With practice we may be eventually able to visit many new places without ever leaving our own backyard.

Every small adjustment in our *vibrational being* generates a brand new experience, even if many of the same people and circumstances remain in our life. As we expand through our personal evolution, in every moment we are forming a new *viewport*. From this new perspective we have the opportunity to interact with others in new and different ways, so we constantly discover new and fresh perspectives. Because of our always-changing new and different perspective, all the people and places we visit will also seem different.

It is conceivable that if we learn to live without unconscious resistance, we will one day be able to freely play with our *vibrational signature* and consciously choose what "song" we want to "sing" in every moment. We could learn how to fully control our movement and travels throughout the *Multiverse* in much the same way as we learn to control any new skill, such as playing an instrument or roller skating. When we first begin to develop any new skill, we typically lack control, so our early successes might seem somewhat accidental or random, but gradually, over time and with practice, our performance improves. However, this ability to move more freely about the *Multiverse* will only become available to us once we are fully available. We can only be available after we first discover those places where the "unexamined" is still blocking the natural flow and expression of our *being,* and we complete the growth necessary to discover how we can clear these blockages.

"New Age" writers and speakers often use the term "higher self." While there are no higher or lower aspects of *self* because all aspects equally contribute to the whole, this naming is an acknowledgment that, within us, we all contain many different aspects, vibrational states, or parallel selves that operate at different levels of awareness. When referring to multi-dimensional space, it is misleading to use physical directions as part of the description, since they can only describe three-dimensional concepts. There is no such thing as our higher, lower, sideways, inner, outer, or in-between *self*. All of our aspects are of equal value and contribute to the whole of our *being*. (This is another way of speaking about our other potential *viewports*.) When we access these different parts within, we then relate to those aspects or "parts" of all other *beings* that *vibrate* in *sympathetic resonance* with these new and different "parts" of ourselves! Referring to the paper-plate model discussed earlier, these "parts" are nothing more than the places our "string of *being*" intersects each different plate or "world." They represent our doppelgangers who are simultaneously experiencing other *viewports*.

As we make these shifts, we might discover that some people from our old world are no longer expressed in their old form within our new *viewport*. After the shift our boss may have retired, or that bully who used to terrorize our kids moved out of town. There will always be a "logically consistent" history associated with any and all of these changes because that is one of the most important characteristics of the Web–it all fits together seamlessly. As we learn how to move about the *Multiverse* more freely, we will discover that there is a logically-consistent history for every *parallel experience*.

However, as we evolve even further, we will, one day, also find that letting go of our need for even this "logical consistency" moves us closer to freedom. Logic is a very three-dimensional concept, and these concepts can make it more difficult for us to freely travel within the *Multiverse* while still "living" within our bodies. The brain is the organ that requires this type of logical consistency, and the brain will always remain "time bound." Needing a logical and timely history will, therefore, always limit our possibilities. Miracles are created outside of logic. As long as we rely on logic and consistency, we will automatically be pulled back towards the more familiar and, therefore, more-limited experience.

NO GUILT

Our existing culture has been built upon a deep and widespread foundation of guilt. We are trained well to blame ourselves for the things we did along with things we should have done. We are also trained to feel guilty about our thoughts and our desires, and if all of this weren't enough, the dominant and pervasive corporate media is constantly trying to convince us that we still are not doing the right things, the right way. We are told that we don't take the proper medications, believe in the correct things, tithe enough, buy our children the best toys, own the perfect hybrid car, or live in the right green house. The composite weight of things we are being programmed to feel guilty about is overwhelming. We were also taught that we must accept this guilt because we are human, and that there is little we can do about it except confess and continue to tithe the proper organizations. We are also taught that we will one day be judged harshly and have to pay for all our sins and transgressions and, if we are lucky and behave the "right" way, we may be rewarded–but only after our death.

The Multiverse does not operate this way; there is never an element of judgment entering into any of its processes. Any judgments that we carry are only our own concepts; ideas that have no real purpose within the *Multiverse* other than possibly providing another new opportunity to learn about judgment itself.

In the Multiverse we are always only "who we are" in each and every moment. The past only matters because it informs the present, but since the present also informs the past, our "history" is changed the moment our *vibrational* state changes. In each now moment, there is no past–it is as if it never existed. All that matters is the present expression of *being*. Guilt about our past is only something that our egos generate within our limited, three-dimensional, conceptual minds.

Since we can instantly change who we are at the deepest levels of *being*, from this "moment" of change everything about our lives becomes new and different. After the change we interact with a different part of the *Multiverse* in a brand-new way. Those events that once generated guilt now provide us with more experience and a fresh opportunity to deepen our wisdom and understanding. We learn more about guilt being only a product of the culture in which we were raised. These opportunities to experience and release guilt are important steps on our path to freedom.

Every moment we begin anew, so there is no reason to ever carry old guilt. *We are fully reborn in each and every moment.*

WHAT THIS MEANS TO US

What does this all mean for our families, our friends, our world and us? For most of us this is the only thing that really matters! We all want to know what really happens where the "rubber meets the road."

The bottom-line truth is that everything we can imagine, and so much more, already exists in every combination of forms, shapes, colors, flavors and sizes. Each and every one of us can access and experience any and all of these other realities by expanding our thinking, actions and, eventually, our core being so we then become free to vibrate fully and resonantly within the Multiverse. As we grow to resonate with greater portions of the Multiverse, our view expands, our options multiply, and our birthright of freedom becomes more realized. Today, our conceptual imagination is limited by familiar forms, shapes, colors, flavors and sizes, but at some point in our evolution we will be able to leave even these behind and step into the unimaginable. Evolutionary growth can seem like a long and slow process when experienced from our realm of time, but it is really an instantaneous, timeless and yet eternal process. We all are beginning a new leg of our wonderful and amazing journey towards a new way of experiencing freedom and being. Together we are all becoming Love, One Love.

PART SEVEN–SUMMARY

From within our three-dimensional reference frame, absolute or clear answers to our most profound questions–those about the deeper nature of life–are not fully accessible or expressible. If there are such answers, they must first emerge from realms that lie beyond our present ability to comprehend. From our current *viewport*, we will never really understand or be able to explain creation. It unfolds in levels far beyond the abilities of our best minds, and it is also a living process–creation is always changing because it, too, is constantly evolving.

However, we can still observe, understand and more clearly express what we are not. From careful observation of what we are not, we can then develop a better idea of who and what we are. Combining this awareness of "that which we are not" with my personal life experience and our most recent science, I have assembled a list of suggestions that all point to a new way of living on our planet. This new way of living changes everything about how our lives appear in this realm. These techniques, and others like them, have served my friends, many others, and me in extraordinary ways for many years, and they will continue to serve to help make our lives more purposeful, exciting and joyful. What follows is a re-worded and re-ordered summary of some of the more practical and useful key points from this book.

- *This world, exactly as it appears before us right now, is absolutely perfect. It is perfect because it always precisely reflects our current state of being. It is a flawless mirror.*

- *We live in a three-dimensional, conceptual reference frame, which we call our universe. Our frame of reference naturally limits the extent of our interaction with the much more comprehensive, interactive and infinite extent that we call the Multiverse. The Multiverse is more expansive than we could ever imagine and the vast majority of it lies far beyond our senses, instruments and comprehension. At this stage in our evolution, we do not possess the conceptual tools to even begin to understand its true depths.*

- *The three-dimensional space that we occupy is only one sub-level of our Multiverse, which is constructed from at least 11 dimensions. All dimensional levels are completely interrelated and functional parts of the whole, and there is no hierarchy or order of importance between dimensional levels. Every part of the Multiverse is equally important and necessary, including our familiar three-dimensional realm.*

- *We have generally been unable to see, experience or understand what lies beyond our three-dimensional conceptual space. We live in a kind of "dimensional fog" or veil. This is not really a limitation because it serves us well. It allows us to focus on our present purpose and work.*

- *All of us have occasional occurrences in our lives that at least partially penetrate this fog. These experiences allow us to have a fleeting sense of what lies beyond.*

- *At least 99 percent of our physical, three-dimensional universe within our "cosmic horizon" can't be seen directly with our eyes or instruments. Even "empty" space has mass, and almost all the mass of the universe that we can measure is found in this "empty" space. Scientists have no real idea what this is, and why it is there! This means that most of the physical universe that we pretend to know and understand is completely mysterious to us.*

- *Everything that we see or experience in our three-dimensional world is just the "shadow" cast from other dimensions beyond. None of what we experience is solid or real. Thinking of our world as a dream is much closer to the truth.*

- *Everything in the physical universe can be reduced to a discussion about the movement of energy in some form. Matter is only energy that is being expressed in a different form.*

- *Time, as we understand it, does not really exist at all. We only need the concept of time to help organize our thinking brains.*

- *Everything, which did happen, could have ever happened, is happening right now, or could happen in the future, already exists right now at this precise moment within the infinitely and intimately-woven fabric of the Multiverse.*

- *Every possibility is always present and available to us as a "cloud of possibilities." Anything can happen. Absolutely anything! Our presence, focus, thoughts, attention, and our resulting core vibration causes this "cloud" to "solidify" around one of these realities. Only then does the potential outcome suddenly appear as "real." The deeper truth is that this expressed outcome is no more real than any other possibility.*

- *The entire Multiverse is fundamentally built from vibration. The expression of form as we understand it, is secondary.*

- *At our deepest place, the source of our individual being, there resonates a beautiful vibrational "song." Our lives are vibratory symphonies resonating through many dimensions. We all play our individual parts within a grand orchestra that produces the greater symphony of life.*

- *Our fundamental individual and cultural vibratory "song" determines what part of the infinite universe we interact with in any moment. What we see and experience is entirely determined by how we vibrate, which is always only a reflection of who we are at that moment. If we change how we resonate by changing our deep core thoughts and beliefs, especially those parts that are still "dark" within the subconscious, the outside world is then seen from a different perspective, so it also appears to completely change.* We can only change the world by changing ourselves.

- *Thoughts by themselves are not enough to create this change or movement. To change our world, there needs to be a deeper shift at the level of our resonant core vibration, or our personal, inner "song of life." Although this process of deep change can begin with a thought, this type of change cannot be achieved at the level of thinking.*

- *Our life purpose is to gain experience so we may evolve to understand and embrace "all that is," and thus discover that all "this" is ultimately who we really are. We learn most deeply through direct experience. All types of human experience are necessary for the completion of this purpose.*

- *We can always influence the appearance of our reality, for at some level we do "create it" by shifting our viewport with every thought, breath and feeling! Every personal experience is the direct result of the natural expression of our core vibrational state. As we evolve and drop resistance, the universe does not change, but our experience of it does.*

- *Each of us, everyone else and everything else, exists in an infinite number of "parallel worlds" simultaneously. Because of the way space, time and consciousness work, we are usually only aware, or think we are only aware, of one of these existences. All these different "selves" are fully connected and continuously share information. This exchange of information between all "selves" and things in the Multiverse is instantaneous.*

- *These universes can be thought of as being stacked so that identical or similar universes are always directly adjacent and accessible–they seem to blend with each other. All universes, even very different parallel ones, are intimately interconnected. This quality, where all parts of multi-dimensional space are always directly adjacent to every other part, is called enfoldment.*

- *All the information about the Multiverse and everything in it is stored holographically. This means that the complete information describing everything is expressed everywhere and is instantly accessible. The interconnectedness of everything in the Multiverse is absolute.*

- *We are able to travel between these parallel universes, and we continuously and constantly do. Most of these "other" universes we visit are so similar that we usually don't notice any difference unless we pay very close attention!*

- *As we dance through these different but always-adjacent universes, over "time" we may notice that the "outside" world that we experience has changed or shifted in some way. The universe that we are experiencing right now is not the same as the one we existed in earlier in the day. Some of the players and scenes may have changed.*

- *All things have the quality of beingness! This beingness is communicated through vibration. At some deeper level that exists beyond our conceptual horizon, all beings and things are fully connected. At another, even deeper level, everything is only "one"! At this level we are all aspects of this single "Being." At the very deepest level of existence there isn't even a "one" for ultimately there is "No-Thing," which is forever birthing the Multiverse and all that it contains.*

- *Our full embrace of everything in existence, including the good, the bad, the happy, the sad, the saint and the sinner, is a necessary, life-changing and world-changing step along our personal path of spiritual growth. Pushing anything away, especially the unpleasant, creates a reaction that makes it more powerful, and its effects become even greater. Instead if we pull it in, accept it, forgive it, and Love it–then we will heal it as we heal our self and our world. The key to transformation is to integrate rather than segregate. We grow by expansion, not exclusion. This is our most direct pathway to freedom.*

- *In the Multiverse, there is no such thing as death. Death is a time-based phenomenon. Time is not real in any absolute sense because time is only a human concept. If "time" isn't real, what becomes of that moment in "time" that we call death? Death is also form-based, and we now understand that form is also not real. Form is only what our experience of a deeper truth looks like as it passes through our 3D realm.*

- *When we "die," we drop our physical bodies along with all the physical blocks that have been accumulated through our egoic bodies. Our soul will then naturally and freely flow through the Web to its perfect resonant place in the Multiverse. We will organically manifest the existence that best matches our natural resonance at that moment. The closing door of one existence is also the welcoming door of the next.*

343

- *Our new existence will always be an accurate reflection of how we resonate deep within at any and every moment. In fact, everything that we see and experience is always only a reflection of what and where we are within our own process of evolution. Knowing and trusting this is a key to freedom.*

- *Everything we experience adds to our being and the greater Being. No matter how any experience looks or feels in the moment, it is always a positive experience for our growth and evolution. This even includes those events that our body does not survive.*

- *Within our dimensional level, our physical form is required for the work of change. At our stage of development, growth and evolution only occur through our physical form because certain types of evolutionary growth can only happen in this realm of 3D form. The work we do in our bodies is critical to the greater evolution of Being. Our 3D realm is a wonderful gristmill for our collective soul.*

- *Once we become comfortable with how all this works, much more dramatic shifts can occur, and we can begin to play more freely with our beingness; and we can do this while we are still in our bodies! This is great fun!*

- *The world we see as "out there" is interpreted entirely through the filtering created by our viewpoint, which can be called our viewport. When we change our viewport, this "out there" also changes. This is the only effective way to change how the external world appears.*

- *There is no point in trying to change the behavior of "others." In the physical realm, "others" will only change when they are ready! Besides, at deeper levels of existence, there are no "others." We only need to change ourselves to change how all these "others" appear to us.*

- *Everything we are experiencing right now is from our personal perspective. It is always subjective because it is filtered, processed and then remembered by our minds. It is our story! There is no such thing as an objective story at the three-dimensional level of human expression!*

- *We only see what we are prepared experience. We change "our world" only by expanding the scope of what we are prepared to experience. We do this by discovering, embracing, healing and integrating all that we resist.*

- *From our perspective, our journey towards Truth is gradual and evolving. What is true for us today will not necessarily be true tomorrow. As our perspective or viewport changes, so does our truth. In our realm, everything is impermanent–even the truths. If we hold on to a relative truth beyond its usefulness, it then becomes an anchor that prevents us from growing or evolving. Being able to shed old ideas and being open to new levels of truth are important to our ability to dance freely within the Web.*

- *If we do what feels "right" in every moment, our lives will unfold beautifully and fluidly because of the geometry of the Multiverse. Discerning true feelings from our old, habitual, fearful and self-destructive response is our contribution to this process. Clearing the shadows and fearful blocks is where we all must start. Only then can our own feelings become our most trusted advisors.*

- *We each create our unique but constantly shifting perspective within the Multiverse through birth, death, living and thinking, interacting, vibrating and being. If we don't like what we see, we can change it through a process that begins with examination of our core beliefs, fears, resistances and deep inner thinking. We need to remember to fully embrace whatever we are experiencing in each and every "right now" because it is always fully resonant with who and what we are in that moment. Through this work, our inner resonance will change and, subsequently, our experience of the universe will change.*

- *In the end there is really nothing to do except to be consciously aware of the "present moment" without any resistance; become a hollow being. Watch, observe and be a passerby; love, compassion, freedom and a peaceful joy naturally follow!*

- *At some level we are all one, so living life with this awareness helps make life more fluid and joyful. It is important to realize that we are always connected at this deep level, no matter what the surface of our lives may look like.*

- *Fear is a human concept that prevents us from experiencing the flow of eternal and ever-present Love. If we are fearful, we cannot be free. Fear is the opposite of Freedom.*

- *As long as we identify with our physical form, we will embody fear. When we come to understand that we are not our bodies–that we are so much more than these bodies–then the fear spontaneously evaporates. Once we learn that we can fully occupy these bodies without identifying with them, we can begin to live our lives to their maximum potential. Only then can spirit fully express itself.*

- *Love always "is." Love is the sea that we dwell within. Love is a place of connection that we can always visit. Love has no opposite. We don't give or share love. Instead, we open ourselves to be within the Love that is always and everywhere present.*

- *Freedom means no longer identifying with our body and ego because we recognize the temporary, illusionary nature of our form.*

- *The deepest expression of Love is to live fully and express our uniqueness without any internal resistance.*

CLOSING

Having lived a very full life, now I can look back and reflect on how far I have come. I always had a strong desire to experience, touch and understand everything in our world and I have tried my best to accomplish this. Along the way I unexpectedly found that for every new experience that I was able to understand, I discovered greater parts that were strange, new and untouchable; with all my explorations, the mystery only grew. I was learning all about my single small piece of the jig-saw puzzle, only to discover that my small piece was only a tiny part of a far greater puzzle.

As we explored and evolved, we learned more about ourselves and our special relationship to the universe; we also inadvertently discovered that those unknown parts of creation have actually expanded to become, by far, the most dominant component of our vision. Not only does this vast unknown represent an enormous void in our understanding, but this large portion also seems to grow exponentially every time we expand our vision.

We now know that the *Multiverse* can never be understood or explained using the language of our minds; relying on structural relationships that exist beyond our three-dimensional universe, it is far too *infinite* to be contained by our limited concepts or words. Any "thinking" about it will only lead to misconceptions; this book, which must be built upon thoughts and words, may even encourage some of these misconceptions. Our "ideas" about this expanse can never be accurate and these ideas can even become limiting concepts that bind us to this realm and restrict our freedom; our words and concepts, at best, can only be pointers that help guide us towards a greater truth.

Our brains function by building upon that which we already understand. Because the Multiverse is so far outside of our conceptual space, any direct comparison to known things and ideas will always miss the mark; often it is more effective to demonstrate what the Multiverse is not. I had to rely on our familiar ideas to build my models, but these only provide hints to help us understand small aspects of the vast unknown. However, just becoming aware that we are not presently capable of comprehending the full *Multiverse* is a significant realization; one that helps us to begin to let go of our confining need to "understand." It is only from remaining open to these other possibilities that we can begin to glimpse this ever-evolving greater truth.

As we continue to let go of old concepts and open to our *infinite* possibilities, we will discover many new ways to explore, occupy and enjoy our ever-evolving and expansive *Multiverse*. This evolutionarily expansive journey of our amazing collective *Being* has always been, and will always be, our ultimate destiny.

RESOURCES
Please feel free to recommend other resources.

PHYSICS, MATH AND QUANTUM PHYSICS

Albert Einstein
Essays in Physics
1950, Philosophical Library

Out of My Later Years
1956, Citadel Press

Joseph Schwartz and Michael McGuiness
Einstein for Beginners
1979, Pantheon Books

Francis S. Collins, head of Human Genome Project
The Language of God
2006, Free Press

Brian Greene
The Elegant Universe: Superstrings, Hidden Dimension, and the Quest for the Ultimate Theory

The Fabric of the Cosmos: Space, Time and the Texture of Reality
2004, Knopf

The Hidden Reality: Parallel Universes and the Deep Laws of the Cosmos
2011, Alfred A. Knopf

Michio Kaku
Beyond Einstein
1997, Oxford University Press

Visions
1999, Oxford University Press

Hyperspace
1994, Oxford University Press

Timothy Ferris
The Whole Shebang: A State of the Universe(s) Report
1997, Simon and Schuster

Bertrand Russell
The ABC of Relativity
1958, George Allen

Lawrence Krauss
Lecture "A Universe from Nothing"
You-Tube

ASTRONOMY AND COSMOLOGY

William J. Kaufmann, III
Discovering the Universe
1987, W.H Freeman and Company

Carl Sagan
Cosmos
1980, Random House

ANTHROPOLOGY

Robert Ardrey
African Genesis
1961, Macmillan

Territorial Imperative
1966, Kodansha Globe

META PHYSICS

Fritjof Capra
The Tao of Physics
1975, Bantam Books

The Web of Life
1996, Anchor Books-Doubleday

The Turning Point
1982, Bantam Books
Movie titled "Mindwalk" directed by Bernt Capra

David Darling
Equations of Eternity
1993, Hyperion

Frank J Tipler
The Physics of Immortality
1994, Doubleday

Frank Wilczek with Betsy Devine
Longing For the Harmonies
1987 W.W. Norton Co.

Fred Alan Wolf Ph.D.
Many books, including:

The Dreaming Universe
1994, Simon and Schuster

Eagle's Quest
1991, Touchstone-Simon and Schuster

Parallel Universes
1988, Touchstone

Paul Davies
Many books, including:

Are We Alone
1995, Orion Publications

The Mind of God
1992, Orion Productions

Space and Time in the Modern Universe
1977, Cambridge University Press

PHILOSOPHY OF SCIENCE

Gary Zukav
The Seat of the Soul
1989, Fireside

The Dancing Wu Li Masters
1979, Bantam

Robert M Pirsig
Zen and the Art of Motorcycle Maintenance
1974, Bantam

Ken Wilber
A Brief History of Everything
1996, Shambahla

The Holographic Paradigm
1982, New Science Library

Eugene Pascal Ph.L.
Jung to Live By
1992, Warner Books

Krista Tippett -Interviews
Einstein's God-Conversations about Science and the Human Spirit
2010, Penguin

Steve McIntosh
Integral Consciousness
2007, Paragon House

PSYCHOLOGY

Stanislav Grof M.D.
The Holotropic Mind: Three Levels of Human Consciousness
1993, Harper-San Francisco

Brian L. Weiss M.D.
Same Soul, Many Bodies
2004, Free Press

Many Lives, Many Masters
1988, Simon and Schuster

Only Love Is Real
1997, Grand Central Publishing

RESEARCH SCIENCE

Rollin McCraty, Ph.D., Executive Vice President and Director
The Institute of HeartMath
Numerous research papers
Quoted in Movie "I Am"

Lewis Thomas
The Lives of a Cell
1974, Viking Press

J. Konrad Stettbascher
Making Sense of Suffering
1993, Meridian

MUSIC

Robert Jourdain
Music, the Brain and Ecstasy
1997, Bard Press

Daniel J. Levitin
This Is Your Brain on Music
2006, Plume

FICTION

Edwin A Abbott
Flatland
1952, Dover Publications

Michael Murphy
Golf in the Kingdom
199,7 Arkana

Jacob Atabet
1977, Jeremy P. Thacher

NON-FICTION

Carol Riddell
The Findhorn Community
1990, Findhorn Press

Elizabeth Gilbert
Eat, Pray, Love
2007, Penguin Books

POETRY AND ART

Kahlil Gibran
Between Morning and Light
1972, Philosophical Library

The Prophet
1923, Alfred A Knopf

SPIRITUALITY AND RELIGION

Western

Elaine Pagels
The Gnostic Gospels
1979, Vintage Books

Michael Wise, Martin Abegg Jr. and Edward Cook, editors and translators
Dead Sea Scrolls
1996, Harper: San Francisco

James M. Robinson, editor
The Nag Hammadi Library
1978, Harper and Row

Stephan A Hoeller
Jung and the Lost Gospels: *Insights into the Dead Sea Scrolls*
1989, The Theosophical Publishing House

Kyriacos C. Markides
Riding with the Lion:The Search of Mystical Christianity
1995, Penguin

Mathew Fox
One River, Many Wells
2000, Tarcher/Putnam

The Coming of the Cosmic Christ
1988, Harper Collins

Rupert Sheldrake with Matthew Fox
The Physics of Angels: Where Science and Spirit Meet
1996, Harper: San Francisco

Eckhart Tolle
The Power of Now
1999, New World Library

The New Earth: Awakening to Your Life's Purpose
2005, Dutton Publishing

Anthony deMello
Awareness
1990, Doubleday

The Way of Love: The Last Meditations of Anthony deMello
1991, Doubleday

William Dych. S.J., editor
Anthony DeMello writings
1999, Orbis Books

Edward Conze, editor and translator
Buddhist Scriptures
1959, Penguin Books

Jack Kornfield
After the Ecstasy, the Laundry: How the Heart Grows Wise on the Spiritual Path
2000, Bantum

Stephen Mitchell, editor
The Enlightened Heart, sacred poetry
1989, Harper and Row

Paul Ferrini
Reflections of the Christ Mind
2000, Doubleday

Nicole Gausseron
The Little Notebook: *The Journal of a Contemporary Woman's Encounters with Jesus*
1995, Harper San Francisco

Joan Borysenko Ph.D.
The Ways of the Mystic: 7 Paths to God
1997, Hay House

Sam Keen
To a Dancing God
1970, Harper

Helen Schucman and William Thetford
A Course in Miracles
1975, Foundation for Inner Peace

Eastern

Thich Nhat Hanh
Peace Is in Every Step:The Path of Mindfulness in Everyday Life
1991, Bantam

Swami Prabhavananda and Christopher Isherwood, editors and translators
How to Know God: the Yoga Aphorisms of Patanjali
1953 & 1981,Vendanta Press

Christopher Isherwood
Vendanta for the Western World
1945, Vendata Society of Southern California

Paramahansa Yogananda
The Autobiography of a Yogi
1946, Self-Realization Fellowship

J. Krishnamurti
Krishnamurti's Journal
1982, Harper and Row

Think on These Things
1981, Harper One

You Are the World
2001, Krishnamurti Foundation

Freedom from the Known
1975, Harper Colins

Stuart Holroyd
Krishnamurti: The Man the Mystery & the Message
1991, Element

Lao Tzu
Tao Te Ching
1997, Wordsworth Editions

Birgitte Rodriguez
Glimpses of the Divine: Working with the Teachings of Sai Baba
1993, Samuel Weiser

Howard Murphet
Sai Baba Man of Miracles
1971, Samuel Weiser Inc.

Ramana Maharshi
The Spiritual Teaching of Ramana Maharshi
1972, Shambala Publications

Kahil Gibran
The Prophet
1979, Alfred A. Knopf

The Voice of the Master
1958, Bantam

Satyam Nadeen
From Onions to Pearls: A Journal of Awakening and Deliverance
1996, Hay House

From Seekers to Finders
2000, Hay House

Gopi Krishna
Living With Kundalini: The Autobiography of Gopi Krishna
1993, Shambahla

Paul Lowe
In Each Moment: A New Way to Live
1998, Looking-Glass Press

The Experiment Is Over
1989, New York

Shri Nisargadatta Maharaj
I Am That
1982, Acorn Press

Ram Dass
Be Here Now
1971, Lama Foundation

Still Here
2000, Riverhead Books

The Path of Service, audio book
1990, Sounds True Recordings

Bubba Free John
The Knee of Listening
1972, Dawn Horse Press

Nirmala-Daniel Erway
Nothing Personal: Seeing Beyond the Illusion of a Separate Self
2001, Endless Satsang Press

Sri H.W.L. Poonja-Papaji
THIS: Prose and Poetry of Dancing Emptiness
2000, Samuel Weiser

Eli Jaxon-Bear, editor
Wake Up and Roar: Satsang with H.W.L. Poonja
1992, Gangaji Foundation

Thomas Byrom
The Heart of Awareness: A Translation of the Ashtavakra Gita
1990, Shambhala

CROP CIRCLES

Freddy Silva
Secrets in the Fields
2002, Hampton Roads

Steve and Karen Alexander
Crop Circles, Signs, Wonders and Mysteries
2006, Arcturus Publishing
Website-www.temporarytemples.co.uk

PHILOSOPHY

Immanuel Kant
Observations on the Feeling of the Beautiful and Sublime
1764

Pain and Healing Philosophy

Deepak Chopra M.D.
Ageless Body, Timeless Mind
1998, Harmony Books

Quantum Healing
1989, Bantam Books

+ many others: one of the most trusted and informed writers about alternative healing

David Deida
Enlightened Sex: Finding Freedom and Fullness Through Sexual Union
Audio book
2004, Sounds True

Bill Moyers
Healing and the Mind
1993, Doubleday

Andrew Weil M.D.
Spontaneous Healing
1995, Knopf

Michael J. Tamura
You Are the Answer
2002, Star of Peace Publishing

Jill Bolte Taylor
My Stroke of Insight
2008, Penguin

Larry Dossey MD
Meaning & Medicine
1991, Bantam

Reinventing Medicine
1999, Harper

Space, Time & Medicine
1982, Shambhala

Beyond Illness
1984, New Science Library

HEALING SELF-HELP

Louise L. Hay
You Can Heal Yourself
1984, Hay House

W. Brugh Joy M.D.
Joy's Way, A Map for the Transformational Journey: An Introduction to Potentials of Healing with Body Energy
1979, Tarcher Putnam

Thorwald Dethlefsen and Rudiger Dahlke M.D.
The Healing Power of Illness
1990, Element Books

HEALING SELF-HELP THERAPY

Chris Jarmey and John Tindall
Acupressure
1991, Gaia Books, London

Ben E. Benjamin, Ph.D.
Listen to Your Pain
1984, Penguin

Barbara and Kevin Kunz
Complete Reflexology for Life
2007, DK Publishing

Bonnie Prudden
Pain Erasure
1980, Ballantine Books

Moshe Feldenkrais
Awareness Through Movement
1972, Harper San Francisco

Pete Egoscue
Pain Free
1998, Bantam

MODERN SPIRITUAL SELF-HELP

Marianne Williamson
A Return to Love
1992, Harper Collins

Neale Donald Walsch
Conversations with God (3 Volumes)
1995, G.P. Putnam's Sons

Rhonda Byrne
The Secret
2006, Atria Books

Gary R. Renard
The Disappearance of the Universe
200,2 Hay House

Charlotte Kasl, Ph.D.
If the Buddha Married: *Creating Enduring Relationships on a Spiritual Path*
2001, Penguin Compass

SHAMANISTIC BOOKS

Michael Harner
The Way of the Shaman
1980, Harper San Francisco

Olga Kharitidi, MD.
Entering the Circle
1996, Harper San Francisco

Sandra Ingerman
Soul Retrieval
1991, Harper Press

TECHNOLOGIES AND WORKSHOPS

Richard Bartlett, DC, ND
Matrix Technology: The Physics of Miracles
1990, Atria (Simon and Schuster)

Michael Brown
The Presence Process: A Journey into Present Moment Awareness
2005, Beaufort Books

Betty Edwards
Drawing on the Right Side of the Brain
workshops and a book
1979, Penguin Books

MOVIES

Tom Shadyac
I Am
2011, Shady Acres Entertainment

Rhonda Byrne
The Secret
2006, Prime Time Productions

William Arntz, Betsy Chase, Mark Vecente
What the Bleep
2004, Roadside Attractions

Bernt Capra
Mindwalk
1981, New Yorker Films

Louis Malle

1981, New Yorker Films

ONGOING MEETING PLACES FOUND IN AUSTIN, TEXAS

Ecstatic Dance Austin
507 Calles, Austin Texas 78702
www.ecstaticdanceaustin.net

Austin Body Choir
www.Bodychoir.org

Five Rhythms-Gabriel Roth
Various cities around country

Contact Improv
Various locations throughout country

Nia Space
Dance, Therapy and Workout
Various Locations around country

Casa de Luz
Macrobiotic Community Center and Meeting Place
1701 Toomey Rd. Austin Tx. 78704
512-476-2535
www.casadeluz.org

Amala Foundation
Transformational Programs and Service
1006 S. 8th St. Austin, Tx. 78704
512-476-8884
info@amalyfoundation.org

ABOUT THE AUTHOR

Tim Cross is a residential and light-commercial architect who has been practicing building design and construction in Austin, Texas since 1980. He is also a trained ecologist. Before turning his attention to architecture, he taught high school physics and worked in the field of environmental science. He served in the Peace Corps and then in the late 1970s as the Environmental Advisor to the Government of Fiji. However, throughout all his adventures, his primary passion has always been to learn as much as possible about this amazing experience called life. This book began as a simple letter to his two daughters, but quickly grew into something unexpected.

Though Tim is an architect, this is not a book about architecture. It is, instead, a book about personal and cultural freedom and how the actual architecture of our universe fully supports our journey towards freedom. He defines freedom as letting go of those things in our lives that block us from experiencing our birthright, which is living fully within the flow of this infinite creation that is shaped and interconnected by Love. He is at a place in his life where his only remaining desire is to allow his experience of Love to deepen. The Architecture of Freedom is his personal journal, describing what he has learned about living in this universe.

Comments or corrections to:
tim@thearchitectureoffreedom.com

BOOK DESCRIPTION-

Do you wonder about the way your life appears? Are you looking for a way to dramatically change your life? Have you tried to change many times only to find that over time you always revert to old patterns?

"The Architecture of Freedom" is full of fresh insights that are designed to help create a more permanent type of change. Exploring modern physics, personal experience, and spirituality, this book outlines a radically different way of understanding our lives, our universe and our being. While not a quick read or easy fix, once understood, the ideas in this book will forever change your life.

Whether or not we are aware of it, what the majority of us most desire is peace of mind in each and every moment. This experience becomes available to all of us when we learn how to live our lives without "resistance" so that we can then use our unique gifts to follow our most personal and joyful path. Due to our deeply held fears, we all create "resistance" to the natural and organic flow that would otherwise effortlessly move our lives. Near the root of these fears is the fear that we will one day die and then cease to exist. However, because of the way our universe is built, this fear of death is completely unfounded. "The Architecture of Freedom" explains why death, or our passing into a state of nonexistence, is impossible.

Freedom is living our lives without this fear or "resistance," so that we are fully available for all the amazing possibilities that then will begin to flow forth. Learning to live this way is about learning how to live in the "present moment" or "now." When we live fearless lives in the "now," we become directly connected to a different and amazing way of being–our birthright. In this way we access the deeper parts of our being to share a type of universal awareness that is healing for each individual and for our entire planet.

Imagine a universe where everything is possible and every idea is fully realized. Everything–all that we consider good or bad, saintly or evil, beautiful or ugly–already exists along with anything else that any person or being could ever dream or imagine. What if you could choose from all of these things to construct your perfect life? Amazingly, this is much closer to the true form of creation than the world that we usually imagine. All of these possibilities are happening at once and we all have the ability to choose which parts of this "everything" that we will experience. We cannot choose using our brains or even our minds; instead, we choose with the entirety of our vibrational being. It is not easy for us to understand this type of choosing because so much of our universe exists and operates in realms that we can't directly access with our minds or five senses. Even though we don't have full access to the full extent of this amazing space, it is always fully interactive with our lives–it helps create everything that we do and experience.

A large part of life's beauty derives from this mystery, which only exists because, in our present form, we are not yet capable of understanding the infinite nature of creation. If we could understand the full extent of creation, we would see clearly that we are all one being, that time is an illusion, that we never will die, and that everything that happens is exactly perfect for the evolution of our soul. We are not here to understand creation–that is not our purpose. We are here to gain experience by fearlessly participating in every aspect of life and living our lives fully. This is true freedom.

Understanding more about the real structure of creation can help eliminate many of our common fears; it is these fears that prevent us from living our lives in freedom. I have devoted a large part of my life to exploring the nearest, and occasionally visible, edges of this truth. This book describes my personal adventure and the process that brought me to this realization. It is my hope that this book might serve others as a helpful guide for this, our common journey.

Made in the USA
Charleston, SC
12 March 2015